HISTORICAL DICTIONARY OF THE 1920s

HISTORICAL DICTIONARY OF THE 1920s

From World War I to the New Deal, 1919–1933

JAMES S. OLSON

Greenwood Press
New York • Westport, Connecticut • London

Library of Congress Cataloging-in-Publication Data

Olson, James Stuart, 1946–
  Historical dictionary of the 1920s.

  Bibliography: p.
  Includes index.
  1. United States—History—1919–1933—Dictionaries.
I. Title.
E784.044 1988   973.91   87–29987
ISBN 0–313–25683–7 (lib. bdg. : alk. paper)

British Library Cataloguing in Publication Data is available.

Library of Congress Catalog Card Number: 87–29987
ISBN: 0–313–25683–7

First published in 1988

Greenwood Press, Inc.
88 Post Road West, Westport, Connecticut 06881

Printed in the United States of America

The paper used in this book complies with the
Permanent Paper Standard issued by the National
Information Standards Organization (Z39.48–1984).

10   9   8   7   6   5   4   3   2   1

To Randy Roberts

CONTENTS

PREFACE

Occasionally in American history, certain periods have an almost schizophrenic quality to them, an indecisiveness about priorities and the nature of social and political change. The 1920s was one of those periods. Caught between the disillusionment of World War I and the economic malaise of the Great Depression, the decade was a watershed between an old and a new America. Although most Americans wanted to retreat back into an isolationist shell and disregard world affairs, they had acquired global territorial and economic interests which required protection. Instead of being a country of farms and villages, the United States had become a country of factories and cities, precipitating an identity crisis. Tradition gave way to innovation as a modern society emerged. Older Victorian values and conservative religion seemed threatened by secularism, urbanism, industrialism, and bureaucracy. The 1920s ushered the United States into the modern age.

In the *Historical Dictionary of the 1920s* I have provided brief essays on the most prominent individuals, social movements, organizations, legislation, treaties, political events, and ideas of the era. They are arranged in alphabetical order, with brief bibliographical citations. Cross-references from one entry to another are indicated by an asterisk after a person or event is discussed in a separate entry. The essays generally cover the period between 1919 and 1933—from the opening of the Paris peace talks ending World War I to the inauguration of Franklin D. Roosevelt as president of the United States. The dictionary also includes a chronology of events between 1919 and 1933 and a selected bibliography about the decade.

Librarians at the Newton Gresham Library at Sam Houston State University were unfailingly courteous and helpful in supplying me with the necessary reference materials.

THE DICTIONARY

A

ABBOTT, EDITH. Edith Abbott was born on September 26, 1876, in Grand Island, Nebraska, to a socially and politically active family. Her father encouraged her ambitions. She graduated from the University of Nebraska in 1901, and then she received a Ph.D. in economics from the University of Chicago in 1905. Abbott studied at the London School of Economics in 1906 and taught at Wellesley College in 1907. In the fall of 1908 she joined her sister Grace Abbott* at Hull House in Chicago, and she lived and worked there until 1920. Together they formed a close relationship with Jane Addams.* The Abbott sisters were strong advocates of women's rights, an end to child labor, maximum hours legislation for women, and improved housing for poor people.

Edith Abbott focused her energies on social research, and the results were hundreds of articles and reports, as well as two landmark books: *Immigration: Select Documents and Case Records* (1923) and *Historical Aspects of the Immigration Problem* (1926). During the 1920s and 1930s she wrote widely, particularly in the *Nation* and the *New Republic,* calling for public works spending and social legislation for the poor. Abbott retired as dean of the School of Social Service Administration at the University of Chicago in 1942 but continued to write and speak. She died on July 28, 1957. (Lela B. Costin, *Two Sisters for Social Justice: A Biography of Grace and Edith Abbott,* 1983.)

ABBOTT, GRACE. Born on November 17, 1878, in Grand Island, Nebraska, Grace Abbott played an influential role in women's issues throughout the 1920s and 1930s. She came from a politically active family: Her father had been involved in Nebraska politics and her mother had worked actively for women's suffrage and abolition of slavery. Abbott graduated from Grand Island College in 1898 and then took a master's degree in political science at the University of Chicago in 1909. Her own interests in reform followed closely those of her parents, except hers were directed more at the problems of poverty among the urban lower classes. Along with her sister Edith Abbott,* she worked at Hull House in Chicago and was influenced by the ideas and attitudes of Jane Addams.* In 1917 she joined the Children's Bureau of the Department of Labor. In 1919

Abbott left the bureau to work for the Illinois State Immigrants Commission, but she came back to Washington, D.C., in 1921 as head of the Children's Bureau.

The 1920s was an inhospitable time for social reform campaigners. The "normalcy" of presidents Warren G. Harding* and Calvin Coolidge* emphasized free enterprise and the resources of the private sector, but of any agency of the federal government, the Children's Bureau had the highest profile among urban social welfare reformers, emphasizing an end to child labor, the need for social welfare legislation, and equality in the workplace for women. She pushed hard to enforce the Sheppard-Towner Act* in hopes of reducing infant and maternal mortality and was especially upset in 1929 when Congress let the law lapse. Abbott was also active in the National Consumers' League and the National Conference of Social Work. Close to Eleanor Roosevelt* as well as several other influential women in the northeastern wing of the Democratic Party,* Abbott continued her campaign quietly until 1933, when the New Deal went into effect. Abbott served on the Consumers' Advisory Board of the National Recovery Administration in 1933 and 1934, and after she left the Children's Bureau to teach at the University of Chicago, President Franklin D. Roosevelt* appointed her to the Committee on Economic Security. There Abbott played an important role in the creation of the Social Security Act of 1935. Grace Abbott died in Chicago on June 19, 1939. (Lela B. Costin, *Two Sisters for Social Justice: A Biography of Grace and Edith Abbott,* 1983; Susan Ware, *Beyond Suffrage: Women in the New Deal,* 1981.)

ABBOTT, ROBERT SENGSTACKE. Robert Abbott was born on November 28, 1868, on St. Simon's Island, Georgia. He graduated from the Hampton Institute in 1896 and studied under Booker T. Washington. In 1899 he earned a law degree from the Kent College of Law in Chicago. Abbott worked for several newspapers but in 1904 founded the *Chicago Defender,* a small weekly newspaper catering to the black community of Chicago. The newspaper was a spectacular success. In its pages, Abbott urged southern blacks to move to the North, where jobs were more plentiful and oppression less intense. By 1918 the *Chicago Defender* had a circulation of 125,000 and was widely distributed in black communities throughout the country. Abbott became a millionaire and one of the leading blacks in the country during the 1920s. During the 1930s, although a Republican, Abbott openly supported Franklin D. Roosevelt* and the New Deal, telling blacks that whatever debt they had once owed to Abraham Lincoln and the GOP had long since been repaid. Robert Abbott died on February 29, 1940. (Roi Ottley, *The Lonely Warrior,* 1955; Allen Spear, *Black Chicago,* 1967.)

ABBOTT, WILLIS JOHN. Willis Abbott was born on March 16, 1863, in New Haven, Connecticut. He took a law degree at the University of Michigan in 1863 but then began a lifelong career in journalism. He wrote for the *New*

York Times-Democrat between 1884 and 1886 and the *New York Tribune* in 1867, when he became co-owner of the *Kansas City Evening News*. The paper declared bankruptcy in 1889, and after writing editorials for the *Chicago Times* and *Evening Mail*, Abbott went to work for the Hearst chain as an editor for the *New York Journal*. In 1913 Abbott wrote *Panama and the Canal in Picture and Prose*, a book which became a bestseller. In 1922 Abbott became editor of the *Christian Science Monitor* and remained there for the rest of his career. Throughout the 1920s he advocated United States entry into the World Court* and the League of Nations,* a position he advocated forcefully in the Democratic Party,* the Foreign Policy Association,* and the Council on Foreign Relations.* Willis Abbott died on May 19, 1934. *(New York Times,* May 20, 1934.)

ADAMS, CHARLES FRANCIS. Charles Francis Adams was born in Quincy, Massachusetts, on August 2, 1866, to one of America's most distinguished families. He graduated from Harvard in 1902, was admitted to the Massachusetts bar in 1903, and practiced law in Boston. In 1929 President Herbert Hoover* appointed Adams to the cabinet post of secretary of the navy, where he served until the end of the administration in 1933. During his tenure as secretary of the navy, Adams played a critical role in the development of the London Naval Treaty* of 1930. Charles Francis Adams died on June 10, 1954. (David Burner, *Herbert Hoover: A Public Life,* 1979; Martin L. Fausold, *The Presidency of Herbert Hoover,* 1985; Robert H. Ferrell, *American Diplomacy in the Great Depression: Hoover-Stimson Foreign Policy, 1929–1933,* 1957; *New York Times,* June 11, 1954.)

ADDAMS, JANE. Jane Addams was born on September 6, 1860, in Cedarville, Illinois. Her father was a Quaker who believed in public service and helped found the Republican Party.* Because of ill health she had to drop out of the Women's Medical College in Philadelphia, and after tours of Europe in 1883 and 1887 she decided on a career in social work, in particular a career directing a settlement house. She had been deeply influenced by London's Toynbee House. In 1889 she moved into a home, formerly owned by Charles Hull, on South Halsted Street in Chicago. Hull House quickly became a major social force in Chicago's immigrant community and in the social work profession. At Hull House, Addams trained a generation of influential social workers while sponsoring lectures, women's clubs, day nurseries, music lessons, and health and nutrition projects.

Jane Addams became a nationally recognized reformer as the influence of Hull House grew. She became active in labor relations and municipal reform movements, and after the Spanish-American War of 1898 Addams was a prominent peace advocate. In 1909 Addams became president of the National Conference of Charities and Correction, and from that position of influence she promoted a variety of progressive causes, including Theodore Roosevelt's ''Bull Moose'' campaign for the presidency in 1912. Addams was reluctant about World

War I, and because of her pacifism and her liberal social ideas, critics labeled her either pro-German, pro-communist, or both. Between 1915 and 1929, she served as international president of the Women's International League for Peace and Freedom. In 1931, Jane Addams received the Nobel Peace Prize. She was the author of a number of books, including *Democracy and Social Ethics* (1902), *Newer Ideals of Peace* (1907), *The Spirit of Youth and City Streets* (1909), *Twenty Years at Hull-House* (1910), *A New Conscience and an Ancient Evil* (1911), *Peace and Bread in Time of War* (1922), and *The Second Twenty Years at Hull-House* (1930). Jane Addams died on May 21, 1935. (Jane Addams, *Twenty Years at Hull-House*, 1910; *The Second Twenty Years at Hull-House*, 1930; Allen F. Davis, *American Heroine: The Life and Legend of Jane Addams*, 1973; Daniel Levine, *Jane Addams and the Liberal Tradition*, 1971.)

ADJUSTED COMPENSATION ACT OF 1924. By 1921 the idea of a bonus payment to American veterans was gaining momentum, especially among farm bloc* congressmen. Conservative Republicans opposed the idea as a raid on the federal treasury quite inconsistent with their goal of cutting federal spending and balancing the budget. Late in 1921 some congressmen, looking ahead to the 1922 elections, joined the bandwagon. In March 1922, by a vote of 332 to 70, the House passed a bonus bill but did not provide any funding. The Senate took the matter up later in the summer, debating where to get the estimated $4 billion to fund a bonus. Democrats had a field day politically accusing the Republican administration of forsaking the men who had fought for freedom in Europe. In August the Senate developed a measure and passed it in September, and, after going through a conference in the middle of the month, the Adjusted Compensation Act was passed on September 15. The bill provided each honorably discharged veteran with a certificate worth $1 for each day served and $1.25 for each day served overseas. If the certificates were held for twenty years, they would triple in value. On September 19, 1922, President Warren G. Harding* vetoed the bill. On September 20, 1922, the House overrode the veto by 258 to 54, but the Senate vote of 44 to 28 fell four votes short of the override. The veto stood.

But the idea was hardly dead. In March 1924 the House passed another bonus bill, and the Senate followed suit in April. President Calvin Coolidge* vetoed it on May 15, but both houses of Congress overrode the veto. The Adjusted Compensation Act of 1924 provided the same cash value as the previous bill, but it was in the form of a twenty-year endowment against which the veteran could borrow up to 25 percent of its value. Cash payment would again become an issue when the economy collapsed in 1931, leading to the "Bonus Army* Riots" of 1932 and the Adjusted Compensation Act of 1936. (David Burner, *Herbert Hoover: A Public Life*, 1979; Donald R. McCoy, *Calvin Coolidge: The Quiet President*, 1967; Eugene P. Trani and David L. Wilson, *The Presidency of Warren G. Harding*, 1977.)

ADKINS v. *CHILDREN'S HOSPITAL* (261 U.S. 525). In 1918 Congress passed legislation permitting the Wage Board of the District of Columbia to set a minimum wage for women. The Children's Hospital in Washington, D.C., employed women on the general cleaning and labor staff and paid them at a rate below the established minimum wage. A supervisor fired a female elevator operator in order to avoid penalty under the act; the operator filed suit and won. Children's Hospital then countered in the federal courts, and the case reached the Supreme Court in 1923 as *Adkins* v. *Children's Hospital.* In its decision, the Supreme Court ruled the act unconstitutional. Writing for the majority, Justice George Sutherland argued that the act violated the Fifth Amendment property rights of business owners by forcing them to pay each worker a minimum wage regardless of whether the employee was worth that much to him and whether the employee needed that level of compensation. Sutherland went on to argue that a contract containing a clause designating a minimum wage was unfair to the employer since no account of the worker's ability to produce or of the business's ability to survive is given in such a contract. The law also failed to state that the employee must compensate the employer by producing an equal amount of work for her pay. Typical of the prevailing judicial philosophy of the 1920s, the case of *Adkins* v. *Children's Hospital* outlawed minimum wage contracts until 1937, when the Supreme Court upheld such arrangements in the case of *West Coast* v. *Parrish.* (Alpheus Thomas Mason, *The Supreme Court from Taft to Warren,* 1958; Joel Francis Paschal, *Mr. Justice Sutherland: A Man against the State,* 1951.)

AGRICULTURAL CREDITS ACT OF 1923. Troubled by huge surpluses and falling prices, farmers in the 1920s searched for a solution to their economic plight, and one program they focused on was the expansion of the federal farm credit establishment. Pro-business Republicans in Congress generally supported such measures because they seemed to satisfy the farm bloc* without leading to price fixing schemes. One such measure was the Agricultural Credits Act of 1923. At the time, Federal Land Banks made long-term loans to farmers while Federal Reserve Banks made short-term loans. The Agricultural Credits Act of 1923 established twelve Federal Intermediate Credit Banks (FICBs), each with $5 million in capital, to make loans of from six to thirty-six months. The FICBs lent the money to cooperative associations, which then relent it to farmers. Although the new credit system helped some farmers, it did nothing to address the real source of the agricultural crisis—gross overproduction. (Freda Baird and Claude L. Benner, *Ten Years of Federal Intermediate Credit,* 1933; Claude L. Benner, *The Federal Intermediate Credit System,* 1926; James H. Shideler, *Farm Crisis, 1919–1923,* 1957.)

AGRICULTURAL MARKETING ACT OF 1929. During World War I American farmers experienced a dramatic rise in commodity prices because of the loss of production in Europe. Responding to rising prices, they increased the amount of land in production, confidently and naively assuming that demand would remain high after the war. Soon after the end of the war, late in 1919, however, commodity prices started down and never recovered until World War II. During the 1920s American farmers were victims of their own success, experiencing the "poverty of abundance" as overproduction depressed prices.

Farm organizations devised a number of schemes during the 1920s; one of them was government-sponsored cooperative marketing. President Herbert Hoover* adamantly opposed the McNary-Haugen Bill* and export debenture plan,* and he proposed the Agricultural Marketing Act of 1929 as an alternative. The bill, which became law on June 15, 1929, established a Federal Farm Board* of eight members and the office of secretary of agriculture to promote the sale of farm products through agricultural cooperatives and stabilization corporations. The law provided a revolving fund of $500 million to provide low-interest loans to agencies involved in the sale of farm products. The goal of the legislation was to stabilize farm prices by helping farmers establish cooperative marketing associations for each major crop and to set voluntary production quotas to prevent overproduction. In 1930, the Federal Farm Board established the Cotton Stabilization Corporation, the Grain Stabilization Corporation, and the Wool Stabilization Corporation to purchase crop surpluses on the open market and hold them during cyclical price declines and sell them when prices were higher.

The Agricultural Marketing Act was too little too late. By 1931 it was burdened with commodities it could not sell except at a loss and continuingly declining prices. They had spent more than $180 million by the end of 1931 and had done nothing to address the farm crisis. The Federal Farm Board stopped purchasing surpluses and confined its activities to short-term loans. A more dramatic approach to the agricultural depression would have to wait for the programs of the New Deal. When they began in 1933, the Commodity Credit Corporation took up where the stabilization corporations left off—providing hundreds of millions of dollars in loans to individual farmers to assist them in marketing their crops. (Van L. Perkins, *Crisis in Agriculture: The Agricultural Adjustment Act and the New Deal, 1933*, 1969; Theodore Saloutos and John D. Hicks, *Agricultural Discontent in the Midwest, 1900–1939*, 1951; James Shideler, *Farm Crisis, 1919–1923*, 1957.)

AIKEN, CONRAD. Conrad Aiken was born in Savannah, Georgia, in 1889, but he spent most of his boyhood and young adulthood in Cambridge, Massachusetts. The year he was born, his father murdered his mother and then committed suicide, shaping Aiken's personal philosophy for the rest of his life. Both poet and novelist, he had a remarkable versatility and was especially adept at stream-of-consciousness writing. Included in his major works are *The Charnel Rose* (1919), *The Coming Forth by Day of Osiris Jones* (1931), and *Time in the Rock* (1936), all poetry; the novels *Great Circle* (1933), *King Coffin* (1935), and *Conversation* (1940); and short story collections *Bring! Bring!* (1925), *Costumes by Eros* (1928), and *Among the Lost People* (1934). His most famous short story was "Silent Snow, Secret Snow," the tale of a child's development of schizophrenia. Aiken's most successful work was *A Heart for the Gods of Mexico* (1939). Conrad Aiken died on August 17, 1973. (Martin Seymour-Smith, *Who's Who in Twentieth Century Literature*, 1976.)

AIR-CONDITIONING. See CARRIER, WILLIS HAVILAND

AIR MAIL ACT OF 1925. In 1918 the Post Office Department began air mail service, and in 1925 Congress passed the Kelly Act, or Air Mail Act. Consistent with the pro-business, anti-government atmosphere of the 1920s, the Air Mail Act turned air mail contracts over to commercial carriers holding government contracts. Although the contracts were awarded to the low bidders, government subsidies to help companies cover huge operating costs were common by the late 1920s. By 1931 the federal government was awarding contracts without competitive bidding. A congressional investigation led by Senator Hugo Black of Alabama revealed the scandal in 1933. President Franklin D. Roosevelt* blamed the previous administrations, and, in February 1934, he turned air mail carrying over to the U.S. Army Air Corps. Republicans accused him of trying to "socialize" America, and their charges became more hostile when several army pilots died in crashes while carrying the mail. In May 1934 Roosevelt returned air mail to private carriers, and in June Congress passed new legislation requiring competitive bidding on all contracts. (Thomas T. Spencer, "The Air Mail Controversy of 1934," *Mid-America* 62 [1980], 161–72.)

ALEXANDER, GROVER CLEVELAND. Grover Cleveland Alexander, one of the most famous baseball* pitchers of the 1920s, was born on a farm in St. Paul, Nebraska, in 1887. In 1906 Alexander lost his job as a telephone lineman and began pitching semi-professional baseball. He signed his first professional contract in 1909 with Galesburg in the Illinois-Missouri League. In 1910 he won twenty-nine games with Syracuse in the New York State League, and in 1911 the Philadelphia Phillies brought him up to the major leagues, where he won twenty-eight games as a rookie. He pitched for the Phillies until 1918, winning thirty or more games in 1915, 1916, and 1917 and posting a 1.22 earned-run average in 1915. Alexander was traded to the Chicago Cubs in 1918, but he missed the season because of a stint in the army which took him to France during World War I. In 1919 and 1920 he returned to baseball and led the National League in earned-run average each year. Alexander played well in 1921 and 1922, but, by 1923, his chronic alcoholism was affecting his game. After spending some time in a sanitarium in 1925, he was traded to the St. Louis Cardinals. Alexander won twenty-one games in 1927 and sixteen in 1928. More bouts with alcoholism ended his baseball career in 1929. The rest of his life was spent barnstorming with exhibition baseball teams and circus sideshows. Grover Cleveland Alexander died on November 4, 1960. (Martin Appel and Burt Goldblatt, *Baseball's Best: The Hall of Fame Gallery*, 1980.)

ALGER, GEORGE WILLIAM. George Alger was born on November 12, 1872, in Burlington, Vermont. Alger grew up amidst progressive political ideas and a Puritan's love for thrift and efficiency. He graduated from the University of Vermont in 1892. He taught school in New York and then received a law degree from the New York University Law School in 1895. Alger was immediately attracted to social issues, and in 1902 he founded the New York Child Labor Committee, a lobbying organization he worked with for the next forty years. He was president between 1920 and 1932. Alger drafted more than forty child labor laws which New York state enacted, as well as the New York Employers' Liability Act of 1902 and the Workmen's Compensation Act of 1910. He was a close friend of Florence Kelley,* Ray Stannard Baker, and Lillian Wald.* In the field of corporate law, Alger became widely regarded for his expertise. His legal work brought him the respect and friendship of Charles Evans Hughes,* Louis Brandeis,* John W. Davis,* and Benjamin Cardozo.* Alger was a true progressive—pragmatic and committed to the legislative solution of social problems. George Alger died on April 19, 1967. (Jeremy P. Felt, *Hostages of Fortune: Child Labor Reform in New York State,* 1965; *New York Times,* April 20, 1967.)

ALIEN PROPERTY CUSTODIAN SCANDAL. One of the major scandals of the Warren Harding* administration involved the office of the Alien Property Custodian. First established in 1917 to manage German-owned property in the United States, the Alien Property Custodian office worked to dispose of German property after the war. Colonel Thomas W. Miller, a war hero and former congressman from Delaware, became the new Alien Property Custodian in 1921. Although Miller's reputation was impeccable—a founder of the American Legion* as well as a member of the Yale Club, the National Press Club, and the Union League Club. But, in September 1921, he agreed to transfer the American Metal Company, a German-owned company, to a syndicate chaired by Richard Merton. In return, the syndicate provided a payment of $50,000 to Miller as well as a payment of $224,000 to Jesse Smith, Attorney General Harry Daugherty's* assistant in the Department of Justice. Smith placed $50,000 in a bank account for Daugherty.

When news of the transaction leaked out, a federal grand jury indicted Miller and Daugherty. The case did not come to trial until September 1926. By that time, Smith had committed suicide. Daugherty and Miller stood trial, but because the bank records of the deposits had been destroyed, the jury could not reach a verdict. Daugherty refused to testify. A second trial was held in February 1927, and Miller was convicted and sentenced to eighteen months in jail and fined $5,000. The jury could not decide on a verdict for Daugherty, and the case against him was dropped. Miller served thirteen months of his sentence. (Robert K. Murray, *The Harding Era: Warren G. Harding and His Administration,* 1969.)

ALTMEYER, ARTHUR JOSEPH. Arthur J. Altmeyer was born in De Pere, Wisconsin, on May 8, 1891. He graduated from the University of Wisconsin in 1914, and, after working as a teacher and principal, he accepted appointment as statistician for the Wisconsin Tax Committee. Altmeyer became chief statistician in 1920. He wrote *The Industrial Commission* in 1932 and *General Accident Statistics for Wisconsin* in 1933. By that time, he had become a nationally recognized expert in labor law administration. In 1933 President Franklin D. Roosevelt* named him to head the National Recovery Administration's Compliance Division, and in 1935 Altmeyer went to work for the Committee on Economic Security, which drafted the Social Security Act of 1935. While on the committee, which he headed after 1937, Altmeyer advocated an unemployment insurance program coordinated with employment agencies, temporary disability programs, and continued expansion of social security to include more and more workers. Altmeyer served as a member of the Social Security Board between 1935 and 1937, and as chairman of the board between 1937 and 1946. His title was changed to commissioner of social security in 1946, and he continued in that position until 1953. After leaving the federal government, Altmeyer served on a number of international social insurance commissions and taught at the University of Chicago and the University of Wisconsin. He died on October 17, 1972. (Arthur Joseph Altmeyer, *The Formative Years of Social Security,* 1968; *New York Times,* October 18, 1972.)

AMERICAN ASSOCIATION FOR LABOR LEGISLATION. See ANDREWS, JOHN BERTRAM

AMERICAN ASSOCIATION FOR OLD AGE SECURITY. The American Association for Old Age Security was established in 1927 by Abraham Epstein* to promote comprehensive old-age social insurance at the federal level. Epstein had spent years as director of the Pennsylvania Old Age Pension Commission, and he was convinced that federal legislation was necessary. Through research, publication, advertising, and lobbying model bills in Congress, the American Association for Old Age Security hoped to implement a social security program for older citizens. The political atmosphere in the 1920s was most inhospitable for social security legislation, but the coming of the New Deal in the 1930s and the strength of Dr. Francis Townsend's campaign for federal pensions gave the American Association for Old Age Security the momentum it needed to help bring about passage of the Social Security Act of 1935. (Roy Lubove, *The Struggle for Social Security, 1900–1935,* 1968.)

AMERICAN CIVIL LIBERTIES UNION. The American Civil Liberties Union (ACLU) was established in 1920, during the Red Scare,* by a group of concerned civil libertarians which included John Dewey,* Clarence Darrow,* Felix Frankfurter, Jane Addams,* Helen Keller, John Ryan,* Norman Thomas,* and Oswald Garrison Villard.* Norman Thomas and Roger Baldwin* had started an American Civil Liberties Bureau in 1917 to provide legal assistance to conscientious objectors refusing to enter the military during World War I. The ACLU was formed specifically to counter the effects of Attorney General A. Mitchell Palmer's* crusade against what he called American radicals. During the 1920s, the ACLU also provided legal assistance for Nicola Sacco* and Bartolomeo Vanzetti* (1920–1927), John Scopes* (1925), the "Scottsboro* boys" (1931), and veterans arrested during the Bonus Army* march (1932). Generally, the American Civil Liberties Union took a broad, liberal view of the First Amendment and was willing to defend all individuals and groups whose rights to freedom of religion, speech, press, assembly, and petition were being violated. By the 1930s the American Civil Liberties Union had become the most well-known civil rights organization in the United States. (Morris L. Ernst, *The First Freedom*, 1946; Charles L. Markmann, *The Noblest Cry*, 1965; Robert K. Murray, *Red Scare: A Study in National Hysteria, 1919–1920*, 1955.)

AMERICAN COALITION OF PATRIOTIC SOCIETIES. The American Coalition of Patriotic Societies (ACPS) was founded in 1929 by John B. Trevor to promote immigration restriction. In 1922 Trevor had established the Citizen's Committee on Immigration Legislation, which campaigned for the National Origins Act of 1924.* After 1929 Trevor and the ACPS demanded that total immigration to the United States be limited to 150,000 people annually. Although the ACPS membership remained quite small, the organization has survived into the 1980s; it still campaigns against communism and for limiting immigration, against issuing Social Security cards to illegal immigrants, and for strengthening the Federal Bureau of Investigation and the Central Intelligence Agency. (Robert Divine, *American Immigration Policy, 1924–1952*, 1957.)

AMERICAN COUNTRY LIFE ASSOCIATION. One of the major themes of social life in the United States during the 1920s was the rural-urban split. In the mid-1920s, for the first time, more Americans lived in cities than on farms, and rural American underwent an identity crisis, primarily because so much historical tradition had venerated the lifestyle of independent, "yeoman farmers." In 1919, Kenyon L. Butterfield, then president of Massachusetts Agricultural College, founded the American Country Life Association (ACLA) to celebrate and improve the quality of rural living in the United States. During the 1920s the ACLA campaigned for better farm-to-market roads, more bank credit, a parcel post service, better federal extension work, reduced railroad freight rates, and the creation of a Federal Farm Board.* Presidents Warren G. Harding* and Calvin Coolidge* did little to respond to ACLA demands, but President Herbert Hoover* implemented the Federal Farm Board with the Agricultural Marketing Act of 1929.* Not until the New Deal of Franklin D. Roosevelt*, however, did farmers and rural Americans get much of the legislation the ACLA wanted. After World War II, ACLA influence declined rapidly. (William L. Bowers, *The Country Life Movement in America, 1900–1920*, 1975.)

AMERICAN FARM BUREAU FEDERATION. The American Farm Bureau Federation (AFBF) was established in 1920 by leaders of state farm bureaus and prominent agricultural spokesman. In 1914 Congress passed the Smith-Lever Act providing for federal support of state extension services, and county agents then led a movement to organize farm bureaus in counties throughout the country. Henry C. Wallace,* editor of *Wallace's Farmer* and soon to become secretary of agriculture under President Warren G. Harding,* was the prime mover in establishing the American Farm Bureau Federation as a national body composed of all the state bureaus. James R. Howard served as national president of the AFBF until 1923, when Edward A. O'Neal of Alabama took over. Farm Bureau membership stood at 325,000 in 1921 but declined under the impact of the farming depression to just 163,000 in 1933. The organization represented large commercial farmers, generally the more prosperous ones, and its chief goal was ''parity''—the re-establishment of the purchasing power of farmers to what it had been between 1909 and 1914. During the 1920s the American Farm Bureau Federation vigorously supported the McNary-Haugen Bill*, which President Calvin Coolidge* vetoed two times. During the Great Depression, the AFBF continued to demand support for McNary-Haugen but also came around to the domestic allotment idea which was institutionalized in the Agricultural Adjustment Act of 1933. (Samuel R. Berger, *Dollar Harvest: The Story of the Farm Bureau,* 1971; Christiana M. Campbell, *The Farm Bureau and the New Deal: A Study of the Making of National Farm Policy, 1933–1940,* 1962.)

AMERICAN FEDERATION OF LABOR. During the 1920s, the American Federation of Labor (AFL) was the largest and most powerful labor union in the United States. Thirteen national unions formed the American Federation of Labor in 1886, with Samuel Gompers* serving as president. Unlike earlier national unions, like the National Labor Union or the Knights of Labor, the American Federation of Labor did not function as a political party, nor did it attempt to organize unskilled workers. Instead of working to reshape the basic institutions of American life, like socialists were trying to do, the American Federation of Labor had more conservative goals: higher wages, better working conditions, and shorter work weeks. Early in the 1900s, the American Federation of Labor even joined the National Civic Federation,* an employer-dominated group dedicated to resolving labor disputes without disruptive strikes. It was a conservative union under Gompers's leadership.

In 1920, AFL membership stood at 3,260,000 people, but despite the growth of the economy during the 1920s, AFL membership remained stable. The economy expanded rapidly in such mass-production industries as automobiles, rubber, chemicals, and utilities, but because the AFL confined its membership to skilled workers, it made few gains among those new workers. Also, the union had to deal with the open shop movement* of the 1920s, in which employers tried to hurt existing labor unions by forming company unions and shop committees. Samuel Gompers's leadership of the AFL gave way to William Green* in 1924, but the conservative nature of the union remained intact. When the depression hit, AFL membership fell to just over two million members in four years, its lowest total since the turn of the century. Not until the Norris–La Guardia Labor Relations Act of 1932* and the New Deal labor legislation of the 1930s would AFL membership start to grow again. (Irving Bernstein, *The Lean Years: A History of the American Worker, 1920–1933,* 1960.)

AMERICAN LEGION. The American Legion was founded in 1919 in Paris, France, by a number of American veterans of World War I who were concerned about the morale of homesick troops and about the presence of revolutionary sentiments in Europe. Theodore Roosevelt, Jr., had called the assembly. Later in the year they held their first convention in St. Louis, Missouri. The legion outlined its purposes as fostering the interests of veterans, promoting "one hundred percent Americanism,"* and protecting democracy in general and in the United States in particular. Congress gave the American Legion a formal charter late in 1919, and the organization went on to become the most powerful veterans' lobby in American history, working to influence American foreign policy as well as various domestic legislation. It kept alive some of the hatreds of the war, especially toward Germans, aliens, conscientious objectors, and radicals, particularly the International Workers of the World. During the 1920s, the American Legion helped secure passage of the National Defense Act of 1920, the Adjusted Compensation Act of 1924,* and the National Origins Act of 1924.* Generally, the legion took a conservative position on domestic legislation, supporting immigration restriction and the Red Scare,* and an activist position on foreign affairs, always insisting that the United States remain in a position of military preparedness. In 1921 the American Legion was instrumental in getting November 11 declared as Armistice Day. By the 1980s the membership of the American Legion had reached more than three million people. (Roscoe Baker, *The American Legion and American Foreign Policy,* 1954; Richard S. Jones, *A History of the American Legion,* 1947.)

AMERICAN PLAN. See OPEN SHOP MOVEMENT

AMERICAN PROTECTIVE ASSOCIATION. See CATHOLICS

AMERICAN PROTECTIVE LEAGUE. The American Protective League was founded in 1917 by A. M. Briggs, a Chicago advertising executive. Complete with secret oaths and fraternal organization, the American Protective League served as a semi-official auxiliary to the Justice Department, assisting the attorney general in finding subversives. The American Protective League quickly mushroomed in size, growing to 250,000 members in 1,200 local associations. They even had official duties to investigate individuals the federal Bureau of Investigation or the War Department's Military Intelligence Division referred to them. During the war, the league looked for people unwilling to purchase war bonds, draft evaders, and food ration violators. After the war, the league formally dissolved, although many local chapters enthusiastically participated in the Red Scare* of 1919–1921 and maintained close ties with the Ku Klux Klan* in the mid-1920s. (John Higham, *Strangers in the Land: Patterns of American Nativism 1860–1925,* 1965.)

AMERICAN VIGILANT INTELLIGENCE FEDERATION. Formed in 1923 by Harry A. Jung, the American Vigilant Intelligence Federation was an intensely anti-Jewish, anti-immigrant organization. Convinced that there was an international plot by "international Jewish financiers" to take over the world, Jung called for a variety of immigration restriction measures and anti-Semitic legislation. The federation frequently distributed the phony "Protocols of the Elders of Zion," which supposedly were the plans for the great Jewish conspiracy. During the 1930s, Jung was convinced that Franklin D. Roosevelt* and the New Deal were pawns of the international Jewish cabal. (George Wolfskill and John A. Hudson, *All but the People: Franklin D. Roosevelt and His Critics, 1933–1939,* 1969.)

"AMOS AND ANDY SHOW." The "Amos and Andy Show" was one of the country's most popular radio* programs in the 1920s, 1930s, and 1940s. It evolved out of a blackface vaudeville act of Freeman F. Gosden, who played Amos, and Charles J. Carroll, who played Andy. In 1926, they started the "Sam and Henry Show" on WGN radio in Chicago, which was a precursor of the black dialogue, situation comedy which became known as the "Amos and Andy Show" on NBC radio in 1929. Amos Jones and Andrew H. Brown were Harlem blacks who owned the Fresh Air Taxi Company, whose "fleet" of cars consisted of one broken-down taxi. Amos was the hardworking family man who kept the company together; Andy was the gullible ne'er-do-well. The character of George Stevens, the "Kingfish," was not added to the program until 1943. "Amos and Andy" is widely regarded by radio historians as the first great radio broadcast with wide national appeal. Throughout much of the 1930s, it was a fifteen-minute nightly serial, and movie houses would often stop their films at the appropriate time and turn on the "Amos and Andy" broadcast. Pepsodent toothpaste sponsored the show until 1937, when Campbell Soup took over. (John Dunning, *Tune in Yesterday: The Ultimate Encyclopedia of Old-Time Radio, 1926–1976.* 1976.)

ANARCHISM. See SACCO AND VANZETTI CASE

ANDERSON, CLAIRE. Claire Anderson was born in Detroit, Michigan, in 1896. As a child and adolescent, she danced in vaudeville; in 1914, she went to work for Triangle Studios as one of its Mack Sennett Bathing Beauties. They were a stock company of ingenues capable of precision line dancing as well as acting in Keystone Kop movies. Eventually, Anderson became a star for Triangle

Studies, and her best-known films were *Cinders of Love* (1916), *The Lion and the Girl* (1916), and *His Baby Doll* (1918). Anderson left Triangle in 1920 and worked as a dancer, actress, and comedienne for several other studios. Her most well-known films in the 1920s were *The Yellow Stain* (1922) and *The Clean-Up* (1923). Anderson never made the transition to sound films. She died on March 23, 1964. (Barbara Naomi Cohen-Stratyner, *Biographical Dictionary of Dance*, 1982.)

ANDERSON, MARY. Mary Anderson was born in Lynkoping, Sweden, on August 27, 1872, and immigrated to the United States in 1889. Her family settled in Chicago, and Anderson went to work in the garment and shoe industries there and became active in union politics. The crusade against exploitation of working women became her lifelong obsession. In 1902 Anderson joined the Women's Trade Union League (WTUL), and she was active in the WTUL for the rest of her life. In 1919 President Woodrow Wilson* appointed her director of the new Women's Bureau of the Department of Labor, and she headed the bureau until 1944. Anderson was passionately committed to the minimum wage, government-sponsored retirement program, and to national medical insurance—causes which found little support in the Republican-dominated 1920s but more credibility during the New Deal of the 1930s. Anderson supported such major New Deal programs as the National Recovery Administration, Social Security, and the Fair Labor Standards Act of 1938. She retired from government service in 1944 and died on January 29, 1964. An irony of her career was that her passionate commitment to protective legislation for women put her at odds with feminists pushing an equal rights amendment. (Mary Anderson, *Woman at Work: The Autobiography of Mary Anderson as told to Mary N. Winslow,* 1951; J. M. Daly, ''Mary Anderson, Pioneer Labor Leader,'' Ph.D. Dissertation, Georgetown University, 1968.)

ANDERSON, SHERWOOD. Sherwood Anderson was born in Camden, Ohio, on September 13, 1876. He fought with the United States Army in the Spanish-American War in 1898 and then pursued a business career until 1912, when he began full-time writing in Chicago and working in a paint factory to support himself. Desperate to express his feelings about America and modern life and feeling trapped in a weak marriage, Anderson had a nervous breakdown, walked out of the paint factory where he worked, and moved to Chicago. His first two novels—*Windy McPherson's Son* (1916) and *Marching Men* (1917)—were not successful, but he came to the attention of literary critics and a broader public in 1919 with his novel *Winesberg, Ohio.* Influenced by Carl Sandburg* and several other Chicago writers, Anderson was able in *Winesberg, Ohio* to describe the small-town world in which he had been raised. During the 1920s, Anderson wrote newspaper editorials as well as his autobiography *The Story-Teller's Story* (1925) and the novels *Dark Laughter* (1925) and *Beyond Desire* (1931). Sensitive to criticism, Anderson eventually felt abandoned by most American writers, whom he thought had turned against him, and his second and third marriages failed as well. Sherwood Anderson died on March 8, 1941. (Sherwood Anderson, *The Story-Teller's Story,* 1925; Rex Burbank, *Sherwood Anderson,* 1964; Ray Lewis White, *The Portable Sherwood Anderson,* 1949.)

ANDREWS, JOHN BERTRAM. John B. Andrews was born on August 2, 1880, in South Wayne, Wisconsin. He graduated from the University of Wisconsin in 1904 and received a master's degree in economics from Dartmouth in 1905. Andrews returned to the University of Wisconsin and studied economics under the tutelage of John R. Commons,* receiving a Ph.D. in 1908. For Commons, Andrews was one of the best students he had ever supervised. Since Commons was active in the American Association for Labor Legislation (AALL), Andrews followed him into the organization, becoming its executive secretary in 1909. Andrews held that position for the rest of his life, transforming the AALL from an academic organization studying labor and social problems to a strong lobbying organization demanding labor standards legislation, workmen's compensation, health insurance, and old age pensions. Between 1910 and 1942, Andrews also edited the AALL's journal—the *American Labor Legislation Review.* Along with Paul Kellogg's* *Survey,* it was the most influential publication in the social work field. When the New Deal passed the Social Security Act of 1935 and the National Labor Relations Act of 1935, the AALL lost some of its momentum because it had achieved many of its aims. John Andrews stayed with the organization until his death on January 4, 1943. (Clarke Chambers, *Seedtime of Reform: American Social Service and Social Action, 1918–1933,* 1963; *New York Times,* January 5, 1943.)

ANNENBERG, MOSES LOUIS. Moses Louis Annenberg was born February 11, 1875, in Kalwischen, East Prussia, to a German-Jewish family. He immigrated to the United States in 1885 and lived in Chicago. Desperately poor, Annenberg worked as a bartender, Western Union messenger, and laborer in a livery stable; in 1900, he began to sell subscriptions to the *Evening American,* a Hearst newspaper. He was so successful that when William Randolph Hearst* started a morning paper, the *Examiner,* in Chicago in 1904, Annenberg was named head of circulation. Annenberg was ruthlessly competitive, even given to violence, in trying to drive other morning newspapers out of business. In 1919 Hearst brought Annenberg to New York to become circulation manager for the entire Hearst chain. When Hearst acquired the *New York Mirror* in 1924, he named Annenberg president. Annenberg left the Hearst enterprises to establish his own business empire, one built upon the *Daily Racing Form* and the *New York Morning Telegram,* both racing newspapers, and a wire service which supplied information on horse races all over the country. By 1930 his Nationwide News Service had a monopoly on the business. In 1934 he established the *Miami Tribune* and in 1936 purchased the *Philadelphia Inquirer.* In 1940 Annenberg was convicted of evading more than $5 million in income taxes, and he spent two years in a federal prison. He died on July 24, 1942, several weeks after being released from prison. (Gaeton Fonzi, *Annenberg*, 1970; *New York Times*, July 25, 1942.)

ANTI-DEFAMATION LEAGUE. The Anti-Defamation League (ADL) of B'nai B'rith was founded in 1913 by Sigmund Livingston. Livingston served as president of the ADL for the next thirty-three years, always campaigning to stop the negative stereotyping of Jews in the press, radio, movies, and vaudeville. At the same time, the ADL was committed to fair treatment and individual civil rights for all Americans, regardless of race, color, religion, or national origins. During the 1920s, the Anti-Defamation League campaigned against the Ku Klux Klan,* anti-Semitism, the Red Scare,* and immigration restriction, especially the quota-based National Origins Act of 1924.* The ADL also spent a great deal of energy fighting the "Protocols of the Elders of Zion," an anti-Semitic document claiming there was a global Jewish conspiracy to take over the world. The ADL correctly showed that the "Protocols" had actually been forged by tsarist secret police in 1905 to justify a Russian anti-Jewish campaign. When Adolf Hitler came to power in Germany in 1933, the ADL vigorously opposed all Nazi anti-Semitic propaganda. (Oscar Handlin, *Danger in Discord: Origins of Anti-Semitism in the United States,* 1948: Carey McWilliams, *A Mask for Privilege: Anti-Semitism in America,* 1948.)

ANTI-SALOON LEAGUE OF AMERICA. The Anti-Saloon League of America was founded in 1895 by an interdenominational group of Protestant and Roman Catholic clerics, including Reverand Howard Russell, Reverend A. J. Kynett, Methodist Bishop Luther B. Wilson, and Roman Catholic Archbishop John Ireland. The Anti-Saloon League was a one-issue lobbying group totally committed to prohibition.* The league was led by the Reverend Purley A. Baker between 1903 and 1924 and the Reverend Francis Scott McBride* between 1924 and 1933. Enormously successful, the Anti-Saloon League had a unique slogan— "Agitation, Legislation, and Law Enforcement"—as it campaigned against alcohol in the United States. It had branch offices in every state and in most large cities. Most of its financial backing came from evangelical churches, especially in the South. The Anti-Saloon League played a central role in getting Congress to pass the Eighteenth Amendment* in 1917 and in securing ratification of the amendment in 1920. The league also saw to it that Congress passed the Volstead Act of 1919* and the Jones Act of 1929, which imposed more severe fines and jail sentences for bootlegging liquor. During the election of 1928,* the league endorsed Herbert Hoover's* candidacy because he had upheld prohibition and because Democratic candidate Al Smith* had openly called for repeal. But it was the Great Depression that doomed prohibition and the Anti-Saloon League. The financial resources dried up, and they failed to stop the election of Franklin D. Roosevelt* or the ratification of the Twenty-First Amendment.* The Anti-Saloon declined in membership and in 1933 split into different factions. (Norman

H. Clark, *Deliver Us from Evil: An Interpretation of American Prohibition*, 1976; J. Austin Kerr, *Organized for Prohibition: A New History of the Anti-Saloon League*, 1985; Peter Odegard, *Pressure Politics: The Story of the Anti-Saloon League*, 1928.)

ARBUCKLE, ROSCOE "FATTY." Roscoe "Fatty" Arbuckle was born on March 24, 1887, in Smith Center, Kansas, and was raised in Indiana. His mother died when he was a child, and his father abandoned him shortly thereafter. Arbuckle began to sing and dance at a local theater, impersonating women and black minstrels, and he developed a slapstick comedy routine. Arbuckle performed in vaudeville and then made it into silent films, becoming one of the Keystone Cops, an associate of Charlie Chaplin,* and the quintessential hilarious fat man. By 1920 he was commanding a salary of $1,000 a day. His own rise to fame paralleled the rise of Hollywood—the public's fascination with film stories as well as their revulsion from the dizzying stories of wealth, power, and sex. Groups like the Women's Vigilance Committee began calling for censorship of Hollywood, and Arbuckle found himself the symbol for all of America's misgivings about life in the 1920s.

On September 5, 1921, at the St. Francis Hotel in San Francisco, Arbuckle sponsored a party on behalf of a fashion designer. Virginia Rappe, a guest at the party, drank heavily, removed some of her clothing, and went into Arbuckle's bathroom to vomit. Rappe died several days later in a San Francisco hospital, and Arbuckle was charged with manslaughter in her death—that he had raped her with a coke bottle. The newspapers of William Randolph Hearst* plastered the stories all over the front pages for months, and circulation rose dramatically. Arbuckle stood trial three times for the alleged crime. During those trials, it became clear that Virginia Rappe had a history of prostitution and had had five abortions between the ages of fourteen and sixteen. The first two juries could not reach a verdict, and the third acquitted Arbuckle. But by that time his career was ruined. Unjustly, Fatty Arbuckle had become the nation's infamous symbol for the decadence of Hollywood values and the self-doubts America was experiencing in the 1920s. Fatty Arbuckle died on June 29, 1933. (David Yallop, *The Day the Cheering Stopped: The True Story of Fatty Arbuckle*, 1976.)

ARMOUR, JONATHAN OGDEN. J. Ogden Armour was born on November 11, 1863, in Milwaukee, Wisconsin, to the wealthy meat-packing family which had founded Armour & Company. Armour attended Yale for several years in the early 1880s but soon joined the family firm. When his father Philip died in 1901, J. Ogden Armour assumed management of the firm, and, during the next twenty years, corporate sales increased from $200 million a year to more than $1 billion. Armour stepped down as chief executive officer in 1923 at a time when the company employed more than 40,000 people. J. Ogden Armour died in London on August 16, 1927. (J. C. Carroll, *Armour and His Times*, 1938; *New York Times*, August 17, 1927.)

ARMSTRONG, LOUIS. Louis Armstrong was born in New Orleans, Louisiana, on July 4, 1900. A gifted musician, he learned to play the bugle, trumpet, and clarinet before he was fifteen years old, and in 1917 he became a professional musician with King Ory's band. By 1922, Armstrong was playing the coronet with the King Oliver Band in Chicago. He formed his own band in 1925 in Chicago, and, at the same time, he switched from the coronet to the trumpet. After completing a 1925 tour of the United States, Armstrong took his group to Europe, where he played the Palladium in London and took England by storm. Known as "Satchmo," Armstrong became the leading jazz musician in the United States.

Jazz was a musical tradition developed by blacks in New Orleans in the late nineteenth century. Unlike other music, which confined a performer to the restrictions of a written score, jazz placed a premium on improvisation. Although a jazz musician may use written music to provide a basic theme, he or she extends it through syncopation, chord changes, addition of notes into the basic melodic structure, or alternations of melodic variations. Jazz musicians will manipulate the basic conflict between a regular, ongoing beat and a performer's personal rhythmic expressions. Musicologists view jazz as a uniquely American contribution to modern music and Louis Armstrong as its most adept practitioner. From the mid-1920s until his death in July 1971, Louis Armstrong epitomized the jazz tradition in the United States. (James L. Collier, *Louis Armstrong: An America Genius,* 1983.)

ARTICLE X. Article X was part of the covenant of the League of Nations* which called for collective security to stop aggression. Opponents of the league in the United States Senate argued that Article X would supersede the congressional war-making power and involve America in wars all over the globe. In response, President Woodrow Wilson* argued that Article X imposed only a moral, not a legal, obligation on the United States. Article X was an important reason for the United States Senate not ratifying the Treaty of Versailles and bringing the country into the League of Nations. (Thomas A. Bailey, *Woodrow Wilson and the Great Betrayal,* 1945; Warren F. Kuehl, *Seeking World Order: The United States and World Organization to 1920,* 1969; John C. Vinson, *Referendum for Isolation: Defeat of Article Ten of the League of Nations Covenant,* 1971.)

ASH CAN PAINTERS. By the early twentieth century, American literature was coming to reflect the naturalistic themes of people like Theodore Dreiser,* and that trend manifested itself in art with the appearance of the Ash Can School. Centered at first in Philadelphia's Pennsylvania Academy and later in New York City, the Ash Can School emphasized democratic art and exploring the everyday life of ordinary people, especially those living in the new urban centers. They were led by Robert Henri (*Laughing Children* and *The Masquerade Dance).* The school included such other painters as William Glackens (*Chez Mouquin*), Everett

Shinn (*London Hippodrome*), George Luks (*The Wrestlers* and *Hester Street*), George Bellows* (*Stag at Star Key's*), and John Sloan (*The Haymarket*). By the 1920s the Ash Can School had become recognized as one of the prominent trends in American art. (Milton W. Brown et al., *American Art,* 1979.)

ASSOCIATION AGAINST THE PROHIBITION AMENDMENT. Although the Association Against the Prohibition Amendment (AAPA) began meeting informally in 1918 during the ratification process for the Eighteenth Amendment,* it was not formally organized until 1920. Its founder was William H. Stayton, a former naval captain with conservative political views. The major political philosophy of the AAPA was that prohibition* was dangerous—not because it outlawed alcohol, but because it represented a centralizing force which destroyed state and local rights. By 1926 the AAPA had a membership of more than 700,000 people in twenty-five states, and it focused most of its energy on lobbying activities. John J. Raskob,* chairman of the Democratic National Committee, and Jouett Shouse, head of the Democratic National Committee's executive council, were prominent members of the AAPA. Shouse became head of the association in 1932 and campaigned for the election of Franklin D. Roosevelt.* After the Democratic landslide of 1932, the AAPA pressured Congress for approval of the Twenty-First Amendment* and for legalization of beer and wine with less than 3.2 percent alcohol content. The AAPA version of the Twenty-First Amendment was the one passed, and twenty-five states used AAPA instructions for ratification. The day after the Twenty-First Amendment was ratified, the AAPA directors formally dissolved the organization. Many of them, however, later joined the American Liberty League, an anti–New Deal group, when they became convinced that Franklin D. Roosevelt was doing more than any other individual in American history to destroy state and local initiatives. (David E. Kyvig, "In Revolt against Prohibition: The Association Against the Prohibition Amendment and the Movement for Repeal, 1919–1933," Ph.D. dissertation, Northwestern University, 1971.)

ASSOCIATIONALISM. Between 1870 and 1920, virtually every section of American society, in trying to cope with the Industrial Revolution, began to look outward and to form certain communities of interest. In less than fifty years, American workers, for example, had organized and replaced the feeble Knights of Labor with the more formidable railroad brotherhoods, the United Mine Workers, and the American Federation of Labor. During the same half century, a new middle class had emerged: doctors, lawyers, professors, teachers, and social workers all organized into professional associations. The American Bar Association, the American Medical Association, the American Historical Association, the National Education Association, and the National Conference on Social Work sought to represent the interests of their constituents. Finally, businessmen formed trade associations, chambers of commerce, and marketing cooperatives to enhance their position in the national economy. "Associationalism" was the term given to the organizational revolution which swept through the United States.

By the 1920s, a number of prominent Americans, especially Secretary of Commerce Herbert Hoover,* saw the formation of the private associations as the dawn of a new, more rational economic system that synthesized individual entrepreneurship and corporate enterprise. Each of the associations, although confined to a particular sector of the economy, had a national perspective and realized that the structural dynamics of the modern economy required cooperative action among like-minded groups. With their faith in scientific management, technology, precision, efficiency, and order, the associations could eliminate destructive competition, enhance research and development, and improve productivity. Finally, the associational movement provided a form of self-regulation to the economy. In emphasizing professional standards, ethical codes of conduct, and rational problem solving, the private associations were self-disciplining and self-improving, and as they policed themselves internally they contributed to social harmony and reduced the need for government intervention. There was no need for an oppressive regulatory state; instead, the federal government would promote economic prosperity by mediating disputes between the major interest groups, providing reliable statistical data for corporate use, and promoting the formation of more and more associations. Associationalism seemed a perfect solution to the challenges of the modern economy: Individual freedom and entrepreneurial enterprise would survive, and voluntary self-regulation of a national economy would continue automatically. (Ellis W. Hawley, "Herbert Hoover, the Commerce Secretariat, and the Vision of an 'Associative State,' " *Journal of American History* 61 [June 1974], 116–40.)

ASSOCIATIVE STATE. See ASSOCIATIONALISM

ASTAIRE, ADELE. Adele Astaire was born on September 10, 1898, in Omaha, Nebraska. Along with her younger brother Fred,* Adele Astaire went to New York in 1907 and spent the next ten years dancing for vaudeville studios. In 1917 the Astaires broke into Broadway as a dance team. They specialized in exhibition ballroom dancing, and producers used their talents in a variety of Broadway shows during the 1920s. Fred and Adele Astaire were featured in *Over the Top* (1917), *The Passing Show of 1918* (1918), *Apple Blossoms* (1919), *The Love Letter* (1921), *For Goodness Sake* (1922), *The Bunch and Judy* (1922), *Lady, Be Good* (1924), *Funny Face* (1927), *Smiles* (1930), and *Band Wagon* (1931). Adele Astaire retired in 1932. She died in Arizona on January 25, 1981. (Fred Astaire, *Steps in Time,* 1967; Barbara Naomi Cohen-Stratyner, *Biographical Dictionary of Dance,* 1982.)

ASTAIRE, FREDERICK AUSTERLITZ. Fred Astaire was born on May 10, 1899, in Omaha, Nebraska. With his older sister Adele,* Astaire went to New York in 1907 and spent ten years dancing before vaudeville audiences. The two

Astaires began performing their ballroom and tap dancing routines on Broadway in 1917 and appeared in a number of popular shows. After Adele retired in 1932, Fred began a film career which teamed him with a series of dancing partners, including Ginger Rogers in the 1940s, Eleanor Powell and Rita Hayworth in the 1950s, and Lucille Bremer, Cyd Charisse, and Barrie Chase in the 1960s and 1970s. Later in his career, he performed in several films which did not require his dancing skills. By the 1980s, Astaire was one of the most beloved figures in Hollywood. He died on June 22, 1987. (Fred Astaire, *Steps in Time,* 1967; Stanley Green and Burt Goldblatt, *Starring Fred Astaire,* 1973; *New York Times,* June 23, 1987.)

AUTOMOBILE. During the 1920s, the automobile became for the first time a mass consumption product in the United States. Henry Ford's* low-priced, assembly-line produced Model T, introduced in 1908, had been copied by other automobile manufacturers, and suddenly the automobile had become affordable to millions of families. The use of installment buying* also made the purchase of an automobile a real possibility for most families. First introduced in 1918, installment buying accounted for 70 percent of new car sales by 1922. The results were astounding. New car sales increased from 4,100 in 1900 to 63,500 in 1908, 461,500 in 1913, 1,951,000 in 1920, and 4,500,000 in 1929. The number of registered automobiles in the United States increased from 9,200,000 in 1920 to 26,700,000 in 1929.

The economic and social impacts of the "car culture" were inestimable. Production of steel, glass, rubber, and petroleum boomed to supply the apparently insatiable demands of the automobile factories in the early 1920s. Road and highway construction was unprecedented, bringing full employment to civil engineers, architects, and construction workers. New industries appeared to take advantage of the mobility enjoyed by Americans who owned automobiles. Hotels, motels, service stations, car repair shops, and resorts all boomed, providing jobs to hundreds of thousands of Americans. By 1925, the automobile industry was number one in the United States in terms of the gross value of its product and number three in terms of its export value. It had become the backbone of twentieth-century American economy.

The social impact of the automobile was no less dramatic. What can only be described as a "car culture" appeared in the United States during the 1920s. Like no other product in the history of the world, the automobile provided freedom to individuals to go when and where they wanted. Residential patterns changed. Families were able to relocate to less crowded, less polluted suburbs, with workers commuting to the jobs; isolated school districts were able to consolidate with larger districts to save money and offer broader curricula; farmers in rural areas were able to conduct their personal financial business in larger towns and cities, eroding the economic foundation of small banks and general stores; and young people were able to travel widely, altering dating patterns and often eliminating chaperons. Once a luxury, the automobile in the 1920s came to be seen as a necessity by most Americans, and the country would never be the same again. (James J. Flink, *The Car Culture,* 1975.)

AVERY, SEWELL LEE. Sewell Avery was born on November 4, 1873, in Saginaw, Michigan. He attended the Michigan Military Academy and in 1894 earned a law degree from the University of Michigan. Sewell immediately went to work for his father's firm, a gypsum company, and in 1901 he formed the United States Gypsum Company. Sewell served as president of U.S. Gypsum until 1936, building it into one of the largest construction products companies in the world. In 1932, Avery was named chairman of the board of the Montgomery, Ward and Company. Sewell helped save the company from bankruptcy in the 1930s, at the same time bitterly opposing the New Deal and union organization activities. During World War II he refused to obey government orders that the company negotiate with the United Mail Order, Warehouse and Retail Employees Union, and eventually the federal government seized control of Montgomery, Ward. Avery stepped down from the chairmanship of Montgomery, Ward in 1955. He died on October 31, 1960. (*Current Biography,* June 1944; *New York Times,* November 1, 1960.)

AWALT, FRANCIS GLOYD. Francis G. Awalt was born in Laurel, Maryland, in 1895. He graduated from the Baltimore Polytechnic Institute in 1914 and then earned a law degree from the University of Maryland in 1917. Awalt practiced law in Baltimore, and between 1920 and 1927 he served as a special assistant to Secretary of the Treasury Andrew Mellon.* At the time, he was also general counsel to the office of the comptroller of the currency. During the Herbert Hoover* administration, Awalt was deputy comptroller of the currency, and he played a conspicuous role in the banking crisis of 1932–1933 in his role as acting comptroller of the currency. Awalt blamed mismanagement, low capitalization, and lax state regulation for the mess the banking system found itself in during the 1920s and early 1930s, and it was Awalt who urged a nationwide banking holiday during the closing days of the Hoover administration. After Franklin D. Roosevelt* was inaugurated president early in March 1933, Awalt stayed on in Washington to advise the new administration on how to reopen the thousands of banks closed by the banking holiday Roosevelt imposed. Francis G. Awalt died on December 30, 1966. (Francis G. Awalt, "Recollections of the Banking Crisis of 1933," *Business History Review* 43 [Autumn 1969], 347–71; *New York Times,* December 31, 1966.)

B

BABBITTRY. Taken from the title of Sinclair Lewis's* 1922 novel *Babbitt,* the term ''Babbittry'' became synonymous during and after the 1920s with the parochialism, stodginess, crass materialism, and smug complacency of small-town business life in America, typifying the ''chamber of commerce'' mentality. (Elizabeth Stevenson, *Babbitts & Bohemians: The American 1920s,* 1967.)

BABY ROSE MARIE. ''Baby Rose Marie'' was the first national child star of radio, debuting on NBC radio* in 1926 when she was three. Born in New York City in 1923, Rose Marie Curley's voice had an amazingly adult sound to it which delighted radio audiences. In 1931 she began to appear on the ''Rudy Vallee* Show,'' and in 1932 she had her own fifteen-minute Sunday show. The show had faded by 1934, but she was back in 1938 with another radio show. Her adult years have been spent as a standup comedienne and as a supporting actress in the popular ''Dick Van Dyke Show'' of the 1960s. (John Dunning, *Tune in Yesterday: The Ultimate Encyclopedia of Old-Time Radio, 1925–1976,* 1976.)

BACHE, JULES SEMON. Jules S. Bache was born on November 9, 1861, in New York City. After studying at the Charles Institute in New York and in Frankfort, Germany, Bache returned to the United States and worked for a time in his father's glass manufacturing plant. In 1880 he went to work as a cashier for Leopold Cohn and Company, his uncle's brokerage firm. He became a partner in the firm in 1886 and the president in 1892, the year his uncle retired. That year he renamed the firm J. S. Bache and Company. During the next generation, Bache had the company form branches throughout the country to serve the needs of small investors, building the business into one of the most successful brokerage houses in the country. Early in 1929 Bache decided the stock market had entered a dangerously speculative period, so he reduced his volume of brokers' loans by more than $200 million during that year. When the stock market collapsed late in 1929, Bache's firm survived easily. That year he was also named vice-president of Chrysler Corporation. J. S. Bache died on March 24, 1944. (*Current Biography,* May 1944; *New York Times,* March 25, 1944.)

BAILEY, BILL. Bill Bailey was born on May 25, 1878, in Richmond, Virginia. A protégé of Bill "Bojangles" Robinson,* Bailey became one of the most well-known black tap dancers of his time. He debuted with Robinson's vaudeville group in 1908 and became a headliner on the black vaudeville circuit, using "Bill Bailey Won't You Please Come Home" as his theme song. During the 1930s, Bailey performed in a number of films with Robinson, including such Shirley Temple films as *The Little Colonel* (1935), *Dimples* (1936), and *Rebecca of Sunnybrook Farm* (1938). Bill Bailey died on November 25, 1949. (Barbara Naomi Cohen-Stratyner, *Biographical Dictionary of Dance,* 1982.)

***BAILEY v. DREXEL FURNITURE COMPANY* (259 U.S. 20).** In 1922, the Supreme Court handed down its decision in the *Bailey* v. *Drexel Furniture Company* case, and it became a leading constitutional symbol in the use of federal taxing authority to regulate child labor. During the progressive period, a number of states had outlawed child labor; in the process, those states without such legislation, especially in the South, acquired competitive advantages in labor costs. Northern manufacturers began demanding federal legislation to equalize labor standards throughout the country, and in 1916 Congress passed the Child Labor Act. Known as the Keating-Owen Act, the law forbade the interstate shipment of products of child labor, defining child labor in nonagricultural industries as production by people less than fourteen years of age. In 1918 the Supreme Court, in *Hammer* v. *Dagenhart,** had overturned the law on the grounds that it violated Tenth Amendment guarantees of states' rights. Congress responded with the Child Labor Tax Act of 1919, which imposed a 10 percent tax on the profits of businesses employing workers under the age of fourteen.

Drexel Furniture Company received a tax bill from the Internal Revenue Service for employing a boy under fourteen. The company paid the tax under protest and sued in the federal courts. In 1922, the Supreme Court heard the case of *Bailey* v. *Drexel Furniture Company* and by an 8 to 1 decision found in favor of the company. Chief Justice William Howard Taft* wrote the majority opinion arguing again that the measure violated Tenth Amendment civil rights guarantees. Binding child labor legislation had to wait for the New Deal of the 1930s, when changes in personnel on the Supreme Court gave the federal government more latitude in social and economic legislation. (Donald E. Anderson, *William Howard Taft,* 1973; Alpheus Thomas Mason, *The Supreme Court from Taft to Warren,* 1958.)

BAKER, NEWTON DIEHL II. Newton D. Baker was born on December 3, 1871, in Martinsburg, West Virginia. He attended the Episcopal High School near Alexandria, Virginia, and graduated from Johns Hopkins in 1892. While at Johns Hopkins, he took a class from Woodrow Wilson,* who periodically lectured there, and lived in the same boarding house where Wilson stayed during his visits to Baltimore. Baker received a law degree from Washington and Lee University in 1894. After a brief period of practicing law in Martinsburg, Baker took a job in Washington, D.C., as private secretary to Democratic Congressman William L. Wilson of West Virginia, who was postmaster general in the second Grover Cleveland administration. Baker lost that job in 1897 when the Republicans took over the White House. He returned to law practice. In 1899 Baker moved his practice to Cleveland, Ohio.

In Cleveland, Baker became involved in local Democratic politics and supported the progressive reforms of Mayor Tom Johnson. Baker became city solicitor under Johnson in 1901 and remained there until 1912, when he won the mayoralty race. He had also been a vigorous supporter of Woodrow Wilson that year. Four years later, Wilson named Baker as secretary of war in his cabinet, a position he held until 1921. During the 1920s, Baker advocated the entry of the United States into the World Court* and League of Nations,* and, after the defeat of John W. Davis* in 1924, Baker became a prominent figure in Democratic presidential politics, frequently mentioned in the same company as Al Smith* and Franklin D. Roosevelt* as a possible candidate. A moderate on domestic policy and an internationalist in foreign affairs, he was active in party affairs during the 1920s. With the onset of the Great Depression, he began giving some reluctant thought to running for the presidency, but his interests had shifted from domestic to foreign policy over the years, and he did not project a clear public image on economic questions. In 1932 Baker assumed the role of dark horse candidate, but he could not stop Franklin D. Roosevelt's nomination. Baker campaigned for Roosevelt, but he found the New Deal disturbing. He was too much a Cleveland Democrat—committed to sound money, fiscal conservatism, tariff reduction, and small government. Newton D. Baker died of heart failure on December 25, 1937. (C. H. Carmer, *Newton D. Baker: A Biography,* 1961.)

BALCH, EMILY GREENE. Emily Balch was born on January 8, 1867, in Jamaica Plain, Massachusetts, to a prominent Boston family. She graduated from Bryn Mawr in 1889 with a degree in economics and sociology. She met Jane Addams,* who became Balch's role model, at a social work conference in 1892. Following Addams's lead, Balch founded Denison House, a settlement, in Boston late in 1892. By that time, Balch was a confirmed progressive and social worker, with special interests in the needs of poor working-class people. She studied economics at Radcliffe and at the University of Chicago between 1892 and 1896, and then joined the staff of Wellesley College, where she taught until 1918. She specialized in economics and immigration, and in 1910 she published *Our Slavic Fellow Citizens,* a classic in immigration history.

After World War I, Emily Balch dedicated her life to the world peace movement. At a conference in Zurich in 1919, Balch played a central role in the creation of the Women's International League for Peace and Freedom. She was elected its first international secretary and editor of its journal. Balch served in that position between 1919 and 1922 and again between 1934 and 1935. She spent the rest of her life travelling the world on behalf of world peace and won the Nobel Peace Prize in 1946. Emily Balch died on January 9, 1961. (*New York Times*, January 10, 1961; Mercedes M. Randall, *Improper Bostonian: Emily Green Balch*, 1964.)

BALDWIN, ROGER NASH. Roger Baldwin was born on January 21, 1884, in Wellesley, Massachusetts, to an old New England family. From his childhood, Baldwin's family was interested in social reform, and he grew up amidst discussions of progressivism, individual rights, and liberty. He graduated from Harvard in 1904 and earned a master's degree in anthropology there in 1905. Baldwin moved to St. Louis, headed a settlement house there, and became head of the local juvenile probation office. Between 1910 and 1917, Baldwin was executive secretary of the St. Louis Civic League, which investigated charges of political corruption. Baldwin's interest in civil liberties was stimulated when St. Louis police refused to allow Margaret Sanger* to give a birth control lecture in 1916. In 1917, Baldwin became director of the American Union Against Militarism, and as part of that he established the National Civil Liberties Union, which became known as the American Civil Liberties Union* (ACLU) in 1920. He spent a year in prison in 1918 for refusing to sign up for the draft, and upon his release Baldwin worked for a while as a labor organizer for the Industrial Workers of the World.

Baldwin then dedicated himself to the work of the ACLU, which he headed until 1950. During the 1920s, the ACLU worked to end censorship of James Joyce's *Ulysses,* helped in the defense and appeals of Nicola Sacco* and Bartolomeo Vanzetti,* opposed the Red Scare,* financed Clarence Darrow's* 1925 defense of John Scopes* in the famous "Monkey Trial," and secured the rights of Jehovah's Witness children not to salute the flag. The ACLU was also a vigorous defender of labor union rights. During the 1920s, Baldwin participated in a number of leftwing united front organizations promoting Soviet interests, but, during the 1930s, Baldwin became increasingly disillusioned with them. Baldwin also opposed the incarceration of 110,000 Japanese Americans during World War II. He retired from the ACLU in 1950. Roger Baldwin died on August 26, 1981. (Peggy Lamson, *Roger Baldwin,* 1976; *New York Times,* August 27, 1981.)

BALLANTINE, ARTHUR ATWOOD. Arthur A. Ballantine was born on August 3, 1883, in Oberlin, Ohio. He graduated from Havard in 1904 and took a law degree there in 1907. Ballantine practiced law in Boston, specializing in tax issues, and in 1918 he became solicitor of internal revenue for the federal government. He served as an economic consultant to the Joint Committee of Congress on Internal Revenue Taxation in 1927, and in 1931 President Herbert

Hoover* named him assistant secretary of the treasury. He served there a year before Hoover named him undersecretary of the treasury in 1932. Ballantine played a critically important role in the banking crisis of 1932–1933, advising Herbert Hoover and then staying on for several weeks after the inauguration of Franklin D. Roosevelt* to advise the new president on how to deal with the crisis. Ballantine strongly urged a nationwide banking holiday, which Roosevelt declared two days after entering the White House, and federal legislation allowing for government investment in troubled banks, which Roosevelt submitted to Congress during his first week in office. Ballantine then returned to private law practice. He died on October 10, 1960. (Arthur Ballantine, "When All the Banks Closed," *Harvard Business Review* 26 [1948], 129–43; *New York Times,* October 11, 1960.)

BANKING. By 1920 banking in the United States had become a haphazard mix of competing institutions. In addition to over 30,000 separate commercial banks, thousands of savings banks, building and loan associations, investment companies, private banks, industrial banks, credit unions, and finance companies existed, complicating the picture. Marked by instability and irregularity, the money market consisted of nearly 50,000 separate units, almost all of which served limited constituencies. The number of banks at the beginning of the 1920s far exceeded the nation's credit requirements. In rural areas especially, state banking authorities had been far too liberal in granting bank charters. Many communities with fewer than five hundred people had two or more banks that competed for the same clientele, and, not surprisingly, they failed to earn enough from their assets to survive. Suspensions occurred most often in states with low population–bank ratios. The country was alarmingly overbanked, particularly in rural communities, and the United States was about to reap the disastrous harvest of its disintegrated money market.

Rural banks suffered from other problems as well. Besides undercapitalization and lack of sound management, demographic changes severely weakened them. Urban growth was depopulating the countryside at the same time that the automobile was making it more convenient for people to shop and bank in larger towns or cities. Equally serious for rural banks was the rise of chain and mail-order department stores that drove country stores out of business and caused the banks to lose some of their best customers. Rural banks slowly lost their clientele to more heavily populated areas. Also, the agricultural depression of the 1920s hurt rural banks. With the revival of European agriculture in 1919, farm prices in the United States collapsed, forcing many farmers to default on wartime agricultural loans. Banks seized land as collateral, but since the land had lost much of its value, the banks saw a serious erosion in their assets. Between 1921 and 1929, more than 5,400 rural banks failed in the United States. Nearly 4,000 others had to merge with more stable institutions.

When the stock market crashed in 1929, banks throughout the country faced a tidal wave of panic-stricken depositors wanting their cash. In 1929, 641 commercial banks failed in the United States, and that number increased to 1,350 failures in 1930 and 1,700 in 1931, the year England abandoned the gold standard. Banks were stuck with poor agricultural loans, weakened assets because of catastrophic declines in securities prices, and bad business loans from companies pressed to the brink of bankruptcy by the Great Depression. President Herbert Hoover* tried to deal with the crisis by having Congress create the Reconstruction Finance Corporation* (RFC) in January 1932, but, despite $2 billion in loans, the RFC was unable to protect the banking system from collapse. In the late winter of 1933, a chain reaction of panics and failures swept throughout the country, virtually closing every bank in the United States. When President Franklin D. Roosevelt* declared a bank holiday on March 6, 1933, he was just formalizing what the economy had already done. The money markets were in a state of total disarray. (James S. Olson, *Herbert Hoover and the Reconstruction Finance Corporation, 1931–1933,* 1977.)

BARA, THEDA. Theda Bara was born Theodosia Goodman in Cincinnati, Ohio, on July 29, 1890. Bara first appeared on Broadway in a 1908 production known as *The Devil.* In 1915 she was cast by director Frank Powell as ''The Vampire'' in *A Fool There Was.* Her portrayal of ''the vamp'' stuck with her throughout her career, and she played it again and again. The role of the vamp always meant a seductive female who attracted men and then humiliated and debased them. Bara was the first of the Hollywood-manufactured personalities: Publicity agents made up the story of her birth in the Sahara desert to an Egyptian princess and a French artist. Her stage name came from a rearrangement of the letters in ''death'' and ''Arab.'' Bara appeared in forty films between 1915 and 1919, and her publicity photographs always showed a pallid woman peering out of heavily darkened eyes. In some of the photos, the skeleton of a man she supposedly had eaten lay at her feet. By 1920 her film career had run its course, and audiences began to laugh at the sexual fantasies turned to camp. Bara played in one more film in 1926, a Stan Laurel comedy, but her career was finished. She died on April 7, 1955. (Majorie Rosen, *Popcorn Venus,* 1973; James Robert Parish, *The Fox Girls,* 1971.)

BARKLEY, ALBEN WILLIAM. Alben Barkley was born on November 24, 1877, in Grover County, Kentucky. He attended Emory College and the University of Virginia Law School, although he graduated from neither one of them. Barkley studied law privately and was admitted to the bar in 1901. He was elected county prosecuting attorney in 1905 and county judge in 1909. Barkley won election to the House of Representatives and served there between 1913 and 1927. During that term in the House, Barkley was a powerful advocate of the Eighteenth Amendment* and its enforcement, even though Kentucky had a large distilling industry. In 1926, Barkley won a seat in the United States Senate, and by that time the problems with prohibition* were becoming obvious to all but the most ideological observers, and Barkley was politically astute enough to realize that the temperance crusade was declining. In the Senate he did not pursue enforcement of the Eighteenth Amendment and easily went along with the Democratic Party's* decision in 1932 to sponsor the Twenty-First Amendment* repealing prohibition. Barkley went on to a distinguished career, serving as majority leader of the Senate between 1936 and 1947 and as vice-president of the United States under Harry S Truman between 1949 and 1953. He was re-elected to the Senate in 1954 and died on April 30, 1956. (Jane R.Barkley and F. S. Leighton, *I Married the Veep,* n.d.; *New York Times,* May 1, 1956.)

BARNES, JULIUS HOWLAND. Julius H. Barnes was born on February 2, 1873, in Little Rock, Arkansas. Barnes's family moved to Duluth, Minnesota, when he was still a child, and after graduating from high school Barnes went to work on the docks. Gradually he built up his own grain dealing, freight, and shipbuilding business. In 1910 he was made president of the wheat brokerage house of Wardell Ames, and the firm, renamed Barnes-Ames Company in 1914, was the largest grain exporter in the world. Barnes also established the Barnes-Duluth Shipbuilding Company and was president of several other construction and Great Lakes freight companies. During World War I, Barnes was president of the U.S. Food Administration's Grain Corporation. Between 1921 and 1924, Barnes served as president of the Chamber of Commerce* of the United States, where he promoted reduced taxation of corporations and the wealthy, the open shop movement,* high tariffs, and support of Republican candidates. Between 1929 and 1931 Barnes was chairman of the board of the Chamber of Commerce. He died on April 17, 1959. (*New York Times,* April 18, 1959.)

BARRYMORE, JOHN. John Barrymore was born John Sydney Blythe in Philadelphia, Pennsylvania, on February 15, 1882, to an illustrious American theatrical family. He acted in a number of Broadway plays in the early 1900s, and in 1913 he signed his first film contract as one of the Fox Players. After World War I, Barrymore became one of the country's matinee idols, known as "The Great Profile." His role in *Dr. Jekyll and Mr. Hyde* in 1920 made him an international star. Barrymore was associated with the Fox Players until 1922 when he signed with Warner Brothers; in 1926, he moved to United Artists. By 1932, when he joined MGM, Barrymore was commanding $150,000 per film. He had a resonant voice which made his transition to sound films an easy one. A heavy drinker and a womanizer, Barrymore's health began to decline in the 1930s. At the time of his death on May 29, 1942, he had made more than sixty films. (James Card, *The Films of John Barrymore,* 1969; *New York Times,* May 30, 1942; Alma Power-Waters, *John Barrymore, The Legend and the Man,* 1941.)

BARRYMORE, LIONEL. Lionel Barrymore was born Lionel Blythe in Philadelphia, Pennsylvania, on April 28, 1878, to one of the nation's most illustrious theatrical families. He studied at Seton Hall University and the Art Students

League in New York, and he starred in his first film in 1911 *(The Battle)*. In the 1920s, Barrymore starred in dozens of films, including D. W. Griffith's *America* and *Sadie Thompson*. Instead of the dashing ladies' man, however, Barrymore's career in the 1920s took a turn to character roles playing older men. Barrymore won an Academy Award as best actor in 1931 for his part in *A Free Soul*. In the 1930s and 1940s, Barrymore endeared himself to American film audiences as Judge Hardy in the Andy Hardy films and as Dr. Gillespie in the Dr. Kildare films. When he died on November 15, 1954, Barrymore had completed more than 300 film roles in his career. (Lionel Barrymore, *We Barrymores*, 1951; James Hotsilibas-Davis, *The Barrymores: The Royal Family in Hollywood*, 1981; *New York Times*, November 16, 1954.)

BARTON, BRUCE. Bruce Barton was born on August 5, 1886, in Robbins, Tennessee. He graduated from Amherst College in 1907 and went into magazine journalism, working for the *Home Herald* in Chicago and then as editor of *Housekeeper*. In 1912 Barton went to work for the P. F. Collier and Son publishing house as an assistant sales manager; between 1914 and 1918, he served as editor of *Everyweek* magazine. Barton organized the advertising firm of Barton, Durstine and Osborn in 1919 and became its first president. Among Barton's creative accomplishments was the Betty Crocker image for General Mills. At the same time, he contributed widely as a free-lance writer for several popular magazines. Barton became a symbol of the business mentality of the 1920s when he wrote *The Man Nobody Knows* in 1925, which described Jesus Christ as the world's best salesman and as a first-class businessmen who surrounded himself with excellent executives—"the twelve apostles." To Barton, the spread of Christianity around the world was simply the result of excellent advertising and marketing activities. In 1936 Barton won a seat in Congress and became a bitter opponent of Franklin D. Roosevelt* and the New Deal. He left Congress in 1941. Bruce Barton died on July 5, 1967. (Bruce Barton, *The Man Nobody Knows*, 1925; *Current Biography*, February 1961; *New York Times*, July 6, 1967.)

BARUCH, BERNARD MANNES. Bernard M. Baruch was born on August 19, 1870, in Camden, South Carolina. Both of his parents were Jews—his father an immigrant from Germany who earned a medical degree in Virginia and his mother a descendent of Sephardic Jews who settled in South Carolina. The family moved to New York City in 1881. Baruch graduated from the City College of New York in 1889. After working at several jobs, Baruch joined A. A. Hausman and Company, a brokerage firm, as an office boy. He became a full partner in 1896. He parlayed a small investment into a million dollars by 1900, when he purchased a seat on the New York Stock Exchange. In his investments, Baruch specialized in copper, sulphur, gold, and rubber companies. Also interested in politics, Baruch was a generous contributor to Democratic causes and a major supporter of Woodrow Wilson* in the election of 1916. Wilson named

Baruch head of the War Industries Board in 1918, which put him in a position to supervise American industrial mobilization during the war. In the process, Baruch became one of the most influential Democrats in the country. Wilson also named him a member of the Supreme Economic Council which met at Versailles in 1919. During the 1920s, Baruch was active in politics and advised the American Farm Bureau Federation* and the United States Grain Growers Corporation. Between 1926 and 1932, Baruch had been a behind-the-scenes politician, helping to put together in Congress the Democratic-Republican coalition which passed the Reconstruction Finance Corporation* Act. According to many observers, especially Franklin D. Roosevelt,* Baruch "owned sixty congressmen." Baruch hoped to be named secretary of state in the Roosevelt administration in 1932, but it was not to be. The new president did not want any rivals in the administration. Instead, Baruch became an elder statesman, alarmed about the bureaucratic direction of the New Deal but resigned to it as a political necessity. Bernard Baruch died on June 20, 1965. (Jordan A. Schwarz, *The Speculator: Bernard M. Baruch in Washington, 1917–1965*, 1981.)

BASEBALL. The history of baseball in the 1920s began inauspiciously at best with revelations of the Black Sox scandal* of 1919 when several players on the Chicago White Sox conspired to lose the World Series to the Cincinnati Reds. Baseball was widely regarded as an American game symbolic of American values: pristine, pastoral, and competitive. When news of the Black Sox scandal hit the press in September 1920, in the midst of the Red Scare,* it precipitated an identity crisis for millions of Americans. In response, major league owners named Judge Kenesaw Mountain Landis* as baseball commissioner. He banned the guilty players from baseball for life and then ruled the game with an iron hand.

Some observers credit Landis with "saving" baseball, as if the Black Sox scandal would have destroyed the game. Americans are more resilient than that. Actually, baseball thrived as never before in the 1920s for three primary reasons. First, the decade was a difficult era culturally for the United States, a time of great social conflict over religion, race, ethnicity, and moral values. Baseball became a cultural currency on which all Americans related to one another.

Second, in 1922, the Supreme Court exempted baseball from the antitrust laws in the Baltimore Federal League antitrust suit against the National and American Leagues. A unanimous court ruled that baseball was not really a business and that its activities across state lines were only incidental. Baseball owners could then contract players for indefinite periods of time and conspire to prevent new leagues from entering the game. The court decision underwrote baseball's prosperity during the 1920s.

Third, and most important, George Herman "Babe" Ruth* transformed the techniques of the game. Until the 1920s, baseball was the game of "Ty" Cobb*—defense, base hits, and stolen bases. Ruth changed it all in 1919 when he hit twenty-nine home runs, the most ever in a single season, and an astonishing fifty-four home runs in 1920. The Yankees doubled their gate that year to 1,289,422 fans. The other owners got the message: In 1920, they outlawed spitballs and, in 1921, they required frequent changes of scuffed balls so that pitchers could not throw bizarre pitches. New technology also enabled a tighter winding of the internal woolen threads of the baseball and a "livelier" ball. The results were dramatic. In 1915 there were 384 home runs in the major leagues; that total had increased to 1,565 in 1930. Major league batting averages were 45 points higher in 1925 than they had been in 1915. Between 1911 and 1920, there had been 26,734 stolen bases; that total dropped to 13,759 between 1921 and 1930. Babe Ruth and home runs, not Mountain Landis, saved baseball in the 1920s and made it the national pastime. (Harold Seymour, *Baseball: The Golden Years*, 1971.)

BATHING BEAUTIES. One symbol of the sexual liberation of the 1920s was the change in swim wear for women and the appearance in movies and at the beach of the "bathing beauties." The term was used to describe women who had abandoned the traditional bathing suit—high necks, long sleeves, skirt, and ankle-length pantaloons—for the new form-fitting, low-neckline and low-back-line style with shoulder straps and a tiny skirt or shorts cut at the upper thigh. Many Americans found the new swimsuits scandalous, and, for a few years in the early 1920s, some women were arrested on grounds of indecent exposure. (Paul Sann, *The Lawless Decade*, 1957.)

BATHTUB GIN. During the years of prohibition,* the term "bathtub gin" was used to describe alcoholic beverages manufactured at home. (Paul Sann, *The Lawless Decade*, 1957.)

BAUER, CHARLES CHRISTIAN. Charles Bauer was born on November 17, 1881, in Springfield, Ohio. He went into the advertising business after high school, and in 1919 he became head of the Community Councils of New York. From 1922 to 1923 and from 1925 to 1929, Bauer served as executive director of the League of Nations Non-Partisan Association. Bauer was an admirer of Woodrow Wilson* and of his internationalism, and during the 1920s he actively campaigned for American participation in the League of Nations* and the World Court.* His leadership of the League of Nations Non-Partisan Association made it the leading internationalist organization in the country. He was dedicated to the peace movement, although he was not a doctrinaire pacifist. During World War II, Bauer was a strong advocate of the creation of a United Nations with active American participation. He died on March 15, 1947. (Charles De Benedetti, *Origins of the Modern American Peace Movement, 1915–1929*, 1979; *New York Times*, March 16, 1947.)

BEARD, CHARLES AUSTIN. Charles Beard was born on November 27, 1874, in Knightstown, Indiana. He received a bachelor's degree from DePauw University in 1898, and, after attending Oxford and Cornell, he earned his Ph.D. in history at Columbia in 1904. Between 1904 and 1917, he taught at Columbia, and in 1913 he wrote his epic *An Economic Interpretation of the Constitution,* which argued that the Founding Fathers had pecuniary interests at stake when they wrote the U.S. Constitution. A confirmed isolationist, Beard was uncomfortable with U.S. intervention into World War I, and in 1917 he resigned from the Columbia faculty when university trustees tried to stifle his criticism of the declaration of war. During the 1920s, Beard spoke widely against an activist foreign policy and condemned American participation in World War I. During the 1930s, he became even more outspoken, supporting the America First Committee and arguing after World War II that Franklin D. Roosevelt* had conspired with the Japanese to attack Pearl Harbor as a means of entering World War II with popular support. Charles Beard died on September 1, 1948. (Mary Beard, *The Making of Charles Beard,* 1955; Richard Hofstadter, *The Progressive Historians,* 1968.)

BEHN, HERNAND. See BEHN, SOSTHENES

BEHN, SOSTHENES. Sosthenes Behn was born on January 30, 1882, in St. Thomas, Virgin Islands. His older brother Hernand, with whom he had a lifelong business relationship, had been born on February 19, 1880. In 1906 the two brothers formed Behn Brothers, a brokerage house in Puerto Rico which financed sugar crops. When the sugar crop failed in 1914, Behn Brothers seized control of the Puerto Rican Telephone Company, which had been posted as collateral for one of their loans. They built the company into a stable enterprise and also purchased a half-interest in the Cuban Telephone Company of Havana, linking the two companies to each other by cable and to the mainland. In 1919 they formed the International Telephone and Telegraph Company (IT&T) to finance their cable expansion. With Hernand as president and Sosthenes as chairman of the board, IT&T expanded rapidly during the 1920s, reaching into thirty countries and increasing its assets from $38 million to $535 million. In 1922 they created a telephone system for Spain, and in 1925 they bought the International Western Electric company from American Telephone and Telegraph to serve their construction and maintenance needs. The company weathered the economic storm of the 1930s, but not without sustaining large losses, especially after the Spanish Civil War and the coming of World War II to Europe. Hernand Behn died on June 6, 1933, and his brother Sosthenes died on June 6, 1957. (Anthony Sampson, *The Sovereign State of I.T.&T.,* 1973.)

BELL, JAMES "COOL PAPA." James "Cool Papa" Bell was born on May 17, 1903, in Starkville, Mississippi. Bell moved with his four brothers to St. Louis in 1916, attended high school for two years, and then went to work in a packinghouse, playing sandlot baseball* on the side. In 1922 he signed a contract with the St. Louis Stars of the Negro National League. He played with the Stars until 1933, becoming very popular among black baseball fans in the United States. Between 1933 and 1946, Bell played for the Kansas City Monarchs, Homestead Grays, Chicago American Giants, and several Mexican and Dominican Republic teams. Bell was known for his speed as a baserunner and his ability to hit resulting in an average which frequently exceeded .400 for the 200–game Negro National League season. Bell scouted for several major league teams in the late 1940s and early 1950s, but then he settled down in Cleveland and worked as a night watchman until his retirement in 1970. He was inducted into the Hall of Fame in 1974. (Martin Appel and Burt Goldblatt, *Baseball's Best: The Hall of Fame Gallery,* 1980.)

BELLOWS, GEORGE WESLEY. George Wesley Bellows was born in Columbus, Ohio, on August 12, 1882. He graduated from Ohio State University in 1903 and then studied painting under Robert Henri in New York. Bellows pursued a realist style and became part of the Ash Can School* in American painting, emphasizing city life, crowds, and boxing, especially in *42 Kids* (1907) and *Stag at Sharkey's* (1907). Between 1910 and 1919, Bellows taught painting at the Art Students League in New York, and from 1919 to 1925, he taught at the Art Institute of Chicago. Bellows's later paintings included *Edith Cavell* (1918), *The Return of the Useless* (1918), and *The Pic-Nic* (1924). He died on January 8, 1925. (Milton W. Brown et al., *American Art,* 1979; *New York Times,* January 9, 1925.)

BENET, STEPHEN VINCENT. Stephen Vincent Benet was born on July 22, 1898, in Bethlehem, Pennsylvania. He graduated from Yale in 1919, by which time he had already published several books. Benet became known as the premier narrative poet of his time, as well as a skilled, if not gifted, novelist. His work had a special ability to evoke a diverse variety of American themes. In 1928, Benet won a Pulitzer Prize for his long poem *John Brown's Body.* His other books and collections of stories included *Heavens and Earth* (1920), *The Beginning of Wisdom* (1921), *Spanish Bayonet* (1926), *Ballads and Poems* (1931), *The Devil and Daniel Webster* (1937), and *Johnny Pye and the Fool-Killer* (1938). Stephen Vincent Benet died on March 13, 1943. (Charles A. Fenton, *Stephen Vincent Benet: The Life and Times of an American Man of Letters, 1898–1943,* 1958.)

BENNETT, FLOYD. See BYRD, RICHARD EVELYN

BERGER, VICTOR LUITPOLD. Victor Berger was born in Nieder-Rehbach, Austria, on February 28, 1860. He immigrated to the United States in 1878, worked at a variety of jobs, and moved to Milwaukee in 1880 where he taught German in the public schools. Berger then went into journalism, editing the

Milwaukee Daily Vorwaerts between 1892 and 1898. In 1900 Berger became editor of the *Social Democratic Herald,* which became a daily in 1911 and was renamed the *Milwaukee Leader.* Berger was an active socialist and, as a member of the International Typographical Union, was a critic of the conservatism of the American Federation of Labor.* Along with Eugene Debs,* Berger helped found the Social Democratic Party in 1897 and the Socialist Party of America* in 1901. He served on the executive council of the Socialist Party until 1923. In 1910, Berger became the first Socialist ever to be elected to the United States Congress, and, when World War I broke out, he was a bitter opponent of American intervention. Because of his opposition to the war, Congress refused to seat him in 1919. Berger was convicted under the Espionage Act in 1921 and sentenced to twenty years in prison, but the United States Supreme Court overturned the conviction. In 1922 Berger returned to Congress, and he was reelected in 1924 and 1926, but he lost his seat in the election of 1928.* Victor Berger died on August 7, 1929. (Sally M. Miller, *Victor Berger and the Promise of Constructive Socialism, 1910–1920,* 1973; *New York Times,* August 8, 1929; James Weinstein, *The Decline of American Socialism, 1912–1925,* 1967.)

BERKELEY, BUSBY. Busby Berkeley was born on November 29, 1895, in Los Angeles, California. His parents were both actors in travelling stock theater companies, so he was raised in show business. During World War II, Berkeley was an entertainment officer in the United States Army, and in 1918 he made his theatrical debut in New York in *The Man Who Came Back.* In the 1920s Berkeley began choreographing dance numbers, and he debuted as a dance director in *A Connecticut Yankee* in 1927. He developed a close professional relationship with Richard Rogers. In 1928 he performed in and staged *Present Arms* (1928), and was soon recognized as one of the best young choreographers in the country. Berkeley's work on *The International Revue* in 1930 brought him to the attention of Eddie Cantor, who had Berkeley choreograph the dance scenes in his film *Whoopee.* During the 1930s Berkeley staged dance scenes for RKO and United Artists films, including *Palmy Days* (1931), *Bird of Paradise* (1932), *Roman Scandals* (1933), and *42nd Street* (1933). Eventually, Berkeley choreographed more than fifty films. (Barbara Naomi Cohen-Stratyner, *Biographical Dictionary of Dance,* 1982.)

BERLIN, IRVING. Irving Berlin was born Israel Baline in Russia on May 11, 1888. He immigrated to the United States with his family when he was five years old. Captivated by music, he became a singing waiter in several New York City restaurants after graduating from high school, but his reputation as a songwriter was first established in 1911 when "Alexander's Ragtime Band" was published. Within a few years, he was writing the music for Broadway plays, including *Watch Your Step* (1914), *The Century Girl* (1916), *Yip Yip Yaphank* (1918), the *Ziegfeld Follies* (1911, 1919, 1920, and 1927), and *The Music Box Revue* (1921, 1922, 1923, and 1924). Berlin was also a prolific producer of popular tunes, composing more than 800 of them during his career. He endeared himself to the American public with such beloved tunes as "Oh, How I Hate to Get up in the Morning," "God Bless America," "Always," "Easter Parade," and "White Christmas." During the 1930s, Berlin wrote music for a number of motion pictures, including *Top Hat* (1935), *On the Avenue* (1937), and *Second Fiddle* (1939). In 1942 he wrote and produced *This is the Army*. No other composer has written any music more familiar to the general American public. (Barbara Salsini, *Irving Berlin: Master Composer of Twentieth Century Songs*, 1972.)

BERLIN TREATY OF 1921. When the Senate refused to ratify the Treaty of Versailles ending World War I, the United States technically remained in a state of war with Germany. The Treaty of Berlin, signed on August 25, 1921, formally ended hostilities between the two countries. In addition, the Treaty of Berlin stipulated that confiscated German property in the United States would be applied against American claims against Germany. (Arnold A. Offer, *The Origins of World War II*, 1975.)

BERRY, GEORGE LEONARD. George L. Berry was born in Lee Valley, Tennessee, on September 12, 1882. Orphaned at the age of seven, Berry ran away from the orphanage where he had been living when he was nine years old, and he went to work as a newsboy for the Jackson, Mississippi, *Evening News*. In 1899 Berry became active in the International Printing Pressmen's and Assistants' Union of North America; he was elected international president of the union in 1907. In 1914 Berry made an unsuccessful bid for governor of Tennessee, and in 1917–1918 he served with the American Expeditionary Force in France. Berry returned to labor politics after the war and in 1919 was one of the founding members of the American Legion,* where he led the movement for immigration restriction and "one hundred percent Americanism."* At the 1924 Democratic National Convention, Berry narrowly lost the vice-presidential nomination to Charles W. Bryan.* Berry was an avid supporter of Franklin D. Roosevelt* and the New Deal during the 1930s, and he served for two years as a United States Senator from Tennessee between 1937 and 1939. George Berry died on December 4, 1948. (Elizabeth F. Baker, *Printers and Technology: A History of the International Printing Pressmen and Assistants' Union*, 1957; *New York Times*, December 5, 1948.)

"BIG FOUR." The term "Big Four" was used in 1919 by journalists to describe the Council of Four at the Versailles negotiations ending World War I. Those four individuals were Woodrow Wilson* of the United States, David Lloyd George of Great Britain, Georges Clemenceau of France, and Vittorio Orlando of Italy. Throughout the negotiations, they met at least daily to shape the Treaty of Versailles. (Thomas A. Bailey, *Woodrow Wilson and the Lost Peace*, 1944.)

BIRDSEYE, CLARENCE. Clarence Birdseye was born on December 9, 1886, in Brooklyn, New York. He attended Amherst College for two years but then left school to work for the United States Biological Survey as a field naturalist. In 1912 he went to Labrador in Canada to work as a fur trapper, where he travelled many miles on dog sleds in icy backcountry. At the time, he became interested in quick-freezing a winter's supply of wild game. During World War I, Birdseye returned to the United States and became a purchasing agent for the U.S. Housing Corporation. From 1918 to 1922, he was an administrative assistant to the head of the United States Fisheries Association. Finally, in 1924, after borrowing on his life insurance policy, Birdseye founded the General Seafoods Company. Using a new method of quick-freezing meat by pressing it between refrigerated metal plates, Birdseye began to market fresh frozen haddock. It was an immediate success. In 1929, Goldman Sachs & Company, an investment firm, reorganized the company with more than $23 million in investment capital and renamed it General Foods. Birdseye then turned his attention to the process of quick-drying food. He died on October 7, 1956. *(Current Biography,* March 1946; Alex Groner, *History of American Business and Technology,* 1972; *New York Times,* October 9, 1956.)

BIRTH CONTROL. See SANGER, MARGARET

"BLACK BOTTOM." The "Black Bottom" was a dance of the 1920s whose popularity was surpassed only by the "Charleston."* It originated among southern blacks, and came to the attention of whites only after the large-scale black migration to northern cities during World War I and the 1920s. Characterized by a genteel slapping of the backside along with forward and backward hopping, the "Black Bottom" was introduced on stage in Irving C. Miller's 1924 production of *Dinah.* (Lynne Fauley Emery, *Black Dance in the United States from 1619 to 1970,* 1972.)

BLACK, JOHN DONALD. John D. Black was born on June 6, 1883, in Jefferson County, Wisconsin. With a keen interest in agricultural economics, he took all of his degrees at the University of Wisconsin, receiving a B.A. in 1909, an M.A. in 1910, and a Ph.D. in 1918. He held a number of academic posts before joining the staff of Harvard University in 1927. Shortly thereafter, Black published his influential *Agricultural Reform in the United States* (1929), a book which proposed acreage reductions as a means of lifting farm commodity prices. The book became extremely popular among liberal agricultural economists and became the basis for the Agricultural Adjustment Act of 1933. Black's other books included *The Dairy Industry and the AAA* (1935), *Parity, Parity, Parity* (1942), and *Three Years of the AAA* (1938). Black retired from Harvard in 1956 as Henry Lee Professor of Economics and continued to write and consult on agricultural problems. He died on April 12, 1960. *(New York Times,* April 13, 1960.)

"BLACK MONDAY." The term "Black Monday" refers to Monday, October 28, 1929, when the stock market dropped 49 points on 9,250,000 shares of trading. On that day, the great crash of 1929 reached full-blown proportions. (John Kenneth Galbraith, *The Great Crash 1929*, 1955.)

BLACK SOX SCANDAL. In the 1919 World Series, the underdog Cincinnati Reds defeated the Chicago White Sox, but there was no hint of scandal until the end of the 1920 season when Charles Comiskey, owner of the White Sox, summarily suspended pitchers Eddie Cicotte and Claude Williams, left fielder "Shoeless" Joe Jackson, center fielder Oscar Felsch, shortstop Charles Risberg, pinch hitter Fred McMullin, first baseman Chick Gandil, and third baseman George Weaver. Cicotte, Jackson, Williams, and Felsch had admitted to a grand jury that in return for a bribe they had purposely lost the 1919 series to the Cincinnati Reds. All eight athletes stood trial in the summer of 1921, and, although a jury acquitted them of all charges, baseball* commissioner Judge Kenesaw Mountain Landis* suspended them for life from the game. Court records indicated that the eight players received $70,000 for losing the series five games to three.

The scandal rocked baseball and American culture. In its pastoral simplicity, baseball seemed a throwback to the country's rural, village past, and the scandal seemed symbolic of what was happening to America as a whole under the impact of mass industrialization and urbanization. Although many predicted that baseball would not recover from the scandal, it survived and thrived. Judge Landis developed a reputation for brutal honesty, restoring integrity to the game, and the home runs of Babe Ruth* brought baseball into the modern era of big hitting and offense. Nevertheless, the so-called Black Sox scandal—along with the Teapot Dome,* the Alien Property Custodian,* and the Veterans' Bureau scandals*; the sexual notoriety of Fatty Arbuckle,* Aimee Semple McPherson,* and the Hall-Mills murder case*; and the organized crime of prohibition*—helped characterize the 1920s as the "lawless decade." (Paul Sann, *The Lawless Decade,* 1957.)

"BLACKSTONE PLANTATION." "Blackstone Plantation" was a popular radio* program starring Frank Crumit and Julia Sanderson. They permiered on CBS in 1929, sponsored by Blackstone Cigars, and spent the next fifteen years on radio, either for CBS or NBC, featuring light talk, soft jokes, music, and cheerful give-and-take between the husband and wife team. (John Dunning, *Tune in Yesterday: The Ultimate Encyclopedia of Old-Time Radio, 1925–1976,* 1976.)

"BLACK THURSDAY." "Black Thursday" was the name given to October 24, 1929, when the stock market traded a record 12,894,650 shares. Although the index fell only from 384 to 372, the number of shares traded indicated the beginning of the panic, which reached full-blown proportions on "Black Monday''*—October 28—and ''Black Tuesday''—October 29, 1929. (John Kenneth Galbraith, *The Great Crash 1929*, 1955.)

"BLACK TUESDAY." ''Black Tuesday'' was the name given to October 29, 1929, when the stock market collapsed. Ever since late in September, the stock exchange had been experiencing selling waves, and, on October 24, a bankers' syndicate led by the House of Morgan had tried to intervene and buy stock, but they managed to stem the tide for only a few days. On ''Black Tuesday,'' the bottom fell out of the stock market, with 16 million shares traded that day and the *New York Times* stock index declining by 43 points. ''Black Tuesday'' became a symbol of the catastrophe that struck the American economy between 1929 and 1940. (John Kenneth Galbraith, *The Great Crash,* 1955; Robert Sobel, *The Great Bull Market: Wall Street in the 1920s,* 1968.)

BLISS, TASKER HOWARD. Tasker Howard Bliss was born on December 31, 1853, in Lewisburg, Pennsylvania. He graduated from the United States Military Academy at West Point in 1875. Bliss was a career army officer who rose to chief of staff of the U.S. Army in 1917. In 1918 he became the official American military representative to the Inter-Allied Supreme War Council and a delegate to the Paris Peace Conference of 1919.* While in Europe, Bliss became convinced that modern warfare was unacceptable because of the enormous destruction it wrought. At the Paris conference, Bliss became a powerful advocate of arms control and a balance of power in Europe. He opposed harsh measures and high reparations* against Germany after the war because he was convinced it would upset the balance of power and lead to another war. During the 1920s, Bliss strongly advocated American membership in the League of Nations,* and he was a founding member of the Council on Foreign Relations.* Bliss also believed that the World Court* had an important role in adjudicating disputes, and he called for American participation. Tasker Howard Bliss died on November 9, 1930. *(New York Times,* November 10, 1930; Frederick Palmer, *Bliss, Peacemaker: The Life and Letters of General Tasker Howard Bliss,* 1934.)

BOBBED HAIR. During the 1920s it became fashionable for women to sport ''bobbed-hair,'' hair cut short just below the ear. Irene Castle, the famous ballroom dancer who led the rebellion against long tresses and wrapped bun hairstyles, was credited with starting the fashion fad. She claimed that some of her hair had burned accidentally and she had had to cut it short. Bobbed-hair quickly became a symbol of sexual freedom of women from the traditional role expectations of the past. (Paul Sann, *The Lawless Decade,* 1957.)

BOHEMIANISM. During the 1920s, a counterculture appeared among the artistic elites and intelligentsia in many American cities, but especially in Greenwich Village of New York City. By 1920 Greenwich Village had become a bohemia—a cultural haven for artists amidst the poverty of the surrounding black and Italian tenements. Although the village had become a tourist trap by mid-decade, its small artistic and literary elite promoted the image of bohemianism: rebellion against authority and tradition; the quest for the ideal life; a celebration of freedom, even anarchism; and a healthy skepticism about morality, convention, and propriety. Although confused about the merits of political rebellion, bohemianism criticized middle-class life as insensitive and parochial and celebrated art as the proper lens through which to interpret American society. (Albert Parry, *Garrets and Pretenders: A History of Bohemianism in America*, 1933; Caroline F. Ware, *Greenwich Village, 1920–1930*, 1935.)

BOK, EDWARD WILLIAM. Edward Bok was born on October 9, 1863, in Helder, Netherlands, and he immigrated to the United States with his family in 1870. When he was nineteen, he was a writer for the *Brooklyn Eagle;* in 1887, he became head of advertising for Charles Scribners Sons. In 1889 Bok was appointed editor-in-chief of the *Ladies Home Journal,* a position he held until 1919. During his tenure with the magazine, Bok openly advocated prohibition,* women's rights,* progressive reform, and environmental safety. Bok also readily addressed such issues as venereal disease and birth control, which other publications thought too controversial. Under his leadership, the *Journal* thrived. After he left the *Journal,* Bok spent the rest of his life advocating international peace and United States membership in the League of Nations.* He died on January 9, 1930. (Edward Bok, *The Americanization of Edward Bok,* 1921; *New York Times,* January 10, 1930.)

BOLSHEVISM. ''Bolshevism'' was the term used in the 1920s to describe the revolutionary political philosophy emanating from the Soviet Union after the Russian Revolution of 1917. The Bolsheviks were Communists and followers of Vladimir Lenin, who believed that Marxism would eventually triumph throughout the industrial world. Because early Bolsheviks had a missionary zeal for exporting their revolution, large numbers of Americans in the late 1910s and early 1920s saw Bolshevism as a threat to religion, capitalism, democracy, and individualism—in short, a threat to the American way of life. Those fears led to the famous Red Scare.* (Robert Murray, *Red Scare: A Study in National Hysteria, 1919–1920,* 1955.)

BOMBINGS. See RED SCARE

BONUS ARMY. In 1924 Congress passed the Adjusted Compensation Act* providing for a cash bonus to World War I veterans with a lump payment in 1945. As the depression worsened after 1929 and hundreds of thousands of veterans were thrown out of work, veterans groups began to demand that they not have to wait until 1945 to receive payment. Instead, they lobbied Congress for new legislation allowing for immediate enactment of a bill providing for loans of up to 50 percent on the bonus certificates awarded in 1924. Congress quickly passed the bill, but President Herbert Hoover* vetoed it on February 26, 1931. In Hoover's view, it was a federal budget buster which would provide money to veterans who did not need it as well as to those who did. The next day, Congress overrode the veto. At the end of 1931, Democratic leaders, anticipating the upcoming election year, began to call for the total payment of the bonuses.

With the Democrats calling for immediate payment of the bonuses, veterans groups sponsored a march on Washington, D.C., to dramatize their demands. Late in May 1932, approximately 1,000 veterans arrived in Washington, and, in June, another 16,000 members of the ''Bonus Expeditionary Force'' joined them. They camped at Anacostia Flats on the outskirts of the city and downtown in empty government buildings. In mid-June, Congressman Wright Patman of Texas sponsored a new bonus bill providing $2.4 billion in fiat money to redeem the bonus certificates, and, although the House passed the bill, the Senate refused. President Hoover then saw to it that Congress passed a bill providing $100,000 to help pay the expenses for the bonus marchers to return home. About 15,000 of them had left Washington by early July, but 2,000 refused to go.

Late in July the District of Columbia police tried to evict the remaining Bonus Army marchers from government buildings, but a riot occurred when the marchers resisted. The riot left two veterans and two policemen dead. Secretary of War Patrick Hurley* asked Hoover to declare martial law, but the president refused. He sympathized with the veterans and did not want to attack them. The president told Hurley to have General Douglas MacArthur* use federal troops to move the occupants from the government buildings to their camps nearby. Hurley, however, told General MacArthur to move the marchers out of the buildings and across the river to Anacostia Flats. Using army troops, MacArthur went further himself and decided to drive the bonus marchers—with tanks, tear gas, rifle fire, sabers, and torches—out of Anacostia Flats as well. On July 29, 1932, MacArthur's troops attacked the Bonus Army and dispersed them, but the photographs and newsreels of American soldiers attacking former soldiers flashed across the newspapers and theater screens of the United States. Hoover was appalled at what had happened and privately blamed both Hurley and MacArthur for acting precipitously; publicly, he shouldered the blame and even argued that the bonus marchers had posed a real threat of insurrection.

The Bonus Army episode was a political disaster for the president. In the middle of an election year, the United States Army had attacked a group of unemployed, hungry veterans and their wives and children. Democratic charges that Hoover was insensitive to the suffering of the poor seemed confirmed by the Bonus Army incident. Franklin D. Roosevelt,* the Democratic candidate for president, remarked upon hearing the news of the Bonus Army incident, ''Well, this will elect me.'' (Roger Daniels, *The Bonus March: An Episode of the Great Depression,* 1971; Donald J. Lisio, *The President and Protest: Hoover, Conspiracy, and the Bonus Riot,* 1974.)

BOOTLEGGER. During the years of prohibition,* the term ''bootlegger'' was used to describe people who illegally marketed alcohol. The term originated with people who hid small flasks of alcohol inside their boots. (Paul Sann, *The Lawless Decade,* 1957.)

BORAH, WILLIAM EDGAR. William Borah was born on June 29, 1865, in rural southern Illinois, near Fairfield. He attended public schools in Illinois and Kansas before entering the University of Kansas at the age of twenty. Because of trouble with tuberculosis and financial difficulties, he was not able to finish his freshman year, and, instead, he began to read law privately in his brother-in-law's office. He passed the bar exam in 1887. Soon after, Borah decided to move west, and in 1890 he settled in Boise, Idaho. Quickly establishing himself as a criminal lawyer and special prosecutor and named chairman of the Republican State Central Committee, Borah rapidly rose to prominence in Idaho.

Elected to the United States Senate in 1906, Borah established himself as a Progressive Republican. He sponsored legislation to create the Department of Labor, an eight-hour day for government contracts, and better working conditions in the steel industry. A dedicated opponent of the big trusts, he fought for the income tax and the direct election of senators amendments. Although his progressivism waned somewhat under Woodrow Wilson,* he claimed it was because Wilson tried to create a greater bureaucracy and centralize too much power in the federal government. During the 1920s, Borah was chairman of the Senate Foreign Relations Committee. An avowed isolationist, he fought United States entry into the League of Nations* and the World Court,* but he did play an instrumental role in the Washington Naval Conference* of 1921, which reduced naval arms, and the Kellogg-Briand Pact.* On domestic policy, he maintained his progressivism, opposing Republican tariff and taxation policies, but he also turned down an offer to run for vice-president on the Progressive Party* ticket in 1924. During the 1930s, Borah gave considerable support to New Deal legislation, but he opposed Franklin D. Roosevelt* on foreign policy. Borah thought Roosevelt was too willing to entangle the United States in foreign commitments. He flirted with seeking the Republican presidential nomination in 1936, but he did not actively seek the position. William Borah died on January 19, 1940. (Claudius O. Johnson, *Borah of Idaho,* 1965; Marian C. McKenna, *Borah,* 1961.)

BOSTON POLICE STRIKE OF 1919. In 1919, in the midst of the labor agitation and political unrest endemic to the United States, the police in Boston formed a labor union and affiliated themselves with the American Federation of Labor* (AFL). They demanded a pay raise significantly above their minimum of $1,100 a year. When the city of Boston refused their request and suspended nineteen police officers for being active in union organization, the police went out on strike on September 9, 1919. Burglaries, looting, and violence escalated immediately in Boston, and Massachusetts governor Calvin Coolidge* called in the national guard. The police commissioner began to recruit new police officers. When AFL president Samuel Gompers* complained to Coolidge that Boston officials were being too heavy-handed, the governor replied that there was "no right to strike against the public safety by anybody, anywhere, anytime." The city pressed amateur policemen into service, who along with the national guardsmen, were able to maintain order. Because of public fear of radicalism at the time, the police strike was very unpopular and collapsed. Calvin Coolidge became a national hero. One year later, the Republican Party* picked him to run for vice-president. (Donald R. McCoy, *Calvin Coolidge: The Quiet President,* 1967.)

BOULDER CANYON PROJECT ACT OF 1928. See HOOVER DAM

BOW, CLARA. Clara Bow was born in Brooklyn, New York, on July 29, 1905. Bow won a beauty contest in 1921 in which the first prize was a screen test, and she soon found herself in Hollywood making movies. Her dance talent, especially the "Charleston"* and the "Black Bottom,"* usually played an important part in her characterizations. Among her most popular films were *Dancing Mothers* (1926), *Kid Boots* (1926), *The Wild Party* (1929), and *Love among the Millionaires* (1930). Those roles were all produced by Paramount/Famous Players–Laskey Studios. Her most celebrated film came in 1927 and earned her the nickname the "It Girl." Entitled *It,* the movie, based on the novel by Elinor Glyn, tried to demonstrate that sex appeal could only be expressed through dancing. Bow was the premier "flapper"* star of the 1920s, portraying liberated women who smoked, drank, and caroused in a rejection of the repressed Victorian lives their mothers had supposedly lived. The flappers, full of neurotic energy, were characterized by bobbed hair*; pallid skin colors; flattened, boyish breasts; and lips painted into narrow Cupid's bows. Her private life matched her film roles, and by the late 1920s Bow was afflicted by serious neuroses and her career declined. She tried a film comeback in the 1930s, but it was a failure. Clara Bow retired to a ranch in Nevada where she died on September 26, 1965. (Joe Morella and Edward Epstein, *The "It" Girl: The Incredible Story of Clara Bow,* 1976; Marjorie Rosen, *Popcorn Venus,* 1973.)

BRANDEIS, LOUIS DEMBITZ. Louis Brandeis was born in Czechoslovakia in 1856 and immigrated to the United States with his family in 1864. His father Adolf established a successful grain commission business in Louisville, Kentucky. Louis Brandeis attended school in Louisville and then in Dresden, Germany, before entering Harvard Law School in 1875. He stayed on there as a law professor after graduating. His brilliance was immediately apparent. Brandeis viewed the Constitution as a flexible instrument that allowed people to govern themselves democratically. In order for the courts to interpret the Constitution properly, they had to consider legal precedents, common sense, and social realities. This method of jurisprudence came to national attention in 1908 when

Brandeis submitted to the Supreme Court what came to be known as a Brandeis brief. In *Muller v. Oregon*, Brandeis persuaded the Supreme Court to accept sociological statistics as evidence in upholding a law.

While arbitrating the New York garment workers' strike in 1910, Brandeis discovered his Jewish identity and eventually became head of the powerful American Zionist movement. He saw Zionism as an extension of the American ideal. Brandeis was also a fervent believer in freedom of business enterprise. He felt that the great enemy of freedom was monopoly and special privileges, such as tariffs and subsidies. He also opposed union demands for closed shops. To force laborers to join a union in order to work violated his ideas of democracy.

In 1912 Woodrow Wilson* asked Brandeis to serve as his campaign adviser. Brandeis helped the future president shape a program that they called the "New Freedom." It called for regulating competition and creating a federal trade commission to supervise business practice. Wilson appointed Brandeis to the Supreme Court in 1916. He served on the Supreme Court for twenty-three years, during the administrations of five presidents. For almost that entire time, his views were expressed in minority opinions. The Great Depression* brought a new popularity to his opinions. Inexpensive editions of his book *Other People's Money* were published during the presidential election campaign of 1932, and Franklin D. Roosevelt* frequently referred to the book in his fireside chats. During the New Deal, Brandeis criticized the early emphasis on national economic planning but felt especially comfortable with the anti-trust nature of the later New Deal. Brandeis suffered a heart attack in January 1939 and retired from the Supreme Court in February 1939. He died on October 5, 1941. (Melvin I. Urofsky, *Louis D. Brandeis and the Progressive Tradition*, 1981.)

BREADLINES.   After 1929 the term "breadline" was used to describe the line outside soup kitchens or government relief offices where unemployed men and women waited for food. (Paul Sann, *The Lawless Decade*, 1957.)

BRICE, FANNY. Fanny Brice, born Fannie Borach on October 29, 1891, in New York City, was a comedienne, singer, and dance satirist. Although she had no formal training, Brice sang while a teenager at Keeney's Theater in Brooklyn and in Burtwig and Simon burlesque shows. In 1910 Florenz Ziegfeld* signed her to perform in the Ziegfeld Follies, which she did in 1910, 1911, 1913, 1916, 1917, 1920, 1921, and 1923. Her best-known songs and routines were the "Sadie" and "Becky" series about girls from the Lower East Side of Manhattan who wanted to be dancers on Broadway. During the late 1920s and 1930s, Brice continued to perform, often in such Billy Rose productions as *Music Box Revue of 1924*, *Sweet and Low* (1930), and *Crazy Quilt* (1931). Late in the 1930s, Brice left the stage for work in radio. She died in Los Angeles on May 29, 1951. (Barbara Naomi Cohen-Stratyner, *Biographical Dictionary of Dance*, 1982.)

BROOKINGS, ROBERT SOMERS. Robert S. Brookings was born on January 22, 1850, in Cecil County, Maryland. In 1867 Brookings became a store clerk in St. Louis, Missouri, and by 1872 he was managing the company. He branched out into real estate, lumbering, and transportation, becoming in the process a well-known business figure in the Midwest. In 1895 he built Cupples Station, a twelve-block private railway terminal in downtown St. Louis, which became a model for railway distribution sites in the United States. In 1896 Brooking's life took a different course when he decided to compensate for his own lack of education by committing himself to higher education. He donated Cupples Station to Washington University and then vigorously raised funds for the university. Brookings was especially committed to the medical school.

The commitment to education brought Brookings inevitably into research and philanthropy. In 1910 he was appointed to the board of the Carnegie Endowment for International Peace,* and in 1916 he founded the Institute for Governmental Research to investigate administrative and political practices in the United States. During World War I, Brookings worked for the War Industries Board (WIB) and became a close associate of Bernard Baruch.* Experience on the WIB gave Brookings a new interest in economics and industrial cooperation. In 1922 he founded the Institute for Economics and in 1924 the Robert Brookings Graduate School of Economics and Government. In 1928 the three organizations he had founded were merged into the Brookings Institute for Government Research, one of the most important research centers and think tanks in American history. One of its first studies concerned the ''Indian problem'' in America. Summarized in the Meriam Report,* the study advocated a change of direction in U.S. Indian policy, one which would return Indian land, allow full expression of Indian culture, and recognize tribal sovereignty once again. Robert Brookings died on November 15, 1932. (Donald T. Critchlow, *The Brookings Institution, 1916–1952: Expertise and the Public Interest in a Democratic Society,* 1985; Herman Hagedorn, *Brookings: A Biography,* 1936; *New York Times,* November 16, 1932.)

BROOKS, VAN WYCK. Van Wyck Brooks was born in Plainfield, New Jersey, on February 16, 1886. He graduated from Harvard in 1907, and except for two years teaching English at Stanford in 1911–1913, he spent his entire career as a writer. Brooks was particularly interested in the literary origins of American culture. Although he had a negative view of the Puritan heritage, he eventually came to appreciate their contribution to American values. Brooks's major works were *The Wine of the Puritans* (1909), *America's Coming-of-Age* (1915), *The Ordeal of Mark Twain* (1920), *The Flowering of New England* (1936), *New England: Indian Summer* (1940), and *The Confident Years* (1952). During the 1920s, Van Wyck Brooks was an influential critic of the works of the Lost Generation.* Brooks was also known as a successful biographer, editor, and French translator. He died on May 2, 1963. (James Hoopes, *Van Wyck Brooks: In Search of American Culture,* 1977.)

BROUN, HEYWOOD CAMPBELL. Heywood Broun was born in Brooklyn, New York, on December 7, 1888. Broun attended Harvard between 1906 and 1910, but he did not graduate, preferring to work as a reporter for the *New York Morning Telegraph*. He joined the *New York Tribune* in 1912, and in 1917 went with the American Expeditionary Force to France as a war correspondent. In 1921 Broun joined the *New York World* and became widely known throughout the United States because of his column "It Seems to Me." In that column, Broun was highly critical of the Red Scare* and the crusade against Nicola Sacco* and Bartolomeo Vanzetti* during the 1920s. His defense of Sacco and Vanzetti was so strong that the *New York World* fired him.

In 1928 Broun went to work for the Scripps-Howard newspaper syndicate, and, in the early 1930s, he was a founder of the New York Newspaper Guild and the American Newspaper Guild, of which he was the first president. He wrote a number of books, including *Pieces of Hate and Other Enthusiasms* (1922) and *Gandle Follows His Nose* (1926). Heywood Broun died on December 18, 1939. (Daniel J. Leab, *A Union of Individuals: The Formation of the American Newspaper Guild, 1933–1935,* 1970; *New York Times,* December 19, 1939; Richard O'Connor, *Heywood Broun: A Biography,* 1975.)

BROWN, WALTER FOLGER. W. F. Brown was born on May 31, 1869, in Massillon, Ohio. He graduated from Harvard in 1901 and received a law degree there in 1903. Brown then returned to Ohio where he joined his father's Toledo law firm and became active in state Republican politics, eventually rising to leadership of the state party organization. In 1921 President Warren G. Harding* asked Brown to chair a special study of the federal government, and in 1924 President Calvin Coolidge* appointed him secretary of commerce. Brown served as secretary of commerce until Coolidge left office in March 1929; then he became President Herbert Hoover's* postmaster general, a position in which he served until Franklin D. Roosevelt* and the Democrats came to power in 1933. Brown then returned to his law practice in Toledo, where he died on January 26, 1961. (Martin L. Fausold, *The Presidency of Herbert Hoover,* 1985; Donald R. McCoy, *Calvin Coolidge: The Quiet President,* 1967; *New York Times,* January 27, 1961.)

BRUERE, HENRY. Henry Bruere was born on January 15, 1882, in St. Charles, Missouri. He graduated from the University of Chicago in 1901 after studying under Thorstein Veblen,* and he studied law and politics at Harvard, New York University, and Columbia. He then had a diverse career, one switching back and forth between business and social welfare. Bruere spent the time between 1903 and 1905 working for International Harvester Company, but then he returned to New York and established the Bureau of Municipal Research. Over the next decade, Bruere served as city chamberlain of New York, head of the Mayor's Pension Committee, and president of the city's Board of Child Welfare. After directing the state division of the United States Employment Service in

1918, Bruere returned to the business world, first as a vice-president of the Metropolitan Life Insurance Company and after 1931 as president of the Bowery Savings Bank, the largest savings bank in the country. He remained at that position until his retirement in 1949. During the 1920s, Bruere was an influential figure in New York politics. His business credentials were strong but so was his commitment to social welfare. He advised governors Al Smith* and Franklin D. Roosevelt* of New York, and he was a leading figure in the campaign for public works and unemployment relief programs. Henry Bruere died on February 17, 1958. *(New York Times,* February 18, 1958; also see the Henry Bruere File in the Oral History Research Office at Columbia University.)

BRYAN, CHARLES WAYLAND. Charles W. Bryan was born on February 10, 1867, in Salem, Illinois. Although his own life was overshadowed by the public career of his older brother, William Jennings Bryan,* Charles W. Bryan was an influential figure in his own right. He attended the University of Chicago and Illinois College, but he did not graduate from either one of them. Bryan settled in Lincoln, Nebraska, in 1891, and immediately became active in farm politics. By 1892 Bryan was an active Democrat with strong populist sympathies. Between 1901 and 1923, he served as editor of *The Commoner,* a political journal. He held a number of political offices in Lincoln, including mayor, and he served terms as governor of Nebraska in 1923–1925 and 1931–1935. In the election of 1924, Bryan was the vice-presidential running mate of Democratic nominee John W. Davis.* Charles Bryan died on March 4, 1945. *(New York Times,* March 5, 1945.)

BRYAN, WILLIAM JENNINGS. William Jennings Bryan was born in Salem, Illinois, on March 19, 1860. He graduated from Illinois College in 1881 and then took a law degree from the Union College of Law in Jacksonville, Illinois, in 1883. Bryan practiced law in Jacksonville for four years before moving his practice to Lincoln, Nebraska. There Bryan became active in Democratic politics and won a seat in Congress in 1890. By that time, the economic life of midwestern farmers was deteriorating under the pressure of massive overproduction and high railroad freight rates. Bryan was re-elected to Congress in 1892 and associated himself with the silver bloc—a coalition of farmers and some industrial workers who believed silver inflation would cure the country's economic ills. He was unsuccessful in 1894 in his bid for a United States Senate seat. After leaving politics, Bryan became head of the editorial staff of the *Omaha World-Telegram* and an extremely popular speaker on the Chautauqua circuit. He toured the country advocating free coinage of silver.

Bryan rocketed to national prominence in 1896 at the Democratic National Convention in Chicago, where he delivered his famous "Cross of Gold" speech and won the party's presidential nomination. The Populist Party then nominated him as their candidate, and Bryan campaigned against the Republican nominee, William McKinley, on the free silver platform. Unable to put together a national coalition of workers and farmers, Bryan lost the election by 7,035,638 votes to 6,467,946. He sought the presidency again in 1900, using anti-imperialism as the issue against McKinley, but Bryan lost again, this time 7,219,530 votes to 6,358,071. Bryan ran again in 1908, but he lost to Republican William Howard Taft* by 7,679,006 votes to 6,409,106.

In 1912 Bryan actively supported the presidential candidacy of Woodrow Wilson,* and when Wilson won the election, Bryan was rewarded with the cabinet position of secretary of state. While at the State Department, Bryan negotiated thirty separate treaties with other nations providing for arbitration of international disputes, but he resigned from the cabinet in 1915 when he felt Wilson was reacting too aggressively to the sinking of the *Lusitania*. Bryan believed strictly in absolute neutrality, and he could not morally continue to serve under Wilson.

William Jenning Bryan's last public role proved to be an ironic one in the 1920s. For all of his career, he had been viewed by many as a radical—for his advocacy of free coinage of silver and for his neutrality during the months preceding American entry in World War I. But Bryan was also a fundamentalist in religion who bitterly opposed the teaching of evolution. Early in the 1920s he delivered hundreds of speeches across the country calling for state legislation prohibiting the teaching of evolution* in public schools, and in 1925, when John T. Scopes of Dayton, Tennessee, was indicted for violating such legislation, Bryan came to town to assist the prosecution. Famed criminal attorney Clarence Darrow* came from Chicago to defend Scopes, and in the subsequent "Monkey Trial" Bryan took the witness stand to defend a literal interpretation of the Bible, only to wither under Darrow's brutal cross-examination. Bryan, known as the "Great Commoner," had ended an illustrious career as a buffoon, at least in the mind of urban America. He died in Dayton, Tennessee, on July 26, 1925, shortly after the end of the trial. (Kendrick A. Clements, *William Jennings Bryan: Missionary Isolationist,* 1982; Lawrence W. Levine, *Defender of the Faith: William Jennings Bryan: The Last Decade, 1915–1925,* 1965.)

"BUBBLES." Born John Sublett on February 19, 1902, in Louisville, Kentucky, "Bubbles" was just seven years old when he began to perform with Ford Lee Washington as the "Buck and Bubbles" tap dancing team. They became an extremely popular dance team during the 1920s, performing on Broadway in *The George White Scandals of 1920* and the *Ziegfeld Follies of 1921*. Both of them were also cast in George Gershwin's *Porgy and Bess,* in which Sublett played the role of "Sportin' Life." "Buck and Bubbles" also worked the black vaudeville and theater circuits and frequently performed at the Apollo Theater. During the 1930s, they danced together in a number of popular films, including *Varsity Show* (1937). The two men danced together until their retirement in 1953. (Barbara Naomi Cohen-Stratyner, *Biographical Dictionary of Dance,* 1982.)

BUCARELI AGREEMENT OF 1923. In 1917 the Mexican Constitution stated that all subsurface mineral deposits were Mexican property, not the property of any foreign corporations that may have negotiated such rights in the past. American companies, especially oil companies, with mineral rights in Mexico were outraged and put pressure on the United States government to remedy the situation, which led to a severing of diplomatic relations between the two countries. In 1921, the Mexican government, under Alvarao Obregon, was interested in seeking American loans and realized that the dispute needed to be resolved. The United States was also interested in resolving the dispute because of predictions that domestic oil shortages were looming on the horizon. An American negotiating team went to Mexico City, where discussions took place on the Calle Bucareli. Mexico agreed to honor American claims against her arising since 1868 if the United States would extend recognition to the Obregon government and recognize Mexican title to all subsurface minerals. The treaty was signed by both parties, and, on August 31, 1923, the United States and Mexico resumed diplomatic relations. (Howard F. Cline, *The United States and Mexico,* 1953; L. Ethan Ellis, *Republican Foreign Policy, 1921–1933,* 1968.)

"BUCK." See "BUBBLES"

BUDGET AND ACCOUNTING ACT OF 1921. Shortly after his inauguration, President Warren G. Harding* called Congress into special session. The new administration was committed to reducing government spending as well as using business methods in government operations, and one target of "normalcy"* was the arcane budgeting process. Under the old system, each government agency annually appeared independently before Congress to appeal for funds. Congress individually appropriated money, but because of the process there was no comprehensive system for allocating money or estimating total expendtures. On June 10, 1921, President Harding signed the Budget and Accounting Act into law. It established a Bureau of the Budget under the direction of the president to prepare an annual budget and a General Accounting Office, with a comptroller general, to audit government accounts. Harding appointed John Raymond McCarl the comptroller general and Chicago banker Charles Dawes* the director of the budget. Between 1922 and 1923, after a whirlwind of activity, Dawes submitted a federal budget of only $3.5 billion, which provided a surplus at the end of the year. (Charles Dawes, *The First Year of the Budget of the United States,* 1923; Fritz M. Marx, "The Bureau of the Budget: Its Evolution and Present Role," *American Political Science Review* 39 [April 1945], 653–84; Robert K. Murray, *The Politics of Normalcy: Government Theory and Practice in the Harding-Coolidge Era,* 1973; Frederick Paxson, *Postwar Years, Normalcy, 1918–1923,* 1948.)

BULL MARKET. Perhaps the most distinguishing feature of the 1920s, at least in the minds of the historical public, was the unprecedented stock market increases and the subsequent crash of 1929. In 1921, the composite average of stocks on the New York Stock Exchange was 54; it increased to 65 in 1923, 106 in 1924, 245 in 1927, and 449 in 1929, nearly a fivefold gain. The gains were, quite literally, unbelievable, as was the crash of 1929, which brought the composite index down to 51 in 1931 and 37 in 1932. Except for minor adjustments, the market had made steady gains throughout the 1920s. More important, those gains were not really tied to dividends or corporate profits. Investors were interested in capital gains, quick ones at that, rather than long-term growth and dividends. Business profits increased quite modestly during the decade, so dividends expectations did not fuel market expansion.

Historians looking back on the extraordinary increases in stock values offer several explanations. One of them is the World War I profits which American investors poured into the stock market. The United States emerged from the war with the strongest economy in the world and huge gains in capital. Some of that money found its way to Wall Street, fueling early stock market gains. Republican tax policies had a similar effect. Secretary of the Treasury Andrew Mellon* was committed to tax reductions for the affluent, and the Revenue Acts of 1921,* 1924,* 1926,* 1928,* and 1929* all reduced general tax and surtax rates. Billions of dollars, which would have gone to the federal government, were left in the hands of investors, who put large amounts into the stock market, driving stock prices higher. Mellon was also committed to paying off the national debt. As he did, government bonds were retired, and investors had to find other outlets for their investment capital. Wall Street was the primary recipient of these funds. By the middle of the decade, with stock prices rising precipitously, corporations began to postpone reinvestment in their own businesses and channeled excess funds into the stock market. Those price increases then attracted smaller investors into the market. The combination of huge volumes of new money entering the market led to extraordinary price increases. Faulty monetary assumptions on the part of Federal Reserve officials prevented the government from exerting any restraining influence. Finally, the creation of investment trusts and margin buying drove the market to unheard of heights. In 1928 and 1929, with so much speculative money coming into the stock market, creative stock manipulators began creating investment trusts and issuing stock on the new companies. Hundreds of those trusts, issuing millions of shares of stock, appeared in 1928 and 1929, driving stock market prices even higher. The problem, of course, was that the values of those stocks were grossly inflated since they did not represent real economic assets. The subsequent stock market crash of 1929 illustrated that dilemma. As for margin buying, investors could put up a small down payment on a stock, take out a call loan from a broker or bank, and purchase the stock using the stock itself as collateral for the loan. As long as securities values in general were rising, margin buying allowed for enormous profits, but when prices declined, margin calls required investors to put up more cash to cover the declining value of the collateral. The demand for cash triggered a wave of selling and helped precipitate the crash of 1929. (John Kenneth Galbraith, *The Great Crash,* 1955; Robert Sobel, *The Great Bull Market: Wall Street in the 1920s,* 1968.)

BURNS, WILLIAM JOHN. William John Burns was born on October 19, 1861, in Baltimore, Maryland. He grew up in Ohio, graduated from a local business college, and became a detective after his father had been named police commissioner of Columbus, Ohio. Burns was highly skilled as an investigator. In 1889 he joined the United States Secret Service where he specialized in finding counterfeiters. In 1903, the Department of the Interior had Burns investigate a massive land fraud scheme in the western states, where he implicated United States Senator John H. Michelet in the case. In 1909, after three years of field work, Burns obtained the evidence necessary to convict San Francisco mayor Abraham Ruef of political graft. Later that year, Burns founded the William J. Burns National Detective Agency, and he quickly ran up a string of successes, solving the 1910 bombing of the Los Angeles *Times* building, investigating municipal corruption in Detroit and Atlantic City in 1912, and proving the innocence of Leo Frank in Georgia in 1914. By that time, his agency had become the most famous in the country. In 1921 Attorney General Harry Daugherty* named Burns head of the Federal Bureau of Investigation, where he vigorously pursued aliens and radicals, including the arrest of 1,200 people during the abortive railroad strike of 1922. Burns had to leave the Justice Department in 1924 when the scandals of Warren G. Harding* and his ''Ohio gang''* came to light. William Burns died on April 14, 1932. *(New York Times,* April 15, 1932; Richard Gid Powers, *Secrecy and Power: The Life of J. Edgar Hoover,* 1987.)

BURROUGHS, EDGAR RICE. Edgar Rice Burroughs was born in Chicago, Illinois, on September 1, 1875. After leaving high school, he worked at a variety of jobs—a clerk for Sears, Roebuck and Company, a gold miner in Idaho, a policeman in Salt Lake City—but he burst into the American consciousness in 1914 when he wrote *Tarzan of the Apes,* a runaway bestseller. During the next twenty years, Burroughs wrote more than forty other novels, most of them about Tarzan.* Burroughs was one of the country's most popular novelists during the 1920s. For an America concerned about urbanization, industrialization, and bureaucratization, the adventures of a lone white man in ''dark Africa'' revived the spirit of the frontier and individualism. His novels inspired cartoons, films, and comic book adventures, and they had a powerful, enduring quality in American popular culture. Edgar Rice Burroughs died on March 14, 1950. (Irwin Rogers, *Edgar Rice Burroughs: The Man Who Created Tarzan,* 1975.)

BURSUM BILL. See PUEBLO LAND ACT OF 1924

BURTON, THEODORE ELIJAH. Theodore Burton was born on December 20, 1851, in Jefferson, Ohio. He graduated from Oberlin College in 1872, and, after reading law privately, he gained entrance to the bar in 1875 and practiced law in Cleveland. Burton won a seat as a Republican in Congress in 1888, lost in 1890, and won again in 1894, serving until 1908. He was elected to the United States Senate for a term in 1908 but failed to be re-elected in 1914. Burton was a progressive on domestic matters and an internationalist in foreign affairs. He won a seat in Congress again during the Warren G. Harding* landslide of 1920 and served there until he won a United States Senate seat in 1928. During the 1920s, Burton supported the League of Nations,* opposed high tariffs, and campaigned for the Kellogg-Briand Pact* outlawing war. Between 1924 and 1928, Burton also served as president of the American Peace Society. He died on October 28, 1929. (Forrest Crissey, *Theodore E. Burton: American Statesman,* 1958.)

BUSINESS CONFERENCES OF 1929. When the stock market collapsed late in 1929, President Herbert Hoover* was prepared to implement the macroeconomic management ideas he had developed in the 1920s. He was at first convinced that the crash, by bursting the speculative bubble, would release capital for legitimate investment and stimulate the economy. The key was confidence. If the leaders of the major corporations would resist panicky retrenchment and maintain wages and investment, the economy would recover quickly. Therefore, during November 19–23, 1929, Hoover convened conferences of leading executives in the business, finance, railroad, construction, and public utilities industries to organize cooperative private sector initiatives. Out of the meetings came three permanent programs: the National Business Survey Conference, a Chamber of Commerce* organization of 170 trade associations whose purpose was to maintain wages and stimulate new investment; the National Building Survey Conference,* which sought to stimulate new construction; and a new Division of Public Construction in the Department of Commerce to accelerate federal building projects. Eventually, however business leaders were not nearly as system oriented as Hoover had assumed. Disastrous quarterly earnings reports in 1930 triggered massive corporate retrenchment and layoffs, just what Hoover initially had wanted to avoid. (Martin Fausold, *The Presidency of Herbert C. Hoover,* 1985; Ellis W. Hawley, *The Great War and the Search for a Modern Order, A History of the American People and Their Institutions, 1917–1933,* 1979.)

BUSINESS CYCLE COMMITTEE. Chaired by General Electric executive Owen D. Young,* the Business Cycle Committee was composed of a number of forward-looking businessmen and economists. Inspired by the Unemployment Conference of 1921,* the committee was formed in 1923 to disseminate the

latest information about business cycle theory and proposals for economic stabilization. In particular, the committee wanted to help businessmen make rational
economic decisions free of speculation on the one hand and desperate retrenchment on the other. Although the committee was suspicious of government measures, they did promote a number of private sector initiatives to help stabilize the
economy during down cycles: unemployment insurance, wage maintenance,
export management, and construction "reserves" to guarantee capital investment
during slack periods. Eventually, the federal government adopted each of those
stabilizers, contrary to what the Business Cycle Committee had originally envisioned, but at least the committee's work had helped prepare policymakers for
the emergence of such economic management. (Evan B. Metcalf, "Secretary
Hoover and the Emergence of Macroeconomic Management," *Business History
Review* 49 [Spring 1975] 60–80.)

BUTLER, NICHOLAS MURRAY. Nicholas Murray Butler was born in Elizabeth, New Jersey, on April 2, 1862. He was educated at Columbia University
where he received his Ph.D. in 1884. Between 1885 and 1900, Butler taught at
Columbia and served as dean; in 1901, he became president of the university,
a post he held until 1945. Butler was a conservative Republican and political
adviser to Theodore Roosevelt, William Howard Taft,* Warren G. Harding,*
and Calvin Coolidge.* In 1910 Butler played a critical role in convincing Andrew
Carnegie to establish the Carnegie Endowment for International Peace.* Between
1925 and 1945, Butler served as president of the Carnegie Endowment for
International Peace and played a central role in implementing the Kellogg-Briand
Pact* on a world scale. During the 1920s, Butler promoted United States membership in the World Court* and limited cooperation with the League of Nations.*
In 1931 he was awarded the Nobel Peace Prize for his work in promoting
international understanding. Butler died on December 7, 1947. (Nicholas Murray
Butler, *Across the Busy Years,* 1939–1940; *New York Times,* December 7, 1947.)

BYRD, RICHARD EVELYN. Richard Byrd, the famous American explorer,
was born on October 25, 1888, in Winchester, Virginia, to one of the state's
most prominent families. He graduated from the United States Naval Academy
in 1912, but, because of an ankle injury, he resigned his commission in 1916.
With war clouds on the horizon, however, Byrd was called back into the navy,
and he graduated as a pilot in 1917. Byrd helped develop the first drift indicator,
allowing a pilot to measure an airplane's deviation from course because of winds,
and he helped plan the navy's first aerial crossings of the Atlantic in 1919 in a
large Curtiss aircraft. During the early 1920s, Byrd continued with a variety of
navy assignments, including a 1925 flying expedition to Greenland, which intrigued Byrd and inspired him with the idea of Arctic exploration. Late in 1925,
with backing from the National Geographic Society, John D. Rockefeller, Jr.,
and Edsel Ford, Byrd began to plan a flight over the North Pole.

On May 9, 1926, after arriving by ship at Kongsfjorden, Spitsbergen, Byrd and his associate Floyd Bennett took off in a Fokker trimotor aircraft named *Josephine Ford*. He completed the flight that day and came to national attention. In 1927, Byrd flew across the Atlantic with three other men in another Fokker trimotor plane. In August 1928, Byrd set sail for Antarctica, where he made his most important contribution to geographic knowledge. Early in January 1929, Byrd established his base camp, which came to be known to the world as "Little America." On November 28–29, 1929, Byrd navigated the flight over the South Pole. Byrd became the most famous explorer and adventurer of the 1920s. He returned to Antarctica in 1934 and 1935 to gather more scientific data, and again in 1940 and 1946. Richard Byrd died on March 11, 1957. (Richard Evelyn Byrd, *Alone,* 1938; Edwin P. Hoyt, *The Last Explorer: The Adventures of Admiral Byrd,* 1968.)

C

CAGNEY, JAMES. Jimmy Cagney was born on July 17, 1899, in New York City. Although he had no formal dance training, Cagney debuted in vaudeville as a female impersonator, and in 1920 appeared on Broadway as a speciality dancer in *Pitter Patter*. After two years on the vaudeville circuit, Cagney returned to Broadway for *Ritz Girl of 1922* and *Snapshots of 1923*. His other Broadway plays in the 1920s included *Outside Looking In* (1925), *Broadway* (1926), and the *Grand Street Follies of 1928*. His 1929 appearance in *Grand Street* resulted in a movie contract from Warner Brothers.* During the 1930s, Cagney moved back and forth from gangster movies to musicals. His most famous crime movie was *The Public Enemy* (1931), which made him a national star; the most remembered musical was *Yankee Doodle Dandy,* the story of George M. Cohan.* Cagney appeared in many more films during the 1950s and 1960s; the most famous one was *Mr. Roberts* in 1956. Cagney's last film performance was in 1983 in *Ragtime*. Jimmy Cagney died on March 30, 1986. (Michael Freedland, *James Cagney,* 1974; Ron Offen, *Cagney,* 1972.)

CAMELS. In 1913, the R. J. Reynolds Tobacco Company released Camel cigarettes, which became an immediate success. Richard J. Reynolds, head of Reynolds Tobacco, made extraordinary gains in marketing Camels during World War I when he provided free cigarettes to American soldiers fighting in Europe. By the end of the war, Camels accounted for one-third of all cigarettes produced in the United States. In 1921, Reynolds began vigorously advertising the cigarette, using the slogan "I'd walk a mile for a Camel," and by 1924 half of all American smokers were smoking Camels. By 1930 the R. J. Reynolds Tobacco Company had made the jump to radio advertising of the product. Camel cigarettes had become the most recognizable cigarette in the country. (Richard B. Tennent, *The American Cigarette Industry,* 1951.)

CANNON, JAMES, JR. James Cannon was born on November 13, 1864, in Salisbury, Maryland. He graduated from Randolph-Macon College in 1884 and earned a master's degree at Princeton in 1889. The year before, he had completed a divinity degree at the Princeton Theological Seminary, and in 1903 he received a doctorate in divinity from Randolph-Macon. Between 1884 and 1894, he was a Methodist minister, and he served as president of the Blackstone College for Girls between 1894 and 1911, and again between 1914 and 1918. During the years before and after World War I and in the 1920s, Cannon was one of the country's most articulate exponents of prohibition.* Between 1894 and 1920, he was also editor of several publications, including the *Methodist Recorder,* the *Baltimore and Richmond Christian Advocate,* the *Richmond Virginian,* and the *Christian Advocate.* Using those editorial forums, Cannon campaigned for the Eighteenth Amendment* and its enforcement once adopted. He was also appointed a bishop in the Methodist Church in 1918. In the presidential election of 1928,* Cannon led the temperance crusade against the candidacy of Governor Al Smith* of New York. His influence declined after 1929 when he was charged with adultery and misuse of church funds. Even though a church tribunal acquitted him of those charges, Cannon's days as a religious leader were over. Cannon spent the rest of his life trying to revive prohibition after its repeal in 1933. He died at a meeting of the Anti-Saloon League of America* on September 6, 1944. (Thomas M. Coffey, *The Long Thirst: Prohibition in America, 1920–1933,* 1975; Virginius Dabney, *Dry Messiah: The Life of Bishop Cannon,* 1949; Richard L. Watson, ed., *Bishop Cannon's Own Story,* 1955.)

CANTOR, EDDIE. Born Edward Israel Iskowitz in New York City on January 31, 1892, Eddie Cantor became a renowned American vocalist, comedian, and personality. By World War I, Cantor had broken into Broadway where he repeatedly played the role of a young man awakening to the wonders of women, alcohol, and culture. Throughout the 1920s, he appeared in several *Ziegfeld Follies,* and, early in the 1930s, he began to star in Busby Berkeley films, including *Whoopee* (1930), *Palmy Days* (1931), *The Kid from Spain* (1932), and *Roman Scandal* (1933). Cantor was also an early radio* star. He appeared on the "Rudy Vallee* Show" in 1930; and, in 1931, his own show, "The Eddie Cantor Show," opened on NBC and quickly became the most popular show on radio. By the 1950s Cantor had moved out to Hollywood, California, where he starred in his own weekly television show, a mixture of talk format and variety. Eddie Cantor died on October 10, 1964. (Barbara Naomi Cohen-Stratyner, *Biographical Dictionary of Dance,* 1982; John Dunning, *Tune in Yesterday: The Ultimate Encyclopedia of Old-Time Radio. 1925–1976,* 1976; *New York Times,* October 11, 1964.)

CAPONE, ALPHONSE. Al Capone was born on January 17, 1899, in Brooklyn, New York, and he grew up to become the most recognized criminal in the United States. Capone left school when he was fourteen and worked at a variety of jobs, including bartender and bouncer in several saloons. During one altercation with a drunken customer, Capone was cut with a knife in the face, and thereafter he bore the nickname "Scarface." Capone moved to Chicago early in 1920 and rapidly rose to leadership in the underworld, creating a huge operation in bootlegging (see also bootlegger) as well as in prostitution and gambling. Capone controlled an elaborate network of breweries, distilleries, and liquor distributorships by the 1920s, and he also controlled a number of influential Chicago politicians and police. He was ruthless in expanding his organization and in eliminating, literally, his competition. Capone was implicated in hundreds of murders during the so-called beer wars as he reduced the power of rival gangs. The most famous incident was the St. Valentine's Day Massacre in 1929 when Capone's mob machine-gunned seven people of the North Side Gang. By the late 1920s, Capone's organization was making more money from its gambling syndicates than from bootlegging, and, at the same time, they went into labor racketeering. In 1930 Capone was arrested, tried, and sentenced to one year in prison for carrying a concealed weapon in Philadelphia, and the next year the federal government charged him with income tax evasion and conspiracy to violate federal prohibition* laws. He was sentenced to eleven years in prison, and he served time in the federal penitentiaries in Atlanta and on Alcatraz. When prison physicians discovered that Capone was suffering from syphilis of the brain, he was released in 1939. Al Capone died on January 25, 1947. (John Kobler, *Capone,* 1971; *New York Times,* January 26, 1947.)

CAPPER, ARTHUR. Born on July 14, 1865, in Garnett, Kansas, Arthur Capper graduated from high school in 1884 and went to work for the *Topeka Daily Capital.* He reported on local and state politics and joined the Republican Party.* In 1891 he became the Washington, D.C., correspondent for the *Capital.* Two years later, Capper purchased the *Topeka Mail,* a small weekly, and over the years built a midwestern business empire by prudent purchases of ailing newspapers. By the early 1900s, his progressive Republicanism was being echoed in the editorial policies of the Capper newspapers. He ran for governor in 1912 on the Republican ticket, maintaining open sympathy for Theodore Roosevelt's Bull Moose candidacy. He lost a close election to Democrat George H. Hodges, but then overwhelmingly defeated Hodges in the 1914 election. In 1918 Capper won a seat in the United States Senate. He emerged as a leader of the farm bloc* in the 1920s, sponsored legislation to ease the marketing of farm products, and unsuccessfully tried to promote the McNary-Haugen Bill.* Capper was known also as a foreign policy isolationist and a critic of Republican presidents during the 1920s. He found them too conservative. During the 1930s, Capper was an early supporter of the New Deal, especially its work relief, agricultural, and Social Security measures. He became known as a Republican New Dealer, even though he remained loyal to his own party. Capper became somewhat critical of President Franklin D. Roosevelt* after 1936 because of the "court-packing" scheme and the drift toward an internationalist foreign policy. Arthur Capper remained in the Senate until 1949. He died on December 19, 1951. (Homer E. Socolofsky, *Arthur Capper: Publisher, Politician, and Philanthropist,* 1962.)

CAPPER-TINCHER ACT OF 1921. Also known as the Future Trading Act, the Capper-Tincher Act was a product of the farm bloc's* demand for reform. At the time, farmers were suffering from the postwar collapse of commodity prices, and many of them continued the old Populist refrain that middlemen were reaping huge profits while farmers starved. The act provided for federal regulation of the large grain exchanges by imposing a prohibitive tax on all speculative transactions. Farmers wanted to make sure they were getting a "real price" for their crops, not one artificially manipulated by eastern speculators. (R. R. Enfield, *The Agricultural Crisis, 1920–1923*, 1924; Theodore Saloutos and John D. Hicks, *Agricultural Discontent in the Middle West, 1900–1939*, 1951; James H. Shideler, *Farm Crisis, 1919–1923*, 1957.)

CAPPER-VOLSTEAD ACT OF 1922. Becoming law on February 18, 1922, the Capper-Volstead Act, or the Cooperative Marketing Act, was known at the time as the Magna Carta of cooperative marketing. Conservative Republicans joined the farm bloc* in supporting the measure because they hoped it would avert the mounting pressure for some type of federal price-fixing scheme. By marketing their crops through cooperatives, farmers could save substantial amounts of money on storage, handling, and commissions, benefitting from economies of scale. Farmers agreed to sell their crops exclusively through the cooperatives, and the cooperatives claimed the right to enforce the agreements. The Capper-Volstead Act exempted the cooperatives from antitrust laws in the interstate marketing of commodities. In 1926 Congress also established a Division of Co-operative Marketing in the Bureau of Agricultural Economics. (Theodore Saloutos and John D. Hicks, *Agricultural Discontent in the Middle West, 1900–1939*, 1951; Homer E. Socolofsky, *Arthur Capper: Publisher, Politician, and Philanthropist*, 1962.)

CARDOZO, BENJAMIN NATHAN. Benjamin N. Cardozo was born in New York City on May 24, 1870, to an old-line Jewish family. He received undergraduate, masters, and law degrees from Columbia University, and then concentrated on commercial law. He quickly gained the respect of the legal establishment because of the brilliance of his legal briefs, advice, and scholarly writings. In 1913 Cardozo was elected to the New York Supreme Court, but he was soon appointed to the New York Court of Appeals. In 1926 Cardozo won an unopposed election as chief judge of the court of appeals. Under Cardozo's leadership, the New York Court of Appeals came to be regarded as one of the most distinguished legal bodies in the country, second only to the United States Supreme Court. In 1932, President Herbert Hoover* nominated Cardozo to fill the Supreme Court vacancy created by the retirement of Oliver Wendell Holmes, Jr.* During the 1930s, Cardozo became part of the liberal wing of the Supreme Court, which viewed the Constitution as a living document capable of evolving and changing with the times. He died July 9, 1938. (Leonard Baker, *Back to*

Back: The Duel Between FDR and the Supreme Court, 1967; *Dictionary of American Biography,* supp. 2 [1958]; 93–96.)

CARNEGIE ENDOWMENT FOR INTERNATIONAL PEACE. The Carnegie Endowment for International Peace was established in 1910 by billionaire Andrew Carnegie, who wanted to promote world peace. Elihu Root,* the prominent Republican attorney and politician, was its first president. Nicholas Murray Butler* and James T. Shotwell,* both of Columbia University, were also involved in its founding. Although the Carnegie Endowment promoted world peace, it was not an ideological pacifist organization. Instead, it promoted international agreements which would be conducive to world peace. During the 1920s, the Carnegie Endowment endorsed United States membership in the League of Nations* and the World Court* and worked diligently to bring about the Kellogg-Briand Pact* of 1928, an international agreement renouncing war as a means of settling disputes, and the various conferences of the 1920s and early 1930s held to bring about arms reduction or disarmament. (Nicholas Murray Butler, *Across the Busy Years,* 2 vols., 1939–1940.)

CARRIER, WILLIS HAVILAND. Willis H. Carrier was born on November 26, 1876, in Angola, New York. He graduated from Cornell University with a major in electrical engineering in 1901 and immediately went to work for the Buffalo Forge Company. He stayed with the company until 1915, becoming chief engineer, but that year he decided to go into business for himself and established the Carrier Engineering Corporation. As an engineer, Carrier specialized in climate control, and he was responsible for a number of important inventions. While still with Buffalo Forge, Carrier had invented systems for humidifying and dehumidifying air and for moving air through large factories, and he had invented a dew point control system. When Carrier left Buffalo Forge in 1915, he was focusing his creative energies on a new refrigeration apparatus— the centrifugal compressor to cool air using nontoxic chemical refrigerants. In 1924 Carrier installed an air-conditioning system at the J. L. Hudson Department Store in Detroit. Four years later, he put similar systems in Washington, D.C., for the Senate and the House of Representatives. Air-conditioning systems also became very popular in the great theater palaces of the 1920s. By 1930 Carrier had installed air-conditioning systems in more than 300 theaters. During the 1930s, Carrier developed the process for air-conditioning high-rise buildings by piping chilled air from a central cooling station out to individual rooms. Willis Carrier retired in 1948 and died on October 7, 1950. (Carrier Corporation, *Twenty-Five Years of Air Conditioning,* 1947; M. Ingels, *W. H. Carrier: Father of Air Conditioning,* 1927; *New York Times,* October 8, 1950.)

CARSTENS, CHRISTIAN CARL. Carl Carstens was born in Bredstedt, Schleswig-Holstein, Germany, on April 2, 1865. When he was still a child, Carsten's family immigrated to the United States and settled in Iowa. Carstens graduated from high school in Davenport, Iowa, and he received a bachelor's degree from Grinnell College in 1891. He taught school for several years in Iowa and then received a master's degree from the University of Pennsylvania in 1900. Specializing in social work, Carstens received a Ph.D. at the University of Pennsylvania in 1903. Between 1903 and 1907, Carstens was assistant secretary of the New York Charity Organization Society, and then he was appointed director of the Massachusetts Society for the Prevention of Cruelty to Children; it was in the area of children's social needs that Carstens made his mark. Between 1921 and 1923, he was president of the American Association for Social Work, and, from 1921 to his death, he was director of the Child Welfare League. Under Carsten's direction, the Child Welfare League established professional standards for child welfare agencies throughout the United States, not only in the areas of adoption and child placement, but also in family counseling, foster care, and the needs of the retarded. When he died on July 4, 1939, Carstens was the most influential American in the field of child welfare. *(Bulletin of the Child Welfare League of America,* November 1939; Peter Romanofsky and Clarke Chambers, eds., *Social Service Organizations,* 1978.)

CARTER, AMON GILLES. Amon G. Carter was born on December 11, 1879, in Crafton, Texas. When he was still only twelve, Carter quit school and went to work selling newspapers, snacks, and lunches to railroad passengers. He held a variety of jobs until 1899 when he went to San Francisco and began to sell advertising. Upon his return to Texas in 1905, Carter got a job with the *Ft. Worth Star,* and in 1907 he was named advertising manager. That same year, Carter helped negotiate a merger of the *Ft. Worth Star* and the *Ft. Worth Telegram,* and he became vice-president of the new *Ft. Worth Star-Telegram.* He became president of the newspaper in 1923. He got in on the ground floor of the radio* business by establishing station WBAP in Fort Worth in 1922, and he was a founder of American Airlines in 1930. Carter made a fortune in the Texas oil business during the 1920s as well. Amon G. Carter died on June 23, 1955. *(National Cyclopedia of American Biography,* 1961, 43:486; *New York Times* and *Ft. Worth Star-Telegram,* June 24, 1955.)

CASTLE, WILLIAM RICHARDS, JR. William R. Castle was born on June 19, 1878, in Honolulu, Hawaii. He graduated from Harvard in 1900, and, between 1906 and 1917, he worked for Harvard. Castle joined the American Red Cross in 1917, and in 1919 he went to work for the State Department. In 1927 Castle became assistant secretary of state and in 1931 underscretary of state. He played important roles in drafting the agreements on the Hoover moratorium* in 1931 and the London Naval Conference of 1930.* An internationalist but also a Republican anti-Communist, Castle opposed American recognition of the Soviet Union in 1933 and eventually became an isolationist on the eve of World War II. Castle died on October 13, 1963. (L. Ethan Ellis, *Republican Foreign Policy, 1921–33,* 1968; *New York Times,* October 14, 1963.)

CATHER, WILLA SIBERT. Willa Cather was born in Winchester, Virginia, on December 7, 1876. In 1884 her family moved to Nebraska, and in 1895 she graduated from the University of Nebraska. She taught school for several years and took up journalism, working as a drama critic in Pittsburgh and as managing editor of *McClure's* between 1907 and 1912. In 1905 she published a book of short stories, *The Troll Garden,* and her first novel, *Alexander's Bridge,* was published in 1912. She then returned to Nebraska to devote herself fulltime to writing. Cather's works struck a responsive chord in American society because she evoked rural, agrarian values at a time when the United States was rapidly making the transition to an urban, industrial country. Her most important novels—*O Pioneers!* (1913), *The Song of the Lark* (1915), *My Antonia* (1918), and *One of Ours* (1922)—had a graceful, lyrical style and stressed the virtues of the rural past and the supremacy of moral and spiritual values over modern consumer culture. A large segment of American society in the 1920s had a nostalgic yearning for an earlier time, and Cather's novels became very influential over them. Willa Cather died on April 24, 1947. (Mildred R. Bennett, *The World of Willa Cather,* 1961; Edward K. Brown, *Willa Cather, A Critical Biography,* 1961.)

CATHOLICS. During the 1920s, Roman Catholics played a conspicuous role in American political and social life, not so much because of anything they intentionally tried to do, but because of the social and economic changes occuring in America which inspired a wave of nativism and ethnocentrism. Roman Catholics had been a tiny minority in the American population until the late 1840s, when the Irish potato famine sent several million immigrants to the United States. Irish Catholics settled primarily in the cities and inspired a powerful strain of nativism in the 1850s, symbolized by the rantings of the Know-Nothing Party. Anti-Catholicism then subsided until the 1890s, when new waves of Italian and Slavic Catholics poured into the country during what historians have since called the "new immigration." By the 1920s, there were more than 23 million Catholics living in the United States. They had become the largest denomination in the country.

For many native American Protestants, the growth of the Catholic Church was just a symbol of larger changes occuring in the United States. In 1920 the census department announced that, for the first time in American history, more people were living in cities than on farms. Not only did Protestantism seem on the decline, but so did rural life—both of them were succumbing to the waves of new, urban immigrants pouring into the country. Rural Protestants reacted strongly to the changes in America. They pushed prohibition* as a moral crusade, and they were enraged that Roman Catholics refused to see drinking as a moral issue. They campaigned for immigration restriction to stem the tide of Catholic and Jewish immigrants. The Ku Klux Klan* appeared again for the first time since Reconstruction, spreading into the north and targeting Catholics and Jews as well as blacks.

The struggle for power between an urban, Catholic North and a rural, Protestant South found expression in the politics of the decade, especially in the Democratic Party.* In the election of 1924,* the Democrats split badly. Rural Protestants, supporting immigration restriction, the Ku Klux Klan, and prohibition, backed William Gibbs McAdoo* for the presidential nomination; urban Catholics from the North, who opposed the Klan, prohibition, and immigration restriction, supported Al Smith.* The convention met in New York City and deadlocked for 102 ballots, ending only when John W. Davis* emerged as a moderate candidate. Incumbent Calvin Coolidge* destroyed the Democrats in the November elections. Four years later, Al Smith won the Democratic nomination, but because he was an Irish Catholic, southerners deserted the party in droves. Herbert Hoover* and the Republicans won easily. Catholicism and anti-Catholicism had been persistent themes throughout the 1920s, and the cultural disputes surrounding Roman Catholicism did not subside until the Great Depression* gave millions of Americans new problems to concern them. (James S. Olson, *Catholic Immigrants in America*, 1987.)

CATT, CARRIE CHAPMAN. Carrie Chapman Catt was born on January 9, 1859, in Ripon, Wisconsin. She graduated from Iowa State College in 1880 and then went to work in the public schools, teaching and serving as principal and eventually as superintendent. In the 1890s, she became interested in the women's suffrage movement, and in 1900 she was named chair of the organization committee of the National American Woman Suffrage Association,* a post she held between 1900 and 1904 and again between 1915 and 1920. Along with Jane Addams,* Catt founded the Woman's Peace Party in 1915, and in 1917 she urged women to support the war effort so as not to set back the suffrage movement. During the 1920s, Catt dedicated herself to women's issues and the peace movement. She founded and served as first president of the League of Women Voters,* established the Women's Joint Congressional Committee,* and lobbied for protective legislation for women. Catt also served as chair of the Committee on the Cause and Cure of War between 1925 and 1932. Her pacifism during the 1920s brought the criticism of conservatives in the United States, but she persisted in her commitment until German treatment of Jews in the 1930s forced her to moderate her position. Carrie Chapman Catt died on March 9, 1947. (*New York Times*, March 10, 1947; Mary Gray Peck, *Carrie Chapman Catt*, 1944.)

CENTRAL AMERICAN TREATY OF 1923. Between December 1922 and February 1923, representatives of the United States and Central American countries met in Washington, D.C., and drafted the General Treaty of Peace and Amity, which upheld the decision of the participating nations not to recognize any government in Central America in which power was achieved through revolution. (Dana G. Munro, *The United States and the Caribbean Republics, 1921–1933*, 1974.)

CHAMBER OF COMMERCE. The United States Chamber of Commerce was established in 1912 by Charles Nagel, the secretary of commerce and labor for President William Howard Taft.* It quickly evolved into one of the most powerful interest groups in the country, and became the recognized spokesman for the business community. Harry A. Wheeler, a banker with the Union Trust Company in Chicago, served as its first president. During the 1920s, Julius H. Barnes* was its most prominent leader. The chamber really came into its own then, primarily because its objectives fit so nicely with those of the Republican Party,* which dominated the federal government. The Chamber of Commerce tried to secure legislation outlawing labor union strikes, opposed government ownership of the railroads, and helped push through Congress the Transportation Act of 1920,* which returned the railroads to private control. The chamber successfully worked to limit the authority of the Federal Trade Commission,* backed the high Fordney-McCumber* and Hawley-Smoot* tariffs, and provided support for the open shop movement.* At the same time, the chamber supported the associationalism* being promoted by Secretary of Commerce Herbert Hoover.* When the Great Depression spread across the United States after 1929, the chamber kept calling it a temporary phenomenon, and initially it supported the New Deal's efforts through the National Recovery Administration to deal with the economic decline. By 1935, however, the Chamber of Commerce was thoroughly disgusted with the anti-business, pro-labor philosophy of the New Deal and the mounting deficits. (Robert M. Collins, "Positive Business Response to the New Deal: The Roots of the Committee for Economic Development, 1933–1942," *Business History Review* 52 [1978], 369–91.)

CHANDLER, HARRY. Harry Chandler was born on May 17, 1864, in Landaff, New Hampshire. Although he came from a well-to-do family, his health forced him to move west in 1882, where he worked for a farmer outside of Los Angeles. In 1885 he got a job as a clerk for the *Los Angeles Times,* and in 1892 he married the daughter of Harrison Gray Otis, the owner of the paper. Over the years, Chandler built the *Times* into the most powerful newspaper on the west coast, while also building himself a real estate empire of hundreds of thousands of acres of farmland in the Imperial Valley, in deep southern California near the Mexican border, and in the San Fernando Valley north of Los Angeles. Using the *Times* as the information vehicle of his economic crusade, Chandler convinced southern California voters in 1903 and 1907 to pass large bond issues bringing water out of the Sierra Nevada mountains to the San Fernando Valley. As these plans were being developed, Chandler secretly bought up large ranches in the area. Eventually, Chandler acquired more than 60 million acres, which he divided up into real estate subdivisions. To bring new settlers to southern California, Chandler used the *Times* as a promotion, advertising entity. During winter months in the 1920s, he circulated special editions of the *Times* in the Midwest. During much of the 1920s, the *Los Angeles Times* had more advertising space sold than any other newspaper in the country.

Chandler's politics were quite conservative, and he was especially opposed to labor unions. A strong supporter of the open shop movement,* Chandler hated labor unions and militantly fought them. The enmity between him and labor leaders was so great that, in 1910, the *Times* building was dynamited, killing twenty employees. To keep the unions away, Chandler paid high wages, adopted the forty-hour week, rarely laid off loyal workers, and recognized the importance of seniority. Chandler was a conservative Republican, always opposed to the ideas of Senator Hiram Johnson, and a bitter opponent of the New Deal in the 1930s. Harry Chandler resigned from the newspaper in 1941 and died on September 23, 1944. (David Halberstam, *The Powers That Be,* 1979; *New York Times,* September 24, 1944.)

CHAPIN, ROY DIKEMAN. Roy Chapin was born in Lansing, Michigan, on February 23, 1880. Chapin studied for a while at the University of Michigan but quit in 1901 to work for the Olds Motor Works in Detroit. By 1904 he was general sales manager of Olds, and in 1906, with his friend Howard E. Coffin,* he founded the E. R. Thomas–Detroit Company. They both got financial backing from Joseph L. Hudson, owner of a chain of Detroit department stores, and founded the Hudson Motor Company. Chapin became president of the Hudson Motor Company in 1909 and remained in that position until 1923, when he became chairman of the board. After World War I, Hudson marketed the ''Essex,'' one of the most popular car models of the 1920s. In August 1932 Chapin became temporary secretary of commerce under President Herbert Hoover,* and he served permanently in that position between December 1932 and March 1933. Chapin returned to Hudson Motor Company and became president in 1934. He died on February 16, 1936. (David Burner, *Herbert Hoover: A Public Life,* 1979; John C. Long, *Roy D. Chapin,* 1945; *New York Times,* February 17, 1936.)

CHAPLIN, CHARLES SPENCER. Charlie Chaplin was born in London, England, on April 16, 1889, to a theatrical family. Because of his father's alcoholism and his mother's frequent bouts with mental illness, Chaplin spent his childhood on the London streets. He began performing on stage in 1897 in pantomine, and by the time he was twenty, he was the star of the Fred Karno Pantomine Group, a well-known international act. On their second tour of the United States in 1913, a representative of Keystone Films saw Chaplin's act and signed him to a contract. Chaplin moved to Burbank, California, in 1914 and began making Keystone films. An immediate success, he made thirty-five films in 1914 for a salary of $7,800, fourteen films for $67,000 in 1915–1916, and eleven films for $1 million in 1916–1917. In 1919, along with Mary Pickford,* Douglas Fairbanks,* and D. W. Griffith,* Chaplin founded United Artists Films.

During the 1920s, Chaplin became the first international media star in world history. His face, characterizations, screen antics, and offscreen life were disseminated around the world to a single audience. Along with radio,* films were the vehicle for the beginning of a global culture, and the silent films of Chaplin were understood by audiences around the world. The character he played was that of the "Tramp"—a little man with a derby hat, cane, floppy shoes, baggy pants, and tight coat. It was a physical comedy in silent films, and Chaplin was a gifted comedian. In the Keystone films, the Tramp was small but witty, able through physical and mental ingenuity to escape the attacks of larger, bumbling figures. There was also a sexual pathos to the character because the Tramp was always too small or too different to have much masculine appeal to women characters. In the 1931 film *City Lights,* through kindness, the Tramp restores the sight of a blind flower girl, who had previously imagined him to be a tall, strong, and handsome man, instead of the tiny, vulnerable man she now sees in front of her.

Chaplin made three sound films in the 1930s but then he retired. The rest of his life was one of great controversy caused by his own sexual adventures, divorces, outspoken support of liberal causes, and his refusal to take out American citizenship. During the Red Scare of the 1950s, Chaplin was accused of being a Communist, and in 1952 the State Department refused to allow him back inside the United States when he was returning from a trip to London. He settled in Switzerland and did not visit the United States for the next twenty years, refusing to allow any of his films to be distributed in the United States. In 1972 he did finally return to the United States to accept a special Oscar from the Motion Picture Academy. Charlie Chaplin, the world's first global superstar, died on December 25, 1977. (Charlie Chaplin, *Charlie Chaplin's Own Story,* 1916; Charlie Chaplin, *My Life in Pictures,* 1974; Pierre Leprohon, *Charles Chaplin,* 1970; Roger Manvell, *Chaplin,* 1974.)

"CHARLESTON." The "Charleston" was the most popular dance of the 1920s. It originated among black workers on the wharves of Charleston, South Carolina, and migrated north when those workers headed for jobs in World War I factories. Characterized by feet twisting and rapid forward and backward kicking steps, the "Charleston" appeared first in the black theater but by 1924 had made the jump to white audiences. In popular culture, the "Charleston" became the symbol of the "flapper"* and the rebellious abandon of the 1920s. (Lynne Fauley Emery, *Black Dance in the United States from 1619 to 1970,* 1972.)

"CHEERIO." "Cheerio" was a thirty-minute radio* program which ran daily on NBC from 1927 to 1940. Its star was Charles K. Field, who used the British greeting "Cheerio" to start each program, which then consisted of inspirational messages, uplifting stories, and good news. (John Dunning, *Tune in Yesterday: The Ultimate Encyclopedia of Old-Time Radio, 1925–1976,* 1976.)

CHESTER, COLBY MITCHELL. Colby M. Chester was born on July 23, 1877, in Annapolis, Maryland. He graduated from Yale in 1898, and in 1900 he received his law degree from the New York Law School. Chester quickly organized his own law firm, specializing in corporate law until World War I, when he joined the army. After the war, he joined the Postum Cereal Company as assistant treasurer, and in 1924 he was made president. Between 1924 and 1929, he aggressively promoted the company, eventually engineering the corporate merger of Postum with fifteen other companies to form the General Foods Corporation. He was president of General Foods until 1935, and, during those years, General Foods marketed some of the most popular product lines in the United States, including Postum, Post Toasties, Jell-O, Sanka coffee, and Maxwell House coffee. Chester stepped down from General Foods in 1935; he died on September 26, 1965. (E. L. Fisch, *Lawyers in Industry,* 1956; *National Cyclopedia of American Biography,* 1970, 52:435.)

CHICAGO RACE RIOT OF 1919. By the summer of 1919, racial tensions were mounting in Chicago. Between 1914 and 1919, the black population of the city had increased from 50,000 to 125,000 people as southern blacks left the cotton fields for wartime jobs in the city's factories. But when the war ended in 1918, demand for workers decreased, and job competition between blacks and working-class whites grew more intense. At the same time, there were thousands of black veterans returning home to Chicago after risking their lives in World War I, and they were less patient than ever before with segregation and discrimination. Finally, the country was caught up in the tensions of the Red Scare,* and fear of change and radicalism was at a peak. The tensions erupted into a full-blown race riot during the last week of July, 1919. A black teenager inadvertently swam across the imaginary line separating the white beach from the black beach at Lake Michigan, and a white mob threw stones at him until he drowned. When black bathers asked a policeman to intervene, he refused and protests started. Soon marauding groups of white youths had entered the black community in Chicago, burning buildings and attacking people on the streets. When the riot finally ended three days later, twenty blacks and fourteen whites were dead. The Chicago race riot was symptomatic of similar tensions throughout the country, for there were other serious race riots in the summer of 1919 in Washington, D.C., in New Orleans, and in a number of smaller southern cities. (Arthur I. Waskow, *From Race Riot to Sit-In: 1919 and the 1960s,* 1966.)

CHILD WELFARE CONFERENCE OF 1919. The rise of social work as a profession early in the twentieth century was largely a result of concern about the plight of children in an industrial society. Early progressive reformers campaigned against child labor and for improved orphanages, public schools, foster care, nutrition, and health. The first White House child conference, called in 1909 by President Theodore Roosevelt, led directly to the establishment of the Children's Bureau in the Department of Commerce and Labor. During the next ten years, social reformers continued their crusade, and in 1919 President Woodrow Wilson* convened another children's conference. Participants demanded federal legislation or a constitutional amendment prohibiting child labor as well as federal legislation in the areas of nutrition, infant and maternal health, hygiene, education, and juvenile delinquency. Among other things, the conference led to the passage of the Sheppard-Towner Act of 1921.* (Clarke A. Chambers, *Seedtime of Reform: American Social Service and Social Action, 1918–1933,* 1963; J. Stanley Lemons, *The Woman Citizen: Social Feminism in the 1920s,* 1973.)

CHRYSLER, WALTER PERCY. Walter P. Chrysler was born April 2, 1875, in Wamego, Kansas. Chrysler graduated from high school and worked in a number of odd jobs until he joined the Union Pacific Railroad as a machinist. He proved to be an excellent mechanic and travelled around the country, working for several large railroads. In 1910 Chrysler quit as head machinist for the Chicago and Great Western Railroad and went to work for the American Locomotive Company. By that time, he was already interested in automobiles,* and in 1912 Chrysler went to work for the Buick Motor Company in a management position. He was an immediate success, changing production processes and taking authority away from the older foremen, who were largely holdovers from the carriage-making era. In 1916 Chrysler became president of Buick. He resigned from Buick after an argument with William C. Durant,* the head of General Motors.

It was a fortuitous decision. Chrysler, at a salary of $1 million a year, took over management of the Willys Overland Company, as well as the management of the Maxwell Motor Company. Both of them were near bankruptcy. While working to save those companies, Chrysler was developing a new car with hydraulic brakes and a high-compression engine. He released the car in 1924, and it made immediate profits; Maxwell Motor Company was renamed the Chrysler Corporation. To provide the company with larger production facilities, Chrysler purchased the Dodge Motor Company in 1928, and, in the process, he created one of the most successful automobile companies in the country. He then introduced the Plymouth and DeSoto models. Walter Chrysler retired as president of the Chrysler Corporation in 1935. He died on August 18, 1940. (Walter O. Chrysler, *Life of an American Workman,* 1950; *New York Times,* August 19, 1940; John B. Rae, *The American Automobile Manufacturers,* 1959.)

CITIZENS' COMMITTEE ON IMMIGRATION LEGISLATION. See AMERICAN COALITION OF PATRIOTIC SOCIETIES

CITIZENS' RECONSTRUCTION ORGANIZATION. Because of the banking* crisis, which had developed in the 1920s and intensified after 1929, currency hoarding was creating serious liquidity problems in the monetary system. Since early in 1930, the amount of currency in circulation had grown by more than $1 billion as depositors turned their bank deposits into cash. In January 1932 Congress had established the Reconstruction Finance Corporation* (RFC) to make loans to troubled banks, and in February 1932 President Herbert Hoover* created the Citizens' Reconstruction Organization (CRO), a voluntary association to sponsor an antihoarding campaign. Hoover obtained Frank Knox, owner of the *Chicago Daily News,* to direct the organization, and Hoover and Knox sponsored a national conference at the White House of more than forty private associations to discuss and promote the campaign. Throughout the country, local Citizens' Reconstruction Organization groups were established to support the publicity campaign. Although Hoover placed great faith in the CRO and hoped it would supplement the work of the RFC, it proved to be no more than a Band-Aid because of the immensity of the banking crisis in 1932 and 1933. (James S. Olson, *Herbert Hoover and the Reconstruction Finance Corporation, 1931–1933,* 1977.)

CLARK, JOSHUA REUBEN, JR. J. Reuben Clark, Jr., was born in Grantsville, Utah, on September 1, 1871. He graduated from the University of Utah in 1898 and received a law degree from Columbia University in 1906. He joined the State Department as a solicitor in 1906, served on the staff of the Judge Advocate General during World War 1, was a special counsel to the Washington Naval Conference* of 1921, and was special counsel to Ambassador Dwight Morrow* in Mexico in 1927 and 1928, where he advised Morrow about the legal implications of the oil and agricultural controversies there. In 1928 President Calvin Coolidge* appointed Clark undersecretary of state, after which Clark wrote what became known as the Clark Memorandum. First published in 1930, the Clark Memorandum argued that the Monroe Doctrine did not apply to purely inter-American relations and that the United States should not intervene so frequently in the internal affairs of its Latin American neighbors. The Clark Memorandum became the foundation for the Good Neighbor Policy,* which Hoover* and then Roosevelt implemented in the 1930s. In 1930 Clark succeeded Morrow as ambassador to Mexico. He left the State Department in 1933 when Franklin D. Roosevelt* and the Democrats took control of the government, worked for a while as president of the Foreign Bondholders Protective Council, and spent much of the rest of his life as a leader of the Mormon Church. J. Reuben Clark, Jr., died on October 6, 1961. (Robert H. Ferrell, ''Repudiation of a Reputation,'' *The Journal of American History* 51 [March 1965], 669–73; Ray C. Hillam, *J. Reuben Clark, Jr., Diplomat and Statesman,* 1973.)

CLARK MEMORANDUM. See CLARK, JOSHUA REUBEN, JR.

CLIFFORD, JACK. Jack Clifford was born in San Francisco, California, in 1885. Clifford tried his hand at prize fighting before moving to New York, where Florenz Ziegfeld, Jr.* signed him to a dance contract in 1911. He danced in several Ziegfeld productions and toured the country with Miriam Wills with their *Jaspar Junction* dance and comedy act. Clifford became a leading actor in films during the mid-1920s, usually playing the villain in more than forty westerns. Jack Clifford died on November 10, 1956. (Barbara Naomi Cohen-Stratyner, *Biographical Dictionary of Dance,* 1982.)

COAL STRIKE OF 1919. Although the coal companies had prospered greatly during World War I, coal miners had enjoyed only stable wage levels because of a 1917 agreement freezing their wages for the duration of the conflict. By 1919 miners were demanding wage increases, and when the United Mine Workers (UMW) cautioned them to be patient, a series of wildcat strikes by independent unions erupted throughout the coalfields. Some miners were demanding nationalization of the mines. John L. Lewis,* head of the United Mine Workers and a bitter anti-Communist, rejected nationalization but in September 1919 called for an agreement with the coal operators providing for a 60 percent wage increase, a five-day week, a six-hour day, and a nationwide contract. The coal companies rejected the demands out of hand, and after federal arbitration attempts in October 1919 failed, Lewis called for a strike to begin on November 1, 1919.

The strike call came at the peak of the Red Scare,* when large numbers of Americans were convinced that a radical Communist conspiracy was preparing to overthrow the government. Attorney General A. Mitchell Palmer* was busily rounding up supposed radicals, and President Woodrow Wilson* was not about to accept a crippling strike in the coalfields. At the end of October, a federal court issued an injunction outlawing the UMW strike. The next day, however, more than 400,000 miners went on strike, convincing the American public that radicals really had taken over the coalfields. When another federal court injunction failed to end the strike on November 11, the Justice Department initiated contempt proceedings against John L. Lewis and various UMW officials. President Woodrow Wilson at the same time agreed to a 14 percent wage increase. The strike ended on December 10, 1919. (Robert K. Murray, *Red Scare: A Study in National Hysteria, 1919–1920,* 1955.)

COBB, TYRUS "TY" RAYMOND. Ty Cobb was born on December 18, 1886, in Narrows, Georgia. He signed a professional baseball* contract in 1904. In 1905 his mother shot and killed his father in an accident while he was trying to catch her with a lover. Ty Cobb never really regained his emotional composure and spent the rest of his life dealing with a psychological rage over the killing. He began to play with the Detroit Tigers in 1905, and although he became extraordinarily successful as a player, accumulating a lifetime batting average of .367, he was a loner despised by opponents and teammates alike. Until Cincinnati Reds star Pete Rose passed him by in 1985, Cobb's record of 4,191 lifetime hits seemed unbeatable. Cobb was released by the Tigers in 1926 in a move which stunned the sports world. Investigators found out that Cobb had been accused of intentionally losing a game in 1919 to the Cleveland Indians in return for a kickback. Although he was subsequently exonerated, he was a beaten man. Cobb played in 1927 and 1928 for the Philadelphia Athletics, but he retired at the end of the season. By that time, the game of baseball had changed dramatically, moving away from the emphasis on defense, speed, and base hits to the power hitting and run scoring abilities of sluggers like Babe Ruth.* An early investment in Coca-Cola stock made Cobb a fortune, but he lived out the rest of his life in a miserable loneliness that matched that of his playing days. Ty Cobb died on July 17, 1961. (Charles C. Alexander, *Ty Cobb*, 1984.)

COCA-COLA. See WOODRUFF, ROBERT WINSHIP

COFFIN, HOWARD EARLE. Howard Coffin was born on September 6, 1873, near West Milton, Ohio. Off and on between 1893 and 1902, Coffin worked and attended the University of Michigan, although he never graduated. He was fascinated with gasoline and steam automobiles, and in 1902 Coffin joined the Olds Motor Works as an engineer. In 1906 he and Roy Chapin* formed the E. R. Thomas-Detroit Company, which in 1910 evolved into the Hudson Motor Company. Coffin concentrated on engineering new cars; Chapin focused his energy on sales and administration. President Woodrow Wilson* named Coffin head of the Council of National Defense during 1917 and 1918. By that time Coffin was also interested in aircraft and aeronautics, and he left the automobile business except for occasional consulting assignments. In 1923 he founded and served as president of the National Aeronautical Association, and in 1925 he established the National Air Transport Company, which later became United Air Lines. Coffin served as president of National Air Transport from 1925 to 1928 and chairman of the board from 1928 to 1930. He retired in 1930, and he died on November 21, 1937. (Charles Kelly, Jr., *The Sky's the Limit*, 1963; *New York Times*, November 22, 1937.)

COHAN, GEORGE MICHAEL. George M. Cohan was born on July 4, 1878, in Providence, Rhode Island. Since his parents used the family in its touring vaudeville act *Four of a Kind*, Cohan was performing before stage audiences as a small child. He formed a partnership with Sam Harris, and together they produced a number of shows in the 1910s. Cohan managed his own theaters, which was unheard of at the time. He danced, staged, and owned his own productions and became one of the most well-known Broadway performers of the 1920s and 1930s. In fact, Cohan became known as "The Man Who Owned Broadway," and he even performed in a minstrel show of that title. Cohan performed in many silent films, including *The Phantom President* (1923), *Seven Keys to Baldpate* (1925), and *Broadway Jones* (1926). George M. Cohan died on November 5, 1942. (George M. Cohan, *Twenty Years on Broadway*, 1925; John McCabe, *George M. Cohan: The Man Who Owned Broadway*, 1973; Ward Morehouse, *George M. Cohan, The Prince of the American Theatre*, 1943.)

COLBY, BAINBRIDGE. Bainbridge Colby was born on December 22, 1869, in St. Louis, Missouri. He graduated from Williams College in 1890 and from the New York Law School in 1892. Between 1892 and 1936, Colby practiced law in New York City and helped found the Progressive Party in 1912. He ran unsuccessfully for governor of New York in 1912 and for the United States Senate in 1914 and 1916. After Theodore Roosevelt lost the presidential election in 1912, Colby supported the Woodrow Wilson* administration. Wilson named him vice-president of the U.S. Shipping Board in 1917. Colby replaced Robert Lansing* as secretary of state in 1920, and the supported the League of Nations.* During his tenure as secretary of state, he helped established the nonrecognition policy toward the Soviet Union, and his 1920 trip to Central America helped set the stage for the Good Neighbor Policy* later in the 1920s. Colby returned to the Republican fold in 1921. During the 1930s, he was a bitter opponent of the New Deal. Bainbridge Colby died on April 11, 1950. (*New York Times,* April 12, 1950; Daniel Smith, *Aftermath of War: Bainbridge Colby and Wilsonian Diplomacy, 1920–21,* 1970.)

"COLLIER HOUR." The "Collier Hour" was radio's* first nationally broadcast dramatic show. Between 1927 and 1932, NBC Radio broadcast the program weekly, using stories dramatized from *Collier's* magazine. Its most popular broadcasts were the stories of the "Fu Manchu" series, based on the Oriental criminal created by British writer Sax Rohmer. (John Dunning, *Tune in Yesterday: The Ultimate Encyclopedia of Old-Time Radio, 1926–1976,* 1976.)

COLLIER, JOHN. John Collier was born on May 4, 1884, in Atlanta, Georgia. Although he was raised amidst prosperity, it was a childhood marred by tragedy. Collier's mother died when he was thirteen, and his father committed suicide three years later. Collier attended Columbia University between 1902 and 1904, and between 1904 and 1906 he worked in Atlanta as a social worker and journalist. After travelling throughout Europe in 1907, Collier returned to New York City and went to work for the People's Institute, an organization trying to improve the lot of recent immigrants. Between 1908 and 1916, Collier also played a central part in the burgeoning national community center movement, although he was in a distinct minority because he insisted on cultural pluralism rather than on assimilation as the focus of social work. After World War I, Collier moved to California and taught at San Francisco State Teacher's College and served as state director of adult education.

    Fearing that Collier was too bolshevik, the state legislature eliminated the position in 1920, and Collier moved to New Mexico, where he lived for several months with the Pueblo Indians. Collier realized that these people had been able to maintain their culture, and he spent the rest of his life working on Indian affairs. In 1922 he became research agent for the Indian Welfare Committee of the General Conference of Women's Clubs, and in 1923 he founded and became executive director of the American Indian Defense Association, a group which called for the termination of the Dawes Severalty Act, for the preservation of Indian cultures, and for civil rights for Indians. For the next ten years, Collier continued his efforts to help Indian people, and in April 1933 Franklin D. Roosevelt* named him commissioner of Indian affairs. Collier, who held the position until 1945, was responsible for the "Indian New Deal," which returned some land to Indians and encouraged the preservation of tribal culture. After he resigned as commissioner of Indian affairs in 1945, Collier taught at the City College of New York and at Knox College. He died on May 8, 1968. (Lawrence C. Kelly, *The Assault on Assimilation: John Collier and the Origins of Indian Policy Reform,* 1983; Kenneth R. Philp, *John Collier's Crusade for Indian Reform, 1920–1954,* 1977.)

COLLINS, FLOYD. Floyd Collins was born on a farm in Barren County, Kentucky, in 1890. Floyd Collins was a thirty-five-year-old spelunker whose death received international attention in 1925. On January 30, 1925, Collins entered the Sand Cave in Barren County, Kentucky, just a few miles from Mammoth Caves. He was 125 feet down into the cave when he lost his footing and became tightly lodged in a small crevice about twelve feet long and only eight inches deep. The temperature was only 16 degrees. For the next sixteen days, the world listened on radio as rescuers tried to reach Collins. More than 20,000 spectators descended on central Kentucky, along with more than fifty reporters, three film crews from motion picture* studios, and dozens of radio* broadcasters. A circus atmosphere, complete with hot dog and soda pop sales- men, prevailed all around the cave, and Americans throughout the country lis- tened to their radios and read the newspapers trying to find news about Collins's fate. On two occasions, interviewers got close enough to Collins to interview him, heightening the tension and the ballyhoo. Sometime between February 12 and February 16, Collins died, ending the media carnival. The death of Floyd Collins in 1925 illustrated the power of the radio to link the entire country together in a common experience. (Michael Lesy, ''Dark Carnival: The Death and Transfiguration of Floyd Collins,'' *American Heritage* 27 [October 1976], 34–45.)

COMISKEY, CHARLES ALBERT. Charles Comiskey was born on August 15, 1859, in Chicago to a family of famine Irish immigrants. His father rose to enjoy some power in Chicago city politics, but Comiskey devoted himself to his only passion—baseball.* In 1878 he began playing for the Dubuque Rabbits, and in 1882 his contract was purchased by the St. Louis Browns of the American Association. He was a player-manager for the Browns late in the 1880s, and in 1890 he purchased the Chicago franchise of the Players League. The league folded the next year, and in 1892 Comiskey was manager of the Cincinnati Reds of the National League. By 1900 Comiskey was owner of a new American League franchise team in Chicago—the White Sox. He borrowed enough money to build Comiskey Park in 1910, and it became the model for other symmetrical baseball stadiums in the country. The real tragedy of Comiskey's life came with the Black Sox scandal* of 1919 when eight of his players allegedly conspired to lose the World Series in order to receive payoffs from gamblers. When news of the fix hit the press, baseball commissioner Kenesaw Mountain Landis* banned the players from baseball for life. Comiskey was heartbroken, and the franchise was shattered. His health deteriorated shortly after the scandal and he retired.

He died on October 26, 1931. (Gustav Axelson, *"Commy": The Life Story of Charles A. Comiskey,* 1919; *New York Times,* October 26, 1931.)

COMMITTEE FOR PROGRESSIVE POLITICAL ACTION. See CONFERENCE ON PROGRESSIVE POLITICAL ACTION

COMMITTEE OF FORTY-EIGHT. After the debacle of the election of 1912, most progressive Republicans abandoned the Bull Moose party and returned to the GOP fold, but a small number of them still hoped to effect a major political change in the United States with a progressive third party. Most regular Republicans wanted nothing to do with them; when Theodore Roosevelt and the Bull Moosers had left the party in 1912, it had guaranteed the election of Woodrow Wilson* and the Democrats. But in 1919 a number of former Bull Moosers, led by J.A.H. Hopkins of New Jersey, formed the Committee of Forty-Eight, who tried to build a coalition of workers and farmers to support Senator Robert M. La Follette* for president. La Follette realized the organization was hopelessly weak, and he refused to accept their nomination. In 1924, however, members of the Committee of Forty-Eight joined forces with the Conference for Progressive Political Action* and nominated La Follette for president. La Follette accepted the nomination of what became known as the Progressive Party* and ran for president against Republican Calvin Coolidge* and Democrat John W. Davis* in the election of 1924.* La Follette won only 16.6 percent of the popular vote; Coolidge won the election. The Committee of Forty-Eight then dissolved. (Kenneth MacKay, *The Progressive Movement of 1924,* 1947.)

COMMITTEE ON MILITARISM IN EDUCATION. The Committee on Militarism in Education was established in 1925 by a group of pacifists and isolationists, which included Oswald Garrison Villard.* The committee's major objective in the 1920s was the elimination of Reserve Officer Training Corps (ROTC) programs in high schools and colleges. The committee vigorously supported disarmament, the Kellogg-Briand Pact* of 1928, and the Neutrality Acts of the 1930s. The Committee on Militarism in Education disbanded after the Japanese attack on Pearl Harbor in 1941. *(New York Times,* 1925–1941.)

COMMONS, JOHN ROGERS. Born on October 13, 1862, in Hollendsburg, Ohio, John R. Commons graduated from Oberlin College in 1888 and received his A.M. there in 1890. He studied at Johns Hopkins and, between 1890 and 1904, he taught economics and sociology at Wesleyan, Indiana, Oberlin, and Syracuse. He began his career at the University of Wisconsin in 1905. An optimistic utilitarian, Commons believed that capitalism was capable of delivering the greatest good to the largest number of people. Since large organizations had assumed control of the economy, the key to stability and prosperity was government mediation between competing interest groups. His scholarship and political activities encouraged his view of capitalism. Commons served actively in the National Civic Federation* and in the American Association for Labor Legislation.* He wrote a plan for unemployment insurance using individual corporate reserves, which Wisconsin enacted in 1932. Between 1913 and 1915, Commons was a member of the U.S. Commission on Industrial Relations, where he advocated corporate planning and cooperation with the government. Pragmatic and committed, Commons played a crucial role in the 1920s in promoting the ideas of industrial responsibility, social welfare, and federal government coordination of the economy, which reached fruition in the New Deal of the 1930s. John R. Commons died on May 11, 1944. (Lafayette Harter, *John R. Commons*, 1962.)

COMMUNIST LABOR PARTY. See COMMUNIST PARTY

COMMUNIST PARTY. In 1919 John Reed and a number of other American radicals gathered in Chicago and established the Communist Labor Party. They named Alfred Wagenhaupt as their executive secretary. At the same time, a rival faction met in Chicago and established the Communist Party of America, with Louis C. Fraina as national secretary. Although both were Marxist, both supported the Bolshevik revolution, and both sought recognition from the Soviet Union, they differed on tactics. The Communist Labor Party believed in collaboration with such groups as the Socialists and International Workers of the World; the Communist Party wanted nothing to do with any groups that were not ideologically pure. When Vladimir Lenin urged Marxist groups around the world in 1921 to cooperate with the trade union movement, representative American Communists gathered in New York to reorganize the Communist Party of America. William A. Weinstone was selected as national secretary, and the next year he was replaced by Jay Lovestone. In 1922 the Communist Labor Party and the Communist Party of America met in a joint convention to patch up their differences, and, out of the meeting, came the United Communist Party. All during the early 1920s, the various Communist factions had been harassed by government agents pursuing their Red Scare* agenda.

In 1924, in order to establish themselves as a legal political entity, the United Communist Party formed the Workers Party of America and nominated William Z. Foster* as president and Benjamin Gitlow as vice-president. The party's ticket called for nationalization of all major industries, the end of all antilabor injunctions, the release of all political prisoners, an end to American imperialism, independence for all American colonies, and diplomatic recognition of the Soviet Union. Foster and Gitlow won 36,386 votes. The next year, the United Communist Party changed its name to the Communist Party of the United States of America. In 1928, Foster and Gitlow again ran for the presidency and vice-presidency, but this time they won only 21,181 votes. When the stock market crashed in 1929 and the country slipped into the Great Depression, the Communist Party was convinced that the collapse of capitalism, predicted by Karl Marx, was imminent, and they expected millions of unemployed workers to join their ranks. It was not to be. In the election of 1932, William Z. Foster again ran for president, this time with James W. Ford as his running mate. Out of more than 40 million votes cast, they won only 102,785. The Communist dream of revolution and redistribution of wealth, even in the depths of the Great Depression, was no match for the American ideology of freedom, opportunity, and progress. (Irving Howe and Louis Coser, *The American Communist Party: A Critical History,* 1957.)

COMPANY UNIONS. See OPEN SHOP MOVEMENT

CONFERENCE FOR PROGRESSIVE POLITICAL ACTION. A number of progressive protest groups functioned during the 1920s, protesting the pro-business atmosphere in Washington, D.C., and the suffering of workers and poor people. In 1922 the leaders of the railroad brotherhoods formed the Committee for Progressive Political Action, which became the Conference for Progressive Political Action (CPPA) after its first convention in 1922. During the congressional and gubernatorial elections of 1922,* the CPPA endorsed a number of candidates, many of whom won their elections. Senator Robert M. La Follette* of Wisconsin emerged as the leader of the CPPA, and under his direction its constituency broadened out from the railroad brotherhoods to include other labor unions, social welfare workers, Socialists, and antitrust advocates. In 1924 the CPPA secured the support of the American Federation of Labor* (AFL) and launched the Progressive Party* to challenge Calvin Coolidge* for the White House. The Progressive Party called for public control of all natural resources, elimination of all monopolies, increased taxes on the rich, elimination of child labor, minimum wages and rights to collective bargaining for labor, prohibition of anti-labor federal court injunctions, and an outlawry of war. Robert M. La Follette ran for president with Senator Burton K. Wheeler* of Montana as his running mate. They managed only 4.8 million votes out of the 28.6 million cast, and only thirteen electoral votes. Republican prosperity doomed them. The Conference for Progressive Political Action met in Chicago in 1925, and after hearing that the AFL would never again endorse a third party effort, they dissolved the organization. The deaths of Robert M. La Follette in 1925 and of Eugene V. Debs* in 1926 removed whatever influence a charismatic leader might have had on a revival of the organization. The Conference for Progressive Political Action was dead. (Kenneth C. MacKay, *The Progressive Movement of 1924,* 1947; James Weinstein, *The Decline of Socialism in America, 1912–1925,* 1967.)

CONFESSION MAGAZINE. One of the major publishing trends of the 1920s was the expansion in subscriptions and sales of the ''confession magazines.'' The rise of the city, the liberation of women, and the impact of the movie industry had all relaxed the Victorian sexual standards, and into the vacuum came the confession magazines—borderline pornography which titillated millions of readers with stories of romantic success and failure, divorce, fantasy, and adultery. Writers were able to grind out the stories in formula fashion, always surviving the cuts of the censors by couching their stories in moral didacticisms and by counseling readers to avoid similar mistakes in their own lives. The most successful of the confession magazines was Bernard Mac-Fadden's *True-Story*, whose subscription list soared from 10,000 buyers in 1919 to two million in 1926. What television soap operas did for American in the 1980s, confession magazines did in the 1920s. (Frederick Lewis Allen, *Only Yesterday: An Informal History of the 1920s,* 1931.)

COOLIDGE, CALVIN. Calvin Coolidge was born in Plymouth Notch, Vermont, on July 4, 1872. Plymouth Notch was the quintessential New England village, and Coolidge was raised amidst the Puritan virtues of thrift, caution, simplicity, and reserve. He graduated from Amherst College in 1895 and began practicing law in Northampton, Massachusetts, in 1897. A Republican, Coolidge became active in local politics and was elected to the state legislature in 1907. He served a term as mayor of Northampton in 1910 and 1911, won a seat in the state senate in 1912, and was elected lieutenant governor of Massachusetts in 1915. Coolidge won election as governor of Massachusetts in 1918 and rocketed to national attention in 1919 when he defiantly refused to accept the Boston police strike of 1919.* When Coolidge called out the National Guard to enforce law and order, he gained a reputation as a tough opponent of radicalism. He seemed a perfect running mate for Republican presidential nominee Warren G. Harding* in the election of 1920,* and together they handed the Democrats an unprecedented defeat. Calvin Coolidge became vice-president of the United States in 1921.

Fate then rescued Coolidge from obscurity. Warren G. Harding died of a stroke on August 2, 1923, and Coolidge became the thirtieth president of the United States. He assumed office at a difficult time. The various scandals of the Harding administration, especially Teapot Dome,* had recently come to light, destroying public confidence in elected officials. But Coolidge's New England reputation for honesty became a real asset. His simplicity and integrity contrasted sharply with the corrupt shenanigans of the "Ohio gang,"* and Coolidge became a reassuring symbol of stability to large numbers of Americans. He ran for the presidency on his own merits in the election of 1924* and defeated Democrat John W. Davis* and Progressive Robert M. La Follette.*

Coolidge had a limited view of the federal government. He firmly believed in free enterprise and business as the backbone of American culture, and he felt strongly that the federal government was to assist, but not to regulate or control, private business. Coolidge sustained the high tariffs of his precedessor and vigorously promoted Secretary of the Treasury Andrew Mellon's* campaign to reduce taxes on the rich. The results were the Revenue Acts of 1924,* 1926,* 1928,* and 1929.* Coolidge did not accept the theories behind the McNary-Haugen Bill* for farmers, and when it passed Congress in 1927 and 1928, the president vetoed it both times. The farm bloc* could not override the vetoes.

As far as Coolidge was concerned, the federal government had no business injecting itself so deeply into the private economy. When Congress passed a bill in May 1928 creating a federal corporation to develop hydroelectric power in the Tennessee Valley at Muscle Shoals,* Coolidge vetoed it. He also allowed the Sheppard-Towner Act* to be extended in 1927, but only with the provision that it would be discontinued in 1929.

On the social issues of the day, Coolidge charted a middle course. Republican businessmen were concerned about the waves of Catholic and Jewish immigration from southern and eastern Europe, but at the same time they did not want to hurt such a source of cheap labor. Coolidge eventually supported the National Origins Act of 1924* limiting immigration through fixed nationality quotas, but the measure also allowed for unlimited immigration from the Western Hemisphere. The president stood firmly behind prohibition.*

In foreign affairs, Coolidge was not as conservative. He supported American participation in the World Court* and cooperation with the League of Nations,* and he promoted the Kellogg-Briand Pact* of 1928, which outlawed war. Because Coolidge wanted the naval limitations of the Washington Naval Conference* extended to noncapital ships, he called the Geneva Naval Conference of 1927* to consider the measure. Although the conference broke up without an agreement, it nevertheless exposed Coolidge's commitment to disarmament. Coolidge was also anxious to improve U.S. relations with Latin America, and some historians pinpoint the beginning of the Good Neighbor Policy* in his administration. Coolidge decided not to run for re-election in 1928. He died on January 5, 1933. (Donald R. McCoy, *Calvin Coolidge: The Quiet President,* 1967.)

CORRIGAN v. *BUCKLEY* (271 U.S. 323). By a unanimous vote on May 24, 1926, the United States Supreme Court ruled that civil rights are not protected by the Fifth, Thirteenth, or Fourteenth Amendments against discrimination by private individuals. The case developed out of privately imposed residential covenants restricting neighborhoods to whites. The court ruled that the victims of such discrimination had not experienced the loss of any guaranteed civil rights. (Congressional Quarterly, *Guide to the U.S. Supreme Court,* 1979.)

COSTIGAN, EDWARD PRENTICE. Edward P. Costigan was a leading figure in Colorado progressivism for three decades. Born on July 1, 1874, in King William County, Virginia, he moved to Colorado with his family when he was still a boy. In 1897 he graduated from Harvard and then practiced law in Denver and Salt Lake City. Costigan early established his credentials as a progressive, serving as an attorney for the Denver Honest Election League and the Anti-Saloon League of America in the early 1900s and president of the Denver Civil Service Reform Association. Costigan helped found the Progressive Party in Colorado in 1912, endorsed the Bull Moose campaign, and failed to win the governorship in 1912 and 1914. In 1916 he endorsed Woodrow Wilson* for the presidency, and Wilson rewarded him with an appointment to the Tariff Commission in 1917. Costigan held the position until 1928, always campaigning for flexible, and usually lower, tariff schedules. He resigned in protest of Republican protectionism in 1928, and in 1930 he won a seat in the United States Senate as a Democrat. Costigan supported the candidacy of Franklin D. Roosevelt* in 1932 and became an avid New Dealer, aligning himself in the Senate with such progressives as George Norris,* Robert Wagner,* and Robert La Follette.* Ill health kept him from running for re-election in 1936, and he died on January 17, 1939. (New York Times, January 18, 1939.)

COTTON STABILIZATION CORPORATION. See FEDERAL FARM BOARD

COUNCIL ON FOREIGN RELATIONS. Formed in 1921 by the merger of several pro-League of Nations* groups and the American Institute of International Affairs, the Council on Foreign Relations was designed to serve as an educational organization informing the public on foreign policy issues. The leading figures in the original Council on Foreign Relations were General Tasker H. Bliss,* Professor Archibald Coolidge of Harvard University, Professor James T. Shotwell* of Columbia University, Professor George Beer of Columbia University, and financier Thomas Lamont.* The council limited its membership to 650 people and acquired an elitist reputation. It was strongly internationalist in its commitment. Beginning in 1922, the council began publishing the journal *Foreign Affairs,* and in 1931 it began to issue annually its *The United States in World Affairs.* (Council on Foreign Relations, *The Council on Foreign Relations: A Record of Twenty-Five Years,* 1947.)

COUZENS, JAMES JOSEPH. James Couzens was born on August 26, 1872, in Chatham, Ontario, Canada. Couzens attended public schools, and after he graduated he took courses at a local business college while working at several different jobs, including a stint in his father's soap factory. In 1890 Couzens went to work as a checker with the Michigan Central Railroad and in 1895 as a bookkeeper for the Malcomson Fuel Company. Alex Y. Malcomson, the owner of the company, was a personal friend of Henry Ford,* and together they founded the Ford Motor Company in 1902. Couzens wanted to be a part of it, so he borrowed $2,500 from Malcomson and invested in the stock. It was the financial decision of a lifetime. In 1903 Ford forced Malcolmson out of the company and made Couzens business manager and then a partner. Couzens resigned as business manager in 1915 after having personal differences with Ford; in 1919, he sold out his 11–percent stock interest for more than $30 million.

Couzen's interests had turned more political anyway. Between 1913 and 1915, he had served as Detroit Street Railroad Commissioner, and then he won a series of elections—police commissioner in 1916, mayor of Detroit in 1918, and mayor again in 1921. A Republican, Couzens was appointed to the United States Senate in 1922 to fill a vacated seat. In the Senate, Couzens opposed the conservatism and tax policies of the Harding* administration and generally allied himself with the progressivism of Senator Robert M. La Follette.* Couzens was re-elected in 1924 and 1930. In 1933 hé was a strong supporter of the New Deal, but he failed in his 1936 bid for re-election. James Couzens died on October 22, 1936. (Harry Barnard, *Independent Man: The Life of Senator James Couzens*, 1958; Allan Nevins and F. E. Hill, *Ford: The Times, The Man, and the Company,* 1954.)

COX, JAMES MIDDLETON. James M. Cox was born on March 31, 1870, in Jacksonburg, Ohio. After leaving high school, Cox went into the newspaper business and eventually established the Cox newspaper chain. He was elected to Congress as a Democrat in 1908 and served until 1913, when he became governor of Ohio, a post he held between 1913 and 1914 and again between 1917 and 1921. In the election of 1920,* Cox was the Democratic nominee for president, and his running mate was Franklin D. Roosevelt.* They campaigned on a theme of continuing Wilsonian internationalism and American entrance in the League of Nations,* but they could not compete with the return to normalcy* plea of Republican candidates Warren G. Harding* and Calvin Coolidge,* and they went down to one of the worst defeats in American political history. After the defeat, Cox continued to campaign for internationalism, a reduction of war reparations on Germany, and U.S. membership in the League of Nations. Although he did not support Franklin D. Roosevelt's candidacy for the 1932 Democratic presidential nomination, Cox actively campaigned for Roosevelt in the general elections of 1932, 1936, 1940, and 1944. James M. Cox died on July 15, 1957. (James E. Cebula, "James M. Cox, Journalist and Politician," Ph.D. dissertation, University of Cincinnati, 1972.)

CRANE, HART. Hart Crane was born in Garrettsville, Ohio, in 1899. During his brief life, he became one of America's most important poets. Crane's difficult childhood was characterized by enormous tension between his parents. The family moved to New York in 1916, and for the rest of his life Crane fought with alcoholism and sexual ambiguity, a confusion over his own bisexuality. His collected works of poetry include *White Buildings* (1926) and *The Bridge* (1930). Although his personal life was often a shambles, Crane's poetry was neither pessimistic nor absurdist, but instead was an affirmative search for the meaning of life. In his own life, he never found it. Crane went to Mexico in 1931 on a Guggenheim fellowship, and, during his return voyage, on April 26, 1932, he committed suicide. (Frederick J. Hoffman, *The 1920s: American Writing in the Postwar Decade,* 1949; *New York Times,* April 27, 1932.)

CRASH OF 1929. During the 1920s, the stock market in the United States underwent extraordinary, unprecedented expansion. The country was caught up in a speculative euphoria, and, between 1925 and 1929, confidence and optimism were transformed into a cult of unlimited expectations. The *New York Times* stock index stood at 65 in 1921 and rose to 134 at the end of 1924, 180 at the end of 1926, 245 at the end of 1927, and 331 at the end of 1928. On the last day of August 1929, the index stood at 449. That was the peak. The Great Crash of 1929 was about to ensue. During September 1929, even though stock prices declined modestly, broker loans had increased by $670 million, indicating that the speculative fever had not diminished; on October 23, the index dropped from 415 to 384, and on October 24, "Black Thursday,"* the rout became a panic. A record of 12,894,650 shares changed hands, and the index dropped to 372. Only massive, organized buying by major banks and investment companies saved the day. On "Black Monday,"* October 28, the panic resumed. The *Times* industrial index fell 49 points that day on more than 9,250,000 shares. The next day, "Black Tuesday,"* saw the index fall another 43 points on 16,400,000 shares. The slide continued off and on until mid-November, when the stock index hit 224. Eventually, in July 1932, it bottomed out at 58. Instead of rising apace with corporate profits and productivity, the bull market of the 1920s had been fueled by Republican tax and budget policies, Federal Reserve irresponsibility, margin buying, an infusion of corporate and bank funds, and the creation of hundreds of bogus investment trusts, each issuing huge amounts of its own stock. The collapse of the stock market, along with the other weaknesses of the economy, sent the country into a tailspin from which it did not recover until the outbreak of World War II. (John Kenneth Galbraith, *The Great Crash 1929*, 1955; Robert Sobel, *The Great Bull Market: Wall Street in the 1920s*, 1968.)

CROLY, HERBERT DAVID. Herbert D. Croly was born on January 23, 1869, in New York City. Over the years, he studied at Harvard University and finally received a degree there in 1910. Croly served as editor of the *Architectural Record* between 1900 and 1906, and as founding editor of *The New Republic* in 1914. Croly's fame in American history came as the result of his 1914 book *The Promise of American Life,* in which he became the philosophical father of progressivism in general and of Theodore Roosevelt's "New Nationalism" in particular. Croly advocated a strong central government to stop the abuses of corporate power and to provide a variety of social welfare programs. During the 1920s and the New Deal, liberals looked to Croly as their intellectual progenitor. Herbert Croly died on May 17, 1930. (Herbert Croly, *The Promise of American Life*, 1914; *New York Times*, May 18, 1930.)

"CUCKOO HOUR." The "Cuckoo Hour" was one of radio's* earliest comedy and variety shows. Created by Raymond Knight, it came to NBC radio in 1930 and was loaded with satire, one-liners, and zany situations, with Knight starring as Ambrose J. Weems, manager of mythical radio station KUKU. "Cuckoo Hour" ran weekly on NBC radio through 1932. (John Dunning, *Tune in Yesterday: The Ultimate Encyclopedia of Old-Time Radio, 1925–1976*, 1976.)

CUMMINGS, E. E. E. E. Cummings was born in Cambridge, Massachusetts, in 1894 and was educated at Harvard University. During World War I, he served in an ambulance corps and was mistakenly imprisoned by the French for a short time. An account of his imprisonment appeared in 1922 when he wrote *The Enormous Room,* which attacked the consequences of bureaucracies and authoritarianism in modern society. Cummings was most popular for his lyrical love poems, which were comic and bawdy; his work was distinguished by his habit of writing only in lower case letters. In 1927, Cummings wrote his best play—*Him.* His collected works of poetry include *Tulips and Chimneys* (1923), *XLI Poems* (1925), *IS 5* (1926), and *No Thanks* (1935). E. E. Cummings died in 1962. (E. E. Cummings, *E. E. Cummings: A Miscellany,* 1958; Martin Seymour-Smith, *Who's Who in Twentieth Century Literature,* 1976.)

CURTIS, CHARLES. Charles Curtis was born in North Topeka, Kansas, on January 25, 1860. He studied law privately in Topeka and gained entrance to the Kansas bar in 1881. Curtis was prosecuting attorney for Shawnee County from 1885 to 1889, and he won a seat as a Republican in Congress in 1892. Curtis stayed in the House of Representatives until 1907, when he was sworn in as a United States Senator from Kansas. He failed to win re-election in 1912 but then was elected again in 1914. Curtis won subsequent terms in 1920 and 1926. Between 1924 and his resignation from the Senate in 1929, Curtis served as majority leader. Curtis was Herbert Hoover's* running mate in the election of 1928,* and he served as vice-president until March 1933. Charles Curtis died on February 8, 1936. *(New York Times,* February 9, 1936.)

CURTIS, CYRUS HERMANN KOTZSCHMAN. Cyrus Curtis was born on June 18, 1850, in Portland, Maine. He quit school in 1863 to work as an errand boy and salesman, but late in the 1860s he began to sell advertising space for several publications. In 1872 he established the *People's Ledger,* a weekly magazine. He sold the magazine in 1878 and became advertising manager for the *Philadelphia Press.* The next year, he established the *Tribune and Farmer,* another weekly magazine. In that magazine, Curtis had had his wife begin a section devoted exclusively to women's concerns; in 1883, he separated it out into a separate magazine—the *Ladies Journal and Practical Housekeeper.* An instant success, it had 25,000 subscribers by the end of the year. Curtis hired Louis M. Alcott to begin writing for the magazine, along with other popular writers, and it grew spectacularly. He renamed it the *Ladies Home Journal,* and circulation went over 700,000 by 1888. He hired Edward W. Bok as editor, and over the next thirty years Bok turned the *Ladies Home Journal* into one of the most influential magazines in the country. The most famous people in the country—politicians, businessmen, writers, and social workers—all contributed articles. By 1893 the circulation exceeded one million.

Curtis was not content with his success, and in 1897 he purchased the *Saturday Evening Post* for only $1,000. Although the *Post* was nearly moribund, Curtis poured money into it and hired George Lorimer as editor. Lorimer stayed in the position until 1936. Circulation went from less than 2,000 in 1899 to more than three million in 1937. The *Post* became for men what the *Journal* had become for women. During the 1920s, the *Saturday Evening Post* and the *Ladies Home Journal* were the dual symbols of the American middle class and its values. It was committed to democracy and capitalism and to business values, although it also supported competition and opposed monopoly. By 1929 the two magazines carried more than 40 percent of all U.S. magazine advertising. Curtis had built an extraordinarily influential empire. He died on June 7, 1933. (Edward W. Bok, *A Man from Maine,* 1923; Frank L. Mott, *A History of American Magazines,* 1938; *New York Times,* June 8, 1933.)

CUTTING, BRONSON MURRAY. Born on June 23, 1888, in Oakdale, New York, to a wealthy family, Bronson Cutting went his own way to become a journalist and United States senator. Cutting attended Groton and entered Harvard with the class of 1910, but, because of ill health, he moved to the New Mexico territory. Troubled by the social and economic problems of the region as well as by the political corruption of the territorial administration, Cutting adopted a progressive political philosophy. Mastering the Spanish language, he became a champion of the Spanish-speaking people of New Mexico. Cutting purchased a newspaper, the *Santa Fe New Mexican,* in 1912 and also published a Spanish edition, *El Nuevo Mexicano.* He used both as forums for his commitment to good government and democracy. Cutting supported Theodore Roosevelt's Bull Moose candidacy in 1912 and remained in the Progressive Party until 1916, when he returned to the Republican fold. His progressive credentials, however, remained intact. During World War I, Cutting served as assistant military attaché at the United States embassy in London. He was chairman of the New Mexico state penitentiary board in 1925 when Governor Richard C. Dillon appointed Cutting to fill the unexpired term of Senator Andricus A. Jones. Cutting was elected in his own right in 1928 and again in 1934. He was an avid supporter of the New Deal until his untimely death in an airplane crash on May 6, 1935. *(New York Times,* May 7, 1935.)

D

DARROW, CLARENCE. Clarence Darrow was born in Kinsman, Ohio, on April 18, 1857. He attended Allegheny College and the University of Michigan Law School and was admitted to the Ohio bar in 1878. In 1887 Darrow moved to Chicago and joined the law firm of John Peter Altgeld. An opponent of capital punishment, Darrow earned a reputation as one of the country's most successful trial lawyers, especially in first-degree murder cases. Among his more prominent clients were Eugene V. Debs,* William "Big Bill" Haywood,* Nathan Leopold, and Richard Loeb (see entry under Loeb-Leopold case). Darrow became an expert in the use of psychiatric evidence. He also gained national attention in 1925 when he defended John Scopes and squared off against William Jennings Bryan* in the famous "Monkey Trial"* in Dayton, Tennessee (see also entry under evolution). By 1933 Darrow was known throughout the country as a defender of the poor and oppressed. In 1934 he headed a special government commission investigating the National Recovery Administration (NRA), and, in his final report, Darrow concluded that the NRA was indeed dominated by monopolies and that only a planned economy with socialized ownership would ever resolve the problem. Clarence Darrow died on March 13, 1938. (Arthur Weinberg and Lola Weinberg, *Clarence Darrow: A Sentimental Rebel,* 1980.)

DAUGHERTY, HARRY MICAJAH. Harry Daugherty was born in Washington Court House, Ohio, on January 26, 1860. He graduated from the University of Michigan with a law degree in 1881, and in 1890 he won a seat as a Republican in the state legislature. Harry Daugherty had a singularly losing record as a politician, failing to win election as attorney general in 1894, as congressman in 1896, as governor in 1897, and as United States Senator in 1902, 1908, and 1916. What he did have was a close personal relationship with Senator Warren G. Harding,* and, when Harding became president in 1921, Daugherty was appointed attorney general.

As attorney general, Daugherty presided over what became known in Washington, D.C., as the "Ohio gang,"* the group of Harding's cronies who received top-level appointments in the new administration. Jesse Smith, Daugherty's close personal friend, committed suicide in 1923 when news began to leak out that he had been deeply involved in bribery and kickbacks involving the Alien Property Custodian's Office.* Daugherty was indicted as well, but he was acquitted of those charges in a trial in 1927. Nevertheless, President Calvin Coolidge* forced Daugherty to resign from the Cabinet in 1924. Harry Daugherty died on October 12, 1941. (Thomas Dixon, *The Inside Story of the Harding Tragedy,* 1932; *New York Times,* October 13, 1941; Eugene P. Trani and David L. Wilson, *The Presidency of Warren G. Harding,* 1977.)

DAVIES, MARION. Marion Davies was born Marion Cecillia Douras in Brooklyn, New York, on January 3, 1897. After graduating from high school in 1916, she attended the Theodore Kosloff Ballet School and then several acting schools in New York City. She had a featured role in Jerome Kern's* 1914 *Nobody Home* and in the *Ziegfeld Follies* of *1916.* Davies signed a contract with William Randolph Hearst's* Cosmopolitan Studios in 1918 and soon after began her long affair with the newspaper tycoon. The Hearst papers began an extraordinary publicity campaign in 1919 which eventually became the first example of overexposure. Davies's first film hit was *When Knighthood Was in Flower* in 1922. Davies had a fine comedic talent which Hearst's exhaustive, constant media blitz eventually destroyed, at least in the public's mind. Davies made several films after the appearance of sound films, including *Blondie of the Follies* (1932) and *Page Miss Glory* (1933), but her career faded after that. She retired from films in 1937 and lived out her life as a caricature of the Hollywood princess in the castle Hearst built for at San Simeon, California. Marion Davies died on September 23, 1961. (Fred Guiles, *Marion Davies: A Biography,* 1972; *New York Times,* September 24, 1961.)

DAVIS, ARTHUR VINING. Arthur V. Davis was born on May 30, 1867, in Sharon, Massachusetts. He graduated from Amherst College in 1888 and went to work with Charles Martin Hall, the inventor of aluminum; together they formed the Pittsburgh Reduction Company. They renamed it the Aluminum Company of America (Alcoa) in 1908. Aluminum was the perfect product for the industrial age, especially when the rise of aviation put a premium on light metals. Davis became president of Alcoa in 1910 and chairman of the board in 1928. Alcoa completely dominated the aluminum industry, and, throughout the 1910s and 1920s, Davis was fighting off Department of Justice antitrust suits. His business was closely associated with the interests of Andrew Mellon* and Richard Mellon, and Andrew Mellon's influence as secretary of the treasury in the 1920s undoubtedly helped Davis succeed in maintaining the corporate integrity of the company. By the time he retired as Alcoa's chairman of the board in 1957, Davis had accumulated a personal fortune approaching $500 million. He was also a major land owner and real estate developer in Dade County, Florida, during the 1950s. Arthur Davis died on November 17, 1962. (Charles Carr, *Alcoa: An American Enterprise,* 1952; *New York Times,* November 18, 1962.)

DAVIS, CHESTER CHARLES. Chester C. Davis was born near Linden, Iowa, on November 17, 1887. He attended Grinnell College and, after graduating in 1911, he began a career in journalism, agricultural economics, and government service. Davis served as managing editor of *The Montana Farmer* from 1917 to 1921 and then went into the state civil service as commissioner of agriculture and labor. Davis specialized in grain production and marketing, and in 1925 he went to work as director of grain marketing for the Illinois Agricultural Association. Along with George Peek,* Davis became one of the leading advocates of the McNary-Haugen plan* to dump farm surpluses abroad after they had been purchased from farmers at fair market value by the federal government. In 1928 Davis endorsed Al Smith* for president and played a critical role in getting the Democratic National Convention to endorse McNary-Haugenism. Soon after, Davis became enamored with the domestic allotment ideas of Professors John Black* and Milburn Wilson to raise farm prices by restricting production. Between 1929 and 1933, Davis was vice-president of the Maizewood Products Corporation. He then joined George Peek, who had been head of the new Agricultural Adjustment Administration (AAA). When Peek resigned at the end of 1933, Davis became the new head of the AAA. In 1936 Davis left the AAA to accept a position on the board of governors of the Federal Reserve Board. He became president of the Federal Reserve Bank of St. Louis in 1941. Davis retired from that position in 1951 to become a director of the Ford Foundation. He died on September 25, 1975. (Dean Albertson, *Roosevelt's Farmer: Claude R. Wickard in the New Deal,* 1961; *New York Times,* September 26, 1975; Edward L. Schapsmeier and Frederick H. Schapsmeier, *Henry A. Wallace of Iowa: The Agrarian Years, 1910–1940,* 1968.)

DAVIS, DWIGHT FILLEY. Dwight F. Davis was born in St. Louis, Missouri, on July 5, 1879. He graduated from Harvard in 1900 and took a law degree at Washington University in 1903. Davis served in a number of appointive offices in St. Louis while practicing law there, and he was an unsuccessful Republican candidate for the United States Senate in 1920. President Warren G. Harding* appointed Davis to the board of the War Finance Corporation* in 1921, and named him assistant secretary of war in 1923. Calvin Coolidge* named Davis secretary of war in 1925, where he served until 1929, when President Herbert Hoover* named him governor general of the Phillippines. Davis returned to private life in 1932. He died on November 28, 1945. (Donald R. McCoy, *Calvin Coolidge: The Quiet President,* 1967; *New York Times,* November 29, 1945.)

DAVIS, JAMES JOHN. James J. Davis was born on October 27, 1873, in Tredegar, South Wales. He immigrated with his parents to the United States in 1881 and went to work in the steel mills of Pittsburgh and the surrounding area at the age of eleven. Davis moved to Elwood, Indiana, in 1893 and continued working in steel and tin plate mills. In 1898 he became city clerk for Elwood and in 1903 recorder for Madison County, Indiana. A Republican and a member of the Amalgamated Association of Iron, Steel, and Tin Workers, Davis served as secretary of labor in the cabinets of Warren G. Harding,* Calvin Coolidge,* and Herbert Hoover.* Davis was a strong advocate of federal public works construction as a way of dealing with unemployment problems. He resigned as secretary of labor in 1930 and successfully ran for the United States Senate. He was re-elected in 1932 and 1938. During the 1930s, Davis was an advocate of minimum wages, maximum hours, collective bargaining, and unemployment assistance, but he strongly opposed Franklin D. Roosevelt's* attempt to pack the Supreme Court in 1937, and he criticized the size of the federal bureaucracy. James J. Davis left the Senate in 1945 and died on November 22, 1947. (James J. Davis, *The Iron Puddler,* 1922; *New York Times,* November 23, 1947; Francis Russell, *The Shadow of Blooming Grove: Warren G. Harding in His Times,* 1968.)

DAVIS, JOHN WILLIAM. John W. Davis was born on April 13, 1873, in Clarksburg, West Virginia; he received undergraduate and law degrees from Washington and Lee University in 1892 and 1895. After teaching law for two years at Washington and Lee, Davis went into private practice and became active in local Democratic politics. He served one term in the West Virginia legislature in 1899 and one term as a United States congressman between 1911 and 1913. He left the House of Representatives when President Woodrow Wilson* named him solicitor general. Because of his intense hatred of Germany and his personal friendship with Secretary of State Robert Lansing,* Davis was named ambassador to Great Britain in 1918, a post he held until 1921. Widely recognized as a moderate Democrat, Davis was a dark-horse candidate for president in 1924. When the Democratic National Convention at New York City deadlocked between William Gibbs McAdoo* and Al Smith* and after it failed to reach a decision after 102 ballots, Davis emerged as a compromise candidate and won the nomination. In the general election, however, he could not overcome the prevailing prosperity and Calvin Coolidge's* ''squeaky clean'' reputation. Davis lost the election. He returned to private law practice after the election, and, during the 1930s, Davis became deeply alienated from Franklin D. Roosevelt* and the New Deal. As a fiscal conservative, Davis could not tolerate the increased power of the federal government or the deficit spending. His opposition was so bitter that he helped organize the American Liberty League to oppose Roosevelt in 1934, and in 1940 he endorsed the presidential candidacy of Republican Wendell Willkie. John W. Davis died on March 24, 1955. (William Henry Harbaugh, *Lawyer's Lawyer: The Life of John W. Davis,* 1973.)

DAVIS, KATHARINE BEMENT. Katharine Davis was born on January 15, 1860, in Buffalo, New York. Her family had a long history of support for feminism, abolition, and civil rights. Davis graduated from the Free Academy of Rochester, New York, with a degree in science in 1879 and then taught high school science. She earned a degree from Vassar College in 1892. Between 1892 and 1897, Davis worked for the St. Mary's College Settlement in Philadelphia, and then she went to graduate school at the University of Chicago, where she studied under economist Thorstein Veblen.* Davis received a Ph.D. in economics and social work in 1900. She then entered the field of corrections, serving as director of the women's reformatory at Bedford Hills, New York, between 1900 and 1914, and then as commissioner of corrections for New York City. She took over the city's parole commission in 1916. Between 1918 and her retirement in 1928, Davis was general secretary of the Rockefeller Foundation's Bureau of Social Hygiene, where she advocated an end to prostitution and improvements in public health and sex education. At times heavy-handed in her approach to moral and sexual problems, Davis nevertheless was one of the leading figures in the public health and corrections field during the 1910s and 1920s. She died on December 10, 1935. (Estelle Freedman, *Their Sisters' Keepers: Women's Prison Reform in America, 1830–1930,* 1981; Rebecca Deming Moore, *When They Were Girls*, 1937.)

DAVIS, NORMAN HEZEKIAH. Norman H. Davis was born August 9, 1878, in Normandy, Tennessee. Although he never graduated from college, he attended Vanderbilt and Stanford, and in 1905 he organized the Trust Company of Cuba. Davis was a successful financier, and he became prominent in Wall Street circles; in 1920 he was appointed by Woodrow Wilson* as undersecretary of state. Frustrated about the drift toward isolationism, Davis left the State Department in 1921 and throughout the 1920s campaigned for disarmament and American entry in the League of Nations* and the World Court.* He served as a delegate to the Geneva Economic Conference of 1927 and the World Disarmament Conference of 1932. Davis was one of the founders of the Council on Foreign Relations* in 1921.

When the Democrats returned to power in 1933, President Franklin D. Roosevelt* appointed Davis an ambassador-at-large, where he served as chairman of the American delegations to the London Naval Conference of 1935 and the Brussels Conference of 1937. Between 1938 and 1944, Davis headed the National American Red Cross. He died on July 1, 1944. (*New York Times*, July 2, 1944.)

DAWES, CHARLES GATES. Charles G. Dawes was born in Marietta, Ohio, on August 27, 1865. He graduated from Marietta College in 1884 and earned a master's degree there in 1887. In 1886 Dawes received a law degree from the Cincinnati Law School. Until 1894 he was a lawyer in Lincoln, Nebraska, and then he went into the electric utility industry. Dawes managed the Illinois election campaign of William McKinley in 1896, and in 1897 President McKinley appointed him comptroller of the currency. Dawes remained in that post until 1902, when he left government service to become president of the Central Republic Bank and Trust Company of Chicago. In 1921, President Warren G. Harding* named Dawes the first director of the budget after passage of the Budget and Accounting Act of 1921.* In 1924 he became the chief architect of the Dawes

Plan,* which reorganized the German reparations* debt to the allied nations. Dawes received the Nobel Peace Prize in 1925 for his work. Calvin Coolidge* selected Dawes as his running mate in the election of 1924,* and Dawes served as vice-president of the United States between 1925 and 1929. In 1932 President Herbert Hoover* appointed Dawes to head the Reconstruction Finance Corporation.* He left that position later in 1932 when the Central Republic Bank and Trust Company faced collapse during the banking crisis. Charles G. Dawes died on April 23, 1951. (Stephen A. Schuker, *The End of French Predominance in Europe: The Financial Crisis of 1924 and the Adoption of the Dawes Plan,* 1976; Bascom N. Timmons, *Portrait of an American: Charles G. Dawes,* 1953.)

DAWES PLAN. By the mid-1920s, the German economy was in ruins. The Reparations Commission of World War I had imposed a debt of $33 billion on Germany—their bill for the damage and death they had "caused" during the war. Between 1921 and 1925, Germany was to pay $375 million each year, and after 1925 the annual payments would rise to $900 million until the debt was paid in full. The reparations* burden crushed the German economy, triggering a runaway inflation, destroying the middle class, and all but undermining the Weimar Republic. The Reparations Commission declared Germany in default in 1923, and the French army moved into the industrialized Ruhr Valley to take its share of German assets.

In the United States, Secretary of State Charles Evans Hughes* realized that normal international trade patterns depended on the revival of the German economy. But as long as the reparations burden rested on the Germany economy, there would be no recovery. So in 1922 Hughes suggested the creation of an international commission to re-evaluate the entire reparations question. The French agreed to the idea in 1923, and in 1924 the Reparations Commission appointed a special committee, headed by Charles G. Dawes,* to propose solutions to the German currency, debt, and budget problems. To stabilize the German economy, the Dawes Commission proposed an international loan of $200 million to Germany and the issuance of a new reichsmark valued at nearly twenty-four United States cents. The German Reichsbank would be reorganized under allied supervision. The Dawes Plan also reduced the debt payments to $250 million for 1925, increasing gradually to $625 million in 1929. In 1925 and 1926, Germany could make its reparations payments out of the loan proceeds. To prevent damage to exchange rates, the German payments could remain inside Germany until economic conditions made the currency transfers feasible.

The Dawes Plan was accepted by Germany and the allied powers and went into operation on September 1, 1924. As part of the agreement, Belgian and French troops withdrew from the Ruhr Valley. The $200 million loan was extended, and an American, S. Parker Gilbert* of J. P. Morgan and Company, was appointed agent general of reparations to supervise the plan. Although the Dawes Plan relieved some of the economic pressure on Germany, it would not prove to be enough, and, later in the 1920s, the Young Plan* would again deal with the currency, reparation, and debt problem. (E. H. Carr, *International Relations between the Two World Wars, 1919–1939,* 1947; Harold G. Moulton and Leo Pasvolsky, *World War Debt Settlements,* 1926; Bascom N. Timmons, *Portrait of an American: Charles G. Dawes,* 1953.)

DAY, WILLIAM RUFUS. William Day was born on April 17, 1849, in Ravenna, Ohio. He graduated from the University of Michigan in 1870 and then earned a law degree there. In 1872 he returned to Ohio and set up a law practice in Canton. His practice was a prosperous one, and he became close friends with another Canton attorney—William McKinley. Both were active in Republican party politics, and Day became a confidant and adviser to McKinley. In 1897 President William McKinley appointed Day assistant secretary of state, and he became secretary of state in the president's cabinet in 1898. President Theodore Roosevelt appointed Day to the United States Supreme Court in 1903. He occupied that position as a conservative who strictly interpreted the Constitution. William Day resigned from the Supreme Court in 1922 and died on July 9, 1923. (*New York Times,* July 10, 1923.)

"DEATH VALLEY DAYS." "Death Valley Days" was radio's* earliest and longest running western adventure show. It debuted on NBC radio in 1930 and remained a weekly fixture until 1941, when CBS picked it up. Ruth Cornwall Goodson, a Vassar graduate and pure-bred easterner, wrote the true stories and maintained extensive research contacts with western life, although all the stories were written in New York. The show was sponsored by the Pacific Coast Thorax Company. (John Dunning, *Tune in Yesterday: The Ultimate Encyclopedia of Old-Time Radio, 1925–1976,* 1976.)

DEBS, EUGENE VICTOR. Eugene V. Debs was born in November 5, 1855, in Elmhurst, Illinois. He went to work for the Terre Haute & Indianapolis Railroad in 1870 and soon joined the local of the Brotherhood of Locomotive Fireman. Honest, committed, and unwaveringly trustworthy, Debs rose through the ranks of the railroad brotherhood, becoming national secretary and treasurer in 1880. In 1893, Debs became a founder and the first president of the American Railway Union, and from that position he promoted the cause of industrial unionism with unwavering passion. Debs led the American Railway Union in its famous strike against the Pullman Company in 1894, and he eventually spent six months in jail for defying court orders to call off the strike. When Debs came out of the federal prison, he was a confirmed Socialist.

In 1897, Debs founded the Social Democratic Party of America, and in 1900 he united it with portions of the Socialist Labor Party* to create the Socialist Party of America.* Debs ran for president on the Socialist ticket in 1900, 1904, 1908, 1912, and 1920, winning nearly 900,000 votes in the election of 1912. Debs had a vision of an industrial America in which the government owned the means of production in the major industries and provided a social welfare safety net for all families. Unlike other radicals of his generation, Debs insisted that socialism must come to America through the ballot box, not through revolution. He opposed American entry into World War I, and in 1918 he was sentenced to ten years in prison for sedition. His final run for the presidency was headquartered in 1920 in his federal prison cell in Atlanta. President Warren G. Harding* ordered Debs's release from jail in 1921. Widely known as the conscience of industrial America, Eugene V. Debs died on October 20, 1926. (Ray Ginger, *The Bending Cross: A Biography of Eugene Victor Debs,* 1949.)

DEMILLE, CECIL BLOUNT. Cecil B. DeMille was born on August 12, 1881, in Ashfield, Massachusetts. Between 1898 and 1900, he studied at the American Academy of Dramatic Arts in New York City, and then he made his acting debut on stage. But his real gift was as a director and scriptwriter, and between 1914 and 1956, he made more than 100 films. DeMille was known for his epic films—stories loosely tied to historical events, and often with Biblical themes, such as *The Ten Commandments* (1923) and *King of Kings* (1927) or *Cleopatra* (1934) and *The Sign of the Cross* (1932). DeMille's films in the 1920s also had great appeal because he frequently mixed Victorian themes with sex and violence, or extolled Christian virtues while portraying a wide range of sins. DeMille also made great artistic advances during the 1920s in film editing, moving away from the action scenes when individuals exit the screen on the right and enter again on the left in favor of more psychological space. Cecil B. DeMille was one of Hollywood's great directors and a giant figure in the film industry during the 1920s. He made his last film in 1956 and died on January 21, 1959. (Charles Higham, *Cecil B. DeMille,* 1973; Gene Ringgold and DeWitt Bodeen, *The Films of Cecil B. DeMille,* 1969.)

DEMOCRATIC PARTY. During the 1920s, the Democratic Party went through an important political and social transformation which reflected important changes simultaneously sweeping through the United States. Throughout its history, the Democratic Party had enjoyed a strong rural base among farmers in the South and the West. Generally, they opposed the tariff and banking policies of first the Federalists and then the Whigs and Republicans in the nineteenth century. Except for the devotion of the Irish Catholics in the cities after 1850, Democrats did not have an urban base in the Northeast.

But new waves of immigration changed all that late in the nineteenth century and early in the twentieth century. Millions of people from southern and eastern Europe poured into the cities of the Northeast and Midwest between 1880 and 1920, as did millions of southern blacks fleeing the ravages of the boll weevil in 1913 and seeking factory jobs during and after World War I. Northern cities became polyglot enclaves of immigrant groups bound together by the economic loyalties of a blue-collar existence. They joined labor unions and viewed the Republican Party* as the representative of corporate management. The black and European immigrants became faithful members of the Democratic Party.

The problem, of course, was that they did not fit well into the social and religious framework of the existing Democratic Party. Whereas most Democrats in 1900 lived in the South, the new immigrants settled in the North. Whereas most Democrats were farmers, the new immigrants were urban workers. Whereas most Democrats lived in a rural setting, the new immigrants were urbanites concentrated into huge, crowded tenements. Finally, whereas most Democrats were Protestants of a fundamentalist bent, the new immigrants were either Roman Catholics* or Jews. By 1920, they were two Democratic parties, one centered in the rural South and the other in the urban North.

The growing population of the North created an identity crisis for the South. The northern cities seemed to have become enclaves for Jews, Catholics, blacks, labor radicals, and secularism. Southern culture reacted during the 1920s with an aggressive assertion of its values and hatreds. The Ku Klux Klan* resurrected itself and spread into some of the northern cities, attacking immigrants, Catholics, Jews, and blacks and demanding immigration restriction. Southern Protestants insisted on enforcing the Eighteenth Amendment* and guaranteeing the survival of prohibition* and condemned the teaching of evolution.* The Democratic Party became the national stage upon which these conflicts were played out.

As for politics, the Democrats were the minority party during the 1920s. Disillusionment with the outcome of World War I had given Republicans both the White House and the Congress in the election of 1920.* Democrats made massive gains in the elections of 1922,* winning seventy-eight extra seats in the House and eight in the Senate, but the Republicans were still in control of Congress. In the election of 1924,* the Democrats self-destructed: The party's nominating convention was a bitter struggle between the northern and southern wings of the party—Governor Al Smith* of New York against William Gibbs McAdoo.* In the end, the Democrats turned to John W. Davis,* a compromise candidate, and lost the election to Republican Calvin Coolidge,* who ran on a platform of more prosperity. Congress remained solidly Republican. In the election of 1926,* the Democrats made some headway, reducing the Republican majorities modestly in both houses. It was the election of 1928,* however, which clearly showed how the Democratic Party was shifting. During the 1920s, the party's strength in the urban precincts of the North had grown enormously, and those gains were reflected in the decision to nominate Al Smith—an Irish Catholic, prohibition-hating opponent of the Ku Klux Klan. The South defected and supported the Republican candidate Herbert Hoover,* and Hoover won easily, but, in Congress, the Republican majority was 267 to 163 in the House and 56 to 39 in the Senate.

Once the Great Depression set in after 1929 and the Republicans lost the issue of prosperity, the Democrats were poised to make up for lost time. In the congressional elections of 1930,* they took control of the House for the first time since World War I. What they needed for 1932 was a presidential candidate who could win support from both the white South and the immigrant North. That candidate proved to be Governor Franklin D. Roosevelt* of New York.

Over the years, he had cultivated machine politicians and immigrants in New York City while at the same time maintaining his personal interests in farming, conservation, and water development. In Franklin D. Roosevelt, the Democrats had a perfect candidate. He put together the coalition of immigrants, workers, southern Protestants, intellectuals, Catholics, and Jews which dominated American politics for the next generation. It was during the 1920s, when the Democratic Party made its transition from a rurally based organization to a complex, national political institution, that it became the majority party in the United States. (David Burner, *The Politics of Provincialism: The Democratic Party in Transition, 1918–1932*, 1968.)

DEMPSEY, JACK. Jack Dempsey was born William Harrison Dempsey on June 24, 1895, in Manassa, Colorado, to Irish immigrant parents. He began boxing professionally in 1911 as "Kid Blackie," fighting in saloons and mining camps where he was also working. Dempsey had fought eighty professional fights before his shot at the heavyweight championship of the world in 1919. On July 4, 1919, he delivered an unmerciful beating to Jess Willard; the fight was stopped in the third round when the champion could not continue. Dempsey was not the most popular champion at first, primarily because of an incident which occurred during World War I. He did not serve in the military supposedly because he had an essential job at the Philadelphia shipyards. A photographer took a picture of Dempsey working a riveting gun in overalls, but the photo also showed that he was wearing expensive, patent leather shoes, making his claims to be working look ludicrous. Eventually, however, Dempsey overcame the public skepticism. He defended his title several times, and against Georges Carpentier in 1920, he fought before boxing's first "million dollar gate"— 80,183 fans paid $1,789,238 to see the fight. Dempsey, also known as the "Manassa Mauler," became one of the athletic stars of the 1920s, along with George Herman "Babe" Ruth,* Harold "Red" Grange,* Bobby Jones,* Bill Tilden,* and Walter Hagen.*

Jack Dempsey lost the title in 1926 to James Joseph "Gene" Tunney.* The fight remains one of the most controversial in sports history. Dempsey knocked Tunney down in the seventh round, but when Dempsey did not move to a neutral corner, referee Dave Barry stopped the count, escorted Dempsey to where he should have gone, and then resumed the count. Tunney had fourteen seconds, instead of nine, to recover, and he did, ultimately winning the decision and the championship. Dempsey spent the rest of his life as a prominent figure in the sporting world and as the owner of a popular New York City restaurant. He died on May 31, 1983. (Randy Roberts, *Jack Dempsey: The Manassa Mauler*, 1979.)

DENBY, EDWIN. Edwin Denby was born in Evansville, Indiana, on February 18, 1870. He took a law degree at the University of Michigan in 1896 and practiced law privately in Detroit. Denby won a seat as a Republican in Congress in 1904 and served there until 1911, where he chaired the House Naval Affairs Committee. He returned to private life after losing a bid for re-election in 1910, served in the Marine Corps during World War I, and then was appointed secretary of the navy in President Warren G. Harding's* cabinet in 1921. Shortly after joining the cabinet, Denby accepted Secretary of the Interior Albert Fall's* argument that the naval oil reserves at Teapot Dome* in Wyoming and at Elk Hills in California should be transferred from the jurisdiction of the Navy Department to the Department of the Interior. When it became clear three years later that Fall had leased those reserves to private interests in return for substantial kickbacks, Denby's reputation was ruined. He resigned as secretary of the navy in 1924. Denby was indicted in the scandal, but the Supreme Court later exonerated him. He returned to Detroit to practice law and died there on February 8, 1929. *(New York Times,* February 9, 1929; Burl Noggle, *Teapot Dome: Oil and Politics in the 1920s,* 1962.)

DEPRESSION OF 1920–1921. Beginning in 1920, the economic boom of World War I and the immediate postwar period turned to a bust. The index of wholesale prices for all commodities fell from 228 in 1920 to 151 in 1921, with raw materials and farm goods leading the way. Retail prices fell 13 percent during the same period. The gross national product fell from $40.1 billion to $37.6 billion, and 4,754,000 people were thrown out of work. The change in the economy had been very abrupt.

The economic decline resulted from several postwar changes in public policy and the end of the war. In farming, European production had fully revived from its World War I hiatus, cutting the demand for American products and reducing farm prices. Individual farmers, heavily in debt to finance wartime production increases, had severe cash flow problems. The only way they could cope with the combination of their debt payments and falling prices was to increase production, hoping that more volume would give them the income they needed to meet their needs. But as millions of farmers used that same approach in 1920 and 1921, over-production became even more and commodity prices fell further. The farm depression, which began in 1920, continued throughout the decade and reached catastrophic proportions in the early 1930s.

Government policy also contributed to the decline. In the last half of 1918, government spending had exceeded income by more than $9 billion, providing enormous purchasing power to the economy and creating millions of jobs. But when the war was over, the government began cancelling its war contracts. During the first half of 1920, government income exceeded spending by $831 million, imposing a net decline in purchasing power on the economy. The Revenue Act of 1919 had also raised the corporate income tax to 12 percent and the individual income tax rate to 8 percent for people making more than $4,000 a year. Tax policy also removed purchasing power from the economy. Finally, the Federal Reserve system raised the rediscount rate from 4.75 percent in 1919 to 7 percent in 1920, which reduced the money supply just when the government fiscal policy was eroding consumer purchasing power. The result was the depression of 1920–1921. (George Soule, *Prosperity Decade: From War to Depression: 1917–1919,* 1947.)

DePRIEST, OSCAR STANTON. Oscar DePriest was born on March 9, 1871, in Florence, Alabama, to a family of former slaves. His father was a farmer who supplemented family income by working as a teamster, and his mother worked part-time as a laundress. In 1878 the family left Alabama for Kansas, and in 1889 DePriest left home and settled in Chicago. He worked as a painter and contractor for several years and became active in local Republican politics. In 1904 DePriest was elected to the Cook County Commission. He was re-elected in 1906, defeated in 1908, and then became a successful real estate developer. In 1915, DePriest became the first black alderman in Chicago history. His star in the Republican Party* rose quickly, and in 1928 DePriest was elected to Congress from the Illinois 3rd Congressional District. Black voters put him in Congress and kept him there until 1935.

In Congress, DePriest was an advocate of Howard University and managed to get a law passed outlawing racial discrimination in the Civilian Conservation Corps in 1933. He unsuccessfully supported the federal antilynching law as well as the right of black government employees to be served in the House restaurant. DePriest was an outspoken opponent of communism, but he also condemned the conviction of the Scottsboro defendants. Black Democrat Arthur W. Mitchell defeated DePriest for re-election in 1934. DePriest then returned to his real estate business in Chicago. Between 1943 and 1947, DePriest served on the Chicago City Council. He died on May 12, 1951, after being hit by an automobile. (Maurine Christopher, *America's Black Congressmen,* 1971; Harold F. Gosnell, *Negro Politicians: The Rise of Negro Politics in Chicago,* 1967; *New York Times,* May 13, 1951.)

DEWEY, JOHN. John Dewey was born on October 20, 1859, in Burlington, Vermont. He received a bachelor's degree from the University of Vermont in 1879 and a Ph.D. from Johns Hopkins University in 1884. Dewey spent the rest of his life teaching philosophy at the University of Michigan (1884–1888 and 1889–1894), the University of Minnesota (1888–1889), the University of Chicago (1894–1904), and Columbia University (1904–1930). As a philosopher of education, Dewey applied the prevailing progressive theories of politics and jurisprudence to public and higher education, arguing for education based on practical experience rather than on authoritarian models. Following the philosophy of psychologist William James, Dewey believed in pragmatism—that truth was established through successful application. Dewey also opposed purely vocational education, which he found too narrow.

During the 1920s, Dewey became more prominent in the United States because of his internationalism and his commitment to the peace movement. Although he had supported American intervention in World War I, Dewey became an advocate of the outlawry of war in the early 1920s. He was active in the Committee on Militarism in Education,* opposing ROTC programs in schools. He also opposed the drift toward war in the 1930s and the passage of the Selective Service Act of 1940. A believer in the rationality of mankind, Dewey was always convinced that war could be eliminated as an act of national policy. John Dewey died on June 1, 1952. (George Dykhuizen, *The Life and Mind of John Dewey,* 1973; Charles F. Howlett, *Troubled Philosopher: John Dewey and the Struggle for World Peace,* 1977.)

DEWSON, MARY WILLIAMS. Mary W. Dewson was born February 18, 1874, in Quincy, Massachusetts. She was raised in a politically active home which supported the women's suffrage movement. Dewson graduated from Wellesley College in 1897 and then worked as an economic researcher for the Women's Educational and Industrial Union in Boston until 1900. Between 1900 and 1912, Dewson served as superintendent of the Massachusetts Girls' Parole Department. In 1911, she formed a friendship with Florence Kelley* and became active in the minimum wage movement of the National Consumers' League. From 1912 to 1917, she operated an experimental, scientific dairy in Massachusetts. When World War I broke out, Dewson left the dairy and became a zone chief in charge of immigrant refugees for the American Red Cross in Europe. Upon her return, she joined the National Consumers' League as a research secretary, and in 1925 she became president of the Consumers' League of New York. In that post, Dewson was a tireless campaigner for women's rights, national health insurance, minimum labor standards, and social security. An intimate friend of the Franklin D. Roosevelt* family, Dewson worked closely with Eleanor Roosevelt,* organizing women's groups in the Democratic Party* in the 1920s. In 1933 she became head of the Women's Division of the Democratic National Committee. In 1934 President Franklin D. Roosevelt appointed her to the Committee on Economic Security, which drafted the Social Security Act of 1935, and in 1937 the president named her a member of the Social Security Board. Ill health forced her to resign in 1938. Mary Dewson died on October 24, 1962. *(New York Times,* October 25, 1962; Paul C. Taylor, *Notable American Women: The Modern Period,* 1980; Susan Ware, *Beyond Suffrage: Women in the New Deal,* 1981.)

DINWIDDIE, COURTENAY. Courtenay Dinwiddie was born in Alexandria, Virginia, on October 9, 1892. He graduated from Southwestern University in 1901, and then did some graduate work at the University of Virginia until 1903. In 1905 Dinwiddie moved to New York City and became a secretary to the board of the Bellevue Hospital. Over the next several years, he worked for a variety of social welfare agencies, including the New York City Visiting Committee of the New York State Charities Aid Association (1906–1910), the Duluth City Board of Public Welfare (1910–1912), and the Associated Charities of Duluth (1912–1913). In 1913 Dinwiddie went to Cincinnati to head the Anti-Tuberculosis League. There he met Edward N. Clopper and developed a lifelong interest in the problem of child labor. In 1920 Dinwiddie became executive secretary of the National Child Labor Committee,* and after several years as director of the American Child Health Association and the Commonwealth Fund, he was elected general secretary of the National Child Labor Committee. His leadership of the committee lasted from 1930 to 1943. In his work, he focused on the lack of state regulation of child labor, the weakness of reported statistics, and the preference of employers to hire children rather than unemployed adults. Dinwiddie played a critical role in the adoption of the Fair Labor Standards Act of 1938, which severely restricted child labor. Dinwiddie died on September 13, 1943. (*New York Times,* September 14, 1943; Walter Trattner, *Crusade for the Children: A History of the National Child Labor Committee and Child Labor Reform in America,* 1970.)

DISABLED AMERICAN VETERANS. The Disabled American Veterans (DAV) was established in 1921 by Judge Robert S. Marx, a veteran of World War I who had sustained a permanent, war-related handicap. Marx founded the organization to lobby for greater government benefits to armed forces veterans suffering from war-related disabilities. The DAV was a highly patriotic organization which insisted on improvements in medical care for veterans, good employment programs, and rehabilitation. The Disabled American Veterans played an important part in the creation of the Veteran's Bureau (now the Veterans Administration) after World War I. (Edward L. Schapsmeier and Frederick H. Schapsmeier, *Political Parties and Civic Action Groups,* 1981.)

DOAK, WILLIAM NUCKLES. William N. Doak was born near Rural Retreat, Virginia, on December 12, 1882. He went to work for the Norfolk and Western Railroad in 1900 and joined the Brotherhood of Railroad Trainmen in 1904. Doak rose up through the union ranks, and in 1916 he was elected vice-president of the Brotherhood of Railroad Trainmen and served as a lobbyist in Washington, D.C. Doak made an unsuccessful bid for a Republican Senate seat in 1924, and in 1928 he became the managing editor of *The Railroad Trainmen.* In 1929, President Herbert Hoover* named Doak to the cabinet post of secretary of labor. Doak served until Hoover left office in March 1933. He died on October 23, 1933. (Walter F. McCaleb, *Brotherhood of Railroad Trainmen, with Special Reference to the Life of Alexander F. Whitney,* 1936; *New York Times,* October 24, 1933.)

DOHENY, EDWARD. Edward Doheny was born on August 10, 1856, near Fond du Lac, Wisconsin. He left home in 1872 for work as a mule driver in Arizona and New Mexico. Doheny worked at a variety of jobs, especially gold prospecting, for the next twenty years, but in 1893 he successfully drilled an oil well in Los Angeles, California. In 1900 Doheny bought leases on 250,000 acres of land in Tampico, Mexico, and when the market for oil eroded early in the 1900s he went into the manufacture of asphalt, selling contracts for half of the paved roads in Mexico City. The development of the automobile in the United States soon increased demand for petroleum products, and Doheny organized the Mexican Petroleum Company of California, which controlled most of the Tampico oil fields. In 1922 Doheny received the contract from the United States Navy to build a large naval fuel depot at Pearl Harbor in Hawaii. Later that year, after bribing Secretary of the Interior Albert Fall* with $100,000, Doheny received drilling rights on 32,000 acres of naval oil reserve land in Wyoming and California. It became known in the 1920s as the Teapot Dome* scandal. Although Fall was convicted of taking a bribe, Doheny was acquitted of the charges of offering the bribe. He claimed it was a loan. Nevertheless, the government cancelled his oil leases. His reputation ruined, Doheny sold his oil interests to Standard Oil of Indiana in 1925. Edward Doheny died on September 8, 1935. (*New York Times,* September 9, 1935; Burl Noggle, *Teapot Dome: Oil and Politics in the 1920s,* 1962.)

DOHERTY, HENRY LATHAM. Henry Doherty was born on May 15, 1870, in Columbus, Ohio. When his father died in 1882, Doherty had to go to work as an office boy at the Columbus Gas Company. Doherty rose steadily in the company, eventually to chief engineer and general manager. In 1898 he helped form a new holding company—American Light and Traction Company—of which he was the president. Seven years later, Doherty formed his own company, Henry L. Doherty and Company, which provided consulting services to utilities companies. Doherty established the Cities Services Company in 1910 by purchasing three utility operating companies, and by 1913 he had acquired fifty-three more of them. Doherty helped reorganize the weak companies, and in 1931 he built the first high-pressure gas line from Amarillo, Texas, to Chicago. During the 1920s Doherty built Cities Services into a huge utility. By 1932, its total assets exceeded $1.25 billion and included more than 200 natural gas and oil properties. To help rationalize the industry, Doherty helped found the American Petroleum Institute in 1919, and he served on its board of directors until 1931. Henry Doherty died on December 26, 1939. (*New York Times,* December 27, 1939.)

DORRANCE, ARTHUR CALBRAITH. See DORRANCE, JOHN THOMPSON

DORRANCE, JOHN THOMPSON. John T. Dorrance was born in Bristol, Pennyslvania, on November 11, 1873. He received an undergraduate degree from the Massachusetts Institute of Technology in 1895 and then earned a Ph.D. in chemistry from the University of Goettingen in 1897. That year he went to work for the John Campbell Preserve Company in Philadelphia, and two years later he invented the method for condensing soup by removing the water. The Campbell product became an immediate success, not only because the public liked it, but also because it could be shipped for so much less than competitive soups, which required the packing of water in the cans. By 1905 Campbell's Soup was selling five million cans a year. John Dorrance became president of Campbell's in 1914 and remained there until his death on September 21, 1930. His brother, Arthur Dorrance, had been born in Bristol in 1893 and had graduated from MIT with a degree in chemical engineering in 1914. He was vice-president of Franco-American Foods, a Campbell's subsidiary; when his brother died in 1930, Arthur became the new president of Campbell's Soup, where he served until his death on September 21, 1946. (Earl C. May, *The Canning Clan,* 1937; *New York Times,* September 22, 1930 and September 23, 1946.)

DOS PASSOS, JOHN RODERIGO. John Dos Passos was born on January 14, 1896, in Chicago, Illinois. He graduated from Harvard in 1916, full of Victorian optimism, but World War I transformed his intellectual outlook, as it did that of the entire world. Dos Passos was astonished at the brutality and meaningless of the war, especially the hatreds it created and the peace it failed to achieve. His first novels, *One Man's Initiation* (1919) and *Three Soldiers* (1921), argued that war was absurd, destroying not only the art and architecture of human history but also its values. During the 1920s, Dos Passos was disgusted with the rise of consumer culture, the politics of business conservatism, and the fear of social change. He was active in the defense of Nicola Sacco* and Bartolomeo Vanzetti,* and after their execution he began work on his famous U.S.A. trilogy: *The 42nd Parallel* (1930), *1919* (1932), and *The Big Money* (1936). The themes of his work revolved around the absurdities of materialism, violence, and fear in American culture. Dos Passos completed a second trilogy —*District of Columbia*—which included *Adventures of a Young Man* (1939), *Number One* (1943), and *The Grand Design* (1948). During his lifetime, Dos Passos gradually moved from left-wing socialism to Jeffersonian liberalism; the transformation represented his own growing skepticism about the human potential. John Dos Passos died on September 28, 1970. (Virginia Spencer Carr, *Dos Passos: A Life,* 1984; Townsend Ludington, *John Dos Passos: A Twentieth Century Odyssey,* 1980.)

DREISER, THEODORE. Theodore Dreiser was born in Terre Haute, Indiana, on August 27, 1871, to a poor, Roman Catholic family. He was the last of eleven children. After graduating from high school, Dreiser spent a year at Indiana University and then went to work as a journalist in Chicago, St. Louis, Toledo, and New York. His first novel, *Sister Carrie,* published in 1900, was a financial failure, even though literary historians came to view it as the classic example of naturalist literature. His 1911 novel *Jennie Gerhardt* was more of a financial success, and it established Dreiser's contemporary reputation. In 1912, 1914, and 1915, Dreiser published the trilogy about financier Frank Cowperwood: *The Financier, The Titan,* and *The Genius.* Ten years later, in 1925, Dreiser produced *An American Tragedy,* which made him a rich man. Dreiser's major theme was that individuals were caught up in impersonal social and economic forces beyond their control, that the bureaucracies, cities, and factories of modern society converted individuals into parts of complex social machines. Dreiser had a highly deterministic view of life.

Later in the 1920s, Dreiser joined the Communist Party* and travelled to the Soviet Union, which he wrote about in 1928 in *Dreiser Looks at Russia*. His writings also included several autobiographical works—*Dawn* (1931), *A Book about Myself* (1922); and *A Hoosier Holiday* (1916). Theodore Dreiser died on December 28, 1945. (Philip L. Gerher, *Theodore Dreiser,* 1964; Lawrence E. Hussman, Jr., *Dreiser and His Fiction: A Twentieth Century Quest,* 1983.)

"DRY." During the 1920s, the term ''dry'' came to refer to any individual who supported prohibition* and the Eighteenth Amendment* as well as any restaurant or night club that honored the law. Individuals who opposed prohibition and establishments which defied the law by serving alcohol were known as ''wet.''* (Norman H. Clark, *Deliver Us from Evil: An Interpretation of American Prohibition,* 1976.)

Du BOIS, WILLIAM EDWARD BURGHARDT. W.E.B. Du Bois was born on February 23, 1868, in Great Barrington, Massachusetts. His father abandoned the family when Du Bois was still just a child, and his mother died in 1884. Du Bois worked at odd jobs and was able to graduate from Fisk University in 1888. He then went to Harvard, where he received a bachelor's degree in 1890 and a master's degree in 1891. Du Bois studied at the University of Berlin between 1891 and 1893 and then returned to Cambridge to become, in 1895, the first black to ever receive a Ph.D. from Harvard. Specializing in economics and history, Du Bois joined the faculty of Wilberforce University in 1895 and then Atlanta University in 1897. Because he was raised in New England, Du Bois's experience with racism had been limited, but in Atlanta between 1897 and 1910 he came to know firsthand the pain of discrimination, and it left him with a lifelong resentment of white people and a passion to achieve equality for black people. His academic career was marked by his ground-breaking studies of black people in American history, including *The Souls of Black Folk* (1903), *John Brown* (1909), and *Black Reconstruction in America* (1910).

Du Bois also became active politically when he was in Atlanta. In 1905 he founded the Niagara movement, a black action campaign in opposition to the accomodationist views of Booker T. Washington. Washington told blacks to work hard and to avoid social and political confrontation; Du Bois urged the opposite, telling blacks to demand and work for social and political equality. In 1909 and 1910, Du Bois was a founder of the National Association for the Advancement of Colored People* (NAACP). He served on its board of directors and as editor of its publication, *Crisis,* from 1910 to 1934. During the 1920s, the journal was the leading publication in the movement for black rights, campaigning for a federal antilynching law, justice for the Scottsboro boys,* and full civil rights. Du Bois was also a leading figure in the pan-African movement, heading the Pan-African Congresses which met in Paris in 1919, in London, Brussels, and Paris in 1921, and in London, Lisbon, and New York City in 1923. Du Bois was the leading black activist of the 1920s. He left the NAACP in 1934 to teach at Atlanta University, but he returned to the organization in 1944. Later in his life, despairing of ever changing the racial situation in the United States, Du Bois joined the Communist Party in 1961 and moved to Ghana to live, where he died on August 27, 1963. (Jack B. Moore, *W.E.B. Du Bois,* 1981; Elliott M. Rudwick, *W.E.B. Du Bois: Propagandist of the Negro Protest,* 1968; Emma G. Sterne, *His Was the Voice: The Life of W.E.B. Du Bois,* 1971.)

DUFFY, FRANK. Frank Duffy was born in County Monaghan, Ireland, in 1861. He immigrated to the United States in 1881 and went to work in New York City as a carpenter. Duffy was active in union politics with the United Order of American Carpenters and Joiners. In 1900 he was elected to the executive council of the United Brotherhood of Carpenters and Joiners. Duffy became secretary-general of the union in 1901 and remained in that post for the next forty-eight years. He also served as a vice-president of the American Federation of Labor* between 1918 and 1940. Known as a conservative unionist, Duffy wanted improved pay and working conditions for workers but no fundamental change in the social and economic order. His political loyalties were Republican. Duffy retired in 1950 and died on July 11, 1955. (Robert A. Christie, *Empire in Wood: A History of the Carpenters' Union,* 1956; *New York Times,* July 12, 1955.)

DUNCAN, ISADORA. Isadora Duncan was born on May 27, 1878, in San Francisco, California. She was raised in an artistic family caught up in the Greek revivalist culture, which became so popular on the west coast in the 1880s. What set Duncan apart, however, was her unwillingness to be straitjacketed by Hellenism in her dance routines. Duncan abandoned the musical and format restrictions of Greek revivalism and instead used classic and Romantic music and performed her dances in popular theaters as well as before small private audiences. In the early 1900s, she worked with Augustin Daly in Chicago and New York, and then she traveled to Europe where she performed and lectured on "The Dance of the Future." Successful but also extraordinarily controversial, she established dance schools in Moscow and Grunewald and used dance as visualizations of entire musical scores. Duncan became the most influential figure in twentieth-century concert dance. She was blessed with a charismatic personality, a powerful performance style, and an absolute sense of personal independence. She is generally credited with the birth of modern dance. Isadora Duncan died on September 14, 1927, in Nice, France. (Paul Magriel, ed., *Isadora Duncan,* 1947; Francis Steegmuller, *"Your Isadora,"* 1974.)

DUNCAN, ROSETTA. See DUNCAN SISTERS

DUNCAN SISTERS. The Duncan Sisters, including Rosetta and Vivian Duncan, performed in an American theatrical dance act which was popular in vaudeville and on Broadway during the 1910s and 1920s. Rosetta Duncan was born on November 23, 1890, in Los Angeles, California, and her sister Vivian was born there on June 17, 1902. Their stage characters were always children, and they debuted on Broadway with *Doing Our Bit* in 1917. Concentrating on soft shoe and fancy dancing, they became extremely popular to theater audiences. Their greatest hit was *Topsy and Eve* in 1924, a Broadway version of *Uncle Tom's Cabin*. They toured across the United States and Europe performing *Topsy and Eve* between 1926 and 1929. Their last performance was in *New Faces of 1936*, after which they retired. Rosetta Duncan died on December 4, 1959. (Barbara Naomi Cohen-Stratyner, *Biographical Dictionary of Dance*, 1982.)

DUNCAN, VIVIAN. See DUNCAN SISTERS

***DUPLEX PRINTING PRESS COMPANY v. DEERING* (254 U.S. 443).** *Duplex Printing Press Company* v. *Deering* was decided on January 3, 1921, by a six to three vote of the United States Supreme Court. Justices Brandeis, Holmes, and Clarke dissented. The decision, consistent with the prevailing conservative business and political philosophy of the 1920s, interpreted the Clayton Act of 1914 very narrowly, holding that the federal courts were prohibited from issuing injunctions only against legal labor union operations. Illegal strikes and secondary boycotts were still subject to federal court injunctions. (Congressional Quarterly, *Guide to the U.S. Supreme Court*, 1979.)

DUPONT, PIERRE SAMUEL. Pierre duPont was born on January 15, 1870, in New Castle County, Delaware, to one of America's most prominent business families. The family made a fortune in chemical manufacturing, finance, and automobiles. Pierre graduated from the Massachusetts Institute of Technology in 1890 and then joined the family business, first in Delaware and then in New Jersey. He played a central role in the development of nitro cellulose, which enabled the production of a smokeless shotgun gunpowder. Pierre duPont left the family business in 1899 to become president of the Johnson Steel Company, but in 1902, through a series of complicated financial maneuvers, he purchased controlling interest in the DuPont Company. He was named president of the corporation in 1915 and then managed its huge profits during World War I, when it supplied more than 1.5 billion tons of explosives to the United States military. After the war, duPont purchased an interest in General Motors, and he served as president of General Motors from 1920 to 1923, and as chairman of the board until 1929. He also turned the family business away from production of explosives to a broader range of synthetic chemical products. Although he was a Republican, duPont at first cooperated with Franklin D. Roosevelt* and the New Deal, but he was soon disaffected by its spending policies, bureaucracy, and anti-business attitude. In 1934 duPont helped found the American Liberty League, an anti-Roosevelt lobbying group. Pierre duPont died on April 5, 1954. (Alfred D. Chandler, Jr., and Stephen Salsbury, *Pierre S. duPont and the Making of the Modern Corporation*, 1971; *New York Times*, April 6, 1954.)

DURANT, WILLIAM CRAPO. William C. Durant was born on December 8, 1861, in Boston, Massachusetts. Although he came from a well-to-do family, Durant left home in 1877 to work in his grandfather's lumberyard and at other odd jobs. In 1881 he was named manager of the Flint Water Works in Flint, Michigan. At the time, Flint led the nation in the manufacture of carriages and wagons, and Durant gradually fell into the business. In 1887 he established the Durant-Dort Carriage Company and became, in the next four years, the leading manufacturer of horse-drawn carriages in the United States. Durant established separate companies specializing in the production of timber, wheels, and spokes, and he used assembly-line techniques to put the carriages together. Durant stayed with the business until 1914, but, as far back as 1904, he had also been in the automobile business after buying the Buick Motor Car Company. Under Durant's leadership, Buick became the leading automobile manufacturer in the country. In 1908 he formed the General Motors Company by buying the Buick, Cadillac, Pontiac, and Oldsmobile motor companies; by bringing the Weston-Mott Axle Company from Utica, New York, to Flint; and by financing Albert Champion's design of a new porcelain spark plug.

Durant was pushed out of General Motors when the company came on hard times in 1910 after he had overproduced cars, so in 1911 he joined with Louis Chevrolet, a mechanic and race car driver, and together they established the Chevrolet Motor Car Company. This company was so successful that Durant began to acquire General Motors stock, and in 1916, with the financial help of John J. Raskob* and Pierre S. duPont,* he had enough stock to take control of General Motors again. The company came on hard times again during the depression of 1920–1921, when Durant again let automobile inventories accumulate too rapidly. Company stock prices sagged badly, and when Durant tried to maintain the price by margin buying, he became overextended. Pierre duPont then took control of the company in 1920 and Durant resigned. Durant tried again, this time forming the Durant Motor Company, but the Great Depression* destroyed the venture. Durant filed for bankruptcy in 1935. He died on March 18, 1947. (Lawrence R. Gustin, *Billy Durant*, 1973; Alfred P. Sloan, Jr., *My Years with General Motors*, 1969.)

E

EASTMAN, JOSEPH BARTLETT. Joseph B. Eastman was born on June 26, 1882, in Katonah, New York. He graduated from Amherst College in 1904 and received a fellowship to work at South End House in Boston. He took the position of secretary to the Public Franchise League in Boston in 1905 and remained there until 1913, when he began to assist Louis Brandeis* in investigations of the Boston Elevated Railway Company and the New York, New Haven & Hartford Railroad. Between 1913 and 1915, he served as adviser to the Electric Street Railway Employees' Union as a wage arbiter, and in 1915 he accepted appointment to the Massachusetts Public Service Commission, where he earned a reputation as an independent progressive who was willing to judge rate cases on their merits and who always considered the public welfare. In 1919 President Woodrow Wilson* appointed Eastman to the Interstate Commerce Commission (ICC), a position he held for the rest of his life.

During the 1920s, Eastman realized before anyone else that the railroads were in a desperate, long-range crisis. They were burdened by heavy debt structures and high, long-term fixed payments, and they were steadily losing freight volume to the expanding trucking industry. When World War I had ended, Eastman had urged the government not to turn the railroads back to private management but to bring about a forced consolidation of duplicated services. He also opposed wage increases to railroad workers because he believed that the railroads could not afford them. By 1933 Eastman was widely recognized as the most liberal mind in the transportation field. He helped draft the Emergency Railroad Transportation Act of 1933, and he accepted appointment under it as federal coordinator of transportation. Although Eastman believed the only answer to railroad troubles was massive reorganization and consolidation, as well as possible nationalization, he was unable as federal coordinator or later as chairman of the ICC (1939–1942) to bring about these goals. Joseph B. Eastman died on March 15, 1944. (Claude M. Fuess, *Joseph B. Eastman,* 1952.)

EDERLE, GERTRUDE. See KELLY, ALVIN "SHIPWRECK"

EDGE ACT OF 1919. See WEBB-POMERENE ACT OF 1918

EDGE, WALTER EVANS. Walter E. Edge was born in Philadelphia on No-
vember 20, 1873. Edge spent his early career in journalism. An active Republican, Edge won a seat in the New Jersey legislature in 1910 and then served in
the state senate between 1911 and 1916, when he won the governorship of New
Jersey where he served until 1919, when he entered the United States Senate.
He campaigned vigorously for international trade expansion, authored the Edge
Act of 1919,* and in 1929 was named ambassador to France by President Herbert
Hoover.* Edge returned to the United States in 1933 and served for years as a
political consultant for the Republican Party.* In 1944 he began another term
as governor of New Jersey and remained there until 1947. Walter Edge died on
October 29, 1956. (Walter Evans Edge, *A Jerseyman's Journal: Fifty Years of
American Business and Politics,* 1948; *New York Times,* October 30, 1956.)

EIGHTEENTH AMENDMENT. See PROHIBITION and VOLSTEAD ACT
OF 1919

ELECTION OF 1918. During World War I, both political parties had tried to
promote a bipartisan approach to the war, and the congressional elections of
1918 at least started out in that same spirit. Democrats had gained and maintained
control of Congress since the election of 1912, when Theodore Roosevelt and
William Howard Taft* had split the Republican vote, but in the intervening years
the GOP made up some of that lost ground. They were waiting for an opportunity
to attack the Wilson administration, and, on October 25, 1918, the president
gave them their chance. Concerned about having a strong bargaining position
when he went to Paris to help negotiate a formal treaty ending World War I,
President Woodrow Wilson* made the following appeal to voters: "If you have
approved of my leadership and wish me to continue to be your unembarrassed
spokesman in affairs at home and abroad, I earnestly beg that you will express
yourself unmistakenly to that effect by returning a Democratic majority to both
the Senate and House of Representatives."
    Republican leaders were outraged and sensed a real political opportunity. They
appealed for Republican unity at the polls, called for an "unconditional" surrender of Germany, accused Wilson of wanting to be easy on Germany, and
expressed distrust at the league of nations idea the president was promoting.
Voters also resented the president's attempt to control the outcome of the election,
and when the votes were in, the Republicans had gained six seats and control
of the Senate (48 to 47), and twenty-one seats in the House (237 Republicans
to 191 Democrats). Republicans also began looking with anticipation toward
1920 when they hoped to regain the White House. (Cortex A. M. Ewing,
Congressional Elections 1896–1944, 1947; W. Stull Holt, *Treaties Defeated by*

the Senate, 1933; William E. Leuchtenburg, *The Perils of Prosperity, 1914– 1932,* 1958.)

ELECTION OF 1920. The re-election of Woodrow Wilson* in 1916 had rested primarily on the theme of pacifism. The notable progressive reforms of his first term were overshadowed by his foreign policy, which Democrats claimed had kept the United States out of World War I. But war proved inevitable. Wilson took the oath of office on March 4, 1917, and Congress declared war on April 6. By the time of the peace treaty eighteen months later, Wilson's political position was deteriorating. Republicans made significant gains in Congress during the election of 1918, and in 1919 refused to ratify the Treaty of Versailles* and place the United States in the League of Nations.* Wilson, an intellectual and an idealist, refused to offer any compromise on the League of Nations and hoped that the election would serve as a referendum on the League. It became instead a rejection of the Democrats and internationalism and an endorsement of Americanism, nostalgic isolationism, and what Warren Harding* would dub "normalcy."*

The Democratic nominating convention met in San Francisco on June 28, 1920, and, after forty-four ballots, selected Governor James M. Cox* of Ohio as its presidential nominee. His running mate was Assistant Secretary of the Navy Franklin D. Roosevelt.* Cox was openly a reformer and a supporter of the League of Nations, and the party drafted a Wilsonian platform. Still, Democrats spent little on the campaign and lacked the leadership Wilson would have provided had he been in good health.

The Republicans assembled in Chicago with three front-running candidates, and, after four ballots, when an impasse appeared to be developing, convention chairman Henry Cabot Lodge* adjourned the convention. During the night, in a "smoke-filled room" at the Blackstone Hotel, a deal was struck giving favorite son Senator Warren G. Harding* of Ohio the best chance to become the GOP nominee. Party bosses summoned Harding during the night, and, after getting reassurances that there were no scandals in his background (except for later revelations about extramarital affairs and an illegitimate child), they decided to nominate him. The convention nominated him on the tenth ballot. Calvin Coolidge* of Massachusetts became Harding's running mate. The Socialist Labor Party nominated W. W. Cox for president and August Gilhaus for vice-president, and the Socialist Party* again nominated Eugene V. Debs.* The Farmer-Labor Party* selected Parley P. Christensen for president; the Single Tax Party named Robert Macauley for president; and the Prohibition Party chose A. S. Watkins.

Harding's qualifications suited the climate of 1920. He campaigned almost exclusively from his front porch in Marion, Ohio, emphasizing the image of a small-town self-made businessman. His speeches were soothing, informal, and banal, although one reporter called them "nothing so much as a string of sponges." Cox campaigned strongly for the League of Nations; Harding sidestepped the issue, leaning more toward isolationism. Most Americans, however,

just voted their resentments. They were homesick for a secure world, and they
looked to Harding to provide it. In the voting, Harding defeated Cox by a total
of 16,152,200 popular votes to 9,147,353. Of the other candidates, Debs received
919,799; Watkins, 189,408; Social Laborite Cox, 31,175; Christensen, 265,411;
and Macauley, 5,837. In the electoral college, Harding won 404 votes, James
Cox, 127. Republicans also swept Congress, winning 300 (they eventually seated
303) out of the 435 seats in the House and 59 seats in the Senate. It was a
landslide and proof that most Americans wanted to forget about the previous
three years. (Paul F. Boller, *Presidential Campaigns,* 1984; Robert K. Murray,
The Harding Era: Warren G. Harding and His Administration, 1969; Eugene
H. Roseboom and Alfred E. Eckes, *Presidential Elections: Strategies of American Electoral Politics,* 1964.)

ELECTION OF 1922. The congressional elections of 1922 were important to
the Democrats, who wanted to regain seats lost in 1920. Circumstances and
issues seemed in their favor. The 67th Congress had been overwhelmingly Republican. The House seated 303 Republicans out of 435, the largest majority in
party history. The Republican majority in the Senate was equally large—fifty-
nine Republicans to thirty-seven Democrats. But the Republican majority was
not a unified one. The huge majority guaranteed at least some intraparty disputes,
and President Warren Harding's* interpretation of executive-congressional relations contributed to the lack of unity. He believed that it was not the executive's
place to propose detailed legislation; that was the business of Congress. But the
Old Guard* leadership was not up to the task, and the 67th Congress lacked
leadership.

Issues did not help the Republicans either. The winter of 1921–1922 was
unhappy for many people. The postwar depression was lingering, business failures were up, and the farm crisis was turning into a disaster, with crop prices
slumping and foreclosures occurring at unprecedented rates. Unions were responding to pay cuts, membership losses, and high unemployment. Republican
policies, which had meant high tariffs and tax cuts for the rich, did not endear
the GOP to large numbers of Americans.

The election was more than a slight move away from Harding's "normalcy."*
The majority the Republicans enjoyed vanished in an unparalleled off-year defeat.
The 68th Congress seated only 225 Republicans and 207 Democrats, and the
GOP majority in the Senate fell from 59 to 37 to 51 to 43. Domination of the
Senate was also precarious because two senators were progressives elected on
the Farmer-Labor Party* ticket. A number of prominent Senators, including
Frank Kellogg* of Minnesota, Joseph Frelinghuysen of New Jersey, and Harry
S. New of Indiana, were defeated. Democrats looked forward to new gains,
including even the White House, in the election of 1924.* (Congressional Quart-
erly, *Guide to U.S. Elections,* 1985; Eugene P. Trani and David L. Wilson, *The
Presidency of Warren G. Harding,* 1977.)

ELECTION OF 1924. The election of 1924 was one of the most complicated political campaigns in American history. Calvin Coolidge* was president, having entered the White House a year before after the sudden death of Warren G. Harding.* Coolidge and the Republicans were riding the crest of a wave of economic prosperity, claiming that Secretary of the Treasury Andrew Mellon's* tax and budgetary policies were responsible. But the Republicans were also vulnerable because of the Harding administration scandals. Throughout late 1923 and 1924, congressional investigating committees had exposed the Teapot Dome,* Veteran's Bureau,* and Alien Property Custodian* scandals, and had implicated such close Harding associates as Secretary of the Interior Albert Fall,* Attorney General Harry Daugherty,* Secretary of the Navy Edwin Denby,* and Veteran's Bureau head Charles Forbes. The Democrats were comfortable claiming that the Harding administration had been one of the most corrupt in American history. The Republican Party* nominated Calvin Coolidge for president and Charles G. Dawes* for vice-president.

The Democratic Party* proved unable to take advantage of the Harding scandals. Coolidge's reputation was still intact, and the Democrats' intense squabbles doomed them to defeat. At their nominating convention in New York City, Al Smith* and William Gibbs McAdoo* fought to a stalemate for 102 ballots. At the time, the party was basically divided between its northern, urban wing, which drew strength from new immigrants and Roman Catholics,* and its lily white, solid southern wing. Raised in Hell's Kitchen in New York, Al Smith represented the northern wing. He opposed prohibition,* the Ku Klux Klan,* and immigration restriction. Smith was also an Irish Catholic. McAdoo, a southerner and the son-in-law of former president Woodrow Wilson,* represented the southern wing of the party. He favored prohibition and immigration restriction, and he acquiesced in the anti-Catholicism of the Ku Klux Klan. Ultimately, the Democrats had to abandon both Smith and McAdoo, compromising on the nondescript John W. Davis,* a Wall Street lawyer. Charles W. Bryan* of Nebraska was his running mate. The Democratic platform condemned the Ku Klux Klan and called for low tariffs, lower income tax rates on the middle class, and government regulation of railroad freight rates.

A third party also appeared, emerging out of the progressive protest group, the Conference for Progressive Political Action.* For the most part, they consisted of old Bull Moosers, social welfare advocates, farm bloc* members, labor unionists, and Socialists. The Progressive Party nominated Senator Robert M. La Follette* for president and Senator Burton K. Wheeler* for vice-president. They demanded a variety of progressive legislation, including the McNary-Haugen Bill,* collective bargaining for labor, the end of antilabor injunctions, higher income taxes on the rich, federal development of Muscle Shoals,* and eventual government ownership of the railroads.

In the end, neither Davis nor La Follette could compete with prosperity, and Calvin Coolidge won the election. He took 15,725,016 popular votes compared to 8,385,586 for Davis, and 4,822,856 for La Follette. In the electoral college,

Coolidge won 382 votes compared to 136 for Davis and 13 for La Follette. Coolidge also carried Republican majorities on his coattails into Congress. When the new Congress convened, Republicans outnumbered Democrats 55 to 40 in the Senate, with 1 Farmer-Laborite, and 247 to 183 in the House, with 2 Socialists and 2 Farmer-Laborites. The Republican Old Guard was in complete control. (Kenneth C. MacKay, *The Progressive Movement of 1924*, 1947.)

ELECTION OF 1926. The 1920s was a decade of Republican Party* political control, but in the election of 1926 the Democratic Party* narrowed the GOP congressional margin, gaining twelve seats in the House and seven in the Senate. The issues of 1924—the power of the Ku Klux Klan,* prohibition,* immigration restrictions, and the Teapot Dome* scandal—exerted substantially less impact on voters in 1926. President Calvin Coolidge* and Republican candidates made sure that the issue before the voters was solely the question of prosperity, and that high tariffs, fiscal restraint, and tax cuts had been responsible. The Democrats claimed that the Republican administration was controlled by big business and was insensitive to the needs of workers and farmers. In the end, it was the prosperity issue that captured the voters' attention. Republican losses in both the House and the Senate were normal for an off-year election by the party controlling the White House and Congress.

When all the ballots were counted, the Republicans controlled the Senate with 48 members to 47 for the Democrats and 1 for the Farmer-Laborites. In the House, Republicans had a strong majority—237 members to 195 Democrats, 2 Farmer-Laborites, and 1 Socialist. In the state houses, Republican governors outnumbered Democrats by 26 to 22. (Congressional Quarterly, *Guide to U.S. Elections*, 1974; Alvin M. Josephy, Jr., *The American Heritage History of the Congress*, 1975; Arthur M. Schlesinger, Jr., ed., *History of American Presidential Elections, 1789–1968*, 1977.)

ELECTION OF 1928. The presidential election of 1928 was one of the most controversial in American history. At the time, most people correctly gave the Democrats no chance of victory. Throughout the 1920s, the party had been badly divided between its rural and urban wings—southern Protestants who supported the Ku Klux Klan,* prohibition,* and states rights were aligned against northern, urban Democrats who hated the Klan and prohibition and supported the social legislation demanded by Catholics* and recent immigrants. By 1928 the urban wing of the Democratic Party* was gaining strength over the rural faction, but internecine warfare still weakened the party. In contrast, the Republican Party* was riding high on the wave of unprecedented prosperity. They played upon a fear that a Democratic victory would destroy the economy. In August 1927 President Calvin Coolidge* announced that he would not seek re-election, and Herbert Hoover,* long-time secretary of commerce, won the nomination in his stead. Senator Charles Curtis* of Kansas was selected as Hoover's running mate.

The Democrats nominated Governor Alfred E. Smith* of New York for president, and Senator Joseph T. Robinson* of Arkansas ran for vice-president.

The election was one of the most colorful in American history, dubbed by some historians as "The Brown Derby Campaign" because of the derby hat Al Smith often wore. Hoover promised the electorate that with four more years of Republican government the country would bring comfort and material progress to every American; he even went so far as to say that the end of poverty was in sight. By eliminating waste in government, by increasing production while reducing economic costs, everyone would benefit. A Quaker by birth, Hoover supported prohibition and appealed to native, traditional voters.

Smith, on the other hand, epitomized the new America of cities, immigrants, and social welfare. A devout Roman Catholic, schooled in the rough and tumble background of New York City machine politics, Smith outspokenly demanded an end to prohibition, condemned the Ku Klux Klan, and opposed immigration restriction. Instead of reaching out to rural America where he needed voter support, Smith alienated them by emphasizing his urban roots, immigrant heritage, and Catholic faith. Throughout the South, where support for the Democratic Party was almost an act of faith, Smith's Roman Catholicism was highly suspect, as was his call for repeal of the Eighteenth Amendment,* and he lost what should have been a major area of support.

In the election of 1928, five other parties ran candidates. The Prohibition Party nominated William F. Varney for president and James A. Edgerton for vice-president; the Farmer-Labor Party* nominated Frank E. Webb for president; the Socialist Labor Party nominated Verne L. Reynolds for president; the Socialist Party* nominated Norman Thomas* for president; and the Communist Party* picked William Z. Foster* as their candidate. None of them stood a chance of even a nominal run for office.

When the ballots were counted, Hoover had received 21,392,190 popular votes compared to Smith's 15,016,443. Among the other candidates, Norman Thomas received 267,420 votes; Foster, 48,770; Reynolds, 21,603; Varney, 20,106; and Webb, 6,390. The electoral vote stood at 444 for Hoover and 87 for Smith. Because of anti-Catholic sentiment against Smith, Hoover won five southern states. In other ways, however, the election was not such a Republican victory. They kept control of the House by 267 votes to 163, and in the Senate, by 56 to 39. Whatever gains the Republicans had made in the South were only temporary aberrations based on the anti-Catholic vote. Even more significant for the future, the Democrats carried the twelve largest cities in the country and brought 122 counties, formerly Republican, in the industrial northeast, into their column. They had laid the groundwork for their urban-based coalition, which would soon come to dominate American politics. (Allan J. Lichtman, *Prejudice and the Old Politics; The Presidential Election of 1928;* 1979; Edmund A. Moore, *A Catholic Runs for President: The Campaign of 1928,* 1956.)

ELECTION OF 1930. Election day in 1930 was on November 4. Usually, the off-year elections enjoyed only a low voter turnout, but such was not the case in 1930. The stock market crash in 1929 had struck fear throughout the country, and in 1930 unemployment had gone beyond five million people. The election of 1930 was the first chance voters had to pass judgment on the incumbent politicians since the onset of the depression, particularly on the policies of Herbert Hoover.* Hoover had been elected by a landslide in 1928, and Republicans controlled the Senate by 56 votes to 39 for the Democrats and the House by 267 to 163. What had appeared to be a guarantee of legislative tranquility in Congress became, under the impact of mass unemployment and social distress, tremendous political conflict.

Nine million fewer people voted in the elections of 1930 than had voted in 1928, and the Republican majorities shrank. In the Senate, the GOP margin slipped to 48 votes to 47 for the Democrats and 1 Farmer-Laborite, and when the Farmer-Laborite sided with the Democrats, the ensuing balance of power could be broken only by the tie-breaking vote of Vice-President Charles Curtis.* The Republican majority in the House dropped from 218 votes to 216. After the election, but before the first session convened on December 7, 1931, fourteen vacancies occurred in the House, and, in the special elections that followed, the make-up of the House changed even more—219 Democrats, 214 Republicans, and 1 Farmer-Laborite. In New York, Governor Franklin D. Roosevelt* was re-elected, setting the stage for his presidential run against Herbert Hoover in 1932. (Congressional Quarterly, *Guide to U.S. Elections,* 1974; Arthur M. Schlesinger, Jr., ed., *History of American Presidential Elections, 1789–1968,* 1977; Jordan A. Schwarz, *The Interregnum of Despair: Hoover, Congress, and the Depression,* 1970.)

ELECTION OF 1932. In the summer of 1932, when perhaps twelve million people were unemployed, the Democrats eagerly expected to win the presidency. Most Republicans sensed their fate. Governor Franklin D. Roosevelt* of New York formally announced his candidacy in January 1932 after supporters James Farley and Louis Howe had conducted an extensive letter-writing campaign in several states and had travelled widely to find Roosevelt supporters everywhere. By the time the Democratic Convention opened in Chicago on June 27, Roosevelt had the largest bloc of supporters, although not enough to secure the nomination. Former Senator James A. Reed of Missouri and Maryland Governor Albert Ritchie were two of the hopefuls encouraged by Al Smith,* the unsuccessful Democratic candiate in 1928. Favorite son candidates abounded, including Governors George White of Ohio and William "Alfalfa Bill" Murray of Oklahoma, Senator James H. Lewis of Illinois, and Speaker of the House John Nance Garner* of Texas. Garner was more than a Texas favorite son; publisher William Randolph Hearst,* chairman of the California delegation, dragged him into the contest, giving the crusty old Texan all the votes of the two delegations. Garner did not attend the convention and clearly was the least active of the major delegates.

Struggles over the contested delegations, rules of nomination, and the convention chairmanship were all won by Roosevelt majorities but not by the two-thirds rule needed to nominate. At the end of an all-night, three-ballot session, Roosevelt was eighty-nine votes shy of nomination. Garner's agreement then to release the Texas delegation from its obligation to vote for him also freed the California delegation. California's forty-four vote switch to Roosevelt created the bandwagon effect, putting him over the top. Garner accepted the second spot on the ticket. In a precedent-breaking move, Roosevelt asked the convention to remain in session so that he might fly to Chicago to deliver an acceptance speech. There he pledged a "new deal" for the American people.

The Roosevelt campaign focused largely on domestic reforms and economic recovery. Except for outright opposition to prohibition* and a call for a balanced budget, Roosevelt's campaign was intentionally vague, focusing on Republican failures and the problems created by the Great Depression without really offering any specific Democratic solutions. The personalities of the two leading candidates were as different as day and night. Herbert Hoover* attacked his opponent; Roosevelt ignored the president. Hoover's speeches went "thud-thud-thud;" Roosevelt's radiated charisma. Roosevelt seemed to draw energy from the crowds; his voice was perfect for radio. He conveyed the feeling that he knew what he would do when he took over the reins of government. When the votes were counted, Roosevelt had carried forty-two states, had secured 472 of the 531 electoral votes, and had defeated Hoover by more than seven million popular votes (22,809,638 to 15,758,901). The Democratic majority in the House of Representatives increased to 313 to 117. The Republican minority in the Senate was reduced to 36. (Richard Oulahan, *The Man Who . . . : The Story of the Democratic National Convention of 1932*, 1971; Elliot Rosen, *Hoover, Roosevelt, and the Brains Trust: From Depression to New Deal,* 1977.)

ELIOT, CHARLES WILLIAM. Charles W. Eliot was born on March 20, 1834, in Boston, Massachusetts. He graduated from Harvard in 1853 and then took a master's degree there in 1856. Eliot taught mathematics at Harvard between 1858 and 1863 and at the Massachusetts Institute of Technology between 1865 and 1869; he then returned to Harvard as its president, a position he held until 1909. Under Eliot's direction, Harvard made the transition to a modern university, complete with graduate school and Ph.D. programs, using the German model pioneered at Johns Hopkins University. A dedicated internationalist, Eliot believed completely in the capacity of mankind to achieve perfection and of society to eliminate war. His ideas were especially appropriate during the Victorian optimism of pre–World War I America, and, during the 1920s, Eliot continued to advocate internationalism and American participation in the League of Nations,* although his optimism and confidence in human nature had come to appear naive and shortsighted to most observers. In the era of the "Lost

Generation,''* Charles Eliot remained tenaciously loyal to his belief in the perfectibility of mankind, the goodness of human nature, and the guarantee of progress. He died on August 22, 1926. (Hugh Hawkins, *Between Europe and America: The Educational Leadership of Charles W. Eliot,* 1972; Henry James, *Charles W. Eliot: President of Harvard University, 1869–1909,* 1930.)

ELIOT, THOMAS STEARNS. T. S. Eliot was born on September 16, 1888 in St. Louis, Missouri, to a New England family. He enjoyed an Ivy League education, studying at Harvard, the Sorbonne in Paris, and Oxford in England. Eliot settled permanently in England in 1914 and took up British citizenship in 1927. Eliot yearned for the life of a High Anglican gentleman, and he was able to find it in Great Britain. He was an enormously productive poet and critic, and in 1948 Eliot received the Nobel Prize for Literature. In his work, Eliot explored the social decadence of modern consumer culture. His most famous work, *The Waste Land* (1922), a powerful poem, is highly personal in exposing a man lost in a civilization he hated. In *Ash Wednesday* (1930), Eliot portrayed his own conversion to mystical Anglicanism. Other important works by T. S. Eliot included *The Love Song of J. Alfred Prufrock* (1915), *Murder in the Cathedral* (1935), *The Family Reunion* (1939), *The Cocktail Party* (1950), and *The Confidential Clerk* (1950). T. S. Eliot died on January 4, 1965. (Ronald Bush, *T. S. Eliot: A Study in Character and Style,* 1983; Philip Ray Headings, *T. S. Eliot,* 1964.)

EMERGENCY AGRICULTURAL CREDITS ACT OF 1921. Early in 1921, Senator George Norris* of Nebraska devised a proposal to create a government corporation to buy farm surpluses for cash and then sell them abroad for credit. Herbert Hoover,* the secretary of commerce, was to serve as head of the corporation. Although the farm bloc* supported the measure, Republican conservatives believed it smacked of socialism. As a compromise, Hoover and Secretary of Agriculture Henry Wallace* drafted an alternative measure known as the Emergency Agricultural Credits Act, which Senator Frank Kellogg* sponsored in Congress. President Warren G. Harding* signed it into law on August 24, 1921. The law permitted the federal government, through Federal Reserve banks, to purchase short-term agricultural paper, secured by agricultural products, from rural banks; grant loans for breeding, fattening, and marketing livestock; and grant loans to marketing cooperatives and foreign buyers of American commodities. (Robert K. Murray, *The Politics of Normalcy: Governmental Theory and Practice in the Harding-Coolidge Era,* 1973.)

EMERGENCY QUOTA ACT OF 1921. After the end of World War I, the massive immigration to the United States from eastern and southern Europe began again, and American nativists began to call for immigration restriction. Madison Grant's* 1913 book *The Passing of the Great Race* was still in vogue, and large numbers of Americans wanted to stem the tide of immigrants from

Italy, Greece, Austria-Hungary, and Japan. For them, the "true America" was composed of northern and western Europeans—fair-skinned Protestants. In 1920 Senator William P. Dillingham of Vermont sponsored legislation to end the flow of immigrants to the United States. Although his bill said nothing about Asian immigration and allowed unlimited immigration from Mexico and Latin America, primarily because of the need for agricultural laborers in the Southwest, it did limit European immigration to 5 percent of the number of foreign-born of each nationality present in the United States in 1910. The bill passed the Senate, but the House amended it to reduce the quotas to 3 percent. That would have limited European immigration to approximately 350,000 people a year. President Woodrow Wilson,* however, pocket-vetoed the bill. After the inauguration of President Warren G. Harding,* Dillingham resurrected the bill. It passed the House by voice vote and the Senate by a margin of 78 to 1. Harding signed it on May 19, 1921. The Emergency Quota Act was the first absolute numerical limit on American immigration, and it established a quota system guaranteeing that northern and western Europeans would enjoy preferential status. In 1924 it was superceded by the National Origins Act.* (Thomas J. Curran, *Xenophobia and Immigration, 1820–1930*, 1975; John Higham, *Strangers in the Land: Patterns of American Nativism, 1860–1925*, 1963.)

EMERGENCY RELIEF AND CONSTRUCTION ACT OF 1932. By the spring of 1932, the economy was reaching bottom, with 25 percent of the work force unemployed. President Herbert Hoover* had established the Reconstruction Finance Corporation* (RFC) in January 1932, and he desperately hoped that its $2 billion in loan funds would stimulate the economy. But it was also an election year, with important politicians clamoring for federal relief programs to ease the suffering of the unemployed. Liberal Democrats like Senator Robert Wagner* of New York were joining with progressive Republicans like Senator Robert M. La Follette, Jr.,* of Wisconsin in promoting a variety of relief bills. In the congressional election of 1930,* the Republicans had lost eight seats in the Senate and majority control of the House, so the likelihood of a successful federal relief program making its way through Congress was good. Hoover worried about the federal government taking over relief programs; he greatly preferred to leave them to local government and private charities. Since that was no longer possible in 1932, and to prevent Congress from passing irresponsible, budget-busting legislation, Hoover decided to sponsor his own law.

His proposal was a modest one, calling for an expansion of RFC lending power. The bill authorized the RFC to loan up to $1.5 billion to state and local governments for the construction of self-amortizing public works projects—toll roads and bridges, sewage and water systems, hydroelectric projects, and so on. It also allowed the RFC to loan up to $300 million to state relief commissions for distribution to the poor. Finally, the bill allowed the RFC to loan money to a variety of financial institutions for reloaning to farmers. Speaker of the House John Nance Garner* added an amendment requiring publication of all RFC bank loans. On July 14, 1932, the House passed the bill 296 to 46, and two days later the Senate passed it by voice vote. The president signed it on July 21, 1932. It was too little, too late. The $1.5 billion in public works construction projects was not spent at all in 1932 because the lead time for beginning such complicated construction was so long. And when the RFC tried to equitably distribute $300 million in relief money when ten times that amount was needed, it became a political nightmare. (James S. Olson, *Herbert Hoover and the Reconstruction Finance Corporation, 1931–1933,* 1977.)

EMERGENCY TARIFF ACT OF 1921. Although American farmers prospered during World War 1, the end of the war soon brought hard times. As European production revived, demand for American farm products fell. So did commodity prices. Heavily in debt to finance wartime production increases, farmers were hard-pressed to satisfy the bankers, and by 1920 they were mired in a severe depression. In the farm belt, people began demanding tariff increases as a way of bringing relief. It was a naive hope. American farm prices were down not because of foreign competition but because of overproduction. High tariffs on foreign commodities would do nothing to raise prices. Woodrow Wilson* had already vetoed one such bill, but when Warren G. Harding* entered the White House, tariff revisionists had their hopes raised. With Harding's blessing, Congress came back with a new measure—the Emergency Tariff Act. President Harding signed it into law on May 27, 1921. The Emergency Tariff Act of 1921 established prohibitive rates on twenty-eight agricultural products. Although the law helped raise sugar and wool prices, it had little effect on other commodities. The Emergency Tariff Act of 1921 was succeeded in 1922 by the Fordney-McCumber Tariff.* (Frank William Taussig, *The Tariff History of the United States,* 1931; Eugene P. Trani and David L. Wilson, *The Presidency of Warren G. Harding,* 1977.)

EPSTEIN, ABRAHAM. Born in Russia on April 20, 1872, Abraham Epstein immigrated to the United States in 1910 and settled in Pittsburgh. He graduated from the University of Pittsburgh in 1917, spent a year in graduate school, and then went to work as research director of the Pennsylvania Commission on Old-Age Pensions, which had been established in 1917. He was also a leading figure in the establishment of the American Association for Old Age Security,* which became the American Association for Social Security in 1933. Throughout the 1920s, Epstein worked to create a statewide system of old age insurance in Pennsylvania but failed to secure legislative funding and became an advocate of a federal program. Only then could a uniform, equitable system of social security be established throughout the country. He was also a firm believer that any social security plan should be financed by government appropriations, not by individual and employee contributions, which he viewed as hopelessly regressive. On those grounds, Epstein eventually became an outspoken critic of the Social Security Act of 1935. For the rest of his career, he continued to call for federal financing of the program so that economic security would be based on income distribution. Abraham Epstein died on May 5, 1942. (Roy Lubove, *The Struggle for Social Security, 1900–1935*, 1968; *New York Times,* May 6, 1942.)

EQUAL RIGHTS AMENDMENT. See NATIONAL WOMAN'S PARTY

ERLANGER, ABRAHAM LINCOLN. Abraham Erlanger was born on May 4, 1860, in Buffalo, New York, to a Jewish family. He grew up in Cleveland and worked as an apprentice office boy at the Euclid Opera House. During his years travelling as an advance agent for touring New York theatrical groups, Erlanger discovered the need for a centralized booking system to cover the entire country for an entire season, making sure that theaters were booked solid as well as the touring groups. Erlanger pioneered centralized booking. Through his Theatrical Syndicate, Erlanger established a virtual monopoly over theatrical bookings in the United States, at least for New York touring groups. During the 1920s, the Erlanger monopoly was broken by the rise of the Schubert booking agency. Abraham Erlanger died on March 7, 1930. *(New York Times,* March 9, 1930.)

ESCH-CUMMINS ACT OF 1920. See TRANSPORTATION ACT OF 1920

EVANS, ELIZABETH GLENDOWER. Elizabeth Evans was born in New Rochelle, New York, on February 28, 1856. She was raised amidst economic plenty, attended Radcliffe College, and after a tour of England in 1908–1909 she converted to socialism. Between 1910 and 1920, Evans was active in the Women's Trade Union League, for which she participated in a number of strikes in the textile mills, and in the National American Woman Suffrage Association.* After World War I, Evans became the national director of the American Civil Liberties Union* and condemned the Red Scare* of Attorney General A. Mitchell Palmer.* Using personal funds, Evans largely financed the defense fund for Nicola Sacco* and Bartolomeo Vanzetti.* Between their arrest in 1920 and their execution in 1927, Evans unfailingly supported them and befriended them. She also became involved in many other liberal causes, especially the rights of aliens, women, and minorities and in various attempts to obtain social welfare legislation. She died on December 12, 1937. *(New York Times,* December 13, 1937; *Who's Who in America, 1920–1921,* 1920.)

"EVEREADY HOUR." "The Eveready Hour" was radio's* first major variety show. It premiered on WEAF radio in New York City on December 4, 1923, and in 1926, NBC began broadcasting it nationally on Tuesday nights. It was a mix of jazz,* popular, and classical music; stand-up comedy; and dramatic presentations. The program lasted until 1930. (John Dunning, *Tune in Yesterday: The Ultimate Encyclopedia of Old-Time Radio, 1925–1976,* 1976.)

EVOLUTION. During the 1920s, the United States was the scene of a great cultural struggle. Ever since 1607, when the first colonists had settled at Jamestown, American culture had rested on a bedrock of rural, farming, and Protestant values. The beliefs in hard work, progress, and individualism seemed rooted in those origins. But in the 1920s, the Industrial Revolution, urbanization, and secular rationalism caught up with America, sending the country into a major identity crisis. In 1925, for the first time in United States history, more people lived in cities than in rural villages and more worked in factories than on farms. Ruralism, once a synonym for virtue, now became synonymous with backwardness and parochialism. The change brought a powerful backlash from rural Americans, which found expression in the rise of the Ku Klux Klan,* the defense of prohibition,* the restrictions on unlimited immigration, and rampant anti-Catholicism and anti-Semitism. For many Americans, the symbol of the new evil was the theory of evolution, and the symbol of the struggle between an urbane, secular America and its rural, religious past was the famous "Monkey Trial"* of 1925 held in Dayton, Tennessee.

Ever since 1859, when Charles Darwin published his *The Origin of Species* and postulated the evolution of man according to the law of natural selection, fundamental Protestants, committed to the inerrancy of the Bible, had labeled the theory of evolution a blasphemy. But by the 1920s, the theory of evolution had gained scientific respectability among biologists and geologists, who saw confirmation of Darwin's theories at every turn in their field work. At major universities throughout the country, evolution had become science while Genesis had become history at best and folk culture at worst. At the same time, the new discipline of Biblical criticism, which treated the Bible as history, not scripture, was casting doubt on some of Christianity's most cherished stories—the six-day creation, Noah's flood, Jonah's "big fish," and so on. For many Protestants, the antichrist had appeared and had to be destroyed. Some prominent clergymen, like Harry Emerson Fosdick,* even adopted a relativist view of the scriptures, and fundamentalists reacted with passion. Beginning with Oklahoma in 1923, state after state in the South enacted statutes prohibiting the teaching of evolution in public schools. The Tennessee statute became law on March 21, 1925.

Shortly thereafter, John Scopes, a biology teacher in Dayton, Tennessee, decided to test the law in court. He taught the theory of evolution in his high school classroom, widely advertising his decision. Tennessee authorities arrested him and brought him to trial on July 10, 1925. The trial, which lasted ten days, epitomized the fears and frustrations of people throughout the country, becoming a genuine media crisis, with reporters and radio broadcasters from around the world descending on Dayton to report the proceedings. It was dubbed the "Monkey Trial" by journalists looking for a headline. William Jennings Bryan,* the three-time Democratic presidential candidate and former secretary of state, came to Dayton to assist the prosecution. Bryan was an inveterate foe of evolution. To assist defense counsel Dudley Field Malone, Clarence Darrow,* the premier criminal attorney in the country, also came to Dayton. From the beginning, the trial was a spectacular confrontation between Bryan and Darrow—Bryan represented the old America and Darrow the new. In the end, Darrow got Bryan on the stand and subjected him to a withering cross-examination, catching him in a series of contradictions and logical inconsistencies. Eventually, Scopes was convicted legally but vindicated culturally. An appeals court subsequently reduced his fine to $1. The "Monkey Trial" was over. (Willard B. Gatewood, *Preachers, Pedagogues, & Politicians: The Evolution Controversy in North Carolina, 1920–1927*, 1966; Donald B. Meyer, *The Protestant Search for Political Realism, 1919–1941*, 1960; Jerry R. Tomkins, ed., *D-Day at Dayton: Reflections on the Scopes Trial*, 1965.)

EXPATRIATES. After World War I, a number of American artists and writers headed for Europe to practice their crafts. Postwar disillusionment, as well as the postwar American pursuit of materialism and normalcy, had made the United States, at least for many of them, a difficult place for serious exploration of American culture. The exchange rate also made it cheap to live abroad. So, after 1918, dozens of American intellectuals—people like Ernest Hemingway,* Gertrude Stein, and Glenway Westcott—headed for the Left Bank of the Seine in Paris, where bohemianism* thrived on a grand scale. Expatriatism provided a freedom from the artist's own world, an opportunity to criticize that world, and a chance to remake one's life all over again. (Frederick J. Hoffman, *The 20s. American Writing in the Postwar Decade*, 1949.)

EXPORT DEBENTURE PLAN. Because of heavy debt burdens and price-depressing overproduction during the 1920s, American farmers were suffering economically. Not since the 1890s had they faced such enormous difficulties. Among the proposed solutions for the farm crisis was the export debenture plan, which the National Grange* vigorously promoted. Founded in 1867 as an agrarian social organization, the National Grange had by the 1890s evolved into a strong interest group advocating pro-farmer legislation. In the 1920s, the leader of the Grange, Louis J. Taber, campaigned vigorously for the export debenture plan. The plan provided an indirect subsidy for farmers selling crops at a loss on world markets. The federal government would issue debentures to farmers equal to the value of their losses for selling on the world market. Farmers would then sell the debentures to foreign traders, who could use them as legal tender in paying import duties. Farm advocates argued that the program would extend to farmers the same import protection manufacturers enjoyed from protective tariffs. Critics claimed that the plan would not solve the basic farm problem—overproduction— and that American farmers were not suffering from heavy competition from foreign producers. When both Presidents Calvin Coolidge* and Herbert Hoover* rejected the export debenture plan, the farmers felt betrayed. (Martin L. Fausold, "President Hoover's Farm Policies, 1929–1933," *Agricultural History* 51 [April 1977] 362–77; Joan Hoff Wilson, "Hoover's Agricultural Policies, 1921–1928," *Agricultural History* 51 [April 1977], 335–61.)

F

FAIRBANKS, DOUGLAS. Douglas Fairbanks was born Douglas Elton Ulman in Denver, Colorado, on May 23, 1883. He attended the Colorado School of Mines for several years and Harvard University for one semester. He acted with several touring companies when he was a teenager and worked as a clerk on Wall Street for a while. Fairbanks debuted on Broadway in 1902 and starred in his first stage hit in 1906—*The Man of the Hour*. In 1915 Fairbanks signed a contract with D. W. Griffith's* Triangle Film Corporation, and his first film hit came in 1916 with *His Picture in the Papers*. Several years later, Fairbanks joined Mary Pickford,* D. W. Griffith, and Charlie Chaplin* and formed United Artists Company. During the 1920s, Fairbanks played the hero in many swash-buckling films, of which *The Mark of Zorro* was one of the most famous. Other 1920s films in this genre included *The Three Musketeers, The Black Pirate, The Thief of Bagdad,* and *Robin Hood*. In 1927 he served as the first president of the Academy of Motion Pictures. Fairbanks had married Mary Pickford in 1920, and they were Hollywood's most prominent couple. Fairbanks divorced Pickford in 1936, but his film career was over by then. He died on December 12, 1939. (Gary Carey, *Doug and Mary: A Biography of Douglas Fairbanks and Mary Pickford,* 1977; Bernard Eisenschitz, *Douglas Fairbanks,* 1969.)

FALL, ALBERT BACON. Albert Fall was born near Frankfort, Kentucky, on November 26, 1861. When he was eleven years old, Fall went to work in a cotton factory in Nashville, Tennessee; in 1891, after studying law privately, he was admitted to the bar. Fall then moved out west and began practicing law in Las Cruces, New Mexico, where he specialized in mining, lumber, farming, railroad, and real estate issues. Fall won a seat in the territorial legislature in 1891 and 1892 as a Democrat, and, between 1893 and 1911, he held a variety of state judicial posts. Fall switched to the Republican Party* before New Mexico was admitted to the union in 1912, when he became one of the first two United States Senators from the new state. In March 1921 Fall became secretary of the interior in the cabinet of President Warren G. Harding.*

Fall remained in the cabinet until his resignation in March 1923 over the famous Teapot Dome* scandal. In 1921 Fall had convinced Secretary of the Navy Edwin Denby* to transfer jurisdiction over naval oil reserves at Teapot Dome, Wyoming, and Elk Hills, California, to the department of the interior. In 1922 Fall then permitted private oil company leasing of those oil reserves in return for a $100,000 payment. Rumors of the scandal began to surface in Washington in 1923, and congressional investigations then exposed it. Fall was indicted in June 1924, and in October 1929 he was convicted. He served a one-year prison term in 1931–1932, and then he returned to his home in New Mexico. Albert Fall died on November 30, 1944. (Albert Bacon Fall, *The Memoirs of Albert B. Fall*, 1966; Burl Noggle, *Teapot Dome: Oil and Politics in the 1920s*, 1962.)

FARISH, WILLIAM STAMPS. William S. Farish was born on February 23, 1881, in Mayersville, Mississippi. He was awarded a law degree from the University of Mississippi in 1900 and practiced law for a year before moving to Beaumont, Texas. He started in the oil business as a driller and trader and set up his offices in Houston. To protect the interests of small oil entrepreneurs, Farish organized the Gulf Coast Producers Association in 1916, and out of the contacts he made there, Farish helped found the Humble Oil and Refining Company in 1917. At first, Farish was in charge of oil production for Humble Oil, but when the company needed capital, he sought out the Standard Oil Company of New Jersey, which purchased a half-interest in Humble in 1919. In 1922 Farish became president of Humble Oil and Refining Company.

As president of Humble Oil, Farish saw to it that the company diversified and integrated, greatly expanding its drilling of crude oil and its refining production. In 1926, to try to rationalize a rapidly growing industry, Farish founded and became the first president of the American Petroleum Institute, a trade association. In 1933 Farish became chairman of the board of Standard Oil Company of New Jersey. He became president of Standard Oil in 1937 and remained there until his death on November 29, 1942. (*New York Times*, November 30, 1942; Henrietta M. Larson and Kenneth W. Porter, *History of the Humble Oil and Refining Company: A Study in Industrial Growth* 1959; Henrietta Larson et al., *History of the Standard Oil Company (N.J.)*, 1971.)

FARM BLOC. During the 1920s, the prevailing Republican political philosophy worshipped business principles and called for reductions in government spending, high tariffs on imports, tax cuts on the rich and well-to-do, and reliance on local and private initiatives to solve national problems. But at the same time, Congress contained a large number of representatives from farm states in the South and West, most of whom were desperate for some way of dealing with the collapse of farm prices in the 1920s. Only the federal government, they believed, had the resources and the perspective to deal with the farm crisis. These congressmen and senators were known at the time as the "farm bloc."

In the Senate, the farm bloc included William S. Kenyon (R-Iowa), Robert La Follette* (R-Wis.), George Norris* (R-Neb.), Arthur Capper* (R-Kans.), Edwin F. Ladd (R-N.Dak.), Peter Norbeck* (R-S.Dak.), Frank B. Kellogg* (R-Minn.), Robert N. Stanfield (R-Oreg.), Charles L. McNary* (R-Oreg.), John W. Harreld (R-Okla.), Henry F. Ashhurst (D-Ariz.), Claude A. Swanson (D-V.), Morris Sheppard (D-Tex.), and John B. Kendrick (D-Wyo.). In the House of Representatives, the farm bloc was capable of mustering ninety to one hundred votes. Its leaders were George Huddleston (D-Ala.), Charles B. Timberlake (R-Colo.), George M. Young (R-N. Dak.), Willis C. Hawley (R-Oreg.), Lindley H. Hadley (R-Wash.), and James A. Frear (R-Wisc.).

During the 1920s, the farm bloc campaigned for both the export debenture plan* and the McNary-Haugen Bill* as the solutions to the farm crisis, but the Republican administrations of Warren G. Harding,* Calvin Coolidge,* and Herbert Hoover* refused to support the measures. At the same time, since they could not afford to alienate completely the farm bloc, as their voting power in Congress was formidable, the Republican administrations agreed to such farm bloc measures as the Capper-Tincher Act of 1921,* the Capper-Volstead Act of 1922,* and the Agricultural Marketing Act of 1929.* (Robert K. Murray, *The Politics of Normalcy: Governmental Theory and Practice in the Harding-Coolidge Era,* 1973; James H. Shideler, *Farm Crisis, 1919–1923,* 1957.)

FARM HOLIDAY MOVEMENT. See RENO, MILO

FARMER-LABOR PARTY. The Farmer-Labor Party was founded in 1919 by John Fitzpatrick, head of the Chicago Federation of Labor. Its first national chairperson was Edward N. Nockels. At first, the party's name was the Labor Party, with the avowed intention of uniting all left-wing labor movements in the United States under a single banner. Hoping to add farmers to the coalition, they renamed it the Farmer-Labor Party in 1920 and ran a presidential ticket in the election that year. Parley P. Christiansen was nominated for president and Max S. Hayes for vice-president. They campaigned for free coinage of silver, unemployment insurance, a federal public works program, an end to immigration, a $1.00 an hour minimum wage, increased taxes on the rich, tariff reductions, government regulation of the stock exchanges, abolition of the Federal Reserve System, prohibition of yellow-dog contracts and antilabor injunctions, independence for the Philippines, and elimination of child labor and holding companies. They drew less than 1 percent of the electorate, a total of 189,339 votes.

In 1921 the Communists gained control of the national organization, which led to an exodus of Socialists, labor leaders, and liberals. The Farmer-Labor Party soon disintegrated, although the Farmer-Labor Party of Minnesota continued to exist, allying itself increasingly with the Democratic Party after 1933. (Murray S. Stedman and Susan W. Stedman, *Discontent at the Polls: A Study of Farmers and Labor Parties, 1827–1948,* 1967.)

FARRELL, JAMES AUGUSTINE. James A. Farrell was born on February 15, 1862, in New Haven, Connecticut, to an immigrant, Irish Catholic family. Farrell went to work in the steel industry when he was just sixteen, going to night school where he studied drafting and engineering. In 1889 he became a salesman for the Pittsburgh Wire Company, and in 1892 he moved to New York as the company's sales manager. The next year, Farrell became general manager of the company. In 1899 Pittsburgh Wire was bought out by American Steel and Wire, and Farrell became foreign sales manager of the company; in 1901, when United States Steel purchased American Steel and Wire, Farrell became the director of foreign operations for the huge corporation. In 1911, Farrell became president of United States Steel and remained in that position until his retirement in 1932.

Although the company underwent tremendous growth during Farrell's tenure, he did not foresee the impact of the automobile industry on the steel business. United States Steel was not prepared for the enormous demand for light sheet steel products to manufacture automobiles, and during the 1920s the company lost large portions of its market share to smaller, more farsighted steel companies. Farrell was also a bitter opponent of labor unions, and during the great steel strike of 1919, he resorted to violence and intimidation to break the union, which earned him a reputation as a meanspirited corporation man. James A. Farrell died on March 28, 1943. (*New York Times,* March 29, 1943; Gertrude G. Schroeder, *The Growth of Major Steel Corporations,* 1953; Melvin Urofsky, *Big Steel and the Wilson Administration,* 1969.)

FAULKNER, WILLIAM. Born in 1897 in New Albany, and raised in Oxford, Mississippi, William Faulkner spent all of his life in Mississippi, except for occasional travels, until he moved to Virginia just before he died. Raised in the South, Faulkner's novels focused on the tragedy of life there—how the dark impulses in human nature found expression in racial violence and fear. He wrote of a fictional Yoknapatawpha County and inhabited it with the entire range of humanity. Early in the 1920s, he lived for a time in New Orleans and there came under the influence of Sherwood Anderson.* Faulkner's first novel was *Soldier's Pay* (1926), and he followed it in rapid succession with *Sartoris* (1929), *The Sound and the Fury* (1929), *As I Lay Dying* (1930), *Sanctuary* (1931), *Light in August* (1932), *Absalom, Absalom!* (1936), *The Hamlet* (1940), *Intruder in the Dust* (1948), and *Requiem for a Nun* (1951). In 1950 Faulkner won the Nobel Prize for Literature. He died on July 6, 1962. (Frederick J. Hoffman, *The 1920s: American Writing in the Postwar Decade,* 1949; Martin Seymour-Smith, *Who's Who in the Twentieth Century,* 1976.)

FEDERAL AID ROAD ACT. See FEDERAL HIGHWAY ACT OF 1921

FEDERAL BUREAU OF INVESTIGATION. See HOOVER, JOHN EDGAR

FEDERAL FARM BOARD. The Federal Farm Board was Herbert Hoover's* answer to the farm bloc demand for the McNary-Haugen Bill* and the export debenture plan.* Created by the Agricultural Marketing Act of 1929,* the Federal

Farm Board was an eight-member agency equipped with a $500 million revolving loan fund to reduce speculation, control surpluses, and prevent wide fluctuations in prices. The loan money would go to hundreds of farm cooperatives, which would then assist farmers in acting in unison to market their products. For Hoover, the Federal Farm Board was perfect; it represented a federal initiative without federal domination. Alexander Legge,* a former assistant to Bernard Baruch* in the War Industries Board, became the first chairman of the Federal Farm Board.

Almost immediately, the board, working to stimulate the growth of farm cooperatives, generously loaned money at 90 percent of cotton's current market value. More and more farmers joined cooperatives, and the cooperatives became more and more influential. Late in 1929, after the stock market crashed, the Federal Farm Board helped stabilize cotton prices by loaning on the crop at 16 cents a pound. Soon the board was doing the same for wheat, corn, grapes, citrus, dairy products, livestock, and wool. It amounted to price fixing by the federal government. In February 1930, when wheat prices fell to $1.00 a bushel, the Farm Board encouraged the formation of a Grain Stabilization Corporation to stop the price fall by making direct purchases on the open market. In May 1930 a Cotton Stabilization Corporation was formed to perform the same function. Critics charged Hoover with fostering socialism.

Although the Federal Farm Board loaned hundreds of millions of dollars and although the stabilization corporations purchased enormous volumes of commodities, it failed to stem the collapse of prices. Wheat went from $1.02 a bushel in July 1929 to 37 cents a bushel in June 1932; cotton fell from 17 cents to 5 cents a pound; and corn fell from 91 cents to 31 cents a bushel. With no authority to impose compulsory cuts in production or mandate rational marketing, the Federal Farm Board simply did not have the power to deal effectively with the farm crisis. (David Burner, *Herbert Hoover: A Public Life*, 1979; James H. Shideler, "Hoover and the Farm Board Project," *Mississippi Valley Historical Review* 42 [March 1956], 710–29.)

FEDERAL HIGHWAY ACT OF 1921. In 1916 Congress passed the Federal Aid Road Act to assist states in constructing adequate rural roads to improve mail delivery, but the automobile revolution was making it clear that a vastly improved highway system was absolutely necessary. Prodded by the farm bloc* and by the American Automobile Association, Congress passed the Federal Highway Act of 1921. The legislation had the states designate a system of interstate and intercounty roads to receive federal funding. Federal spending for highway construction went from $19.5 million in 1920 to $88 million in 1923. Highway expansion greatly stimulated the automobile industry. (Eugene P. Trani and Daniel L. Wilson, *The Presidency of Warren G. Harding*, 1977.)

FEDERAL HOME LOAN BANK ACT OF 1932. By the summer of 1932, the unemployment rate was reaching catastrophic proportions, and the Hoover administration was desperate to find some means of creating jobs. Because administration officials were convinced that the country was facing a crisis of confidence and severe shortages of credit, they proposed creating a new federal banking system to stimulate the construction industry. President Herbert Hoover* had recommended such a system in his address to Congress on December 8, 1931, and Congress passed the Federal Home Loan Bank Act in July. Hoover signed it into law on July 22, 1932. The law established a five-person Home Loan Bank Board and created a system of government banks to discount home mortgages. The Federal Home Loan Bank received $125 million in capital to discount the home mortgages of building and loan associations, insurance companies, and savings banks. The administration believed that the banks would liquefy the market for mortgages and revive the construction industry. Although the Federal Home Loan Bank system provided some liquidity to the home mortgage market, it did little to revive what had become a moribund construction industry. (David Burner, *Herbert Hoover: A Public Life*, 1979; James S. Olson, *Herbert Hoover and the Reconstruction Finance Corporation, 1931–1933*, 1977.)

FEDERAL INTERMEDIATE CREDIT BANK SYSTEM. On March 4, 1923, President Warren G. Harding* signed into law the Federal Intermediate Credit Act, a bill the farm bloc* had been campaigning for since 1921. The War Finance Corporation* had been providing intermediate credit to troubled farmers, but farmers wanted the program institutionalized. The new law established twelve federal intermediate credit banks, one in each federal reserve district. The Federal Farm Loan Board supervised the new banks. Each had $5 million in capital to make loans of from six months to three years to farm and livestock marketing cooperatives. Private groups could also establish agricultural credit corporations and apply for loan money. (James Shideler, *Farm Crisis, 1919–1923*, 1957.)

FEDERAL POWER COMMISSION. Although the unique political coalition which had given rise to the progressive movement was breaking apart in the 1920s, progressivism still had a great deal of vitality, especially as it was expressed by the farm bloc* and groups that still believed in federal regulation. On June 20, 1920, Congress passed the Water Power Act, which created the Federal Power Commission (FPC) and brought electric utilities under the growing regulatory umbrella. Its original purpose was to exercise general administrative management of water-power sites and similar installations on navigable rivers, public land, and reservations. It issued licenses and permits for the construction of dams, power facilities, reservoirs, transmission lines, and generators. The Federal Power Commission in the 1920s also regulated the operation of power projects. In 1930 Congress strengthened the FPC, giving it more authority over rates, services, and operations; but, until 1935, the commission never made use of its new authority. The Public Utility Holding Company Act of 1935 amended the Water Power Act of 1920 and renamed it the Federal Power Act. After 1935 the FPC had supervisory control over all electric energy transmitted in interstate commerce regardless of whether the power came from water or fuel sources. (Richard Lowitt, "The Federal Power Commission," in Donald Whitnah, ed., *Government Agencies,* 1983.)

FEDERAL RADIO COMMISSION.. When Warren G. Harding* took office in 1921, there were only two commercial radio* stations in the United States; by 1922, there were more than 300, and, during 1922, another 500 started operation. It quickly became obvious that some type of federal regulation was necessary. In 1922 Secretary of Commerce Herbert Hoover* held a conference in Washington, D.C., for radio executives, and they called for government regulation of the airwaves. Subsequent conferences in 1923, 1924, and 1925 led to a voluntary system of licensing through the Department of Commerce and distribution of frequencies in the 500– to 1,500–kilocycle range. Since the continuing proliferation of radio stations made the voluntary program inadequate, Congress passed the Radio Act in February 1927. The law declared that the federal government owned the airwaves and established a five-person Federal Radio Commission to license stations, prohibited censorship except for obscene material, and guaranteed equal access to the airwaves for political candidates. The Federal Radio Commission was superseded by the Federal Communication Commission in 1934. (Erik Barnouw, *A History of Broadcasting in the United States,* vol. 1, *A Tower in Babel: To 1933,* 1966.)

FEDERAL RESERVE BOARD. Federal Reserve Board policies proved to be woefully inadequate during the 1920s. The board might have helped tighten money market conditions by selling government securities in the open market and increasing the rediscount rate, but two problems, along with erroneous assumptions about monetary policy, confused board authorities and left them unable to take decisive action. Part of the problem involved the postwar shift of the world's financial capital from London to New York. Since 1914 the United States had gradually become the principal free gold market in the world; by 1924, the United States held over 40 percent of the world's monetary gold stock. In addition to increasing bank reserves in this country, the huge collections of gold made it more difficult for Great Britain and France to return to the gold standard. During the 1920s, economic leaders in the United States and Europe believed that international financial stability could not be permanently restored until all the major industrial nations returned to the gold standard, which required a credit rate differential between the New York and London money markets sufficient to stimulate American investment in foreign markets and restrict gold imports into the United States. Federal Reserve officials agreed with that assumption, but they were caught on the horns of a dilemma: To discourage the investment boom in the United States, the board would have to raise interest rates, but such restrictive policies would only serve to attract foreign capital to America. Moreover, an easy money policy that lowered domestic interest rates, while pleasing to foreign leaders and conducive to the international resumption of the gold standard, would further stimulate the speculative mania in the United States. Either choice left board officials with an unacceptable problem.

The second problem facing the Federal Reserve Board in the 1920s was the need to discourage securities speculation without simultaneously inhibiting legitimate business growth. The choice that frustrated and preoccupied them throughout the decade was whether to hurt business (and discourage speculation) by easing money market rates. No wonder the Federal Reserve officials were divided and bewildered; as a result, the board followed an ambiguous and confusing set of policies until 1929 and a helpless policy of relative inaction thereafter.

The board first became concerned about the unprecedented securities speculation in 1925. Refusing to tighten credit for fear of depressing commerce and industry, the board simply requested that bankers borrow from Federal Reserve banks only to meet nonspeculative needs. To discourage the importation of more gold and to stimulate a slightly stalled economy, the board lowered the discount rate to 3.5 percent in 1927, which eased credit conditions and naturally stimulated investment and speculation. In 1928, however, worrying about how to stem the speculative tide, the board again embarked on a restrictive policy and returned rates to 4 percent. As securities prices and the volume of brokers' loans continued to increase, the board increased the discount rate to 4.5 percent and then to 5 percent.

However, the fear that business might be injured by restrictive monetary policies generated a contradictory policy in which Federal Reserve banks purchased banker acceptances while discount rates remained high. Federal Reserve officials believed that the funds banks received from the sale of acceptances would be used only for legitimate business needs and not for speculation. They assumed that the method of increasing the money supply determined the uses to which the funds would be put; they failed to understand that the purchase of acceptances increased the volume of excess reserves that could then be invested in the securities markets. The board actually hoped that its high discount rates would discourage speculation while its purchases of bankers' acceptances would stimulate a credit expansion and business growth. That assumption was erroneous. With the fresh infusion of Federal Reserve funds, bankers increased their reserve balances and reduced their Federal Reserve bank indebtedness, negating the impact of the discount rate. Stock prices continued to rise until 1929, when the board concluded that the call loan rate, then running between 7 and 12 percent, was so high and speculation so intense that the manipulation of the discount rate was almost completely ineffective.

Federal Reserve officials did not appreciate the impact that high discount rates had on open market rates: The board stimulated the call money rates and attracted nonbank lenders into the market. Many corporations diverted surplus funds into the call loan market. These funds financed many of the 1928 and 1929 price increases on the exchanges. The Federal Reserve's range of vision was too narrow at that time to include control of nonbank lenders as a legitimate responsibility.

Federal Reserve and bank credit were their only concerns, and they were astonishingly complacent about the enormous power of corporate lenders. The board did not consider itself responsible for controlling the flow and destination of nonbank investment funds. This neglect nullified much of the board's effectiveness over the money market in the last years of the 1920s and contributed substantially to the eventual collapse of the stock market. (Elmus R. Wicker, *Federal Reserve Monetary Policy, 1917–1933,* 1966.)

FEDERAL TRADE COMMISSION. Between 1920 and 1929, the Federal Trade Commission, (FTC) was transformed by the politics of "normalcy"* from a progressive, antimonopoly government agency into a pro-business institution. Established by the Federal Trade Commission Act in 1914, the FTC was originally designed to prohibit all "unfair methods of competition." Progressives like Senators Albert B. Cummins of Iowa and Robert M. La Follette* of Wisconsin hailed the measure as a historic political reform, but when President Warren G. Harding* demanded "less government in business and more business in government," the FTC's days as a progressive institution were numbered. Businessmen were universally condemning the FTC; federal courts were hostile to its activities; and the Republican Congress after 1921 repeatedly called for restrictions on its authority.

The watershed for the FTC came in 1925. In February 1925, President Calvin Coolidge* appointed William E. Humphrey* to the FTC, giving conservatives a majority because of the 1922 appointment of Vernon W. Van Fleet and the 1924 appointment of Charles H. Hunt. The FTC immediately adopted new procedures, ending all sweeping investigations except where definite allegations of unfair practices were evident; proclaiming the need for "informal settlements" rather than costly court suits or agency rulings; and allowing private, preliminary hearings before formal action began. Humphrey's pro-business attitudes also led him to allow business to govern itself through trade association rules. By 1926 business groups were praising the FTC, and progressives were condemning it. Some progressives like Congressman Tom Connally of Texas and Senator William H. King of Utah began to demand abolition of the FTC. The Federal Trade Commission had been completely transformed. (G. Cullom Davis, "The Transformation of the Federal Trade Commission, 1914–1929," *The Mississippi Valley Historical Review* 49 ([December 1962], 437–55.)

FESS, SIMEON DAVISON. Simeon D. Fess was born on a farm in Allen County, Ohio, on December 11, 1861. He graduated from Ohio Northern University in 1889 and received a master's degree in history there two years later. Fess then taught history at Ohio Northern until 1896 and studied at the law school on the side. He received his law degree in 1896 and assumed leadership of the university's law school. In 1900 Fess was named vice-president of Ohio Northern University. He stayed in that position until 1902, when he went to the University of Chicago as a lecturer. In 1907 Fess was named president of Antioch

College, and he remained in that position until 1917. Fess was active in Republican politics in Ohio, and over the years, he became recognized as a leading educator. In the election of 1912, he won a seat in Congress, where he remained until 1923, when he began to serve two terms in the United States Senate. A loyal conservative Republican, Fess supported the high-tariff pro-business atmosphere of the 1920s; in 1930, he became chairman of the Republican National Committee. He was, of course, completely disillusioned by the New Deal. Simeon D. Fess left the Senate in 1935 and died on December 23, 1936. (David Burner, *Herbert Hoover: A Public Life*, 1979; *New York Times*, December 24, 1936.)

FILENE, EDWARD ALBERT. Edward Filene was born on September 3, 1860, in Salem, Massachusetts. His father had opened a small business in Boston in 1881, but declining health forced him to turn it over to Edward in 1882. Specializing in women's fashions, William Filene's Sons Company became one of the leading retail establishments in Boston. Edward concentrated on sales and administrative policy while his brother Lincoln focused on personnel. They invented the idea of the "Bargain Basement" in 1902, placing the articles that did not sell rapidly on basement tables at cut-rate prices. By 1912 Filene's had become the largest specialty store in the world—its store occupyied an entire city block in downtown Boston. The Filene brothers also invented the charge card, which allowed customers to make purchases and be billed one month later. By 1912 sales had reached nearly $8.5 million.

Filene was also known at the time as an enlightened employer. He established a minimum wage for women and allowed the Filene Cooperative Management Association to negotiate and settle disputes between management and labor. Filene's provided paid vacations for employees and in 1924 began to provide paid winter vacations as well. Filene also established the Filene Employees Credit Union, which became a model for the credit union movement throughout the country. In 1919 Filene established the Cooperative League of Boston, which the next year became known as the Twentieth Century Fund, a research group which studied social trends in the United States. Filene was an active Democrat, but his liberal social views precipitated a power struggle in the company during the late 1920s, especially after he expressed his intention to turn over control of the company to the Filene Cooperative Management Association. After 1928, Filene continued as president of the firm, but stockholders had left him with little power. Filene also spent years after the end of World War I campaigning for United States participation in the League of Nations.* Edward Filene died on September 26, 1937. (John William Ferry, *History of the Department Store*, 1960; Stacy Holmes, *Brief History of Filene's*, 1972; Tom Mahoney and Leonard Sloan, *The Great Merchants*, 1955; *New York Times*, September 27, 1937.)

FINLEY, JOHN HUSTON. John H. Finley was born on October 19, 1863, in Grand Ridge, Illinois. He graduated from Knox College in 1887 and then went to graduate school at Johns Hopkins University. At first, he went into social work, serving as secretary of the New York State Charities Aid Association and editor of *Charities Review* between 1889 and 1892. He specialized in the problem of child welfare. In 1892 Finley became president of Knox College and in 1899 editor of *Harper's Weekly*. He served as editor at *Harper's* until 1903 when he became president of the City College of New York. Finley served as commissioner of education for New York between 1913 and 1921; between 1921 and 1938, he was editor of the *New York Times*. John Finley died on March 7, 1940. *(New York Times,* March 8, 1940.)

"THE FIRE CHIEF." "The Fire Chief" was the first comedy show to be broadcast on national radio.* Starring Ed Wynn, it premiered on April 26, 1932, and was sponsored by Texaco. Heard weekly by an audience of thirty million people, the show was very popular in the early 1930s. Wynn pioneered the technique of breaking into commercials with jokes and satire, a talent Jack Benny and Fibber McGee would later raise to an art form. The show lasted until 1935, when people like Jack Benny and Eddie Cantor* eclipsed Wynn. (Jack Dunning, *Tune in Yesterday: The Ultimate Encyclopedia of Old-Time Radio, 1925–1976,* 1976.)

FIRESTONE, HARVEY SAMUEL. Harvey Firestone was born in Columbiana, Ohio, on December 20, 1868. He went to public schools and a business college in Cleveland after graduation. Firestone went to work as a salesman with his uncle's buggy company, but after it went bankrupt in 1896, he decided to go into the business of selling rubber wheels. He set up a company which he sold three years later for $40,000, and he used the money to move to Akron and establish the Firestone Tire and Rubber Company, which manufactured tires for bicycles and buggies. Firestone developed a pneumatic rubber tire to replace the solid rubber tire in 1903, and in 1906 Henry Ford* placed a large order for his automobile* company. The two men became close friends. In 1907 Firestone invented a disposable rim which allowed a flat tire to be changed. Between 1901 and 1913, Firestone sales went from $100,000 a year to $15 million.

During the 1920s, Firestone slashed prices for tires, developed the "baloon tire" which became standard on automobiles, promoted the trucking industry, and bitterly refused to negotiate with labor organizers. In 1928, he also pioneered the "one-stop" service store around the country, where consumers could purchase gasoline, oil, tires, and automobile parts and obtain automobile repairs. By the time of World War II, there were more than 600 of the Firestone stores in the United States. By 1937, despite the Great Depression, Firestone's total sales exceeded $156 million. Harvey Firestone died on February 7, 1938. (Harvey Firestone, *Men and Rubber,* 1926; Alfred Lief, *Harvey Firestone,* 1951; *New York Times,* February 8, 1938.)

"THE FIRST NIGHTER PROGRAM." "The First Nighter Program" was the first radio* program in the United States to offer three-act dramatic plays. It premiered on NBC radio on December 4, 1930, and continued until 1949. Don Ameche was its first star, and the show concentrated on light, romantic comedies. (John Dunning, *Tune in Yesterday: The Ultimate Encyclopedia of Old-Time Radio, 1925–1976,* 1976.)

FISHER, FREDERICK JOHN. Frederick Fisher was born on January 2, 1878, in Sandusky, Ohio. His father was a blacksmith and wheelwright, and, when he was fourteen, Fisher left school and went to work in his father's business. Fisher was adept as a carriage maker. In 1902 he moved to Detroit and took a job as a draftsman for a large automobile* body manufacturer. Five years later, Fisher was the plant superintendent. With his brother Charles, Fisher founded the Fisher Body Company in Detroit in 1908. Instead of adapting carriage bodies for automobiles, Fisher designed bodies for automobiles, and manufactured his products to be sturdy and efficient. By 1916 Fisher Body was manufacturing 370,000 units a year, and in 1919 General Motors bought a controlling interest in the company. During the 1920s, Fisher Body constructed twenty factories around the country and became the most successful of General Motors's divisions. By 1925 they were making 425,000 bodies a year, and the company trademark, "Body by Fisher," was familiar throughout the United States. In 1926 General Motors bought the remaining shares of Fisher Body. By the end of the decade, the assets of the Fisher family—Frederick Fisher and his brothers— exceeded $500 million. Frederick Fisher died on July 14, 1941. *(New York Times,* July 15, 1941; Alfred P. Sloan, Jr., *My Years with General Motors,* 1969.)

FISHER, IRVING. Irving Fisher, a leading economist at Yale University, was born on February 27, 1867, at Saugerties, New York. He earned an undergraduate degree and a Ph.D. in economics at Yale. Fisher's dissertation became a landmark in the development of mathematical economics. Fisher took a position at Yale in 1890 and became a full professor in 1898. Between 1894 and 1899, he published widely in scholarly journals on bimetallism, the theory of utility and prices, interest, and capital. A serious bout with tuberculosis left Fisher with an extraordinary interest in health; he became a crusader for exercise, proper diet, relaxation therapy, and avoidance of tobacco and alcohol. He played an important role in the ratification of the Eighteenth Amendment,* and he campaigned vigorously for the League of Nations.* In 1928 Fisher published *The Money Illusion* to educate laymen about prices and money. The stock market crash of 1929* caught him by surprise, wiped out his personal fortune, and eventually destroyed much of his reputation as a leading economist. In February 1930 he wrote an optimistic book about the crash, *The Stock Market Crash and After,* in which he argued that recovery was just around the corner. Two years later, he had to revise his point of view, arguing in *Booms and Depressions* that devastating shifts in the business cycle could be controlled by the Federal Reserve Board.* The depression could be stopped if the federal government would pursue a policy of ''reflating the price level up to the average level at which outstanding debts were contracted, and maintaining that level unchanged.'' Supported by leading silver monetarists, Fisher urged President Franklin D. Roosevelt* to abandon the gold standard and try to stabilize currency at the 1926 level. The president's ill-fated gold-buying scheme in 1933–1934 was one consequence of Fisher's arguments about manipulating price levels through purchases of hard metal. Eventually, Fisher became a strong critic of the New Deal. Irving Fisher died on April 29, 1947. (W. Fellner et al., *Ten Economic Studies in the Tradition of Irving Fisher,* 1967; Irving Fisher, Jr., *My Father Irving Fisher,* 1956.)

FITZGERALD, FRANCIS SCOTT KEY. F. Scott Fitzgerald was born in St. Paul, Minnesota, on September 24, 1896. He went to Princeton in 1913 but left before graduating in 1917 to enter the army. His first novel, *This Side of Paradise* (1920), exposed the strength of his Roman Catholic moralism, even though he was not at all active in the religion. The irony of Fitzgerald's life was that he respected decency and exposed, in such novels as *The Great Gatsby* (1925) and *Tender Is the Night* (1934), the decadence and materialism of the ''Jazz Age'' of the 1920s, but his own personal life was a shambles. The character Gatsby was destroyed by his own moral irresponsibility, and Fitzgerald was aiming his words at his own life. Between 1924 and 1930, Fitzgerald lived in Europe with his wife Zelda Sayre, who suffered two nervous breakdowns there. They returned to the United States, but Fitzgerald's novels in the 1930s which received negative critiques, were not financial successes. After suffering a nervous breakdown himself, Fitzgerald went to Hollywood as a scriptwriter, and then declined into alcoholism. F. Scott Fitzgerald died on December 21, 1940. (Alfred Kazan, *F. Scott Fitzgerald: The Man and His Work,* 1951; Andre Le Vot, *F. Scott Fitzgerald: A Biography,* 1983; Arthur Mizener, *The Far Side of Paradise: A Biography of F. Scott Fitzgerald,* 1965.)

FIVE-POWER TREATY OF 1922. See WASHINGTON NAVAL CONFERENCE

FLAGPOLE SITTING. See KELLY, ALVIN ''SHIPWRECK''

FLAPPER. The term ''flapper'' was used to describe the avant-garde, sexually liberated woman of the 1920s. World War I had brought about enormous social changes, and new women's fashions symbolized them. The typical flapper had bobbed hair* and cultivated a slender, boyish look. Instead of dark stockings, she wore flesh-colored stockings that exposed the leg, especially since hemlines were up six to ten inches above the ankle. Instead of high laced shoes, the flapper wore low pumps that showed off the ankle. The clothes symbolized the new role of women—vital, experimental, and exciting. (Paul Sann, *The Lawless Decade*, 1957.)

FLOOD RELIEF. See MISSISSIPPI FLOOD OF 1927

FLORIDA BOOM. During the 1920s, no financial event rivaled the stock market for excitement, profit, and crash, except the Florida real estate boom. Early in the 1920s, developers had turned to Florida because of its climate and its accessibility to the money and population of the Northeast, the Coolidge prosperity and credibility of a "get-rich-quick" culture, and the widespread use of the automobile. In 1922 and 1923, they had created whole new residential communities in Coral Gables, Miami Beach, Davis Islands, Tampa, Sarasota, and St. Petersburg. Investors in on the ground floor of those projects made fortunes. As the news spread of the enormous profits to be made in Florida real estate, a host of speculators, crooks, and naive buyers entered the business. People sometimes bought property "site-unseen" based on slick brochures. Land prices doubled and tripled and quadrupled in matters of months.

In the summer of 1926, however, the geometric growth rates began to slow, and the boom collapsed on September 18, 1926, when an enormous hurricane struck South Florida and flooded all the major coastal areas. Housing developments were destroyed, 400 people were killed, and 50,000 people were left homeless. Heavily leveraged and dependent on continuing cash investment, real estate developments collapsed. By 1927 South Florida was besieged with bank failures and real estate bankruptcies. Real estate bonds secured by new buildings under construction were being defaulted, and dozens of Florida cities verged on bankruptcy. The Florida land boom and collapse of the mid-1920s was a rehearsal for the boom and bust that hit the entire economy after 1929. (Frederick Lewis Allen, *Only Yesterday: An Informal History of the 1920s*, 1931.)

FORD, HENRY. Henry Ford was born near Dearborn, Michigan, on July 30, 1863. He attended school until 1878 when he moved to Detroit and worked for several years as a machine-shop apprentice and farm machinery repairman. In the mid-1880s Ford operated a sawmill and in 1887 became the chief engineer for Edison Illuminating Company in Detroit. Ford's personal interests rested on the "horseless carriage," and by 1896 he had constructed his first automobile.* He built the "999" racing car in 1903 and then organized the Ford Motor Company that same year. Ford developed the Model T later in the decade and in 1909 began producing it on a mass scale, using factory assembly methods that brought international acclaim. The Model T was characterized by lightness, durability, efficiency, and low cost. By 1916 Ford was able to sell the Model T for $350 and still make a profit. It was the only model Ford produced. In 1916 Ford was producing 2,000 Model Ts each day. In 1914 Ford became a pioneer in labor relations by introducing the eight-hour day and $5 per day minimum wage as well as a profit-sharing program. Hoping to stave off World

War I, Ford chartered the ship *Oscar II* and carried a large group of pacifists, feminists, and reformers to Scandinavia. Ford made an unsuccessful bid as a Democrat for a United States Senate seat in 1918, campaigning in favor of American entrance into the League of Nations.* By that time, Ford had become bitterly anti-Semitic and blamed the Jews for his election defeat.

During the 1920s, Ford vigorously expanded corporate operations but also faced stiff challenges. He constructed a huge industrial complex at River Rouge in Dearborn, which included a foundry, glass factory, blast furnaces, coke ovens, and assembly facility. He also purchased forests in Michigan, iron resources in Minnesota, coal mines in Kentucky and West Virginia, and a rubber plantation in Brazil. In 1929 he bought the Lincoln Motor Car Company and diversified his product. Diversification was long overdue. Because of new competition from the Chevrolet, which General Motors was producing, the Model T's market share of all automobiles sold in America fell from 56 percent in 1921 to 34 percent in 1926. Ford tried to cut the price on the Model T, but it had little effect. Many consumers were drawn to the Chevrolet because it seemed more stylish, even if it was more expensive. In 1927 Ford shut down production at River Rouge for five months to begin production of the Model A. The Model A had captured 45 percent of the market by 1929, but the depression badly cut into sales and Ford discontinued it in 1931.

Ford's reputation as an enlightened entrepeneur did not survive the 1920s and 1930s. He became a bitter opponent of labor unions and the New Deal. Harboring profascist views, Ford saw the New Deal and the Congress of Industrial Organizations as symbols of radicalism and communism. He saw the "sit-down" strikes of 1937 by the United Automobile Workers (UAW) as the beginning of a revolution, and unlike General Motors he refused to sign a contract with them. Ford resorted to violence-prone strike-breaking hoodlums to cajole workers. Not until 1941, when global war was on the horizon and huge production orders were mounting, did Henry Ford acquiesce and recognize the UAW. Henry Ford died on April 7, 1947. (Allan Nevins, *Ford,* 1954.)

FORDNEY-McCUMBER TARIFF OF 1922. On May 27, 1921, President Warren G. Harding* signed the Emergency Tariff Act,* which raised to protective levels the tariffs on twenty-eight agricultural products. Convinced that American business needed protection from foreign competition as well, the new Republican administration was committed to raising general tariff levels. In the House, the responsibility fell on Joseph W. Fordney, chairman of the Ways and Means Committee. In June 1921 his committee reported out a new tariff bill, which passed by a vote of 288 to 177 along highly partisan lines, Republicans favoring it and Democrats opposing it. In the Senate, Porter J. McCumber* of North Dakota headed the push for tariff legislation, and the bill he finally got to the floor of the Senate contained 2,082 amendments to the House measure, most of them log-rolling increases in tariff schedules. The bill passed the Senate by a vote of 48 to 25 in August 1922. The Fordney-McCumber bill spent the next month in conference committee, but it passed both houses of Congress, and Harding signed it into law on September 21, 1922.

The law raised general tariff levels approximately 25 percent above the protectionist Payne-Aldrich Tariff of 1909 and allowed the United States Tariff Commission to recommend schedule changes by as much as 50 percent without congressional authorization. In the long run, the tariff hurt foreign trade. The U.S. Tariff Commission, under the direction of Republicans in the 1920s, recommended only thirty-seven changes in tariff schedules, and thirty-two of them were increases. By raising tariff schedules to protectionist levels, the Fordney-McCumber Act triggered retaliatory tariffs in Europe against the United States, reduced the availability of foreign markets for American products, and prevented Europeans from generating the revenues they needed to repay their debts to the United States. Along with the Hawley-Smoot Tariff of 1930, the Fordney-McCumber Tariff was a contributing factor in the collapse of the economy after 1929. (Robert K. Murray, *The Politics of Normalcy: Governmental Theory and Practice in the Harding-Coolidge Era,* 1973; Frank W. Taussig, *The Tariff History of the United States,* 1931.)

FOREIGN POLICY ASSOCIATION. The Foreign Policy Association was founded in 1918 by prominent social worker Paul U. Kellogg* to promote international peace and U.S. entrance into the League of Nations.* At first, it was called the League of Nations Association, but the name was changed to the Foreign Policy Association in 1920. Early members included Herbert Croly,* William Durant,* Mary and Charles Beard,* John R. Commons,* John Dewey,* Felix Frankfurter, and Ida M. Tarbell. Norman Hapgood served as its first president. When the League of Nations essentially became a dead issue early in the 1920s, the Foreign Policy Association changed its focus to educating the public on international issues through a speaker's bureau and local debates. It continued to advocate an internationalist foreign policy for the United States. (L. Ethan Ellis, *Republican Foreign Policy, 1921–1933,* 1968.)

FOSDICK, HARRY EMERSON. Harry Emerson Fosdick was born on May 24, 1878, in Buffalo, New York. He graduated from Colgate University in 1900, earned a divinity degree from Union Seminary in New York in 1904, and received a master's degree from Columbia University in 1908. Fosdick was minister of the First Baptist Church of Montclair, New Jersey, between 1904 and 1915, and then he joined the teaching staff of the Union Seminary, a position he held until 1934. At the same time, Fosdick served as a minister of the Riverside Church of New York. During the 1920s, Fosdick became the embodiment of liberal Protestantism and the enemy of fundamentalists throughout the country, especially after 1922 when his sermons were broadcast widely over the radio. Fosdick believed in the divinity of Jesus Christ and in the immortality of the human soul, but he also believed in social action, progressive reform, and the relativity of scriptural interpretation. Fosdick saw no conflict between evolution* and the

Bible—a position that brought William Jennings Bryan* to demand his removal as a Presbyterian minister. Christianity, for Fosdick, was a gospel of love, not sectarian dogma, and he carried those convictions with him until his death on October 5, 1969. (Harry Emerson Fosdick, *The Living of These Days: An Autobiography,* 1956; *New York Times,* October 6, 1969.)

FOSDICK, RAYMOND BLAINE. Raymond Fosdick was born on June 9, 1883, in Buffalo, New York. He graduated from Princeton University in 1905, earned a master's degree there in 1906, and received a law degree from the New York Law School in 1908. Fosdick worked as a legal counsel for New York City between 1908 and 1912 and as comptroller for the Democratic Party* during Woodrow Wilson's* successful presidential bid in 1912, and he served as a researcher for the Bureau of Social Research. During World War I, he chaired the Commission on Training Camp Activities, and in 1919, Fosdick served as a civilian aide to General John Pershing. In 1919 he was appointed undersecretary-general of the League of Nations,* but when the United States refused to join, Fosdick left the organization in 1920. He then spent the next sixteen years in private law practice, but his internationalism was unabated, and between 1923 and 1935, Fosdick was a founder and president of the League of Nations Non-Partisan Association. From that position, and as head of the Rockefeller Foundation between 1936 and 1948, Fosdick became one of the most well-known internationalists in the country. Fosdick was single-minded in his conviction that the United States should join the League of Nations and the World Court,* and although he failed in that endeavor, he became a vigorous supporter of the United Nations after World War II. During the last years of his life, Fosdick was chair of the publications committee of the Woodrow Wilson Foundation and supervised publication of *The Papers of Woodrow Wilson.*Raymond Fosdick died on July 18, 1972. (Daryl L. Revoldt, "Raymond B. Fosdick: Reform, Internationalism, and the Rockefeller Foundation," Ph.D. dissertation, University of Akron, 1981.)

FOSTER, WILLIAM ZEBULON. William Z. Foster was born in Taunton, Massachusetts, on February 25, 1881. Foster held a variety of jobs and became politically active as a young man, joining the Socialist Party of America* in 1901 but abandoning it in 1909 for the International Workers of the World. Foster became an advocate of radical syndicalism and an officer in the Syndicalist League of North America. In 1917 Foster founded the International Trade Union Educational League and led the steel strike of 1919.* In 1921 Foster visited the Soviet Union and joined the Communist Party* of America. Foster was the Communist Party's presidential candidate in the elections of 1924,* 1928,* and 1932,* and he served as national chairman of the party between 1932 and 1957. Indefatigable in his commitment to Marxism, Foster never wavered in his belief that capitalism would inevitably collapse and that revolution would sweep through America. He died in Moscow on September 1, 1961. (William Z. Foster,

Pages from a Worker's Life, 1939; Arthur Zipser, *Workingclass Giant: The Life of William Z. Foster*, 1981.)

FOUR-POWER TREATY. By 1920 most Americans were weary of foreign policy issues. Disillusionment with the achievements of World War I was already setting in, and most people hoped that the geographical isolation of the United States would protect the country in the future as it had in the past. The Republican administrations of Warren Harding* and Calvin Coolidge* during the 1920s officially opposed American participation in the League of Nations* as well as in the World Court.* At the same time, American economic relations existed on a global scale, making foreign policy isolationism a marginal possibility at best. Concern about Japanese expansion in the Far East and Pacific had worried the Wilson administration as far back as 1917, when Woodrow Wilson recognized Japan's special interest in China in exchange for a guarantee of China's territorial integrity and the Open Door policy. At the same time, Wilson had supported allied intervention in Siberia during the Bolshevik revolution in part to limit Japanese expansion there, had opposed any declaration of racial equality in the Treaty of Versailles,* and resisted Japan's claims to the Pacific island of Yap.

To deal with a variety of geopolitical questions, President Warren Harding invited Great Britain, France, Italy, Japan, China, Belgium, the Netherlands, and Portugal to the Washington Naval Conference* of 1921.* After weeks of debate, they agreed to several treaties, including the Four-Power Treaty between Japan, France, the United States, and Great Britain. Each country agreed to respect the sovereignty of one another's island possessions in the Pacific and to meet for discussion if any trouble arose over them. In return for this arrangement, England and Japan promised to abrogate the Anglo-Japanese Alliance of 1902, which had embarrassed the United States and had threatened American interests in the Pacific. The Senate ratified the Four-Power Treaty, but stipulated that the United States would not necessarily defend it by force. Japan eventually became frustrated with what she considered her second-class status after the Washington Naval Conference as well as with the 1924 American immigration laws, which had specifically prohibited Japanese immigration. In 1931 Japan broke the treaties and formally denounced them in 1935. (L. Ethan Ellis, *Republican Foreign Policy, 1921–1933*, 1968; Akira Iriye, *After Imperialism: The Search for a New Order in the Far East, 1921–1931*, 1965.)

FOURTEEN POINTS. The Fourteen Points consisted of the proposals President Woodrow Wilson* made at the Versailles negotiations to end World War I. Wilson spoke before Congress on January 8, 1918, outlining his vision for the postwar world, based on what he called a "new diplomacy." In the first four proposals, Wilson called for open diplomacy, in which no secret deals were concocted and to which the world press was given full access; freedom of the seas to guarantee the flow of commerce; worldwide tariff reductions so that international trade would be stimulated; and disarmament. In the next nine proposals, Wilson proposed redrawing the map of Europe so that political boundaries reflected ethnic and linguistic divisions—only then would Poles, Lithuanians, Czechs, Slovaks, Croatians, Serbians, Ukrainians, and Slovenians enjoy self-determination. Finally, in the fourteenth proposal, Wilson called for the creation of a League of Nations,* believing that collective security would preserve world peace.

The Fourteen Points met with stiff resistance at Versailles. Open diplomacy foundered on the need for secrecy in preliminary negotiations; otherwise, political pressures at home would prevent compromise and treaty development. Freedom of the seas and tariff reductions, to European leaders at least, seemed designed to benefit the United States, which had emerged from the war economically powerful. Disarmament, too, was rejected simply because political insecurities in France and Great Britain were too great. Although Wilson's specific proposals for realignment of the European political map were not enacted, the Treaty of Versailles* did lead to the creation of Poland, Lithuania, Austria, Hungary, Czechoslovakia, and Yugoslavia out of the ruins of Germany, Austria-Hungary, and Russia. Finally European leaders acquiesced to Wilson's demand for a League of Nations, even though they were quite skeptical about its ability to enforce the peace. The irony, of course, was that the United Stated Senate refused to ratify the Treaty of Versailles because of the League of Nations provision. (Thomas A. Bailey, *Woodrow Wilson and the Lost Peace,* 1944.)

FOX, WILLIAMS. William Fox was born on January 1, 1879, in Tulchva, Hungary, to a Jewish family. He immigrated to New York City with his family while an infant, and he attended public schools. Fox worked for a while in the garment district, but in 1904 he scraped together enough money to purchase a nickelodeon theater in Brooklyn. By 1908 he owned fourteen more of them. After 1910 Fox began buying vaudeville theaters and changing half the evening programs to movies. His theaters were large and comfortable, and middle-class attendance at vaudeville programs skyrocketed. In 1912 Fox established the Greater New York Film Rental Company, a distribution enterprise which came into direct competition with Thomas Edison's distribution monopoly—the General Film Company. Fox refused to sell out to Edison, and he prospered as a distributor. He then vertically integrated his business by going into the production of movies, establishing the Fox Film Corporation in 1915. Fox signed Theda Bara* to star in his first production—*Carmen*. In 1919 he began producing films in Hollywood, California, helping make the city the film capital of the world.

During the 1920s and 1930s, Fox had an enormous impact on the film industry. He produced such films as *What Price Glory? (1926), Evangeline* (1929), *Cleopatra (1934),* and *Les Miserables* (1935). Along with Warner Brothers, Fox was an early entrant into sound movies, and he acquired hundreds of movie theaters in the 1920s and 1930s. When the Great Depression* hit, Fox owned properties worth more than $300 million, but he was heavily leveraged financially, and the crash of the stock market ruined him. Fox declared bankruptcy in 1933. Fox

138   FOY, EDDIE, JR.

Film Corporation merged with Twentieth Century Film Corporation in 1935. In 1941, Fox spent a short time in prison for trying to bribe a bankruptcy court judge. Fox died on May 8, 1952. (*New York Times,* May 9, 1952; Upton Sinclair, *Upton Sinclair Presents William Fox,* 1933; Robert Sklar, *Movie Made America,* 1975.)

FOY, EDDIE, JR. Eddie Foy, Jr., born Edwin Fitzgerald Foy, Jr., on February 4, 1910, in New York City, came from a performing family, and his family trained him to tap dance on the vaudeville circuit. The act was entitled "The Seven Little Foys." Foy performed in vaudeville from the time he was five until he was nineteen, when he made his Broadway debut in *Show Girl* (1929). Subsequently, Foy performed in a number of Broadway plays, such as *Smiles* (1930), *At Home Abroad* (1935), and *The Pajama Game* (1954), where he played the role of "Hines." Foy also made a number of films in the 1930s and 1940s, and he became a popular television performer in the 1950s and 1960s. Eddie Foy died on July 15, 1983. (Barbara Naomi Cohen-Stratyner, *Biographical Dictionary of Dance,* 1982; *New York Times,* July 16, 1983.)

FRAZIER, LYNN JOSEPH. Lynn J. Frazier was born near Medford, Minnesota, on December 21, 1874. He moved with his parents to the Dakota Territory in 1881 when they decided to homestead a tract of land in Pembina County. Frazier graduated from the Mayville State Normal School in 1895 and from the University of North Dakota in 1901. He farmed in Pembina County for several years and became active in the politics of the new Non-Partisan League.* Representing the league in the election of 1916, Frazier surprised himself and everyone else by winning the governorship. He was re-elected in 1918 and 1920, but the postwar backlash caught up with his progressive politics, and he was recalled from office in 1921. Frazier then affiliated himself with the Republican Party* and won election to the United States Senate in 1922. In the Senate, Frazier was an isolationist in terms of foreign policy, wanting nothing to do with the League of Nations,* and a progressive in domestic policy, supporting a wide variety of pro-farmer legislation, including the McNary-Haugen Bill.* He was temporarily read out of the Republican Party in 1924 for supporting the presidential candidacy of Robert M. La Follette* and the Progressive Party,* but he was nonetheless re-elected to the Senate in 1928 and 1934. During the New Deal years, Frazier affiliated himself with the progressive wing of the Republican Party, but his isolationism cost him re-election in 1940. Lynn J. Frazier died on January 11, 1947. (*New York Times,* January 12, 1947.)

"FRISCO." See FRISCO, JOE

FRISCO, JOE. Joe Frisco was born Louis Wilson Josephs in 1890 in Milan, Illinois. He worked the vaudeville circuit and was a dancing partner in the act "Coffee and Doughnuts." Frisco came to Broadway in 1924 and became an instant star. He gave birth to the "Frisco," a strut characterized by bent knees, tipped torso, cigar, derby hat, and a stutter, which became widely imitated by other performers. During the 1920s, dance halls throughout the country held "Frisco" contests to see who could best imitate the dance. Frisco was also a popular stand-up comedian. He died on February 16, 1958. (Barbara Naomi Cohen-Stratyner, *Biographical Dictionary of Dance,* 1982.)

FROST, ROBERT. Born in San Francisco, California, on March 26, 1874, Robert Frost moved to New York City with his family in 1884 and grew up there. Eventually, he became the dean of American poetry. By 1912 he had tried his hand at farming, selling eggs, teaching, and assembly-line work, but, frustrated with his marriage, family, and life, he went to England for three years, where he produced his first book, *A Boy's Will* (1913). That was followed in 1914 by *North of Boston.* In his personal life, Frost experienced pain and tragedy. One son committed suicide, one daughter died very young, another daughter was permanently institutionalized for insanity, and a third daughter was completely alienated from him because of the way she perceived he had treated her mother. Frost was full of grief, afraid of insanity, and desperate for happiness. His poetry evoked powerful New England images, not only in environmental scenery but also in a Calvinist sense of depression, loneliness, and pessimism. In 1961, President John Kennedy made Frost the poet laureate of the United States by having Frost read at his inauguration. Robert Frost died on January 29, 1963. (Martin Seymour-Smith, *Who's Who in Twentieth Century Literature,* 1976.)

FULLER, ALFRED CARL. Alfred C. Fuller was born on January 13, 1885, in Wellsford, Nova Scotia. After he graduated from high school, Fuller's family moved to Somerset, Masschusetts. He got a job with the Boston Elevated Railroad Company, and in 1905 he went to work as a salesman for the Somerville Brush Company. The next year, Fuller founded his own company, the Capital Brush Company. In 1910 he changed the company's name to the Fuller Brush Company, and he began to advertise in national magazines and to employ salesmen nationwide to market cleaning brushes. Between 1911 and 1924 company sales increased from $40,000 a year to $12 million—the "Fuller Brush Man" salesmen were ubiquitous, door-to-door salesmen in middle-class America. By 1930 Fuller had 3,600 salesmen combing the countryside, working out of 200 branch offices. In 1943 Fuller stepped down as president, and his son, Alfred, took over but he remained chairman of the board until he died on December 4, 1973. (*Current Biography,* 1950; *New York Times,* December 5, 1973.)

G

GALLAGHER, RICHARD "SKEETS." Antoine Richard Gallagher was born in 1891 in Terre Haute, Indiana. During the World War I period, Gallagher became prominent on the vaudeville circuit dancing in an act entitled "The Magazine Girl," and he appeared as a high-kicking eccentric dancer in several silent films, including *Up in the Clouds* (1921), *'Op She Goes* (1922), *No, No, Nanette* (1924), *Rose Marie, The City Chap* (1925), and *Lucky* (1927). When sound movies came along late in the 1920s, a number of producers discovered that Gallagher also had verbal abilities, and he debuted in a 1927 W. C. Fields film—*The Potters*—with Paramount Pictures. Gallagher made dozens of films in the late 1920s and 1930s, and during the 1940s he returned to the theater in "Good Night Ladies," a burlesque routine. Richard "Skeets" Gallagher died on May 22, 1955. (Barbara Naomi Cohen-Stratyner, *Biographical Dictionary of Dance*, 1982.)

GARBO, GRETA. Greta Garbo was born Greta Lovisa Gustafsson in Stockholm, Sweden, on September 18, 1905. Between 1922 and 1924, she attended the Royal Dramatic Theatre School in Stockholm, working part-time as an extra in several European films to pay her way. Garbo moved to Hollywood in 1925 after signing a contract with Metro-Goldwyn-Mayer films. During the 1920s and 1930s, Garbo became the first "modern woman" star in the film industry. The roles she played always allowed her to be the emancipated woman, choosing rationally her sexual encounters without powerful moral restraints on them. Her major films included *The Temptress* (1926), *Love* (1927), *The Divine Woman* (1928), *The Kiss* (1929), *Anna Christie* and *Romance* (1930), *Susan Lenox* (1931), and *Mati Hari* (1932). Garbo had an especially strong following in Europe. Garbo made the transition to sound films, but her performance in *The Two-Faced Woman* (1941) received bad notices from critics, and she left Hollywood, retreating into a self-imposed exile in Europe. (Alexander Walker, *Greta Garbo: A Portrait*, 1980.)

GARNER, JOHN NANCE. John Nance Garner was born on November 22, 1868, in Red River County, Texas. He had few opportunities for advanced education, but he read law privately and entered the Texas bar in 1890. He practiced law privately until 1898, when he won election to the state legislature. In 1901, Garner was elected to Congress, and he maintained his seat for the next thirty years. During the Republican ascendancy of the 1920s, Garner emerged as a leader of the Democratic Party,* and in 1931 he was elected speaker of the house by the narrow margin of three votes. As leader of the opposition, Garner steered a delicate course, favoring such Herbert Hoover* policies as the Reconstruction Finance Corporation* but offering Democratic alternatives in order to assure the party's success in 1932. He became a favorite-son candidate for the presidency at the Democratic convention in Chicago. Governor Franklin D. Roosevelt* of New York emerged as the front-runner, but he lacked the two-thirds vote necessary for the nomination. On the fourth ballot, Garner released his delegates, principally from Texas and California, in order to avoid the divisive results of the deadlocked Democratic convention that had occurred in the election of 1924.* His move created a stampede to Roosevelt, and, in turn, the party faithful nominated Garner for the vice-presidency by acclamation. During the campaign, Garner offered his Southwestern colloquialisms and straightforward opinions when asked but generally adopted a low profile and let Roosevelt make most of the public appearances.

Garner served two terms as vice-president, but he gradually grew disillusioned with the large bureaucracy and budget deficits of the New Deal. In 1940, Garner made an abortive bid for the Democratic presidential nomination, but he was too conservative for most Democrats, and he lost badly in the primary elections. Garner was not disappointed about not being vice-president anymore; he had once likened it to a "bucket of warm spit." He retired to his family home in Uvalde, Texas, and died on November 7, 1967. (Ovie C. Fisher, *Cactus Jack,* 1978; Bascom N. Timmons, *Garner of Texas,* 1948.)

GARVEY, MARCUS MOSIAH. Marcus Garvey was born on August 17, 1887, in St. Anne's Bay, Jamaica. Garvey attended public schools and in 1901 apprenticed out as a printer. He became active in labor union activities, and, between 1910 and 1914, he travelled widely in Central America and Europe. During those travels, he observed white discrimination against blacks all around the world, and in 1914 Garvey returned to Jamaica and organized the Universal Negro Improvement Association (UNIA) and the African Communities League (ACL). The UNIA was a self-help, benevolent group designed to bring pride to black people, and the ACL was a political organization whose purpose was to bring about independent nationhood on the African continent. Garvey came to the United States on a speaking tour in 1916, and by 1919 he had more than a million followers who were active in more than 700 branches. A gifted speaker with a flamboyant flair, Garvey mesmerized his audiences. In 1918 the UNIA and the ACL merged, and during the 1920s the UNIA provided a number of services to black people: death benefits, correspondence courses, adult classes, lectures, and socials. Garvey also helped blacks establish businesses in their communities, such as laundries, restaurants, and dry goods stores. The UNIA regularly fed thousands of poor blacks, published a weekly newspaper called *The World,* ran the Black Star Line (a steamship company), and constantly preached the same motto—"One God! One Aim! One Destiny!" By the 1920s, Garvey was preaching a racial philosophy of black separatism, black self-improvement, and black unity. His slogan became "Africa for the Africans at Home and Abroad." Garvey preached that God was black, and in 1921 he established the African Orthodox Church to institutionalize that doctrine. By 1922 Garvey headed the most powerful black organization in the world.

Because of that philosophy, Garvey unnerved both black integrationists in organizations such as the National Association for the Advancement of Colored People* and whites worried about black rebellion. Beginning in 1918, the Bureau of Investigation in the Department of Justice put Garvey under surveillance. In 1922 federal agents arrested Garvey for using the mail to market shares in the Black Star Line. He was convicted in 1923 and sentenced to prison in 1925. Without his charismatic leadership, the UNIA lost much of its vitality. Garvey was deported from the United States in 1927 and died in London on June 10, 1940. (Edmund D. Cronon, *Black Moses: The Story of Marcus Garvey and the Universal Negro Improvement Association,* 1955; Adolph Edwards, *Marcus Garvey, 1887–1940,* 1967.)

GARY, ELBERT HENRY. Elbert Gary was born on October 8, 1846, in Wheaton, Illinois. He attended the Illinois Institute and served briefly in the Union army during the Civil War; in 1865, he began to read law privately. Gary entered the Union College of Law in Chicago in 1866, and, after graduating in 1868, he began to practice law, specializing in railroad cases; over the years, he accumulated a number of influential friends in corporate America. In 1898, J. P. Morgan convinced Gary to leave his law practice and assume the presidency of the Federal Steel Company. During the next three years, Gary played a central role in Morgan's creation of the United States Steel Corporation. Gary was chairman of the board of U. S. Steel from 1903 until 1927. As head of a huge corporation, Gary cultivated relations with important politicians, especially Theodore Roosevelt and William Howard Taft,* always working to prevent antitrust action against the company. Through what he called the "Gary Dinners," he also met frequently with leading steel executives throughout the country where they discussed and informally set steel prices. When intense competition from smaller firms hit the steel industry in the 1910s, Gary developed his "umbrella concept," which set a general price level for all firms, allowing a place in the market for smaller companies. As for labor relations, Gary believed in high wages, safe working conditions, long hours, and absolutely, positively no union representation for employees. During the steel strike of 1919,* Gary crushed steelworkers with an iron hand, employing intimidation, violence, and accusations of Communist infiltration to defeat the workers. The strike lasted more than three months until the union called it off in January 1920. Gary's reputation as a benevolent corporate leader did not survive the strike. He died on August 15, 1927. (Frederick Lewis Allen, *The Lords of Creation,* 1935; *New York Times,* August 16, 1927; Ida Tarbell, *Life of Elbert Gary,* 1925.)

GAVIT, JOHN PALMER. John P. Gavit was born on July 1, 1868, in Albany, New York. He went to work as a cub reporter for the *Albany Evening Journal* in 1885, and, between 1890 and 1893, he earned a degree at the Hartford Theological Seminary. Gavit spent the next nine years working in various settlement houses in the Northeast. In 1902 he went back into journalism and worked for the Associated Press as a reporter and eventually as bureau chief in Washington, D.C. Gavit became editor of the *New York Evening Post* in 1912. In 1918 he went back into social work, this time as director of research for the Carnegie Institute's project on immigration. In his book *Americans by Choice* (1920), Gavit argued that the popular ideas about the inferiority of the newer immigrants from southern and eastern Europe were simply racist myths. Gavit predicted they would assimilate quickly and peacefully into American life. Gavit returned to the *Post* between 1920 and 1924, spent time writing about American life, and in 1927 joined Paul Kellogg's* *Survey* as a columnist. Gavit stayed with the magazine for the next twenty-seven years. He died on October 27, 1954. *(New York Times,* October 28, 1954.)

GEHRIG, HENRY LOUIS. Lou Gehrig was born on June 19, 1903, in New York City, to a German immigrant family. He graduated from high school in 1921 and enrolled at Columbia University, where he studied and played baseball* for a year until it was discovered that he had played the summer before for a professional team—Hartford in the Eastern League. He was declared ineligible for college athletics, so he signed a contract with the New York Yankees. He played with Hartford until 1924 when the Yankees called him up to the majors. In 1925 Gehrig began to play regularly, and he never left the Yankee lineup for the next fourteen years, playing in 2,130 consecutive games. A polite, respectful, and kind man, Gehrig was also very strong physically and a talented hitter. Although he always played in the shadow of George Herman "Babe Ruth",* Gehrig was highly respected by his teammates, and he served for years as captain of the Yankees. During his career, he hit 493 home runs with 1,991 runs-batted-in and a lifetime batting average of .340. During the 1920s and 1930s, Gehrig was a symbol of propriety and stability in a changing world. In June 1939, physicians at the Mayo Clinic discovered that Gehrig was suffering from amyotrophic lateral sclerosis. He died of the disease on June 2, 1941. (Martin Appel and Burt Goldblatt, *Baseball's Best: The Hall of Fame Gallery,* 1980; *New York Times,* June 3, 1941.)

GENEVA ARMS CONVENTION OF 1925. To gain some sense of control over the international market for weapons, the major powers gathered in Geneva in 1925 for the International Conference for the Supervision of the International Trade in Arms and Munitions. The United States delegation was headed by Theodore Burton,* a Republican congressman from Ohio, and Hugh S. Gibson,* the United States minister to Switzerland. The treaty resulting from the conference provided for nations to make quarterly reports on arms exports. The United States Senate ratified the treaty in 1935. (Robert A. Divine, *The Illusion of Neutrality*, 1962.)

GENEVA CONFERENCE OF 1932. One of the dominant trends in international foreign policy during the 1920s was the theme of disarmament and arms reduction, and several conferences met during the decade to work on the problem: the Washington Naval Conference,* the Geneva Arms Convention of 1925,* the Geneva Naval Conference of 1927,* and the London Naval Conference of 1930.* The Preparatory Commission on Disarmament of the League of Nations* planned further arms reductions, and on February 2, 1932, a general disarmament conference met at Geneva, Switzerland. The United States offered a proposal for eliminating all offensive weapons, but the idea died a quick death. President Herbert Hoover* then instructed the American delegation to propose a 30 percent reduction in offensive weapons, but before any agreement was reached, the conference adjourned in July 1932. The meetings reconvened in February 1933, adjourned in disagreement again in June 1933, and tried again in October 1933, but by that time Germany had left the League of Nations. The Geneva Conference of 1932 dissolved permanently in April 1934 without achieving any arms reduction treaties. (L. Ethan Ellis, *Republican Foreign Policy, 1921–1933*, 1968.)

GENEVA NAVAL CONFERENCE OF 1927. Although the Washington Naval Conference* of 1921–1922 had established limits on battleship construction, it precipitated an arms race in cruiser construction, which had not been limited by the treaty. The United States and Great Britian immediately ran into an impasse: The British insisted on ''absolute need'' and no formulas, and the American delegation strove to impose ratios on the participating nations. The conference broke up without reaching any conclusion. (L. Ethan Ellis, *Republican Foreign Policy, 1921–1933*, 1968.)

GERBER, DANIEL FRANK, JR. Daniel Gerber was born in Fremont, Michigan, on May 6, 1898. After graduating from high school, he served in the army during World War I and then returned and completed a year of study at a business college. In 1920 Gerber joined the family business—Fremont Canning Company. Early in the 1920s, Gerber began to urge his father to go into the business of producing strained baby food, a novel idea at the time because conventional wisdom said that infants were to have a liquid-only diet until they were a year old. In 1928 his father agreed, and Gerber took out advertisements in large-circulation women's magazines, complete with coupons. Instead of selling baby food at pharmacies, which was the practice in the 1920s, Gerber marketed them through grocery stores. The "Gerber Baby" picture of a healthy, red-cheeked infant became a symbol for the company, and within a few years it was recognized throughout the country. By the start of World War II, the company had dropped all of its adult food products and concentrated exclusively on the baby food market. In 1941 he changed the name of the company to Gerber Products Company. Daniel Gerber died on March 16, 1974. (*New York Times,* March 18, 1974.)

GERSHWIN, GEORGE. George Gershwin, America's most gifted modern composer, was born in Brooklyn, New York, on September 26, 1898. He studied piano under Charles Hamburg, and, by the time he was twenty-one, he was already composing music for musical comedies, Broadway plays, and serious classical and operatic performers. Gershwin's compositions were peculiarly American, taking native folk and ethnic themes and putting them to serious music. Beginning with "La La Lucille" in 1919, Gershwin composed a host of popular musical pieces for Broadway, including "Our Nell" in 1923, "Sweet Little Devil" in 1923, "Lady, Be Good!" in 1924, the music for all of George White's "Scandals" (1920–1924), and "An American in Paris" (1928). His "Of Thee I Sing" won a Pulitzer Prize in 1931. Gershwin's operatic compositions included "Blue Monday" (1922) and "Porgy and Bess" (1935). Among his serious compositions were "Rhapsody in Blue" (1923) and "Concerto in F Major for the New York Symphony Society" (1925). George Gershwin died of a brain tumor on July 11, 1937. (Barbara Mitchell, *George Gershwin,* 1987; *New York Times,* July 12, 1937.)

GIANNINI, AMADEO PETER. A. P. Giannini was born on May 6, 1870, in San Jose, California. He quit school in 1883 to go to work in the family produce business, and by 1891 he owned half-interest in the firm. Giannini retired in 1901 with a small fortune. When his father-in-law died in 1902, family members asked Giannini to manage the estate, including shares in Columbus Savings and Loan Society. Giannini encouraged the institution to cultivate the favor of small borrowers and depositors. When they refused, he resigned and organized the Bank of Italy in 1904, with assets totaling $ $300,000. The bank's clientele consisted almost exclusively of Italian merchants, laborers, and small businesses. When the California legislature passed a statute in 1909 permitting branch banking, Giannini quickly expanded, and by 1918 had twenty-four branches in addition to the headquarters in San Francisco. In 1927 Giannini merged his banking interests into the Bank of Italy National Trust and Savings Association, which became the Bank of America. Giannini, a loyal Democrat, was progressive in his political philosophy, criticizing the tax policies of Republican administrations in the 1920s and praising the New Deal of Franklin D. Roosevelt* in the 1930s. A. P. Giannini died on June 3, 1949. (Marquis James and Bessie R. James, *Biography of a Bank: The Story of the Bank of America, NT & SA,* 1954; *Los Angeles Times,* June 4, 1949.)

GIBSON, HUGH SIMONS. Hugh Gibson was born on August 16, 1883, in Los Angeles, California. He graduated from the Ecole Libre des Sciences Politiques in 1907 and entered the diplomatic corps in 1908. Gibson had a number of assignments until 1919, when he became minister to Poland, a position he held until 1924 when he became minister to Switzerland. Beginning in 1924, Gibson chaired the United States delegation preparing for the Geneva Arms Convention of 1925,* and he also chaired the American delegation to the Geneva Naval Conference of 1927.* Between 1927 and 1933, Gibson served as ambassador to Belgium and, between 1933 and 1937, as ambassador to Brazil. A strong internationalist, Gibson believed firmly that, as the world became more integrated economically, it would have to develop new forms of political cooperation. He was an especially strong advocate of American participation in the League of Nations.* Gibson represented the United States at most of the disarmament conferences in the 1920s and 1930s, and he believed the Kellogg-Briand Pact* was a strong move toward international peace. After World War II, Gibson was active in several international relief commissions. He died on December 12, 1954. (Perrin C. Galpin, ed., *Hugh Gibson, 1883–1954,* 1956; Ronald E. Swerczek, "The Diplomatic Career of Hugh Gibson, 1908–1938," Ph.D. dissertation, University of Iowa, 1972.)

GIFFORD, WALTER SHERMAN. Walter S. Gifford was born on January 10, 1885, in Salem, Massachusetts. He graduated from Harvard in 1905 and went to work for the Western Telephone Corporation, part of American Telephone and Telegraph (AT&T). Three years later, Gifford went to work for AT&T and in 1918 became controller. He was named vice-president of finance in 1919 and president in 1925. In 1931 he became head of the President's Organization on Unemployment Relief,* a voluntary group established by President Herbert Hoover* to relieve unemployment problems around the country. Gifford, who remained with AT&T until 1949, was responsible for building it into the corporate giant it eventually became, increasing its annual revenues from $657 million to $2.25 billion. In 1950 President Harry S Truman named Gifford ambassador to Great Britain. Walter S. Gifford died on May 7, 1966. (John Brooks, *Telephone: The First Hundred Years,* 1976; N. R. Danielian, *AT&T: The Story of an Industrial Conquest,* 1939; *New York Times,* May 8, 1966.)

GILBERT, SEYMOUR PARKER. Seymour P. Gilbert was born on October 13, 1892, in Bloomfield, New Jersey. He received his bachelor's and master's degrees from Rutgers in 1912 and 1916, and a law degree from Harvard in 1915. Gilbert practiced law privately for a few years, but in 1920 he became assistant secretary of the treasury for fiscal affairs. During the Harding administration Gilbert served as undersecretary of the treasury. He left public life in 1923 to practice law but returned in 1924 as agent-general for reparations payments, a position created by the Dawes Plan* to advise the German government on financial questions and to see to the proper investment and conversion into foreign currencies of reparations payments. By 1927 Gilbert was convinced that revision of the reparations* schedule was essential, and his views led to the Young Plan* of 1930, which abolished his position. Gilbert then left public life again, this time for a partnership in J. P. Morgan & Company. Seymour Gilbert died on February 23, 1938. *(Dictionary of American Biography,* 1958, supp. 2:234.)

GIMBEL, BERNARD. Bernard Gimbel was born on April 10, 1885, in Vincennes, Indiana, to the famous retailing family. His father Isaac had founded the Gimbel chain of department stores in the 1860s. Bernard Gimbel graduated from the University of Pennsylvania in 1907 and was named vice-president of Gimbel Brothers Department Stores in 1909. In 1910 he supervised construction of the ten-story Gimbel's store in midtown Manhattan, which became a symbol for the company. Under his direction, the company bought out Saks and Company in 1923, and in 1925 he was named president of the company, a position he held until 1953. Between 1925 and 1953, annual sales increased from $15 million to $500 million. Bernard Gimbel died on September 29, 1966. (Leon Harris, *Merchant Princes,* 1979; *New York Times,* September 30, 1966.)

GISH, LILLIAN DIANA. Lillian Gish, one of the great actresses of the American stage and screen, was born on October 14, 1896, in Springfield, Ohio. She was raised in a theatrical family and began to tour with her mother and sister when she was only six years old. Gish debuted in 1912 for D. W. Griffith* in his film *An Unseen Enemy* and then starred in a variety of Griffith productions, the last one in 1922—*The Orphans of the Storm.* It was his famous film *The Birth of a Nation* which established Gish as a screen star. In 1924 Gish signed an $800,000 contract with Metro-Goldwyn-Mayer. She made her first sound film—*One Romantic Night*—in 1930, and she won an Academy Award in 1946 for her performance in *A Duel in the Sun.* During the 1920s, her screen persona was the lovely, suffering heroine blessed with great inner strength. Audiences loved her. From her frail, haunting appearance she radiated great emotional strength. Gish continued to perform throughout much of her life, and in 1984 she received the Life Achievement Award of the American Film Institute. (Anthony Slide, *Lillian Gish: Actress,* 1969 and *The Griffith Actresses,* 1973.)

GITLOW v. *NEW YORK* **(268 U.S. 652).** By a seven to two vote, with Justices Brandeis and Holmes dissenting, the United States Supreme Court decided on June 8, 1925, that the First Amendment prohibition against government limitations on freedom of speech applies to the states as well as to the federal government. The Fourteenth Amendment to the Constitution, the court ruled, extended First Amendment prohibitions to the states. (Congressional Quarterly, *Guide to the U.S. Supreme Court,* 1979.)

GLASS, CARTER. Born in Lynchburg, Virginia, on January 4, 1858, Carter Glass was the son of Robert Henry Glass and Augusta Christian. His father was a newspaper editor, so Glass grew up in a political atmosphere. He attended school until he was fourteen; then he went to work as a printer's apprentice for the *Lynchburg Daily Republican*. Glass also worked for several years as an auditor for the Atlantic, Mississippi, and Ohio Railroad, but in 1880 he became a reporter and writer for the *Lynchburg Daily News,* a paper he purchased later in his life. Between 1881 and 1901, Glass was clerk for the Lynchburg city council; he held a seat in the state senate between 1899 and 1902; and he served in the United States House of Representatives from 1902 until 1918. As chairman of the House Committee on Banking and Currency, Glass was the sponsor and acknowledged "father" of the Federal Reserve Bank Act in 1913. For the rest of his life, Glass treated the Federal Reserve System as one of his own family, tenaciously guarding its independence. Between 1918 and 1920, Glass served as secretary of the treasury under Woodrow Wilson.* He resigned that position in 1920 to accept appointment to the United States Senate, filling the seat vacated by the death of Thomas S. Martin of Virginia. Glass was re-elected to the Senate in 1924, 1930, 1936, and 1942, and he served as president pro tempore of the Senate between 1941 and 1945.

As a conservative Democrat, Glass was suspicious of progressive schemes in the 1920s to solve the farm problem, guarantee the right of labor to bargain collectively, and implement a variety of social welfare legislation. During the 1930s, Glass disliked the massive bureaucracy and largescale spending of the New Deal. In Glass's mind, social workers and lawyers had taken over the Democratic Party* in the 1930s. He was responsible for passing the Glass-Steagall Act of 1932,* but, in general, he opposed tinkering with the country's financial apparatus. Stubborn, independent, and rigidly committed to states rights politics, Glass never made the transition from the progressivism of Woodrow Wilson to what he called the "radicalism" of Franklin D. Roosevelt.* Carter Glass died on May 28, 1946. (Norman Beasley, *Carter Glass: A Biography,* 1939; *New York Times,* May 29, 1946.)

GLASS-STEAGALL ACT OF 1932. Because of the severe weaknesses in the banking* system and the rash of bank failures that had plagued the country throughout the 1920s, the United States was experiencing a rash of gold withdrawals from foreign investers and hoarding of gold by American citizens. The situation was so serious that Secretary of the Treasury Ogden Mills* feared the country would have to abandon the gold standard. To restore confidence in the money markets and avert any need to abandon the gold standard, President Herbert Hoover* had called for the creation of a Reconstruction Finance Corporation* (RFC), which Congress established in January 1932. The RFC was designed to loan money to banks which would then expand their commercial loans and stimulate a revival of the economy. As part of that general objective, Congress passed the Glass-Steagall Act, and Hoover signed it on February 27,

1932. Sponsored by Senator Carter Glass* of Virginia and Representative Henry Steagall of Alabama, the bill amended the Federal Reserve Act, which at the time required that all Federal Reserve currency issues be backed by 40 percent in gold and 60 percent in securities eligible for discounting. The Glass-Steagall Act broadened the classes of securities eligible for discounting and permitted the use of government securities to back Federal Reserve currency issues beyond the 60–percent level. The law released approximately $750 million of the government gold supply to be used for credit expansion.

The Federal Reserve Board* was reluctant, however, to use government securities as collateral for currency issues, primarily because Senator Carter Glass, "father of the Federal Reserve System," did not like the provision. He had sponsored the Glass-Steagal Act only because Hoover had put so much pressure on him. It was not until May 1932 that the Federal Reserve Board began to use the securities as collateral. In the long run, however, the Glass-Steagall Act did little to stimulate the economy. The collapse of the banking system late in 1932 and early 1933 rendered the bill useless. (Lester V. Chandler, *American Monetary Policy, 1928–1941,* 1971.)

GLENN, JOHN MARK. John M. Glenn was born in Baltimore, Maryland, on October 28, 1858, to a wealthy, socially prominent family. He graduated from Washington and Lee University in 1878, took a master's degree there in 1879, and earned a law degree at the University of Maryland in 1882. Glenn worked for the Baltimore Charity Organization Society and married its director, Mary Wilcox. Glenn rose to prominence in the American social welfare movement, serving for a time as president of the National Conference of Charities and Corrections. In 1906, he became director of the Russell Sage Foundation, a new philanthropic organization devoted to social welfare research. Glenn was president of the foundation until 1931. During his tenure, the Russell Sage Foundation financed hundreds of research projects and the establishment of social work schools at major American universities. John Glenn stayed with the board of directors of the foundation until 1948. He died on April 20, 1950. (Shelby M. Harrison, "John Mark Glenn," *Survey* [June 1950], 64–68; Roy Lubove, *The Professional Altruist, The Emergence of Social Work as a Career, 1880–1930,* 1965; *New York Times,* April 21, 1950.)

"THE GOLDBERGS." "The Goldbergs" was one of radio's* most popular programs between 1931 and 1934, when Pepsodent sponsored it. It originated in 1929 when Gertrude Berg brought "Effie and Laura" to CBS, who carried it only for one week before she took it to NBC. By 1931 NBC presented "The Goldbergs" as a nightly serial. It was a fictionalized comedy of life with "The Goldbergs," a Jewish family who lived in New York City. Rich in Jewish dialect and ethnic humor, the program survived in one form or another until 1945. (John Dunning, *Tune in Yesterday: The Ultimate Encyclopedia of Old-Time Radio, 1925–1976,*1976.)

GOLDMAN, EMMA. Emma Goldman was born in Kovno, Lithuania, on June 27, 1869. She moved with her family to Germany in 1877 and then to St. Petersburg, Russia, in 1882; three years later, they immigrated to the United States, settling in Rochester, New York. Goldman worked in a series of textile mills and sweat shops in New York and New England, and gradually she became interested in labor and then, in radical politics. The Haymarket riots and subsequent trials of the anarchists in 1886 raised her political consciousness another level, and she soon became an avowed anarchist. In 1889 Goldman moved to New York City and soon was seen frequently as a speaker at various radical meetings. She spent a year in prison for urging workers to steal food if they could not earn it, and in 1895 she toured Europe, where she lectured widely on American radicalism.

By the time she returned from Europe, Goldman had become one of the country's most visible radicals. During the late 1890s, she worked diligently to establish connections with European anarchist movements, and between 1906 and 1917 Goldman served as editor of *Mother Earth,* a monthly anarchist newspaper. She hit the campus lecture circuit, expounding on her favorite topics— radicalism, theater, and birth control. Goldman bitterly opposed World War I and the preparedness campaigns, and when the United States entered the conflict in 1917, she worked to opposed the selective service law. She spent 1918 and 1919 in a federal prison after being convicted of obstructing the draft. After her release from prison, Goldman became a target of the Red Scare,* and in January 1920 Attorney General A. Mitchell Palmer* saw to it that Goldman left the United States on the ''Soviet Ark.''* Except for a brief visit in 1934, she never returned to the United States, although she was equally displeased with the Soviet Union. Goldman spent the rest of her career promoting a variety of radical causes. Known to most Americans as ''Red Emma,'' Goldman symbolized radicalism and xenophobic insecurity during the 1920s. She died on May 14, 1940, in London. (Emma Goldman, *Living My Life,* 1931; Charles A. Madison, *Critics and Crusaders: A Century of American Protest,* 1947.)

GOMPERS, SAMUEL. Samuel Gompers was born in London, England, on January 27, 1850. His parents were working-class Jews, and the family immigrated to the United States in 1863. They settled in New York City, and Gompers went to work as a cigarmaker and attended school at night. When he was fourteen, he joined the Cigarmakers' International Union and became president of his own local in 1875. Gompers then rose through the union ranks; he became vice-president of the Cigarmakers' International Union in 1886 and president in 1896. Gompers served as president of the union until his death in 1924. Gompers was also a leading figure in the formation of the American Federation of Labor,* of which he served as president between 1886–1895 and 1896–1924.

Samuel Gompers epitomized responsible, conservative craft unionism. He opposed organizing unskilled, industrial workers because he believed management then held the advantage in labor disputes. Unskilled workers were too easily replaced. Gompers was committed to craft unionism—organization of skilled workers—and craft autonomy. He also felt that American workers should avoid any hint of radicalism, try to win the confidence of management through business unionism, and use strikes only as a last resort.

During the 1920s, Gompers represented a middle road in the American labor movement. He avoided the radical left by insisting that all economic and political change must come through established channels; Gompers even opposed government-mandated workmen's compensation laws, eight-hour days, old-age pensions, and comprehensive health insurance. On the other hand, he opposed the open shop movement* of the 1920s and the spread of company unions.* Gompers was an advocate of legislation outlawing child labor and guaranteeing the right of collective bargaining. Among prominent conservative businessmen, Gompers was viewed as a stable, sensible adversary. Samuel Gompers played the key role in the rise of the American Federation of Labor to the pinnacle of power in the United States labor movement. He died in San Antonio, Texas, on December 13, 1924. (Stuart B. Kaufman, *Samuel Gompers and the Origins of the American Federation of Labor, 1848–1896,* 1973; Howard Livesey, *Samuel Gompers and Organized Labor in America,* 1978.)

GOOD, JAMES WILLIAM. James W. Good was born in Cedar Rapids, Iowa, on September 24, 1866. He graduated from Coe College in 1892 and then took a law degree at the University of Michigan in 1893. Good practiced law privately in Indianapolis, Indiana, and in Evanston, Illinois, between 1893 and 1928, and served four terms in Congress as a Republican between 1909 and 1921. In the election of 1924,* Good managed Calvin Coolidge's* campaign in the western states, and in 1929 President Herbert Hoover* selected Good to serve as secretary of war. Good died on November 18, 1929. (Martin L. Fausold, *The Presidency of Herbert C. Hoover,* 1985; *New York Times,* November 19, 1929.)

GOOD NEIGHBOR POLICY. In the years before World War I, the United States had aggressively asserted its authority over the entire Western Hemisphere. President Theodore Roosevelt had fomented revolution in Panama in order to secure an isthmian canal, much to the embarrassment and anger of Colombia. In 1904, the president had also issued the so-called Roosevelt Corollary to the Monroe Doctrine, asserting the United States's right to intervene in the internal affairs of hemispheric nations in order to prevent European intervention. The corollary happened to justify his 1904 intervention in the Dominican Republic to ensure that the country paid its bills. Under President William Howard Taft,* the United States pursued what became known as "Dollar Diplomacy"—an aggressive protection of American corporate interests abroad. In 1911, Taft sent 2,500 marines into Nicaragua to protect American life and property there during a revolution. Most of the troops were withdrawn in 1912, but a small contingent of them remained until 1925. President Woodrow Wilson* eventually sent American troops into Haiti, the Dominican Republic, and Mexico.

By the 1920s, Latin American nations were thoroughly disgusted with what they called "the colossus of the north." Although Secretary of State Charles Evans Hughes* removed the troops from the Dominican Republic in 1924 and Nicaragua in 1925, the troops went back into Nicaragua in 1926 during renewed fighting between various political factions. In April 1927, Henry L. Stimson* went to Nicaragua at President Calvin Coolidge's* request and brought about a negotiated settlement and free elections. That same year, Dwight Morrow,* the new ambassador to Mexico, helped settle the tensions between Mexico and the United States by getting President Plutarco Calles to stop his bitter anti-Catholic* campaign and to recognize the oil rights of American companies doing business in Mexico before 1917. Some historians pinpoint the Mexican settlement as the real beginning of the Good Neighbor Policy.

Shortly after his election in November 1928, President-elect Herbert Hoover* went on a seven-week goodwill tour of Latin America and proclaimed the willingness of the United States to re-evaluate its traditional role in hemispheric foreign policy. In 1930 Hoover approved the Clark Memorandum* on the Monroe Doctrine, a document written by Undersecretary of State J. Reuben Clark, Jr.,* which repudiated the right of the United States to intervene in the internal affairs of Latin American countries. Hoover backed his promise with actions. When revolutionaries took over the government of Brazil in 1930, the State Department extended immediate diplomatic recognition. Hoover removed the marines from Haiti in 1932 and from Nicaragua in 1933.

The Good Neighbor Policy received its real fulfillment late in 1933 at the Seventh International Conference of American States, which met in Montevideo, Uruguay. At the conference, the new secretary of state, Cordell Hull, announced to a stunned audience that "no state has the right to intervene in the internal or external affairs of another." In May 1934 President Franklin D. Roosevelt* signed a treaty ending the Platt Amendment and its controls over Cuba. Historians generally attribute the loyalty of Latin American countries to the allied powers during World War II to the improved relations with the United States resulting from the implementation of the Good Neighbor Policy during the late 1920s and 1930s. (Alexander DeConde, *Herbert Hoover's Latin American Policy,* 1951; E. O. Guerrant, *Roosevelt's Good Neighbor Policy,* 1950; Dexter Perkins, *A History of the Monroe Doctrine,* 1955.)

GORDON, ANNA ADAMS. Anna Gordon was born on July 21, 1853, in Boston, Massachusetts. She attended the Mount Holyoke Seminary and earned a master's degree at the Lasell Seminary in 1875. Devoutly religious, Gordon spent the years between 1877 and 1898 as the private secretary to temperance crusader Frances E. Willard. Willard headed the Women's Christian Temperance Union between 1879 and 1898, and in the process Gordon acquired national influence in the temperance movement. In 1914 Anna Gordon became president of the Women's Christian Temperance Union, a position she held until 1925. She was a vigorous supporter of the Eighteenth Amendment* and of enforcement of prohibition* during the 1920s. She was also deeply interested in child welfare issues. Between 1922 and 1925, she served as president of the international Women's Christian Temperance Union. Anna Gordon retired in 1925 and died on June 15, 1931. (Julia Freeman Deane, *Anna Adams Gordon: A Story of Her Life,* 1935; Helen E. Tyler, *Where Prayer and Purpose Meet: The W.C.T.U. Story,* 1949.)

GRAHAM, MARTHA. Martha Graham, an American pioneer of modern dance, was born on May 11, 1894, in Allegheny, Pennsylvania, and raised in Santa Barbara, California. She trained to dance in Los Angeles, and between 1916 and 1923 she was a member of several Ruth St. Denis and Ted Shawn dance companies. During the early 1920s, she was a partner to Shawn in *Xochit* (1921), *Dance* (1921), *Malaguena* (1921), and *Lantern Dance* (1922). She left the Denishawn school in 1923 and joined the *Greenwich Village Follies.* Between 1924 and 1926, Graham taught at the Eastman School of Music in Rochester, New York. Her first solo recital came in 1926, and from that date on, she was the leading figure in American modern dance. During the 1920s and 1930s, she choreographed short solo and group works for all-female companies, works based on pre-Raphaelite art. Some of her more important works then were *Vision of the Apocalypse* (1929), *Lamentation* (1930), and *Primitive Mysteries* (1931). Later in her life, Graham continued her artistic innovations, moving into universal characterizations based on grand religious and mythological themes. She has been the major figure in American dance not only because of her artistic creations but also because she has trained two full generations of dancers and choreographers. (Barbara Naomi Cohen Stratyner, *Biographical Dictionary of Dance,* 1982.)

GRAIN STABILIZATION CORPORATION. See FEDERAL FARM BOARD

GRANGE. See EXPORT DEBENTURE PLAN

GRANGE, HAROLD. Harold "Red" Grange was born on June 10, 1903, in Wheaton, Illinois. He attended the University of Illinois, and, as a halfback of the university's football team, Grange captured national attention in 1923, 1924, and 1925. Known as the "Galloping Ghost," he was a gifted runner—fast, nimble, and able to make the cuts and turns necessary for long gains. In 1926, Grange signed a professional contract with the Chicago Bears, and the team immediately launched a barnstorming "Red Grange Football Tour," playing ten games in seventeen days all over the country. Stadiums in major cities were filled to watch Grange perform, and in the process he gave professional football a media boost which launched it into major spectator sports status in the United

States. In 1927 and 1928, Grange played for an independent football team, the New York Yankees, but he returned to the Bears in 1929 and finished his playing career with them. Grange then spent the rest of his life as a sports announcer for radio and television. (Gene Schoor, *Red Grange, Football's Greatest Halfback*, 1952.)

GRANT, MADISON. Madison Grant was born on November 18, 1865, in New York City, to a distinguished upper-class family. He received his bachelor's degree from Yale in 1887 and then took a law degree at Columbia University in 1890. A bachelor all of his life, Grant had patrician instincts befitting his upbringing. He was concerned with the natural world and the environment, and he expressed those concerns through official positions in such groups as the New York Zoological Society, the American Museum of Natural History, and the Save the Redwoods League. But Grant's interests were not confined to preserving the natural world; he also became one of the most articulate spokesmen for upper-class Anglo-Saxon culture in the United States. An avid genealogist and charter member of the Society of Colonial Wars, Grant believed fervently in the prevailing doctrines of Anglo or Nordic superiority—that the explanation of American success in the world was a racial or ethnic one. Grant, active in the Eugenics Research Association and in the Immigration Restriction League, feared that American institutions would be destroyed by the influx of new immigrants in the late nineteenth and early twentieth centuries.

Grant's point of view gained national attention in 1916 when he wrote *The Passing of the Great Race*. The book made Grant the leading spokesman for nativist intellectuals. Arguing that Nordic institutions were the political, economic, and military genius of the world, Grant said that Nordic mixture with Jews, east Europeans, and southern Europeans would dilute American culture and send the United States into a decline from which it would never recover. He also made the case for aristocracy as well as racial purity; democracy would only give power to inferior immigrants and accelerate the decline of American society. Couched in the language of science, *The Passing of the Great Race* played an important role in the immigration restriction legislation which reached fruition in the National Origins Act of 1924. Madison Grant died in New York City on May 30, 1937. (Madison Grant, *The Passing of the Great Race*, 1916; John Higham, *Strangers in the Land: Patterns of American Nativism, 1860– 1925*, 1963; *Who Was Who in America*, I [1943], 477.)

GRANT, WILLIAM THOMAS. William T. Grant was born on June 27, 1876, in Stevensville, Pennsylvania. He was raised in Malden, Massachusetts, but he quit school to work at a variety of odd jobs. In 1895 he became a shoe salesman; from there he worked in the department store business until he decided in 1906 to open his own store. He had a novel idea: He would establish a discount department store in which no item sold for more than 25 cents. The first Grant department store opened in Lynn, Massachusetts; a second one was opened in

1908 in Waterbury, Connecticut. It was a popular marketing idea, and the stores thrived. Grant opened a New York City store in 1913, and by 1918 there were more than thirty stores. At that time, he raised the maximum price on his products to $1. During the 1920s, the Grant chain expanded rapidly until it was the most familiar name in discount retailing. By 1940 there were stores all over the country. When W. T. Grant died on August 6, 1972, there were more than 1,150 stores in the chain. The irony, of course, was that the company went bankrupt in 1975. Over the years, it had been caught in a squeeze by the expansion of Sears' and Penney's, on the one hand, and by new discount houses like Wal-Mart and K-Mart, on the other. (Godfrey Lebhar, *Chain Stores in America, 1859–1959,* 1959; *New York Times,,* August 7, 1972.)

GREAT DEPRESSION. Historians have debated the causes of the Great Depression for a half-century now, and although the various interpretations are still controversial, they have identified a number of key problems. Because of ignorance and ineptitude on the part of the Republican administrations and the Federal Reserve Board,* the bull market* on the stock exchanges got out of hand, attracting capital which should have been invested in other areas of the economy. The banking* system was hopelessly overbuilt and undercapitalized, and the failure of thousands of banks in the 1920s and early 1930s destroyed consumer confidence and inhibited the flow of working capital to legitimate businesses. Gross overproduction in the farming sector, combined with heavy debt structures and fixed payments, drove commodity prices down and millions of farmers out of business. Federal trade legislation, especially the Fordney-McCumber Tariff of 1922 and the Hawley-Smoot Tariff of 1930, stifled international trade. Between 1929 and 1933, the gross national product declined dramatically and unemployment increased to approximately 25 percent of the workforce.

   Throughout the 1920s, Republicans had taken responsibility for the economic prosperity which had almost become legendary. In his inaugural address in March 1929, President Herbert Hoover* had even promised Americans that they would soon see the day when poverty would be eliminated. Seven months later, the stock market crash* occurred, and the economy went into its worst tailspin in United States history. Most people held Hoover and the Republicans responsible, and as a result the Democratic Party* dominated American politics for the next generation. (James S. Olson, *Saving Capitalism: The Reconstruction Finance Corporation and the New Deal, 1933–1940,* 1988.)

GREEN, WILLIAM. William Green was born in Coshocton, Ohio, on March 3, 1873. For two generations, his family had worked as coal miners, and in 1889 Green did the same. He also became active in union politics, and he rose through the ranks of the United Mine Workers. In 1906 Green became head of the Ohio unit of United Mine Workers, and between 1910 and 1913 he served in the Ohio State legislature, where he labored successfully for passage of the

1911 workmen's compensation law. Between 1912 and 1922, Green was secretary-treasurer of the United Mine Workers as well as a member of the executive
council of the American Federation of Labor.* When Samuel Gompers died in
1924, Green was elected president of the AFL.

During the 1920s, Green was indefatigable in his support for federal labor
standards legislation, social security, and an end to labor injunctions and yellow-
dog contracts. He worked closely with Senator George Norris* and Representative Fiorello La Guardia* in their successful development of the Norris–La
Guardia Labor Relations Act of 1932.* A devoted Baptist and a bitter anti-
Communist, Green felt labor must be disciplined and responsible for winning
management confidence. During the 1930s, Green put the full weight of the AFL
behind the National Industrial Recovery Act of 1933, the National Labor Relations Act of 1935, and the Social Security Act of 1935. He left the United
Mine Workers in 1937 during the split between the AFL and the Congress of
Industrial Unions over the question of industrial unionism. Throughout World
War II, Green supported a no strike pledge from labor to keep production lines
operating at full speed. He opposed the Taft-Hartley Act of 1946 as a slave labor
law, and in 1949 he organized the International Confederation of Trade Unions.
William Green died on November 21, 1952. (Max D. Danish, *William Green*,
1952; Melvyn Dubofsky and Warren Van Tine, *John L. Lewis: A Biography*,
1977; Philip Taft, *The A.F. of L. from the Death of Gompers to the Merger*,
1959.)

GREW, JOSEPH CLARK. Joseph C. Grew was born on May 27, 1880, in
Boston, Massachusetts. He graduated from Harvard in 1902 and entered the
Foreign Service in 1904. Grew held a series of overseas diplomatic assignments,
and in 1919 he accompanied the American delegation to the Paris peace talks
ending World War I. He was a delegate to the Lausanne Conference in 1922–
1923, and he served as undersecretary of state between 1924 and 1927. President
Calvin Coolidge* appointed Grew ambassador to Turkey in 1927, and he remained at that post until 1932, when Herbert Hoover* named him ambassador
to Japan. Grew held that post until the United States severed diplomatic relations
with Japan after Pearl Harbor in 1941. He retired in 1945 after a brief stint as
temporary secretary of state. Joseph Grew died on May 25, 1965. (Joseph C.
Grew, *Turbulent Era*, 1952; Waldo H. Heinrichs, Jr., *American Ambassador:
Joseph C. Grew and the Development of the U.S. Diplomatic Tradition*, 1966.)

GREY, ZANE. Zane Grey was born on January 31, 1875, in Zanesville, Ohio.
His father was a dentist. As a child, Zane Grey was addicted to baseball and
adventure novels. He hated academic studies, but he loved to read, and in 1896
he completed a dental degree at the University of Pennsylvania. Grey opened a
practice in Brooklyn, but he could barely stand the work, so he started to write
at night. His first novel, *Betty Zane* (1903), which was privately published, was
based on the lives of his mother's family. After Grey's second novel, *Spirit of*

the Border (1906) was published and sold well, he began to contribute articles regularly to *Field and Stream* magazine. In 1910 Grey sold his first novel to *Harper's—The Heritage of the Desert*, a romantic novel about Mormons—but it was not until 1912 that he really achieved fame with *Riders of the Purple Sage*, a runaway bestseller which made Grey financially independent for the rest of his life. Grey had an outstanding narrative style and descriptive ability, and his subsequent novels were based on a tried but true formula: lots of romance, lots of action, and a moralistic struggle between good and evil, all put in a frontier setting. Grey's villains were universally greedy, dishonest, and immoral, and his heroes were just the opposite.

During the 1920s, Grey was the most well-known writer of popular fiction in the United States. He was a permanent fixture on the bestseller lists. It was a decade when Americans were realizing that the country's frontier heritage was rapidly slipping into history, and Grey's novels struck a nostalgic chord. Between 1918 and 1933, he wrote twenty-four books, including *Man of the Forest* (1920), *The Mysterious Rider* (1921), *The Wanderer of the Wasteland* (1923), *The Thundering Herd* (1925), *Nevada* (1928), and *The Wolf Tracker* (1930). Literary critics were hard on his work, describing it as superficial and weak on characterization, but the public loved it. Zane Grey died on October 23, 1939. (Richard W. Etulain, ''A Dedication to the Memory of Zane Grey 1872–1939,'' *Arizona and the West* 12 [Autumn, 1970], 217–220.)

GREYHOUND. See WICKHAM, CARL ERIC

GRIFFITH, DAVID WARK. D. W. Griffith was born on a farm in Oldham County, Kentucky, on January 22, 1875. After graduating from high school, he performed with a variety of local and regional stock companies until 1895 and then spent four years as a reporter for the Louisville *Courier Journal*. Griffith's real love, however, was acting, and he returned to the stage in 1906, to play a lead role in *The Clansman* in New York. In 1908 Griffith went to work for the American Mutoscope and Biograph Company, and, between 1908 and 1913, he directed nearly 500 one- and two-reel films for them. Between 1915 and 1920, Griffith reached the height of popularity in the United States, when he released the films *The Birth of a Nation* (1915), *Intolerance*, (1916) *Hearts of the World* (1918), *Broken Blossoms* (1919), and *Way Down East* (1920). Griffith was no ideologue, and he could juxtapose Victorian morality and modern sexuality, white supremacy and liberal tolerance, with ease. In 1920, he joined with Charlie Chaplin,* Mary Pickford,* and Douglas Fairbanks* to form United Artists Company. He left United Artists in 1925 and went to work for Paramount, but his late 1920s films did not have the same impact as those he produced between 1915 and 1920. Griffiths made only two sound films, *Abraham Lincoln* (1930) and *The Struggle* (1931). He died on July 23, 1948. (Iris Barryk and Eileen Bowser, *D. W. Griffith: American Film Master*, 1965.)

H

HAGEN, WALTER. Walter Hagen was one of the most prominent sports figures of the 1920s. He was born in Rochester, New York, on December 21, 1892, and he debuted as a professional golfer in the 1912 United States Open, finishing third. Hagen won the United States Open tournament in 1914, and, before his retirement in 1929, he won sixteen other major titles, including the United States Open again in 1919, the PGA championship in 1921, 1924, 1925, 1926, and 1927, and the British Open in 1922, 1924, 1928, and 1929. Well dressed and dapper, Hagen was an extremely popular figure who made golf a sport of widespread appeal in the 1920s. After his retirement, he continued to play exhibition matches, and he served as the dean of American professional golfers. Walter Hagen died on October 6, 1969. *(New York Times,* October 7, 1969.)

HALL, JOYCE CLYDE. Joyce Clyde Hall was born on December 29, 1891, in David City, Nebraska. After the death of his father in 1897, Hall went to work part-time in a local stationery store, and, when he was fourteen, he pooled several hundred dollars with money of his two older brothers and opened a company selling greeting cards. Five years later, he was attending a business college in Kansas City and maintaining a healthy business on the side as a jobber for greeting cards. In 1913, he and his brother Rollie established the ''Hallmark'' label to market Christmas cards. Convinced that people wanted more personalized greeting cards in general, they bought their own printing plant in 1916 and began producing them. They struggled along for a year until World War I created an enormous demand for cards to send overseas to soldiers. Through widespread advertising on radio and in magazines during the early 1920s, they gave Hallmark cards a national reputation. An innovative marketing tool, the ''Eye Vision Display Fixture,'' which put cards at eye level to customers in stores and markets, greatly boosted sales after 1924. They expanded nationwide by establishing independent Hallmark shops; by 1958, there were more than 6,000 stores selling nearly two million cards a day. Joyce Clyde Hall died on October 29, 1982. (Milton Moscowitz et al., *Every-Body's Business,* 1980; *New York Times,* October 30, 1982; *Who's Who in America,* 1978–1979.)

HALL-MILLS MURDER CASE. On September 16, 1922, Reverend Edward Hall of the Protestant Episcopal Church of New Brunswick, New Jersey, and Eleanor Mills, the soloist in the church choir, were found murdered on a rural road. Both had been shot; their bodies had been arranged into an intimate position; and their love letters had been scattered around the murder scene. The case became one of the most famous of the 1920s—replete with sex, religion, scandal, and murder. Four years later, the case went to trial. Hall's wife Francis, whom the press dubbed the "Iron Widow," was charged with the crime, along with her brothers, Willie and Henry Stevens. The subsequent trial lasted nearly a month, with the press hanging on every word. They nicknamed the chief prosecution witness "The Pig Woman" because she raised pigs for a living. Despite the sensationalism, a jury acquitted the defendants after five hours of deliberation. (Paul Sann, *The Lawless Decade,* 1957.)

HAMMER v. *DAGENHART* **(247 U.S. 251).** In 1916 Congress passed the Keating-Owen Act, which prohibited the interstate shipment of products made by child labor. Although long advocated by social reformers, the abolition of child labor also found support among northern textile manufacturers. State laws in New England already regulated child labor in the textile mills, making it difficult for northern producers to compete with unregulated southern mills. National legislation was an attempt by social reformers to abolish child labor for moral reasons, but it was equally a crusade by northern textile owners to regulate labor markets across the country. Southern mill owners protested the legislation and carried their objections to the United States Supreme Court. In 1918, by a five to four vote, the Supreme Court overturned the legislation in the *Hammer* v. *Dagenhart* case on the grounds that it was really a regulation of local labor relations practices rather than a genuinely interstate commerce issue. Justice Oliver Wendell Holmes, Jr.,* wrote the minority opinion upholding the right of federal courts to enforce the commerce clause. Congress responded to the decision in 1919 with the Child Labor Relations Act, which imposed a heavy tax on all products in interstate commerce made with the assistance of child labor. In 1922 the Supreme Court overturned it in *Bailey* v. *Drexel Furniture Company.** Not until the New Deal in the 1930s would permanent prohibitons on child labor be enacted on the federal level. (Alpheus Thomas Mason, *The Supreme Court from Taft to Warren,* 1958; Henry F. Pringle, *The Life and Times of William Howard Taft,* 1939.)

HAMMETT, SAMUEL DASHIELL. Samuel Dashiell Hammett was born in Baltimore, Maryland, on May 29, 1894, and was raised there and in Philadelphia. In 1908 he quit school, and, after spending several years at a variety of jobs, he joined the Pinkerton Detective Agency as a private investigator. He served in the army during World War I, returned to Pinkerton for three years, and then set out on his own to write fiction. By the late 1920s, Hammett was one of the most popular writers in America, the leading detective novelist in the country.

His four best novels were *Red Harvest* (1929), *The Dain Curse* (1929), *The Maltese Falcon* (1930), and *The Glass Key* (1931). In 1934 he wrote *The Thin Man*. Left-wing in his politics, Hammett was always concerned about the need for economic justice in the world; he was a member of the American Communist Party during the 1920s and 1930s. He drank heavily and died of lung cancer on January 10, 1961. (Martin Seymour-Smith, *Who's Who in Twentieth Century Literature,* 1976.)

"THE HAPPINESS BOYS." "The Happiness Boys" was a regular, comedy radio* program which played on Friday nights on NBC between 1926 and 1939. Starring Billy Jones and Ernie Hare as "The Happiness Boys," the program was sponsored by Happiness Candy. The program ended when Hare died on March 9, 1939. (John Dunning, *Tune in Yesterday: The Ultimate Encyclopedia of Old-Time Radio, 1925–1976,* 1976.)

HARDING, WARREN GAMALIEL. Warren G. Harding was born on November 2, 1865, in Corsica, Ohio. He attended Ohio Central College for three years, studied law, and in 1884 he bought the *Marion Star,* a local newspaper. An active Republican, Harding was elected to the state senate in 1900 and to the lieutenant governorship in 1904. He lost a run for governor in 1910, but in 1914 Harding was elected to the United States Senate, where he earned a reputation for party discipline and loyalty. In 1920, the Republican National Convention deadlocked in its presidential balloting between Leonard Wood* and Frank O. Lowden.* Warren G. Harding became the perfect compromise candidate, and, in what historians later called the deal made in "a smoke-filled room," Harding won the party's nomination.

Party officials thought Harding would be the perfect candidate—handsome, midwestern, and noncontroversial. They tabbed Calvin Coolidge,* governor of Massachusetts, as the vice-presidential running mate because of the reputation for toughness Coolidge had earned in dealing with the Boston police strike of 1919.* In the election, they faced Governor James M. Cox* of Ohio for president and assistant secretary of the navy Franklin D. Roosevelt* for vice-president. Campaigning on a platform of "normalcy"*—higher tariffs, reduced federal spending, and a pro-business atmosphere—Harding handily defeated Cox by a count of 16,152,200 popular votes to 9,147,353, and 404 to 127 in the electoral college.

A congenial man given to backslapping, jokes, card games, womanizing, and drinking, Harding was a peculiar president who was destined to go down as one of the most inept in American history. When he came into the White House, he had no real agenda beyond restoring America to its former tranquility before Woodrow Wilson,* the Democrats, and World War I had changed everything. Neither an intellectual nor a reformer, Harding came to the presidency with a detached style, hoping the people he selected to his cabinet would allow him to effect the "return to normalcy" as well as enjoy the limelight of the White

House. His personnel decisions proved to be almost schizophrenic, brilliant in certain instances and incredibly shortsighted in others. Both the accomplishments and the catastrophes of the Harding administration can be attributed to those men. As for the president, he was almost an innocent bystander.

As secretary of state, Harding selected Charles Evans Hughes,* the brilliant Republican attorney and former justice of the Supreme Court. Because the Treaty of Versailles* was still a hot issue capable of bringing down the wrath of the Republican isolationist wing, Hughes could do little about getting the United States to join the League of Nations* or the World Court.* But he was committed to foreign policy activism, and that commitment was reflected in the Washington Naval Conference* of 1921–1922, the Five-Power Treaty of 1922,* the Nine Power Treaty,* and Naval Arms Reduction Treaty. As secretary of the treasury, Harding picked Andrew W. Mellon,* one of the richest men in the country. Mellon was committed to restoring a pro-business atmosphere conducive to increased capital investment and productivity. He reduced federal spending enough to produce budget surpluses and retire the national debt, saw to tariff reductions through the Fordney-McCumber Tariff of 1922,* and decreased federal income taxes, especially on the rich, through the Revenue Acts of 1921,* 1924,* 1926,* 1928,* and 1929.* Finally, as secretary of commerce, Harding chose Herbert C. Hoover,* the now famous Republican leader who had risen to fame in the United States by helping American refugees get out of Europe at the beginning of World War I, organizing the relief effort to feed millions of starving people in Europe during and after the war, and directing the Food Administration for Woodrow Wilson. Hoover used his position as secretary of commerce to boost associationalism, promote research and development, and promote business-labor cooperation.

But in the end, the work of Hughes, Mellon, and Hoover was compromised by the corruption of Harding's other appointees. He surrounded himself in Washington with cronies known as the "Ohio gang,"* and it was those old friends who eventually destroyed the administration. Charles Forbes, head of the Veteran's Bureau,* was caught taking kickbacks on hospital construction contracts, hospital site sales, and purchases of medical equipment. Albert B. Fall,* the secretary of the interior, engineered the Teapot Dome* scandal in which Secretary of the Navy Edwin Denby* turned over government naval reserves to the Interior Department and Fall then leased the reserves out for private development, all in return for lucrative contracts. Harry Daugherty,* the attorney general of the United States, had to resign after it became clear that he had been part of the scandals in the Alien Property Custodian Office,* in which former German properties in the United States were sold at below market value in return for kickbacks. Just as the scandals were first being revealed, Harding suffered a heart attack in San Francisco and died on August 2, 1923. (Robert K. Murray, *The Harding Era: Warren G. Harding and His Administration,* 1969; Francis Russell, *The Shadow of Blooming Grove: Warren G. Harding in His Times,* 1968; Andrew Sinclair, *The Available Man: The Life Behind the Masks of Warren*

Gamaliel Harding, 1965; Eugene P. Trani and David L. Wilson, *The Presidency of Warren G. Harding,* 1977.)

HARDY, OLIVER. See LAUREL, STANLEY

HARLEM RENAISSANCE. Between 1914 and 1920, dramatic changes took place in the black community, inspired primarily by the mass migration of southern blacks to northern cities during World War I to acquire jobs in defense industries. The demographic shift produced a political and cultural revolution. In the major cities of the North, blacks became a new political force in the Democratic Party,* and because of their huge numbers in cities like New York, Philadelphia, Chicago, and Boston, they began to express the richness of their culture in new, more visible ways. The fact that 400,000 blacks had served in the military during the war also produced a greater aggressiveness in asserting basic civil rights. In New York City, the flowering of black culture became known as the Harlem Renaissance.

The major theme behind the Harlem Renaissance was a sense of racial pride and recognition of African roots. The black press had become an increasingly powerful force in America, and newspapers like the *Pittsburgh Courier,* the *Chicago Defender,* and the *New York Amsterdam News* became the primary vehicles for the expression of black values. Periodicals like the National Association for the Advancement of Colored People's* *Crisis,* the National Urban League's *Opportunity,* and the Socialist journal *The Messenger* lobbied for equality of opportunity. Prominent individuals like Marcus Garvey* and his back-to-Africa movement popularized black pride. Writers like Langston Hughes,* Countee Cullen, Claude McKay, and Jean Toomer produced a new black literature. New York City's Harlem became recognized nationwide as the center of black art and literature. Not until the economic devastation of the 1930s did the Harlem Renaissance run its course. By then, Harlem would forever be known as the symbol of black society in the United States. (Joseph R. Conlin, *Our Land, Our Time,* 1986; Margaret Perry, *The Harlem Renaissance Bibliography,* 1982; Charles Scruggs, *The Sage in Harlem,* 1984.)

HART, WILLIAM SURREY. William S. Hart was born in Newburgh, New York, on December 6, 1865. After leaving school, he worked in the post office for several years; during those years, he also studied acting part-time. Hart toured with several dramatic companies in the 1890s, and he gained wide recognition for his role as Massala in *Ben Hur* (1899). In 1905, Hart came to Broadway as the cowboy star of *The Squaw Man.* After that, he continued to play the lead in a number of western productions. Hart made his first film in 1914, and in 1915 he signed a contract with the Triangle Film Group, where he was directed by D. W. Griffith.* Hart became the country's first cowboy film star in the 1920s, and his best-known films were *O'Malley of the Mounted* (1921), *Travelin' On* (1922), *Wild Bill Hickok* (1923), and *Singer Jim McKee* (1924). Hart's popularity fell after that because of a notorious paternity suit, and he made his last film, *Tumbleweeds,* in 1925. William S. Hart died on June 23, 1946. (Diane Koszanski, *The Complete Films of William S. Hart: A Pictorial Record,* 1980; *New York Times,* June 24, 1946.)

HAUGEN, GILBERT NELSON. Gilbert N. Haugen was born on April 21, 1859, in Rock County, Wisconsin. He quit school at the age of fourteen and worked at several odd jobs until he bought a farm in 1877 in Worth County, Iowa. Haugen studied at night school. In 1890 he helped organize the Northwood Banking Company and was named president, a position he held until 1899. Haugen served in the state legislature between 1887 and 1893, and he was elected as a Republican to the United States House of Representatives in 1899. Haugen served there with distinction for the next thirty-four years, earning a reputation as a progressive Republican passionately concerned about the plight of the American farmer. Haugen is best remembered in the 1920s for his sponsorship of the McNary-Haugen Bill,* a congressional measure designed to assist American farmers by government purchase of surpluses and disposal of them in foreign markets. The measure was vetoed twice by President Calvin Coolidge* and never became law. Gilbert Haugen died on July 18, 1933. *(New York Times,* July 19, 1933.)

HAUPTMANN, RICHARD BRUNO. Richard Bruno Hauptmann was born in Germany in 1899. He attended trade school and learned to be a carpenter. When World War I broke out, Hauptmann was drafted into the Germany army, and he served there until 1918. After the war, Hauptmann was convicted several times of burglary in Germany, and between 1920 and 1923 he served time in prison. Two months after he was released from prison, Hauptmann was arrested and charged with several other burglaries, and to avoid prosecution, he fled to the United States illegally in 1923. In 1934, Hauptmann was arrested and charged with the kidnapping and murder of Charles A. Lindbergh, Jr., the son of the aviator Charles Lindbergh and his wife Anne Morrow. The Lindbergh kidnapping was, at the time, considered the "crime of the century," and the murder trial of Bruno Hauptmann in 1935 attracted extraordinary media interest. A jury convicted Hauptmann of the crime and sentenced him to death.

Hauptmann insisted that he was innocent, and even though the governor of New Jersey, Harold Hoffman, offered to commute his sentence to life in prison if he confessed to the crime, Hauptmann refused, and on April 3, 1936, he was executed in the New Jersey electric chair. Although many people claimed that Hauptmann was innocent, the most recent study of the crime concluded that Hauptmann was guilty of the kidnapping and murder of Charles Lindbergh, Jr. (Jim Fisher, *The Lindbergh Case,* 1987.)

HAVANA CONFERENCE OF 1928. The Havana Conference of 1928 was the Sixth International Conference of American States. Because of continuing American controversies with Nicaragua and Mexico, the Havana Conference had a decidedly anti-United States flavor to it. Latin American nations tried to draft a treaty denouncing United States intervention in hemispheric affairs, but the treaty was postponed. Former Secretary of State Charles Evans Hughes* headed the American delegation to the Havana Conference. The conference agreed to hold a special meeting later in the year to discuss arbitration issues, and at that meeting, which met during December 1928 to January 1929, an arbitration treaty was worked out, although the United States would not ratify it without a clause requiring Senate approval before any formal action under the arbitration treaties. (Samuel Inman, *Inter-American Conferences,* 1965.)

HAWES-CUTTING ACT OF 1933. In 1916 Congress passed the Jones Act, which expressed the American intention to grant full independence to the Philippines sometime in the future. By 1932 American sugar and dairy companies were pushing for Filipino independence so that cane sugar and coconut oil would compete with United States products. Labor unions were also interested in independence so that the Philippines would fall under immigration restriction legislation. On January 13, 1933, Congress passed the Hawes-Cutting Act, which provided for Filipino independence in 1945 while reserving to the United States the option of maintaining military bases there and reviewing the decisions made by Filipino courts. The Philippines government rejected the act in 1933, and independence legislation had to wait another year until the Tydings-McDuffie Act of 1934. (Dorothy Borg, *The United States and the Far Eastern Crisis, 1933–1938,* 1964.)

HAWLEY-SMOOT TARIFF. When President Herbert C. Hoover* came into office in 1929, he was committed to tariff reform, but, in the legislative process, the logrolling principle eventually created one of the highest tariffs in United States history. The original sponsor of the tariff was Congressman Willis C. Hawley of Oregon, but he quickly lost control of the measure. In the Senate, Reed Smoot* of Utah was in charge of the bill, but he was strongly inclined toward protectionism, especially for farm goods (a futile gesture given the huge surpluses being produced) in general and Utah sugar in particular. Senator Joseph R. Grundy of Pennsylvania, former head of the Pennsylvania Manufacturers' Association, enthusiastically agreed to the demands of farm state senators for high agricultural duties, and they, in turn, supported his call for high duties on industrial goods.

In Congress, insurgent Republicans and some Democrats tried to keep the duties reasonable, and inserted provisions supporting the export debenture plan* for agriculture and amending the Fordney-McCumber Act* requiring Congress rather than the president to approve any schedule revisions. President Hoover opposed both the amendments and threatened to veto the measure. Both of the amendments were removed from the bill. Congress debated the bill throughout the spring of 1930, and on June 13, 1930, the Senate passed it by a vote of 44 to 42. The House followed suit on June 14 by a vote of 222 to 153. The strongest support for the bill came from the industrial Midwest and Northeast. Hoover signed the bill on June 17, 1930.

The Hawley-Smoot Tariff raised the duties on raw materials between 50 and 100 percent above the Fordney-McCumber levels; its average ad valorem rates were 40 percent compared to 33 percent for Fordney-McCumber. The tariff increases for the most part attracted universal condemnation from economists who feared it would destroy international trade, increase the cost of living, subsidize wasteful and inefficient production, and inspire retaliatory tariffs from foreign competitors. They were right. After the stock market collapse of October 1929, the economy was sliding into the worst depression in American history, and the Hawley-Smoot Tariff only accelerated the decline. (Martin L. Fausold, *The Presidency of Herbert C. Hoover*, 1985.)

HAYS, ARTHUR GARFIELD. Arthur Garfield Hays was born on December 12, 1881, in Rochester, New York. He graduated from Columbia University in 1902 and earned a master's degree and a law degree there in 1905. Hays went into private practice, specializing in international law and civil rights cases. His own commitment to First Amendment liberties and individual equality was unequivocal. After World War I, Hays played an important role in establishing the American Civil Liberties Union* (ACLU), and he served a term as national director of the ACLU. During the 1920s and early 1930s, Hays was directly involved in a host of civil rights: issues assisting the National Association for the Advancement of Colored People in its suit against segregation in the city of Detroit, working to overturn the conviction and death sentences of Nicola Sacco* and Bartolomeo Vanzetti,* helping to defend John Scopes in the "Monkey Trial"* of 1925, and aiding the the defense of the "Scottsboro boys."* Hays's life was a consistent struggle on behalf of free expression and equal treatment before the law. He died on December 14, 1954. (*New York Times,* December 15, 1954.)

HAYS, WILLIAM HARRISON. William Hays was born in Sullivan, Indiana, on November 5, 1879. He graduated from Wabash College in 1900 and took a master's degree there in 1904. Hays studied law privately and was admitted to the bar in 1904. He practiced law and became active in county and state Republican committees, chairing the Republican state committee between 1914 and 1918. Between 1918 and 1921, Hays was chairman of the Republican National Committee. President Warren G. Harding* appointed Hays to his cabinet as postmaster-general in 1921, and Hays served in that post until 1922, when he resigned to become president of the Motion Picture Producers and Distributors of America. Hays died on March 7, 1954. (*New York Times,* March 8, 1954; Francis Russell, *The Shadow of Blooming Grove: Warren G. Harding in His Times,* 1968.)

HAYWOOD, WILLIAM DUDLEY. William ''Big Bill'' Haywood was born in Salt Lake City, Utah, on February 4, 1869. He went to work as a miner when he was fifteen and spent ten years laboring in Nevada and Utah before moving to Silver City, Idaho, in 1894. Haywood became active in a new union, the Western Federation of Miners,—and in 1899 he was elected to the executive board. He became national secretary-treasurer of the union in 1900 and helped lead a number of strikes in 1901 and 1902. Haywood was astounded at the anti-union attitudes of mine operators and their willingness to resort to violence to block organization attempts. Over the years, Haywood's politics became more and more radical; he went through a political and philosophical transition, from a militant trade unionist to a revolutionary. In 1905 Haywood helped establish the new Industrial Workers of the World (IWW), or the ''Wobblies.'' Tall, gruff, and militant, Haywood became the symbol of radical unionism in the United States, especially after his trial in 1907 for the murder of a former Idaho governor. Haywood was acquitted.

He abandoned the IWW in 1908 because of its factionalism, and he spent the next four years travelling around the country on behalf of the Socialist Party of America,* but eventually he tired of its conservative, moderate approach to industrial problems. Haywood came back to the Industrial Workers of the World in 1912. In 1917 he was arrested on charges of violating the Espionage Act, i.e., opposing American entry into World War I. Haywood was convicted and spent the next two years in prison. When he was released in 1919, he immediately became a target for Attorney General A. Mitchell Palmer's* ''Red Scare''*—a bitter, nationwide crusade against political radicalism. Haywood abandoned the United States for the Soviet Union in 1921, where he hoped to view the results of revolution firsthand. Haywood stayed in the Soviet Union for the rest of his life and died in Moscow on May 18, 1928. (Joseph R. Conlin, *Big Bill Haywood and the Radical Union Movement,* 1969; Frederick C. Giffin, *Six Who Protested: Radical Opposition to the First World War,* 1977; William D. Haywood, *Bill Haywood's Book: The Autobiography of William D. Haywood,* 1929.)

HEARST, WILLIAM RANDOLPH. William Randolph Hearst was born in San Francisco, California, on April 29, 1863. He studied at Harvard from 1882 to 1885, and he was awarded an LL.D. degree from Oglethorpe in 1927. His interest in politics was deep, if erratic, and he served two terms in Congress (1903–1907) as a Democrat from New York. Although he ran for mayor of New York City and later for governor of New York, his influence was primarily the result of his ownership of such important newspapers and magazines as the *San Francisco Examiner,* the *Los Angeles Examiner,* the *Los Angeles Herald and Express,* the *Chicago Herald-American,* the *Boston American,* the *Boston Record,* the *New York Journal-American,* the *New York Mirror,* the *Baltimore News-Post,* the *Pittsburgh Sun-Telegram,* the *Detroit Times,* and the *Milwaukee Sentinel.* He had inherited $5 million from his mother, and used the money in 1895 to buy the *New York Journal;* and he then built a reputation for crude, sensational "yellow journalism" in his competition with the Joseph Pulitzer newspapers. Using new technology and mass circulation, Hearst built his newspaper empire by driving the competition out of business.

By the 1920s, Hearst owned ninety newspapers, three radio stations, and such magazines as *Good Housekeeping* and *Harper's Bazaar,* but, in the process of creating his empire, Hearst had become a thoroughly despised man. His political failures tended to make him more and more conservative, even by the standards of the 1920s. He had opposed American entry into World War I, and he bitterly opposed the nomination of Al Smith* as the Democratic presidential candidate in 1928. During the 1930s, he was absolutely convinced that Franklin D. Roosevelt* was leading the country down the road to communism. In the election of 1936, all of his newspapers pushed the candidacy of Republican nominee Alf Landon, but when Roosevelt defeated Landon in a landslide, Hearst gradually withdrew from the political arena. Out of touch with the ambitions and beliefs of most Americans, Hearst held opinions increasingly regarded as extreme. He died on August 14, 1951. (Rodney P. Carlisle, *Hearst and the New Deal: The Progressive as Reactionary,* 1982; William A. Swanberg, *Hearst, Citizen Hearst,* 1961.)

HEMINGWAY, ERNEST. Ernest Hemingway was born in Oak Park, Illinois, on July 21, 1899. After leaving high school, he worked as a reporter for the *Kansas City Star* until 1917, when he volunteered as an ambulance driver in France during World War I. While overseas, he enlisted in the Italian army. After the war, Hemingway went back to the newspaper business, working as a correspondent in the Middle East for the *Toronto Star*. In 1922 Hemingway settled in Paris among the Lost Generation* of American expatriates,* where he began his writing career. His first novel, *The Sun Also Rises,* was published in 1926, and in 1929 he followed it up with *A Farewell to Arms.* Hemingway placed a great value on toughness and "manly virtues," and he was fascinated with sports and athletic challenges. Blessed with a terse, laconic writing style, he had great influence on two generations of American writers, as did the themes of his novels—the meaninglessness of death, the need for courage, and the importance of stoically facing the absurdities of the universe. Hemingway's other novels included *To Have and Have Not* (1937), *For Whom the Bell Tolls* (1940), and *The Old Man and the Sea* (1952). Ernest Hemingway died on July 2, 1961, of a self-inflicted gunshot wound. (Frederick Hoffman, *The 1920s: American Writing in the Postwar Decade,* 1949; *New York Times,* July 3, 1961; Martin Seymour-Smith, *Who's Who in Twentieth Century Literature,* 1976.)

HILL, DAVID JAYNE. David J. Hill was born in Plainfield, New York, on June 10, 1850. He graduated from what today is Bucknell University in 1874 and received a master's degree there in 1877. He taught at Bucknell and was named president of the university in 1879. He moved on to the presidency of the University of Rochester in 1888, where he stayed until 1896 when he went abroad for two years of travel and study. In 1898 Hill was appointed assistant secretary of state by President William McKinley. He fulfilled a number of diplomatic assignments until he was named ambassador to Germany in 1908. Although Hill formed a close relationship with the Kaiser, he had to resign the post in 1911 because of Republican party politics. Between 1914 and 1917, Hill was a strong advocate of military preparedness and was an equally strong supporter of American entry into the war. After the war, Hill became an outspoken opponent of American participation in the League of Nations.* He thought its outlines for collective security were too vague, and he also disliked Woodrow Wilson* enough to oppose the League of Nations out of spite. Throughout the 1920s, Hill campaigned widely for world peace, even though he continued to oppose American membership in the League of Nations and the World Court.* David Hill died on March 2, 1932. (Aubrey Parkman, *David Jayne Hill and the Problem of World Peace,* 1975.)

HILL, GEORGE WASHINGTON. George Washington Hill was born on October 22, 1884, in Philadelphia, Pennsylvania. The family moved to New York City before his father became president of American Tobacco Company. George studied at Williams College for two years before joining American Tobacco. In 1907, with the assistance of his father, he purchased the tobacco firm of Butler and Butler, and he became president of the firm. Hill aggressively marketed the company's principal product—Pall Mall cigarettes—and made it one of the most successful brands in the country. He rejoined American Tobacco as vice-president and sales manager in 1912, and in 1916 he introduced a new cigarette named Lucky Strike. Between 1916 and 1931, Hill transformed Lucky Strike into the number one cigarette in sales in the country. He became president of American Tobacco Company. His advertising campaigns, which consumed more than $250 million between 1921 and 1938, became legendary for their success as well as their questionable ethics. To attract women smokers in the 1920s, Hill launched the "Reach for a Lucky instead of a sweet" campaign, which compared beautiful, thin women smoking Lucky Strikes with obese women eating candy. On radio,* Hill sponsored the Walter Winchell shows. Hill also broadcast and printed testimonials from physicians that Lucky Strike was a "smoother," and supposedly more healthy, cigarette. Lucky Strike sales, despite the outraged protests of antismoking reformers, jumped from $12 million in 1920 to $40 million in 1924. During the 1930s, Hill maintained Lucky Strike sales and American Tobacco Company profits by sponsoring Frank Sinatra, Ethel Smith, the "Jack Benny Show," and "Your Hit Parade." George Hill died on September 13, 1946. (*New York Times,* September 14, 1946; Robert Sobel, *They Satisfy,* 1978; Richard Tennant, *The American Tobacco Industry,* 1950.)

HILLQUIT, MORRIS. Morris Hillquit was born in Riga, Latvia, on August 1, 1869. His family immigrated to the United States in 1886, and Hillquit went to work in a shirt factory in New York City. In 1890 he joined the Socialist

Labor Party* and became active in radical politics, studying law at the same time at the New York Law School, where he graduated in 1893. Hillquit left the Socialist Labor Party in 1899 because he disagreed with the increasingly revolutionary militancy of its leader, Daniel DeLeon. In 1901 Hillquit became an early member of the Socialist Party of America,* primarily because he believed its tactics—nonviolent political action—were more compatible with the American environment. He was active in organizing workers for the United Hebrew Trades, and in 1913 Hillquit became general counsel for the International Ladies Garment Workers Union. He remained there until 1933. In 1917 Hillquit actively opposed United States entry into World War I. He established the American Conference for Democracy and Terms of Peace in 1917 to promote his views. He served as chairman of the national committee of the Socialist Party of America between 1913 and 1933. Hillquit was indefatigable in laboring on behalf of poor workers and immigrants, and he opposed the paranoia of the Red Scare* in 1919 and 1920. In 1924 Hillquit endorsed the presidential candidacy of Robert M. La Follette* and the Progressive Party.* He resented the business philosophy that dominated national politics in the 1920s, and after 1929 he viewed the depression as an opportunity for socialism to make real gains in American politics; however, Hillquit did not live to see how Franklin D. Roosevelt* and the New Deal prevented American Socialists from exploiting the suffering of the Great Depression. Hillquit died on October 7, 1933. (Morris Hillquit, *Loose Leaves from a Busy Life,* 1934; *New York Times,* October 8, 1933; Norma F. Pratt, "Morris Hillquit (1869–1933): A Political Biography of an American Jewish Socialist," Ph.D. dissertation, University of California at Los Angeles, 1977.)

HINES, WALKER DOWNER. Walker Hines was born on February 2, 1870, in Russellville, Kentucky. He graduated from Ogden College in Bowling Green, Kentucky, in 1888; worked at a number of jobs for several years; and then studied law at the University of Virginia, receiving his degree in 1893. Hines joined the legal staff of the Louisville and Nashville Railroad, and in 1901 he was named vice-president of the company. In 1906 Hines became general counsel for the Atchison, Topeka, and Santa Fe Railroad, and in 1916 he was named chairman of the board. When World War I broke out, Hines was named assistant to William Gibbs McAdoo,* director general of the railroads. Together they organized the United States Railroad Administration, which took control of the railroads, and when McAdoo resigned as head of the agency in 1919, Hines took over. Unlike McAdoo, Hines wanted the railroads returned to private control as soon after the war as possible, and he vigorously supported the Transportation Act of 1920,* which brought that return about. Hines then resigned as head of the United States Railroad Administration. He practiced law during the remainder of the 1920s and served as president of the Cotton Textile Institute. Walker Hines died on January 14, 1934. (Austin Kerr, *American Railroad Politics,* 1968; *New York Times,* January 15, 1934.)

HOLBROOK, DAVID HELM. David H. Holbrook was born on February 9, 1867, in Lake Geneva, Wisconsin. He graduated from Ripon College in 1901, and, for the next fourteen years, he taught social studies in Wisconsin public schools. Between 1914 and 1918, he was head of counseling for the Minneapolis school district, and in 1918 he took a social work position with the American Red Cross. Holbrook moved to New York City in 1920 to become executive secretary of the American Association for Organizing Family Social Work, and in 1925 he became executive secretary of the National Social Work Council (NSWC). For the next twenty years, as a leader of the NSWC, Holbrook urged social work agencies to concentrate on people, not administration, and he urged politicians to view social work as a social investment in people rather than a business decision. Holbrook retired in 1949 and died on August 27, 1962. *(New York Times,* August 28, 1962.)

HOLMES, JOHN HAYNES. John Holmes was born on November 29, 1879, in Philadelphia, Pennsylvania. He graduated from Harvard in 1902 and then took a degree from the Harvard Divinity School in 1904. Between 1904 and 1919, Holmes was a Unitarian minister in Massachusetts and New York City, and, at the same time, he was a leading spokesman for the social gospel—the responsibility of people, through their local, state, and national governments, to care for the sick, orphaned, and unemployed. In 1909 Holmes was a founder of the National Association for the Advancement of Colored People,* and in 1918 he played a central role in establishing the American Civil Liberties Union.* Holmes became editor of *Unity,* a weekly publication of the Chicago settlement house, Abraham Lincoln Center. He edited the weekly for the next twenty-six years. Holmes was an active pacifist during the 1920s, calling on all nations to turn away from war as a means of achieving national objectives. Holmes was uncompromising in his commitment to individual liberty. Oddly enough, he opposed both the Versailles Treaty* and the League of Nations* because he felt they were instruments of the major powers. Between 1929 and 1932, Holmes worked against the corrupt government of Mayor Jimmy Walker in New York City, eventually bringing about the Seabury investigations which forced Walker's resignation in 1932. John Holmes died on April 3, 1964. (John H. Holmes, *I Speak for Myself: The Autobiography of John Haynes Holmes,* 1959; Carl H. Voss, *Rabbi and Minister: The Friendship of Stephen S. Wise and John Haynes Holmes,* 1964.)

HOLMES, OLIVER WENDELL, JR. Oliver Wendell Holmes, Jr., was born on March 8, 1841, in Boston, Massachusetts. He graduated from Harvard College in 1861. After graduation, he was commissioned a second lieutenant in the Massachusetts Twentieth Volunteers, and he was wounded in battle during the Civil War. He returned to Harvard after the war and earned his law degree there in 1866. For the next fifteen years, Holmes practiced law in Boston and taught at the Harvard Law School, specializing in constitutional law. In 1882 he was appointed an associate justice of the Massachusetts Supreme Court. During the next twenty years, Holmes adopted a progressive philosophy on labor and industrial issues, writing more than 1,000 opinions and often incurring the wrath of corporate interests. When Horace Gray retired from the United States Supreme Court in 1902, President Theodore Roosevelt offered the vacancy to Holmes. Holmes, although a lifelong Republican, proved to be pragmatic and fiercely independent on the court. During the 1920s, Holmes frequently offered minority opinions, along with Justices Louis Brandeis* and Harlan Fiske Stone,* because he basically accepted the right of the people, through the federal government, to regulate large corporations. Holmes interpreted the commerce clause of the Constitution liberally and wanted to protect the rights of labor. In 1932, at the age of ninety-one, Holmes retired from the Supreme Court. He died on March 6, 1935. (Alpheus Thomas Mason, *The Supreme Court from Taft to Warren,* 1958; *New York Times,* March 7, 1935.)

HOLT, HAMILTON. Hamilton Holt was born on August 19, 1872, in Brooklyn, New York. He graduated from Yale in 1894 and then did graduate work at Columbia between 1894 and 1897. Holt joined the staff of New York City *The Independent* in 1894 and became managing editor in 1897 and editor and owner in 1913. Holt became interested in international political organization and world peace in the early 1900s, and he was a founder of the New York Peace Society in 1906. Holt spent the years before World War I actively campaigning for creation of some international peacekeeping organization. When the world went to war in 1914, Holt set in motion the process that led to creation of the League to Enforce Peace* in 1915. Its major purpose was to ensure that an international peacekeeping organization would be established as a result of World War I. When the United States refused to join the League of Nations* in 1919 and 1920, Holt abandoned his membership in the Republican Party* because of its isolationist position. In 1922 he helped found the League of Nations Non-Partisan Association to campaign for American membership. Holt made an unsuccessful bid for a United States Senate seat in 1924. In 1925 he became president of Rollins College, a position he held until 1949. Hamilton Holt died on April 26, 1951. (Warren F. Kuehl, *Hamilton Holt: Journalist, Internationalist, Educator,* 1960.)

HOOVER DAM. After years of negotiations among Arizona, Utah, Colorado, Nevada, and California over the development and use of the waters of the Colorado River, Congress passed the Boulder Canyon Project Act on December 21, 1928, authorizing construction of a huge federal dam near Boulder City, Nevada. The purpose of the dam was to provide water control, irrigation, hydroelectric power, and flood control along the Colorado River. The dam was situated at Black Canyon on the Colorado River, approximately twenty-five miles southeast of Las Vegas, Nevada. Construction began in 1931 and was completed in 1936. The dam was considered to be the world's most monumental engineering achievement—726 feet high and 1,244 feet long. It was dedicated in honor of President Herbert Hoover,* although the name reverted to Boulder Dam for a while until 1947, when the federal government again officially recognized it as Hoover Dam. (Norris Hundley, *Water for the West,* 1974.)

HOOVER, HERBERT CLARK. Herbert Clark Hoover was born on August 10, 1874, in West Branch, Iowa. Orphaned as a child, he was shuttled back and forth between several relatives before he moved to Oregon. Hoover graduated from Stanford University in 1895 with a major in mining and metallurgical engineering. He worked around the world as an engineer between 1895 and 1913, and he accumulated a personal fortune. Hoover came to public notice in 1914 when World War I broke out and he worked out a successful method of getting American citizens out of Europe and back to the United States. During the war, Hoover headed the Commission for the Relief of Belgium, which shipped millions of tons of food to relieve starving in the Low Countries. In the process, he built a global reputation as a humanitarian sensitive to the suffering of the poor and as an administrator capable of solving problems. President Woodrow Wilson* appointed Hoover head of the U.S. Food Administration in 1917, and between 1918 and 1922 Hoover headed the American Relief Association, a humanitarian group providing food and medicine to war-torn areas of Europe and the Soviet Union.

Hoover was popular enough in 1920 that both political parties courted him as a presidential candidate, but he announced himself as a Republican and decided not to run, instead choosing to accept a spot in Warren G. Harding's* cabinet as secretary of commerce. In that post, Hoover was the most active secretary of commerce in United States history. He believed firmly in what he called the ''associative state''—a national economy governed by organized interest groups and assisted by the federal government. Hoover encouraged the formation of trade associations, farm cooperatives, marketing groups, and labor unions because he believed those groups were capable of negotiating differences and improving competition as well as providing professional standards, expert planning, and efficiency. Hoover served as secretary of commerce under both Presidents Warren G. Harding and Calvin Coolidge.*

As for foreign affairs, Hoover had a global perspective based on his personal exeriences. He had a Jeffersonian idealism which fused nationalism and internationalism. Hoover at first favored United States membership in the League of Nations,* believing that Woodrow Wilson's vision of a world order was the only way to prevent another global conflagration. Reluctantly, he supported the Treaty of Versailles* with the reservations of Henry Cabot Lodge,* only because he thought it was politically necessary to get ratification. During the 1920s, he walked a political tightrope in the Republican Party,* avoiding much talk about the League of Nations but supporting the disarmament conferences. By 1928, Hoover was the heir apparent for the Republican Party presidential nomination, which he pursued after Calvin Coolidge decided not to seek re-election. In a controversial campaign against Governor Al Smith* of New York, Hoover won the presidential election of 1928.*

His success in the election rested on two public perceptions: that he was a genuine humanitarian and that he had been responsible for much of the Republican prosperity of the 1920s. With the stock market crash of 1929* and the Great Depression, the second assumption was dashed, and when Hoover delayed again and again in providing large-scale federal relief programs, the prevailing belief in his humanitarianism died too. In his inaugural address, Hoover had predicted the ultimate demise of poverty in the United States, but less than a year later the country was in desperate and worsening circumstances.

Hoover's response to the economic crisis was to try to marshall the voluntary resources of the country to provide relief, rely on benevolent corporate leaders to maintain employment, and use the federal government to coordinate recovery efforts. Hoover was not a laissez-faire president. The Agricultural Marketing Act of 1929* created government stabilization corporations to purchase some crop surpluses; the Reconstruction Finance Corporation* of 1932 provided up to $2 billion in federal loan money to prop up the banking system; the Federal Home Loan Bank Act of 1932* provided $500 million to shore up weakened savings and loan associations; and the Emergency Relief and Construction Act of 1932* appropriated $3.3 billion for relief and public works loans. Hoover's problem was that the programs did not stimulate the economy. Like most followers of classical economics, Hoover thought that a massive infusion of credit into the economy would automatically lead to increased consumer demand, production, and employment. But the Great Depression was primarily a problem of consumer purchasing power, not credit availability. During his administration, the unemployment problem grew steadily worse, finally reaching 25 percent in 1932. That was the kiss of death in an election year. Worse yet, Hoover was perceived as the man who led the government riot against the Bonus Army* marchers in the summer of 1932, further convincing the public that he was mean spirited and insensitive. In the election of 1932,* Franklin D. Roosevelt* and the Democrats delivered an unprecedented defeat to Hoover and the Republicans, driving the president out of the White House and routing the Republicans in Congress.

Hoover then spent the rest of his life as an elder statesman, criticizing the New Deal and the steady growth of the federal government, which he felt was dangerously bureaucratic, inefficient, and stifling. Late in the 1940s, Hoover presided over a commission studying the federal government, and he recommended sweeping consolidations in federal agencies. Herbert Hoover, once the great humanitarian and later the symbol of the suffering of the Great Depression, died on October 20, 1964. (David Burner, *Herbert Hoover: A Public Life,* 1979; James S. Olson, *Herbert Hoover and the Reconstruction Finance Corporation, 1931–1933,* 1977.)

HOOVER, HERBERT WILLIAM. Herbert William Hoover was born on October 30, 1877, in New Berlin, Ohio. After finishing high school, he studied for two years at Hiram College and then entered the family harness and tannery business. The family prospered by adapting the business to new consumer interests, shifting away from horse collars and harnesses early in the 1900s to leather for belts, purses, coats, and automobile straps. World War I provided them with multimillion-dollar government contracts for what became known as the W. H. Hoover Company, named after Herbert's father Henry William. In 1908 Hoover and his brother Frank decided to provide financial backing for one of their janitors, who had invented an electric sweeper by mounting a small engine on a Bissell carpet sweeper. William and Herbert Hoover established the Electric Suction Sweeper Company to market the new product. Herbert Hoover placed advertisements in the *Saturday Evening Post* and *Ladies Home Journal,* and demand for the "Hoover vacuum cleaner" was immediate. Hoover established dealerships across the country just before and after World War I, and by the 1920s the product had a national reputation. Hoover became president of the Hoover Suction Sweeper Company in 1922, by which time, he had developed newer, lighter vacuum cleaners and had introduced door-to-door salesman and home demonstrations, which also increased sales. He died on September 16, 1954. (Frank G. Hoover, *Fabulous Dustpan,* 1955; *New York Times,* September 17, 1954.)

HOOVER, JOHN EDGAR. J. Edgar Hoover was born in Washington, D.C., on January 1, 1895. He graduated from George Washington University in 1916 and earned a law degree there in 1917. Hoover immediately went to work for the Department of Justice, and in 1919 he was named special assistant to Attorney General A. Mitchell Palmer,* in which position he actively pursued the Red Scare.* In 1921, Hoover was named assistant director of the Bureau of Investigation, serving under William J. Burns.* He became director of the new Federal Bureau of Investigation (FBI) in 1924 after Butler resigned in the wake of the Teapot Dome* scandal. Hoover directed the FBI for the rest of his life. During the 1930s, he became a household word in the United States as FBI agents, known as "G-men," went after gangsters like John Dillinger. During the late 1930s and throughout World War II, Hoover used the FBI to pursue Nazi collaborators and spies; during the 1950s and 1960s, he resumed his crusade against communism, writing *Masters of Deceit* in 1958. By that time, Hoover was one of the most powerful people in the federal government because of the widespread support and reputation he had cultivated throughout his career. He died on May 2, 1972. (Richard G. Powers, *Secrecy and Power: The Life of J. Edgar Hoover,* 1987.)

HOOVER MORATORIUM. In the Treaty of Versailles* in 1919, the Allied powers saddled Germany with responsibility for World War I and imposed reparations* of $56 billion on her. The reparations proved disastrous to the

German economy, and the Allied powers eventually agreed to reduce them in the Dawes Plan* of 1924 and the Young Plan* of 1929. By then, the reparations were down to just over $8 billion, but the serious erosion of the world economy in 1931 made further intervention necessary. Germany wanted the reparations reduced or eliminated, but France objected as long as the Allies were still required to repay their war debts* to the United States. In May 1931 the central bank of Austria failed, threatening financial stability throughout the Western world. On June 20, 1931, President Herbert Hoover* proposed a twelve-month moratorium on Allied war debt payments and German reparations payments. The French agreed in July 1931, and the moratorium went into effect. At the Lausanne Conference of 1932,* German reparations were reduced to less than $1 billion. (Edward W. Bennett, *Germany and the Diplomacy of the Financial Crisis,* 1962; Bernard V. Burke, "American Economic Diplomacy and the Weimar Republic," *Mid-America* 54 [October 1972], 211–33; Benjamin Rhodes, "Herbert Hoover and the War Debts, 1919–1933," *Proloque* 6 [Summer 1974], 150–80.)

"HOOVERVILLES." A pejorative term clearly reflecting the public conviction that Herbert Hoover* was responsible for the Great Depression, "Hoovervilles" described the shanty towns sprouting up around the country in the early 1930s. By 1932 the communities of the homeless and unemployed had increased in size and number. With unemployment rates exceeding 25 percent and the number of business failures and farm and home foreclosures increasing, thousands of Americans were migrants, and tens of thousands were homeless. In empty lots, city outskirts, beaches, riverbanks, municipal parks, and garbage dumps, these families erected makeshift shacks of cardboard, scrap metal, and cloth. The largest of the "Hoovervilles" was in St. Louis, where more than 1,000 people lived in makeshift housing. In New York City, hundreds of people lived along the Hudson River between 72nd St. and 100th St. In California, groups of migrant families lived out of their cars while they searched for farm labor. Like "Hoover blankets" (newspapers), "Hoover heaters" (camp fires), and "Hoover hogs" (armadillos), the term "Hooverville" symbolized the suffering wrought by the depression and implied that Herbert Hoover and the Republicans were responsible. (Martin G. Towey, "Hooverville: St. Louis Had the Largest," *Gateway Heritage* 1 [Fall 1980], 4–11.)

HOPKINS, HARRY LLOYD. See TEMPORARY EMERGENCY RELIEF ADMINISTRATION

HORNSBY, ROGERS. Rogers Hornsby was born on April 27, 1896, in Winters, Texas. In 1914 he signed a contract with Hugo, Oklahoma, in the Texas-Oklahoma League, but in 1915 the St. Louis Cardinals purchased his contract. Outspoken and proud of his natural talent, Hornsby considered himself the greatest hitter in baseball*, and he usually proved his claims. His lifetime batting average was eventually .358. Between 1921 and 1925, Hornsby won the batting title with averages of .397, .401, .384, .424, and .403. He was also regularly a leader in total hits, doubles, triples, runs scored, and runs-batted-in. After a dispute with team management, Hornsby was traded to the New York Giants in 1926, and in 1928 they traded him to the Boston Braves. He remained difficult to manage, however, and the Braves traded Hornsby to the Chicago Cubs at the end of the 1928 season. In 1929 baseball commissioner Kenesaw Mountain Landis* criticized Hornsby for his attitude as well as his tendency to gamble, which Landis would not tolerate. Hornsby returned to the Cardinals in 1933, and in mid-year he signed on as manager of the St. Louis Browns, a post he held until 1937. He managed a variety of teams in the minor leagues after that and managed the St. Louis Browns in 1952 and the Cincinnati Reds in 1953. Rogers Hornsby died on January 5, 1963. (Martin Appel and Burt Goldblatt, *Baseball's Best: The Hall of Fame Gallery,* 1980; *New York Times,* January 6, 1963.)

HOUGHTON, ALANSON BIGELOW. Alanson Bigelow Houghton was born in Cambridge, Massachusetts, on October 10, 1863. He graduated from Harvard in 1886 and then went to work in the family business, the Corning Glass Works in Corning, New York. Houghton became president of Corning in 1910. He won a seat as a Republican in Congress in 1918, and in 1923 President Warren G. Harding* named him ambassador to Germany. In 1924 Houghton was instrumental in convincing the German leaders to accept the Dawes Plan.* Calvin Coolidge* named him ambassador to Great Britain in 1925. Houghton returned to the United States in 1928 and was unsuccessful in his attempt to run for the United States Senate. He died on September 16, 1941. (H. C. Allen, *Great Britain and the United States,* 1969; *New York Times,* September 17, 1941.)

HOUSE, EDWARD MANDELL. Edward M. House was born in Houston, Texas, on September 28, 1858. He attended Cornell University and then spent his early adulthood supervising his family's extensive cotton plantations. Active in Democratic politics, House became a close political advisor to Governor James Hoggs of Texas and worked hard to give the Texas delegation to candidate Woodrow Wilson* at the Democratic National Convention of 1912. In return, Wilson named House to serve as his White House deputy. House remained in Wilson's service until 1919. The two men had become estranged over foreign policy issues, particularly since House was advising Wilson to compromise on the Treaty of Versailles* in order to get Senate ratification. In June 1919, House returned to Texas. Periodically, over the next nineteen years, he served as a political consultant to various Democratic politicians; he died on March 28, 1938. (Alexander George and Juliette L. George, *Woodrow Wilson and Colonel House,* 1956; *New York Times,* March 29, 1938.)

HOUSTON, DAVID FRANKLIN. David F. Houston was born in Monroe, North Carolina, on February 17, 1866. He graduated from the College of South Carolina in 1887 and received a master's degree in economics and political science from Harvard in 1892. Houston taught at the University of Texas between 1894 and 1902, serving as dean of the faculty during his last three years in Austin. Houston became president of Texas A&M University in 1902 and returned to Austin as president of the University of Texas in 1905. Between 1908 and 1916, Houston served as chancellor of Washington University in St. Louis, Missouri. A strong supporter of the candidacy of Woodrow Wilson* in the election of 1912, Houston was named secretary of agriculture in 1913. He switched over and became secretary of the treasury in 1920. When President Warren G. Harding* entered the White House in 1921, Houston left the cabinet to become president of Bell Telephone Securities company. David F. Houston died on September 2, 1940. (David Franklin Houston, *Eight Years with Wilson's Cabinet*, 1926; John W. Payne, "David F. Houston: A Biography," Ph.D. dissertation, University of Texas, 1953.)

HOWARD, CHARLES PERRY. Charles Howard was born on September 14, 1879, in Harvel, Illinois. He worked on the railroads between 1897 and 1899 and as a miner between 1900 and 1903, when he went to work as a printer. Howard was active in union politics after joining the International Typographical Union, (ITU) in Tacoma, Washington. He was president of the Portland Central Labor Council between 1916 and 1918, and in 1918 President Woodrow Wilson* appointed him commissioner of conciliation in the Department of Labor. Howard edited the *Railway Maintenance of Way Employees' Journal* between 1919 and 1922, and in 1923 he was elected president of the ITU. He was defeated in 1924 but re-elected in 1926. An outspoken advocate of industrial unionism, Howard became secretary of the Committee for Industrial Organization (CIO) in 1935. Howard, a Republican, served as president of the ITU until 1938. He died on July 21, 1938. (*Dictionary of American Biography,* supp. 2 [1944] 322–23; Seymour Lipset et al., *Union Democracy: The International Politics of the International Typographical Union,* 1956.)

HUGHES, CHARLES EVANS. Charles Evans Hughes was born on April 11, 1862, in Glen Falls, New York. Hughes attended Colgate University between 1876 and 1878, but he transferred to Brown University where he thought academic life would be more rigorous. He graduated third in his class at Brown, taught school for a year, and in 1882 entered Columbia Law School. Hughes earned his law degree in 1884 and then specialized in commercial law. He joined the law faculty of Cornell University in 1891, but then he returned to private practice in New York City in 1893. During the 1890s, Hughes chaired two investigative commissions, one looking into the utilities industry and the other, the insurance industry; in the process, he impressed progressive Republicans, who backed him in his 1906 bid to become governor of New York. Hughes defeated Democratic candidate William Randolph Hearst* by 58,000 votes and entered the governor's mansion in Albany.

Hughes was re-elected in 1908, but, by then, he had alienated important elements in the Republican Party.* He refused to change the state law prohibiting racetrack betting, and he earned the lifelong wrath of Theodore Roosevelt when he rebuffed the president's friendly attempts to intervene in a bitter fight to oust Hughes's superintendent of insurance. Hughes decided not to seek re-election, and in 1910 President William Howard Taft* nominated him to fill a vacancy on the United States Supreme Court. As a justice, Hughes was widely regarded as a liberal activist, upholding the right of Congress to control interstate commerce and upholding the rights of labor and minorities. In 1916 the Republican Party persuaded Hughes to resign his court post and challenge Woodrow Wilson* for the White House. Because Wilson had preempted many of the progressive reform issues, Hughes had a difficult time defining his campaign, and he lost the election.

Out of politics, Hughes returned to his law practice in New York and continued to speak out on the issues. On the question of the League of Nations,* he was a moderate reservationist who basically supported the idea of American participation. In 1921 President Warren G. Harding* appointed Hughes secretary of state, in which position he presided over the Washington Naval Conference* of 1921–1922, which developed a series of treaties on naval arms reduction, restrictions on submarine warfare, the Open Door policy, and the balance of power in the Pacific. Hughes also played a central role in developing the Dawes Plan,* which scaled down and refinanced German reparations* payments. Hughes's administration at the State Department was also noted for the Berlin Treaty of 1921,* the Santiago Conference of 1923,* and his advocacy of American entry into the World Court.*

Hughes resigned as secretary of state in 1925 and returned to private law practice, but in 1930 President Herbert Hoover* nominated him to succeed Chief Justice William Howard Taft. There he presided over the court during its battles with President Franklin D. Roosevelt* and the New Dealers. Critics have unjustly assailed Hughes as a conservative on the court, when he was actually quite moderate; after 1935, he usually opposed the conservative faction and provided the swing vote in confirming New Deal legislation. Hughes resigned from the court in 1941, and he died on August 29, 1948. (Betty Glad, *Charles Evans Hughes and the Illusions of Innocence,* 1966; *New York Times,* August 30, 1948; Merl J. Pusey, *Charles Evans Hughes,* 1951.)

HUGHES, JAMES LANGSTON. Langston Hughes was born in Joplin, Missouri, on February 1, 1902. His family moved frequently between 1902 and 1915, and eventually he graduated from high school in Cleveland, Ohio. A published poet at the age of nineteen, Hughes studied at Columbia University briefly in 1921, but then he left school and travelled widely around the world. He returned to the United States in 1924 and was publishing poetry widely by

1925, especially in such black journals as *The Crisis* and *Opportunity*. In 1926 he entered Lincoln University. During the 1920s, Hughes gained recognition as an important black artist, and he was a major figure in the Harlem Renaissance. He published several books of poetry during the 1920s, including *The Weary Blues* (1926) and *Fine Clothes to the Jew* (1927). During the late 1930s, Hughes was a columnist for the *Baltimore Afro-American,* and in 1943 he began his long-term commitment as a columnist for the *Chicago Defender.* By the 1950s, he was travelling widely throughout the United States reading his poetry and lecturing. Langston Hughes died of congestive heart failure on May 22, 1967. A poet, playwright, anthologist, novelist, and songwriter, Hughes was one of the most gifted and prolific writers in American history. (Donald C. Dickinson, *A Bio-Bibliography of Langston Hughes,* 1967; James A. Emanuel, *Langston Hughes, 1902–1967,* 1967; *New York Times,* May 23, 1967.)

HULL, CORDELL. Cordell Hull was born on October 2, 1871, in Overton County, Tennessee. He attended the National Normal University in Lebanon, Ohio, in 1888 and 1889, and then he studied law at the Cumberland Law School, where he received his degree in 1891. After practicing law, he entered the political arena in 1893 and was elected to the Tennessee legislature and served there until 1897. Hull returned to his private law practice until 1903, when he was appointed to fill a judgeship in the 5th Judicial Circuit of Tennessee. In 1907 he was elected to the United States House of Representatives, where he served continuously (except for 1921–1922) until his election to the Senate in 1931. In Congress, Hull was a leading progressive, authoring the Federal Income Tax Act (1913), the Revised Federal Income Tax Act (1916), and the Federal Inheritance Tax Act (1916).

During the 1920s, Hull advocated low tariffs to stimulate world trade, disarmament, United States membership in the League of Nations,* and revision of United States interventionist policies in Latin America. In 1933, President Franklin D. Roosevelt* selected Hull to join his cabinet as secretary of state, and in that position Hull was responsible for the Reciprocal Trade Agreements Act of 1934 and the development of the Good Neighbor Policy.* Next to Roosevelt, Hull became one of the most popular Democrats in the country during the 1930s. During World War II, Hull concentrated his efforts on creation of the United Nations and in 1945 he received the Nobel Peace Prize for his efforts. Hull retired from the State Department in 1944 and died on July 23, 1955. (Cordell Hull, *The Memoirs of Cordell Hull,* 1948; *New York Times,* July 24, 1955; Julius W. Pratt, *Cordell Hull, 1933–1944,* 1964.)

HUMPHREY, DORIS. Doris Humphrey was born on October 17, 1895, in Oak Park, Illinois. She began her dance training in Chicago but eventually moved to Los Angeles to train at the Denishawn School of Ruth St. Denis and Ted Shawn. She joined them at the time of their transition to abstractionism, and Humphrey danced and choreographed several of their works, including *Second*

Arabesque (1919), *Valse Brilliante* (1922), and *Scherzo Waltz* (1924). In 1927 she broke with the Denishawn School and set up her own New York studio; over the next sixteen years, she staged more than eighty major works, including such innovative creations as *Water Study* in 1928 and the *Life of the Bee* in 1929. Because of arthritis, she retired as a performer in 1943, leaving a legacy as one of the great dance abstractionists of the twentieth century. Doris Humphrey died on December 29, 1958. (Barbara Naomi Cohen-Stratyner, *Biographical Dictionary of Dance,* 1982.)

HUMPHREY, WILLIAM EWART. William E. Humphrey was born near Alamo, Indiana, on March 31, 1962. He graduated from Wabash College in 1887 and practiced law at Crawfordsville, Indiana, between 1888 and 1893. Humphrey moved to Seattle, Washington, in 1893 to practice corporate law, and there he specialized in the timber industry. A conservative Republican, Humphrey was a member of Congress between 1903 and 1917, and in 1924 he was campaign manager for President Calvin Coolidge's* successful re-election bid. Because the Federal Trade Commission* (FTC) had repeatedly investigated the northwestern timber industry, Humphrey was a bitter opponent of the FTC; and in 1925, with the clear hope that he would transform the agency into a pro-business institution, Coolidge appointed him to a six-year term as a commissioner. There Humphrey dominated the conservative majority and essentially changed the FTC from a progressive body working to guarantee free competition into a pro-business, conservative body. President Herbert Hoover* reappointed him in 1931.

During the early New Deal, however, President Franklin D. Roosevelt,* James M. Landis, and Felix Frankfurter saw Humphrey as a hopeless reactionary. Roosevelt fired Humphrey in 1933 in a decision that the commissioner fought in the courts. Two years later, after Humphrey's death in 1934, the Supreme Court handed down its decision in *Humphrey's Executor (Rathbun)* v. *United States,* overturning the firing on the grounds that the president did not have the authority to remove officials of regulatory agencies for political reasons before their scheduled reappointment. (G. Cullom Davis, "The Transformation of the Federal Trade Commission, 1914–1929," *The Mississippi Valley Historical Review* 49 [December 1962], 437–55; Donald A. Ritchie, *James M. Landis: Dean of the Regulators,* 1980.)

HURLEY, PATRICK JAY. Patrick J. Hurley was born in Choctaw, Indian Territory of present-day Oklahoma on January 8, 1883. He graduated from the National University in Washington, D.C., in 1908 and then received a law degree at George Washington University in 1913. Hurley practiced law in Tulsa, Oklahoma, until his 1929 appointment as secretary of war in the Herbert Hoover* administration. As secretary of war, Hurley played an aggressive role in the Bonus Army* march on Washington, D.C., and even disobeyed Hoover's counsel for moderation in telling General Douglas MacArthur* to disperse the marchers. The Bonus Army incident in 1932 proved to be a political disaster for President Hoover. Hurley returned to his law practice in 1933 and remained in Oklahoma until 1942, when President Franklin D. Roosevelt* asked him to serve as his personal representative at the Moscow Conference of 1942 and the Teheran Conference of 1933. In 1944 Hurley became ambassador to China. After World War II, Hurley publicly condemned the Yalta agreements of 1945 and blamed the Roosevelt administration for the fall of China to the Communists in 1949. Patrick J. Hurley died on July 30, 1963. (Russell Buhite, *Patrick J. Hurley and United States Foreign Policy,* 1973.)

HYDE, ARTHUR MASTICK. Arthur M. Hyde was born in Princeton, Missouri, on July 12, 1877. He graduated from the University of Michigan in 1899 and then earned a law degree at the University of Iowa in 1900. Hyde practiced law in Princeton until 1915. A progressive Republican, Hyde served a term as mayor of Princeton between 1908 and 1912, and in 1920 he won election as governor of Missouri. He stayed in the governor's mansion until 1925, when he became president of the Sentinel Life Insurance Company. In 1929, President Herbert Hoover* appointed Hyde secretary of agriculture, in which position he worked to establish the programs of the Federal Farm Board.* In 1933 Hyde went into private law practice in Kansas City, Missouri. He died on October 17, 1947. (Eugene Lyons, *Herbert Hoover: A Biography,* 1964; *New York Times,* October 18, 1947.)

I

IMMIGRATION RESTRICTION. See NATIONAL ORIGINS ACT OF 1924

IMMIGRATION RESTRICTION LEAGUE. The Immigration Restriction League was founded in 1894 by a group of upper-class Yankee elitists alarmed about the influx of southern and eastern European immigrants. The original founders included former Senator George F. Edmunds of Vermont, philanthropist Robert T. Paine, and prominent historian John Fiske. Prescott Hall, a Boston attorney, was named executive secretary. The Immigration Restriction League quickly evolved into one of the most influential lobbying groups in the country. It played a central role in securing passage of the Immigration Act of 1903, which excluded anarchists; the Immigration Act of 1907, which prohibited Japanese immigration from Hawaii; the Immigration Act of 1917, which required a literacy test of all prospective immigrants; the Immigration Act of 1920, which provided for the deportation of radical aliens; and the Emergency Quota Act of 1921,* which discriminated against immigrants from southern and eastern Europe. When Congress passed the National Origins Act of 1924,* imposing a formal quota system on future immigration, the Immigration Restriction League had achieved its major objective, and disbanded in 1924. (Thomas J. Curran, *Xenophobia and Immigration, 1820–1930,* 1975.)

INDIAN CITIZENSHIP ACT OF 1924. See SNYDER ACT OF 1924

INDUSTRIAL CONFERENCES OF 1919 AND 1920. In 1919 there were 3,374 labor strikes in the United States, including the spectacular Boston police strike* and the great steel strike,* as well as widespread racial unrest and rioting. The country was in the midst of the Red Scare,* and fear of radicalism was widespread. Labor unions were suspect, despite the conservatism of Samuel Gompers* and the American Federation of Labor,* because they threatened to organize society along class lines. In preparation for the election of 1920* and in an attempt to reestablish the progressive credentials of his administration, President Woodrow Wilson* convened the National Industrial Conference in

Washington, D.C., between October 6 and 24, 1919, with Secretary of the Interior Franklin Lane* presiding. Representatives of management and labor met to discuss collective bargaining and trade unionism. Because the conference met in the middle of the steel strike, feelings between the two groups were tense, and the conference broke up without any general agreement.

Wilson then convened a second National Industrial Conference on December 1, 1919, under the leadership of Secretary of Labor William B. Wilson* as chairman and Herbert Hoover* as vice-chairman. The second conference focused its attention on the settlement of industrial disputes, but labor representatives were suspicious because they felt that the conference was more interested in resolving disputes than in discovering the source of those disputes. The conference met on and off until March 6, 1920, when it finally recommended establishment of a National Industrial Board to investigate, but not arbitrate, management-labor disputes, and the establishment of shop committees in every company where workers and supervisors could discuss matters of mutual concern.

The second industrial conference did not achieve any lasting reforms. Corporate leaders were already embarking on the open shop movement* of the 1920s, campaigning against independent trade unionism and trying to convert shop committees into company unions.* At the same time, the Red Scare quickly disappeared in 1920 and 1921, reducing public fears about labor radicalism and relieving the necessity for establishing some sort of formal negotiating process between workers and management. (Gary Dean Best, "President Wilson's Second Industrial Conference, 1919–1920," *Labor History* 16 [Fall 1975] 505–20; Haggai Hurvitz, "Ideology and Industrial Conflict, President Wilson's First Industrial Conference of October, 1919," *Labor History* 18 [Fall 1977], 509–24.)

INSTALLMENT BUYINGS. One of the most remarkable financial developments of the 1920s was the birth of installment plans as a way of purchasing consumer goods. In 1919 the volume of installment debt in the United States totaled less than $100 million; by 1927, that number had grown to more than $7 billion. Several thousand new credit institutions—finance companies—had appeared to assist consumers in purchasing automobiles, furniture, radios, and electrical appliances. The traditional practice of saving up enough money to buy a product gave way to a new doctrine in consumer culture—buy now and pay later. Installment buying had an immediate impact on the economy of the 1920s. Suddenly, large numbers of consumers were able to purchase goods they had only dreamt about before. Demand for automobiles and furniture grew geometrically in the early 1920s as consumers rushed to get in on the technological wonders and the credit miracle. The automobile and furniture industries expanded plant capacity to deal with the demand. The real problem, however, came later in the decade. By that time, the consumer market had become saturated, at least in terms of the entrance of new buyers. Instead of large volumes of new demand, replacement of existing automobiles and furniture became the norm, as did purchases of used products. The automobile and furniture companies found themselves with an excess capacity by 1927, and they began to lay off workers. Well before the stock market crash in 1929,* the industrial economy was already softening. (Wilbur C. Plummer and Ralph A. Young, *Sales Finance Companies and Their Credit Practices,* 1940.)

INSULL, SAMUEL. Born in London on November 11, 1859, Samuel Insull, after attending fine private schools, went to work in 1874 for an auctioneering company. In 1879 he became secretary to Colonel George E. Gouraud, the European representative for Thomas A. Edison's electric power industry. Several of Insull's reports to the United States impressed Edison, and in 1881 he brought Insull to the United States as his secretary. Edison soon put Insull in charge of the Thomas A. Edison Construction Company. In 1892 Insull became president of Chicago Edison. By 1929 Insull had built an unparalleled utility empire in the Midwest by corporate combinations and use of holding companies. The Insull empire consisted of five great corporate systems with more than 150 subsidiaries, 4.5 million customers, and $2.5 billion in assets. At the top of the holding company empire were two companies, the Insull Utility Investments, Inc., and Corporation Securities Company of Chicago. Revenue from the operating companies sustained the holding companies, but any interruption in those revenues immediately would threaten the corporate superstructure. When the stock market crashed in 1929,* Insull was unable to keep the empire liquid. By December 1931, Insull Utilities Investment was in the hands of creditors; and in 1932, when Middle West Utilities failed to secure refinancing credit, the company and its 111 subsidiaries went into receivership. Insull resigned from sixty corporations and fled to Europe. In September 1932 Franklin D. Roosevelt,* then Democratic nominee for president, attacked Insull publicly; and politicians used the collapse of Insull's empire to illustrate business corruption and the evil forces at work that caused the Great Depression.* Insull was indicted and tried but acquitted of charges of embezzlement, mail fraud, and violation of the Bankruptcy Act, and he died in France on July 16, 1938. The publicity surrounding his career, the spectacular collapse of his corporate empire, and the public outrage over the suffering caused by the Great Depression led to unprecedented demands for reform. Those demands eventually led to significant portions of the Banking Act of 1933, the Corporate Bankruptcy Act, and the Wagner-Connery Act, as well as the Public Utility Holding Company Act of 1935, the Securities and Exchange Commission, the Tennessee Valley Authority, and the Rural Electrification Administration. (Forrest McDonald, *Insull,* 1962.)

INTERNATIONAL LABOR ORGANIZATION. The International Labor Organization (ILO) was created by the Treaty of Versailles* in 1919 to promote equitable labor standards throughout the world. It was headquartered at Geneva, Switzerland. Consistent with its post–World War I suspicion of internationalism, the United States did not join the ILO until 1934. In 1945 the ILO became part of the United Nations, but the United States withdrew from it in 1977 after concluding that the ILO had become a tool of the Communist bloc countries. (Anthony Alcock, *History of the International Labor Organization,* 1971.)

"IRRECONCILABLES." The term "irreconcilables" was used by journalists and later by historians to describe the group of from thirteen to sixteen United States Senators who were uncompromisingly opposed to ratification of the Treaty of Versailles.* Generally, they were suspicious of internationalism and they preferred to pull the United States back behind the two oceans that had historically protected her from European and Asian conflicts. Included in the group of "irreconcilables" were William Borah* of Idaho, Robert M. La Follette* of Wisconsin, Frank B. Brandegee of Connecticut, George H. Moses* of New Hampshire, Medill McCormick of Illinois, George W. Norris* of Nebraska, Hiram Johnson* of California, Joseph I. France of Maryland, Philander C. Knox* of Pennsylvania, Bert M. Fernald of Maine, Albert Fall* of New Mexico, Miles Poindexter of Washington, and Henry Cabot Lodge* of Massachusetts. During the 1920s, the "irreconcilables" continued to campaign against United States membership in the League of Nations* and the World Court.* (Thomas A. Bailey, *Woodrow Wilson and the Great Betrayal,* 1945; Ralph A. Stone, *The Irreconcilables,* 1970.)

ISOLATIONISM. "Isolationism" is a term used to describe the strong tendency in American foreign policy to abstain from an active role in international affairs. Ever since George Washington's warning that the United States should avoid "entangling alliances," Americans have debated the merits of internationalism. During the nineteenth century, isolationism reigned supreme, as it did during the years between World Wars I and II when the United States refused to join the League of Nations* or the World Court* and passed the Neutrality Acts in the 1930s to stay out of war. World War II ended permanently any serious American commitment to isolationism, even though the Vietnam War did give many people in the United States serious doubts about internationalism. Nevertheless, after World War II, the United States had global economic, political, and strategic interests, and isolationism was no longer a reasonable means of shaping foreign policy. (Selig Adler, *The Isolationist Impulse,* 1957; Robert E. Osgood, *Ideals and Self-Interest in America's Foreign Relations,* 1953.)

J

JARDINE, WILLIAM MARION. William M. Jardine was born in Oneida County, Idaho, on January 16, 1879. He graduated from the Agricultural College of Utah in 1901, and, between 1901 and 1918, he taught at the College of Utah, Lafayette College, and Kansas State College. Between 1918 and 1928, he was president of Kansas State University. During those years, he was highly visible in American agriculture, particularly through positions he held with the American Bankers' Association, the American Society on Agronomy, and the National Research Council. Jardine was secretary of agriculture in the Calvin Coolidge* cabinet from February 1928 to March 1929. Jardine then returned to private life and served as president of the Municipal University of Wichita from 1934 to 1939. He died on January 17, 1955. (Donald R. McCoy, *Calvin Coolidge: The Quiet President,* 1967; *New York Times,* January 18, 1955.)

JARRETT, MARY CROMWELL. Mary Jarrett, the founder of psychiatric social work, was born on June 21, 1877, in Baltimore, Maryland. She graduated from Goucher College in 1898 and taught school for two years before going to Boston as a caseworker for the Boston Children's Aid Society. She consulted frequently with E. E. Southard, the famous Boston social psychiatrist, and in 1913 she went to work with him at the Boston Psychopathic Hospital as head of the social services department. She initiated a training program for psychiatric caseworkers, and in 1918, anticipating the return of hundreds of thousands of emotionally traumatized soldiers from Europe, Jarrett founded a training program at Smith College. In 1922 she coauthored, with Southard, the book *Kingdom of Evils,* which argued that such social problems as vice, crime, and poverty were vulnerable to social and psychological reform. In 1920, Jarrett founded what became the American Association of Psychiatric Social Workers and continued her crusade, arguing that, since more than half of all people needing the assistance of social workers were suffering from mental disorders, psychiatric social work was the only approach society could take to deal with their problems. During the rest of the 1920s and 1930s, Jarrett worked for the United States Public Health Service and the Welfare Council of New York City, where she specialized in the problems of chronically ill people. Her 1933 book *Chronic Illness in New York City* was considered a classic. Jarrett retired in 1943 and died on August 4, 1961. (Frederick P. Gay, *The Open Mind: Elmer Ernest Southard,* 1938; Vida S. Grayson, "Mary Jarrett," in *Notable American Women,* 1980.)

JARROTT, JOHN. John Jarrott was born in Jacksonville, Florida, in 1893. He was raised on the steamboat circuit along the Mississippi River; his father was a professional gambler and his mother, a prostitute. When Jarrott was thirteen, his mother committed suicide and his father abandoned him to a touring prizefighter, who used him as a tap dancer to attract customers to exhibitions. By 1912 Jarrott was dancing in Chicago cabarets, and in the process he became one of the most successful ballroom dancers in the country, inventing or introducing the "Grizzley Bear," the "Turkey Trot," and the "Yankee One Step," which became popular during and after World War I. By 1923 Jarrott was hopelessly addicted to barbituates, opium, and cocaine, and he remained a drug addict for the rest of his life. John Jarrott died in Bellevue Hospital, in New York City, on June 15, 1955. (Barbara Naomi Cohen-Stratyner, *Biographical Dictionary of Dance,* 1982.)

JAZZ. See ARMSTRONG, LOUIS

JEFFERS, JOHN ROBINSON. Robinson Jeffers was born in Pittsburgh, Pennsylvania, on January 10, 1887 into a deeply religious, Presbyterian home; during the 1920s, he was recognized as one of the most important playwrights and poets in the United States. His father was a minister, and Jeffers was raised in an atmosphere of moralistic Calvinism; his poetry and dramas reflected a strong sense that God had abandoned humanity, that only pessimism was possible given the plight of the world, and that man had no power to influence his own fate. Among Jeffers's most important works were *Tamar* (1924), *The Women at Point Sur* (1927), and *Medea* (1946). Robinson Jeffers died on January 20, 1962. (Martin Seymour-Smith, *Who's Who in Twentieth Century Literature,* 1976.)

JEWS. By the 1920s, the Jewish population of the United States had reached approximately 3,500,000 people. The first Jews to come to America were Sephardic immigrants who settled in Boston, New York, and Philadelphia during the colonial period. They were few in number—perhaps 2,500 people at the time of the American Revolution—and were accepted relatively well by the surrounding Protestants, especially by Puritan New Englanders who viewed them as an Old Testament community. During the nineteenth century, the American Jewish community expanded greatly with the immigration of 225,000 German Jews. Well-educated, anxious to assimilate, and loyal to the tradition of Reform Judaism, the German Jews also settled in the major American cities. The last great wave of Jewish immigration to the United States began in the 1880s and continued until the early 1920s. During that period, nearly 2,500,000 Jews came to the United States from Russia, Austria-Hungary, and Romania. Primarily Orthodox in their spiritual inclinations, they crowded into large ethnic ghettoes in the Northeast, especially in New York City.

The influx of Roman Catholics* from southern and eastern Europe, along with the immigration of several million Jews, precipitated a wave of anti-Catholicism and anti-Semitism in the United States during the 1920s. Groups such as the Ku Klux Klan* openly campaigned for immigration restriction and sometimes even violently intimidated Catholics and Jews. Various Jewish organizations, such as the Anti-Defamation League, began to campaign just as actively for civil rights for all Americans. In 1924, Congress responded, however, to nativist demands by passing the National Origins Act,* which strictly limited immigration from those areas of Europe from which most Jews had come. (Henry L. Feingold, *Zion in America: The Jewish Experience from Colonial Times to the Present,* 1974; James S. Olson, *The Ethnic Dimension in American History,* 1979.)

JOHNSON, HIRAM WARREN. Hiram Warren Johnson was born on September 2, 1866, in Sacramento, California. Grover Johnson, his father, an attorney who handled many cases for the Southern Pacific Railroad, which was the dominant force in California politics, was a conservative Republican who was elected to the state legislature in 1877 and to the United States Congress in 1894. Hiram attended public school in Sacramento and began reading law after three years at the University of California at Berkeley. In 1894 Hiram managed his father's congressional campaign, but, while working in the family law firm, he became estranged, both personally and politically, from his father. Hiram gained a reputation as a progressive Republican. In 1901 he supported the reform candidate for mayor of Sacramento, and in 1906 he worked to oust Abraham Ruef, the machine mayor of San Francisco. In 1910 Hiram Johnson ran for governor of California and won the election. He quickly established his reputation as a progressive by establishing a civil service system, regulating railroads and public utilities, enacting workmen's compensation, and obtaining an eight-hour day for women and children. He ran in 1912 as Theodore Roosevelt's vice-presidential running mate with the Bull Moose party. Though defeated, he was re-elected governor of California in 1914. Two years later, he won a seat in the United States Senate.

In the Senate, Johnson earned a reputation as a progressive in domestic affairs and an isolationist in foreign affairs. He supported a wide variety of social welfare, labor, and pro-farmer legislation, as well as the McNary-Haugen Bill* and federal development of Muscle Shoals.* He also intensely opposed American participation in the League of Nations.* In 1932, Johnson openly endorsed Franklin D. Roosevelt* for president, rejecting the candidacy of Republican Herbert Hoover.* He supported Roosevelt until the late 1930s, by which time Johnson thought the president was leading the country into another war. Johnson openly opposed naval expansion, conscription, and lend-lease. In July 1945, Johnson cast one of only two dissenting Senate votes against the charter of the

United Nations. He died on August 6, 1945. (Ronald L. Feinman, *Twilight of Progressivism: The Western Republican Senators and the New Deal*, 1981; George Mowry, *California Progressives*, 1951; *New York Times*, August 7, 1945.)

JOHNSON-REED IMMIGRATION ACT. See NATIONAL ORIGINS ACT of 1924

JOLSON, AL. Al Jolson was born Asa Yoelson on May 26, 1886, in Srednike Russia. He immigrated with his family to the United States, and, as a child he began to sing and dance soft-shoe in vaudevillian productions, much to the consternation of his Jewish parents. The first Broadway shows he appeared in were in Schubert Brothers productions at the Winter Garden Theater in New York, where he played in blackface as a servant to the principal characters. By 1913, although he was still playing the servant role, Jolson was a hit with the audiences, especially in the musical *Honeymoon Express*. The acting persona that he best projected on Broadway was that of the sentimental, devoted son, and his song "Mammy" became the symbol of that role. In 1927, Jolson came to national attention in the first commercially successful sound film, *The Jazz Singer*. He later starred in a number of films, including *The Singing Fool* (1929) and *Mammy* (1930). Jolson never learned to act because his audiences wanted to see him play Jolson, not anybody else. His voice and face became known to millions of Americans in the late 1920s and 1930s. Al Jolson had a desperate need to be loved and noticed, and those needs eventually destroyed three marriages. He died in San Francisco, California, on October 23, 1950. (Michael Freedland, *Jolson*, 1972.)

JONES, ROBERT TYRE, JR. Bobby Jones was born in Atlanta, Georgia, on March 17, 1902. He received a degree in mechanical engineering from the Georgia School of Technology in 1922, and then he earned a bachelor's degree from Harvard in 1924. After studying law at Emory University in 1926 and 1927, Jones was admitted to the Georgia bar in 1928, and he practiced law in Atlanta for the rest of his career. During the 1920s, however, Jones was known as the greatest golfer of his era, even though he played as an amateur. He won the United States Amateur Championship in 1924, 1925, 1927, 1928, and 1930; the British Amateur Championship in 1930; the United States National Open Championship in 1923, 1926, 1929, and 1930; and the British National Open Championship in 1926, 1927, and 1930. From his Atlanta base, Jones also became the father of the Master's Championship. Bobby Jones died on December 18, 1971. (Oscar Keeler, *The Bobby Jones Story*, 1953; *New York Times*, December 19, 1971.)

JONES, RUFUS MATTHEW. Rufus Jones was born on January 25, 1863, in South China, Maine. He graduated from Haverford College in 1885 and earned a master's degree there in 1886. After studying at the University of Heidelberg and the University of Pennsylvania between 1887 and 1895, Jones attended Harvard University and earned a master's degree there in 1901. He was a devout Quaker and an equally devout advocate of world peace. He played a leading role in the formation of the Americans Friends Service Committee in 1917 and became its first chairman. The Quaker organization was dedicated to peace, overseas relief, and alternative national service for conscientious objectors. Jones was chair of the American Friends Service Committee from 1917 to 1928 and again from 1935 until 1944. He worked closely with Herbert Hoover* in providing food for starving children in Germany in 1919 and 1920, and then he worked with the American Relief Administration in its famine relief program in the Soviet Union in 1922 and 1923. Jones also wrote widely during his career, specializing in themes of Christian mysticism; his works include *The Church's Debt to Heretics* (1924) and *New Studies in Mystical Religion* (1927). Rufus Jones died on June 16, 1948. (Elizabeth Gray Vining, *Friend of Life, the Biography of Rufus M. Jones,* 1958.)

JONES, WESLEY LIVSEY. Wesley L. Jones was born on October 9, 1863, in Bethany, Illinois. He graduated from Southern Illinois College in 1886, studied law privately, and was admitted to the bar in 1890. Jones moved to the Washington Territory to practice law and devoted himself as well to Republican politics. In 1898 he won a seat in Congress and served there until 1909, when he entered the United States Senate. He was re-elected to the Senate in 1914, 1920, and 1926. Jones earned a reputation as a moderate progressive, although he was very careful politically to maintain a middle-of-the-road position. He was, however, a strong advocate of women's suffrage and an uncompromising supporter of prohibition.* The Anti-Saloon League of America* and the Women's Christian Temperance Union put Jones on their temperance lecture circuit, and he campaigned for prohibition until the Eighteenth Amendment* was ratified. During the 1920s, Jones campaigned for vigorous enforcement of the Volstead Act,* and in 1929 he authored and secured passage of the Jones Act, which provided for a five-year jail term and a $10,000 fine for people violating the Volstead Act. The law was too harsh, however, and Jones became the object of intense criticism from the enemies of prohibition. He died on November 19, 1932. (Mark Edward Lender and James Kirby Martin, *Drinking in America: A History,* 1982; *New York Times,* November 20, 1932.)

K

KEATON, BUSTER. Buster Keaton was born Joseph Francis Keaton in Piqua, Kansas, on October 4, 1895, to a theatrical family. Harry Houdini gave him the name "Buster" in 1896 after the sixth-month-old Keaton fell down a flight of stairs without hurting himself. He joined his parents' vaudeville act in 1898, and they performed together as "The Three Keatons" until 1917. Keaton then met Roscoe "Fatty" Arbuckle* and joined the Comique Film Corporation making silent comedies. Between 1917 and 1919, he appeared in fifteen two-reel films, with time out for a stint in the army in 1918. By the 1920s, Keaton rivaled Charlie Chaplin* as a comic genius. Unlike Chaplin, Keaton had little to do with exploring moral ambiguities or exposing the dark, ironic side of life in his films. Keaton was more optimistic, confident, and naive. He made more two-reelers between 1920 and 1923, including *Daydreams* and *Cops,* and, between 1923 and 1929, Keaton made two feature films a year. *The General* and *Steamboat Bill* were completed during this period.

Keaton's problems began with the transition to sound films. His voice did not translate well into the new medium, and, as his popularity waned, his personal life deteriorated. For twenty years, he drank heavily while appearing in a series of situation comedy films as a straight man to Jimmy Durante. His career revived somewhat in 1950 when he appeared in Charlie Chaplin's *Limelight*. He stopped drinking altogether and appeared in a number of feature films before his death on February 1, 1966. (Tom Dardis, *Keaton: The Man Who Wouldn't Lie Down,* 1979; Buster Keaton, *My Wonderful World of Slapstick,* 1960; David Robinson, *Buster Keaton,* 1968.)

KEITH, MINOR COOPER. M. C. Keith was born on January 19, 1848, in Brooklyn, New York. He left school in 1864 and worked at various jobs until 1871 when he went to Costa Rica to help his brother build a railroad. When his brother died in 1874, Keith finished the project against enormous political, engineering, and financial odds, although the road from the Caribbean inland to San Jose was not operational until 1890. During the years he was building the railroad, Keith was also investing in banana plantations. In the 1890s, Keith also invested in banana plantations in Panama and Nicaragua. By 1899 Keith dominated the banana industry in Central America and was exporting huge volumes of bananas to the United States. That year, he merged his interests with the Boston Fruit Company to form the United Fruit Company. Keith then spent the rest of his life building railroads in Central America, developing banana plantations along the routes to make sure that United Fruit could ship its crops to market. In 1912 Keith established the International Railways of Central America, and he served as president of the company. When he died on June 14, 1929, Keith was the most well-known American in Central America. (Thomas McCann, *An American Company: The Tragedy of United Fruit,* 1976; *New York Times,* June 15, 1929.)

KELLEY, FLORENCE. Florence Kelley was born in Philadelphia, Pennsylvania, on September 12, 1859. She graduated from Cornell University in 1882, and, after being refused admission to graduate school at the University of Pennsylvania because she was a woman, Kelley went abroad to the University of Zurich. In Switzerland, she became acquainted with radical students and soon became an avid Socialist. When Kelley returned to the United States in 1886 she became a member of the Socialist Labor Party,* and she spent the next several years translating the works of Friedrich Engels and Karl Marx into English. Kelley eventually left the Socialist Labor Party because of theoretical differences with Daniel DeLeon over violence and revolution. In 1891 Kelley moved to Chicago and lived at Jane Addams's* Hull House, where she became active in reform politics.

In 1892 she went to work for the Illinois Bureau of Labor Statistics investigating working conditions in the garment industry. After campaigning actively on behalf of an end to child labor, limited working hours for women, and government regulation of sweatshop labor, Kelley was appointed chief factory inspector for Illinois by Governor John Peter Altgeld. She attended law school at night at Northwestern University and earned her degree in 1894. In 1899 Kelley returned to live in New York City and became general secretary of the National Consumers' League, a position she held for the rest of her life. In 1909 she was a founding member of the National Association for the Advancement of Colored People.* During the 1920s, Kelley continued her fight against child labor and also began to campaign for old age pensions, federal labor standards legislation, and women's rights. She died on February 17, 1932. (Dorothy Rose Blumberg, *Florence Kelley: The Making of a Social Pioneer,* 1966; Josephine Goldmark, *Impatient Crusader: Florence Kelley's Life Story,* 1953.)

KELLOGG-BRIAND PACT. An antiwar treaty, the Kellogg-Briand Pact was the culmination of the peace movement of the 1920s. The passion for peace after World War I became the preeminent theme in American foreign policy for two decades. The number of peace organizations, such as the Carnegie Endowment for International Peace,* had increased greatly. In 1923 publisher Edward Bok* sponsored a contest offering $100,000 for the best peace plan. Twenty-two thousand Americans, including such prominent people as William Jennings Bryan* and Franklin D. Roosevelt,* submitted ideas. The movement to outlaw war was launched by Simon Levinson, a wealthy Chicago lawyer. Levinson distributed his "Plan to Outlaw War" to politicians, peace organizations, and the public. One of his converts was James Shotwell,* a professor of history at Columbia University. In March 1927, Shotwell persuaded Aristide Briand, the French foreign minister, to support the idea. Brian saw an opportunity to tie the United States informally to the French system of alliances. A treaty outlawing war between the two countries was sent to President Calvin Coolidge* and Secretary of State Frank B. Kellogg* in June 1927.

Isolationist pressures in Congress, however, were too strong, and the treaty resembled an alliance; Kellogg therefore proposed a multilateral treaty outlawing war. Brian did not like the counterproposal, but France could not find a way to refuse. So, on August 27, 1928, fourteen nations met in Paris to sign the treaty. In the ensuing years, another forty-eight countries signed it. The treaty, which simply renounced war as an instrument of national policy, had no teeth and had to rely on the force of moral sanction to enforce its provisions. The United States signed the treaty with certain exceptions, particularly exempting the Monroe Doctrine and any self-defense issues. A prominent United States senator scoffed at the idea, claiming it would be as effective in preventing war "as a carpet would be to smother an earthquake." Still, the Kellogg-Briand Pact was popular with the American public and it was a concession to peace groups. Relying solely on the force of world moral opinion to enforce its provisions, the treaty became an institution of ridicule when World War II erupted. (L. Ethan Ellis, *Republican Foreign Policy, 1921–1933,* 1968; Robert H. Ferrell, *Peace in Their Time: The Origins of the Kellogg-Briand Pact,* 1952.)

KELLOGG, FRANK BILLINGS. Frank B. Kellogg was born in Potsdam, New York, on December 22, 1856. When he was still an infant, his parents moved the family to a farm in Minnesota. Kellogg had little formal schooling, but he read law privately and passed the bar exam in 1877. He practiced law for ten years and then moved to Minneapolis where he joined a large law firm. Kellogg stayed with the firm for the next twenty years and built up a national reputation in antitrust law. He was elected president of the American Bar Association in 1912, and in 1916 he won a seat as a Republican in the United States Senate. Kellogg was a moderate internationalist on foreign policy and wanted the United States to ratify the Treaty of Versailles* with mild reservations. Calvin Coolidge* appointed Kellogg ambassador to Great Britain in 1923, and he played a role in developing the Dawes Plan* of 1924. When Charles Evans Hughes* left the cabinet in 1925, Coolidge brought Kellogg home and named him secretary of state.

As secretary of state, Kellogg saw to it that the United States intervened in Nicaraguan affairs. The marines had been removed in 1925, but when revolution broke out shortly thereafter, Coolidge and Kellogg sent the marines back to supervise free elections. The Latin American countries did not view the intervention as justified, and Kellogg was roundly criticized. What Kellogg is most remembered for historically, however, is the Kellogg-Briand Pact,* an international agreement renouncing war as an instrument of national policy. Kellogg was awarded the Nobel Peace Prize for his efforts. He left the Department of State in 1929 and then served between 1930 and 1935 as an associate justice of the Permanent Court for International Justice. Frank Kellogg died on December 21, 1937. (L. Ethan Ellis, *Frank B. Kellogg and American Foreign Relations, 1925–1929,* 1961; Robert H. Ferrell, *Peace in Their Time: The Origins of the Kellogg-Briand Pact,* 1952.)

KELLOGG, PAUL UNDERWOOD. Paul Kellogg was born in Kalamazoo, Michigan, on September 30, 1879. After graduating from high school, Kellogg worked on the editorial staff of the *Kalamazoo Daily Telegraph,* but in 1901 he left Kalamazoo to attend Columbia University. In 1902 he went to work on the editorial staff of *Charities,* the journal of the Charity Organization Society. In 1907 and 1908, Kellogg led the research group that produced the famous Pittsburgh Survey, a six-volume series on social and economic life in Pittsburgh. An early model of sociological research, the survey called for a shorter work week, better housing, and worker's compensation programs. When he returned to New York City, Kellogg converted *Charities,* which had become *Charities and the Commons,* into the *Survey.* It quickly became the major publication in the emerging field of social work. Kellogg became editor-in-chief in 1912.

Kellogg used the *Survey* to promote improved housing, urban recreational facilities, urban renewal, social welfare legislation, regional planning, public health programs, and conservation. A gifted journalist and a dedicated social reformer, Kellogg was the major figure behind the *Survey* until it ceased publication in 1952. During those years, in addition to his work on the *Survey,* Kellogg served on the National Conference of Charities and Corrections, the Committee to Secure a Federal Commission on Occupational Standards, the Foreign Policy Association,* the National Federation of Settlements, the American Association of Social Workers, the National Conference on Social Welfare, and the Committee on Economic Security. Paul Kellogg died on November 1, 1958. (Clarke Chambers, *Paul Kellogg and the Survey: Voices for Social Welfare and Social Justice,* 1971.)

KELLOGG, WILL KEITH. Will K. Kellogg was born on April 7, 1860, in Battle Creek, Michigan. Kellogg left school when he was fourteen, and in 1899 he moved to Texas where he worked selling brooms. A devout Seventh Day Adventist and a vegetarian, Kellogg wanted to find some way of marketing grains and nuts. In 1895, along with his brother, he decided to try to sell wheat flakes as a breakfast food. When it proved to be too late for the wheat flakes industry, because Charles William Post had already cornered it, Kellogg turned his attention to corn flakes. In 1905 he established the Battle Creek Toasted Corn Flake Company. By advertising in *Ladies Home Journal* and using redeemable coupons, Kellogg built the company quickly, and by 1909 he was selling over one million cases of corn flakes a year. In 1921 he changed the name of the company to Kellogg Company, and during the 1920s Kellogg's Corn Flakes became one of the most recognizable consumer products in the country. Kellogg stepped down from active leadership of the company in 1939; he died on October 6, 1951. (*New York Times,* October 7, 1951; H. B. Powell, *The Original Has the Signature,* 1952.)

KELLY, ALVIN "SHIPWRECK." Alvin "Shipwreck" Kelly was born in New York City in 1901. He gained temporary notoriety in 1927 by sitting on top of a flagpole in Baltimore, Maryland, for twenty-three days and seven hours. Food and drink were hauled up to him by bucket, and other items were removed in the same way. Kelly's flagpole sitting was mimicked by dozens of others in 1927 and 1928. Historians looking back at the 1920s see a "hero culture" emerging, a new way of worshipping individualism in an increasingly industrial, urban, and bureaucratic society. Kelly's flagpole sitting was one example; another was Gertrude Ederle's swim across the English channel in 1926. Charles Lindbergh's* famous flight across the Atlantic in 1927 augmented the hero culture in a spectacular way. (Frederick Lewis Allen, *Only Yesterday: An Informal History of the 1920s,* 1931.)

KENT, FRANK RICHARDSON. Frank R. Kent, the famous conservative columnist during the 1920s and 1930s, was born in Baltimore, Maryland, on May 1, 1877, and educated in public and private schools. He went to work as a reporter for the *Baltimore Reporter* in 1898 and the next year he joined the staff of the *Baltimore Sun.* Kent was a political reporter for ten years and a Washington correspondent for the *Sun* for two years before being named managing editor of the paper in 1911. After serving as managing editor for ten years, Kent became the paper's London correspondent between 1922 and 1923. After returning to the United States, Kent became a syndicated political columnist whose articles regularly appeared in more than one hundred daily newspapers. Kent was the author of a number of books, including *The Story of Maryland Politics* (1911), *The Great Game of Politics* (1923), *History of the Democratic Party* (1925), and *Political Behavior* (1928). Kent's basic political philosophy was conservative, based on faith in local government rather than on federal bureaucracies, but he was by no means a slavish supporter of Republican politicians in the 1920s. During the New Deal of the 1930s, he did criticize the drift toward big government and the tendency to use relief jobs as patronage for building big-city political machines. Frank Kent died on April 14, 1958. (Eugene W. Goll, "Frank Kent's Opposition to Franklin D. Roosevelt and the New Deal," *Maryland Historical Magazine* 63 [June 1968], 158–71; *New York Times,* April 15, 1958.)

KENYON, WILLIAM SQUIRE. William S. Kenyon was born on June 10, 1869, in Elyria, Ohio. He studied at Iowa College, took law classes at Iowa State University, and was admitted to the bar in 1891. Kenyon opened a law practice in Fort Dodge, Iowa, that year, and in 1893 he became prosecutor for Webster County. He was appointed a district judge in Iowa in 1897 and served in that capacity until 1899. Kenyon was active in Republican politics and won a seat in the United States Senate in the election of 1910. A progressive Republican as well as a strong temperance advocate, he sponsored the Webb-Kenyon Act of 1913, which made it a crime to transport alcohol from a "wet"* state into a "dry"* state. Kenyon campaigned actively for the Eighteenth Amendment* to the Constitution, as well as for federal antitrust action and labor reform. He resigned from the Senate in 1922 to accept President Warren G. Harding's* appointment to the federal bench as a circuit court judge. As a judge, Kenyon voided the Teapot Dome* oil leases, and he served on the Wickersham Commission* which investigated enforcement of the Volstead Act.* Kenyon died on September 9, 1933. *(New York Times*, September 10, 1933.)

KERN, JEROME. Jerome Kern was born in New York City on January 27, 1885. Musical historians recognize Kern as the father of the modern musical comedy. Between 1912 and 1939, he wrote dozens of commissioned numbers, operettas, and revues. He became widely known for his *Miss 1917* and *Kitchy-Koo of 1920,* and he then achieved national fame for such musicals as *Sally* (1920), *Sunny* (1925), and *Show Boat* (1927). He carefully integrated social and ballroom dance with his operettas, and he was widely considered to be a genuine American musical talent. In the 1930s, Kern's works made it into films with the dancing ability of Fred Astaire* and Ginger Rogers. The number "Smoke Gets in Your Eyes," a duet for the film *Roberta* in 1935, was especially popular. Jerome Kern died in New York City on November 11, 1945. (Gerald Boardman, *Jerome Kern,* 1981; David Ewen, *The World of Jerome Kern,* 1960.)

KNIGHTS OF COLUMBUS. The Knights of Columbus was founded in 1882 by Father Michael J. McGivney. Its primary purpose was to provide a fraternal fellowship for Roman Catholic* men similar to that provided for Protestant men by the Masonic Lodges. Like immigrant aid associations, the Knights of Columbus also provided insurance to its members. By the 1920s, the Knights of Columbus was actively working to counter anti-Catholic propaganda, especially that issued by the Ku Klux Klan.* In 1922, the Knights of Columbus provided the financial support necessary to test a 1921 Oregon law outlawing parochial schools. The case, known as *Pierce* v. *Society of Sisters,* reached the Supreme Court in 1922, where the Oregon statute was declared unconstitutional. The Knights of Columbus also worked to repeal prohibition* and to stop the anti-Catholic bias built into various immigration restriction* legislation. (Christopher J. Kauffmann, *Faith and Fraternalism: The History of the Knights of Columbus, 1882–1982,* 1982.)

KNOX, PHILANDER CHASE. Philander C. Knox was born in Brownsville, Pennsylvania, on May 6, 1853. He graduated from Mount Union College in Ohio in 1872, and in 1875 he was admitted to the bar and began practicing law. Knox moved to Pittsburgh and became a leading corporate attorney. In 1901 President William McKinley named him attorney general of the United States. Knox won a seat in the United States Senate in 1904 and served there until 1909, when President William Howard Taft* named him secretary of state. While at the State Department, Knox aggressively promoted American business interests abroad; his zeal to promote capitalism abroad earned American foreign policy during his tenure the name ''Dollar Diplomacy''—the United States government placed its political and military might behind her corporate investments abroad. Knox also settled disputes with Great Britain over the Atlantic fisheries and helped negotiate a series of arbitration treaties. He left the State Department in 1913 and practiced law for four more years, but in 1916 he won a seat again in the United States Senate, where Knox earned a reputation as one of the ''irreconcilables''* who opposed American entry into the League of Nations* at all costs. Philander Knox died on October 12, 1921. (Samuel F. Bemis, *American Secretaries of State and Their Diplomacy,* 1929; *New York Times,* October 13, 1921.)

KNUDSEN, WILLIAM. William Knudsen was born on March 25, 1879, in Copenhagen, Denmark. He immigrated to the United States in 1900 after studying drafting and engineering in Denmark. Knudson worked in several machine tool factories before joining the John R. Keim Mills in Buffalo, New York, which manufactured crankcases and rear axle casings for the Ford Motor Company. In 1911 Ford Motor bought out the company. By 1913 Knudsen was in charge of designing assembly-line operations for all of Henry Ford's* plants, and by the time of World War I, Knudsen was recognized as the premier expert in the country on mass production in heavy industry. Because of a personality conflict, Ford fired Knudsen in 1921, and Knudsen went to General Motors, where Alfred P. Sloan put him in charge of Chevrolet Motors. Between 1924 and 1926, Knudsen redesigned Chevrolet. Chevrolet sales jumped from just under 73,000 in 1921 to more than 720,000 in 1926; in 1927, it outsold Henry Ford's Model T.* Knudsen became vice-president of General Motors in 1933 and president in 1937. When World War II broke out, Knudsen joined the army as a lieutenant general to serve as an adviser to the undersecretary of war. He retired from the army in 1945 and died on April 27, 1948. (Nathan Beasley, *Knudsen: A Biography,* 1947; John B. Rae, *American Automobile Manufacturers,* 1959.)

KRAFT, JAMES LEWIS. James Kraft was born on November 11, 1874, in Fort Erie, Ontario, Canada. He immigrated to the United States in 1903 after finishing high school and working for several years as a clerk, and he settled in Buffalo, New York. In 1904, Kraft moved to Chicago, where he immediately started his own business wholesaling cheese to small food stores, and then, with his two brothers, he founded J. L. Kraft Brothers and Company in 1909. At the time, cheese was difficult to market because it spoiled so quickly, but in 1916 Kraft managed to produce natural cheese through a pasteurization process which made it possible to package it in small amounts which could be stored for longer periods of time. Kraft then established his business on a firm footing by selling millions of four-ounce cans of cheese to the United States Army during World War I. Gross sales went from $2 million a year in 1917 to more than $28 million a year in 1926. Kraft cheese products were sold throughout the country, and per capita consumption of cheese grew dramatically. National Dairy Products bought out Kraft in 1930, but James Kraft continued to head the subsidiary. He died on February 16, 1953. (*National Cyclopedia of American Biography* 41 [1956], 240; *New York Times,* February 17, 1953.)

KRESGE, SEBASTIAN SPERING. Sebastian Kresge was born on July 31, 1867, in Bald Mount, Pennsylvania. After graduating from high school, Kresge attended business college in Poughkeepsie, New York, and he taught school for a while. In 1889 he moved to Scranton, Pennsylvania, where he worked as a clerk and bookkeeper. He left that job in 1892 and spent the next fifteen years as a travelling salesman hawking hardware. Some of his customers were small variety stores. In 1897 Kresge joined with one of his clients and opened two variety stores, one in Memphis and the other in Detroit. The partnership split up in 1899, and Kresge became sole owner of the store in Detroit. Kresge joined with his brother-in-law, Charles J. Wilson, and formed Kresge and Wilson, Company, which began opening new "5 and 10 cent" stores. By 1907 they had stores in eight northeastern cities. They incorporated as S. S. Kresge in 1907 with a total of eighty-five stores. Kresge served as president of the company, and he continued during World War I and the early 1920s to open new stores. When he retired in 1925, the chain had 600 stores in the United States and gross annual sales of nearly $160 million. Kresge spent the rest of his life involved in a number of charitable concerns; he died on October 18, 1966. (Godfrey M. Lebhar, *Chain Stores in America,* 1963; *New York Times,* October 19, 1966.)

KU KLUX KLAN. The Ku Klux Klan (KKK) was founded in 1866 in Pulaski, Tennessee, by several ex-Confederate soldiers concerned about the direction of Reconstruction. Nathan Bedford Forrest, a former Confederate general, emerged as the KKK leader in 1867. The Klan became a terrorist organization which used violence and intimidation to restore the white ruling class to power in southern state governments and to disfranchise black voters. After the removal of the last Union troops from the South in 1877, the Ku Klux Klan gradually disbanded.

In 1915 film producer D. W. Griffith* released *The Birth of a Nation,* a film which celebrated the efforts of the Ku Klux Klan during Reconstruction. The film inspired William Joseph Simmons to revive the Klan, a revival which began in 1915 with a large cross-burning ceremony on top of Stone Mountain, Georgia.

Because of the impact of immigration from southern and eastern Europe and the influx of large numbers of Roman Catholics* and Jews,* most of whom settled in northern cities, and because of the migration of southern blacks to northern cities during World War I, the Ku Klux Klan was able to establish a powerful base in the North during the 1920s. In 1925 the Ku Klux Klan reached a total membership of more than 5 million people, an extraordinary number given the fact that the total American population was just over 100 million people. At the Democratic National Convention of 1924, nearly 400 delegates were Klansmen who blocked the nomination of Governor Al Smith* of New York. The convention bitterly debated whether to condemn the Klan. In 1928, again, the Klan opposed Al Smith's candidacy for president because he was a Roman Catholic. Convinced that the southern and eastern Europeans pouring into the United States after 1900 were inferior to native white Protestants, the Klan also campaigned for the National Origins Act of 1924.* The Klan often resorted to violence and intimidation in its attacks on Catholics, Jews, and blacks.

Late in the 1920s, revelations of financial corruption in the Ku Klux Klan's national headquarters damaged its reputation among followers, as did news of sexual improprieties by several Klan leaders. In 1940 the Klan took a pro-Nazi stand and allied itself with the German-American Bund. When the United States went to war with Germany late in 1941, the Klan's friendship with the Nazis was the proverbial "kiss of death." The Klan was dissolved in 1944 when the Federal Bureau of Investigation began to investigate it as a subversive organization, but it was revived again during the civil rights movement of the 1960s and 1970s. (David M. Chalmers, *Hooded Americanism: Ku Klux Klan, 1865– 1965,* 1965; Kenneth T. Jackson, *The Ku Klux Klan in the City, 1915–1930,* 1967; Arnold S. Rice, *The Ku Klux Klan in American Politics,* 1962.)

L

LA FOLLETTE, ROBERT MARION. Robert M. La Follette was born on June 14, 1855, on a farm in Primrose Township, Wisconsin. He was raised on the farm and in a neighboring town after his father died and his mother remarried; in 1873, she moved the family to Madison so that Robert could attend the University of Wisconsin. He was an extremely popular student there, and he graduated in 1879 after teaching school part-time, editing the student newspaper, and becoming a Republican. La Follette took some classes at the law school in the fall of 1879, read law privately, and passed the state bar examination in 1880. That year, he was also elected district attorney for Dane County. Four years later, he was elected to Congress, but he was swept out in the Democratic resurgence of 1890.

During the early stages of his political career, La Follette was a fairly typical Republican, believing in high tariffs, business subsidies, and the self-made man culture of capitalism. At the local level, however, he avoided ethnoreligious disputes. He practiced law in the 1890s but turned to progressive insurgency during the depression of 1893 and the Populist agitation of 1895–1896. Riding the crest of progressivism, La Follette was elected governor of Wisconsin in 1900 and re-elected in 1902 and 1904. During his tenure in the state house, he pushed tariff reform, direct primary elections, conservation, and railroad property taxes. In 1905 the Wisconsin legislature elected La Follette to the United States Senate.

In the Senate, La Follette aligned himself with other progressive insurgents, particularly Albert Beveridge, Jonathan Dolliver, Moses Clapp, Joseph Bristow, and Albert Cummins. He promoted railroad regulation, tariff reform, pure food and drug legislation, honesty in government, and what became the "Wisconsin Idea"—the use of experts on government commissions to deal with economic and social problems. Interested in seeking the presidency, La Follette launched the National Progressive Republican League in 1911, but he then battled both Theodore Roosevelt and William Howard Taft* for the 1912 Republican nomination. When Taft won the nomination and Roosevelt bolted the party, La Follette retreated to the sidelines, endorsing no candidate but privately hoping for Woodrow Wilson's* victory. La Follette was re-elected to the Senate in 1910, 1916, and 1922.

His relationship with Woodrow Wilson soured over foreign policy. La Follette became convinced that American foreign policy was becoming more and more the tool of large corporations out to aggrandize their own interests, and he was also convinced that Wilson was leading the country down the road to war. In April 1917, La Follette voted against the declaration of war and similarly opposed conscription legislation and the Espionage Act. The war, in his mind, was oppressing civil liberties and enthroning big business as the most powerful force in the economy.

During the 1920s, La Follette continued his progressive crusade. He opposed the Transportation Act of 1920* as a windfall for railroads by legalizing pooling and exempting them from the antitrust laws, and he hated the Water Power Act of 1920* and the Mineral Leasing Act for giving private corporations access to public domain resources. La Follette was also an outspoken opponent of Secretary of the Treasury Andrew Mellon's* tax policies and a major figure in the Senate investigation of the Warren G. Harding* scandals. In the election of 1924,* La Follette won the presidential nomination of the Progressive Party,* but he won only 16.5 percent of the popular vote and only Wisconsin's electoral votes. Republican Calvin Coolidge* took 54 percent of the vote to Democrat John W. Davis's* 28.8 percent. The election drained La Follette, and he died of a heart attack on June 18, 1925. (David P. Thelan, *Robert M. La Follette and the Insurgent Spirit,* 1976; idem, *The Early Life of Robert M. La Follette, 1855–1884,* 1966.)

LA FOLLETTE, ROBERT MARION, JR. Born on February 6, 1895, in Madison, Wisconsin, Robert Marion La Follette, Jr., was raised in one of the most politically prominent families in America. His father, Robert M. La Follette,* served as a congressman, governor, and United States senator, and his name became synonymous with early twentieth-century progressivism—a political philosophy committed to good government, regulation of monopolies, conservation, and popular control of political institutions. Robert M. La Follette, Jr., who entered the Senate in 1925 and served until 1946, was a transitional figure linking progressivism with the urban liberalism of the New Deal. He entered the University of Wisconsin in 1913, but he never graduated; he quit school in 1916 and went to work as a clerk in his father's Senate office. He became his father's personal secretary in 1919; when Robert M. La Follette died in 1925, Robert, Jr., won the special election to fill the vacant seat.

He did not emerge from his father's shadow until after the stock market crash of 1929.* Until then, he had been preoccupied with the traditional issues of progressivism. After 1929 La Follette became an outspoken critic of Herbert Hoover,* despite their shared Republican party affiliation. He demanded direct relief for the unemployed, a massive expansion of public works, and national economic planning. He became recognized as one of the most liberal members of the Senate. During the New Deal, La Follette consistently charged Franklin D. Roosevelt* with not moving fast enough or far enough in restoring the mass purchasing power or protecting collective bargaining rights for labor. On virtually every labor, relief, public works, and taxation issue of the 1930s, La Follette tried to push the president farther to the left. Robert M. La Follette, Jr., was defeated for re-election in 1946 by Joseph McCarthy, and he committed suicide in February 24, 1953. (Jerold S. Auerbach, *Labor and Liberty: The La Follette Committee and the New Deal*, 1966; Patrick J. Maney, *"Young Bob" La Follette: A Biography of Robert M. La Follette, Jr., 1895–1953*, 1978.)

LA GUARDIA, FIORELLO HENRY. Fiorello La Guardia was born in New York City on December 11, 1882. He received his early education in Arizona, and he wrote articles for the *Phoenix Morning Courier*. La Guardia was a war correspondent for the *St. Louis Post-Dispatch* during the Spanish-American War. Master of seven languages, he had travelled widely as a young man, serving with the American consulate in Hungary and Austria between 1901 and 1906 and working as an interpreter at Ellis Island for incoming immigrants between 1907 and 1910 while studying for his law degree at New York University. A progressive Republican, La Guardia opposed Tammany Hall in New York City and served as deputy attorney general of New York between 1915 and 1917. La Guardia was elected to the 65th and 66th Congresses as a Republican, resigned in 1918 to serve with the army air corps during World War I, and upon his return was elected president of the Board of Aldermen of New York City. La Guardia was re-elected to Congress in 1922 and remained there until 1933, when he became mayor of New York City. In Congress during the 1920s, La Guardia doggedly opposed Republican Party* tax cuts on the rich and high tariffs and fought for legislation to protect the rights of labor. He coauthored the Norris–La Guardia Labor Relations Act of 1932,* which outlawed the indiscriminate use of court-ordered injunctions to break labor strikes. La Guardia served as mayor of New York until 1945. He died on September 20, 1947. (*New York Times,* September 21, 1947.)

LAMONT, THOMAS WILLIAM. Thomas William Lamont was born on September 30, 1870, near Albany, New York. He obtained his preparatory education at Phillips Exeter Academy, and he graduated from Harvard in 1892. He received a position as secretary to the Cushman Brothers, a food distributing firm; and, when they approached bankruptcy in 1898, they asked Lamont to reorganize and manage the business. His success was immediate, and in 1903 he joined the Bankers' Trust Company, becoming vice-president in 1905. In 1911 Lamont became a partner with J. P. Morgan and Company. During World War I, Lamont coordinated wartime finances among the Allied countries for President Woodrow Wilson,* helped assist with the Dawes* and Young plans* for payment of German reparations,* and served as President Herbert Hoover's* secretary of commerce. Lamont was a lifelong Republican, but he was also an internationalist, and throughout the 1920s he worked through economic diplomacy and international banking circles to try to create some global machinery for managing politics. His objective was a sincere, if naive, one. When the stock market crashed in 1929,* Lamont tried unsuccessfully to stabilize the market by establishing a banking consortium. He consistently believed that the depression was a crisis of confidence and would be short-lived. During the 1930s, Lamont was an open critic of the New Deal. When J. P. Morgan* died in 1943, Lamont succeeded him as chairman of the board. Thomas Lamont died on February 2, 1948. (*Dictionary of American Biography,* suppl. 4 [1974], 469–71; Michael J. Hogan, "Thomas W. Lamont and European Recovery: The Diplomacy of Privatism in a Corporate Age," in Kenneth Paul Jones, ed., *U.S. Diplomats in Europe, 1919–1941,* 1981; *New York Times,* February 3, 1948.)

LANDIS, KENESAW MOUNTAIN. Kenesaw Landis was born on November 20, 1866, in Millville, Ohio. His parents named him after Kennesaw Mountain in Georgia, where his father had been wounded during the Civil War. Landis was raised in Delphi, Indiana, and then in Logansport, Indiana. He was especially interested in baseball and bicycling. Landis graduated from the Union Law School in Chicago in 1891 and then opened his own practice. In 1893 Landis became the private secretary of Secretary of State Walter Q. Gresham, and in 1905 President Theodore Roosevelt appointed him to the federal bench—as judge for the northern district of Illinois. In 1907 Landis became a national figure when he fined John D. Rockefeller, Jr.,* and Standard Oil a total of $29 million in a freight rebate case. The Supreme Court overturned the decision, but Landis's reputation for toughness had been forever established.

In 1920, when the Black Sox scandal* tarnished the reputation of baseball,* the owners wanted to appoint a commissioner who would restore integrity to the game. When the owners offered him the job, Landis accepted on the condition that he be given absolute power in governing baseball. They agreed. He immediately banned for life the players involved in the Black Sox scandal and prohibited club owners from having any gambling interests, even horse racing. Landis ruled baseball with an iron hand for the next twenty-five years, suspending Babe Ruth* for the first forty games of the 1922 season for playing in a forbidden exhibition after the 1921 World Series. That Landis could make that decision stick against the popularity of Ruth and the power of Yankee club owner Jacob Ruppert clearly demonstrated his control over baseball. While still commissioner of baseball, Landis died on November 17, 1944. (*New York Times,* November 18, 1944; J. G. Taylor Spink, *Judge Landis and Twenty-Five Years of Baseball,* 1947.)

LANE, DENNIS. Dennis Lane was born in Chicago, Illinois, in 1881. A Roman Catholic, he had to leave school when he was ten years old and go to work in the Chicago stockyards. Soon after, he joined the Amalgamated Meat Cutters and Butcher Workmen of North America. Because of his active support of union organization, Lane was blacklisted by the major meat-packing companies, and he spent several years as a door-to-door salesman. In 1913 Lane was elected to the executive board of the Amalgamated Meat Cutters, and in 1917 he became head of the union and he dominated it for the next quarter of a century. Lane watched organization drives in the meat-cutting industry succeed during World War I but then languish during the depression of 1921–1922.* Unwisely, Lane called a butchers' strike in 1921, which management easily crushed, setting the union back a decade. After that, Lane simply worked to consolidate the union, and he campaigned on behalf of industrial unionism. During the 1930s, he refused to bolt the American Federation of Labor* (AFL) for the Congress of Industrial Organization, and the Amalgamated Meat Cutters remained firmly in the AFL. Dennis Lane died on August 10, 1942. (*The Butcher Workman,* September 1, 1942 [newspaper published by Amalgamated Meat Cutters and Butcher Workmen of North America]; David Brody, *The Butcher Workmen: A Study of Unionization,* 1964.)

LANE, FRANKLIN KNIGHT. Franklin Lane was born near Charlottetown, Prince Edward Island, Canada, on July 15, 1864. He spent two years at the University of California at Berkeley and then studied law part-time at the Hastings Law School in San Francisco. Lane was admitted to the bar in 1888. He immediately went into journalism, becoming the New York correspondent for the *San Francisco Chronicle.* In 1891 Lane became editor of the *Tacoma Daily News,* and he stayed with that job until 1895 when he opened a law office in San Francisco. Lane was elected city and county attorney for San Francisco in 1899 on the Democratic ticket. He was defeated in 1902 in his bid for the California governorship, despite the endorsement of the Non-Partisan League. In 1906, President Theodore Roosevelt appointed Lane to the Interstate Commerce Commission. President Woodrow Wilson* selected Lane as his secretary of the interior in 1913, and Lane remained in that position until his resignation in 1920. Franklin Lane died on May 18, 1921. (Franklin K. Lane, *The Letters of Franklin K. Lane,* 1922; *New York Times,* May 19, 1921.)

LANSING, ROBERT. Robert Lansing was born in Watertown, New York, on October 17, 1864. He graduated from Amherst in 1886, read law privately, and was admitted to the bar in 1889. Between 1889 and 1907, Lansing practiced in the family law firm in Watertown, and during those years he fulfilled a number of diplomatic assignments, including serving as counsel for the United States in the Bering Sea Arbitration of 1892–1893, counsel for the Chinese and Mexican delegations in Washington, D.C., and counsel for the United States Bering Sea Claims Commission in 1896–1897. He was a specialist in international law, and when William Jennings Bryan* resigned as secretary of state in 1915, Lansing was appointed by Woodrow Wilson* to fill the post. He remained in the Wilson cabinet until 1920. Lansing served as secretary of state during a critical period in American history, taking the State Department through World War I and the

Treaty of Versailles* negotiations. Lansing signed the Treaty of Versailles in 1919 and was strongly in favor of American entry into the League of Nations.* In 1920, Wilson asked Lansing to resign. Lansing had independently convened the cabinet in Wilson's absence during the president's long recuperation from a stroke, and Wilson felt the secretary of state had tried to usurp his authority. Lansing returned to his private law practice, and he died on October 30, 1928. (*New York Times,* October 31, 1928; Daniel Molloy Smith, *Robert Lansing and American Neutrality,* 1958.)

LATHROP, JULIA CLIFFORDE. Julia Lathrop was born on June 29, 1858, in Rockford, Illinois. Both of her parents were committed feminists, which meant suffragists in the mid-nineteenth century. Julia Lathrop graduated from Vassar College in 1880, and, after working as a secretary for ten years, she went to Hull House in Chicago and formed a lifelong friendship with Jane Addams.* In 1893 Governor John Peter Altgeld appointed Lathrop as the first woman on the State Board of Charities. She travelled widely throughout the state visiting poor houses, county farms, and charitable houses. She resigned from the board in 1901 when a new governor began to use the state charitable agencies as patronage appointments, but she rejoined it again in 1905 when Governor Charles Deneen took office. Lathrop also became a strong advocate of improved care for the mentally ill.

In 1912, when Congress established the Children's Bureau in the Department of Commerce and Labor, President William Howard Taft* appointed Lathrop to head the new agency. She was the first woman bureau chief in the history of the federal government. Because her funds were limited, Lathrop had to choose carefully the work of the Children's Bureau, and at first she concentrated on the problem of infant mortality and maternal mortality, both of which led to the Sheppard-Towner Act of 1921.* She then retired from public life but first ensured that President Warren G. Harding* would appoint Grace Abbott* in her place, guaranteeing that the Children's Bureau would not be politicized. Julia Lathrop died on April 15, 1932. (Jane Addams, *My Friend, Julia Lathrop,* 1935; Lela B. Costin, *Two Sisters for Social Justice: A Biography of Grace and Edith Abbott,* 1983; Jacqueline K. Parker and Edward M. Carpenter, "Julia Lathrop and the Children's Bureau: The Emergence of an Institution," *Social Service Review* 55 [March 1981], 60–77.)

LAUREL, STANLEY. Along with Oliver Hardy, Stan Laurel was one of the most popular comics in American history. Laurel was born Arthur Stanley Jefferson in Ulverston, England, on June 16, 1890; Hardy was born Norvell Hardy, Jr., on January 18, 1892, in Harlem, Georgia. Both men toured with theatrical and vaudeville troupes as young men and went into the movies in 1914. Laurel eventually made seventy films, most of them with Oliver Hardy as his comic partner, between 1926 and 1956. Unlike Charlie Chaplin,* Buster Keaton,* or W. C. Fields, Laurel and Hardy never portrayed or projected alienation in their comedy. Above all else, their films expressed middle-class, bourgeois values put to slapstick. At the same time, their comedy always culminated in accidents, destruction, Freudian slips, misunderstandings, and physical pain, providing an unconscious parody of middle-class materialism. Often, they were victims of avaricious, aggressive wives, who make constant demands that the two men were unable to meet. During the 1920s, and ever since, Laurel and Hardy were the first and probably the most popular comedy team in America. Oliver Hardy died on August 7, 1957, and Stan Laurel died on February 23, 1965. (Charles Barr, *Laurel and Hardy,* 1967; John McCabe, *Laurel and Hardy,* 1975.)

LAUSANNE CONFERENCE OF 1932. The Lausanne Conference of 1932, convened simultaneously with the World Disarmament Conference, brought the United States, Great Britain, and France together to deal with the continuing problem of German reparations,* issues formerly confronted by the Dawes Plan* and the Young Plan.* The global depression had all but eliminated Germany's ability to meet its reparations payments, and the allied nations were falling behind in their own debt payments to the United States. The conference agreed to cut German reparations by more than 90 percent, down to $715 million, contingent upon the allied nations continuing their own debt payments to the United States.

The Lausanne Agreement was never ratified because the United States was unwilling to yield on the debt question. The World War I debts, because of the depression, had become uncollectible. The allied debt was an issue in the election of 1932, and politicians stayed away from the controversy because most Americans viewed the debt as sacrosanct. In 1932 and 1933, all the allied nations except Finland defaulted on their debts. Germany, of course, did not make the required reparations payments to Great Britain and France. (Robert Ferrell, *American Diplomacy in the Great Depression,* 1957; Joan Hoff Wilson, *American Business and Foreign Policy, 1920–1933,* 1971.)

LEAGUE FOR INDEPENDENT POLITICAL ACTION. The League for Independent Political Action (LIPA) was founded in 1929 by a group of liberals and Socialists hoping to form a new, left-wing political party. The group included John Dewey,* Oswald Garrison Villard,* Paul H. Douglas, W.E.B. Du Bois,* and Reinhold Niebuhr. They were discouraged about the unwillingness of either the Republican Party* or the Democratic Party* to promote real social change and with the inability of the Socialist Party of America* to attract a following. The League for Independent Political Action hoped to bring all the left-wing factions into a new third party. The league demanded a massive federal public works program, nationalization of major industries, higher taxes on the rich and on corporations, a six-hour day for workers, workmen's compensation, a federal antilynching law, and disarmament. In the election of 1932,* the league endorsed Norman Thomas,* the presidential candidate of the Socialist Party. In the election, two LIPA members won elections: Elbert Thomas of Utah won a seat in the United States Senate, and Marion Zionchek of Washington won a seat in the House of Representatives. The coming of the New Deal, however, stole the LIPA's thunder. By 1936, with the New Deal shifting considerably to the left, many of the original LIPA demands had been achieved. When Franklin D. Roosevelt* was re-elected in the 1936 landslide, the League for Independent Political Action dissolved. (Paul H. Douglas, *The Coming of a New Party,* 1932; Donald R. McCoy, *Angry Voices, Left-of-Center Politics in the New Deal Era,* 1958.)

LEAGUE OF NATIONS. The League of Nations, established as part of the Treaty of Versailles* in 1919, formally went into operation on January 10, 1920. Between that first meeting in 1920 and its last meeting on December 14, 1939, the League of Nations enjoyed the membership of sixty-three countries, with the notable exception of the United States. Because of strong isolationist sentiment in the Senate and the unwillingness of President Woodrow Wilson* to compromise and allow the insertion of various reservations, the Treaty of Versailles was never ratified. Consequently, the league focused its attention primarily on European affairs. The league had an assembly composed of all member nations and an executive council of several permanent and nonpermanent nations. Included in the League of Nations were such auxiliary bodies as the World Court,* the Permanent Court of International Justice, and the International Labor Organization.* During the 1930s, the League of Nations was totally helpless in stopping Japanese aggression in East Asia, German aggression in Europe, and Italian aggression in North Africa. The League formally dissolved on April 18, 1946. (F. P. Walters, *A History of the League of Nations,* 1952.)

LEAGUE OF WOMEN VOTERS. In 1920 the National American Woman Suffrage Association* held its last convention. With the Nineteenth Amendment* to the Constitution ratified, the organization had achieved its purposes, so it dissolved and launched a new group—the League of Women Voters. The primary purpose of the new league was to serve as a nonpartisan organization dedicated to increasing female participation in politics. Between 1920 and 1947, the league's honorary national president was Carrie Chapman Catt.* The first president was Maud Wood Park. Throughout the 1920s, on the national and local levels, the League of Women Voters worked to improve election honesty and integrity in the United States and to increase the number of women active in politics. (Mary Gray Peck, *Carrie Chapman Catt,* 1944.)

LEAGUE TO ENFORCE PEACE. The League to Enforce Peace was founded in 1915 by Hamilton Holt and members of the New York Peace Society. Former president William Howard Taft* served as its first president. The main purpose of the league was to bring about creation of an international organization capable of collective security efforts in order to maintain world peace. When the Treaty of Versailles* contained provisions for the League of Nations,* the members of the League to Enforce Peace felt they had fulfilled their objectives, but they were bitterly disappointed when the United States refused to join the new international organization. The League to Enforce Peace quickly broke apart and ceased to function after 1920. (Ruhl J. Bartlett, *The League to Enforce Peace,* 1944; Warren F. Kuehl, *Seeking World Order: The United States and International Organization to 1920,* 1969.)

LEE, IVY LEDBETTER. Ivy Ledbetter Lee was born on July 16, 1877, in Cedartown, Georgia. He graduated from Princeton in 1898 and then attended Harvard Law School for a year before taking a job as a reporter for the *Morning Journal* in New York City. He studied English at Columbia University until 1903, supporting himself by working for the *Morning Journal* as well as the *New York Times* and the *New York World.* In 1903 Lee became a press agent for Seth Low, who was running for mayor of New York City, and after the election Lee established his own public relations firm. The age of national advertising was just appearing in the United States, and Lee found his niche in the public relations side of the field. By 1904 he was representing the Democratic National Committee as well as several large corporations. His real break came in 1915 when the Rockefeller family hired him to contain the adverse publicity coming from the Ludlow labor massacre in Colorado. Lee's modus operandi in such circumstances was to have company leaders simply tell the truth because the public would find it out in the long run anyway. The strategy worked. The Rockefellers opened their financial books concerning the Colorado mining operations to journalists, explained their point of view, and in the end managed to contain the adverse publicity. After that, Lee became a public relations adviser to the country's most prominent people, including Charles Schwab, Walter Chrysler,* the Rockefellers, Harry F. Guggenheim, and Charles Lindbergh,* as well as dozens of large corporations. During the 1920s, Lee was widely recognized as the "father of public relations." He died on November 9, 1934. (Eric F. Goldman, *Two-Way Street: The Emergence of the Public Relations Counsel,* 1948; Ray E. Hiebert, *Courtier to the Crowd,* 1966; *New York Times,* November 10, 1934.)

LEE, WILLIAM GRANVILLE. William G. Lee was born in La Prairie, Illinois, on November 29, 1859. He finished grammar school before going to work as a carpenter, and, in 1879, Lee got a job as a brakeman with the Atchison, Topeka, and Santa Fe Railroad. Subsequently, he worked for the Wabash Railroad and the Missouri Pacific. Lee joined the Brotherhood of Railroad Trainmen (BRT) in 1890 and then went to work as a brakeman and freight conductor for the Union Pacific. He established a branch of the BRT in Kansas City, Missouri, in 1892, and in 1895 he was elected vice grand master of the national BRT. In 1909 Lee became president of the Brotherhood of Railroad Trainmen, a position he held until 1928. A Republican, Lee endorsed his party's candidates in presidential elections, and it was through his efforts that the union finally achieved the eight-hour day, but not before he called a nationwide strike in 1917. In the election of 1924,* Lee broke with other railroad labor leaders and refused to endorse the Progressive Party* candidacy of Robert M. La Follette.* William G. Lee died on November 2, 1929. (*New York Times,* November 3, 1929; Joel Seidman, *The Brotherhood of Railroad Trainmen: The Internal Political Life of a National Union,* 1962.)

LEGGE, ALEXANDER. Alexander Legge was born on July 13, 1866, in Dane County, Wisconsin. His family moved to a ranch in Nebraska in 1876, and in 1883 Legge quit school and found a job as a cowboy in Wyoming. In 1891, Legge became a bill collecter for the McCormick Harvesting Machine Company, and he proved very successful at it. By 1898 he was branch manager of the McCormick office in Council Bluffs, Iowa. He went to corporate headquarters in 1899, and in 1902, when International Harvester purchased the company, Legge became sales manager for the new company. Legge then rose through the corporate hierarchy of International Harvester, becoming senior vice-president of the company in 1918. During World War I, Legge was an assistant to Bernard Baruch* on the War Industries Board, and in 1918 and 1919 he helped draft the economic sections of the Treaty of Versailles* for Woodrow Wilson.* Legge returned to International Harvester in 1919 and in 1922 was named president of the company. Under Legge's direction, International Harvester survived the farm depression of the 1920s and staved off a major government antitrust suit. President Herbert Hoover* chose Legge to serve as chairman of the Federal Farm Board* in 1929. Created by the Agricultural Marketing Act of 1929,* the purpose of the Federal Farm Board was to encourage the formation of marketing cooperatives, establish commodity stabilization corporations to deal with farm surpluses, and make loans to farmers to assist them in marketing their crops. Alexander Legge died on December 3, 1933. (Robert D. Cuff, *The War Industries Board,* 1973; *New York Times,* December 4, 1933.)

LEOPOLD AND LOEB CASE. See LOEB-LEOPOLD CASE

LEVERMORE, CHARLES HERBERT. Charles H. Levermore was born in Mansfield, Connecticut, on October 15, 1856. He graduated from Yale in 1879 and earned a Ph.D. in history at Johns Hopkins in 1886. Levermore taught history at the University of California at Berkeley and at the Massachusetts Institute of Technology until 1893, when he moved to Brooklyn to serve as principal of the Adelphi Academy and, between 1896 and 1912, as president of Adelphi College. In 1914 Levermore abandoned academe to devote his life to a quest for world peace. Until his death on October 20, 1927, Levermore was one of the country's most visible peace advocates, urging the United States to join the World Court* and to actively engage in constructive, international efforts to prevent war. (*Dictionary of American Biography* 6 [1933], 199–200; *New York Times,* October 22, 1927.)

LEVINSON, SALMON OLIVER. Salmon O. Levinson was born in Nobles-ville, Indiana, on December 29, 1865. He graduated from Yale in 1888 and then earned a law degree at the Chicago College of Law in 1891. Levinson practiced law in Chicago, but, shortly before World War I, he left his legal practice to campaign full-time on behalf of world peace, especially to try to implement an international agreement to outlaw war. Levinson tried to get a prohibition against war written into the covenant of the League of Nations,* and when he failed he became a bitter opponent of the Treaty of Versailles.* He organized the American Committee for the Outlawry of War in 1922 and worked diligently to achieve his goal between 1922 and 1927. Levinson became a strong supporter of what became the Kellogg-Briand Pact* of 1928. Levinson condemned the military aggression that became so common in the 1930s. He died on February 2, 1941. (Robert Ferrell, *Peace in Their Time: The Origins of the Kellogg-Briand Pact,* 1952; John E. Stoner, *S. O. Levinson and the Pact of Paris,* 1943.)

LEWIS, HARRY SINCLAIR. Sinclair Lewis was born in Sauk Centre, Min-nesota, on February 7, 1885. He graduated from Yale in 1908, but only after spending some time in one of Upton Sinclair's socialist Communities and trav-elling in Latin America, especially Panama, where he watched some of the construction of the Panama Canal. Lewis tried his hand at journalism, working for the *Courier* in Waterloo, Iowa, the *San Francisco Bulletin,* the Associated Press, and *Adventure* magazine, between 1908 and 1914. Lewis's writing first came to the attention of a broad audience when his short stories began to appear in *Saturday Evening Post* in 1915. In 1920, Lewis published his first major novel, *Main Street,* which sarcastically described the ''virtues'' of small-town life in the United States. In 1922 Lewis wrote *Babbitt,* for which he won the Nobel Prize for Literature in 1930. *Babbitt* added a new adjective to the language of the 1920s, and ''Babbittry''* became synonymous with materialism, con-formity, and middle-class complacency. During his literary career, Lewis wrote a total of twenty-three novels, including *Arrowsmith,* (1925), *Elmer Gantry* (1927), *Dodsworth* (1929), and *It Can't Happen Here* (1935). Sinclair Lewis died in Rome, Italy, on January 10, 1951. (Mark Schorer, *Sinclair Lewis: An American Life,* 1961.)

LEWIS, JOHN LLEWELLYN. John L. Lewis was born in Lucas, Iowa, on February 12, 1880. His father was a coal miner, and in 1896 Lewis went into the mines himself, digging coal, lead, and silver in a variety of western mines. In 1909 he was elected president of the Panama, Illinois, local of the United Mine Workers (UMW) union. Between 1909 and 1920, Lewis held a number of important union positions, including chief statistician, business manager of the *United Mine Workers Journal,* and UMW vice-president. In 1920 Lewis became international president of the United Mine Workers of America. The decade was a difficult time for the union. Between 1920 and 1933, UMW membership dropped from more than 500,000 to less than 75,000, with overproduction in the industry responsible for falling prices, declining wages, and serious unemployment. Lewis was a ruthless leader, crushing all opposition and centralizing union control in the headquarters office. During the 1930s, Lewis rallied labor support for the New Deal. He supported the National Industrial Recovery Act of 1933 and saw to it that, within a few months of its passage, more than 90 percent of American coal miners were in the United Mine Workers Union. In 1935 Lewis established the Committee for Industrial Organization (CIO) within the American Federation of Labor* to organize mass-production industrial workers. In 1936 Lewis became the first president of the CIO. Although he was a Republican, Lewis endorsed the re-election of Franklin D. Roosevelt* in 1936 and saw to it that the CIO contributed $500,000 to the campaign. In the election of 1940, disillusioned with Roosevelt's leadership, Lewis returned to the Republican fold and endorsed GOP candidate Wendell Willkie. John L. Lewis remained at the helm of the United Mine Workers until his retirement in 1960. He died on June 11, 1969. (Melvyn Dubofsky and Warren Van Tine, *John L. Lewis: A Biography,* 1977; Charles K. McFarland, *Roosevelt, Lewis, and the New Deal,* 1970.)

LIBBY, FREDERICK JOSEPH. Frederick Libby was born on November 24, 1874, in Richmond, Maine. He graduated from Bowdoin College in 1894, studied at the universities of Berlin, Heidelberg, Marburg, and Oxford, and earned a divinity degree from the Andover Theological Seminary in 1902. Libby was a minister for the Congregational Church in Maine between 1905 and 1911, taught at Phillips Exeter Academy from 1912 to 1915, worked with the American Friends Service Committee during the war years, and then returned to Phillips Exeter in 1919. Libby worked for the American Friends Service Committee again in 1920 and 1921, and in 1921 he founded the National Council for Prevention of War, an organization he headed for the next half century. Libby had strong Republican leanings and supported the Washington Naval Conference* of 1921–1922, the Kellogg-Briand Pact,* the World Court,* membership in the League of Nations* (with reservations on Article X*), and the neutrality acts of the 1930s. He endorsed the Stimson Doctrine* when Japan invaded Manchuria in 1931. The National Council for Prevention of War reached its peak of influence in the mid-1930s and then declined as Nazi and Japanese aggression became more blatant. During World War II, Libby opposed the idea of unconditional surrender, blamed Franklin D. Roosevelt* for precipitating the attack on Pearl Harbor, and called for creation of a United Nations. Libby remained executive secretary of the National Council for Prevention of War until his death on June 26, 1970. (Peter Marabell, ''Frederick Libby and the American Peace Movement, 1921–1941,'' Ph.D. dissertation, Michigan State University, 1975.)

LIBERAL PARTY. The Liberal Party was founded in 1932 by Socialist Frank E. Webb, who thought socialism was the only answer to the economic problems brought on by the Great Depression. The Liberal Party ran a presidential slate in the election of 1932.* William H. Harvey of Arkansas, the old-line Populist who had written *Coin's Financial School* in 1894, was nominated for president and Frank F. Hemenway for vice-president. Calling for nationalization of all industry, they won only 53, 199 votes and disbanded after Franklin D. Roosevelt* was inaugurated. (Donald R. McCoy, *Angry Voices, Left-of-Center Politics in the New Deal Era,* 1971.)

LIFE-SAVERS. See NOBLE, EDWARD JOHN

LINDBERGH, CHARLES. Charles Lindbergh was born on February 4, 1902, in Detroit, Michigan. He grew up in Little Falls, Minnesota, where his father was an isolationist congressman. Lindbergh attended the University of Wisconsin between 1920 and 1922, but he left to serve as a barnstorming and airmail pilot. He came to the attention of the world on May 20, 1927, when he flew a single-engine airplane, *The Spirit of St. Louis* from New York to Paris. His success in making the solo flight across the Atlantic made him a global hero. In the United States, Lindbergh's feat struck an extraordinarily responsive chord, a great act of individual courage in an age of urbanization, industrialization, and bureaucratization. In 1930, Lindbergh married Anne Spencer Morrow, the daughter of banker and diplomat Dwight Morrow.*

Lindbergh's fame soon came to haunt him. In 1932, in what became one of the most widely publicized crimes and trials of the twentieth century, Charles and Anne's son was kidnapped and murdered. Bruno Hauptmann* was arrested, convicted, and executed for the crime, but the atmosphere of the judicial process was almost circus-like. The Lindberghs never really emotionally overcame the death of their little boy. Between 1935 and 1939, they lived in seclusion in Europe; when World War II broke out, Lindbergh took an isolationist stand, even becoming a member of the America First Committee. He came under intense criticism in 1941 when he accused the Jews* of trying to bring the United States into the war. After Japan bombed Pearl Harbor, however, Lindbergh supported the war effort. After the war, Lindbergh served as a director of Pan American Airways and worked in various wildlife preservation causes. He died on August 26, 1974. (Wayne S. Cole, *Charles A. Lindbergh and the Battle against American Intervention in World War II,* 1974; *New York Times,* August 27, 1974.)

"LINDY HOP." The "Lindy Hop" was a popular dance of the 1920s. Like the "Charleston,"* it came to white audiences by way of migrating southern blacks settling in northern cities during World War I and the 1920s. The "Lindy Hop" was popularized at the Savoy Ballroom in Harlem. It was characterized by shimmying hip movements, strutting, shuffling steps, head shaking, and undulating body movements. Also like the "Charleston," the "Lindy Hop" became a symbol of the cultural rebellion against Victorian restraints which occurred in the United States during the 1920s. (Lynne Fauley Emery, *Black Dance in the United States from 1619 to 1970,* 1972.)

LIPPMANN, WALTER. Walter Lippmann was born on September 23, 1889, in New York City. He graduated from Harvard in 1909 and began a career in journalism. In 1910 he worked as a reporter for the *Boston Common,* and between 1910 and 1912 Lippmann was an assistant to Lincoln Steffans at *Everybody's Magazine.* Lippmann joined the *New Republic* as associate editor in 1912 and remained there until 1917. During World War I, Lippmann strongly advocated American entry into the conflict as a means of saving Anglo democracy and guaranteeing a just peace in Europe. In 1917 and 1918, Lippmann was a member of the Inquiry, a group which helped draft Woodrow Wilson's* Fourteen Points* peace proposal for the conference at Versailles. Early in his political career, Lippmann was a Socialist, but, after World War I, he gradually became more conservative. He joined the editorial staff of the *New York World* in 1922 and at the same time adopted his lifelong crusade for a more peaceful world. Lippmann was disillusioned by the war and the emergence of fascism in the 1920s. He had little faith in the League of Nations,* believing instead that balanced power politics was the only realistic way of preserving peace. Lippmann did take comfort in the naval arms reductions of the 1920s but thought little of the Kellogg-Briand Pact.* In 1923, he joined the Republican *New York Herald Tribune,* where he remained for the rest of his career. Lippmann's syndicated column began in 1931. During the 1930s, Lippmann was an intelligent but cautious internationalist who ultimately advocated American intervention when Nazi aggression became so blatant. After the war, Lippmann called on the United States to recognize the Soviet spheres of influence in Eastern Europe and warned the United States against intervention in Southeast Asia. Walter Lippmann died on December 14, 1974. (Marquis Childs and James Reston, *Walter Lippmann and His Times,* 1959; Ronald Steele, *Walter Lippmann and the American Century,* 1980.)

"LITTLE ORPHAN ANNIE." "Little Orphan Annie" was one of the most popular comic strips and juvenile radio* shows of the 1920s and 1930s. The comic strip, created and written by Harold Gray, came to radio in April 1931 and was the forerunner of the children's serials format. The radio program survived until 1943 and the comic strip into the 1980s. (John Dunning, *Tune in Yesterday: The Ultimate Encyclopedia of Old-Time Radio, 1925–1976,* 1976.)

LOCARNO TREATY. The Locarno Treaty of 1925 was designed to enhance French security. Ever since the end of World War I, France had been preoccupied with fears of a German military revival, and the Treaty of Locarno guaranteed the existing borders between France and Germany and Belgium and Germany; established arbitration treaties between Germany and France, Belgium, Czechoslovakia, and Poland; and provided a treaty of mutual guarantee between France, Czechoslovakia, and Poland. The involved nations signed the treaty on December 1, 1925. The United States regarded the Locarno Treaty as a symbol of European stability, hopefully enabling Europeans to settle their own disputes without violence and without involving the United States. As a symbol of European hope for the future, the Treaty of Locarno also provided for German entry into the League of Nations* in 1926. Ten years later, Adolf Hitler repudiated the treaty and reoccupied the Rhineland. (E. H. Carr, *International Relations between the Two World Wars, 1919–1939*, 1947; Gordon Craig and Felix Gilbert, eds., *The Diplomats, 1919–1939*, vol. 1, 1965.)

LODGE, HENRY CABOT. Henry Cabot Lodge was born on May 12, 1850, in Boston, Massachusetts. He graduated from Harvard in 1871, earned a law degree there in 1874, and then received a Ph.D. in 1876. After working for the *North American Record* between 1873 and 1878 and teaching at Harvard between 1876 and 1889, Lodge began his political career as a Republican state legislator. He served in the Massachusetts legislature between 1880 and 1883 and then won a seat in the United States House of Representatives, where he served between 1887 and 1893. In 1892, Lodge was elected to the United States Senate. He remained there for the rest of his life.

In the Senate, Lodge concentrated his energies on foreign policy questions. He drafted the Philippine Organic Act, supervised ratification of the second Hay-Pauncefote Treaty in 1901, and was a member of the Alaska Boundary Tribunal in 1903. Lodge was personally close to President Theodore Roosevelt. During the later stages of his career, Lodge became known as an isolationist, primarily because of his opposition to Woodrow Wilson,* the Treaty of Versailles,* and the League of Nations.* As chairman of the Senate Foreign Relations Committee between 1919 and 1924, Lodge kept the United States out of the League of Nations, primarily because he was convinced that membership would limit American foreign policy alternatives. During the early 1920s, Lodge was a delegate to the Washington Naval Conference,* supported the Thomson-Urrutia Treaty of 1921* giving Colombia $25 million in payment for its Panama claims, and consistently fought all attempts to get the United States into the World Court.* Henry Cabot Lodge died on November 9, 1924. (John Garraty, *Henry Cabot Lodge*, 1953.)

LOEB-LEOPOLD CASE. On May 21, 1924, Bobby Franks, a fourteen-year-old Chicago boy, was found murdered. Police found a pair of eyeglasses near Franks's body and traced them to Nathan Leopold, a nineteen-year-old graduate of the University of Chicago and the son of a millionaire transport executive. Leopold claimed to have spent the day with Richard Loeb, an eighteen-year-old graduate of the University of Michigan and the son of a Sears, Roebuck executive. When police also traced a ransom note to Leopold's Underwood typewriter, Loeb confessed that they had murdered Franks for the "fun of it," just to see if they could commit a perfect crime.

The 1924 trial was a national spectacle. The Loeb and Leopold families retained Clarence Darrow* for the defense, and the state of Illinois asked for the death penalty. Darrow offered a unique defense: The two men had killed

Bobby Franks, but they were mentally ill. Leopold, he claimed, was a manic depressive paranoiac and Loeb, a dangerous schizophrenic. Emotionally, they were both children living in a fantasy world. Darrow prevailed when the jury found them both guilty and sentenced each to life plus ninety-nine years in prison, avoiding the death penalty. Richard Loeb was stabbed to death by a fellow inmate on January 28, 1936, at the Illinois State Penitentiary. Nathan Leopold died of a heart attack on August 30, 1971, in San Juan, Puerto Rico. He was paroled in 1958 and then worked at a mission in Puerto Rico for a church. (Paul Sann, *The Lawless Decade,* 1957.)

LOEW, MARCUS. Marcus Loew was born May 7, 1870, in New York City. Because of poverty, he left school when he was ten years old and went to work for a firm which colored maps. Loew tried his hand in the fur business and went bankrupt when he was a young man, but by 1900 he had reached prosperity through timely investments in New York apartment houses. In 1903 he joined with Adolph Zukor and David Warfield in establishing the Automatic Vaudeville Company, which ran the penny arcades and nickelodeons so popular in New York. In 1904 he formed Loew's Enterprises to set up nickelodeons outside the city. He was joined in the enterprise by William Fox.* Nickelodeons were small theaters, usually converted stores or shops, in which films and vaudeville acts were presented. The primary clientele of the nickelodeons comprised poor immigrants in the major cities. By 1915, Loew was trying to attract more well-to-do, middle-class audiences, so he began to purchase much larger, more luxurious theaters and to present handsomely produced films with elaborate plots. He was a success. By 1919 Loew owned more than one hundred theaters. During the 1920s, the trend in the movie industry was for vertical integration, and Loew realized he would need movie production facilities if he was going to guarantee a constant supply of new films for his theaters to show. So, in 1920, he purchased Metro Films, a bankrupt production company, and, in 1924, Loew purchased independent film production companies from Samuel Goldwyn and Louis B. Meyer. Metro-Goldwyn-Meyer immediately became a corporate giant in the film industry. Marcus Loew died on September 5, 1927. (*New York Times,* September 6, 1927; Leo C. Rosten, *Hollywood,* 1941; Robert Sklar, *Movie-Made America,* 1975.)

LONDON, MEYER. Meyer London was born in Suwalki, Russia, on December 29, 1871. He immigrated with his family to the United States in 1891, and they settled in New York City, where London studied law at night and passed the bar examination in 1898. He joined the Socialist Labor Party* in 1896 but soon left the party because of philosophical differences with chief Daniel De Leon, whom London accused of being too radical and too violent. In 1901 London was a founding member of the Socialist Party of America.* For nearly thirty years, London served as legal counsel to the Amalgamated Clothing Workers. He won a seat in Congress as a Socialist in 1914 and was re-elected in 1916.

London lost his seat in the election of 1918* because of his vote against the declaration of war against Germany in 1917. He was re-elected in 1920 but defeated in 1922. During his congressional career, London earned a reputation as a vigorous advocate of a federal antilynching bill, old age pensions, national health insurance, and an end to child labor. He died on June 6, 1926. (Melech Epstein, *Profiles of Eleven,* 1965; *New York Times,* June 7, 1926.)

LONDON NAVAL CONFERENCE OF 1930. At the instigation of President Herbert Hoover* and British Prime Minister Ramsey MacDonald, delegations from the United States, Great Britain, France, Italy, and Japan met in London in 1930 to discuss naval arms limitations. Hoover selected Secretary of State Henry Stimson* to head the American delegation, and he was accompanied by Senators Joseph T. Robinson* and David A. Reed,* Charles G. Dawes,* Charles F. Adams,* and Hugh S. Gibson.* Italy did not stay at the conference because of her traditional enmity toward France, and France insisted on new anti-German security measures. When the United States and Great Britain refused to go along with the measures, France withdrew from the conference, making it a three-way conference. The conference agreed to alter modestly the tonnage limitation of the Washington Naval conference* from 5:5:3 to 10:10:7, which gave Japan a slightly higher cruiser ratio. The Japanese also got parity with the United States and Great Britain in destroyers and submarines. The conferees agreed to extend the capital ship holiday to 1936; granted permission for the United States to exceed its ratio if the other countries did so as well; and limited the 10:10:7 ratio to 1936. The Senate ratified the treaty on July 21, 1930, by a vote of 58 to 9. (Robert H. Ferrell, *American Diplomacy in the Great Depression: Hoover-Stimson Foreign Policy, 1929–1933,* 1957.)

LONDON NAVAL TREATY. See LONDON NAVAL CONFERENCE OF 1930

LONGWORTH, NICHOLAS. Nicholas Longworth was born on November 5, 1869, in Cincinnati, Ohio. He graduated from Harvard in 1891, spent a year at the Harvard Law School, and then earned a law degree from the Cincinnati Law School in 1894. Longworth opened a private law practice and quickly became involved in state Republican politics. He served in the state legislature between 1899 and 1903, and, in the election of 1902, Longworth was elected to Congress. His politics were conservative and predictable. In the election of 1912, he lost his seat because of the split in Republican ranks between the regulars and the Bull Moose progressives, but he regained the seat in 1914 and kept it until his death on April 9, 1931. Longworth served as speaker of the house between 1925 and 1931, where he presided over the business politics of the Calvin Coolidge* and Herbert Hoover* administrations. *(Who Was Who in America,* I [1943], 744.)

LOST GENERATION. The term "lost generation" was coined by critic Gertrude Stein to describe the young intellectuals, poets, artists, and novelists of the 1920s. Disillusioned by the cynical outcome of World War I, disturbed by the consumer culture of the 1920s, and outraged by the conservative politics of the Warren Harding* and Calvin Coolidge* administrations, they virtually withdrew from American society, figuratively and physically, many of them fleeing to the Left Bank in Paris to come to terms with themselves. Profoundly alienated, they thought it was impossible to find meaning and personal fulfillment in the materialistic, impersonal jungle of American values. The Lost Generation included such people as H. L. Mencken,* Ernest Hemingway,* F. Scott Fitzgerald,* John Dos Passos,* T. S. Eliot,* Eugene O'Neill,* Thomas Wolfe,* and Ezra Pound.* They turned inward, rebelled against middle-class values, and then produced the finest literature in American history. (Malcolm Cowley, *Exiles Return,* 1934; Frederick T. Hoffman, *The Twenties,* 1949; Edmund Wilson, *The Twenties,* 1975.)

LOVEJOY, OWEN REED. Owen Lovejoy was born on September 9, 1866, in Jamestown, Michigan. He graduated from Albion College in 1891 and then entered the Methodist ministry. Lovejoy was pastor at several Michigan churches for the next thirteen years, but, in 1904, he decided to leave the ministry to begin a career in social work. For several years before making the decision, he had been increasingly interested in social welfare issues, and those concerns shaped the sermons he delivered to his congregations. His first assignment was as an investigator for the newly formed National Child Labor Committee.* In 1907 Lovejoy was appointed executive secretary of the National Child Labor Committee, and he remained in that post until his resignation in 1926. He proved to be a tireless crusader in the battle against child labor. In 1920 he was elected president of the National Conference of Charities and Corrections, and in 1922, the president of the American Association of Social Workers. Lovejoy left the National Child Labor Committee in 1926, primarily out of discouragement when Congress refused to pass the child labor amendment. He worked for the New York Children's Aid Society until 1935, when he became associate director of the American Council on Education. Lovejoy retired in 1939. He died on June 29, 1961. (*New York Times,* June 30, 1961; Walter I. Trattner, *Crusade for Children: A History of the National Child Labor Committee and Child Labor Reform in America,* 1970.)

LOWDEN, FRANK. Frank Lowden was born on January 26, 1861, in Sunrise City, Minnesota. He graduated from Iowa State University in 1885 and then took a law degree at the Union College of Law in 1887. Lowden practiced law in Chicago between 1887 and 1906, while also teaching law at Northwestern University. Active in state Republican politics, Lowden made an unsuccessful bid for the party's gubernatorial nomination in 1904 but then won a seat in Congress in 1906, where he served until 1911. Lowden became governor of

Illinois in 1917 and pushed through a reform agenda which included increased state aid to public schools, consolidation of government departments, and increased funding for the University of Illinois. He was also an outspoken opponent of racial and religious discrimination. Lowden decided not to seek re-election in 1920, retiring to his farm and law practice. In 1924 he let his name be put in nomination for the presidency, but he turned down an offer from the eventual nominee, John W. Davis,* to run for vice-president. Frank Lowden died on March 20, 1943. (William T. Hutchinson, *Lowden of Illinois: The Life of Governor Frank O. Lowden,* 1957.)

LUCKY STRIKE. See HILL, GEORGE WASHINGTON

LYNCHING. Throughout the late nineteenth and early twentieth centuries, vigilante action against alleged black criminals was widespread throughout the United States, especially in the South. Between 1889 and 1918, nearly 3,000 blacks were lynched in the United States, and black organizations like the National Association for the Advancement of Colored People* (NAACP) and the National Urban League campaigned actively against it. In the summer of 1919, when anti-black race riots occurred in a number of American cities, particularly in Chicago and Washington, D.C., the NAACP decided on more formal action, and sponsored a national conference on lynching. Charles Evans Hughes* was the keynote speaker. In 1919 and 1920, more than one hundred more blacks were lynched in the United States, and the NAACP convinced Congressman L. C. Dyer of Missouri to sponsor a federal antilynching bill in the House. The bill passed by a vote of 230 to 119 in the House of Representatives, over widespread southern opposition. In the Senate, however, it did not have a prayer: a well-organized filibuster by southern senators doomed it, and President Warren G. Harding* would not take a strong stand in favor of the bill. It died there. Periodically throughout the 1920s and 1930s, the NAACP managed to get new antilynching bills into the congressional docket, but none of them survived the southern filibusters in the Senate. Nevertheless, the NAACP felt that the campaign against lynching had helped reduce the problem. The number of black lynchings fell to twenty-nine in 1923 and to sixteen in 1924, after which it remained fairly constant, until the late 1940s, when it dropped dramatically and disappeared. (Walter White, *Rope and Faggot, A Biography of Judge Lynch,* 1929.)

M

McADOO, WILLIAM GIBBS. William Gibbs McAdoo was born near Marietta, Georgia, on October 31, 1863. His father, an attorney, moved the family to Tennessee, where he taught at the University of Tennessee. McAdoo studied there between 1879 and 1882, but he withdrew to take up a clerkship in the federal circuit court in Chattanooga. He studied law at night and was admitted to the bar in 1885. McAdoo moved to New York in 1892, and, although his law practice was only marginal financially, he organized the Hudson and Manhattan Railroad Company, and, with financial assistance from several New York bankers, he completed the first tunnel under the Hudson River in March 1904. The tunnel made McAdoo famous in New York. He became active in New York Democratic politics, and in 1912 McAdoo vigorously supported the candidacy of Woodrow Wilson.* When Wilson won, he named McAdoo secretary of the treasury. Two years later, McAdoo married Wilson's daughter, Eleanor Randolph Wilson. During his six years in the cabinet, McAdoo also served as chairman of the Federal Reserve Board,* head of the Federal Farm Loan Board, head of the War Finance Corporation,* and director of the nation's railroads during World War I.

At the Democratic convention in 1920, McAdoo was widely considered the front-runner and heir to Wilson's presidency. When Wilson did not endorse him, McAdoo did not seek the nomination; instead, he waited until the election of 1924,* when he contested the nomination with Governor Al Smith* of New York. The convention deadlocked—McAdoo enjoyed the support of southerners, the Ku Klux Klan,* Protestant fundamentalists, and prohibitionists; Smith had the support of city dwellers, northerners, Catholics*, immigrants, and opponents of prohibition.* Eventually, the convention turned to John W. Davis* as a compromise candidate. McAdoo returned to Los Angeles, where he had lived since 1922. In the area of foreign policy, McAdoo advocated American entry into the League of Nations,* lower tariffs, and disarmament. In 1932, he won election to a United States Senate seat from California. He supported the New Deal of Franklin D. Roosevelt.* In 1938, McAdoo failed in his bid for re-election. He died on February 1, 1941. (Otis L. Graham, ''William Gibbs

McAdoo,'' in *Dictionary of American Biography*, suppl. 3 [1973], 479–82; *New York Times,* February 2, 1941.)

MacARTHUR, DOUGLAS. The child of a military family, Douglas Mac-Arthur was born on January 26, 1880, on an army base near Little Rock, Arkansas. He graduated from West Point in 1903, and then served with distinction in the Philippines and in Mexico and with the Rainbow Division in World War I. After the war, MacArthur became commandant of West Point and was promoted to general in 1930. In 1932, when he was army chief of staff, MacArthur came to national attention when he dispersed the Bonus Army* of poverty-stricken veterans who were demanding payment of their cash bonuses. President Herbert Hoover* asked Secretary of War Patrick Hurley* to move the veterans out of several federal buildings they were occupying in Washington, D.C. Hurley went one step beyond Hoover's instructions and told General Douglas MacArthur to move the demonstrators out of the business district and all the way back to their hovels at Anacostia Flats. MacArthur then far exceeded his authority by using tanks, guns, and tear gas to evict the demonstrators and destroy their camp. Photographs of American soldiers attacking poverty-stricken American veterans flashed across newspapers in July 1932 and all but destroyed Hoover's chances of being re-elected.

In 1935, MacArthur went to the Philippines as a military adviser, and during World War II he was commander-in-chief of army forces in the Pacific. After the war, MacArthur virtually ruled Japan as head of the occupation force. He drafted the new Japanese constitution and then established a democratic government there. In 1950 MacArthur took command of United Nations forces in Korea and stayed there until 1951 when President Harry Truman fired him for insubordination. Douglas MacArthur died on April 5, 1964. (William Manchester, *American Caeser: Douglas MacArthur 1880–1964*, 1978.)

McBRIDE, FRANCIS SCOTT. Francis McBride was born on July 29, 1872, in Carroll County, Ohio. He graduated from Muskingum College in 1898 and then received a theology degree from the Allegheny Theological Seminary in 1901. Between 1901 and 1912, McBride was a Presbyterian minister for several congregations in Illinois, but his real passion was the temperance movement, and in 1912 he became state superintendent of the Illinois Segment of the Anti-Saloon League* of America. From the very beginning, he established a reputation as a temperance militant who believed that a constitutional amendment, rather than education and persuasion, was the only way of eliminating the influence of alcohol in American society. Once the Eighteenth Amendment* was ratified, McBride was a strong advocate of tough enforcement measures. In 1924, he was named superintendent of the Anti-Saloon League of America, a position he held until 1936. During his tenure with the Anti-Saloon League, the league itself was divided between advocates of militant enforcement and advocates of education and persuasion. In the election of 1928,* McBride came out strongly in favor of Herbert Hoover* and against Governor Al Smith* of New York. He also marshalled the evangelical churches and the supporters of prohibition* behind Hoover. Victory in that election, however, was the peak of the Anti-Saloon League's efforts. The Great Depression eroded its financial resources, and the public's patience with prohibition, leading to ratification of the Twenty-First Amendment* in 1933. Francis McBride died on April 23, 1955. (Ernest Cherrington, *History of the Anti-Saloon League,* 1913; *New York Times,* April 24, 1955.)

McCORMICK, ROBERT RUTHERFORD. Robert R. McCormick was born on July 30, 1880, in Chicago, Illinois, to a prominent family whose fortune had been made in the farm implements industry. McCormick attended Groton and graduated from Yale in 1903. He studied law at Northwestern University in Chicago, and although he did not finish a degree he was nevertheless admitted to the bar in 1908. McCormick was active as a Republican in local Chicago politics, and in 1912 he supported the progressive candidacy of Theodore Roosevelt for president. In 1914, McCormick gained financial control of the *Chicago Tribune,* and over the next two decades he transformed it into one of the most influential newspapers in the country. McCormick vertically integrated the newspaper by acquiring hundreds of thousands of acres of Canadian forests for pulp and two Canadian paper mills. During World War I, McCormick joined the United States Army and earned the rank of colonel while serving with the American Expeditionary Force, and upon his return to the United States in 1918 he made the *Tribune* a pulpit for his own views. McCormick became a doctrinaire isolationist during the 1920s, opposing any American entanglement with the corrupt politics of Europe, and he was also a vigorous opponent of prohibition.* During the 1930s, McCormick fought Franklin D. Roosevelt* and the New Deal at every turn, and after World War II he was an intense anti-Communist. Robert R. McCormick died on April 1, 1955. (*Chicago Tribune,* April 2, 1955.)

McCUMBER, PORTER JAMES. Porter J. McCumber was born on February 3, 1858, in Crete, Illinois. He received a law degree from the University of Michigan in 1880 and then opened up a law practice in North Dakota. A Republican, McCumber served in the territorial legislature in 1885 and 1887 and as state's attorney for Richland County in 1897 and 1898; in the election of 1898, he won a seat in the United States Senate, an office he held until 1923. Unlike many other midwestern Republican senators, McCumber was an internationalist who supported the League of Nations* after World War I. In fact, he was the only Republican on the Senate Foreign Relations Committee who favored the Treaty of Versailles* as President Woodrow Wilson* had submitted it. McCumber helped sponsor the Fordney-McCumber Tariff of 1922, which raised tariff rates. He was not re-elected in 1922, and, between 1925 and 1933, he served as a member of the International Joint Boundary Commission. McCumber died on May 18, 1933. (*New York Times,* May 19, 1933.)

MACK, CONNIE. Cornelius McGillicuddy was born on December 22, 1862, to an Irish immigrant family in East Brookfield, Massachusetts. "Connie" went to work in the textile mills when he was nine years old, but even while working he found time to play baseball.* By the time he was eighteen, Mack was playing professionally in the New England leagues, and he made it to the majors in 1886 as a catcher for Washington. He tried to buy a franchise in the new Player's League in 1890, but when the league folded, Mack lost his life savings. The next year, he played for Pittsburgh in the National League. He stayed with Pittsburgh until 1896, when he became manager of the Milwaukee franchise in the Western League. When the Western League became the American League in 1900, Mack was awarded ownership of the Philadelphia Athletic franchise, and he also became manager. He managed the club for the next half century, helping to change baseball's image in the process. Soft-spoken and gentle, Mack drank moderately and never smoked, and he wore a business suit when he managed the club. By the 1920s he was the symbol of baseball's integrity and pastoral significance, despite the impact of the Black Sox scandal.* He retired from baseball in 1950 as a national sports hero. Connie Mack died on February 8, 1956. (Martin Appel and Burt Goldblatt, *Baseball's Best: The Hall of Fame Gallery,* 1980; *New York Times,* February 9, 1956.)

McKENNA, JOSEPH. Joseph McKenna was born on August 10, 1843, in Philadelphia, Pennsylvania, to Irish immigrant parents. They moved to California when he was still a child to get away from anti-Catholic, anti-Irish prejudice in Philadelphia. McKenna graduated from the Benicia Collegiate Institute with a law degree in 1865 and was admitted to the California bar in 1866. Active in Republican politics, he served as district attorney for Solano County between 1866 and 1870, spent one term in the California legislature in 1875–1876, and served four terms in Congress between 1885 and 1892. In 1892, President Benjamin Harrison appointed McKenna to the U.S. ninth judicial circuit, and in 1897 President William McKinley named him to the cabinet as attorney general. Later that year, McKinley appointed him to the United States Supreme Court. On the court, McKenna was a rigid, doctrinaire conservative, and he served in the post until his retirement in 1925. He was the judicial symbol of right-wing business conservatism. Joseph McKenna died on November 21, 1926. (*New York Times,* November 22, 1926.)

McNARY, CHARLES LINZA. Charles McNary was born on June 12, 1874, near Salem, Oregon. He was raised in a large farm family until his parents died during his early teens and he left to live with an older sister. He attended Stanford University from 1896 to 1898. Too poor to finish, McNary returned to Salem in 1898, studied law privately, and served a two-year term on the state supreme court between 1913 and 1915. He became chairman of the Oregon Republican State Committee in 1916, and in 1917 he was appointed to complete the unexpired term of Senator Harry Lane. McNary was re-elected to full terms in 1918, 1924,

1930, 1936, and 1942. In 1926 he became chairman of the Senate Agriculture committee, and during the 1920s he sponsored the McNary-Haugen Bill* to dump American farm surpluses abroad after the federal government had purchased them from farmers. A leading progressive Republican in the Senate, McNary was able, because of his pragmatism, to maintain strong ties with liberals as well as conservatives. During the 1930s, McNary supported such New Deal legislation as the National Industrial Recovery Act and the Agricultural Adjustment Act, but he opposed the gold-buying scheme and the wages and hours legislation. In 1940 Wendell Willkie selected McNary to run as vice-president on the Republican ticket. Charles McNary died on February 25, 1944. (Ronald L. Feinman, *Twilight of Progressivism: The Western Republican Senators and the New Deal*, 1981; *New York Times,* February 26, 1944.)

McNARY-HAUGEN BILL. After the end of World War I, the industrial sector of the American economy surged ahead, but agriculture went into a depression which did not really end until the outbreak of World War II. Huge surpluses were deflating commodity prices while farmers were stuck with large, fixed-debt payments they had incurred during the war. Between 1920 and 1932, one farm in every four was sold for debt or taxes. Republicans and Democrats from farming states tried to organize in Congress, and they proposed a variety of schemes to relieve their constituents. The proposal that gained the most attention was the McNary-Haugen Bill, named after Senator Charles McNary* of Oregon and Representative Gilbert N. Haugen* of Iowa. The bill was actually the brainchild of George N. Peek,* head of the Moline Illinois Plow Company. Peek had served under Bernard Baruch* on the War Industries Board, and he had faith that the federal government could do something to help farmers cope with the economic crisis.

In its particulars, the McNary-Haugen Bill proposed the creation of a government Agricultural Credit Corporation to buy farm surpluses on the American market at a ratio price computed to commodity prices between 1905 and 1914. The Agricultural Credit Corporation would then sell the surpluses on the world market at whatever price it could get and then charge an equalization tax on farmers for the crops they sold themselves in the United States to make up the difference. McNary and Haugen submitted the bill to Congress in 1924, but it did not reach a vote until 1927. By that time, the bill had changed somewhat. It covered only five crops—cotton, wheat, corn, rice, and hogs—with a twelve-member Federal Farm Board* to administer the program. The equalization fee would not be imposed on producers but upon processors, transporters, and retailers. After suffering defeats in both the House and the Senate, the McNary-Haugen Bill finally passed through Congress in February 1927, only to receive a stinging veto from President Calvin Coolidge* on the grounds that the federal government had no business entering the agriculture markets and setting prices. In April 1928 the bill again passed the Senate, by a vote of 53 to 23, and the House in early May, by a vote of 204 to 121. Coolidge vetoed it again on the grounds that it approved price fixing, that it would only make the surpluses worse, and that it was an unconstitutional use of the taxing power. The McNary-Haugen Bill was dead. (Gilbert C. Fite, *George N. Peek and the Fight for Farm Parity,* 1954; Frederic L. Paxson, "The Agricultural Surplus: A Problem in History," *Agricultural History* VI [April 1932], 51–58.)

McPHERSON, AIMEE SEMPLE. Aimee Elizabeth Kennedy was born on October 9, 1890, in Ingersoll, Canada. As a teenager, she became interested in the Salvation Army, but in 1908, at a Pentecostal revival led by the Reverend Robert J. Semple, she converted to evangelical religion as the focus of her life. She married Semple later that year. The two of them went to China in 1909 as missionaries, and Robert Semple died there within two months. Aimee returned to the United States to continue her evangelical revivals. She married Harold S. McPherson in 1912, but it was an unhappy union which ended in divorce in 1921. During those years, Aimee held tent revivals all over Canada and the United States.

In 1923 she finished constructing her International Church of the Foursquare Gospel in Los Angeles, and using flamboyant dress and a theatrical flair, she began to gain a real following in the 1920s. She began broadcasting her revivals over the radio* and establishing new Foursquare churches throughout the United States—400 of them by 1935. The Foursquare Gospel emphasized the ministry of Jesus Christ in four ways: (1) the Savior of the world, (2) the Baptizer of the Holy Spirit, (3) the Healer of human sickness, and (4) the returning King of Kings. Aimee McPherson's new denomination emphasized a personal salvation based on love, forgiveness, and the healing power of Jesus Christ.

In 1926, she became embroiled in a scandal when she disappeared while swimming at a California beach. When she reappeared several weeks later, she claimed to have been kidnapped, but enterprising journalists claimed she had spent the time on a love tryst with her business manager. The scandal made headlines for weeks. McPherson returned to her ministry and continued her work, despite a nervous breakdown in 1930 and another failed marriage in 1935. She died of an overdose of barbituates on September 27, 1944. (Nancy B. Mavity, *Sister Aimee,* 1931; *New York Times,* September 28, 1944; Lately Thomas, *Storming Heaven,* 1970.)

MAH JONG. Mah Jong was a popular board game during the 1920s. In 1920 some American travellers brought the game to the United States from China, and in 1922 W. A. Hammond, a California lumber merchant, began to import sets of the game on a large scale. He sold thousands of the sets, and by 1923 it had become a national fad, even including the establishment of the Mah Jong Society of America. (Frederick Lewis Allen, *Only Yesterday: An Informal History of the 1920s,* 1931.)

MANCHURIA. See STIMSON, HENRY LEWIS

MARATHON DANCING. The marathon dance craze came to the United States at the depths of the depression in 1932. They were basically theatrical circuses in which advertisers offered prize money, in return for radio* time and newspaper space, to couples capable of dancing together for days on end. The marathon dances were actually endurance contests; dancers were eliminated only when both of them fell asleep and collapsed. Rules permitted them to sleep fifteen minutes out of every hour and to sleep in the partner's arms as long as one of them kept moving. To unemployed people, the marathon dance halls offered some protection from the cold and several days of food, as long as they could hold out. To audiences, they often provided a grotesque entertainment, a way of forgetting about the troubles of the larger world. (Agnes DeMille, *America Dances,* 1980.)

MARBURG, THEODORE. Theodore Marburg was born on July 10, 1872, in Baltimore, Maryland. He graduated from Johns Hopkins University in 1890 and later did graduate work at Oxford University and at Heidelberg University. Late in the 1890s, Marburg was active as a progressive in Baltimore politics, campaigning for honest government, municipal efficiency, and social reform. He also became active in the world peace movement, and in 1912 President William Howard Taft* appointed Marburg minister to Belgium, where he served until 1914 and was outraged at German treatment of Belgium during World War I. After the war, Marburg left the Republican Party* when Senator Henry Cabot Lodge* opposed entrance into the League of Nations* and when President Warren G. Harding* upheld that position. Marburg spent the 1920s working for American entrance into the League of Nations, trying to achieve fair treatment for Germany, and opposing the disarmament conferences of the decade, which he felt were destabilizing events for world peace when no international peacekeeping body was in place. When Germany turned to aggression again in the 1930s, Marburg advocated decisive action by the allied powers against Germany and called for an American declaration of war on Germany as early as 1939. He died on March 3, 1946. (Henry Atkinson, *Theodore Marburg: The Man and His Work,* 1951.)

"THE MARCH OF TIME." "The March of Time" debuted on CBS radio* on March 6, 1931, and it became the most popular news documentary in radio history. Produced and sponsored by *Time* magazine, it was designed to resemble the Movietone newsreel, featuring daily interviews and "news of the day" broadcasts. Early broadcasters included Harry Von Zell, Ted Husing, and Westbrook Van Voorhis. The program lasted until 1945. (John Dunning, *Tune in Yesterday: The Ultimate Encyclopedia of Old-Time Radio, 1925–1976,* 1976.)

MASTERS, EDGAR LEE. Edgar Lee Masters was born on August 23, 1869, in Garnett, Kansas. He was raised in Illinois in a family committed to Populism, and in his poetry, Masters evoked images of the Midwest and rural life. His most important work was *Spoon River Anthology,* in which the inhabitants of a cemetary in Illinois make comments about their lives and homes. It was full of satiric opinions about the hypocrisy of life and how nature and selfishness defeat people. Although none of Masters's subsequent writings had anywhere near the influence of *Spoon River Anthology,* he was an important intellectual and artist of the 1920s. Masters died on March 5, 1950. (John T. Flanagan, *Edgar Lee Masters: The Spoon River Poet and His Critics,* 1974.)

MAYER, LOUIS BURT. Louis B. Mayer was born on July 4, 1885, in Minsk, Russia, and he immigrated with his family to New Brunswick, Canada, in 1888. He left school in 1899 and worked for several years in his father's ship salvage business, but, fascinated by motion pictures, in 1907 Mayer moved to Haverhill, Massachusetts, where he bought an old theater. Mayer started buying up other theaters and established his own production company in 1914; in 1915 he established Metro Pictures to distribute films. In 1918 Mayer decided to devote his energies to producing films, and he moved to Los Angeles, California, where he established the Louis B. Mayer Pictures Corporation. In 1924, Marcus Loew* purchased Mayer's companies and formed Metro-Goldwyn-Mayer (MGM) Corporation, which soon became a corporate giant in the film industry. Mayer was named vice-president of the new company. Over the next twenty-five years, Mayer brought a galaxy of film stars to MGM and personally became known as the "czar of Hollywood" because of his power in the industry. When MGM's business fortunes declined with the nationwide drop in movie attendance after World War II, Mayer was moved out of his position with the company. Louis Mayer, one of the founders of the movie industry in the United States, died on October 29, 1957. (Bosley Crowther, *The Lion's Share,* 1957; *New York Times,* October 30, 1957; Leo Rosten, *Hollywood,* 1945.)

MAYTAG, FREDERICK LOUIS. Frederick L. Maytag was born on July 14, 1857, in Elgin, Illinois, to German immigrant parents. He spent only a few months in school, working instead on the family farm. In 1880 Maytag became a salesman for a farm implements dealer in Newton, Iowa, and in 1890 he went into lumber retailing. Maytag invested money in a small farm implements company in 1893, and then lost money on some railroad and automobile* investments. But in 1907 he started to manufacture washing machines, and he founded the Maytag Company in 1909. Because of the increasingly widespread use of electricity, the demand for electrical appliances was mushrooming, and Maytag was perfectly timed to exploit the new demand. In 1922, his company invented the "gyrafoam washer," which cleaned clothes through rough water rather than by rubbing movements. The washing machine was an instant hit. Sales increased from $2 million in 1921 to $53 million in 1926. Frederick Maytag was president of the company until 1921 and chairman of the board until 1937. During the 1920s, the term "Maytag" became synonymous with washing machines and was one of the most recognizable consumer items in the country. Frederick Maytag died on March 26, 1937. (Charles Kelly, Jr., *The Sky's the Limit,* 1963; *National Cyclopedia of American Biography,* 27 [1939], 361; *New York Times,* March 27, 1937.)

MELLON, ANDREW WILLIAM. Andrew Mellon was born in Pittsburgh, Pennsylvania, on March 24, 1855. Mellon attended the Western University of Pennsylvania, but he did not graduate since he left in 1872 to establish his own construction and building supply business. In 1874 Mellon joined his father's banking firm and he became owner of it in 1882 when his father retired. Mellon then built a business empire in Pittsburgh. He organized the Union Trust Company in 1889 and later went into the oil business, helping to organize the Gulf Corporation. Mellon was also a founder of the Aluminum Company of America. By the time of World War I, Mellon had become one of the wealthiest men in the United States. President Warren G. Harding* made Mellon secretary of the treasury on March 4, 1921.

As secretary of the treasury, Mellon was one of the most influential people in Washington, D.C., during the 1920s. He came to the office with his own vision of what "normalcy"* meant. Mellon was convinced that the extravagant spending and confiscatory income taxes of the Woodrow Wilson* administration, although necessary to the prosecution of the war effort, would be disastrous in a peacetime economy. Consequently, Mellon was determined to reduce federal spending, to balance the budget and eventually produce a surplus, to retire the national debt, and to reduce substantially income taxes, especially those levied on rich and well-to-do individuals. He was convinced that the rich, with more income at their disposal, would then increase investment in the economy and guarantee a decade of prosperity.

Although he appeared frail and old at sixty-five in 1921, Mellon proved to be determined and powerful. He served as secretary of the treasury under Warren G. Harding, Calvin Coolidge,* and Herbert Hoover,* and, during his tenure, his budget cuts produced a net surplus of $8 billion, which he used to reduce the national debt. Mellon also brought about substantial tax reductions in the Revenue Acts of 1921,* 1924,* 1926,* 1928,* and 1929.* Critics charged that those tax reductions personally saved Mellon $800,000 a year. Mellon resigned from the Department of the Treasury in 1932 to accept Herbert Hoover's appointment as ambassador to Great Britain. In 1933 Mellon returned home to Pittsburgh. He died on August 26, 1937. (Martin L. Fausold, *The Presidency of Herbert C. Hoover,* 1985; Donald R. McCoy, *Calvin Coolidge: The Quiet President,* 1967; Harvey O'Conner, *Mellon's Millions,* 1933; Eugene P. Trani and David L. Wilson, *The Presidency of Warren G. Harding,* 1977.)

MENCKEN, HENRY LOUIS. H. L. Mencken, the iconoclastic journalist and social critic, was born in Baltimore, Maryland, on September 12, 1880. He graduated from the Polytechnic Institute and immediately went into newspaper work, serving as police reporter and then as city editor of the *Baltimore Morning Herald* until 1906 when he joined the staff of the *Baltimore Sun*. During the 1920s, Mencken's cynicism about American materialism made him enormously popular in literary circles, and he played an important role in boosting the careers of people like Theodore Dreiser,* D. H. Lawrence, and Sherwood Anderson.* Mencken served as editor of the *American Mercury* between 1925 and 1933. Mencken was especially critical of religious piety in the 1920s, which he called "tin-pot moralism." During the John Scopes* trial in Dayton, Tennessee, Mencken portrayed religious fundamentalism as hopelessly myopic and superficial and William Jennings Bryan* as a buffoon. During the 1930s and World War II, when his debunking cynicism no longer seemed appropriate, Mencken lost much of his popularity, particularly after he described Franklin D. Roosevelt* and the New Deal as "the sorriest mob of mountebanks ever gathered together at one time. . . . " Roosevelt was just too popular with the general public and with most intellectuals. H. L. Mencken died on January 29, 1956. (Carl Bode, *Mencken,* 1969; William Manchester, *Disturber of the Peace,* 1951.)

MERCHANT MARINE ACT OF 1920. Because of the activities of the United States Shipping Board during World War I, the United States enjoyed one of the largest merchant fleets in the world during the 1920s. Second only to that of Great Britain, the United States merchant fleet was carrying more than half of all goods entering or leaving American ports by 1920. Most of the fleet, however, was government owned, and, in the shift to "normalcy,"* the transition back to private ownership had to occur. On June 5, 1920, President Woodrow Wilson* signed the Merchant Marine Act into law. It repealed all emergency war legislation concerning shipping, extended the tenure of the United States Shipping Board, ordered the sale of government-owned ships to private companies, and provided a fund of $25 million from the sales to supply capital for private builders to construct new ships. The United States Shipping Board was given the authority to designate shipping routes and to operate government ships until the shift to private control was completed. (John B. Hutchins, "The American Shipping Industry Since 1914," *Business History Review* 28 [June 1954], 109–21.)

MERIAM REPORT. In 1926, at the request of the Bureau of Indian Affairs, Secretary of the Interior Hubert Work asked the Institute for Government Research, later known as the Brookings Institution, to conduct a study of Indian affairs. Oil magnate John D. Rockefeller* agreed to finance it. Dr. Lewis Meriam, a social scientist working for the institute, headed the study. After spending seven months on a field trip and nearly another year in writing the report, the commission published *The Problem of Indian Administration,* commonly known as the Meriam Report, in 1928. The report charged that Indians suffered from poverty, poor health, poor educational levels, and widespread discrimination. The culprit, they charged, was the Dawes Severalty Act of 1887, which had systematically reduced Indian landholdings and destroyed the governing structures of the reservations. The Meriam Report recommended that the practice of "alloting" Indian land by taking it from the tribe and giving it to individual Indians and whites be stopped; that appropriations for the Bureau of Indian Affairs be increased; and that the federal government end its attempts to wipe out tribal government and tribal cultures. The Meriam Report paved the way for the "Indian New Deal" of the 1930s. (James S. Olson and Raymond Wilson, *Native Americans in the Twentieth Century,* 1984.)

MEYER, EUGENE, JR. Eugene Meyer was born on October 31, 1875, in Los Angeles, California. Meyer graduated from Yale in 1895 and then spent several years working in international banking houses in Paris, London, and Berlin with friends of his father. On a whim, he left the family banking firm in 1901, established the Eugene Meyer, Jr., and Company, and spent every penny he had purchasing a seat on the New York Stock Exchange. It was a fortuitous decision because there he met and formed a friendship with Bernard Baruch.* Through judicious investments, Meyer became a real power in the American copper industry by the time of World War I, as well as a major stockholder in Allied Chemical. In 1917, Baruch brought Meyer to Washington as a division head in the War Industries Board, and in 1918 President Woodrow Wilson* named him managing director of the War Finance Corporation* (WFC). Meyer remained with the WFC until it was dissolved late in 1925. Meyer helped reorganize the Federal Farm Loan Board in 1927. In 1930 President Herbert Hoover* appointed him governor of the Federal Reserve Board,* a move progressive Republicans bitterly resented because of Meyer's strong Wall Street connections, and in 1932 Hoover made him chairman of the new Reconstruction Finance Corporation* (RFC). Meyer resigned from the RFC after the election of Franklin D. Roosevelt,* and in 1933 he purchased the *Washington Post.* Meyer used the *Post* as a vehicle to criticize the New Deal and to urge an internationalist foreign policy on Franklin D. Roosevelt. In 1941 the president named Meyer to the National Defense Mediation Board. Five years later, Meyer was appointed president of the World Bank. He died on July 17, 1959. (*New York Times,* July 18, 1959; James S. Olson, *Herbert Hoover and the Reconstruction Finance Corporation, 1931–1933,* 1977; Merlo Pusey, *Eugene Meyer,* 1974; Chalmers Roberts, *The Washington Post: The First 100 Years,* 1977.)

MILLS, OGDEN LIVINGSTON. Ogden Mills was born in Newport, Rhode Island, on August 23, 1884. He graduated from Harvard in 1904 and received a law degree there in 1907. Mills practiced law in New York City, served in the state legislature as a Republican between 1914 and 1917, and, after a stint in the army during World War I, Mills returned home to win a congressional seat in 1920. He was a member of Congress from 1921 to 1927. Mills failed in his bid for the governorship of New York in 1926, losing to Al Smith,* and in 1927 he was appointed undersecretary of the treasury by President Calvin Coolidge.* In 1932 Herbert Hoover* appointed Mills secretary of the treasury, a post he held until the inauguration of Franklin D. Roosevelt* in March 1933. Mills then returned to his law practice, wrote several books, including *What of Tomorrow* (1935) and *Liberalism Fights On* (1936), and spoke widely on the lecture circuit. Ogden Mills died on October 11, 1937. (David Burner, *Herbert Hoover: A Public Life,* 1979; *New York Times,* October 12, 1937; James S. Olson, *Herbert Hoover and the Reconstruction Finance Corporation, 1931–1933,* 1977.)

MISSISSIPPI FLOOD COMMITTEE. See MISSISSIPPI FLOOD OF 1927

MISSISSIPPI FLOOD OF 1927. In the spring of 1927, after heavy winter snows and then a two-week rainstorm stretching from Minnesota to Louisiana, the Mississippi River flooded an area 1,000 miles long and 40 miles wide. Crops and livestock were destroyed, and 600,000 people were homeless. President Calvin Coolidge* appointed a Mississippi Flood Committee with Secretary of Commerce Herbert Hoover* as chairman. For the next three months, Hoover supervised a federal-state effort involving Illinois, Missouri, Arkansas, Louisiana, Kentucky, and Tennessee. Hoover brought together nearly $50 million in federal and private funds, which built 150 refugee camps and provided food and clothing for 325,000 homeless people, and secured Rockefeller Foundation financing for one hundred county health units in the affected areas. In the process, Herbert Hoover became a national figure and set the stage for his successful campaign for the presidency in the election of 1928.* (Pete Daniel, *Deep 'n As It Comes: The 1927 Mississippi River Flood,* 1976; Bruce Lokof, "Herbert Hoover, Spokesman for Humane Efficiency: The Mississippi Flood of 1927," *American Quarterly* 22 [Fall 1970], 690–700.)

MITCHELL, CHARLES EDWIN. Charles E. Mitchell was born on October 6, 1877, in Chelsea, Massachusetts, and was educated at Amherst, where he graduated in 1899. Mitchell began to work with the Western Electric Company in 1899, became assistant manager in 1904, and went into banking as president of the Trust Company of America in New York in 1907. In 1911 he founded Charles E. Mitchell & Company Investments and became president of National City Bank in 1921. During the 1920s, Mitchell transformed National City into a truly international bank as well as into a modern, full-service retail bank, which included checking accounts, savings accounts, and personal loans. Between 1929 and 1933, Mitchell was chairman of the board of the National City Bank. In 1932 and 1933, the investigations of the Pecora Committee put Mitchell in the national spotlight as a series of bank frauds and shady loan deals to bank officers was exposed at National City Bank. A conservative Republican, Mitchell tried to defend the bank's practices and laissez-faire values by praising private property and individual liberty; but Pecora was relentless in his questioning, and Mitchell's reputation was seriously tarnished, especially after it was learned that he had been speculating in National City Bank stock. He resigned from National City in 1933 and joined the firm of Blyth & Company, an investment banking concern, in 1935. Charles Mitchell died on December 14, 1955. (*New York Times*, December 15, 1955; Ferdinand Pecora, *Wall Street under Oath*, 1939; Giulio Pontecorvo, "Investment Banking and Security Regulation in the Late 1920s," *Business History Review* [Summer 1958], 166–91; Earl Sparling, *Mystery Men of Wall Street*, 1930.)

MITCHELL, WILLIAM DEWITT. William DeWitt Mitchell was born in Winona, Minnesota, on September 9, 1874. He graduated from the University of Minnesota in 1895 and earned a law degree there in 1896. Mitchell practiced law in St. Paul, completed army tours of duty during the Spanish-American War and during World War I, and in 1925 was appointed solicitor general by Calvin Coolidge.* President Herbert Hoover* named him attorney general in 1929. Mitchell served in the cabinet until 1933, when he returned to private law practice, this time in New York. During World War II, he served as chief counsel to the joint congressional committee investigating the Pearl Harbor controversy. William Mitchell died on August 24, 1955. (David Burner, *Herbert Hoover: A Public Life*, 1979; *New York Times*, August 25, 1955.)

MITCHELL, WILLIAM LENDRUM. William Lendrum "Billy" Mitchell was born on December 29, 1879, in Nice, France. He graduated from George Washington University in 1898 and enlisted in the army to fight in the Spanish-American War. Mitchell made a career out of the military, graduating from the Army Staff College in 1909, serving on the Mexican border in 1912, and joining the army general staff in 1913. During World War I, Mitchell became head of aviation for several army units, and in 1919 he was promoted to brigadier general and appointed director of military aviation. In the early 1920s, Mitchell became extremely controversial in the American military because of his outspoken convictions that major naval vessels were vulnerable to air attack. When he accused high-level American military officers of incompetence for ignoring his warnings about the future significance of air power, Mitchell was court-martialed in 1925. He retired from the army in 1926 and spent the rest of his life preaching the gospel of air power. Billy Mitchell died on February 19, 1936. Early in 1942, after the successful Japanese attack on Pearl Harbor, Congress posthumously restored Mitchell to the army and the rank of major general. (Burke Davis, *The Billy Mitchell Affair*, 1967; *New York Times*, February 20, 1936.)

MODEL A. See FORD, HENRY

MODEL T. See FORD, HENRY

"MONKEY TRIAL." See EVOLUTION

MOORE, JOHN BASSETT. John Bassett Moore was born on December 3, 1860, in Smyrna, Delaware. He attended the University of Virginia for two years, read law privately, and gained admission to the Virginia bar in 1883. In 1885 Moore became a clerk in the State Department. Between 1891 and 1924, Moore taught at Columbia University and became a world renowned scholar of international law, writing such books as *History and Digest of International Arbitration* (1898) and *American Diplomacy* (1905). Moore was a member of the negotiating teams that composed the Treaty of Paris of 1898 and the Hay-Pauncefote Treaty of 1901. After World War I, Moore opposed United States entry into the League of Nations* because he was convinced that collective security arrangements actually increased the likelihood of war. On the other hand, he favored American participation in the World Court,* and in 1921 Moore became the first American judge on the court. He remained there until his retirement in 1928. John Moore died on November 12, 1947. (Richard Megargee, "Realism in American Foreign Policy: The Diplomacy of John Bassett Moore," Ph.D. dissertation, Northwestern University, 1963.)

MORGAN, JOHN PIERPONT, JR. The third generation of America's most prominent banking dynasty, John Pierpont Morgan, Jr., was born on September 7, 1867, at Irvington-on-Hudson, New York. He attended St. Paul's school in Concord, New Hampshire, and graduated from Harvard in 1889. He immediately entered the banking business with Jacob C. Rogers and Company in Boston, and in 1891 he joined his father's firm—Drexel, Morgan & Company in New York. Between 1898 and 1905, his banking apprenticeship continued in London as a partner in J. P. Morgan & Company. When his father died in 1913, Morgan became senior partner of J. P. Morgan & Company. For the next two decades, he was a leading figure in the international banking community. During the 1920s, because of strong economic growth and a mass market for new securities, the company prospered. At the same time, Morgan became the world expert on financing government debt, especially recapitalizing national debts. J. P. Morgan & Company floated bond issues for Great Britain, France, Belgium, Italy, Austria, Cuba, Canada, and Germany. Morgan played an important role in the Dawes Plan* of 1924 and in the creation of the Bank for International Settlements and the Young Plan* in 1929. During the stock market crash of 1929,* Morgan tried to put together an investment pool of $30 million to stabilize the market, but he failed.

By the time of the New Deal, J. P. Morgan, Jr., had become the leading symbol of private capitalism in the United States. He at first welcomed the New

Deal, especially when Franklin D. Roosevelt* declared the bank holiday, but Morgan's sympathy was short-lived. The Pecora investigations into banking irregularities had embarrassed Morgan, and the Banking Act of 1933 forced him to separate investment from commercial banking. J. P. Morgan & Company remained a bank, and a new company—Morgan, Stanley & Company—took over the underwriting business. Morgan came to view the New Deal as hopelessly anti-business and narrow-minded, the tool of reform-minded lawyers and economists. In addition, the higher taxes and regulatory legislation cut into his personal income, a fact which did little to endear the New Deal to him. Morgan gradually withdrew from the business and died on March 13, 1943. (John D. Forbes, *J. P. Morgan, Jr., 1867–1943*, 1981.)

MORROW, DWIGHT WHITNEY. Dwight Morrow was born in Huntington, West Virginia, on January 11, 1873. He graduated from Amherst College in 1895 and took a law degree at Columbia in 1899. He specialized in corporate law, and between 1914 and 1927 he worked for the J. P. Morgan* and Company banking firm. In 1927, President Calvin Coolidge* appointed Morrow minister to Mexico, and he served at that post until 1930, earning a reputation as a sophisticated and sensitive diplomat. During his stay in Mexico, Morrow helped negotiate bitter differences between the government and the Roman Catholic* church. Morrow's tact and good judgment allowed President Plutarco Calles of Mexico to improve United States–Mexican relations by protecting American-owned land and subsurface oil rights. Morrow completed his mission to Mexico in 1930 and then served as a delegate to the London Naval Conference of 1930. In November 1930, Morrow was elected to the United States Senate from New Jersey on a Republican slate, but he died suddenly on October 5, 1931. (Mary M. McBride, *The Story of Dwight W. Morrow*, 1930; *New York Times*, October 6, 1931; Harold Nicolson, *Dwight Morrow*, 1935.)

MOSES, GEORGE HIGGINS. George H. Moses was born on February 9, 1869, in Lubec, Maine. He graduated from Dartmouth College in 1890 and then earned a master's degree there in 1893. Moses spent the rest of his life involved in Republican politics. He was private secretary to the governor of New Hampshire from 1889 to 1891 and again in 1905, as well as secretary to the chairman of the state Republican committee in 1890. Between 1893 and 1905, Moses was secretary to the state forestry commission as well as a political consultant to various Republican politicians. In 1918 he won a seat in the United States Senate to fill an unexpired term, and he was reelected to that post in 1920 and again in 1926. During the 1920s, Moses was a member of the Republican "Old Guard"*—an advocate of limited government spending, high protective tariffs, and government assistance to the business community, but a foe of social welfare and labor standards legislation. Moses went down to defeat with other Republicans in the election of 1932.* He died on December 20, 1944. (*Who Was Who in America*, II [1950], 386.)

MOSES-LINTHICUM ACT OF 1931. Sponsored by Senator George Moses* of New Hampshire and Congressman J. Charles Linthicum of Maryland, the Moses-Linthicum Act passed Congress on February 23, 1931, and replaced the Rogers Act of 1924* and the legislative mandate for the Foreign Service. In general, it helped further professionalize the Foreign Service by trying to guarantee impartiality in transfers, assignments, and promotions, and it improved benefits by providing for annual leaves, special living allowances, and regular salary increases. (Warren F. Ilchman, *Professional Diplomacy in the United States, 1779–1939,* 1961.)

MOTION PICTURES. The automobile,* the radio,* and the motion picture were the greatest cultural technological achievements of the 1920s; of these, the motion picture did the most to create a mass culture in the United States. In 1889, Thomas Edison had first developed the kinetoscope, a primitive motion picture apparatus; and in 1896 Thomas Armat invented the vitascope, which projected motion picture images on a wall or screen. *The Great Train Robbery,* the first film narrative, appeared in 1903. By 1908, film entrepreneurs had established 10,000 nickelodeons—small, storefront movie theaters catering to a working-class, ethnic clientele—throughout the country.

Between 1910 and 1927, the movie industry mushroomed. Major studios— Metro-Goldwyn-Meyer, Warner Brothers, Columbia, and RKO—began to produce full-length, high-budget motion pictures, appealing to a more affluent, middle-class audience. By 1920 there were 20,000 theaters in the United States, and that number grew to 28,000 in 1929. Many of the new theaters were huge "palaces" capable of seating from 1,000 to 2,000 people in luxurious splendor. Actors and actresses like Charlie Chaplin,* Buster Keaton,* Fatty Arbuckle,* William S. Hart,* Rudolph Valentino,* Clara Bow,* Theda Bara,* and Douglas Fairbanks* became household figures, familiar to millions of Americans by the 1920s. Producers and directors like Cecil B. De Mille* and D. W. Griffith* produced hundreds of films a year, enough for movie marquees to change every few days.

The cultural impact of motion pictures was enormous. Before the appearance of movies, American culture was sharply divided along ethnic and regional lines. The ethnic theaters, ethnic language newspapers, regional and ethnic dialects, and local legends and heroes predominated. Movies changed all that. All over the country, across ethnic and regional lines, Americans attended the same movies, watched the same stars, laughed at the same jokes, and listened to the same dialects and theater music. Vaudeville and the ethnic theaters rapidly declined, giving way to a new mass culture.

The appearance of sound films only accelerated the trend. Lee De Forest invented the process for placing sound recordings on film celluloid, and in 1927 Warner Brothers produced *The Jazz Singer,* starring Al Jolson.* Music and dialogue made the silent films, and many silent film stars, obsolete and, at the same time, eliminated employment for the theater musicians who played for the silent films.

The rise of Hollywood also had great symbolic, cultural significance in the 1920s. In a society worried about rapid social change, Hollywood came to symbolize all that was wrong with modern America—a fetish of materialism, uninhibited sexuality, divorce, and instability. For rural Protestants intent on reforming America, Hollywood seemed a perfect place to start, and the "scandalous" lives of people like Fatty Arbuckle, Clara Bow, and Rudolph Valentino were proof. In the motion pictures, the modern America of industrialization, secularism, sexuality, and urbanization was portrayed to the entire world. (Lary May, *Screening out the Past: The Birth of Mass Culture and the Motion Picture Industry,* 1980.)

MUKDEN INCIDENT OF 1931. In September 1931, the Japanese blamed the Chinese for destroying a small section of the Southern Manchurian Railroad's track near Mukden, Manchuria. At the time, the Japanese were managing the railroad, but they used the Mukden incident as a pretext for invading Manchuria as a whole and for launching the Greater East Asia Co-Prosperity Sphere. The Mukden Incident precipitated the Manchurian crisis of 1931 and led to the Stimson Doctrine* of 1931. (Robert H. Ferrell, *American Diplomacy in the Great Depression: The Hoover-Stimson Foreign Policy, 1929–1933,* 1957.)

MURPHY, J. PRENTICE. J. Prentice Murphy was born on September 12, 1881, in Philadelphia, Pennsylvania. He attended the University of Pennsylvania for three years, working part-time with the Pennsylvania Society to Protect Children from Cruelty; in 1908 he left college to become general secretary of the Children's Bureau of Philadelphia. Between 1911 and 1920, Murphy had the same position with the Boston Children's Aid Society, where he campaigned vigorously for an end to child labor and a variety of social welfare legislation. In 1921, Murphy was a founding member of the Child Welfare League of America, and between 1932 and 1934 he served as its president. He actively worked in various positions for the National Conference on Social Work between 1911 and 1936. Murphy was a strong supporter of the Sheppard-Towner Act of 1921,* and he focused much of his energy on the creation of foster care, rather than institutional care, for orphaned and abused children. J. Prentice Murphy died on February 3, 1936. ("J. Prentice Murphy," *The Family* 10 [March 1936], 128; E. O. Lundberg, "Pathfinders of the Middle Years," *Social Service Review* 21 [March 1947], 1–34.)

MURRAY, ARTHUR. Born Arthur Murray Teichmann in 1896 in New York City, Arthur Murray was trained in dance at Castle House. He opened his first ballroom dance studio in Asheville, Georgia in 1919, and during the 1920s and 1930s he used a national advertising campaign to market mail-order dance lessons and franchise new dance studios across the country. Arthur Murray's name became a household word during the 1920s in the United States. Using such phrases as "80 days ago they laughed at me . . . " or "How could I go to the party when they knew I couldn't dance" on radio* and in magazines, Murray built a franchise dance empire. He hosted a radio show with his wife Katharine from 1929 to 1949, and between 1950 and 1957 they had a regular television show. Arthur Murray retired from the dance business in 1964. (Barbara Naomi Cohen-Stratyner, *Biographical Dictionary of Dance,* 1982.)

MUSCLE SHOALS. See NORRIS, GEORGE WILLIAM

N

NANKING INCIDENT OF 1927. A diplomatic crisis between the United States and the Nationalist Chinese developed in March 1927 when forces under the control of Chiang Kai-shek entered Nanking and assaulted the foreign community, killing one American and five Europeans. Although the United States threatened economic sanctions against China unless apologies and indemnities were offered, the State Department had no intention of following through with its threats. Isolationist sentiments were still running high in the United States, and any deep political or military involvement in the Far East would not have enjoyed any popularity at home. Eventually, the United States let its protest of the attack remain dormant, and it was soon forgotten in the media. (Warren I. Cohen, *America's Response to China*, 1971; Ethan L. Ellis, *Republican Foreign Policy, 1921–1933*, 1968.)

NATIONAL AMERICAN WOMAN SUFFRAGE ASSOCIATION. The National American Woman Suffrage Association (NAWSA) was founded in New York City in 1890 by a merger of the National Woman Suffrage Association and the American Woman Suffrage Association. Elizabeth Cady Stanton was the first president of NAWSA, and Susan B. Anthony was vice-president; Carrie Chapman Catt* was president between 1900 and 1904 and between 1915 and 1920; and Anna Howard Shaw was president from 1904 to 1915. The National American Woman Suffrage Association, which established branches in every state of the union, was a powerful lobbying organization. After World War I, NAWSA demanded that President Woodrow Wilson* throw the weight of the presidency behind the proposed Nineteenth Amendment* to the Constitution. Congress approved the amendment in 1919 and it was ratified in 1920. When women enjoyed the right to vote throughout the country, the National American Woman Suffrage Association disbanded. (Aileen S. Kraditor, *The Ideas of the Woman Suffrage Movement, 1890–1920*, 1965.)

NATIONAL ASSOCIATION FOR THE ADVANCEMENT OF COLORED PEOPLE. The National Association for the Advancement of Colored People (NAACP) was founded in 1909 by several prominent civil rights leaders, including W.E.B. Du Bois,* Mary White Ovington, Henry Moskowitz, William English Walling, and Oswald Garrison Villard.* Formation of the NAACP was a direct result of the Springfield, Illinois, race riot of 1908, which inspired liberal intellectuals to establish a group dedicated to the elimination of racial discrimination in the United States. The NAACP's major target was legal, de jure discrimination and segregation, and it approached its crusade through legal action in the federal courts, arguing that the First, Fifth, Fourteenth, and Fifteenth Amendments of the Constitution all prohibited legal discrimination against black people. During the 1920s and early 1930s, the NAACP was led by James Weldon Johnson and then Walter White. The NAACP directed its energies during the 1920s and early 1930s to a number of issues: elimination of the lynching* of blacks in the South by passage of a federal antilynching law, which they never succeeded in pushing through Congress; opposition to Herbert Hoover's* nomination of John J. Parker* to the United States Supreme Court, which they succeeded in stopping in 1931; and legal support for the black men arrested in Alabama in the Scottsboro* rape case. The NAACP was primarily a middle-class civil rights organization which sought redress through the federal court system. (Robert L. Jack, *History of the National Association for the Advancement of Colored People,* 1943; Charles F. Kellogg, *History of the National Association for the Advancement of Colored People, 1909–1929,* 1967.)

NATIONAL ASSOCIATION OF MANUFACTURERS. The National Association of Manufacturers (NAM) was founded in 1895 in Cincinatti, Ohio, with the primary purpose of promoting business. Gradually, the NAM came to represent the needs of big business in the United States, and it became, during the 1920s, an inveterate foe of collective bargaining, labor strikes, and union organization. To counter the power of such groups as the United Mine Workers and the American Federation of Labor, the NAM sponsored the American Plan, a system of company unions operating in an open shop* legal atmosphere. During the 1920s, the National Association of Manufacturers opposed the McNary-Haugen Bill,* federal development of Muscle Shoals,* and federal public works programs, and it championed the idea of free enterprise and a minimum of government regulation. The Great Depression dealt a real blow to the NAM. From a high of 5,350 member businesses in 1922, it dropped to only 1,500 businesses in 1933. When the New Deal appeared during the 1930s, the National Association of Manufacturers became a bitter opponent, claiming that New Dealers represented only the needs of radicals and labor agitators. It opposed the candidacy of Franklin D. Roosevelt* in 1932, 1936, 1940, and 1944. (Albert K. Steigerwalt, *The National Association of Manufacturers,* 1964; Richard S. Tedlow, "The National Association of Manufacturers and Public Relations during the New Deal," *Business History Review,* 50 [1976], 25–35.)

NATIONAL ASSOCIATION OF RADIO BROADCASTERS. The National Association of Radio Broadcasters (NARB) was established in 1922 by Eugene F. McDonald, who served as president of the association until 1925. The NARB was committed to intellectual freedom of the radio* waves and to federal regulation, so they campaigned for what became the Radio Act of 1927, which assigned frequencies to private broadcasting stations. In 1951 it changed its name to the National Association of Radio and Television Broadcasters, and in 1957 to the National Association of Broadcasters. (Erik Barnouw, *The Golden Web: A History of Broadcasting in the United States,* 3 vol., 1966, 1968, 1970.)

NATIONAL BUILDING SURVEY CONFERENCE. See BUSINESS CYCLE COMMITTEE

NATIONAL CHILD LABOR COMMITTEE. Established in 1904, the National Child Labor Committee was supported by social work professionals concerned about the educational and social needs of children, as well as by northern industrialists worried about cheap wages in the South. A variety of northern states had already passed laws controlling child labor, but southern states had not, and southern mill owners thus had a competitive advantage in lower labor costs. Comprehensive national legislation was the only answer. Congress first addressed the issue in the Keating-Owen Act of 1916, which provided federal prohibition of child labor to be used to make goods shipped in interstate commerce. In particular, the law prohibited the labor of any child under the age of fourteen. In 1918, however in the *Hammer* v. *Dagenhart** case, the Supreme Court overturned the law. The National Child Labor Committee then helped sponsor a new law, which added a 10 percent federal tax on all goods entering interstate commerce if they had been produced by children. In 1922, in the *Bailey* v. *Drexel Furniture Company** case, the Supreme Court overturned that law, arguing that the tax was an impermissible use of Congress's police power. During the political conservatism of the 1920s, the National Child Labor Committee could do little more than try to educate the public, since serious federal legislation was simply not forthcoming, and success with the child labor issue on the national scale had to wait until the New Deal of the 1930s. (Clarke A. Chambers, *Seedtime of Reform: American Social Service and Social Action, 1918–1933,* 1963.)

NATIONAL CIVIC FEDERATION. The National Civic Federation (NCF) was established in 1893 in Chicago, Illinois. Its leader was Ralph M. Easley, who wanted to provide a means of mediating disputes between labor and management. In 1901 Republican businessmen Mark Hanna became president of the National Civic Federation and Samuel Gompers,* president of the American Federation of Labor,* became vice-president. After World War I, the National Civic Federation became directly involved in the Red Scare,* assisting Attorney General A. Mitchell Palmer* in rounding up radicals, and, in the process, the NCF lost some of its labor support. When Samuel Gompers died in 1924, labor turned away from the mediation efforts of the National Civic Federation because it was convinced that the NCF had become a tool of management. The National Civic Federation disbanded in 1925. (Marguerite Green, *The National Civic Federation and the Labor Movement, 1900–1925,* 1956.)

NATIONAL COMMITTEE ON THE CAUSE AND CURE OF WAR. The National Committee on the Cause and Cure of War was established in 1925 by feminist and peace advocate Carrie Chapman Catt* to promote world peace. Catt served as president of the committee until 1932. During the 1920s, the committee campaigned for American participation in the League of Nations* and the World Court* and disarmament, and during the 1930s it supported the Neutrality Acts. The National Committee on the Cause and Cure of War disintegrated after Germany invaded Poland in 1939. To many people, the idea of collective security had to replace pacifism when the world faced such a malignant enemy as Adolf Hitler; others proclaimed peace regardless of the nature of the military threat. (Mary Gray Peck, *Carrie Chapman Catt,* 1944.)

NATIONAL CONFERENCE OF CHRISTIANS AND JEWS. The National Conference of Christians and Jews was established in 1928 to promote religious understanding and brotherhood. Among its first prominent members were Newton Baker and Roger Straus. Everett R. Clinchy served as its first president. The headquarters were located in New York City. The 1920s had been a time of intense religious misunderstanding in the United States, especially when groups like the Ku Klux Klan* made Jews* and Catholics* the object of persecution. The National Conference of Christians and Jews, through conferences and public relations work, tried to counter that development in the 1920s. (Edward L. Schapsmeier and Frederick H. Schapsmeier, *Political Parties and Civic Action Groups,* 1981.)

NATIONAL COUNCIL FOR PREVENTION OF WAR. The National Council for Prevention of War was established by Frederick J. Libby* in 1921. Libby was head of the Arms Limitation Council, a disarmament group. In particular, the National Council for Prevention of War lobbied for naval arms reductions and worked diligently to influence United States policy at the Washington Naval Conference* of 1921–1922. The council also supported the efforts of the Geneva Naval Conference of 1927,* the Geneva Conference of 1932,* and the London Naval Conference of 1930.* During the 1930s, the council supported the Neutrality Acts to prevent the United States from entering World War II. The National Council for Prevention of War disbanded after the Japanese attack on Pearl Harbor in 1941. (Elton Atwater, *Organized Efforts in the United States towards Peace,* 1963.)

NATIONAL CREDIT CORPORATION. On September 21, 1931, Great Britain went off the gold standard and sent money markets all over the world into a tailspin. In the United States, it only exacerbated the banking* crisis, bringing about the suspension of hundreds of banks when panic-stricken depositors began withdrawing their funds. Committed to voluntarism and the strength of the private sector, Herbert Hoover* wanted the banking community to work out a plan to rescue weak banks. Early in October 1931, Secretary of the Treasury Andrew Mellon* held a meeting at his Washington apartment for a number of prominent New York bankers, and there they organized the National Credit Corporation, a private pool of $500 million to loan out to troubled banks.

The National Credit Corporation was soon an obvious failure. In the first place, the dimensions of the banking crisis dwarfed its meager resources. Not until the New Deal had invested billions of dollars in the banking system would stability return to the money markets. Second, the directors of the National Credit Corporation would loan money only to sound banks able to post adequate collateral, making sure that troubled banks would not have access to its funds. By December 1931, the National Credit Corporation had loaned only $10 million, and President Hoover had to call for the establishment of the Reconstruction Finance Corporation.* (James S. Olson, "The End of Voluntarism: Herbert Hoover and the National Credit Corporation," *Annals of Iowa*, 41 [Fall 1972], 1104–13.)

NATIONAL FEDERATION OF BUSINESS AND PROFESSIONAL WOMEN'S CLUBS. The National Federation of Business and Professional Women's Clubs was founded in Washington, D.C., in 1919. Its major purpose was to promote the economic interests of middle-class women who were pursuing professional careers. During the 1920s, the federation worked primarily to achieve equal pay for women performing the same jobs as men and to secure uniform civil service classifications for women. It achieved the latter goal in 1923 when the United States civil service commission instituted such a system. (NFBPWC, *History of the National Federation of Business and Professional Women's Clubs*, 1961.)

NATIONAL GRANGE. Originally established in 1867 as the Patrons of Husbandry, the National Grange was originally a secret, fraternal organization of farmers designed to meet the social needs of an isolated, rural population. After the panic of 1873, the Grange became more overtly political, lobbying for legislation beneficial to farmers, particularly state regulation of railroads and grain elevators. They lobbied for the Interstate Commerce Act of 1887, which brought the railroads under federal regulation; and, during the 1890s, the Grange movement was closely associated with Populism. After 1900, when the farm economy improved, the Grange campaigned for federal antitrust legislation, for paved roads in rural areas, for a system of government rural credit banks, for parcel post, and for regulation of the securities exchanges and futures markets.

During the 1920s, the Grange campaigned for enactment of the McNary-Haugen Bill* to dump farm surpluses in foreign markets. By the early 1930s, the Grange had come to support crop reduction and soil conservation schemes, and it became an early advocate of the Agricultural Adjustment Administration in the 1930s. Along the with National Farmers' Union and the American Farm Bureau Federation,* the National Grange was the most influential farm lobbying group in the United States during the 1920s. (Solon J. Buck, *The Granger Movement,* 1963; Dennis S. Nordin, *The Rich Harvest: Mainstreams of Granger History, 1867–1900,* 1974.)

NATIONAL ORIGINS ACT OF 1924. Throughout the late nineteenth century, the demands for immigration restriction mounted in the United States. Labor unions, concerned about crowded labor markets and low wages, had long demanded an end to the open door, while employers had just as insistently called for a continuation of unlimited immigration. But in the 1890s, when immigration from southern and eastern Europe began to predominate, a new ethnic dimension strengthened anti-immigrant forces. The new immigrants tended to be Roman Catholic* or Jewish,* and they huddled into huge urban communities. Nativist groups like the American Protective Association* and the Ku Klux Klan* predicted the demise of the white, Protestant, nordic American, as did popular writers like Madison Grant.* Congress had excluded Chinese immigrants in 1882, and in 1903 Congress set up an inspection system for new immigrants and excluded anarchists and prostitutes. Congress had also passed literacy tests for new immigrants in 1896, 1913, and 1915, but Presidents Grover Cleveland, William Howard Taft,* and Woodrow Wilson* had vetoed them.

World War I gave new momentum to the restrictionists. A wave of antiradical hysteria swept through the country, and newer immigrants were suspect in terms of their loyalty to the United States. Also, since the United States was at war with Germany, Italy, and Austria-Hungary, the German, Italian, Polish, Hungarian, Czech, Slovak, Slovenian, and Croatian immigrants were under careful scrutiny. Congress passed a series of laws between 1917 and 1921 limiting immigration: a literacy test, which was passed over Wilson's veto in 1917; a war measure excluding anarchists in 1918; and an act deporting alien enemies and anarchists in 1920.

When the Republicans assumed control of Congress and the White House in 1921, the clamor for restriction had become overwhelming. In May 1921 Congress passed the Emergency Quota Act,* which limited immigration annually to 3 percent of the number of each nationality according to the 1910 census, with no more than 357,000 immigrants admitted each year. The demands of racists, unions, and patriotic societies continued, however, and in May 1924 Congress passed the Johnson-Reed Act, or the National Origins Act, which reduced the total number of immigrants to be admitted each year from 357,000 to 164,000 and limited the annual immigration from any one country to 2 percent of its 1890 American population. The shift in the law from 1910 to 1890 reduced the quota of southern and eastern Europeans in favor of northern and western Europeans. The law stated that in 1927 the maximum annual immigration would drop to 150,000 and the 2 percent apportionment would be based on the 1920 census. That change did not go into effect until 1929. Finally, the National Origins Act excluded all Japanese immigration, which led to mass protests in Japan and the staging of "Humiliation Day" in Tokyo on July 1, 1924. The Japanese were enraged about being singled out in the law. The National Origins Act, in a concession to western farmers, allowed unlimited immigration from the Western Hemisphere, guaranteeing a continued supply of Hispanic farm laborers. The era of unlimited American immigration was over. (Thomas J. Curran, *Xenophobia and Immigration, 1820–1930,* 1975; John Higham, *Strangers in the Land: Patterns of American Nativism, 1860–1925,* 1955; James S. Olson, *The Ethnic Dimension in American History,* 1979.)

NATIONAL WOMAN'S PARTY. In 1912 Alice Paul* and Crystal Eastman formed the Congressional Union for Woman Suffrage; by 1916, it had evolved into the National Woman's Party (NWP), an independent third party committed to the absolute equality of women in the world. Between 1916 and 1920, the NWP resorted to militant demonstrations to secure ratification of the Nineteenth Amendment* to the Constitution. President Woodrow Wilson* opposed women's suffrage, so the National Woman's Party made him and the Democratic Party* their special targets. When the Nineteenth Amendment to the Constitution was ratified in 1920, Paul considered it only a first step. In the 1920s, women could not run for public office or serve on juries in a number of states; surrendered citizenship if they married foreigners; enjoyed few property rights, and rarely got custody of children in divorce cases. To rectify these inequities, the National Woman's Party proposed an Equal Rights Amendment, and, in 1923, Paul introduced it to Congress. She wanted nothing less than absolute equality for women. For example, Paul applauded the Supreme Court's decision in *Adkins* v. *Children's Hospital,** which voided special minimum wage laws for women. If minimum wages were not for men, said Paul, they certainly were not for women.

The Equal Rights Amendment did not make much headway in the 1920s. Membership in the National Woman's Party peaked at 50,000 in 1920 and then declined after ratification of the Nineteenth Amendment. Other women's groups were vigorously pursuing protective legislation. In 1920, the League of Women Voters* created the Women's Joint Congressional Committee, a coalition of ten women's groups (American Association of University Women, American Home Economics Association, General Federation of Women's Clubs, National Consumers League, National Council of Jewish Women, National Federation of Business and Professional Women's Clubs,* National Women's Christian Temperance Union, National Women's Trade Union League, and Daughters of the American Revolution), which altogether claimed ten million members. They wanted federal maternal and infant protection legislation, which they secured in the Sheppard-Towner Act of 1921*; federal aid to education; federal development of Muscle Shoals*; social security, and an end to child labor. Since many of these seemed to be special legislation that benefited only women, the National Woman's Party opposed them, splitting the women's movement during the 1920s. By the mid-1920s, the Women's Joint Congressional Committee was vigorously pursuing the peace movement, and conservative groups like the Daughters of the American Revolution and later the General Federation of Women's Clubs bolted the group. Because of such strong philosophical differences, the women's movement could not unite behind the Equal Rights Amendment, and it failed to secure congressional approval. (William Henry Chafe, *The American Woman: Her Changing Social, Economic, and Political Roles, 1920–1970*, 1972; J. Stanley Lemons, *The Women Citizen: Social Feminism in the 1920s*, 1973; Lois Scharf and Joan Jensen, eds., *Decades of Discontent: The Women's Movement 1920–1940*, 1983.)

NEWBERRY, TRUMAN HANDY. Truman Newberry was born in Detroit, Michigan, on November 5, 1864. He graduated from Yale in 1885, and, because of family connections, Newberry went to work immediately for the the Bay City & Alpena Railway as superintendent of construction. In 1887, his father died, and Newberry was named president of the Detroit Steel and Spring Company, as well as of all other family businesses, a position he held until 1902. Between 1902 and 1905, Newberry was a director of the Packard Motor Company. At the end of 1905, President Theodore Roosevelt named him assistant secretary of the navy and secretary of the navy in 1908, where he served until the end of the Roosevelt administration in 1909. In 1918, running as a Republican against Henry Ford,* who had won the Democratic nomination, Newberry won a seat in the United States Senate. The election campaign had been an ugly one, in which Newberry had attacked Ford as a pacifist and a "Hun lover." When the election was over, Ford unleashed an army of private detectives, who turned up undeniable evidence that Newberry had vastly exceeded Michigan limits on campaign spending. A grand jury indicted Newberry, and he was subsequently convicted and sentenced to prison. In 1922, the Supreme Court overturned the conviction, and Newberry took up his seat in the Senate; however, shortly thereafter, he resigned it. Truman Newberry died on October 3, 1945. *Detroit Free Press*, October 4, 1945; *Dictionary of American Biography*, supp. 3 [1973], 549–55.)

NEWBERRY v. UNITED STATES (256 U.S. 232). By a vote of five to four, the United States Supreme Court held on May 2, 1921, that Truman Newberry's conviction for violating federal statutes against excessive primary campaign spending was unconstitutional because Congress did not have the power to regulate primary campaigns. In the court's opinion, political primaries were not part of the formal election process and therefore were not subject to federal regulation. (Congressional Quarterly, *Guide to the U.S. Supreme Court*, 1979.)

NEW ERA. Frederick Lewis Allen, the noted journalist and popular historian of the 1920s, used the term "New Era" to describe the decade. Because of the unprecedented prosperity of the 1920s, the preoccupation with sex* and morality, the rise of an urban society, the ubiquitousness of the automobile,* and the popular intoxication with radio* and motion pictures,* Allen was convinced that the United States had entered a "New Era." The term seemed appropriate to scholars, and "New Era" became a conventional way of designating the 1920s. (Frederick Lewis Allen, *Only Yesterday,* 1931.)

NICHOLSON, THOMAS. Thomas Nicholson was born on January 27, 1862, in Woodburn, Ontario, Canada. He graduated from Northwestern University in 1892, received a divinity degree that same year from the Garrett Biblical Institute, and earned a master's degree at Northwestern in 1895. Between 1884 and 1903, Nicholson taught school and worked as a principal; from 1903 to 1908, he was president of Dakota Wesleyan University. He joined the Board of Education of the Methodist Episcopal Church as general secretary in 1908, and stayed there until 1916 when he was ordained bishop of Chicago. Nicholson stayed in Chicago until 1924, when he assumed the episcopate of Detroit. Nicholson was a devout campaigner of the temperance movement, and in 1921 he was elected president of the Anti-Saloon League* of America, a position he held until 1932. During the 1920s, Nicholson tried to defend the Eighteenth Amendment* and guarantee enforcement of the Volstead Act,* but his efforts were in vain. The experiment with prohibition* disintegrated into a crime-ridden, moralistic crusade which most urban Americans disdained. Nicholson retired in 1932, by which time he could see that prohibition was doomed. He died on December 20, 1947. (*New York Times,* December 21, 1947.)

NINE POWER TREATY. The Nine Power Treaty, a product of the Washington Naval Conference* of 1921–1922, was signed on February 6, 1922. Nine countries, including the United States and Japan, agreed to respect the territorial integrity and political independence of China. They also pledged to assist China in maintaining political stability and guaranteeing equal commercial access by international corporations to the Chinese market. In essence, the Nine Power Treaty was a reiteration of the Open Door Policy, with nine international powers agreeing to its principles. The United States Senate ratified the Nine Power Treaty in March 1922. (Thomas H. Buckley, *The United States and the Washington Conference, 1921–1922,* 1970; Eugene P. Trani and David L. Wilson, *The Presidency of Warren G. Harding,* 1977.)

NINETEENTH AMENDMENT. The movement for women's suffrage formally began in 1848 at the Woman's Rights Convention at Seneca Falls, New York. It first emerged from the antislavery movement when such women as Lucretia Mott, Susan B. Anthony, and Elizabeth Cady Stanton were outraged when abolitionist men would not treat abolitionist women with any respect at all. They discovered another form of slavery in America—the bondage of women—and they decided to do something about it. The Woman's Rights Convention at Seneca Falls in 1848 was the first step. Former women crusaders in the temperance and antislavery movements flocked to the campaign for women's rights, and the National Woman's Rights Convention at Worcester, Massachusetts, in 1850 was the result. At that and at subsequent conventions in the 1850s, Mott, Stanton, and Anthony demanded property, civil, and voting rights for women.

The Civil War interrupted the movement, but in 1869 Susan B. Anthony formed the National Woman Suffrage Association to campaign for the vote. Stanton and Anthony then spoke and lobbied throughout the country for the rest of their lives trying to achieve the franchise. Their first victories came in the western states, where frontier conditions had a social leveling effect and where women settlers were desperately needed. The territory of Wyoming first gave women the franchise, and it was admitted to the union in 1890. Colorado became a woman suffrage state in 1893, and Utah and Idaho followed in 1896. By that time, Frances Willard and the Women's Christian Temperance Union had joined the crusade.

At the turn of the century, the movement lagged for a time. The older leaders had passed away or were too old to continue the fight, and no one had appeared to take their place. But that vacuum did not last for long. In 1907 Harriot Stanton Blatch formed the Woman's Political Union, and in 1909 Carrie Chapman Catt* formed the Woman Suffrage Party. Also, the progressive movement aided women's suffrage. Once progressivism added a social welfare dimension to its reforms, progressives saw the women's vote as a way of increasing their political power. In 1911 Washington and California added the women's vote, giving the national movement a real boost. Still, women's suffrage was confined to the western states, none of which had any real power in the electoral college and therefore little power to affect presidential elections.

In 1912, Alice Paul* joined the crusade, blaming the Democratic Party* for the failure of women's suffrage to succeed outside of the Far West. Paul demanded a federal constitutional amendment and began holding demonstrations in Washington, D.C. When Woodrow Wilson* would not support the amendment, Paul organized anti-Democrat campaigns throughout the western states in the elections of 1914. In 1916 she founded the National Woman's Party* to promote the woman's vote, and they campaigned against Democrats in all the suffrage states. During World War I, she arranged for constant picketing of the White House, always demanding women's suffrage.

While Paul was militantly protesting, Carrie Chapman Catt had become the president of the National Woman's Suffrage Association. She was an effective lobbyist and worked at the state level to achieve the franchise. In 1914, Illinois, a large electoral state, had accepted women's suffrage, but her great victories came in Rhode Island and New York in 1917. That gave the constitutional amendment tremendous momentum. Democrats now felt vulnerable in large, powerful states. Membership in the National Woman's Suffrage Association had grown from 13,000 in 1893 to more than two million in 1917. On January 10, 1918, the House of Representatives voted for the Nineteenth Amendment,* with two votes to spare. By 1919, thirty-nine states allowed women to vote in at least some elections. That year, the amendment was passed by the Senate, and one year later ratification was complete. Women had the right to vote. (Olivia Coolidge, *Women's Rights: The Suffrage Movement in America, 1848–1920,* 1966.)

NIXON v. *CONDON* (286 U.S. 73). On March 7, 1927, by a unanimous vote in the case of *Nixon* v. *Herndon,* the United States Supreme Court overthrew a Texas law that excluded blacks from voting in the Democratic party primary elections. According to the court, the "white primary" violated the equal protection clause of the Fourteenth Amendment. In response, the Texas legislature passed a law authorizing the state party executive committee to determine voting qualifications, and the party quickly excluded blacks. On May 2, 1932, by a vote of five to four in *Nixon* v. *Condon,* the Supreme Court overturned the law, again arguing that neither state government nor political parties could deprive blacks of their Fourteenth Amendment and Fifteenth Amendment guaranteed right to vote. (Congressional Quarterly, *Guide to the U.S. Supreme Court,* 1979.)

NIXON v. *HERNDON* (273 U.S. 536). See NIXON v. CONDON

NOBLE, EDWARD JOHN. Edward J. Noble was born on August 8, 1882, in Gouverneur, New York. He graduated from Yale in 1905 and then spent several years in the advertising business. Along with partner J. Ray Allen, Noble bought the rights to a mint candy product called Life Savers. They began marketing the product out of New York City, but they were unsuccessful until 1914, when they began using a foil packaging which preserved the product's flavor. In the beginning, they hired young people to go into business for themselves as Life Savers salesmen, and sales jumped from 940,000 packages in 1914 to 6,725,000 in 1915. Sugar shortages hurt the business during World War I, but after the war sales increases were rapid, especially after they added the famous fruit candy line in 1924. By the end of the 1920s, Life Savers was one of the most well-known candy products in the United States. Noble continued as chairman of the board until 1938. In 1940, he purchased WMCA radio* station in New York City, sold it in 1943, and late in 1943 purchased the Blue Network from RCA for $8 million. The Blue Network became the American Broadcasting Company in 1944, and he presided over the early years of the company. During 1938 and 1939, Noble served as the first head of the Civil Aeronautics Authority and briefly in 1940 as secretary of commerce. He died on December 28, 1958. *(New York Times,* December 29, 1958.)

NONPARTISAN LEAGUE. The Nonpartisan League was established in 1915 by Arthur C. Townley at Bismarck, North Dakota, and Townley served as its first president. For years, North Dakota politics had been dominated by the Republican Party,* but Townley believed that the farm bloc needed better political representation. Townley envisioned the Nonpartisan League fielding a slate of candidates sympathetic to farmer needs. The league's basic philosophy was socialistic, calling for state ownership of all grain elevators, processing mills, storage facilities, and meat processing plants, as well as nationalization of the railroads. In 1916, the Nonpartisan League won a major victory when Lynn J. Frazier* was elected governor of North Dakota by a landslide. League candidates also won 81 of 113 seats in the state house of representatives and 19 of 49 seats in the state senate. The Nonpartisan League had reached a membership of nearly 200,000 people by World War I; its main centers were in Minnesota, North Dakota, South Dakota, and Montana. After that, the Nonpartisan League declined in power. During World War I it took, for a time, a pro-German stand, and when the United States declared war on Germany in 1917, the league's reputation was damaged. During the 1920s, its Socialist philosophy did not fit the conservative political temperament of the times, and the league lost members. During the 1930s, despite the Great Depression,* the Nonpartisan League did not make any important gains. Lynn Frazier was by then a United States Senator, and, along with Representative William Lemke, he sponsored the Frazier-Lemke Act of 1934 which placed a moratorium on farm foreclosures. Once again, however, foreign policy issues hurt the league. Its membership was decidedly isolationist during the 1930s, and, when the United States entered the war in 1941, the league was again perceived as potentially subversive group. The Nonpartisan League joined the Democratic Party* in 1956. (Robert L. Moran, *Political Prairie Fire: Nonpartisan League, 1915–1922*, 1955; Charles E. Russell, *The Story of the Nonpartisan League: A Chapter in American Evolution*, 1974.)

NORBECK, PETER. Peter Norbeck, a Progressive Republican from South Dakota, was born on August 27, 1870, near Vermillion. He attended the University of South Dakota and then moved several times within the state between 1900 and 1909 working as a farmer, contractor, and driller of oil and gas wells. Norbeck won a seat in the state legislature in 1909, served as lieutenant governor in 1915 and 1916, and was governor of South Dakota between 1917 and 1921. Norbeck was elected to the United States Senate in 1920, and won reelection in 1926 and 1932. During his nearly sixteen years in the Senate, Norbeck was a leader of the farm bloc,* and he adopted a consistently progressive stand on many issues, promoting the McNary-Haugen Bill* in the 1920s and promoting a host of marketing schemes that resulted in the Agricultural Marketing Act of 1929.* In the 1930s, he played an important role in the coalition of liberal Democrats and progressive Republicans responsible for much of the New Deal legislation. In the election of 1936, Norbeck could not bear to endorse Alf Landon, so he supported

President Franklin D. Roosevelt.* Six weeks later, Norbeck died on December 20, 1936. (*New York Times,* December 21, 1936.)

"NORMALCY." For the past sixty years journalists and historians have used the term "normalcy" to describe the business culture and conservative politics of the 1920s. In May 1920, during a speech in Boston, Massachusetts, Senator Warren G. Harding* called for a return to "not heroism, but healing, not nostrums but normalcy." After years of war, disillusionment, and social strife, most Americans were ready for tranquility, and Harding's use of the term "normalcy" captured the mood of a nation. When Harding won the Republican nomination in 1920, the GOP campaigned on the theme of a "return to normalcy," and, ever since, historians have found the phrase a useful tool for describing American politics in the 1920s. "Normalcy" has become synonymous with pro-business legislation in the form of high tariffs, low taxes, and generous subsidies. (Robert K. Murray, *The Politics of Normalcy: Governmental Theory and Practice in the Harding-Coolidge Era,* 1973; Frederick L. Paxson, *Postwar Years, Normalcy, 1918–1923,* 1948.)

NORRIS, GEORGE WILLIAM. George Norris was born in Sandusky County, Ohio, on July 11, 1861. Tragedy struck the family in 1864 when his father died of pneumonia and his older brother was killed in the Civil War. George worked all through his childhood to help support the family, and he attended Baldwin University for two years. Norris graduated and received a law degree from the Northern Indiana Normal School and Business Institute (later Valpariso University) in 1883. He taught school for two years and then moved to Nebraska to open a law practice. Norris prospered in the 1880s, and in the 1890s he began his public career, serving as the prosecuting attorney for Furnas County (1890–1895) and state judge for the 14th Judicial District (1896–1902). In 1902 he won a seat in Congress as a Republican. Norris quickly evolved into a powerful progressive congressman, favoring railroad regulation, lower tariffs, and political reform. In the election of 1912, he won a seat in the United States Senate and began a career of thirty-three years in the upper house.

In domestic policy, Norris supported most of Woodrow Wilson's* progressive reform program, but he strongly opposed what he regarded as Wilson's adventurism in foreign policy, especially in Mexico. In 1917 he voted against arming American merchant ships and against the declaration of war on Germany. Re-elected in 1918, Norris opposed American entry into the League of Nations.* During the 1920s, Norris was constantly at odds with the business-dominated, conservative Republican administrations. He was increasingly disillusioned with his own party, especially with such scandals as Teapot Dome* and the influence major corporations had on politicians. In foreign policy, he opposed the continued interventions in the Caribbean and Central America and favored recognition of the Soviet Union.

Domestically, Norris was a thorn in Republic sides. No issue was more emotionally charged than that concerning the future of facilities built at Muscle Shoals,* Alabama, during World War I. Norris stood like granite against administration attempts to dispose of the facilities to private interests at virtual giveaway prices. Rather, he demanded that Muscle Shoals' hydroelectric facilities be operated by the government for the welfare of the people of the Tennessee River Valley. By 1928 he succeeded in gaining congressional approval for government operation of Muscle Shoals, only to have it vetoed by President Calvin Coolidge.* A similar bill, passed in 1931, was vetoed by President Herbert Hoover.* Norris did succeed in passing the Twentieth Amendment* to the Constitution and the Norris–La Guardia Labor Relations Act of 1932.*

In the elections of 1928* and 1932,* Norris bolted the Republican Party* and endorsed Al Smith* and Franklin D. Roosevelt* for president. Under a Democratic administration, Norris finally succeeded with his Muscle Shoals plan when Congress passed and Roosevelt signed a bill creating the Tennessee Valley Authority in 1933. Norris also sponsored the Rural Electrification Act of 1936. He was a faithful supporter of Franklin D. Roosevelt. Norris lost his bid for reelection in 1942. He died on September 2, 1944. (Richard Lowitt, *George W. Norris: The Making of a Progressive, 1861–1912,* 1963; idem, *George W. Norris: The Persistence of a Progressive, 1913–1933,* 1971; idem, *George W. Norris: The Triumph of a Progressive, 1933–1944,* 1978.)

NORRIS–La GUARDIA LABOR RELATIONS ACT OF 1932. Early in the 1900s, organized labor viewed "government by injunction" as a new and dangerous form of oppression in which federal judges became at once legislators, judges, and executioners. The courts exercised sweeping controls over unions under the Sherman Antitrust Act of 1890, and they used the antistrike injunction frequently. Progressives brought political pressure on Congress, and the Clayton Act of 1914 pointed out that labor unions did not necessarily come under antitrust laws. It prohibited the use of injunctions unless the court believed that a strike would cause irreparable damage to property, and it made boycotts, strikes, and peaceful demonstrations legal. Samuel Gompers,* head of the American Federation of Labor,* called the Clayton Act the "Magna Carta" of labor. But, despite the law, the federal courts were full of justices from the old school who looked on labor unions with suspicion. In addition, it was the custom of business early in the 1900s to extract from employees a promise not to join a labor union as a condition of employment. Such promises were called "yellow-dog contracts" by workers. The Supreme Court had upheld such agreements.

Organized labor felt the need to deal with the problems of injunctions and yellow-dog contracts, and in 1932 Senator George W. Norris* of Nebraska and Congressman Fiorello La Guardia* of New York submitted legislation to Congress. Professor Felix Frankfurter of the Harvard Law School wrote the measure. It prohibited federal courts from issuing injunctions against ordinary collective-bargaining practices, such as strikes, picketing, and boycotts—and it made yellow-dog contracts unenforceable. Although reluctant about the measure, President Herbert Hoover* signed it on March 23, 1932. Court injunctions could no longer be used against legitimate union activities. The Norris–La Guardia Labor Relations Act of 1932 was one of the few genuinely progressive laws passed since the Woodrow Wilson* administration. (C. O. Gregory and H. A. Katz, *Labor and the Law*, 1979.)

NYE, GERALD PRENTICE. Gerald P. Nye was born in Hortonville, Wisconsin, on December 19, 1892. He graduated from high school in 1911 and moved to Iowa to pursue a career in journalism. Later he moved to North Dakota and bought the *Fryburg Pioneer* in 1919 and the *Griggs County Sentinel-Courier* in 1920. In November 1925 Senator Edwin F. Ladd died, and Nye was appointed to fill the unexpired term. In an extremely close election, Nye won his own seat in 1926. He was critical of the Coolidge* administration, regarding the president as the tool of big bankers and businessmen. During the Hoover* administration, Nye pushed hard for farm relief, and during the New Deal he was an especially vocal critic of the National Recovery Administration and the National Labor Relations Board.

   Nye gained national attention in 1934 by lobbying against the military armaments industry, insisting that a special Senate committee investigate its practices. An ardent isolationist, Nye helped secure the Neutrality Acts of the 1930s. He eventually accused Franklin D. Roosevelt* of intentionally leading the country into World War II. In the election of 1944, Nye suffered a stunning defeat and abandoned his political career. Gerald P. Nye died on July 17, 1971. (Richard S. Kirdendall, *The United States, 1929–1945: Years of Crisis and Change,* 1974; *New York Times,* July 18, 1971.)

O

OCHS, ADOLPH SIMON. Adolph S. Ochs was born on March 12, 1858, in Cincinnati, Ohio. In 1869, Adolph went to work in the offices of the Knoxville *Chronicle*, where he began his lifelong infatuation with the newspaper business. When he was nineteen, he moved to Chattanooga, Tennessee, and in the next year, with $250, he bought controlling interest in a failing newspaper, the *Chattanooga Times*. It was an immediate success, and in 1896, with $75,000, Ochs bought the *New York Times*, which had also come on hard times. Slowly he built the paper into a profit-making venture, as well as the most respected journal in New York City, and in 1902, Ochs purchased the Philadelphia *Public Ledger*. By 1920, the *New York Times* had become one of the most prestigious newspapers in the world; he even made its sports pages journalistically respectable. He was the first American publisher to install direct wireless contacts with Europe. During the 1920s, Ochs, as a follower of Reform Judaism, opposed Zionism and stimulated real controversy among Jews in New York City. Adolph Ochs died on April 8, 1935. (Meyer Berger, *The Story of the New York Times,* 1951; David Halberstam, *The Powers That Be,* 1979; *New York Times,* April 9, 1935.)

O'CONNOR, THOMAS VENTRY. Thomas O'Connor was born in Toronto, Canada, in 1870. When he was still an infant, his family moved to Buffalo, New York, and after leaving home O'Connor went to work on the Great Lakes, eventually becoming a marine engineer and a tugboat captain. In 1908 he was elected president of the International Longshoreman's Association, and he provided conservative leadership of the union for the next thirteen years. A Republican, O'Connor never sanctioned a longshoremen's strike. President Warren Harding* appointed him vice-chairman of the United States Shipping Board in 1921, and in 1924 O'Connor became chairman. Consistent with the philosophy of the time, O'Connor used his position to assist private shipping interests. He died on October 17, 1935. *(New York Times,* October 18, 1935; Maud Russell, *Men along the Shore,* 1966.)

"OHIO GANG." The term "Ohio Gang" was used by journalists and later by historians to describe the presidential appointments of the Warren G. Harding* administration in the 1920s. A native of Marion, Ohio, Harding surrounded himself in Washington, D.C., with cronies from home. Charles "Old Doc" Sawyer of Marion, Ohio, became the White House physician. Ed Scobey, former sheriff of Pickaway County, Ohio, became the new director of the mint. Harding's brother-in-law, the Reverend Heber H. Votaw, became superintendent of federal prisons. Daniel Crissinger, a lawyer and banker from Marion, Ohio, became comptroller of the currency. Harding later sent Crissinger on to bigger and better things—governor of the Federal Reserve Board.* A vacation, card-playing cohort of Harding, Charles R. Forbes, became head of the Veteran's Bureau.* Harding's longtime friend and adviser, Harry Daugherty,* was named attorney general, and Daugherty's intimate friend and confident, Jesse Smith, came along, even enjoying an office at the Department of Justice without a government job. The unofficial headquarters of the "Ohio Gang" was 1625 K Street in Washington, D.C. There Jesse Smith arranged regular parties for card-playing, drinking, and prostitute chasing, pasttimes in which even the president indulged. Because Harding gave so much trust and power to men with so few scruples and with so little integrity, he soon found himself in the midst of the scandals that eventually defined his presidency. (Eugene P. Trani and David L. Wilson, *The Presidency of Warren G. Harding,* 1977.)

O'KEEFFE, GEORGIA. Born on a wheat farm near San Prairie, Wisconsin, on November 15, 1887, Georgia O'Keeffe was the distinguished, female modernist painter of the 1920s. After finishing high school, she studied at the Art Institute of Chicago and in 1907 and 1908 under William Merritt Chase at the Art Students League of New York. From Japanese painters, she gained an appreciation for the abstract, and several winters in Texas provided her with a sense of space and landscape. O'Keeffe met Arthur Steiglitz in 1916, and he arranged for her first exhibition in 1917. During the 1920s, O'Keeffe's work took its modernist turn, enlarging details to such an extent that objects lost their recognizable quality, such as her painting *Yellow Cactus Flowers.* Later in the 1920s, in such works as *Radiator Building—Night, New York* (1927), she went into a period of chilling detail in reconstructing urban landscapes. Beginning in the 1930s, O'Keeffe spent her winters in Santa Fe, New Mexico, and she moved there permanently in 1946. By that time her work had become increasingly abstract, although it still retained her ability to juxtapose mystery and power. Georgia O'Keeffe died on March 6, 1986, at the age of ninety-eight. (Milton W. Brown et al., *American Art,* 1979.)

OLD GUARD. The term "Old Guard" was used by journalists in the 1920s and subsequently by historians to describe the conservative Republican congressional delegation. For the most part, they advocated high tariffs, reduced taxes on the rich, and a pro-business posture by the federal government. The congressmen usually included as members of the "Old Guard" were Boies Penrose (Pennsylvania), Joseph W. Fordney (Michigan), Frank Brandegee (Connecticut), Lewis Ball (Delaware), Medill McCormick (Illinois), Joseph E. Watson (Indiana), Harry S. New (Indiana), Henry Cabot Lodge* (Massachusetts), Joseph S. Frelinghuysen (New Jersey), James W. Wadsworth, Jr., (New York), William M. Calder (New York), Philander Knox* (Pennsylvania), Walter E. Edge* (New Jersey), Joseph I. France (Maryland), Frederick Hale (Maine), and Reed Smoot* (Utah). (Robert K. Murray, *The Politics of Normalcy: Governmental Theory and Practice in the Harding-Coolidge Era,* 1973.)

"ONE HUNDRED PERCENT AMERICANISM." The phrase "one hundred percent Americanism" came into vogue after President Woodrow Wilson* issued his war message to Congress in April 1917. Public opinion was caught up in a jingoistic nationalism which insisted on conformity and loyalty, and which demanded that minority groups—racial, political, and ethnic—identify completely with the American nation. For some groups, such as German Americans or Socialists, the spirit of "one hundred percent Americanism" meant persecution, even when there was no overt justification for it. When the war ended, the spirit of "one hundred percent Americanism" lived on in two forms: anti-radicalism and the Red Scare* of 1919–1921, and the xenophobia which resulted in the National Origins Act of 1924.* Only then did the chauvinism begin to subside. (John Higham, *Strangers in the Land. Patterns of American Nativism 1860–1925,* 1965.)

O'NEILL, EUGENE. Eugene O'Neill was born in New York City on October 16, 1888. In 1914 and 1915 he attended George Pierce Baker's "47 Workshop" at Harvard University, and then he joined the Provincetown Players. Their troupe provided the staging for most of O'Neill's plays. During the 1920s, O'Neill was the most experimental of American dramatists; literary scholars now view him as the greatest dramatist produced by American culture. O'Neill's view of life grew more and more pessimistic, until in *The Iceman Cometh* (1946), his vision of humanity degenerated into meaningless illusion followed by death. O'Neill's great works during the 1920s include *The Emperor Jones* (1921), *Anna Christie* (1922), *The Hairy Ape* (1922), *Desire under the Elms* (1925), *The Great God Brown* (1926), *Strange Interlude* (1928), and *Mourning Becomes Electra* (1931). Eugene O'Neill died on November 27, 1953. (Frederick J. Hoffman, *The 1920s: American Writing in the Postwar Decade,* 1949; Martin Seymour-Smith, *Who's Who in Twentieth Century Literature,* 1976.)

OPEN SHOP MOVEMENT. During the 1920s, American corporations launched a strong movement against union organization. Labor had made important gains during World War I, and a major objective of big business during the 1920s was to set back the clock. To take the sting out of the campaign, businesses worked at improving wages, hours, and working conditions. Real wages went up 26 percent between 1919 and 1929, and workers for the first time began to get paid vacations and modest retirement programs. Business called it "welfare capitalism" and argued that benevolent employers were more capable of meeting workers' needs than labor unions. They even organized company unions, shop committees, and workers' councils to hear worker grievances.

The company union* was the most ubiquitous feature of "welfare capitalism" in the 1920s. Major corporations knew that labor unions were here to stay, and Secretary of Commerce Herbert Hoover* was even encouraging their formation as means of increasing the national organization structure of the American economy. But instead of dealing with such existing unions as the American Federation of Labor* or the United Mine Workers, which seemed to have an adversarial relationship with management, company officers preferred to establish unions within the corporation, which they felt could achieve all the beneficial results of labor organization without the disruptions of strikes and work stoppages. Workers, of course, had little trust in the company unions of the 1920s, which they felt were simply pawns of management.

Beginning in 1919, corporate officials painted unions as dangerous, subversive, and anti-American. The central doctrine of what business called "democratic capitalism" was the "open shop" (where no worker could be forced to join a union in order to keep a job), and in 1920 the National Association of Manufacturers* launched the "American Plan," a nationwide union-busting movement. Federal courts helped, as did the political atmosphere in Washington. In 1921 the Supreme Court declared picketing illegal and upheld the use of anti-union injunctions to break strikes. The Justice Department helped crush the strike of 400,000 railroad workers in 1922. Union membership in the United States has traditionally increased during prosperous times, but the 1920s, because of the open shop movement, was an important exception. Between 1920 and 1929, union membership dropped from 5 million to 4.3 million members. (Irving Bernstein, *The Lean Years: A History of the American Worker, 1920–1933*, 1960; Robert Zenger, *Republicans and Labor*, 1969.)

P

PACKERS AND STOCKYARDS ACT OF 1921. On August 15, 1921, Congress passed the Packers and Stockyards Act, an act that did not exactly fit the pattern of ''normalcy'' prevailing early in the 1920s. Pushed by the farm bloc* in Congress, the act gave the Department of Agriculture the power to prohibit unfair trade practices in the livestock, poultry, and dairy industries. Gross overproduction had drastically reduced commodity prices after World War I, but large numbers of farmers were saddled with high fixed costs because of debts they had undertaken to increase war production. By the early 1920s, a new farm crisis was emerging, and farmers were once again, as they had in the 1890s, blaming middlemen and processors for their plight. The Packers and Stockyards Act forced all operators of stockyards and marketing cooperatives to register with the Department of Agriculture and refrain from artificially manipulating prices. Although the general tone of the legislation was not consistent with normalcy's retreat from government interference in business, conservative Republicans had little choice but to go along with the farm bloc. (James H. Shideler, *Farm Crisis, 1919–1923,* 1957.)

PAGE, WALTER HINES. Walter Hines Page was born on August 15, 1855, in Cary, North Carolina. He graduated from Randolph-Macon College in 1876 and then did graduate work at Johns Hopkins until 1878. Page became a reporter for the *St. Joseph Gazette* in Missouri in 1880, and he worked for the *New York World* between 1881 and 1883. He became editor of *Forum* magazine in 1887, and in 1898 he joined the *Atlantic Monthly* in the position of editor. A close friend of Woodrow Wilson,* Page was appointed ambassador to Great Britain in 1913, where he worked diligently against American neutrality and in favor of American intervention. Page returned to the United States in 1918 and died on December 2, 1918. (Ross Gregory, *Walter Hines Page: Ambassador to the Court of St. James,* 1970.)

PALEY, WILLIAM SAMUEL. William S. Paley was born on September 28, 1901, in Chicago, Illinois, to Russian immigrant parents. His family had made a fortune in the cigar business in the United States, and William graduated from the Wharton School of Finance of the University of Pennsylvania in 1922. He immediately entered the family business as a vice-president. In 1924, Paley signed a contract with WCAU radio* to advertise the "La Palina" cigar line, and in the process he became fascinated with the new medium. In 1928, Paley purchased the United Independent Broadcasters Network, a small radio chain, and in 1929 he changed its name to the Columbia Broadcasting System (CBS). He then pioneered the network system by offering programming free to affiliates in return for the advertising revenues. By 1930 there were seventy radio stations in the CBS network. By the end of the 1930s, CBS consisted of 114 stations, and advertising revenues were twenty times greater than they had been in 1930.

Paley was also the father of broadcast journalism, a new programming which became successful during World War II with Edward R. Murrow's broadcasts from England. With the jump into television in the 1950s, CBS became the largest advertising medium in the world, its revenues exceeding $4 billion in 1983. Paley continued to play a direct role in supervising CBS in the 1980s. (Erik Barnouw, *The Golden Web: A History of Broadcasting in the United States*, 3 vols., 1966, 1968, 1970; Les Brown, *Television: The Business behind the Box,* 1974; David Halberstam, *The Powers That Be,* 1979.)

PALMER, ALEXANDER MITCHELL. A. Mitchell Palmer was born in Moosehead, Pennsylvania, on May 4, 1872. He graduated from Swarthmore College in 1891, studied law privately, and was admitted to the bar in 1893. Palmer worked in private practice and as director of a number of financial corporations, and he served actively in state Democratic politics. He was elected to Congress in 1908 and served until 1915, where he earned a reputation as a progressive and an opponent of child labor. Palmer lost a bid for a United States Senate seat in 1914, and in 1917 President Woodrow Wilson* appointed him head of the Alien Property Custodian's Office.* In 1919 Wilson named Palmer to the post of attorney general.

Although Palmer continued his earlier commitments to an end of child labor and to a restoration of competition to the economy through antitrust laws, his tenure as attorney general is primarily remembered by historians for his vigorous prosecution of the "Red Scare"* attack on Socialists, Communists, anarchists, and labor radicals during 1919 and 1920. Convinced that the widespread labor strikes of 1919 and the bombings that year were part of a large-scale conspiracy, Palmer launched an unprecedented attack on political radicals. Through formal prosecution or private innuendo with employers, Palmer saw to it that suspected radicals were deported, jailed, or deprived of their livelihoods. His public profile in the Red Scare left Palmer with dreams of grandeur, and he tried but failed to secure the Democratic presidential nomination in 1920. When the Republicans came to power in 1921, Palmer retired to his law practice. He died on May 11, 1936. (Stanley Coben, *A. Mitchell Palmer: Politician,* 1963.)

PARAMOUNT PICTURES. See ZUKOR, ADOLPH

PARIS PEACE CONFERENCE OF 1919. On January 18, 1919, representatives of the United States, France, Great Britain, and Italy gathered at Versailles outside of Paris to draft the formal treaties ending World War I. President Woodrow Wilson* headed the American delegation; the other members of the ''Big Four''* were Georges Clemenceau of France, David Lloyd George of Great Britain, and Vittorio Orlando of Italy. Each of them had important demands they expected to be achieved in the final treaty. Wilson came to Europe promoting his Fourteen Points,* which included open diplomacy, free trade, freedom of the seas, national self-determination in Central Europe, and creation of a League of Nations.* The French wanted guarantees that they would be protected from future German aggression as well as enormous, punitive reparations to be imposed on Germany. The Italians insisted on territorial boundary changes which would have given them access to the Brenner Pass, Fiume, and new land on the Adriatic.

After extended negotiations conducted between January and June of 1919, the Big Four drafted the Treaty of Versailles. Among other things, the treaty forced Germany to accept the guilt for World War I and pay a yet-to-be-determined reparations bill; seized from her all German colonies as well as Alsace-Lorraine, the Saar Basin, Posen, and parts of Schleswig and Silesia; and forced Germany to disarm completely. The treaty also created a League of Nations, whose members promised to oppose external aggression of one country against another; impose military and economic sanctions against aggressor nations; reduce armaments around the world; and establish a Permanent Court of International Justice. Wilson's proposals for open diplomacy, free trade, and freedom of the seas were rejected as naive or unworkable.

When the Paris Peace Conference ended on June 28, 1919, President Woodrow Wilson signed the Treaty of Versailles for the United States, but, when he returned, he found that Senate ratification of the treaty would be impossible without major compromises. Isolationist Republicans, known as the ''irreconcilables,''* opposed the treaty completely as a serious compromise of American sovereignty. Another group of Republicans, led by Senator Henry Cabot Lodge* of Massachusetts, favored the treaty if Wilson would make major compromises. Eventually, Wilson refused to make any concessions to the Republicans, and in a number of Senate votes he failed to secure ratification. The United States did not join the League of Nations. Not until July 2, 1921, did the United States, by a joint congressional resolution, formally end the war against Germany and Austria-Hungary. (Thomas Bailey, *Woodrow Wilson and the Lost Peace,* 1944.)

PARKER, JOHN JOHNSTON. John J. Parker was born in Monroe, North Carolina, on November 20, 1885. He graduated from the University of North Carolina in 1907 and took a law degree there in 1908. Parker practiced law in the Greensboro and Charlotte area and was active in Republican politics. In 1920 he won the Republican gubernatorial nomination but lost in the general election. President Calvin Coolidge* appointed Parker to the court of appeals for the fourth district in 1925, and Parker remained there for the rest of his life. He earned a degree of notoriety in 1930 when President Herbert Hoover* nominated him to fill a vacancy on the Supreme Court. Parker's confirmation seemed routine until the American Federation of Labor* (AFL) and the National Association for the Advancement of Colored People* (NAACP) came out against it. The AFL opposed Parker's confirmation because he had written legal rulings upholding antilabor injunctions and "yellow-dog contracts"; the NAACP opposed Parker's confirmation because of a 1920 remark he had made expressing the opinion that blacks were not yet mature enough to hold public office. The debate over the nomination lasted throughout March and April of 1930, but on May 7 the Senate rejected the nomination by a vote of forty-nine to forty-seven. Labor-conscious Democrats and thirteen northern Republicans concerned about the black vote scuttled the nomination. Parker went on to become a distinguished American jurist. He died on March 17, 1958. *(New York Times,* March 18, 1958; Richard L. Watson, Jr., "The Defeat of Judge Parker: A Study in Pressure Groups and Politics," *The Mississippi Valley Historical Review* 50 [September 1963], 213–34.)

PAUL, ALICE. Alice Paul was born in Moorestown, New Jersey, on January 11, 1885. She graduated from Swarthmore in 1905, studied at the New York School of Social Work in 1906, and earned a master's degree in 1907 and a Ph.D in 1912, both of them at the University of Pennsylvania. Paul also earned a law degree from the Washington College of Law in 1922. As a young woman, she became actively engaged in the suffrage movement. In 1912 and 1913, she served as national chairman of the Congressional Committee of the National American Woman Suffrage Association,* and, between 1913 and 1917, she was national chairman of the Congressional Union for Woman Suffrage. She was a leading figure in the formation of the National Woman's Party* in 1917 and served as its chairman until 1921. After the Nineteenth Amendment* became law, Paul continued her crusade, now investing all of her energies in the drive for the Equal Rights Amendment* (ERA). She was a bitter opponent of special protective legislation for women, which she believed prevented passage of the Equal Rights Amendment. Throughout the 1920s, Paul campaigned actively for passage of the Equal Rights Amendment, but in doing so she split the women's movement into two groups: one dedicated to the ERA and the other committed to the passage of social welfare legislation protecting women workers. The ERA did not have much support in the 1920s, primarily because most Americans felt passage of the Nineteenth Amendment was enough and that social welfare legislation, rather than the ERA, was a reasonable approach to the continuing problems. Alice Paul continued to speak up for women's rights until her death on July 9, 1977. *(Who Was Who in America,* VII [1982].)

PEEK, GEORGE NELSON. George N. Peek was born in Polo, Illinois, on November 19, 1873. In 1885 the family moved to a farm near Oregon, Illinois. Peek graduated from high school in 1891 and attended Northwestern University for a year before going to work as a salesman for Deere and Company in Minneapolis, Minnesota. He rose quickly in the company and in 1901 was named general manager of the John Deere Plow Company in Omaha, Nebraska. Within a few years, Peek had transformed the company into a highly profitable concern. He moved to Moline, Illinois, in 1911 to become vice-president of sales for Deere and Company. These were prosperous times for farmers, and Peek's reputation grew. When the United States entered World War I, Alexander Legge,* an executive of International Harvester Company, recommended Peek as the industrial representative to the War Industries Board (WIB). Peek resigned from Deere and served on the board with distinction, gaining national attention and the respect of WIB chairman Bernard Baruch.* In 1918, Baruch had Peek appointed head of the postwar Industrial Board to lower prices and stimulate industrial growth. Frustrated because of the lack of power the Industrial Board had, Peek resigned and returned to Illinois as president of the Moline Plow Company.

Early in the 1920s, the agricultural depression swept through the country, and Peek realized that if farmers in general and Moline Plow in particular were going to prosper, American agriculture had to be made profitable again. In 1922 Peek developed a comprehensive farm relief plan using protective tariffs, marketing cooperatives, government loans, and a domestic price support scheme. He proposed that the federal government purchase surplus crops at a fair price and export them at the world price. An equalization fee for each unit of a commodity sold by the farmer would be collected to make up the difference when the domestic price was higher than the export price. In Congress, the proposal became known as the McNary-Haugen Bill,* and Peek resigned his position at Moline Plow to lobby full-time for the legislation. The bill faced concerted opposition from agricultural processors, middlemen, urban politicians, and conservative Republicans, and, when it passed Congress in 1927 and in 1928, President Calvin Coolidge* vetoed it both times.

Frustrated as a Republican, Peek endorsed Al Smith* for president in 1928 and Franklin D. Roosevelt* in 1932, and, in turn, Roosevelt named Peek head of the Agricultural Adjustment Administration (AAA) in 1933. It was a post Peek hated—he believed in an export solution to the farm crisis, not in production cuts. Peek resigned from the AAA in 1933 and accepted an appointment as head of the Export-Import Bank, but he quit that, too, in 1935. Peek returned to the Republican Party* in 1936. He died on December 17, 1943. (Gilbert C. Fite, *George N. Peek and the Fight for Farm Parity,* 1954.)

PENNEY, JAMES CASH. J. C. Penney was born on September 16, 1875, in Hamilton, Missouri. He graduated from high school in 1893 and went to work in a local dry goods store. Penney worked in several dry goods stores in Ohio and Colorado until 1899, when he moved to Evanston, Wyoming, to work in another dry goods store. He moved to Kemmerer, Wyoming, in 1902 to manage a store, and his bosses allowed him to purchase a one-third interest for $2,000. Penney began buying up other small stores, and in 1904 he established his headquarters in Salt Lake City, Utah. By 1911 J. C. Penney owned twenty-two stores in the intermountain west, and that total increased to forty-eight in 1917, when Penney bought out his partners and moved the corporate offices to New York City. After World War I, Penney expanded his chain store department stores enormously, and by 1929 they totaled 1,450 stores with $209 million in annual sales. When World War II broke out, there were more than 1,600 J. C. Penney department stores throughout the United States, and the company had become the most successful chain store operation in the country. J. C. Penney remained as chairman of the board until 1948 and a member of the board of directors until his death on February 12, 1971. (N. Beasley, *Main Street Merchant: The Story of J. C. Penney,* 1948; *New York Times,* February 13, 1971; James Cash Penney, *Fifty Years with the Golden Rule,* 1950.)

PERKINS, FRANCES. Frances Perkins was born in Boston, Massachusetts, on April 10, 1880. She graduated from Mount Holyoke College in 1902, taught school for five years, and then moved to Chicago, Illinois, where she worked for a while at Jane Addams's* Hull House. Perkins received a master's degree from Columbia University in 1910 and then became secretary of the New York City Consumers' League. In 1912, she became secretary of the New York Committee on Safety, a position which brought her to the attention of state legislators Al Smith* and Robert Wagner,* both of whom shared her concerns about the needs of immigrants and the working poor. She witnessed the Triangle Shirtwaist Fire in New York City in 1911, which killed 146 women laborers, and Perkins spent the rest of her life working on behalf of state and federal labor legislation. In 1919 Governor Al Smith appointed her to the New York State Industrial Commission, which administered the state's labor legislation, and in 1926 she became chairman of the commission. Perkins had also become close to Eleanor Roosevelt* in Democratic Party* activities for women in New York, and in 1929 Governor Franklin D. Roosevelt* appointed Perkins the state industrial commissioner. Four years later, Roosevelt named her secretary of labor— the first woman in American history to hold a cabinet position. In that position, she headed the New Deal's drive for pro-labor legislation and headed the President's Committee on Economic Security, which led to the Social Security Act of 1935. Frances Perkins served as secretary of labor until 1945. Between 1946 and 1953, Perkins was a member of the United States Civil Service Commission. She died on May 14, 1965. (George Martin, *Madame Secretary: Frances Perkins,* 1976; *New York Times,* May 15, 1965.)

PICKFORD, MARY. Born Gladys Mary Smith on April 8, 1893, in Toronto, Canada, Mary Pickford debuted as a child actress in the 1898 play *Bottle's Baby,* and she debuted on Broadway in 1907 in *The Warrens of Virginia.* In 1909 Pickford got a leading role in D. W. Griffith's* *The Violin Maker of Cremona,* and then she made dozens of Biograph films under Griffith's direction, becoming known as "The Biograph Girl with the Curls." In 1913 Pickford signed a contract with Adolph Zukor,* and the next series of films transformed her into "America's Sweetheart." She cultivated a screen image of innocence, virginity, and simplicity, virtues that were held in high regard during the 1920s by a segment of the American public yearning for the rural past. By 1916 Pickford was commanding a salary of $10,000 a week to act in such films as *Poor Little Rich Girl, Tess of the Storm Country,* and *Rebecca of Sunnybrook Farm.* In 1922, Pickford joined with Douglas Fairbanks,* Charlie Chaplin,* and D. W. Griffith to establish United Artists. By then, she had become an American film idol, an eternal child/woman. In that sense, she was just the opposite of Clara Bow* and Theda Bara,* who symbolized the modern materialism of American life in the 1920s. Mary Pickford was a "sweetheart," not a "vamp"* or a "flapper."* Pickford did not really make the transition to sound films, and she retired from acting in 1933, living the rest of her life in self-exile at her Hollywood mansion "Pickfair." Mary Pickford died on May 29, 1979. (Gary Carey, *Doug and Mary: A Biography of Douglas Fairbanks and Mary Pickford,* 1977; Robert Windelin, *Sweetheart: The Story of Mary Pickford,* 1973.)

PINCHOT, GIFFORD. Gifford Pinchot was born on August 11, 1865, in Simsbury, Connecticut. He graduated from Yale in 1889 and studied forestry at the French National Forestry School. Pinchot began his career as a forester with Phelps, Dodge & Company in 1890, and in 1898 he became chief forester for the Department of Agriculture. Primarily interested in conservation, Pinchot had the backing of President Theodore Roosevelt in the creation of the United States Forestry Service and federal regulation of natural resources. Pinchot was also a progressive reformer committed to federal regulation and perhaps even ownership of the railroads, public utilities, mines, and forests. Pinchot was also committed to the prohibition* movement. In 1910 President William Howard Taft* fired Pinchot after he complained that Secretary of the Interior Richard Ballinger was planning to lease Alaska coal reserves to private developers.

Pinchot supported the Bull Moose candidacy of Theodore Roosevelt for president in 1912, and in 1922 the Republican Party* of Pennsylvania nominated him for governor. Pinchot won the election, failed in a subsequent bid for a United States Senate seat, and then was re-elected governor in 1930. From that post in Harrisburg, Pinchot bitterly attacked President Herbert Hoover* for not providing more federal relief to the unemployed. Although Pinchot did not want to see the Eighteenth Amendment* repealed, he nevertheless endorsed Democrat Franklin D. Roosevelt* for president in 1932 because he felt that the suffering of the Great Depression had to be relieved. Gifford Pinchot died on October 4,

1946. (Martin L. Fausold, *Gifford Pinchot: Bull Moose Progressive,* 1961; Harold T. Pinkett, *Gifford Pinchot: Private and Public Forester,* 1970.)

POPPY. See VETERANS OF FOREIGN WARS OF THE UNITED STATES

POUND, EZRA LOOMIS. Ezra Pound was born in Hailey, Idaho, on October 30, 1885. He graduated from Hamilton College in 1905 and then earned a master's degree at the University of Pennsylvania in 1906. In 1907, Pound began travelling widely throughout Europe. His first works of poetry were published then—*Personae* (1909), *Exultations* (1909), *Canzoni* (1911), and *Ripostes* (1912). Pound lived in London between 1917 and 1919 and edited the *Literary Review,* and he moved to Paris in 1920 to serve as correspondent for *The Dial.*

During the 1920s, Pound worked closely with a number of important writers, including T. S. Eliot,* William Butler Yeats, and James Joyce, assisting them in developing their works. All the while, he kept writing and publishing his own poems, which eventually were compiled into *Cantos* (1972). Pound moved to Italy in 1924, and during World War I he broadcast pro-fascist radio programs. Charged with treason, he was extradited to the United States in 1945, where he was hospitalized for insanity. Pound returned to Italy in 1958 and died on November 1, 1972. (Donald Davie, *Ezra Pound: Poet as Sculptor,* 1964; Hugh Kenner, *The Pound Era,* 1971.)

PRESIDENT'S EMERGENCY COMMITTEE ON UNEMPLOYMENT RELIEF. See PRESIDENT'S ORGANIZATION ON UNEMPLOYMENT RELIEF

PRESIDENT'S ORGANIZATION ON UNEMPLOYMENT RELIEF. Late in 1930, as unemployment continued to grow worse, Herbert Hoover* was faced with congressional demands for a vigorous government program of public works construction and work relief. Hoover preferred a private sector initiative, so he established the President's Emergency Committee on Unemployment Relief at the cabinet level to coordinate the work of the federal government, industry, state and local governments, women's groups, and social welfare agencies. Arthur Woods headed the group. A few months later, frustrated by the increasing unemployment problem, Woods proposed a $375 million federal employment program, which Hoover summarily rejected.

Woods then left the committee, and on August 13, 1931, it was absorbed by the new President's Organization on Unemployment Relief. It was headed by Walter S. Gifford,* president of American Telephone and Telegraph. Like its precedessor, it shied away from promoting direct federal relief programs in favor of coordinating private and local government options, but, as unemployment reached 15 percent in 1931 and then 20 percent in 1932, the organization's work appeared hopelessly inadequate, leading to passage of the Emergency Relief and

Construction Act of 1932.* (David Burner, *Herbert Hoover: A Public Life*, 1979; Martin L. Fausold, *The Presidency of Herbert C. Hoover*, 1985.)

PROGRESSIVE PARTY. See CONFERENCE FOR PROGRESSIVE POLITICAL ACTION

PROHIBITION. The crusade against alcohol began as early as the 1790s, but it was not until the 1820s and 1830s that it began to gain momentum. In 1830 the annual per capita consumption of whiskey in the United States had reached ten gallons, and evangelical Protestants had linked the temperance movement with their own revivalism. Justin Edwards and the American Society for the Promotion of Temperance began holding temperance revivals and extracting from people pledges to abstain. By the mid-1830s, more than a million people had made that promise, and by 1850 per capita consumption of alcohol had dropped to 2.1 gallons a year. In 1846 Maine became the first state to outlaw alcohol, and more states followed in the 1850s. For middle-class Protestants, prohibition reflected their own beliefs in personal discipline and social control.

After the 1880s, groups like the Women's Christian Temperance Union and the Anti-Saloon League of America* campaigned for national prohibition, and most southern and western states passed prohibition laws. By the time of World War I, 75 percent of Americans lived in "dry"* counties. Congress submitted the Eighteenth Amendment,* prohibiting the manufacture, sale, and distribution of alcohol, to the states in 1917; it was ratified in January 1919. Later in the year, Congress passed the Volstead Act* defining alcoholic beverages as anything containing more than 0.5 percent alcohol. William Jennings Bryan* proudly announced that liquor was a dead issue, as dead as slavery.

How wrong he was. Prohibition precipitated a cultural crisis in the United States during the 1920s. A whole illegal industry rose up to fill the demand that legitimate businessmen could no longer meet. Illegal distillers and smugglers filled the marketplace; speakeasies flourished; and bootleggers made fortunes from peddling alcohol. Federal agents trying to enforce the Eighteenth Amendment often encountered wholesale resistance from police and local officials in major urban areas. In Chicago, mobster Al Capone* built a multimillion dollar empire, complete with a private army and a ruthless willingness to use violence to enforce his will. By 1924 the vast majority of Americans in urban areas were demanding the repeal of prohibition. Other groups like the Association against the Prohibition Amendment* opposed the Eighteenth Amendment because they considered it an unwarranted intrusion on the prerogatives of local government.

For rural Americans, especially in the South, the issue had a greater cultural meaning, however. Prohibition was wrapped up in ruralism, religious fundamentalism, and isolationism. For them, the north represented a new, secular, immigrant America filled with vices, of which alcoholism was only one. They insisted on enforcing prohibition. In the Democratic Party,* especially during the election of 1924,* the struggle over prohibition found its most intense political expression. Urban Democrats in the north rallied around New York governor Al Smith,* who openly called for repeal; southerners supported William Gibbs McAdoo,* who supported enforcement. In the end, the party turned to John W. Davis,* a weak compromise candidate, because they could not agree on what to do about prohibition.

But the tide was turning in favor of those who wanted prohibition repealed. By the late 1920s, the law was virtually unenforceable, and the organized crime surrounding it was rampant. Al Smith won the Democratic presidential nomination in 1928 on an anti-prohibition platform, and although he lost the election to Republican candidate Herbert Hoover,* he had dealt a death blow to prohibition. Hoover appointed a Commission on Law Observance and Enforcement to investigate the question, and former attorney general of the United States George W. Wickersham* headed it. The report, issued in January 1931, stated clearly that enforcement of the Eighteenth Amendment had broken down completely. Still, the commission did not openly advocate repeal. In the election of 1932,* both the Democrats and the Republicans advocated returning liquor control issues to the states. In February 1933 Congress approved the Twenty-First Amendment* repealing the Eighteenth Amendment. One month later, Congress passed the Beer Tax Act, which legalized beverages with less than a 3.2 percent alcohol content. The Twenty-First Amendment was ratified and went into effect in December 1933. Prohibition was over. (Herbert Asbury, *The Great Illusion,* 1950; Norman H. Clark, *Deliver Us from Evil: An Interpretation of American Prohibition,* 1976; Andrew Sinclair, *The Age of Excess,* 1962.)

PROHIBITION PARTY. Founded in 1869, the Prohibition Party was a third political party in America dedicated to a constitutional amendment abolishing the manufacture and distribution of alcohol in the United States. Beginning with the election of 1872, the Prohibition Party ran a presidential candidate in each election, securing its largest total of 271,111 votes in 1892. After ratification of the Eighteenth Amendment,* the Prohibition Party lost its reason for existence, but, at the party convention of 1920, they decided to continue in order to guarantee enforcement of the Volstead Act.* Prohibition Party candidate Aaron S. Watkins won 189,467 votes in the election of 1920,* and Herman P. Faris won 57,551 votes in the election of 1924.* Problems with prohibition in the 1920s further weakened the party, and in the election of 1928* William F. Varney won only 20,106 votes. When the Twenty-First Amendment* to the Constitution ending prohibition was ratified, it inspired a little more activity from anti-prohibitionists, and William D. Upshaw won 81,869 votes in the election of 1932.* (Norman H. Clark, *Deliver Us from Evil: An Interpretation of American Prohibition,* 1976; James R. Turner, "The American Prohibition Movement, 1865–1897," Ph.D. dissertation, University of Wisconsin, 1972.)

PUEBLO LAND ACT OF 1924. In 1921 and 1922, Senator Holm O. Bursum of New Mexico introduced a bill in Congress to divest the Pueblo Indians, who numbered about 8,000 people, of large sections of their land along the Rio

Grande River in favor of 12,000 white squatters who had settled there. Some of the squatters had purchased the land legally; some had moved there thinking it was part of the public domain; and others had simply encroached on Pueblo property illegally. Secretary of the Interior Albert B. Fall* and Bursum wanted to legalize these settlers' claim to the land. Such groups as the Indian Rights Association, the General Federation of Women's Clubs, and the American Indian Defense Association protested the measure, as did prominent Americans like Zane Grey,* Carl Sandburg,* Edgar Lee Masters,* and John Collier.* In November 1922, the Pueblos formed the All Pueblo Indian Council to fight the Bursum bill. As a compromise, Congress passed the Pueblo Land Act in 1924. It established the Pueblo Lands Board, located in Santa Fe, to determine ownership and to compensate claimants, both Indian and non-Indian. When the board found in favor of a settler, Congress made cash compensation to the Pueblos. Initially, the Pueblo Indians received $600,000 as compensation for the loss of land, but in 1933 Congress passed the Pueblo Relief Act, which gave another $761,958 to the Pueblos and $232,986 to settlers denied their claims. (James S. Olson and Raymond Wilson, *Native Americans in the Twentieth Century,* 1984; Kenneth Philp, ''Albert B. Fall and the Protest from the Pueblos, 1921–1923,'' *Arizona and the West* 12 [Autumn 1970], 237–54.)

R

RADIO. Because of the growing number of radio broadcasts by ship operators, amateurs, and musical performers, Congress passed the Radio Act of 1912, which required station operators to secure licenses from the Department of Commerce. The first station to begin regular broadcasting was WWJ in Detroit in 1920, which began covering election returns. In 1921 WJZ in Newark, New Jersey, broadcast the World Series, and KYW in Chicago presented performances of the Chicago Civic Opera. In 1922 more than 500 new stations began broadcasting, and sales of radios went from $60 million in 1922 to $843 million in 1929. Secretary of Commerce Herbert Hoover* convened a series of radio conferences in the 1920s to deal with problems created by the extraordinary growth, leading up to the Radio Act of 1927, which brought the airwaves under federal control.

American Telephone and Telegraph initiated the first network broadcast in 1923, and Calvin Coolidge's* address on the night before the election of 1924* reached more than twenty million people. The Radio Corporation of America, led by David Sarnoff,* was founded in 1919, and in 1923 it spun off a subsidiary, the National Broadcasting Company. The Columbia Broadcasting System was formed in 1928 and headed by William S. Paley.* Radio's impact on American culture was immediate, especially when regular programming began with such programs as the "Amos and Andy Show"* in 1928. Even before, its potential for bringing the country together had been demonstrated in 1925 with the death of Floyd Collins* in a Kentucky cave. Soon people all across the country were turned into the same programs, recognizing the same kinds of stars and heroes and enjoying a new mass culture only hinted at before in mass-produced books and magazines. (Eric Barnouw, *A History of Broadcasting in the United States*, Vol. 1, *A Tower in Babel: To 1933*, 1966.)

"THE RADIO GUILD." "The Radio Guild" was radio's* first national, hour-long dramatic program. It came to NBC radio in 1929 under the direction of Vernon Radcliffe, and it remained on the air until 1939, always occupying late afternoon, weekday time slots. Those spots became known as "prime soap time." (John Dunning, *Tune in Yesterday: The Ultimate Encyclopedia of Old-Time Radio, 1925–1976,* 1976.)

RAILROAD STRIKE OF 1922. During the 1920s, because of increased competition from long-haul trucks, railroad freight volume declined, as did revenues, and in 1922 the railroads announced an across-the-board wage cut for railway workers. In protest, railway shopmen went on strike. Attorney General Harry Daugherty* was convinced that the strike was a Communist conspiracy, and, over the protests of Secretary of State Charles Evans Hughes* and Secretary of Commerce Herbert Hoover,* he had a federal district court issue a broad restraining order on September 1. Arguing that the railroad brotherhoods had violated the Sherman Antitrust Act, the court prohibited workers from taking any action furthering the strike, including interviews, telephone calls, and planning sessions. President Warren G. Harding* vigorously supported the injunction, and the strike was broken. (Irving Bernstein, *The Lean Years: A History of the American Worker, 1920–1933,* 1960.)

RAILWAY LABOR ACT OF 1926. The Railway Labor Act of 1926 was the only major piece of labor legislation passed at the federal level during the 1920s. The railroad strike of 1922 had proven that the arbitration mechanisms of the Transportation Act of 1920* had failed, and the Railway Labor Act of 1926 was designed to prevent future strikes. The outgrowth of extended negotiations between representatives of the major railroads and the railroad brotherhoods, the bill was sponsored by Senator James Watson of Indiana and Congressman James Parker of New York. Between March and May 1926, it made its way through Congress, and President Calvin Coolidge* signed it on May 20, 1926. The law created a Board of Mediation, a five-member board appointed by the president of the United States, to evaluate contract disputes between railroad workers and railroad management. The board was to investigate disputes, propose solutions, and, if necessary, convince the interested parties to submit to voluntary arbitration. In the end, the measure proved to be a failure, primarily because the railroads were not willing to eliminate their company unions, which the railroad brotherhoods hated and which the Railway Labor Act had seemed to prohibit. Because of that difference of opinion, the Board of Mediation was unable to resolve disputes. Not until the Railway Labor Act of 1934 created the National Railroad Adjustment Board and the New Deal eliminated company unions did real progress occur in negotiating labor disputes in the railroad industry. (Irving Bernstein, *The Lean Years: A History of the American Worker, 1920–1933,* 1960.)

RANDALL, CARL. Carl Randall was born on February 28, 1898, in Columbus, Ohio, where he also studied dance. He attended Ohio State University and supported himself there by performing in midwestern vaudeville theaters. Randall became famous on Broadway as the juvenile lead in musical comedies, the character who "gets the girl" while singing romantic and comic ballads. He had that featured role in many Schubert Brothers' productions, including *Sonny* (1921), *Sunny Days* (1923), *Countess Maritza* (1929), and *Pardon My English* (1933). Later in the 1930s, Randall choreographed such Broadway shows as *The Little Show of 1935* and *Knickerbocker Holiday* (1938). Throughout much of the 1940s, Randall was the resident choreographer for the New York City Opera. He died on September 16, 1965. (Barbara Naomi Cohen-Stratyner, *Biographical Dictionary of Dance,* 1982.)

RANDOLPH, ASA PHILIP. A. Philip Randolph was born in Crescent City, Florida, on April 15, 1889. As a black student, he graduated from the Cookman Institute in Jacksonville, Florida, and moved to New York City, where he worked as a railroad porter and attended the City College. Randolph converted to socialism, and in 1917 he founded the *Messenger,* a Socialist monthly. He was unsuccessful in running as a Socialist for several New York City offices in the early 1920s, but he found his real skill as a labor organizer. In 1925, Randolph founded the Brotherhood of Sleeping Car Porters. Ten years later, they won their first contract, with the Pullman Palace Car Company. In 1941 Randolph led the March on Washington Movement, which forced President Franklin D. Roosevelt* to establish the Fair Employment Practices Committee. In 1947 Randolph founded the League for Nonviolent Civil Disobedience against Military Segregation. When the American Federation of Labor* (AFL) and the Congress of Industrial Organizations (CIO) merged in 1955, Randolph was elected to the executive council and named vice-president of the AFL-CIO. Randolph stayed in the post until his resignation in 1974. He died on May 16, 1979. (Jervis Anderson, *A. Philip Randolph: A Biographical Portrait,* 1972; William H. Harris, *Keeping the Faith: A. Philip Randolph, Milton P. Webster, and the Brotherhood of Sleeping Car Porters, 1927–1937,* 1977.)

RANKIN, JEANNETTE. Jeannette Rankin was born on June 11, 1880, in the Montana Territory. She graduated from the University of Montana in 1902 and spent the rest of her life engaged in the struggle for world peace and women's rights. Early in the 1900s, she became active in the Montana progressive movement, and she played an influential role in securing the right to vote in the state in 1914. She was a member of the Republican Party. In 1916, she became the first woman in United States history to win a seat in Congress, and shortly after her swearing in she voted against the American declaration of war against Germany. Her stand cost her re-election. Rankin was active in the Women's International League for Peace and Freedom in the 1920s, and in 1928 she founded the Georgia Peace Society. Between 1929 and 1939, Rankin was an organizer for the National Council for the Prevention of War, and in 1940 she won a seat in Congress again. In 1941 she cast the only vote against the declaration of war on Japan. She left Congress in 1943. Rankin firmly believed that United States military power should be employed only in a defense of the continental United States. During the 1950s, she opposed Cold War militarism and American involvement in both Korea and Vietnam. She formed the Jeannette Rankin Brigade to oppose the Vietnam War in 1967. Rankin died on May 18, 1973. (Joan Hoff-Wilson, "Peace Is a Woman's Job...', Jeannette Rankin's Foreign Policy," *Montana: The Magazine of Western History* 30 [January 1980], 28–41.)

RANSOM, JOHN CROWE. John Crowe Ransom was born in 1884 in Tennessee and was educated as an undergraduate at Vanderbilt University. He was awarded a Rhodes Scholarship in 1913 and spent a year studying at Oxford University in England. Between 1914 and 1937, he taught at Vanderbilt, and, from 1937 until his death in 1974, he was associated with Kenyon College. During the 1920s, Ransom was a prominent American poet; his work evoked images of the Old South, a nostalgia for an old, premodern order. But, even then, like so many southern writers, Ransom was troubled by the ironies of his vision—the yearning for a simpler society but with a concern about its racism and violence. Ransom's works of poetry included *Poems about God* (1919), *Chills and Fever* (1924), and *Two Gentlemen in Bonds* (1926). Much of his post-1920s career was dedicated to literary criticism, and that included such works as *God without Thunder* (1930) and *The World's Body* (1938). John Crowe Ransom died on July 3, 1974. (*Who's Who in Twentieth Century Literature,* 1976.)

RAPIDAN CONFERENCE OF 1929. In October 1929 President Herbert Hoover* and British Prime Minister Ramsay MacDonald met at Hoover's private retreat in Rapidan, Maryland, to discuss naval issues. While Hoover wanted to seek a reduction in the number of battleships each nation was maintaining, MacDonald wanted to reduce the maximum battleship tonnage from 35,000 to 25,000 tons. Hoover also suggested that Great Britain withdraw from her military bases in the Western Hemisphere. Although no final agreement was reached, the Rapidan Conference paved the way for the London Naval Conference of 1930.* (David Burner, *Herbert Hoover: A Public Life,* 1979.)

RASKOB, JOHN JACOB. Forced to leave school and go to work upon his father's death, John J. Raskob, born on March 17, 1879, in Lockport, New York, went on to become a leading industrialist and a prominent figure in the Democratic Party.* At first a stenographer for the Worthington Pump Company, Raskob soon had a job as a secretary to Pierre S. duPont,* then president of street railway companies in Ohio. Thus, Raskob's association with the duPont family began in 1902 and lasted for years. Raskob rose to assistant to Pierre duPont in Wilmington, Delaware, then treasurer of E. I. duPont de Nemours & Company, and eventually to director and vice-president. At the same time, Raskob was investing in General Motors and became a major stockholder. In the late 1910s, as chairman and director of finance at General Motors, Raskob played a major role in restructuring the company and paving the way for the large-scale installment selling of automobiles. A loyal Democrat, Raskob became

influential in the party, rising to the head of the Democratic National Committee
in 1928 and helping to engineer the Franklin D. Roosevelt* landslide in the
election of 1932.* Also during the 1920s, Raskob had been a prominent member
of the Association against the Prohibition Amendment,* a group that opposed
prohibition* because it represented a concentration of too much power at the
federal level of government. Because of that perspective, Raskob soon became
alienated from the New Deal. Although a Democrat, Raskob had a conservative
political philosophy, and under the New Deal the federal government simply
became too powerful for his tastes. He was alarmed at the anti-business flavor
of the New Deal and the cult following Roosevelt enjoyed. Raskob became a
leading figure in the American Liberty League, an anti-Roosevelt group in the
1930s, and, to eliminate his influence from the party, the Democrats paid off a
$120,000 debt to Raskob in 1934. Late in the 1930s, Raskob completely severed
his connections to the Democratic Party. He died on October 15, 1950. (David
Burner, *The Politics of Provincialism: The Democratic Party in Transition,
1918–1932,* 1968; *New York Times,* October 16, 1950.)

RECONSTRUCTION FINANCE CORPORATION. In December 1932, with
the money markets in a state of collapse and the failure of the National Credit
Corporation,* President Herbert Hoover* appealed to Congress for the creation
of a Reconstruction Finance Corporation (RFC). He wanted the RFC to receive
$500 million and to enjoy the right to borrow up to $2 billion more to make
loans to banks, savings banks, building and loan associations, credit banks,
industrial banks, credit unions, mutual savings banks, and life insurance companies. With those loans, the institutions could meet depositor demands, forestall
the banking* panics which had closed more than 5,000 banks during the 1920s,
lead to an increase in commercial lending, and lift the country out of the depression. Congress responded to his request, and Hoover signed the RFC Act into
law on February 2, 1932. The RFC also had the power to make loans to railroads.
Competition from cars and trucks had seriously eroded railroad freight volume,
as had the economic decline after 1929. Large numbers of railroads could not
meet their bonded indebtedness payments; when they defaulted on their bonds,
the banks and life insurance companies holding such assets were badly hurt.

Under the direction of Charles G. Dawes,* the RFC immediately began making
loans, and for a while in 1932 it stemmed the tide of bank failures. In the process,
however, the RFC encountered tremendous criticism. The bulk of its funds went
to the largest banks—hardly surprising since those banks controlled dispropor-
tionately large shares of money market assets—but Democratic critics had a field
day with RFC loans, accusing the Hoover administration of taking care of big
business while ignoring the suffering of the poor. The attacks grew more intense
in June 1932 when Dawes resigned from the presidency of the RFC to return to
Chicago and see after his own troubled bank—the Central Republic Bank. When
the RFC granted the Central Republic a loan of $90 million to keep it open and
prevent a banking panic in the Midwest, the charges that the Hoover adminis-

tration was pro-rich and pro-business gathered momentum. The fact that the national unemployment rate was reaching 25 percent in an election year only made Hoover's plight worse.

In July 1932, Hoover consented to, and Congress passed the Emergency Relief and Construction Act,* which authorized the RFC to increase its indebtedness to $3 billion and to use the money to provide up to $300 million in relief loans to state and local agencies and $1.5 billion in public works construction. Although the legislation should have been a political plus for Herbert Hoover, it came just one week before the disastrous Bonus Army* riots, which sealed for a generation Hoover's reputation as a miserly, insensitive president.

By early 1933, although the RFC had loaned out all of the $300 million for relief and more than $1 billion to various money market institutions, the nation's economy was on the verge of collapse. Frightened depositors were hoarding huge volumes of currency; businessmen were laying off workers in record numbers; and bankers were accumulating large amounts of excess reserves with Federal Reserve banks. Because all RFC loans had to be paid back, borrowing banks could not enjoy enough time to stabilize their capital structures. By February 1933, banking panics were spreading throughout the country, and it would have taken billions of RFC dollars to even begin to deal with the situation. When Herbert Hoover left office in March 1933, banking holidays were in effect throughout most states, and the Hoover administration was bankrupt. The Reconstruction Finance Corporation, although the largest government agency up to its time in American history, had been unable to deal with the magnitude of the crisis. (James S. Olson, *Herbert Hoover and the Reconstruction Finance Corporation, 1931–1933,* 1977.)

RED SCARE. When the United States entered World War I, a wave of nativist hysteria swept throughout the country, with its primary target German Americans and new immigrants. The Bolshevik Revolution of 1917 in the Soviet Union, especially after the global propaganda campaign predicting the demise of capitalism, created equally powerful strains of antiradicalism. When the war ended, the campaign against German Americans quickly lost its momentum, but the fears of immigrants, Communists, Socialists, and anarchists intensified, leading to the immigration restriction movement and the Red Scare of 1919–1920.

The events of 1919 seemed to confirm fears that a radical conspiracy really was at work in the United States. The country was ripe with labor unrest. Coal and steel strikes,* as well as the Boston police strike,* raised public ire. A series of bloody race riots spread through the country, the worst one in Chicago, leaving 120 people dead and whole sections of cities burned and looted. In the spring of 1919, a series of bombings, including one on Wall Street which killed thirty-eight people, enraged the public.

A. Mitchell Palmer,* the attorney general of the United States, launched a crusade against radicalism late in 1919 and early in 1920, which led to mass arrests and deportations of suspected radicals. He created an antiradical division in the Justice Department and put J. Edgar Hoover* in charge. Palmer also formed quasi-official relationships with groups such as the American Legion* to assist the Justice Department in identifying radicals. On January 2, 1920, alone, Palmer staged a series of raids in thirty-three cities, which led to the arrest of 2,700 people. By May 1920, the raids had stopped, and public opinion began to settle down. The nation's preoccupation with conformity and political conservatism had peaked. (Stanley Coben, *A Mitchell Palmer: Politician,* 1963; Robert K. Murray, *Red Scare: A Study in National Hysteria, 1919–1920,* 1955.)

REED, DAVID AIKEN. David Aiken Reed was born on December 21, 1880, in Pittsburgh, Pennsylvania. He graduated from Princeton in 1900, studied law privately, and was admitted to the bar in 1903. Reed practiced law in Pittsburgh until 1917, when he joined the United States Army as an infantry officer in World War I. Reed resumed his law practice after the war and was active in state Republican politics; in 1922 he was appointed to fill the Senate seat vacated by the death of William E. Crow. Reed was re-elected in 1923 and again in 1928. He was an ally of Gifford Pinchot* in Republican politics in Pennsylvania, and he was also a man of great influence in the Senate, adopting a pragmatic position on domestic legislation and a moderately internationalist view on foreign affairs. Reed played an especially important role in securing the agreements of the London Naval Conference of 1930.* Reed was unsuccessful in his bid for re-election in 1934. He died on February 10, 1953. (L. Ethan Ellis, *Republican Foreign Policy, 1921–1933,* 1968; *New York Times,* February 11, 1953.)

REED, JAMES ALEXANDER. James A. Reed was born on November 9, 1861, in Richland County, Ohio. He moved with his family to Cedar Rapids, Iowa, in 1864. Reed attended Coe College, studied law privately, and was admitted to the bar in 1885. Reed moved to Kansas City, Missouri, to practice law in 1887 and became active in the politics of the local Democratic machine. In 1898 Reed became the prosecuting attorney for Jackson County, and in 1900 he was elected mayor of Kansas City. He served in that post until 1904, resumed his law practice, and in 1910 was elected to a seat in the United States Senate. Reed was reelected in 1916 and in 1922 but did not seek re-election in 1928. He was a consistent critic of Republican tax and tariff policies during the 1920s and a vehement critic of Herbert Hoover* after 1929. James Reed resumed his law practice in 1929 and died on September 8, 1944. (*New York Times,* September 9, 1944.)

RENO, MILO. Milo Reno was born on January 5, 1866, near Agency, Iowa. He attended William Penn College in Oskaloosa but left after deciding not to become a minister. Reno tried selling farm machinery and insurance, and he lived for a time in South Dakota and California. In 1918, inspired by his father's loyalty to the Greenback and Populist parties in the nineteenth century, Reno joined the National Farmers' Union. He proved to be a popular leader, and in

1921 he was elected president of the Iowa division of the union. Reno campaigned consistently on the theme that farmers deserved "the cost of production plus a reasonable profit." Iowa farmers, hit hard by the agricultural depression, elected Reno president of the National Farmers' Holiday Association in 1932 and pledged to keep commodities off the market until they received fair prices for them. The association took a militant stand in August 1932 when it prevented milk and livestock trucks from delivering supplies to market. The strike spread to five states, and Reno became a national figure. Reno called off the strikes when Franklin Roosevelt* was inaugurated in March 1933 in order to give the new president enough time to develop a good farm program. But when the Agricultural Adjustment Act was passed, Reno saw it as a tool of the American Farm Bureau Federation,* which he considered the voice of large commercial farmers in the United States. In September 1933 Reno tried to get the strikes started again, until cost of production and currency inflation were implemented by the administration, but the movement collapsed and Reno returned to relative obscurity. He died on May 5, 1936. (John L. Shover, *Cornbelt Rebellion: The Farmers' Holiday Association,* 1965; Ronald A. White, *Milo Reno: Farmers Union Pioneer,* 1941.)

REPARATIONS. The issue of reparations, or the fines imposed by a conquering nation on its defeated enemy to pay for the war, was central to the diplomatic negotiations at the Paris Peace Conference of 1919.* The Allied nations wanted massive reparation payments imposed on Germany. The Treaty of Versailles* established a Reparations Commission to determine the size of the German obligation and to collect payments. Although the United States took a moderate position on reparations, the Senate refusal to ratify the Treaty of Versailles brought on the expulsion of the United States representative on the commission and the loss of a moderate voice. Initially, the Reparations Commission saddled Germany with a $10 billion debt, but in 1921 added an additional $23 billion to pay for estimated veterans pensions in France and Great Britain. The absurdly high reparations sent the German economy into a tailspin, leading to the Dawes Plan* (1924), the Young Plan* (1929), the Hoover Moratorium* (1931), and the Lausanne Conference of 1932,* each of which reduced the reparations substantially. In 1933 Adolf Hitler renounced all reparations payments. The issue was dead. (Thomas A. Bailey, *Woodrow Wilson and the Lost Peace,* 1954; Philip Mason Burnett, *Reparations at the Paris Peace Conference from the Standpoint of the American Delegation,* 1940.)

REPUBLICAN PARTY. After World War I, the Republican Party found itself in a position of political dominance in the United States. Public disillusionment with the outcome of the peace had inspired a healthy skepticism in the United States about international involvement, and Republican opposition to the Treaty of Versailles,* combined with President Woodrow Wilson's* ideological ineptitude about the League of Nations* issue, gave the Republican Party an extraordinary political momentum. In the congressional elections of 1918,* which Wilson had tried to use as a referendum on Democratic leadership, the Republicans had gained control of both houses of Congress and set the stage for the greater victory in 1920.

As the presidential election of 1920* approached, the Republicans began to call for a "return to normalcy*"—an America of prewar security, isolationism, and prosperity. At the nominating convention in Chicago, the Republicans could not break a logjam between General Leonard Wood* of New Hampshire, Senator Hiram W. Johnson* of California, and Governor Frank Lowden* of Illinois. Senator Warren G. Harding* of Ohio emerged as a compromise candidate and won the nomination, and he selected Governor Calvin Coolidge* of Massachusetts as his running mate. Campaigning on a platform of higher tariffs, lower taxes, lower government spending and expressing great skepticism about Woodrow Wilson's vision of the League of Nations, the Republicans handed a massive defeat to James M. Cox* and Franklin D. Roosevelt,* the Democratic Party* candidates. Harding took more than 60 percent of the popular vote, and Republicans retained both houses of Congress.

The Harding administration then did what it had campaigned to do, passing the Fordney-McCumber Tariff of 1922,* cutting government spending, reducing federal income taxes, and preferring arms reductions through the Washington Naval Conference* to participation in the League of Nations or the World Court.* But there was another side to the Harding administration, one of unprecedented corruption which led to the scandals of Teapot Dome,* the Veterans' Bureau,* and the Alien Property Custodian Office.* Late in 1923, just as news of the scandals began to surface, Warren Harding died of a stroke, and Calvin Coolidge* became president. Throughout 1924, revelations of the scandals made headlines across the country. Given the fact that it was an election year, the scandals could have been a political catastrophe for the Republicans, but the public trusted Coolidge's integrity and appreciated the economic prosperity of the 1920s—two issues the Democrats really could not contest. At the same time, the Democrats were destroying their party in a divisive struggle between their urban and rural branches: Northern, urban Democrats who hated prohibition* and the Ku Klux Klan* supported Governor Al Smith* of New York for president; while rural southern, Protestants who hated Roman Catholics,* immigrants, and cities and who loved prohibition and the Ku Klux Klan supported William Gibbs McAdoo* for president. The Democratic convention in New York deadlocked for 102 ballots between the two men before turning to John W. Davis,* a Wall Street lawyer, as a compromise candidate. In the elections Coolidge took 54 percent of the popular vote and handily defeated Davis. The Republicans kept control of Congress as well.

Four years later, Calvin Coolidge announced he would not seek re-election, and Secretary of Commerce Herbert Hoover* won the Republican presidential nomination. By that time, the urban wing of the Democratic Party had assumed control of the party and nominated Al Smith for president. A city-bred descendent of Irish Catholics, Smith opposed prohibition and hated the Ku Klux Klan. Hoover campaigned on the prosperity theme, promising America four more years of full employment and rising wage levels, while sidestepping the issues of prohibition and religion. Smith could not carry the traditionally Democratic South because of his religion, and Hoover was elected president with 57 percent of the popular vote. Charles Curtis* became vice-president. Republicans controlled both houses of Congress again.

   But then disaster struck the Republicans. They had maintained their political control during the 1920s because of the prosperity of the economy, but when the stock market crashed in 1929 (see crash of 1929) and the country slipped into a terrible depression, the Republicans lost their major issue. President Hoover kept promising that prosperity would return, that the country was just suffering a crisis of confidence. In 1930 Congress passed the Hawley-Smoot Tariff,* a protective tariff designed to protect jobs in the United States but which actually served only to stifle foreign trade and bring on more unemployment. In the congressional elections of 1930,* the Republicans lost eight seats in the Senate and majority control of the House. Unemployment continued to increase; by 1932, more than 25 percent of the work force could not find jobs. Hoover established the Reconstruction Finance Corporation* and passed the Federal Home Loan Bank Act of 1932* to loan money to financial institutions, which he assumed would then reloan it to businesses, but the money never did "trickle down" to consumers. Hoover also resisted federal relief programs because he was philosophically opposed to them, and, in the process, the Republicans appeared stingy and insensitive to the suffering of the poor. Democrats exploited the situation for all it was worth, and in the presidential election of 1932* Franklin D. Roosevelt* handed Hoover one of the worst defeats in American history. Worse still for the Republicans, the composition of the Senate was 59 Democrats to 36 Republicans and 1 Farmer-Laborite; and the House, 313 Democrats to 117 Republicans and 5 Farmer-Laborites. The Democrats would control Washington, D.C., for the next generation. (George H. Mayer, *Republican Party, 1854– 1966*, 1967; Malcom C. Moos, *Republicans: A History of Their Party*, 1956.)

REVENUE ACT OF 1921. A central premise of Republican "normalcy"* early in the 1920s was tax reform, by which Secretary of the Treasury Andrew Mellon* meant reductions for business and well-to-do people. Mellon and other conservative Republicans were convinced that the reductions would encourage capital investment and strengthen the economy. In July 1921 Mellon submitted his proposal to Congress. The existing law provided for a 4–percent tax on the first $4,000 in income and an 8–percent tax on any income above that. There was also a surtax which escalated from 1 percent on incomes over $5,000 to 65 percent on incomes in excess of $1 million. The corporate income tax was 10 percent, and there was also an excess profits tax. Mellon wanted the excess profits tax eliminated, the surtax reduced to a maximum of 32 percent, the corporate tax reduced by an indefinite amount, and the general 4 percent and 8 percent rates to remain the same.

In Congress, the bill encountered a storm of protest from southern and western congressmen as well as from such progressives as Senator Robert M. La Follette* of Wisconsin. Warren G. Harding vacillated on the bill for a while but eventually came out strongly in favor of tax reform, even appearing before the Senate to plead Mellon's case. Progressive Republicans and liberal Democrats did not have the clout to stop the bill altogether, but they did amend it substantially. The excess profits tax was eliminated, but the corporate income tax was raised to 12 percent. The maximum surtax was reduced to 50 percent. General rates were left the same, but low-income people were helped when the head-of-household exemption was raised from $2,000 to $2,500 and the dependent exemptions from $200 to $400, at least for all families with incomes of less than $5,000. The bill also, for the first time, imposed a 12.5 percent tax on capital gains, which previously had been taxed at normal rates. President Harding signed the measure on November 23, 1921. (Roy G. Blakey and Gladys C. Blakey, *The Federal Income Tax*, 1940; Eugene P. Trani and David L. Wilson, *The Presidency of Warren G. Harding*, 1977.)

REVENUE ACT OF 1924. Dedicated to tax reduction as a matter of economic philosophy and in anticipation of the 1924 elections, the Republican administration under Calvin Coolidge* and Secretary of the Treasury Andrew Mellon* wanted badly to follow up on the Revenue Act of 1921* with further reductions. Coolidge signed the Revenue Act of 1924 on June 2, 1924, and the bill was retroactive to January 1. The act replaced the general rates of the Revenue Act of 1921—4 percent on the first $4,000 in income and 8 percent on the rest— with a 2 percent rate on the first $4,000, 4 percent on the next $4,000, and 6 percent on the rest. The maximum surtax was reduced from 50 percent to 40 percent, and the maximum surtax was imposed on income in excess of $500,000, not $200,000 as it had been previously. (Roy G. Blakey and Gladys C. Blakey, *The Federal Income Tax*, 1940; J. F. Sherwood, *Federal Tax Accounting*, 1934.)

REVENUE ACT OF 1926. In keeping with the Republican commitment to tax reduction as a way of boosting capital investment, President Calvin Coolidge* and Secretary of the Treasury Andrew Mellon* in 1926 followed up on the tax reform measures of 1921 and 1924. Because of Republican gains in the election of 1924,* progressives in Congress had no chance of stopping the measure. Mellon pushed it through Congress, and Coolidge signed it into law on February 26, 1926. The Revenue Act of 1926 reduced the maximum inheritance tax and surtax rates to 20 percent and repealed the gift tax outright. The corporate income tax rate, however, was increased from 12 percent to 12.5 percent in 1926 and to 13.5 percent in 1927. Andrew Mellon was convinced that the money left in the hands of investors would be put to better use than the government could ever have imagined. Personal exemptions were raised from $1,000 to $1,500, and from $2,500 to $3,500 for heads of household. The tax rate schedule was 1.5 percent on the first $4,000 of income, 3 percent on the next $4,000, and 5 percent on the rest, compared to the previous rates of 2 percent, 4 percent, and 6 percent. (Roy G. Blakey and Gladys C. Blakey, *The Federal Income Tax*, 1940; Robert K. Murray, *The Harding Era: Warren G. Harding and His Administration*, 1969.)

REVENUE ACT OF 1928. President Calvin Coolidge* signed the Revenue Act of 1928 on May 29, 1928. Consistent with Secretary of the Treasury Andrew Mellon's* goal of reducing the federal deficit, paying off the national debt, and reducing the burden of taxation, the Revenue Act of 1928 decreased the corporation income tax from 13.5 percent to 12 percent. (Roy G. Blakey and Gladys C. Blakey, *The Federal Income Tax*, 1940; J. F. Sherwood, *Federal Tax Accounting*, 1934.)

REVENUE ACT OF 1929. The Revenue Act of 1929 was enacted by a joint resolution of Congress and was confined to the 1929 tax year. For 1929, the resolution reduced the general rate schedule by 1 percent at each level: The first $4,000 in income was taxed at 0.5 percent, the next $4,000 at 2 percent, and the rest at 4 percent. (J. F. Sherwood, *Federal Tax Accounting*, 1934.)

REVENUE ACT OF 1932. The onset of the Great Depression greatly reduced federal tax revenues as demands on the federal budget increased. President Herbert Hoover* wanted to achieve a balanced budget, and the only way to do that was to seek a tax increase. At first, an alliance of southern Democrats and conservative Republicans talked of imposing a 2.5 percent manufacturers sales tax as well as increases in the maximum surtax and general rate schedules in order to raise an additional $1.25 billion. President Hoover endorsed the idea of the sales tax, but a rebellion by insurgent Republicans and liberal Democrats in the House and Senate doomed the proposal. Instead, Congress eventually raised the corporate income tax to 13.75 percent, the maximum surtax from 25 percent to 55 percent, and the general rate schedules to 4 percent and 8 percent. The law also imposed a 5 percent excess profits tax. President Hoover signed the measure on June 6, 1932. (Martin L. Fausold, *The Presidency of Herbert C. Hoover*, 1985.)

"RIN-TIN-TIN." "Rin-Tin-Tin" was one of the earliest radio* adventure programs. It debuted on NBC radio in 1930, sponsored by Ken-L Ration, the dog food, and ran until 1934. The program featured the adventures of a German shepherd who battled bad men in the Old West. (John Dunning, *Tune in Yesterday: The Ultimate Encyclopedia of Old-Time Radio, 1925–1976*, 1976.)

ROBERTS, OWEN JOSEPHUS. Owen J. Roberts was born on May 2, 1875, in Germantown, Pennsylvania. Roberts received his undergraduate and law degrees from the University of Pennsylvania, and his academic work as a student was so brilliant that the law school put him on the faculty right after his graduation. He taught at the University of Pennsylvania for the next twenty years while also practicing as a trial attorney. Between 1903 and 1906, Roberts was first assistant district attorney of Philadelphia. Roberts gained national prominence in the 1920s when he served as special counsel investigating the Teapot Dome* and Elk Hills oil scandal. It was his successful prosecution of the Teapot Dome cases that brought Roberts to the attention of President Herbert Hoover,* who appointed him to the United States Supreme Court in May 1930.

When Roberts assumed office, the Supreme Court was almost evenly divided between liberals and conservatives. On the liberal side were Justices Louis Brandeis,* Harlan F. Stone,* and Benjamin N. Cardozo*; on the conservative side were Justices Willis Van Devanter, James McReynolds, George Sutherland, and Pierce Butler. Chief Justice Charles Evans Hughes* stood in the middle. In his first few terms, Roberts's decisions proved hard to predict, but early into the New Deal he was more often with the conservatives than the liberals, voting to strike down the National Industrial Recovery Act and the Agricultural Adjustment Administration. Later in the New Deal, after President Franklin D. Roosevelt* threatened to pack the Supreme Court, Roberts was the justice who made the "switch in time to save nine" and began to side with the liberals. Roberts chaired the commission investigating the Pearl Harbor disaster of 1941. He retired from the Supreme Court in 1945 and died on May 17, 1955. (Charles A. Leonard, *A Search for a Judicial Philosophy: Mr. Justice Roberts and the Constitutional Revolution of 1937,* 1971; *New York Times,* May 18, 1955.)

ROBINS, MARGARET DREIER. Margaret Dreier Robins was born on September 6, 1868, in Brooklyn, New York, to a wealthy German immigrant family. She did not attend college but immediately after high school began to work for a variety of New York charities. In 1903, she joined the legislative committee of the Women's Municipal League and spent the rest of her life working on behalf of women's rights and social welfare legislation. In 1907 she was elected president of the Women's Trade Union League, while serving in a consulting capacity to the American Federation of Labor. Until she resigned that position in 1922, Robins campaigned tirelessly for labor organization, strike support, women's rights, protective labor legislation, and public education. Robins favored women's suffrage but opposed the Equal Rights Amendment,* fearing it would jeopardize chances for securing protective legislation for women workers. Robins retired in 1922 and died on February 21, 1945. (Gladys Boone, *The Women's Trade Union League in Great Britain and America,* 1942; Nancy Schrom Dye, *As Equals and As Sisters,* 1980.)

ROBINSON, BILL "BOJANGLES." Born Luther Robinson on May 25, 1878, in Richmond, Virginia, Bill "Bojangles" Robinson was the king of American tap dancing. He began performing as a child and continued on the vaudeville circuit. Before World War I, Robinson danced in a number of cabaret and variety acts on the black theater circuit, performing at the Cotton Club and Apollo Theater in New York; and during the 1920s, he was featured in several Broadway hits, including *Lew Leslie's Blackbirds of 1927* and *Brown Buddies* in 1930. Robinson also performed in a number of films, such as *From Harlem to Heaven* (1929), *Dixiana* (1930), and *In Old Kentucky* (1935). His four films with child star Shirley Temple in the 1930s—*The Little Colonel* (1935), *The Little Rebel* (1935), *Rebecca of Sunnybrook Farm* (1938), and *Just around the Corner* (1938)—endeared him to millions of Americans. "Bojangles" Robinson died on May 25, 1949. (Barbara Naomi Cohen-Stratyner, *Biographical Dictionary of Dance,* 1982; Lynne Fauley Emery, *Black Dance in the United States from 1619 to 1970,* 1972.)

ROBINSON, JOSEPH TAYLOR. Joseph T. Robinson was born on August 26, 1872, in Lonoke County, Arkansas. Robinson attended the University of Arkansas and the law department of the University of Virginia and passed the bar exam in 1895. He began practicing law in Lonoke in 1895, the same year that he won a seat in the state legislature. Robinson won a congressional seat in the election of 1902 and remained in the House of Representatives until 1913, when he resigned after winning the governorship of Arkansas. His tenure as governor, however, was shortlived, for he won a seat in the United States Senate on January 28, 1913. Robinson was re-elected in 1918, 1924, 1930, and 1936. During and after World War I, Robinson was a dedicated exponent of Woodrow Wilson's* internationalism, supporting the League of Nations* Covenant and opposing reparations.* Robinson also worked for a restructuring of Germany's war debts which led to the Dawes Plan* and the Young Plan.* He became a prominent figure in the Democratic Party,* serving as chairman of the 1920, 1928, and 1936 conventions and running as Al Smith's* vice-presidential running mate in the election of 1928.* During the 1920s, he had opposed government development of Muscle Shoals,* called for a balanced budget, and warned about the centralization of power in the federal government. When Democrats organized the Senate in 1933, Robinson was elected majority leader. Basically conservative, Robinson assisted Franklin D. Roosevelt* in implementing the early New Deal, even though he worried about its long-range implications. But above all other things, Robinson was the most loyal of Democrats, who viewed party fidelity as an act of faith. He was determined to keep conservative southern Democrats and liberal northern Democrats united against the Republican Party,* under whose thumb he had suffered so long in the 1920s. Joseph Robinson died on July 14, 1937. (Neven E. Neal, "A Biography of Joseph T. Robinson," Ph.D. dissertation, University of Oklahoma, 1957.)

ROCKEFELLER, JOHN DAVISON, JR. John D. Rockefeller, Jr., was born in Cleveland, Ohio, on January 29, 1874. He graduated from Brown University in 1897 and then entered his father's business, Standard Oil of Ohio. Rockefeller served as vice-president of Standard Oil between 1908 and 1911, but, after that, he was primarily concerned with the operation of his father's philanthropic concerns. During the last twenty-five years of his life, John D. Rockefeller gave away more than $550 million, and John D. Rockefeller, Jr., handled the distribution of the money through charitable institutions: the Rockefeller Institute for Medical Research, the General Education Board, the Rockefeller Foundation, and the Laura Spelman Rockefeller Memorial Foundation. Beginning in 1931, Rockefeller supervised construction of the Rockefeller Center in New York City. He was also highly interested in industrial relations, and in 1922 he founded the Industrial Relations Counselors, Inc., to lead the fight against the twelve-hour day in American business. John D. Rockefeller, Jr., died on May 11, 1960. (Raymond B. Fosdick, *John D. Rockefeller, Jr.: A Portrait,* 1956; David Horowitz and Peter Collier, *The Rockefellers,* 1975.)

ROCKNE, KNUTE KENNETH. Knute Rockne was born in Voss, Norway, on March 4, 1888, and he immigrated to the United States with his family in 1893. Although not a Roman Catholic,* Rockne graduated from the University of Notre Dame in 1914 and then accepted a job as head football coach at his alma mater. By the 1920s, Rockne had become the most famous coach in the country, not just because of his 1924 national football championship and the skill of such Notre Dame players as the "Four Horsemen of the Apocalypse" or the "Seven Blocks of Granite," or even for his innovations in the game, including the forward pass and the single-wing formation; instead, the public perceived Rockne as a stalwart, stubborn, committed winner—an immigrant who had made good in the United States. He demanded total commitment from his players, and he promised them that the rewards of absolute dedication would be worth the effort. In the 1920s, when Americans seemed confused about the future and were intoxicated with the consumer culture, Rockne seemed to epitomize the older frontier values—hard work, individual effort, team work, and success. His death in a plane crash on March 31, 1931, shocked the entire country. (Jerry Brondfield, *Rockne: Football's Greatest Coach,* 1976.)

ROGERS ACT OF 1924. Sponsored by Congressman John J. Rogers of Massachusetts, the Rogers Act of 1924 established the modern United States Foreign service. It combined the Diplomatic Service and the Consular Service into one agency, established salary levels for foreign service officers above general civil service levels, provided a retirement program, and set up an entrance by examination system. (John E. Harr, *The Professional Diplomat,* 1960; Warren F. Ilchman, *Professional Diplomacy in the United States, 1779–1939,* 1961.)

ROGERS, WILL. Will Rogers was born on November 4, 1879, in Oologah, Indian Territory. He came to vaudeville in 1905 and became a regular stand-up comedian with the "Ziegfeld Follies"* in 1914. Roger's humor blended self-deprecation, political satire, midwestern truisms, and a healthy, if subtle, dose of American patriotism. Audiences loved him because his humor was always to the point but never malicious. By the 1920s, he was lecturing across the country and appearing periodically in movies as himself. A number of his books, such as *Rogerisms—The Cowboy Philosopher on Prohibition* (1919) and *Rogerisms— The Cowboy Philosopher on the Peace Conference* (1919), were bestsellers. When he died in a plane crash on August 15, 1935, Will Rogers was mourned by the entire country. (C. Peter Rollins, *Will Rogers,* 1984.)

ROOSEVELT, ANNA ELEANOR. Anna Eleanor Roosevelt was born on October 11, 1884, in the Victorian world of New York society. She was raised in a wealthy, prominent family, but her mother rejected her emotionally and her father was an alcoholic. By the time she was ten, both her parents had died. She attended the Allenswood School near London and recovered emotionally from the trauma of her young childhood, and in 1905 she married Franklin D. Roosevelt,* a distant cousin. They had five children, and they moved to Washington, D.C. in 1913 when Franklin became assistant secretary of the navy. Eleanor's husband's affair with her social secretary provided another emotional challenge in her life, which she met by forging an independent identity for herself. After her husband's defeat for the vice-presidency in the election of 1920,* the Roosevelts returned to live in New York, and she became active in the Women's Trade Union League and the women's division of the Democratic Party.* She was also active in campaigns for minimum wage legislation, passage of the child labor amendment, and expansion of the Sheppard-Towner Act.* When her husband was elected governor of New York in 1928, Roosevelt worked diligently to assist women in gaining political appointments. During the 1920s, she was also a foe of the Equal Rights Amendment* because she believed that the role women played in American society at the time demanded protective legislation.

Eleanor Roosevelt's real prominence, however, came after Franklin's election as president of the United States in 1933. Many people considered her the conscience of the New Deal. She was outspoken, although politically sensitive, about the need for social welfare legislation and unemployment relief. Eleanor Roosevelt also became the chief civil rights advocate of the New Deal, insisting that black workers find places in government relief agencies and endorsing a federal anti-lynching law (see lynching). After Franklin's death in 1945, Eleanor became the most well-known woman in the world, campaigning tirelessly against poverty, suffering, and discrimination. Eleanor Roosevelt died on November 7, 1962. (Tamara R. Hareven, *Eleanor Roosevelt: An American Conscience,* 1968; Joseph P. Lash, *Eleanor and Franklin,* 1971; Joan Hoff Wilson and Marjorie

Ligniman, eds., *Without Precedent: The Life and Career of Eleanor Roosevelt,* 1984.)

ROOSEVELT, FRANKLIN DELANO. Franklin D. Roosevelt was born in Hyde Park, New York, on January 30, 1882. An only child, Roosevelt was pampered by an elderly, indulgent father, James Roosevelt, and a loving, doting mother, Sarah Delano Roosevelt. His family's wealth on both sides reached back into commercial and maritime businesses of the early nineteenth century, and Roosevelt's childhood world was one of economic security amidst an atmosphere of gentility common to the "old rich." At the family estate at Hyde Park, he enjoyed servants, pets, limitless toys, money, and family as well as manicured lawns and fields, thick but well-kept forests, and herds of cattle and sheep. The Roosevelts carefully managed their business interests, not as an end in itself but as a means of maintaining the protected, secure world at Hyde Park. Franklin D. Roosevelt grew up with a personality which was at once competitive but not acquisitive. Extremely self-assured from a life of ego reinforcement, Roosevelt was insensitive to the emotional moods of others and at the same time at ease with large numbers of people. His childhood at Hyde Park proved the perfect breeding ground for political success.

Schooled at Groton, Harvard (1904), and the Columbia University Law School, Roosevelt enjoyed a sense of *noblesse oblige,* characteristic of his economic class. His view of life was conventional and conservative, but Roosevelt was also a man of action, willing to try different things without becoming wedded to abstract concepts or fixed positions. His political career began in 1911 when he won a seat in the New York state legislature by opposing Tammany Hall and by advocating open and honest government. Eventually, he made peace with the New York City machine, realizing that its support was essential to any statewide Democratic candidate. Exploiting the family name, he followed Theodore Roosevelt by becoming assistant secretary of the navy, where he served under President Woodrow Wilson* between 1913 and 1920. He ran unsuccessfully for vice-president of the United States, along with presidential candidate James M. Cox, in the election of 1920. A polio attack in 1921 condemned Roosevelt to a wheelchair and confirmed his retreat into private life. The illness brought the first real crisis to Roosevelt, forcing him to retreat to Hyde Park and to evaluate his future. He emerged emotionally unscathed. At the Democratic national conventions in 1924 and 1928, he nominated Al Smith* for president, and in the election of 1928* he won the governorship of New York. Re-elected in 1930, Roosevelt's administration in Albany was noted for its emphasis on conservation, state regulation of public utilities, prison reform, old age pensions, and unemployment relief through the Temporary Emergency Relief Administration.* Because he had remained relatively free from the bitter party fights of 1924 and 1928 and because he had a national reputation, he was a leading figure for the Democratic presidential nomination in 1932. He secured the nomination and, during the Great Depression, swamped President Herbert Hoover* in the election of 1932.* His promise of a "new deal" to end the depression became the theme of his administration. Facing both the Great Depression and World War II, Roosevelt was re-elected in 1936, 1940, and 1944, becoming one of the most influential presidents in American history. He died on April 12, 1945. (James MacGregor Burns, *Roosevelt: The Lion and the Fox,* 1956; Paul Conkin, *The New Deal,* 1967; Frank Freidel, *Franklin D. Roosevelt: Launching the New Deal,* 1973.)

ROOT, ELIHU. Elihu Root was born in Clinton, New York, on February 15, 1845. He graduated from Hamilton College in 1865 and then took a law degree at New York University in 1867. Root practiced law in New York City for sixteen years before becoming the United States attorney for the southern district of New York. Blessed with a brilliant legal mind and an overpowering sense of duty, Root was an enlightened conservative in the late nineteenth and early twentieth centuries. In 1899, he accepted an appointment in William McKinley's cabinet as secretary of war, where he played a major role in the development of the Foraker Act for Puerto Rico, the Platt Amendment for Cuba, and the reorganization of the army during the Filipino rebellion. He became especially close to President Theodore Roosevelt, and in 1905 he became secretary of state. His most important accomplishment while heading the state department was the negotiation of the Root-Takahira Agreement with Japan in 1908, which reaffirmed the idea of an independent China and acknowledged the status quo in the Pacific.

Root won a seat in the United States Senate from New York in 1908, and, as the progressive movement emerged, he found himself increasingly allied with President William Howard Taft,* even breaking with Theodore Roosevelt during the Bull Moose campaign of 1912. He did not seek re-election to the Senate in 1914. The intraparty struggles of the previous three years had been too personally troubling for him. Beginning in 1910, Root served as a member of the international court at The Hague and as president of the Carnegie Endowment for International Peace.* He won the Nobel Peace Prize in 1912.

During the 1920s, Root actively called for United States entry into the League of Nations* and the World Court.* An elder statesman for the Republican Party* in the 1920s, Root adamantly opposed the Eighteenth Amendment* to the Constitution as an unacceptable invasion of individual privacy. He was a delegate to the Washington Naval Conference* of 1921–1922, where he helped draft the Nine Power Treaty.* Root also played an important role in drafting the regulations of the World Court. He supported Herbert Hoover's* candidacy for president and was flabbergasted at the growth of the federal bureaucracy during the years of the New Deal. Elihu Root died in New York City on February 7, 1937. (Richard W. Leopold, *Elihu Root and the Conservative Tradition,* 1954.)

ROSENWALD, JULIUS. Julius Rosenwald was born on August 12, 1862, in Springfield, Illinois, to German-Jewish immigrant parents. After leaving high school, he went into the wholesale clothing business, and in 1895 he purchased a one-quarter interest in Sears, Roebuck and Company, a mail-order firm. Rosenwald rose quickly in the company, becoming vice-president in 1895 and president in 1910. He immediately expanded the company's mail-order business beyond its only products, watches and jewelry, to a wide variety of consumer goods. Exploiting the demand for goods in rural areas, Sears, Roebuck became one of the largest retailers in the United States. In 1925, aware that the automobile was inevitably going to reduce mail-order sales and expand shopping areas, Rosenwald decided to go into direct retailing. He hired Robert E. Wood* away from Montgomery, Ward and put him in charge of sales. Wood opened eight stores in 1926 and sixteen more in 1927. He became president of Sears, with Rosenwald chairman of the board, in 1928; that year, they opened 168 new retail stores. By 1929, when the onset of the depression prevented more expansion, there were 324 retail stores. Gross sales for Sears had gone from $1 million in 1896 to $443 million in 1929. Julius Rosenwald was an enlightened employer, committed to health, dental, and profit-sharing plans for his workers. He died on January 6, 1932. (John E. Jeuck, *Catalogues and Counters: A History of Sears, Roebuck and Company*, 1950; *New York Times*, January 7, 1932.)

ROWE, LEO STANTON. Leo S. Rowe was born in McGregor, Iowa, on September 17, 1871. He graduated from the Wharton School of Finance and Commerce of the University of Pennsylvania in 1890, and received a Ph.D. from the University of Halle in 1892 and a law degree from the University of Pennsylvania in 1895. Between 1895 and 1917, Rowe taught at the University of Pennsylvania and consulted frequently for the Department of State. In 1917 Rowe became an assistant secretary of the treasury, and in 1919 he moved over to the State Department where he headed the Latin American Division. Rowe opposed in principle the practice of American intervention in the affairs of other hemispheric neighbors, and he became a strong advocate of the Good Neighbor Policy.* In 1920 Rowe was named head of the Pan American Union where he worked hard to implement a policy of hemispheric cooperation rather than military confrontation and occupation. He became a moving force behind the emergence of the Good Neighbor Policy in the 1920s and 1930s. Rowe remained as head of the Pan-American Union until his death on December 5, 1946. (*Dictionary of American Biography*, supp. 4 [1974], 705–6; *New York Times*, December 6, 1946.)

RUBINOW, ISAAC MAX. Isaac Rubinow was born in Grodno, Russia, on April 19, 1875. He immigrated to the United States in 1893, and he graduated from Columbia University in 1895 and earned an M.D. degree there in 1898. Rubinow practiced medicine for a few years, but his real interest was biostatistics, particularly after concluding that illness among the poor was as much an economic as a medical problem. Between 1900 and 1913, when he published *Social Insurance*, Rubinow worked on his Ph.D. at Columbia and earned a living as an economist for the federal government. He spent the rest of his life campaigning for social insurance—workmen's compensation, social security, national health insurance, and unemployment insurance. In 1916 Rubinow became executive secretary of the American Medical Association's Social Insurance Commission and, in 1917, the director of the Bureau of Social Statistics for New York City's Department of Public Charities.

During the 1920s, Rubinow was active in Jewish charities. Between 1918 and 1922, he worked in Palestine trying to improve hospital and medical care, and between 1922 and 1927 he was director of the Jewish Welfare Society in Philadelphia. He worked as editor of the *Jewish Social Service Quarterly* between 1925 and 1929. Rubinow wrote *The Care of the Aged* in 1931 and *The Quest for Social Security* in 1934. When the Social Security Act of 1935 finally passed, Rubinow supported it but expressed dismay that it was financed through individual and employer contributions, because he felt it would reduce purchasing power, eliminate federal control, and not play any role in redistributing income. Isaac Rubinow died on September 1, 1936. (W. Andrew Achenbaum, *Old Age in the New Land*, 1978; Roy Lubove, *The Struggle for Social Security, 1900–1935*, 1968; *New York Times*, September 3, 1936.)

RUTH, GEORGE HERMAN. George Herman "Babe" Ruth was born on February 6, 1895, in Baltimore, Maryland. Because he was neglected as a child, Ruth was placed in the St. Mary's Industrial School, a Catholic facility for delinquent boys. He lived there until 1914, when he entered professional baseball* and pitched for the Baltimore and Providence franchises in the International League. Ruth was blessed with great athletic skills, and, even if he did have an unusual physique—he was 6' 2'' and 215 pounds, with a beer belly and thin legs—he was a graceful runner. In 1915, Ruth moved up to the major leagues to play for the Boston Red Sox. He had a record of sixteen wins against eight losses in 1915, twenty-three to twelve in 1916, and twenty-four to thirteen in 1917. Because of his hitting abilities, the Red Sox also had Ruth play outfield on his non-pitching days, so much so that he appeared in fifty-nine games in 1918. Ruth's last year as a pitcher was 1919. Pressed financially, the Red Sox sold Ruth to the New York Yankees, who placed him permanently in right field. Ruth then began a hitting career that changed baseball forever.

Until Ruth began to play in the 1920s, baseball had been a game of base hits, stolen bases, excellent pitching, and fine defense. But Ruth electrified Yankee fans in 1920 by hitting fifty-four home runs and batting .376. It was an extraordinary achievement, since all of the rest of the American League teams combined hit only fifty home runs in 1920. The next year, he came back with fifty-nine home runs and 170 runs-batted-in. In the process, Ruth became a larger-than-life figure, a genuine American hero, despite the fact that he was a known womanizer and a prodigious drinker. What America needed in the 1920s was a new hero, one consistent with an increasingly urban society instead of the rural western heroes so common to the nineteenth century. Ruth filled the bill. He was gregarious, charismatic, and enormously talented. Baseball changed, too, with hitting and home runs becoming more and more important. In 1927 Ruth hit sixty home runs, breaking his own record. His lifetime statistics included 2,174 runs scored, 2,873 hits, 714 home runs, 2,204 runs-batted-in, and a .342 batting average. Ruth's last season with the Yankees was 1934. The next year, Ruth played for the Boston Braves and retired on May 25, 1935, after hitting three home runs in his last game. Ruth died of cancer on August 16, 1948. (*New York Times,* August 17, 1948; Marshall Smelser, *The Life That Ruth Built: A Biography,* 1975.)

RYAN, JOHN AUGUSTINE. John A. Ryan was born on May 25, 1869, in Vermillion, Minnesota, and, like so many other young Irish-American men, he decided to enter the Roman Catholic* priesthood and he graduated from the St. Thomas Seminary in 1892. Shortly after his ordination, Ryan became interested in Populist and labor politics, and he spent the rest of his life campaigning for social justice. He taught at St. Paul Seminary in Minnesota between 1902 and 1915 and at the Catholic University of America from 1915 to 1939. Ryan firmly believed that society and the economy were not independent entities functioning according to natural law but were subject to social control and morality, and he argued that social and labor legislation were the obligations of government. Ryan became a widely read author and tireless campaigner on behalf of minimum wage laws. From 1919 until his death, Ryan also served as director of the department of social action of the National Catholic Welfare Conference. Ryan wrote widely, especially for such journals as *Catholic Action* and the *Catholic Charities Review,* and during the 1920s he began to call for social security, government health insurance, and labor standards legislation. Ryan was the author of several books, including *A Living Wage* (1906), *Distributive Justice* (1916), and *Social Doctrine in Action* (1941). Widely recognized as the leader of the Catholic social justice movement, John Ryan died on September 16, 1945. (Patrick W. Gearty, *The Economic Thought of Monsignor John A. Ryan,* 1953.)

S

SACCO AND VANZETTI CASE. The Sacco and Vanzetti case was the most celebrated criminal trial and liberal crusade of the 1920s. On April 15, 1920, a robbery of a shoe factory in South Braintree, Massachusetts, resulted in the murder of a paymaster and a guard. The crime occurred at the peak of the Red Scare* in the United States, and the justice department had been investigating two Italian immigrants, Nicola Sacco* and Bartolomeo Vanzetti,* because of their avowed anarchism. Justice department officials advised local police authorities of their presence in Massachusetts, and on May 5 they were arrested and charged with robbery and murder. Their trial was presided over by Judge Webster Thayer. Although the prosecution could not really prove conclusively that the two men had committed the crime, their political views were paraded before the jury, and on July 14, 1921, they were convicted and sentenced to death.

Their conviction brought a storm of protest from the Italian-American community and from liberals and civil rights advocates. Sacco-Vanzetti defense funds were established in the United States and Europe, and such distinguished people as Albert Einstein, Felix Frankfurter, H. G. Wells, and George Bernard Shaw protested the sentence and called for a review of the case, claiming that Sacco and Vanzetti had been convicted not because of the evidence but because of their political views. For six years, they were able to secure stays of execution. Early in July 1927, Governor Alvan T. Fuller of Massachusetts appointed a blue-ribbon commission, headed by Harvard president Abbott Lawrence Lowell, to investigate the case, but at the end of the month the commission upheld the conviction. Sacco and Vanzetti, asserting their innocence to the very end, went to the electric chair on August 23, 1927, sending out as their last message the words "This is our career, and our triumph." When word of their death reached Europe, protests as well as attacks on American embassies were widespread. Controversy over the case still survives, and the question of Sacco and Vanzetti's guilt or innocence remains unanswered. (Robert K. Murray, *Red Scare: A Study in National Hysteria, 1919–1920,* 1955; Francis Russell, *Sacco and Vanzetti: The Case Resolved,* 1986.)

296   SACCO, NICOLA

SACCO, NICOLA. Nicola Sacco was born in Torre Maggiore, Italy, on April 22, 1891. He immigrated to the United States in 1908 and went to work in a Milford, Massachusetts, shoe factory. To avoid the draft, Sacco fled to Mexico in 1917 and 1918. He converted to socialism and eventually to philosophical anarchism while working in the shoe factory. Early in 1920, at the peak of the "Red Scare"* hysteria, the paymaster and a guard of a shoe factory in South Braintree, Massachusetts, were murdered during a robbery. Department of Justice agents had been investigating Sacco for his political beliefs for over a year, and in May 1920 he was arrested, along with Bartolomeo Vanzetti,* and charged with the murders. The subsequent Sacco and Vanzetti Case* became a cause célèbre of the 1920s, especially after both men were convicted and sentenced to death. Their supporters argued that the convictions were politically motivated, more a product of anarchist political beliefs than of evidence. Although there was more than reasonable doubt about their guilt, and despite widespread protests, both of them were executed in the Massachusetts electric chair on August 23, 1927. (Felix Frankfurter, *The Case of Sacco and Vanzetti,* 1927; *New York Times,* August 24, 1927.)

SANDBURG, CARL. Carl Sandburg was born in Galesburg, Illinois, on January 6, 1878, to Swedish immigrant parents. He studied at Lombard College in Galesburg, Illinois, between 1898 and 1902 and then began a career in journalism, writing poetry and biography in his spare time. Coming out of a midwestern tradition, Sandburg believed fervently in democracy and Populism. In 1918 he was writing editorials for the *Chicago Daily News.* He was the author of a variety of books of poetry, criticism, and biography, including *Chicago Poems* (1916), *Corn Huskers* (1918), *The Chicago Race Riots, 1919* (1919), a six-volume biography of Abraham Lincoln (1926–1939), and such works as *The American Songbag* (1927) and *Good Morning America* (1928). During World War II, Sandburg wrote a weekly column for the Chicago *Times* Syndicate, and after the war he continued to write poetry, to lecture on the radio, and to speak around the country. Carl Sandburg died on July 22, 1967. (Richard Crowder, *Carl Sandburg,* 1963; *New York Times,* July 23, 1967.)

SANGER, MARGARET. Margaret Sanger was born on September 14, 1879, in Corning, New York. Her father was an atheist and an advocate of the single-tax ideas of Henry George, but the family was beset with poverty, and Margaret decided early in her life that those problems came from the size of the family, which included eleven children. She married in 1902 but became increasingly dissatisfied with life as a housewife. The family moved to New York City, and Sanger became active in the Industrial Workers of the World. She became prominent in America when she began to campaign for sexual reform—sex education, eradication of venereal disease, and family planning and birth control. At the time, Victorian values made her a controversial figure. In 1913 the United States Post Office refused to distribute a copy of the magazine *Call* because it contained Sanger's article on syphilis. After that, Sanger spent the rest of her life trying to remove the stigma attached to the distribution of information on contraceptives.

In 1914, Sanger founded her journal *Woman Rebel,* which was dedicated to legalization of birth control. The Post Office declared it unmailable as well, and in 1914 she was indicted for violating the postal code. She fled to Great Britain and the Netherlands to avoid prosecution, but there she learned more about creating a politically acceptable movement in favor of birth control. She returned to the United States in 1914 and began to campaign for women to open contraceptive advice centers, and she established a model center in Brooklyn. The police closed it down ten days later, but court orders later said that the move was unconstitutional, especially if physicians were involved in the decision to distribute birth control information. Sanger then used the tactic of physician-directed birth control information as the best way politically of securing her goals. In 1921, she established the American Birth Control League, which had evolved into the Planned Parenthood Federation of America by 1942. In 1923, she established the Birth Control Clinical Research Bureau in New York, the first doctor-staffed birth control clinic in the United States. By 1938 she had established more than 300 similar centers thorughout the country. Sanger also fought a number of court battles to overturn the Comstock Act of 1873, which had classified birth control information as obscenity. She was successful in 1936 when a federal court permitted the mailing of birth control information to physicians. After World War II, Sanger continued her crusade—now on a global level—as a means of dealing with the population explosion. She died on September 6, 1966. (*New York Times,* September 7, 1966; James Reed, *From Private Vice to Public Virtue: The Birth Control Movement and American Society Since 1830,* 1978; Margaret Sanger, *Margaret Sanger: An Autobiography,* 1938.)

SANTIAGO CONFERENCE OF 1923. The Santiago Conference of 1923, or the Fifth International Conference of American States, met in Santiago, Chile, on March 25, 1923. Its primary purpose was to discuss the impact of the large-scale entrance of American banks into Latin America since World War I. Generally, the Latin American delegations condemned the United States's refusal to enter the League of Nations.* Despite U.S. objections, the conference also agreed to give credentials to the delegations of countries not enjoying diplomatic recognition with the United States. Finally, the conference urged the establishment of mutual committees of investigation to help mediate hemispheric disputes. The conference adjourned on May 3, 1923. (Samuel Guy Inman, *Inter-American Conferences,* 1965.)

SARNOFF, DAVID. David Sarnoff was born in Uzlian, Russia, on February 27, 1891. He studied the Talmud in Russia before the family immigrated to New York City in 1900, where Sarnoff worked as a paper boy, studied Morse code on his own, and in 1906 got a job as an office boy for the Marconi Wireless

Telegraph Company. He diligently studied technical manuals and took classes at the Pratt Institute of Brooklyn, and in 1913 he was hired to operate a powerful radio* station on top of Wanamaker's Department Store in New York City. In 1914, Sarnoff began receiving news of the Titanic disaster and for three days passed the information on to various news bureaus and newspapers. Sarnoff was an early believer in the consumer potential of home radios, and in 1919 he wrote a long memo to Owen D. Young,* chairman of the Radio Corporation of America (RCA), detailing the future of the radio. RCA had absorbed the Marconi company in 1919. Sarnoff broadcast the Dempsey*-Carpentier fight from Hoboken, New Jersey, into dozens of Marcus Loew's* theaters, where 200,000 people listened to it. In 1921 RCA began to manufacture radio sets, and Sarnoff was named general manager of the company. By 1925, net sales exceeded $85 million, and in 1926, in order to increase the market for radios, RCA launched the National Broadcasting Company, with Sarnoff at its head. Sarnoff eventually became the most important person in American broadcasting. In 1930, he became president of RCA and he headed RCA until 1966 and remained chairman of the board until his death on December 12, 1971. (Carl Dreher, *Sarnoff: An American Success,* 1977; Eugene Lyons, *David Sarnoff,* 1966.)

***SCHENCK v. UNITED STATES* (249 U.S. 47).** In 1917 Congress passed the Espionage Act, which provided fines up to $10,000 and prison terms of up to twenty years for people convicted of aiding the enemy, avoiding the draft, or acting disloyally toward the United States government. The postmaster general had the power to bar treasonous or seditious publications from the mail. In the *Schenck* v. *United States* decision of 1919, the Supreme Court unanimously upheld the law, arguing that wartime conditions justified restraint of freedom of speech and of the press, especially if the speeches or publications posed a "clear and present danger" to public well-being. (Horace C. Peterson and Gilbert C. Fite, *Opponents of War, 1917–1919,* 1957.)

SCHNEIDERMAN, RACHEL ROSE. Rose Schneiderman was born in Savin, Russian Poland, on April 6, 1882. Her father, a Jewish tailor, brought his family to the United States in 1890. Schneiderman went to public schools until she was thirteen, when she went to work in a department store and then in a hat and cap factory. As a teenager, she came to believe in labor union organization, and in 1903 she helped establish Local 23 of the United Cloth Hat and Cap Makers of North America. The next year, Schneiderman was appointed as the first woman to the union's executive board. In 1905 she joined the Women's Trade Union League (WTUL). After working for several years as a national organizer for the WTUL, Schneiderman was appointed to the executive board in 1911. She became a national figure that year after the tragic Triangle Shirtwaist Factory fire in New York City, where 146 sweatshop laborers died in a conflagration. Schneiderman campaigned vigorously for legislation requiring safe working conditions. She was elected president of the New York branch of the WTUL in 1918, served as vice-president of the national WTUL between 1919 and 1926, and then served as president from 1926 to 1950.

A political activist, Schneiderman supported women's rights and fair labor standards legislation. She was nominally a member of the Socialist Party of America,* but she consistently supported Democratic candidates for office after the stock market crash of 1929.* Rose Schneiderman died in New York City on August 11, 1972. (Gladys Boone, *The Women's Trade Union League in Great Britain and the United States of America,* 1942; Gary Endelman, "Solidarity Forever: Rose Schneiderman and the Woman's Trade Union League," Ph.D. dissertation, University of Delaware, 1978.)

SCOPES, JOHN. See EVOLUTION

SCOTTSBORO CASE. In March 1931, nine young black men were arrested in Scottsboro, Alabama, for the alleged rape of two white women on a freight train. The youngest of the blacks was thirteen years old. An all-white jury convicted all nine men of rape, and each of them was sentenced to death. The National Association for the Advancement of Colored People* provided legal assistance to the "Scottsboro boys," as did the Communist Party,* which made an international case out of their plight. The Supreme Court threw out the convictions on the grounds that the young men did not enjoy the benefit of adequate counsel during their trial, and in a subsequent trial they were convicted again and sentenced to up to ninety-nine years in prison. Through legal maneuvering and the parole process, all of the men were eventually freed; the last of them left prison in 1950. (Dan T. Carter, *Scottsboro: A Tragedy of the American South,* 1976.)

SEATTLE GENERAL STRIKE OF 1919. When World War I ended in 1918, federal contracts for the manufacture of war goods disappeared as well, and throughout the country labor unions and workers were concerned about losing many of the gains they had achieved between 1914 and 1918. Labor leaders were militant in their insistence on higher wages, shorter hours, and the right of collective bargaining. From the public perspective, however, such demands were frightening, especially since the Red Scare* and fear of radicalism were gaining momentum in 1919. In the Pacific Northwest, where radical organizers from the Industrial Workers of the World had long been making strident demands, fears of radicalism and subversion were especially acute. On January 21, 1919, 35,000 Seattle shipyard workers went on strike, and the next day the Seattle Central Labor Council, which represented all organized labor in the area, called a general strike of all workers to support the shipyard workers. On February 6, the day of the strike, more than 60,000 workers failed to show up on the job. To a nation frightened of communism and bolshevism, the words "general strike" smacked of Marxism, and the general public had little sympathy for the workers. Mayor Ole Hanson called in federal troops and threatened to take over all the jobs of striking workers and operate them with government help. The public hailed his defiant stand, and the strike was broken. The Seattle general strike of 1919 was the opening event in the Red Scare, which would consume American attention in 1919 and 1920. (Robert K. Murray, *Red Scare: A Study in National Hysteria, 1919–1920,* 1955.)

"SETH PARKER." "Seth Parker" was the radio* creation of Phillips H. Lord. It first appeared in 1929, and by 1933 it was one of NBC radio's most popular programs, occupying a Sunday evening time slot. More than 300 "Seth Parker Clubs" had been formed by 1933 to promote the songs, hymns, and stories presented on the radio program. The character of Seth Parker on the program was that of a kind, grandfatherly figure who tried to find ways of helping poor and troubled people. The program lasted until 1936. (John Dunning, *Tune in Yesterday: The Ultimate Encyclopedia of Old-Time Radio, 1925–1976,* 1976.)

SEX. Without question, the era of the 1920s was a decade of social change and controversy, and the issue of sexuality was no exception. During the 1920s, Victorian values were finally eclipsed, and a new sense of liberation appeared. Several factors contributed to the change. First, the rise of the city—with its mass culture and anonymity—damaged the credibility of many rural virtues. The extraordinary or even the bizarre was more likely to be tolerated in cities than in small towns. Second, the campaign for women's rights, which had culminated in ratification of the Nineteenth Amendment* to the Constitution in 1920, had removed some of the cultural restraints on female behavior, opening new opportunities of expression. Third, the widespread use of the automobile* gave people a mobility and a privacy they had not enjoyed before. Finally, World War I, with its violence, pessimism, and ultimate disillusionment, had fostered a new climate of opinion in America, one less concerned about tradition than experimentation.

The new spirit of sexual freedom was expressed in a variety of ways. Women's fashions exposed more flesh as hemlines rose and necklines dropped. Bobbed hair,* bathing beauties,* and the rapid gyrations of the "Charleston"* on the dance floor became new fads. Chaperoned dating declined, and illegitimate births increased. Margaret Sanger* launched the birth control and family planning movement. Readers avidly consumed the soft-core pornography of the confession magazines.* In Hollywood, sultry film stars like Theda Bara,* Clara Bow,* Rudolf Valentino,* and Douglas Fairbanks* became fantasy lovers to millions of Americans. The news was full of sexual scandals—the Fatty Abruckle* trial, the Aimee Semple McPherson* "kidnapping," and the Hall-Mills murder case.* Sex, like religion, was a preoccupation of the 1920s. (Paula S. Fess, *The Damned and the Beautiful: American Youth in the 1920s,* 1971; James J. Flink, *The Car Culture,* 1975; J. Stanley Lemons, *The Woman Citizen: Social Feminism in the 1920s,* 1973; Elizabeth Stevenson, *Babbitts and Bohemians: The American 1920s,* 1967.)

SHANGHAI INCIDENT OF 1932. Because of resentment over the increasing Japanese presence in Manchuria and China, the Chinese in Shanghai launched a widespread boycott of Japanese goods in 1931. On January 28, 1932, Japanese marines invaded the city, and Japanese aircraft bombed the city. Secretary of State Henry L. Stimson* vigorously protested the attack on the city and hinted that the United States might have to increase its military presence in Guam and the Philippines. On May 5, 1932, China and Japan signed an armistice ending the controversy. (Robert H. Ferrell, *American Diplomacy in the Great Depression: The Hoover-Stimson Foreign Policy, 1929–1933*, 1957.)

SHEPPARD-TOWNER ACT OF 1921. In 1912 President William Howard Taft* created the Children's Bureau in the Department of Labor because the United States had a relatively high rate of infant and maternal mortality. In 1918 the bureau discovered that 16,000 women had died in childbirth and 250,000 children had failed to survive their first year. Under the direction of Julia Lathrop,* the bureau began to campaign for federal programs to improve income levels for all people and to provide hygiene instruction. Despite the opposition of the American Medical Association, which resisted any government involvement in medical care, Warren G. Harding* threw his support behind the program for hygiene instruction. On November 13, 1921, he signed the Sheppard-Towner Maternity and Infancy Protection Act. It appropriated $1.5 million in 1922 for distribution to state hygiene instruction programs, and $1.25 million a year for the years from 1923 to 1927. The Calvin Coolidge* administration did not sustain the legislation, however, and the Herbert Hoover* administration let it lapse in 1929. (J. Stanley Lemons, *The Woman Citizen: Social Feminism in the 1920s,* 1973.)

SHIPSTEAD, HENRIK. Henrik Shipstead was born in Burbank, Minnesota, on January 8, 1881; after graduating from the state college at St. Cloud, he went on to Northwestern University and received a degree in dentistry in 1903. Shipstead practiced dentistry in Glenwood, Minnesota, between 1904 and 1920 and became active in local politics, serving as mayor of Glenwood (1911–1913) and a term in the state legislature (1917). He moved to Minneapolis in 1920 and joined the Farmer-Labor Party,* where his progressive views about government-business relations found a comfortable home. In 1922 Shipstead won a seat in the United States Senate on the Farmer-Labor Party ticket, and during the 1920s he endorsed a host of progressive causes, including the McNary-Haugen Bill,* government development of Muscle Shoals,* and the candidacy of Robert M. La Follette* in the election of 1924.* Shipstead was re-elected to the Senate in 1928 and 1934, and during the New Deal he generally allied himself with the coalition of liberal Democrats and progressive Republicans in the Senate. With the Farmer-Labor coalition disintegrating in the late 1930s, Shipstead declared himself a Republican and won re-election in 1940. He was an unsuccessful candidate for renomination in 1946, and he retired from the Senate. Shipstead died on June 26, 1960. *(New York Times,* June 27, 1960.)

SHOTWELL, JAMES THOMSON. James Shotwell was born on August 6, 1874, in Strathroy, Ontario, Canada. He received his undergraduate degree from the University of Toronto in 1898 and a Ph.D. in history from Columbia in 1903. Shotwell spent the rest of his life teaching history at Columbia and campaigning for world peace. A prominent historian specializing in medieval studies and the development of science and technology, Shotwell became a leading internationalist during World War I, supporting the diplomacy of President Woodrow Wilson.* For Shotwell, the keys to world peace were technical expertise, long-range planning, free trade, and collective, multinational action against aggression. During World War I, he served as chairman of the National Board for Historical Service, and he worked with Walter Lippmann* and Edward M. House* on The Inquiry, a committee which prepared discussions for the peace negotiations of 1918–1919. Wilson appointed Shotwell to the American delegation which went to Paris to negotiate the Treaty of Versailles* in 1919. That same year he supervised the Carnegie Endowment for International Peace* project on the *Economic and Social History of the World War,* which was completed in 1936 with the publication of 152 volumes.

In 1924 Shotwell became director of the division of economics and history of the Carnegie Endowment, a post he held until 1949, when he became president of the foundation. During the 1920s, Shotwell campaigned actively for American entry into the League of Nations,* the World Court,* and the International Labor Organization.* He also suggested to French foreign minister Aristide Briand the idea of a treaty outlawing war in 1927, which was the genesis of the Kellogg-Briand Pact.* Shotwell served as president of the League of Nations Association between 1935 and 1939, but when German aggression became so apparent late in the 1930s, he began to call for collective action, with the support of the United States, against Adolf Hitler. At the end of World War II, Shotwell served as a consultant to the United Nations. He retired as head of the Carnegie Endowment for International Peace in 1950. James Shotwell died on July 16, 1965. (Harold Josephson, *James T. Shotwell and the Rise of Internationalism in America,* 1975; James T. Shotwell, *The Autobiography of James T. Shotwell,* 1962.)

SIBERIAN INTERVENTION of 1918–1920. The Bolshevik Revolution of 1917 threw Europe into a turmoil, especially in 1918 when Russia abandoned France and England and pulled out of the war. France and England were alarmed. They worried that huge arsenals of U.S. arms shipped to Murmansk and Vladivostok would fall into German hands; that the lack of an eastern front would permit Germany to shift troops to France; that a pro-Allied Czech army of 45,000 troops would be trapped by the Germans in Russia; and that Germany might take control of Russia. Both France and Germany wanted the United States to send an army into Russia to prevent those disasters. President Woodrow Wilson* was reluctant, but he did want to see moderate, democratic forces defeat the Bolsheviks in the Russian civil war. Wilson was also concerned that Japan might exploit the power vacuum in Russian and expand her power in Manchuria, Siberia, and China.

Eventually—to contain Japan, to help rescue the Czechs, to prevent a German triumph in Russia, and to assist anti-Bolsheviks—Wilson sent two armies into the Soviet Union. In August and September 1918, a contingent of 5,000 American troops joined British troops in Murmansk in northern Russia. They stayed until July 1919, protecting supply depots and railroad lines and assisting anti-Bolshevik forces. At the same time, a contingent of 9,000 American troops joined a British-Japanese army in Vladivostok in August 1918. They, too, protected supply depots and railroad lines, escorted the evacuating Czech troops out of Vladivostok, and worked to protect the territorial integrity of the Soviet Union against Japanese expansion. Wilson withdrew the American troops in April 1920. The Japanese left in 1922 as part of the agreement at the Washington Naval Conference of 1921.* (Roy Watson Curry, *Woodrow Wilson and Far Eastern Policy, 1913–1920,* 1957; Betty Miller Unterberger, *America's Siberian Intervention, 1918–1920,* 1956.)

SINCLAIR, HARRY. Harry Sinclair was born on July 6, 1876, in Wheeling, West Virginia. He grew up in Independence, Kansas, and, shortly after leaving high school, he began to buy and sell oil leases and wheat futures. He purchased his first oil pump in 1901 and gradually built up a reputation as an independent oil driller. In 1916, he consolidated his interests into the Sinclair Oil and Refining Company. Sinclair came to national attention in the early 1920s over the Teapot Dome* scandal. Sinclair gave Albert Fall,* the secretary of the interior, $233,000 in government bonds, $85,000 in cash, and prime livestock in return for drilling rights to United States naval oil reserves. The scandal made headlines in the United States in 1923 and 1924, and Fall was convicted, fined $100,000, and sentenced to a term in the federal penitentiary. In 1929 a federal jury acquitted Sinclair of conspiring to defraud the government. The oil leases, however, were all cancelled. Sinclair continued to build his oil business, and during World War II he served as a member of the Petroleum Industrial War Council. Harry Sinclair died on November 10, 1956. (Robert Enger, *The Politics of Oil,* 1961; Burl Noggle, *Teapot Dome: Oil and Politics in the 1920s,* 1962.)

SMITH, ALFRED EMANUEL. Born on December 30, 1873, in New York City, Al Smith grew up in the social atmosphere of immigrant Irish-America: Roman Catholic, hardworking, and Democratic. He was a devout Catholic* and he attended parochial school, but when his father died in 1886, Smith had to go to work in a variety of laboring jobs. He also became involved in the religion of politics in New York City's Fourth Ward. Smith dutifully performed the errands of ward politicians as a young man, and in 1903 he won a seat in the state assembly. He proved to be an excellent politician, solicitous of constituent needs, loyal to party leadership, and adept at legislative maneuvering. In 1911 he was named majority leader of the assembly and then speaker of the assembly in 1912. After the Triangle Shirtwaist fire of 1911, Smith became a vocal advocate of strong social welfare responsibilities for the government, including labor standards laws, child labor restrictions, workmen's compensation, and regulation of business monopolies. His political stature grew, and he won the governorship of New York in 1918, lost in 1920, and then won again in 1922, 1924, and 1926. There he presided over a reorganization of New York state government, a conservation program, a comprehensive housing program, work-men's compensation improvements, public health, limits on child labor, and public works job development. In the process, Al Smith became a national figure.

He was a prominent candidate for the Democratic presidential nomination for the election of 1924,* representing the urban, "wet,"* northern wing of the Democratic Party,* struggling against the "dry,"* southern and Ku Klux Klan*-supported candidacy of William Gibbs McAdoo.* Both of them eventually lost out to the dark horse, compromise candidate John W. Davis.* By the election of 1928,* however, the urban wing had come to dominate the Democratic Party, and Smith won the nomination, but his Roman Catholicism, his opposition to prohibition,* and his immigrant sympathies, as well as the prevailing "Repub-lican prosperity," cost him the election, putting Herbert Hoover* in the White House. Smith went into private business after the election but gradually grew resentful of Franklin D. Roosevelt's* growing status as the new governor of New York. He doubted Roosevelt's political convictions and wanted the pres-idential nomination again in 1932, but Roosevelt won the nomination and the presidency, and Smith drifted into alienation. As a 1920s liberal, he had fought for civil liberties, for individual rights, and for freedom from government in-terference in people's lives and against bureaucracy and prohibition. By the 1930s, jealous of Roosevelt and appalled at the New Deal bureaucracy, Smith began to call for a repudiation of the New Deal, joining the anti-Roosevelt American Liberty League and endorsing Republican candidate Alf Landon for president in 1936 and Wendell Willkie in 1940. Al Smith died on October 4, 1944. (Oscar Handlin, *Al Smith and His America,* 1958; *New York Times,* October 5, 1944.)

SMOOT, REED. Reed Smoot was born in January 10, 1862, in Salt Lake City, Utah. He graduated from the Brigham Young Academy in 1879 and entered a business career which brought him into ranching, real estate, insurance, and banking, as well as into the corporate presidencies of the Hotel Utah, the Home Fire Insurance Company, and the Smoot Investment Company. In 1900 Smoot was named an apostle in the Mormon Church, a position he held for the rest of his life. In the election of 1902, Smoot ran as a Republican and was elected to the United States Senate. Evangelical Protestants contested his seating in the Senate because of his ties to the Mormon Church, but after a thorough inves-tigation Smoot was allowed to take the oath of office. For the next thirty years, he was a faithful member of the Republican Old Guard,* becoming, in the 1920s, chairman of the Senate Finance Committee. Smoot favored high tariffs, low taxes on the well-to-do people, reductions in government spending, and an isolationist foreign policy. In 1930, he sponsored in the Senate the Hawley-Smoot Tariff,* which raised tariff rates and, unfortunately, contributed to reductions in foreign trade and employment. In the election of 1932,* Smoot could not stand the tidal wave of support for the Democratic Party,* and he lost his bid for re-election. For the remainder of his life, he devoted his energies to the Mormon Church. Reed Smoot died on February 9, 1941. (*Salt Lake Tribune*, February 10, 1941.)

SNYDER ACT OF 1924. By the time of World War I, a major debate was raging in the United States over the question of citizenship for American Indians. With passage of the Dawes Act of 1887, the members of any tribe agreeing to allotment—the dissolution of tribal authority and distribution of tribal land to individual families—were automatically eligible for citizenship. In 1918 Congress provided that any Indian veteran of World War I was also eligible for citizenship. Many Indians, however, were suspicious of citizenship: Groups like the Iroquois felt that citizenship in the United States was synonymous with the end of tribal existence, so they resisted. Other liberals argued that citizenship would help assimilate American Indians into the body politic. In January 1924, Congressman Homer P. Snyder of New York introduced House Resolution 6355 authorizing the secretary of the interior to grant citizenship to all Native Americans requesting it. The Senate Committee on Indian Affairs then proposed a blanket, immediate citizenship law which raised the ire of many full-blooded Indians who were skeptical about rapid assimilation. Finally, the Snyder Act emerged from a conference committee. It extended citizenship to all American Indians born within the territorial limits of the United States. (Gary C. Stein, "The Indian Citizenship Act of 1924," *New Mexico Historical Review* 47 [July 1972], 312–24.)

SNYDER-GRAY CASE. The Snyder-Gray case was one of the most spectacular trials of the 1920s. In 1927, after a two-year affair, Judd Gray and Ruth Snyder bludgeoned to death her husband, Albert Snyder. They tried to cover up the crime by claiming that a burglar had killed Albert and had tied up Ruth before ransacking their apartment in Queens, New York. But when stolen items that had been hidden in the apartment began to show up, Ruth Snyder and her lover Judd Gray, a travelling corset salesman, confessed to the crime. The trial became a near media circus when testimony revealed that the two defendants had tried many times to kill Albert Snyder with prune juice poisoned with overdoses of sleeping pills. The jury deliberated for less than two hours before convicting Snyder and Gray and sentencing them both to death. They died in the electric chair on January 12, 1928. (Paul Sann, *The Lawless Decade*, 1957.)

SOCIALIST LABOR PARTY. The Socialist Labor Party, founded in 1877, was the first Marxist organization in American history. Its leading figure until his death in 1914 was Daniel DeLeon. The Socialist Labor Party was committed to transforming America into a classless society through revolutionary trade unionism, but it made little headway. DeLeon was a true ideologue with a personality to match. The Socialist Party of America,* led by Eugene V. Debs,* emerged as the leader of responsible, pragmatic Socialists in the United States, while the Socialist Labor Party served as a political home for only a radical fringe. In the election of 1920,* the Socialist Labor Party blamed World War I on capitalists and called for workers to take control of the means of production. Candidate William W. Cox won only 30,418 votes. In the election of 1924,* they nominated Frank T. Johns; he won only 28,368 votes. The election of 1928* was no better; Verne L. Reynolds won 21,608 votes. In the election of 1932,* with the country in the midst of the Great Depression, the Socialist Labor Party expected to do much better, assuming that the country was ripe for the Marxian-expected uprising of the working classes. Instead, candidate Reynolds won only 34,028 votes. America was still a land of small property owners and workers who expected to prosper and succeed. There was no place for socialism in general, let alone the radical socialism of the Socialist Labor Party. (Don K. McKee, "Daniel De Leon: A Reappraisal," *Labor History*, 1 [Fall 1960], 1–12; James Weinstein, *The Decline of Socialism in America, 1912–1925*, 1967.)

SOCIALIST PARTY OF AMERICA. Founded in 1901 by people opposed to the radical socialism of Daniel DeLeon and the Socialist Labor Party,* the Socialist Party of America was led by Eugene V. Debs,* former president of the American Railway Union. From the outside, the Socialist Party adopted the most conservative position among American radicals, insisting that socialism would have to come to the United States through peaceful political campaigning, not by revolution. The Socialist Party proved to be ahead of its time. Its original platform called for woman's suffrage, federal old age pensions, unemployment insurance, an end to child labor, prohibition of the use of force to break up labor strikes, a minimum wage for workers, and a shorter work week, all of which were eventually enacted in the United States. The Socialist Party also called for government ownership of the transportation, communication, and banking systems. Eugene V. Debs was the perennial Socialist candidate for president, and in the election of 1912 he surprised most Americans by winning 6 percent of the vote in the presidential election.

In the election of 1920,* Debs was again the Socialist nominee, but this time he ran for president from the federal penitentiary at Atlanta, where he was serving time for opposing American entry into World War I. The Socialist platform criticized the Woodrow Wilson* administration for suppressing civil liberties during the war and launching the Red Scare* after the war, demanded full civil rights for blacks, abolition of the League of Nations,* and recognition of Ireland as an independent nation. Debs won only 3.4 percent of the vote. In 1924, the

Socialist Party endorsed the Progressive Party* candidacy of Robert M. La Follette* for president, hoping to form a broad-based coalition with other progressives and liberals in the United States, but La Follette polled only 4.8 million votes out of the 29 million cast.

Debs died in 1926, and the mantle of Socialist leadership fell to Norman Thomas.* In the election of 1928,* the Socialist Party called for repudiation of all war debts,* removal of American troops from Nicaragua, independence for the Philippines, diplomatic recognition of the Soviet Union, and the outlawry of war, as well as its traditional domestic issues. Thomas managed to garner only 266,453 votes—the lowest Socialist total in its history. When the Great Depression settled on America after 1929, however, the Socialist Party thought its time had finally come. In the election of 1932,* Norman Thomas called for massive federal relief efforts, public works employment, social security, the right of labor to bargain collectively, repeal of prohibition,* and American entry into the League of Nations and the World Court.* Much to Thomas's dismay, however, he polled only 881,951 votes, just 2 percent of the total cast. The Socialist Party, even in the midst of the Great Depression, had little appeal to the mass of American workers. When the New Deal passed much of the Socialist domestic agenda in the 1930s, the party was left with no real issues, and it declined even further. (Ray Ginger, *The Bending Cross: A Biography of Eugene V. Debs,* 1949; David A. Shannon, *The Socialist Party of America,* 1955; James Weinstein, *The Decline of Socialism in America, 1912–1925,* 1967.)

SOLEMN REFERENDUM. By 1919 President Woodrow Wilson* found himself facing an impasse in the United States Senate. He would not compromise enough on the Treaty of Versailles* to secure the Republican support he needed for ratification, and the Republicans, led by Henry Cabot Lodge,* were not about to back down. Wilson, an admirer of the British parliamentarian system, then hatched a bizarre scheme which only showed just how far his health problem had put him out of the mainstream. He wanted fifty-seven recalcitrant senators to resign and stand immediately for re-election. If they were replaced by pro– League of Nations people, Wilson would have his ratification; if a majority of them were re-elected, Wilson would resign the presidency. At the urging of his advisors he abandoned the scheme, but at the annual Jackson Day dinner on January 8, 1920, Wilson requested that the election of 1920* be a "solemn and grand referendum" on the League of Nations* to decide whether the United States should join. He toyed with the idea of running again but finally decided that his health would not permit it. When Warren G. Harding* and the Republicans triumphed in the election of 1920, Wilson had his referendum, but not what he expected. American participation in the League of Nations was permanently doomed. (Wesley M. Bagby, *The Road to Normalcy: The Presidential Campaign and Election of 1920,* 1962; Kurt Wimer, "Woodrow Wilson's Plan for a Vote of Confidence," *Pennsylvania History,* 28 [July 1961], 279–93.)

SOVIET ARK. At the height of the Red Scare,* Attorney General A. Mitchell Palmer* instituted deportation proceedings against a number of prominent American radicals. On December 22, 1919, the U.S.S. *Buford* sailed out of New York harbor for Hango, Finland, carrying 249 deportees. The United States government had expelled them. Included on board were genuine radicals Emma Goldman* and Alexander Berkman as well as hundreds of others whose radical credentials were marginal at best. Since their eventual destination was the Soviet Union, journalists dubbed the *Buford* the "Soviet Ark." (Robert K. Murray, *Red Scare: A Study in National Hysteria, 1919–1920,* 1955.)

SPEAKEASIES. The term "speakeasies" became common during the 1920s to describe bars, restaurants, saloons, or dance halls where alcohol was illegally sold. The Eighteenth Amendment* and the Volstead Act* had prohibited the sale of beverages with more than 0.5% alcohol content, and when patrons were seeking admittance to an establishment serving alcohol, they had to "speak easy" when requesting entrance so as not to attract attention. The typical speakeasies fronted as ice cream parlors, soft drink establishments, restaurants, and tearooms. Usually at the door, a panel would open to a peephole, and the proprietor would "size up" the prospective patron before letting him or her in. By 1929 there were an estimated 32,000 speakeasies in New York City alone. (Paul Sann, *The Lawless Decade,* 1957.)

STEEL STRIKE OF 1919. Throughout 1919, Americans had been preoccupied with radicalism, social change, and violence. The Bolshevik Revolution had succeeded in the Soviet Union, and Communists around the world were predicting global revolution. Disillusionment with the outcome of World War I was already setting in, and concerns about economic readjustment were becoming common. The Seattle general strike of 1919* had sent a shock wave of concern throughout the country, as had the series of summer race riots, particularly those in Chicago and Washington, D.C. In August 1918, a number of labor leaders had established the National Committee for Organizing Iron and Steel Workers, with Samuel Gompers,* head of the American Federation of Labor,* as honorary chairman, John Fitzpatrick as acting chairman, and William Z. Foster* as secretary-treasurer. The steel companies had resisted all the efforts of the committee to organize steel workers, and in 1919 the fact that Foster was a genuine radical gave rise to rumors that the steel organizing drives were covers for Communist agitation. In June 1919 the committee had asked Elbert H. Gary,* head of United States Steel, to begin negotiations for a wage increase, but he refused to meet with them. Gary would not back down from the long-held open shop* policy of U.S. Steel.

The National Committee for Organizing Iron and Steel Workers then called for a steel strike to begin on September 22. It demanded the right of collective bargaining, reinstatement of all men discharged for union activity, an eight-hour day, seniority rights, abolition of company unions, and higher pay. The strike call came amidst the turmoil over the Boston police strike,* in which public sentiment had been weighted heavily against the police. President Woodrow Wilson* asked for a postponement of the strike; nevertheless, 275,000 workers went on strike on the first day, and by September 25, nearly 400,000 workers were out. Early in October, rioting broke out in a number of American cities between strikers and employer-hired strikebreakers, and state militia were called in to quell the disturbances. Twenty people died in the rioting. At that point, public fears of revolutionary upheaval in the United States doomed the strike. It continued for another two months, but on January 8, 1920, the National Committee ended it. The workers gained absolutely nothing from the companies. (Robert K. Murray, *Red Scare: A Study in National Hysteria, 1919–1920*, 1955.)

STIMSON DOCTRINE. See STIMSON, HENRY LEWIS

STIMSON, HENRY LEWIS. Henry L. Stimson was born on September 21, 1867, in New York City. He graduated from Yale in 1888 and then earned his master's and law degrees from Harvard in 1889 and 1890, respectively. Stimson practiced law with Elihu Root* between 1891 and 1899, and then he established his own firm. In 1906 President Theodore Roosevelt appointed Stimson United States attorney for the southern district of New York, and Stimson focused his attention and energies on railroad antitrust cases. He made an unsuccessful run for governor of New York as a Republican in 1910, but in 1911 President William Howard Taft* named Stimson secretary of war. Stimson served in the army during World War I, and then, during the 1920s, he practiced law and acted as a diplomatic troubleshooter for the Warren G. Harding* and Calvin Coolidge* administrations. Between 1928 and 1929, Stimson was governor-general of the Philippines, and in 1929 President Herbert Hoover* named him secretary of state in his cabinet.

During his tenure as secretary of state, Stimson's major challenge involved the Japanese invasion of Manchuria in 1931. Preoccupied by the Great Depression and in an isolationist mood, most Americans did not want military intervention in Asia on behalf of China, so in January 1932 Stimson proposed what has become known as the Stimson Doctrine—the United States would not recognize any treaty or puppet government in China that violated the Open Door Policy, the Nine Power Treaty* of 1922, or the Kellogg-Briand Pact.* When Japan established the puppet Manchukuo government in Manchuria, most League of Nations* countries adopted the Stimson Doctrine as well, refusing to extend diplomatic recognition. But the Stimson Doctrine was little more than paper, at least as far as the Japanese were concerned: The United States would not recognize their presence in Manchuria, but nor would they interfere with it.

When Franklin D. Roosevelt* took office in 1933, Stimson retired to private life, but Roosevelt brought him out of retirement in 1940 when he named him secretary of war. With World War II looming on the horizon, Roosevelt wanted to take a bipartisan approach to foreign and military policy, and Stimson seemed ideal for the cabinet. Stimson retired again in 1945, and he died on October 20, 1950. (Elting E. Morison, *Turmoil and Tradition: A Study of the Life and Times of Henry L. Stimson,* 1960; Henry L. Stimson, *The Far Eastern Crisis,* 1936.)

STONE, HARLAN FISKE. Harlan Fiske Stone, the eleventh chief justice of the Supreme Court, was born in Chesterfield, New Hampshire, on October 11, 1872. He graduated from Amherst College in 1894 and from the Columbia University Law School in 1898. Stone came from a Republican political tradition, but he developed a flexible pragmatism which later characterized his years on the Supreme Court. He opened a law practice in New York City and became a member of the Columbia law faculty in 1899. He was appointed dean of the law school in 1910 and served there until 1923. President Calvin Coolidge,* amidst the wake of the Harding* political scandals, appointed Stone attorney general of the United States in 1924, and Stone quickly undertook a reform of the Federal Bureau of Investigation, appointing J. Edgar Hoover* as acting director to replace William J. Burns.* Stone also helped reform the federal prison system and the Alien Property Custodian's Office.* In the process, he gained a national reputation as a loyal Republican with impeccable credentials for honesty and scholarship. President Coolidge named him to replace Judge Joseph Mc-Kenna* on the Supreme Court in 1925.

Stone's judicial philosophy was well-developed by the mid-1920s. At Columbia University he had developed a reputation as a defender of civil liberties and as a believer in "sociological jurisprudence"—the conviction that the law must adjust to changing social and economic conditions. A Victorian liberal by instinct and sympathy, Stone resented the rigid, legal formalism of the conservative justices during the 1920s. He came to feel that the Court was too zealous in protecting property rights from legislative encroachment of Congress and state legislatures. Indeed, Stone viewed the Constitution as a living document subject to changing interpretation. It was not a product of rigid, judicial formulas. By the late 1920s and early 1930s, Stone was clearly identified with Justices Oliver Wendell Holmes, Jr.,* and Louis Brandeis* as the "liberal minority" on the Supreme Court. Although he was a close friend of President Herbert Hoover,* Stone grew impatient during the early years of the Great Depression with Republican conservatism. He hated laissez-faire economic principles in the face of massive social and economic dislocation, and he did not agree with the majority decisions of the court that invalidated many state taxation and regulatory statutes in the 1920s. In his view, state legislatures did not automatically violate Fifth Amendment property rights by passing progressive tax laws. During the years of the New Deal, Stone's views became those of the majority, especially after the crisis of 1937 when President Franklin D. Roosevelt* tried to "pack the court." Roosevelt named Stone chief justice of the Supreme Court in 1941. Harlan Stone died on April 22, 1946. (Alpheus Thomas Mason, *Harlan Fiske Stone: Pillar of the Law,* 1956.)

STONE, WARREN STANFORD. Warren Stone was born in Ainsworth, Iowa, on February 1, 1860. He attended Western College of Iowa for two years before going to work as a fireman on the Rock Island Railway in 1879. Stone was promoted to engineer in 1884 and joined the Brotherhood of Locomotive Engineers. He rose to head the union in 1904. Stone was tireless in his efforts to achieve an eight-hour day for railroad workers, and, although he was conservative about the use of strikes, he eventually came to be convinced in government ownership of the railroads. In 1924 Stone served as treasurer of the Conference for Progressive Political Action,* which sponsored the presidential candidacy of Robert M. La Follette.* Stone died on June 12, 1925. (*New York Times*, June 13, 1925; Reed C. Richardson, *The Locomotive Engineer, 1863–1963: A Century of Railway Labor Relations and Work Rules*, 1963.)

SUNDAY, WILLIAM ASHLEY. William Ashley "Billy" Sunday was born on November 19, 1862, in Ames, Iowa. After graduating from high school in 1880, he worked as an undertaker's assistant and as a furniture salesman for three years; he then played professional baseball* for eight years, during which time he became increasingly preoccupied with his own spiritual life. After working for the Young Men's Christian Association, or the YMCA, between 1891 and 1893, Sunday joined the evangelist circuit as a revivalist, assisting several preachers until striking out on his own in 1896. He was ordained a Presbyterian minister in 1903 and became a gifted revivalist preacher, at least in his capacity for religious theater. Sunday was blessed with an extraordinary charisma and stage presence, and his salty, aggressive style appealed to common, working-class people. During the 1920s, Sunday became the premier evangelist in the United States, condemning alcohol, crime, communism, and political corruption. Sunday accepted the endorsement of the Ku Klux Klan* and frequently condemned what he called the "excesses" of blacks and immigrants, but his appeal to white audiences was undiminished. His message was a simple one—a return to the "old-time religion" would solve America's moral crisis—and rural, southern Americans listened intently to what he had to say. Sunday's health began to fail later in the 1920s, and he had to reduce his time on the circuit. He died on November 6, 1935, still the embodiment of rural, evangelical Protestantism. (William G. McLoughlin, *Billy Sunday Was His Real Name*, 1955.)

SWANSON, GLORIA. Gloria Swanson was born Gloria May Josephine Svensson in Chicago, Illinois, on March 27, 1899. Swanson acted in her first film as an extra in 1915—*The Fable of Elvira and Farina and the Meal Ticket*. By 1916 she had signed a contract with Keystone Films and began to act in leading roles; in 1919, she signed a contract with Cecille B. DeMille,* and he turned her into the most famous silent screen star of the 1920s. In his films, Swanson flirted, posed, and discreetly revealed her body, reflecting a powerful sexual innuendo. Those films included *Why Change Your Wife* (1920) and *The Affairs of Anatole* (1921). Swanson's provocative look and affected slouch generated a powerful image as the aggressive female, and her private life fit the pattern. She married and divorced six times, and, during the 1920s, she had an ongoing affair with Joseph P. Kennedy, the Boston financier and father of future President John F. Kennedy. Although her voice was suited to sound motion pictures, her sultry style was more at home in the 1920s than the 1930s. She made several films in the 1930s, including *Indiscreet* (1931) and *Tonight or Never* (1931), but her film career quickly deteriorated. By the 1950s she was doing only cameo shots and advertising health foods on television. (Robert Hudson, *Gloria Swanson,* 1970.)

SWOPE, GERARD. Gerard Swope, a prominent businessman and an early architect of the idea of business and government cooperation, was born in St. Louis, Missouri, on December 1, 1872. In 1895 he graduated from the Massachusetts Institute of Technology with a degree in electrical engineering, and he went to work for the Western Electric Company. Swope rose quickly through the company, becoming general sales manager of the New York office in 1908 and vice-president of the national office in 1913. He was named president of General Electric in 1919 and chairman of the board in 1922, a position Swope kept until his retirement in 1939.

During the 1920s and 1930s, Swope rose to a position of national prominence as a spokesman for business interests, but he was not a typical conservative. A friend of Jane Addams,* he sympathized with the needs of working people. Swope was also a prominent figure in the trade association movement, and he believed in industrial self-regulation. As the first president of the National Electrical Manufacturers Association, Swope believed in the ability of industry to regulate itself. During the 1920s, he became a close associate of Herbert Hoover,* who, as secretary of commerce, worked to encourage trade associations as a means of rationalizing the industrial economy, eliminating wasteful competition, and improving productivity. When the depression swept through the country after 1929, Swope believed its source was overproduction. He urged the federal government to adopt a plan of industrial self-regulation through trade associations, suspension of anti-trust laws, and national economic planning through establishment of codes of ''fair competition.'' His proposals were later embodied in the National Industrial Recovery Act of 1933. During the New Deal, Swope served as a member of the Business Advisory Council, the Coal Arbitration Board, the National Labor Board, and the Committee on Economic Security. He died on November 20, 1957. (David Loth, *Swope of GE—The Story of Gerard Swope and General Electric in American Business,* 1958; *New York Times,* November 21, 1957.)

T

TAFT, WILLIAM HOWARD. William Howard Taft was born on September 15, 1857, in Cincinnati, Ohio. He graduated from Yale in 1878 and received a law degree from the Cincinnati Law School in 1880. Active in Republican Party* politics, Taft served as a collector of internal revenue in Cincinnati in 1882, practiced law privately between 1883 and 1887, and was then appointed a judge of the superior court of Ohio in 1887. In 1889, President Benjamin Harrison appointed Taft solicitor general of the United States and, in 1892, a judge in the federal circuit court. President William McKinley named Taft head of the Philippine Commission in 1900, and Taft served as governor general of the Philippines from 1901 until 1904. He returned to the United States in 1904 when President Theodore Roosevelt named him secretary of war in the cabinet.

As secretary of war, Taft served as a diplomatic troubleshooter for Roosevelt throughout the world, working to promote American economic interests in Latin America and Asia, supporting the Open Door policy, and limiting Japanese influence in the Pacific. By 1908 his national reputation was firmly established, and Taft was elected president of the United States to succeed Roosevelt. Despite the criticisms of many Republicans, Taft accumulated an enviable record as a progressive, but he was defeated for re-election in 1912 when liberal Republicans, led by Theodore Roosevelt, bolted the party, divided the vote, and handed the White House to Woodrow Wilson* and the Democrats. Taft then became a professor of law at Yale.

When the Republicans returned to power in 1921, President Warren G. Harding* appointed Taft chief justice of the United States Supreme Court. His judicial philosophy was a conservative one, which generally extended large powers to the states and narrow ones to the federal government, and upheld property rights as superior to the needs and demands of labor unions and minority groups. Taft wanted badly to be the leader of a united court, but it proved impossible because Oliver Wendell Holmes, Jr.,* Louis Brandeis,* and Harlan Fiske Stone* came to constitute a liberal minority during the 1920s. Still, Taft was not a rigid, doctrinaire ideologue on the Court, preferring a more pragmatic approach to economic and social problems. He voted with the majority in restricting the use of injunctions in labor disputes and upholding minimum wage legislation. Generally, Taft was part of the conservative majority on the court which extended full property rights to businesses, protecting them from legislative interference, unless the business was directly involved in what Taft called the "public interest." Toward the end of his life, Taft became more and more conservative, fearing that America was being taken over by radicals. He died on March 8, 1930. (Henry F. Pringle, *The Life and Times of William Howard Taft*, 1939.)

"TARZAN." In 1932, "Tarzan" came to radio* as the first major syndicated series. Patterned after the hero in Edgar Rice Burroughs's *Tarzan and the Apes*, the program appeared as a fifteen-minute serial three times a week. Burroughs's daughter Joan played the voice of Jane, and Tarzan was played by a series of stars, including James Pierce and Carlton KaDell. The series lasted until 1935, by which time more than 350 segments had been produced. (John Dunning, *Tune in Yesterday: The Ultimate Encyclopedia of Old-Time Radio, 1925–1976*, 1976.)

TEAPOT DOME. The Teapot Dome scandal was the most infamous example of corruption during the Warren G. Harding* administration in the early 1920s. Rumors of graft and corruption began to circulate around Washington, D.C. right after Harding and his "Ohio Gang"* had been installed in power. Senator Thomas J. Walsh,* a Democrat from Montana, decided to launch a special investigation of the Department of the Interior after he heard rumors of graft in the leasing of government oil supplies. The investigation led to revelation of the Teapot Dome scandal.

In 1921, Secretary of the Interior Albert B. Fall* had convinced Secretary of the Navy Edwin Denby* to transfer jurisdiction over the United States naval oil reserves at Elk Hills, California, and Teapot Dome, Wyoming, to the Department of the Interior. Ignorant of the graft behind the transfer, President Harding approved the move. At the time, oilman Edward L. Doheny* had made Fall an interest-free, non-collateral, indefinite loan of $100,000. On April 25, 1922, Fall secretly leased the Elk Hills reserve to Doheny. Fall also leased the Teapot Dome reserves to oilman Harry F. Sinclair* on April 7, 1922, and in March 1923, after he had resigned as secretary of the interior, Fall had received another "loan," this time $25,000 from Sinclair. Fall used the money to buy a ranch in New Mexico.

Early in 1924, Walsh's committee found out about the loans and then the leases. Walsh pushed a joint resolution through Congress condemning the deal and calling on the attorney general to return indictments. In June 1924 a federal grand jury indicted Fall on bribery and conspiracy charges. He was eventually convicted, sentenced to one year in prison, and fined $100,000. In subsequent trials, Sinclair and Doheny were acquitted of the bribery charges, although Sinclair spent nine months in a federal prison for contempt of court. Although the scandal had the potential of ruining the Republican Party's* chances in the election of 1924,* it did not have that outcome. Harding had died on August 2, 1923, before the revelations came out, and the new president, Calvin Coolidge,* had not been involved. Coolidge's reputation for honesty was unimpeachable, and the Republicans weathered the political storm. In the election, the Democrats ruined their chances by divisive struggles between its southern and northern wings. (Burl Noggle, *Teapot Dome: Oil and Politics in the 1920s,* 1962.)

TECHNOCRACY. From June 1932 through early 1933, the technocracy movement intrigued millions of Americans as a possible answer to the Great Depression. Howard Scott, the leader of the movement, claimed that capitalism was dying because increasingly efficient production and decreasing manpower requirements had precipitated the crisis. With the assistance of Columbia University, Scott conducted an exhaustive study of technology in the American economy and finally predicted an era of prosperity after the collapse of capitalism because the natural resources and technological capabilities of the country would be shared through a system of "energy certificates." The certificates, representing the yearly conversion of resources to energy, would be equally distributed among the population. Critics called technocracy socialism, fascism, or communism, and criticized its economic theories. When Scott accused President Franklin D. Roosevelt* in 1933 of trying to lead the country down the road to fascism, he lost much of his support, especially at Columbia University. Journalists then discovered that he had forged his academic credentials. Scott disappeared from public view, although he did establish Technocracy, Inc., which became a proto-fascist group in its own right in the late 1930s. (William A. Akin, *Technocracy and the American Dream: The Technocrat Movement 1900–1941,* 1977.)

TEMPORARY EMERGENCY RELIEF ADMINISTRATION. One of the real criticisms leveled at the Herbert Hoover* administration between 1930 and 1933 was its lack of commitment to a federal relief program to assist the poor and unemployed. That criticism became especially clear after New York, under the leadership of Governor Franklin D. Roosevelt,* had established the Temporary Emergency Relief Administration (TERA) in September 1931 to provide such assistance. Harry L. Hopkins, a Roosevelt aid, was named executive director of the TERA. The TERA relied on a system of matching grants to stimulate local funding and to provide direct assistance to the unemployed. The TERA issued bonds to finance its grants and encouraged cities and counties to develop work relief projects for the jobless. Harry Hopkins also insisted that local TERA committees be staffed by social work professionals. The Temporary Emergency Relief Administration became a prototype for New Deal relief agencies during the 1930s, and at the same time it boosted the presidential chances of Governor Roosevelt by giving him an image of a politician concerned about the plight of the poor and unemployed. (Robert Sherwood, *Roosevelt and Hopkins,* 1948.)

THOMAS, NORMAN MATTOON. Norman Thomas was born in Marion, Ohio, on November 20, 1884. He attended Bucknell College for a year and then graduated from the Princeton Theological Seminary in 1908. Thomas went to work in New York City at the East Side Settlement House and served as an assistant pastor at Christ Church in New York City. He was ordained a Presbyterian minister in 1911 and became pastor of the East Harlem Church. Thomas, however, was not happy in the pastorate. His years in the settlement house had convinced him that drastic change was necessary in the United States before the suffering of poor people could really be addressed, and Thomas joined the Socialist Party of America.* Thomas bitterly opposed American entry into World War I, and when church leaders and members of his congregation criticized his stand, he resigned the pastorate, becoming secretary of the Fellowship of Reconciliation, an antiwar group. He also edited its monthly journal, *World Tomorrow*.

In 1918 Thomas was one of the founders of the American Civil Liberties Union,* and the next year he established the League for Industrial Democracy. He also became an associate editor of *The Nation* in 1919. Thomas promoted the widespread labor strikes of 1919 and opposed the Red Scare.* He became increasingly prominent in Socialist circles during the 1920s, and eventually he inherited the mantle left by Eugene V. Debs.* In each election between 1928 and 1944, Thomas ran for president of the United States on the Socialist Party ticket. During the 1930s, he campaigned widely on behalf of the Southern Tenant Farmers Union and opposed American entry into World War II. Thomas was also an antiwar activist during the Vietnam War. He died on December 19, 1968. (Harry Fleischman, *Norman Thomas: A Biography, 1884–1968*, 1969; Bernard K. Johnpoll, *Pacifist's Progress: Norman Thomas and the Decline of American Socialism*, 1970.)

THOMSON-URRUTIA TREATY OF 1921. The Thomson-Urrutia Treaty was viewed as a final settlement of the United States–Colombian dispute stemming from the Panama controversy of 1903. In the treaty, the United States agreed to pay Colombia a total of $25 million in compensation for Theodore Roosevelt's decision in 1903 to recognize Panamanian independence and seize what later became the Panama Canal Zone. The treaty did not have much chance of being ratified until Colombia agreed to give the United States oil concessions. United States Minister to Colombia Thaddeus A. Thomson had negotiated the treaty with Colombian Foreign Minister Francisco Urrutia in 1914, but few senators were willing to support it as long as former president Theodore Roosevelt was still alive. Roosevelt died in 1919, and the Senate ratified the treaty in 1921. (Gordon Connell-Smith, *The United States and Latin America*, 1974; E. Taylor Parks, *Colombia and the United States, 1765–1934*, 1934.)

TILDEN, WILLIAM TATEM, JR. William "Big Bill" Tilden was born on February 10, 1894, in Germantown, Pennsylvania, to a prosperous family. As a teenager, he became fascinated with tennis, and by 1921 Tilden was the undisputed champion of the world. Tall and angular, and blessed with a fluid game and extraordinary confidence, Tilden went undefeated between 1921 and 1928, repeatedly winning every major tournament in the world. He was personally responsible for bringing tennis out of its cloistered world of the rich and establishing its popularity among the general public. During the 1930s, although not as competitive as he had been in the 1920s, Tilden was still the dean of the game, but his reputation was destroyed in 1946 when he was arrested and convicted of homosexuality and indecency with a child. Tilden spent several months in jail for the offense and was all but blacklisted after his release. He died on June 5, 1953. (Frank Deford, *Big Bill Tilden: The Triumphs and the Tragedy,* 1975.)

TOBIN, DANIEL JOSEPH. Daniel J. Tobin was born in County Clare, Ireland, in April 1875. A Roman Catholic,* he immigrated to the United States in 1890. Tobin worked in a sheet metal factory and went to night school until 1894, when he became a driver and motorman for a Boston street railway company. The next year, Tobin got a job driving a delivery truck for a meat-packing company and joined the local of the International Brotherhood of Teamsters, Chauffeurs, Warehousemen and Helpers of America. Tobin became the Teamsters business manager in 1904 and was elected president of the union in 1907. He remained in that position until 1952. Tobin died on November 14, 1955. (*New York Times,* November 15, 1955; Sam Romer, *The International Brotherhood of Teamsters: Its Government and Structure,* 1962.)

TRANSPORTATION ACT OF 1920. Railroads expanded rapidly across the United States after the Civil War, and as the economy came to depend more and more on the railroads for the distribution of goods, demands for federal regulation from farmers, shippers, and manufacturers increased. Congress passed the Interstate Commerce Act in 1887 to deal with the problem, and it established the Interstate Commerce Commission (ICC) to regulate the railroads. Subsequent legislation strengthened the ICC. In the meantime, railroad construction had created a crazy-quilt, overbuilt transportation system beleaguered by huge debts, new competition from automobiles and trucks, and gross duplication of facilities. During World War I, the government took over the railroads to ensure efficient operation. After the war, the railroads were returned to private control, and the Transportation Act of 1920 was the vehicle for that transition.

Congressman John J. Esch, chairman of the House Committee on Interstate and Foreign Commerce, sponsored the bill in the House, and Senator Albert B. Cummins sponsored it in the other chamber. The bill moved through Congress late in 1919 and early in 1920, gathering support among traditional Republicans and conservative Democrats, but raising the ire of progressives in both parties. After a good deal of arguing in a conference committee, the Esch-Cummins Bill passed both houses of Congress on February 21, 1920. President Woodrow Wilson* signed the bill into law on February 28. The law returned the railroads to private control on March 1, 1920; called on the ICC to draw up a comprehensive plan for railroad consolidation, giving them the blessing of exemption from antitrust laws; authorized the ICC to control pooling arrangements, regulate service, and supervise new issues of railroad securities; and empowered the ICC to evaluate the value of railroad property, set maximum and minimum freight and passenger rates, and establish fair rates of return to railroad stockholders. The bill also guaranteed railroad profits for a six-month period during the transition to private control and provided a recapture clause for all net earnings in excess of 6 percent, the money to return to an ICC pool to be distributed to low-income roads. Finally, the Transportation Act of 1920 established a Railroad Labor Board to adjudicate disputes between management and unions. Although the Transportation Act was a noble attempt to bring order to the industry, declining freight volume, heavy debt structures, and new competition doomed the railroads to long-term economic problems. In just a few years, the depression exposed those weaknesses. (Ari Hoogenboom and Olive Hoogenboom, *A History of the ICC: From Panacea to Palliative,* 1976; K. Austin Kerr, *American Railroad Politics, 1914–1920: Rates, Wages, and Efficiency,* 1968.)

TREATY OF VERSAILLES. See PARIS PEACE CONFERENCE OF 1919

TWENTY-FIRST AMENDMENT. By 1932 the "noble experiment" of prohibition* had become a political and legal nightmare. Enforcement of the Eighteenth Amendment* had proved impossible and organized criminal elements were making fortunes supplying illicit alcohol to millions of consumers. Groups like the Association Against the Prohibition Amendment* were campaigning for repeal of the Eighteenth Amendment, and the Democratic Party* had endorsed that campaign. In its 1932 platform, the Democratic Party called for immediate action by Congress to propose a new amendment to the states. After Franklin D. Roosevelt's* victory in the election of 1932,* the lame-duck Congress submitted a proposed constitutional amendment to the states. The proposal repealed the Eighteenth Amendment. Between February 20 and December 5, 1933, the proposed amendment secured the necessary ratifications of the various states. The Twenty-First Amendment was proclaimed on December 5, 1933. (Alfred H. Kelly and Winfred A. Harbison, *The American Constitution,* 1970.)

TUNNEY, JAMES JOSEPH. James Joseph "Gene" Tunney was born in New York City on May 25, 1897. He started amateur boxing as a teenager, joined the Marine Corps in 1918, and in 1919 won the light heavyweight title of the American Expeditionary Force. He left the service after the war and took up a professional boxing career, winning the light heavyweight championship in 1922. In 1926, Tunney defeated Jack Dempsey* for the heavyweight championship, and their rematch in 1927 became one of the most controversial sporting events in United States history. During the fight, Dempsey hit Tunney with a savage punch that put the champion on the floor for a full fourteen seconds, but, because

Dempsey failed to move to the neutral corner, the referee did not start the count, and Tunney was able to recover. Tunney won the fight and defended the title later against Tom Henney. He retired in 1928 and died on November 7, 1978. (*New York Times*, November 8, 1978; Randy Roberts, *Jack Dempsey: The Manassa Mauler,* 1979.)

TWENTIETH AMENDMENT. The Twentieth Amendment to the Constitution, also known as the "Lame-Duck Amendment," set back the convening of a new Congress from March 4 to January 3, and the inauguration of the new president from March 4 to January 20. It was sponsored by George W. Norris,* a Republican senator from Nebraska. It abolished the lame duck sessions of Congress in which defeated members sat and functioned even while a newly elected Congress, ready to work with a popular mandate, sat around and waited. The last lame duck session opened in December 1932 with 158 defeated members sitting in the House and the Senate. Norris proposed the amendment on March 2, 1932, and it was declared ratified on February 6, 1933. Effective on October 15, 1933, Congress would convene each year on January 3. Franklin D. Roosevelt* was the first president inaugurated under the amendment on January 20, 1937. (*Dictionary of American History,* IV, 1976.)

U

UNEMPLOYMENT CONFERENCE OF 1921. Because of the depression of 1921–1922, the American economy went into a tailspin and unemployment reached alarming levels, hitting 11.9 percent in 1921. Concerned about the long-term implications of massive unemployment, Secretary of Commerce Herbert Hoover* suggested to President Warren G. Harding* that the federal government sponsor a special conference to explore ways of dealing with the problem. With the backing of prominent businessmen like Owen D. Young* and labor leaders like William Green,* the conference opened on September 26, 1921. The emphasis was on voluntary action, not on any federal spending programs. A parade of speakers emphasized the need to build self-respect among the unemployed, the importance of industrial efficiency as a long-range solution to unemployment, the need for individual philanthropy and charitable giving, and the need for local government initiatives. The conference urged higher tariff levels, lower railroad rates, and accelerated work on normally scheduled federal construction projects. Although the conference had no permanent results, Hoover considered it a success. The federal government had provided leadership, not bureaucracy, and it had stimulated private and local activities. It was a vintage Herbert Hoover program. (Carolyn Grin, "The Unemployment Conference of 1921: An Experiment in National Cooperative Planning," *Mid-America* 55 [April 1973], 83–107; Robert H. Zieger, *Republicans and Labor, 1919–1929,* 1969.)

UNIVERSAL NEGRO IMPROVEMENT ASSOCIATION. See GARVEY, MARCUS MOSIAH

UPSHAW, WILLIAM DAVID. William David Upshaw was born on October 15, 1866, in Newman, Georgia. He attended Mercer University for two years before becoming an evangelist and lecturer. By 1906 Upshaw was publisher of the magazine *Golden Age,* a militant Christian journal dedicated to prohibition,* women's suffrage, white supremacy, and the rights of labor. Upshaw was instrumental in achieving Georgia's prohibition law in 1907, after which he gained a national reputation as a prohibition lecturer for the Anti-Saloon League of

America* and the Women's Christian Temperance Union. Running as a Democrat, Upshaw won election to the House of Representatives in 1918, and he served four terms there, always insisting on vigorous enforcement of the Volstead Act.* Upshaw was widely considered the ''driest of the dries.''* He was also a vigorous supporter of the Ku Klux Klan,* an affiliation that hurt him late in the 1920s when the Klan's influence declined in the United States. He lost his bid for re-election in 1926; and, in the election of 1928,* rather than support Al Smith,* who was a leading ''wet,''* Upshaw endorsed the candidacy of Republican Herbert Hoover.* In 1932, Upshaw ran for president under the banner of the Prohibition Party,* but he secured only 81,000 votes. For much of the remainder of his life, Upshaw campaigned against communism and radicalism. He died on November 21, 1952. (*Dictionary of American Biography,* supp. 5 [1977], 701–2; *New York Times,* November 22, 1952; Peter H. Odegard, *Pressure Politics: The Story of the Anti-Saloon League,* 1982.)

V

VALENTINO, RUDOLPH. Born Rodolpho Alfonzo Raffaelo di Valentina d'Antonguolla in Castellaneta, Italy, on May 6, 1895, Rudolph Valentino immigrated to the United States in 1913 and found odd jobs in dance halls and saloons. He worked as an extra in a number of films until he was finally featured in two enormous 1921 hits—*The Four Horsemen of the Apocalypse* and *The Sheik*. With those successes, Hollywood made Valentino into the country's greatest male sex star. Women by the millions consumed news of his stage and private life, and in the process Valentino assumed larger-than-life dimensions in the United States. Several later films were also hits, including *Blood and Sand* (1922) and *Monsieur Beaucaire* (1924). Ironically, it was Valentino's death from peritonitis on August 23, 1926, which guaranteed his status in the history of Hollywood. He was hardly a great actor, and most film historians suspect that his popularity would not have survived the transition to sound films, but in death Valentino achieved a legendary stardom. His funeral was really the first one of a major screen star in the 1920s, and the tens of thousands of people who tried to attend the funeral or passed by his gravesite illustrated the birth of a national pop culture in the United States. It was the timing of his death, not his acting skills, which made Valentino an important figure in the history of Hollywood. (Noel Botram and Peter Donnelly, *Valentino: The Love God*, 1976; Robert Oberfirst, *Rudolph Valentino: The Man Behind the Myth*, 1962.)

VALLEE, RUDOLPH. Born Hubert Prior Vallee on July 28, 1901, in Island Pond, Vermont, Rudy Vallee grew up in Westbrook, Maine, and fell in love with music. After lying about his age to enter the navy during World War I, Vallee was discharged in 1917 and eventually studied music at the University of Maine and Yale. He was an accomplished saxophonist, and he toured with the Vincent Lopez band before starting his own group, the "Connecticut Yankees," where he played at the Heigh-Ho Club in New York City and perfected his trademark greeting of "Heigh-ho, everybody!" On October 24, 1929, the "Rudy Vallee Show" debuted on NBC radio,* and he was a smash hit, playing the saxophone and singing songs in "crooner" style. From the time the show opened, and throughout the 1930s, Vallee was extraordinarily popular in the United States, a radio heart-throb to match Rudolph Valentino's* film stardom. Known as "The Vagabond Lover," his theme song was "My Time Is Your Time." Vallee left NBC radio in 1943 to join the U.S. Coast Guard. In the 1950s and 1960s, Vallee continued to perform, including a hit role in *How to Succeed in Business without Really Trying* and a radio talk show. He died on July 3, 1986. (John Dunning, *Tune In Yesterday: The Ultimate Encyclopedia of Old-Time Radio, 1925–1976,* 1976; *New York Times,* July 4, 1986.)

VAMP. See BARA, THEDA

VANDERBILT, CORNELIUS III. Cornelius Vanderbilt III was born on September 5, 1872, in New York City. He graduated from Yale in 1895 and took a master's degree there in 1899. Heir to the family railroad fortune, Vanderbilt worked for the New York Central Railroad between 1895 and 1899, and then went to London and Paris to analyze their subway systems. After returning to New York, he joined forces with August Belmont in building the Interborough Rapid Transit Company, the city's first subway system, in 1904. Vanderbilt served on the boards of a dozen American railroads and was a symbol during the 1920s of the strength of American industry. An active Republican, Vanderbilt wholeheartedly supported the conservative values of the 1920s and was equally uncomfortable with the political and economic culture of the New Deal. He retired from business in 1939 and died on March 1, 1942. (Alvin F. Harlow, *The Road of the Century: The Story of the New York Central,* 1947; *New York Times,* March 2, 1942.)

VANDERLIP, FRANK ARTHUR. Frank A. Vanderlip was born on November 17, 1864, near Aurora, Illinois. When his father died in 1877, Vanderlip became the sole supporter of the family. He became a lathe operator and studied mathematics, shorthand, and drafting in the evenings. In 1885 he became city editor of the *Aurora Evening Post,* and in 1889 he moved to Chicago to become associate editor of *The Economist.* Vanderlip became private secretary to Secretary of the Treasury Lyman J. Gage in 1897, and later in the year he was appointed assistant secretary of the treasury. Vanderlip made important contacts there, and in 1901 he joined the National City Bank in New York as a vice-president. He became president of National City in 1909 and remained there until 1919, aggressively pushing the bank into international finance. Vanderlip's politics, however, were not conventional. He opposed Calvin Coolidge* for president in the election of 1924,* and he supported the Progressive Party* ticket of Robert M. La Follette* and Burton K. Wheeler,* even though he was a Republican. During the early 1930s, Vanderlip advocated abandonment of the gold standard and devaluation of the currency and praised Franklin D. Roosevelt* when the New Deal did so in 1933. Frank Vanderlip died on June 29, 1937. (*New York Times,* June 30, 1937.)

VAN DYKE, JOHN WESLEY. John Wesley Van Dyke was born on December 27, 1849, in Mercersburg, Pennsylvania. He went to work in the oil fields as a young man, and, when he was twenty-four, he found a job as a mechanic with a subsidiary of Standard Oil. Van Dyke became an expert in refinery engineering and worked his way up through management levels in several refineries. In 1903 he became manager of a plant for the Atlantic Refining Company, and in 1911, when the Supreme Court broke up Standard Oil, Atlantic Refining Company split off and became independent. Van Dyke was named president of the new company that same year and remained in the position until 1927. During those years, he built Atlantic Refining into a fully integrated oil corporation and served for a time as head of the American Petroleum Institute. John Van Dyke died on September 13, 1939. (John G. McLean and R. W. Haigh, *The Growth of Integrated Oil Companies,* 1954; *New York Times,* September 17, 1939.)

VANN, ROBERT LEE. Robert Lee Vann was born on August 27, 1879, in Ahoskie, North Carolina. The son of ex-slaves, he graduated from high school in 1901, attended the Wayland Academy in Richmond, Virginia, between 1901 and 1903, and then entered the Western University of Pennsylvania in Pittsburgh. Vann edited the school newspaper, graduated in 1906, and received a law degree in 1909. To supplement his income, he served as legal counsel to a new black newspaper, *The Pittsburgh Courier,* and in 1910 he became the editor, a position he held until his death in 1940. During the 1920s, the *Courier* became the most prominent black newspaper in the country; and Vann, the most prominent black journalist. A Republican, Vann supported Franklin D. Roosevelt* in the election of 1932* after becoming disenchanted with Herbert Hoover's* "feeble attempts" to relieve the suffering of the depression. Roosevelt rewarded Vann with an advisory role in the New Deal, which made Vann part of the "black cabinet." In 1936 Vann urged black people throughout the country to switch their political allegiances—to "turn Lincoln's picture to the wall. That debt has been paid in full." Robert Vann died on October 24, 1940. (Andrew Buni, *Robert L. Vann of the Pittsburgh Courier: Politics and Black Journalism,* 1974.)

VAN SWEARINGEN, MANTIS JAMES. Mantis James Van Swearingen was born on July 8, 1881, in Wooster, Ohio. After being orphaned at the age of twelve, Van Swearingen moved to Cleveland and became a clerk at a local company. Along with his brother Oris, his senior by two years, Van Swearingen went into the real estate business. The two brothers were virtually inseparable, both bachelors and roommates. In 1900 they purchased 1,400 acres of land on the eastern edge of Cleveland and began to develop it into a residential suburb. Desperate for transportation facilities out to the suburb, they purchased the Nickle Plate Road in 1916 from the New York Central Railroad for more than $8 million. From that base, they built a real estate and railroad empire during the 1920s. During the decade, they bought the Toledo, St. Louis and Western Railroad; the Lake Erie and Western Railroad; the Chesapeake and Ohio Railroad;

the Hocking Valley Railroad; the Erie Railroad; and the Missouri Pacific Railroad.

Because they were heavily leveraged in making the railroad purchases, the stock market crash of 1929* hurt them badly. They could not make their debt payments. Not only had collapsing securities values wiped out much of their asset structure, but also, railroads in general came on hard times. The depression drastically reduced freight volume just as new competition from trucks was doing the same thing. The Van Swearingen railroads were burdened with heavy debt structures and they could not make their fixed payments. When the Reconstruction Finance Corporation* loaned the Missouri Pacific $5 million in 1932, liberals and progressives raised a storm of protest about the federal government bailing out millionaires while poor people starved. The loan did little good. In 1935 the Van Swearingens defaulted on a $48 million loan from J. P. Morgan & Company, and their financial empire crumbled. Mantis James Van Swearingen died on December 12, 1935, and his brother Oris died on November 23, 1936. (Frederick Lewis Allen, *The Lords of Creation*, 1977; Robert Carson, *Main Line to Oblivion*, 1971; Taylor Hampton, *The Nickle Plate Road*, 1947; *New York Times*, December 13, 1935 and November 24, 1936.)

VAN SWEARINGEN, ORIS PAXTON. See VAN SWEARINGEN, MANTIS JAMES

VANZETTI, BARTOLOMEO. Bartolomeo Vanzetti was born in Villafalletto, Italy, on June 11, 1888. He graduated from high school before he immigrated to the United States in 1908. Vanzetti lived first in New York City, but he travelled widely throughout the United States, supporting himself with a variety of jobs. In 1915 he settled in Plymouth, Massachusetts, but then spent 1917 and 1918 in Mexico to avoid being drafted into the United States Army. Vanzetti became enamored of philosophical anarchism during World War I, and he came to know Nicola Sacco.* On April 15, 1920, a payroll robbery in South Braintree, Massachusetts, resulted in the murder of a paymaster and a guard, and in May, Vanzetti and Sacco were arrested and charged with the crime. In the subsequent trial, both were convicted and sentenced to death. Because of the atmosphere of anti-radicalism prevalent at the time, the trial revolved more around Vanzetti's and Sacco's anarchist political philosophy than evidence that they had committed the murder and robbery. The Sacco and Vanzetti case* became an international cause célèbre, and from his jail cell Vanzetti wrote a series of letters proclaiming his political philosophy as well as his innocence. Despite numerous appeals and the support of many prominent Americans, the death sentence against Sacco and Vanzetti was carried out on April 23, 1927, when they died in the Massachusetts electric chair. (Felix Frankfurter, *The Case of Sacco and Vanzetti*, 1927; Fred Somkin, "How Vanzetti Said Goodbye," *Journal of American History* [September 1981], 298–312.)

VEBLEN, THORSTEIN BUNDE. Thorstein Veblen was born on July 30, 1857, in Cato, Wisconsin. He graduated from Carlton College in 1880 and then earned a doctorate in 1884 at Yale. During the course of a distinguished academic career, Veblen taught history and economics at the University of Chicago, Stanford University, the University of Missouri, and the New School for Social Research. Veblen became a leading economic theorist in the United States, specializing in institutional economics and arguing in favor of government regulation of the economy as well as the creation of a social security network. His book *The Theory of the Leisure Class* (1899) argued that modern industrial society revolved around conspicuous consumption. Veblen was convinced that the most powerful forces in modern society were technology, the price system, and the nation state. He wrote and lectured with extraordinary wit and satire, always poking ridicule at the wealthy and at the middle-classes who aped their values. During the 1920s, Veblen was convinced that consumerism and business values had triumphed in the United States, and that the Republican administrations of Warren G. Harding,* Calvin Coolidge,* and Herbert Hoover* reflected that victory. He died on August 3, 1929. (Joseph Dorfman, *Thorstein Veblen and His America*, 1934; Douglas Dowd, *Thorstein Veblen*, 1966.)

VETERANS BUREAU SCANDAL. Along with the Teapot Dome* scandal and the Alien Property Custodian scandal,* the Veterans Bureau scandal contributed to the reputation of the Warren Harding* administration as one of the most corrupt in American history. The scandal first emerged in 1923 and involved Charles R. Forbes, a World War I hero and the director of the Veterans Bureau. A sycophant, Forbes had parlayed card games with Warren G. Harding into the presidential appointment. Early in 1923, Harding became aware that Forbes was illegally selling government supplies and taking kickbacks on hospital building contracts. Harding forced him to resign on February 15, 1923, hoping to keep the scandal private. It was not to be. Early in March, the Senate ordered an investigation of the Veterans Bureau, and on March 15, Charles F. Cramer, general counsel of the bureau, committed suicide.

The Senate investigation which began late in October 1923, revealed that Forbes had worked out a closed bidding system for new veterans' hospitals between himself, the Thompson-Black Construction Company of St. Louis, and the Hurley-Mason Construction Company of Tacoma—each party keeping a third of the profits. Forbes also had the Veterans Bureau purchase hospital sites at exorbitant prices, and then he personally collected kickbacks from the sellers. Finally, it was discovered that Forbes had sold $3 million worth of Veterans Bureau hospital supplies to private companies for only $600,000, taking another kickback himself. Eventually, Forbes was sentenced to two years in prison and fined $10,000. (Robert K. Murray, *The Harding Era: Warren G. Harding and His Administration*, 1969.)

VETERANS COMPENSATION ACT. See ADJUSTED COMPENSATION ACT OF 1924

VETERANS OF FOREIGN WARS OF THE UNITED STATES. The Veterans of Foreign Wars (VFW) was founded in 1899 after the Spanish-American War, but it did not become a major political force until after World War I. In 1920, Robert G. Woodside, head of the VFW, wrote its motto "Honor the Dead by Helping the Living" and launched the fund-raising campaign of selling the buddy poppy, a red crepe-paper poppy, to finance veterans' assistance programs. During the 1920s, the VFW campaigned for immigration restriction, deportment of political radicals, veterans' bonuses, and improvement in Veterans Bureau programs for veterans. It also condemned President Herbert Hoover* for his handling of the Bonus Army* demonstrations in 1932. (See the *VFW Magazine* for the 1920s.)

VIDOR, KING WALLIS. King Vidor was born in Galveston, Texas, on February 8, 1894. In 1909 he began to work in a Galveston theater as a ticket-taker and projectionist; by 1910, he was making local newsreels. Vidor drove to Hollywood in a Model T* in 1915 and found work filming local newsreels there and selling them to Universal Studios. Vidor directed his first feature film, *The Turn in the Road*, in 1918; in 1922 he directed *Peg-O-My-Heart* for Metro-Goldwyn-Mayer. His 1925 film *The Big Parade*, which grossed $18 million, made his reputation, and Vidor became a powerful figure in Hollywood. He made his first sound film, *Hallelujah*, in 1929, and, during the next thirty years, he directed twenty-five more films, including *The Champ* (1932) and *War and Peace* (1956). King Vidor retired from filmmaking in 1959 and died on November 1, 1982. (John Baxter, *King Vidor*, 1976.)

VILLARD, OSWALD GARRISON. Oswald Garrison Villard was born in Wiesbaden, Germany, on March 13, 1872, and he graduated from Harvard in 1893, taking a master's degree there in 1896. He immediately began a career in journalism, first with the *Philadelphia Press* (1896–1897) and then with the *New York Evening Post* (1897–1918). During those years, Villard also served as editor of *The Nation* (1897–1932). Since his grandfather, William Lloyd Garrison, had been a leading abolitionist, and his mother, Fanny Villard, was a prominent suffragette, Villard grew up as a social liberal and as a pacifist. He bitterly opposed the Spanish-American War of 1898 and the jump to imperialism, and he opposed military preparedness before World War I. Because of political compromises made in the negotiations at Paris, Villard was an outspoken opponent of the Treaty of Versailles,* terming it a "covenant with death." During the 1920s, Villard opposed the Red Scare,* supported the campaign to save Nicola Sacco* and Bartolomeo Vanzetti* from the electric chair, and called for creation of a welfare state as a means of dealing with the problems of modern industrialism. He consistently advocated protection of civil liberties. In the 1930s, Villard was comfortable with most of the legislation produced under the New Deal. Late in the 1930s, however, he broke with the Franklin D. Roosevelt* administration because he became convinced that the United States was drifting into World War II. Villard called for only moral condemnation of fascism, not military action, and in the process he alienated himself from most Americans, especially after the Japanese attack on Pearl Harbor. Oswald Garrison Villard died on October 1, 1949. (D. Joy Humes, *Oswald Garrison Villard, Liberal of the 1920s,* 1960; Michael Wreszin, *Oswald Garrison Villard, Pacifist at War,* 1965.)

"THE VOICE OF FIRESTONE." "The Voice of Firestone" was radio's* most consistently popular musical show. Sponsored by Firestone Tire and Rubber Company, it premiered on NBC radio on December 3, 1928, and, for the next twenty-seven years, it occupied the same time slot on Monday evenings at 8:30 P.M., eastern standard time. The seventeen-member orchestra, directed by William Daly, performed classical pieces, marches, show tunes, and popular songs. (John Dunning, *Tune in Yesterday: The Ultimate Encyclopedia of Old-Time Radio, 1925–1976,* 1976.)

VOLSTEAD ACT OF 1919. In December 1917, Congress, succumbing to the political pressure of the prohibition* movement, passed and sent to the states the Eighteenth Amendment* to the Constitution. It prohibited the manufacture, sale, or transportation of alcoholic beverages. The thirty-sixth state ratified the amendment in January 1919, and in October Congress passed the National Prohibition Enforcement Act, or the Volstead Act. President Woodrow Wilson* vetoed the bill on October 27, but Congress overrode the veto the next day. The Volstead Act, which went into effect on January 16, 1920, defined alcohol as any drink with more than 0.5 percent alcohol. The Internal Revenue Bureau supervised enforcement of the law. In November 1923, Congress extended prohibition to Hawaii and the Virgin Islands and reduced the alcohol content of medicines. The Volstead Act was amended by the Beer-Wine Revenue Act of March 22, 1933, which redefined alcohol as any beverage with more than 3.2 percent alcohol content and left enforcement up to the states. (Norman H. Clark, *Deliver Us from Evil: An Interpretation of American Prohibition,* 1976; Andrew Sinclair, *Prohibition: Era of Excess,* 1962.)

W

WADSWORTH, JAMES WOLCOTT, JR. James W. Wadsworth, Jr. was born in Geneseo, New York, on August 12, 1877. He graduated from Yale in 1898, served with an artillery unit in the Spanish-American War, and then became a New York farmer and rancher between 1899 and 1904. Wadsworth served in the state legislature between 1904 and 1910, when he moved to Texas to manage a large ranch. He returned to New York in 1914 to run for the United States Senate, a bid he won. In the Senate, Wadsworth was known as an affable member of the Republican Old Guard,* an advocate of high tariffs, balanced federal budgets, and the prerogatives of business management. Robert F. Wagner* unseated Wadsworth in the election of 1926.* Wadsworth went back to farming for six more years, but he won a seat in Congress in 1932 and stayed there until 1951. During the 1930s and 1940s, he was a bitter opponent of the New Deal and the Fair Deal. James Wadsworth died on June 21, 1952. *(New York Times,* June 22, 1952.)

WAGNER, ROBERT FERDINAND. Robert F. Wagner was born in Hesse-Nassau, Germany, on June 8, 1877. When he was eight, the family immigrated to New York City, and he received his political education in the Tammany machine and developed a political philosophy involving an urban, progressive, pragmatic approach to domestic reform. Wagner won a seat in the state legislature as a Democrat in 1904, and was president pro tem of the state senate by 1911. With House Speaker Alfred E. Smith,* Wagner served on the New York Factory Investigating Commission and guided fifty-six industrial and labor reforms through the legislature by 1914. As a legislator, he emphasized the rights of organized labor and the need for government programs to guarantee economic stability. In 1926 Wagner was elected to the United States Senate, where he quickly earned a reputation as a hardworking, passionate, pragmatic liberal. Wagner specialized in unemployment problems, especially in establishing the principle of federal responsibility for stabilizing the labor markets. He introduced three measures in Congress to deal with employment problems. Herbert Hoover* signed one of the bills, to improve statistics gathering, in early 1930. In 1931

Hoover signed legislation establishing a Federal Employment Stabilization Board. Wagner's third bill, one to reorganize the U.S. Employment Service, was vetoed by Hoover in 1930 and was not passed until June 1933 when it became known as the Wagner-Peyser Act.

When unemployment expanded after 1929, Wagner became a leading advocate in Congress of unemployment relief. In December 1931, he submitted a plan for a $2 billion emergency public works program, part of which was implemented in the Emergency Relief and Construction Act of 1932.* In 1933 Wagner sponsored the Federal Emergency Relief Act, which provided $500 million in relief grants to the states, and the National Industrial Recovery Act of 1933 included Wagner's proposal for a $3.3 billion public works program. He was also instrumental in securing the labor standards provisions of the National Industrial Recovery Act of 1933, as well as the National Labor Relations Act of 1935. Wagner played a central role in passage of the Social Security Act of 1935. Robert Wagner remained in the Senate until 1949, and he died on May 4, 1953. (J. Joseph Huthmacher, *Senator Robert F. Wagner and the Rise of Urban Liberalism,* 1968.)

WALD, LILLIAN. Lillian Wald was born on March 10, 1867, in Cincinnati, Ohio. After graduating from the New York Hospital School of Nursing in 1891 and the Women's Medical College in 1893, she began a career in social service, pacifism, and progressivism. Wald was the founder of the Henry Street Settlement House, patterned after Jane Addams's* Hull House in Chicago. In 1904, along with people like Jane Addams and Florence Kelley,* Wald established the National Child Labor Committee* to campaign against child labor in the United States. When World War I erupted in Europe, Wald immediately began to work to prevent American intervention in the war, staging large-scale demonstrations for peace in 1914. She helped establish the American Union against Militarism in 1914 to promote internationalism and condemn militarism. After World War I, she was active in the Women's Peace Party, and she was targeted for investigation by Attorney General A. Mitchell Palmer* during the Red Scare* of 1919 and 1920. Wald described herself as a ''militant pacifist,'' and late in the 1930s she protested openly the persecution of Jews in Germany. Wald died on September 1, 1940. (Robert L. Duffus, *Lillian Wald: Neighbor and Crusader,* 1938.)

WALGREEN, CHARLES RUDOLPH. Charles Walgreen was born on October 9, 1873, on a farm near Galesburg, Illinois. He attended a business college in Dixon, Illinois; he worked as a bookkeeper for a year; and then he labored in a shoe factory. When he lost part of a finger in an industrial accident, Walgreen decided to apprentice out as a druggist. After moving to Chicago in 1893, he worked in a drugstore during the day and studied pharmacy at night school. Walgreen became a registered pharmacist in 1897 and served in the army during the Spanish-American War. When the war was over, Walgreen returned to Chicago and in 1902 purchased a small drugstore. He formed C. R. Walgreen and Company and began acquiring more stores. The number of stores Walgreen owned grew from 7 in 1916, to 110 in 1927, and to 493 in 1939.

Walgreen pioneered the modern drugstore. He placed lunch counters in the store along with the soda fountain, and he was the first to sell malted milkshakes. Walgreen also introduced modern, self-service retailing in which customers shopped in well-lit stores and carried their own items to a cash register. Merchandise was placed on open shelves instead of behind the traditional showcases. Through a subsidiary company, Walgreen manufactured his own ice cream, candy, and some pharmaceuticals. Charles Walgreen died on December 11, 1939. (*Dictionary of American Biography,* supp. 2 [1944], 688–89; *New York Times,* December 12, 1939.)

WALLACE, HENRY AGARD. Henry A. Wallace was born near Orient in Adair County, Iowa, on October 7, 1888. As a boy, Henry took an interest in the scientific study of plants; and, when he was sixteen, he conducted his first significant experiment with seed corn, embarking on a course of scientific inquiry that eventually earned him worldwide recognition as a plant geneticist. In 1910 Wallace graduated from Iowa State College at Ames. From 1910 to 1933, he helped edit *Wallace's Farmer,* the influential farm journal founded by his father, Henry Cantwell Wallace.* Wallace's genetic experiments with corn culminated in 1923 with the first successful hybrid seed corn for commercial use, which led to the founding, in 1926, of the Hi-Bred Seed Company (later renamed the Pioneer Hi-Bred Seed Company) of which Wallace was president until 1933.

Wallace also had a profound interest in agricultural economics. Influenced by the ideas of Thorstein Veblen* and self-taught in statistical techniques, Wallace probed the economics of farm production and falling farm income in the hard times of the 1920s, frequently making recommendations—for crop storage, collective action, planned production, and government assistance—which boldly challenged the laissez-faire thinking of the day. From 1924 to 1928, Wallace vigorously supported the McNary-Haugen Bill,* a measure designed to boost farm prices by authorizing the government to buy up surpluses and sell them abroad. Though the McNary-Haugenites failed to achieve their purpose, Wallace emerged from the struggle as a seasoned veteran of farm politics and a respected farm leader of national importance. Although a lifelong Republican, Wallace endorsed Al Smith* for president in the election of 1928,* and in 1933 the new president, Franklin D. Roosevelt,* named Wallace secretary of agriculture, where he implemented the Agricultural Adjustment Act's crop reduction program. Wallace served as vice-president of the United States between 1941 and 1945, and then as secretary of commerce between 1945 and 1946. By then, Wallace's politics were leaning more and more to the left, and in 1948 he tried an independent run for the presidency under the banner of the Progressive Party.* After his defeat, he returned to private life and continued his scientific research. Henry A. Wallace died on November 18, 1965. (*New York Times,* November

19, 1965; Edward L. Schapsmeier and Frederick H. Schapsmeier, *Henry A. Wallace of Iowa: The Agrarian Years, 1910–1940*, 1968.)

WALLACE, HENRY CANTWELL. Henry C. Wallace was born in Rock Island, Illinois, on May 11, 1866. He attended Iowa State Agricultural College off and on between 1885 and 1891, and he graduated in 1892. Wallace settled in Ames, Iowa, and became part owner and publisher of the *Farm and Dairy* magazine. Wallace later bought the magazine out completely and changed its name to *Wallace's Farmer*. It became one of the leading farm journals in the United States. Between 1906 and 1920, Wallace also served as national secretary of the Cornbelt Meat Producers Association. In March 1921, he became the new secretary of agriculture in President Warren G. Harding's* cabinet.

As secretary of agriculture, Wallace emphasized the need for farmers to increase their productivity while accepting Department of Agriculture advice in adjusting production to consumption. Wallace's biggest problem while serving as secretary of agriculture was with Secretary of Commerce Herbert Hoover.* For Hoover, farming was changing from a way of life to a business, and farmers needed to adjust to that. While Wallace favored federal subsidies to farmers, Hoover opposed them, hoping improved marketing tactics would do the job. While Wallace campaigned for lower railroad rates, Hoover felt those rates reflected market conditions and that the federal government should not tamper with them. Above all else, Wallace resented the fact that Hoover was so deeply involved in agricultural affairs. It was bureaucratic imperialism. Eventually, President Warren G. Harding sided with Hoover against Wallace in his approach to agricultural problems. Henry C. Wallace died in office on October 25, 1924. Less than nine years later, his son Henry Agard Wallace* became secretary of agriculture under president Franklin D. Roosevelt.* (Donald L. Winters, *Henry Cantwell Wallace as Secretary of Agriculture, 1921–1924*, 1970.)

WALSH, DAVID IGNATIUS. David I. Walsh was born on November 11, 1872, in Leominister, Massachusetts. He received a bachelor's degree from Holy Cross College in 1893 and a law degree from Boston University in 1897. Walsh began practicing law and won a seat as a Democrat in the state legislature in 1900. He was elected lieutenant governor in 1913 and governor of Massachusetts in 1914. In 1918 Walsh won a seat in the United States Senate, a position he lost in the election of 1924.* In 1925 Senator Henry Cabot Lodge* died, and Walsh won the special election to fill Lodge's unexpired term. David Walsh remained in the United States Senate until 1947. During his tenure there, Walsh earned a reputation as an advocate of the rights of labor to minimum wages, maximum hours, and safe working conditions, as well as the right to bargain collectively. Walsh had little success during the 1920s in implementing his point of view, but during the 1930s he played a key role in securing New Deal legislation on behalf of workers and labor unions. David Walsh died on June 11, 1947. (*New York Times*, June 12, 1947.)

WALSH, FRANCIS PATRICK. Francis Walsh was born in St. Louis, Missouri, on July 20, 1864. When his father died in 1874, Walsh had to go to work to help support his eight brothers and sisters. He learned shorthand and accounting, and he was able to work for Western Union and several railroads as a secretary and accountant. Walsh also read law privately and gained entry to the bar in 1889. A skilled trial lawyer, he was active in Kansas City politics with the Democratic Party,* where he opposed the machine organization of Boss Tom Pendergast. Walsh held several posts in city government and became a leading Kansas City progressive. In 1913, President Woodrow Wilson* appointed Walsh chairman of the Commission on Industrial Relations. In 1918 Wilson appointed Walsh co-chairman, along with William Howard Taft,* of the National War Labor Board. During the 1920s, Walsh dedicated his time to civil liberties, especially opposition to the Red Scare,* and to the cause of Irish independence. He was especially active in the defense of Nicola Sacco* and Bartolomeo Vanzetti.* Walsh supported Robert M. La Follette* for president in the election of 1924* but then supported Al Smith* in the election of 1928* and Franklin D. Roosevelt* in the elections of 1932* and 1936. Walsh died on May 2, 1939. (*Dictionary of American Biography,* supp. 2 [1944], 690–91; *New York Times,* May 3, 1939.)

WALSH, THOMAS JAMES. Thomas J. Walsh was born on June 12, 1859, in Two Rivers, Wisconsin. He received a law degree from the University of Wisconsin in 1884, taught school briefly, and began to practice law. Walsh moved to Helena, Montana, in 1890, and continued to practice law. He was active in state Democratic politics, and in the election of 1912 Walsh won a seat in the United States Senate. He was re-elected in 1918, 1924, and 1930. During his tenure in the Senate, Walsh built up a record as a liberal Democrat, favoring women's rights, an end to child labor, protection of union collective bargaining, and American entrance into the League of Nations.* Walsh became a national figure in 1924 when his investigation of the Department of the Interior and the Department of the Navy revealed the Teapot Dome* scandal. He pursued the scandal with a vengeance, eventually exposing the part played by Secretary of the Interior Albert Fall* in leasing United States naval oil reserves to private companies. Walsh also played a leading role in restricting Japanese immigration to the United States and preventing the cancellation of Europe's World War I debts. Late in 1932, President-elect Franklin D. Roosevelt* announced that he was naming Walsh as attorney general in his new cabinet, but, while en route to Washington, D.C., to take his oath of office, Walsh died on March 2, 1933. (J. Leonard Bates, ''Senator Walsh of Montana, 1918–1924,'' Ph.D. dissertation, University of North Carolina, 1952; *New York Times,* March 3, 1933; Burl Noggle, *Teapot Dome: Oil and Politics in the 1920s,* 1962.)

WARBURG, PAUL MORITZ. Paul Warburg was born on August 10, 1868, in Hamburg, Germany, to one of Europe's most prominent Jewish banking families. After graduating from gymnasium in Hamburg, Warburg joined the family firm, M.M. Warburg and Company, and became a partner in 1895. That same year, he married Nina Loeb, daughter of Solomon Loeb, and in 1902 came to New York as a partner in Kuhn, Loeb and Company. Warburg spent the rest of his life investing his energies in the American firm. He specialized in railroad and international finance. After the panic of 1907, Warburg became a leading advocate in the United States of the need for a central bank, and he served as an adviser to Senator Nelson Aldrich's National Monetary Commission. The commission's report led to the Federal Reserve Act of 1913. Warburg was appointed to the board of governors of the Federal Reserve System in 1914, and he resigned from that post during World War I, largely because he feared his German ancestry might create too many political problems for the agency.

Warburg returned to Kuhn, Loeb and Company in the 1920s and headed two of its affiliates while he served as chairman of the Bank of Manhattan Company. By that time, he was a leading figure in American finance, helping arrange the consortium loans which kept the German economy afloat in the later 1920s, calling for more centralization in the Federal Reserve System, and demanding government regulations controlling the speculative mania which eventually brought on the stock market crash of 1929.* Paul Warburg died on January 24, 1932, just a few years before the New Deal enacted many of the economic reforms he had advocated. (David Farrer, *The Warburgs: The Story of a Family,* 1975; *New York Times,* January 26, 1932; E. Rosenberg and A. J. Sherman, *M. M. Warburg & Co., 1798–1938,* 1979.)

WAR DEBTS. During World War I, the United States loaned more than $7 billion to allied nations to assist them in fighting the war; after the war, to assist in reconstruction, the United States expanded those loans by $3.3 billion, bringing the total to $10,350,479,075. Although more than 90 percent of the money had been used to purchase United States agricultural and manufactured goods, creating an unprecedented prosperity, the American public expected repayment in full, at 5 percent interest. At first, the debtor nations seemed willing to pay because they expected to be receiving large reparations* payments from Germany. When the German economy collapsed in 1921 and reparations* were scaled down in the Dawes Plan,* in 1924, and in the Young Plan,* in 1929, the allied nations claimed they would be unable to repay the debt. United States politicians, especially President Calvin Coolidge,* demanded payment, and the Europeans argued that the United States should cancel the debts in the name of world prosperity. For a time, a triangle existed—American bankers loaned Germany more than $2 billion in the late 1920s, the Germans made reparations payments, and the allied nations then made approximately $2 billion in debt payments—but it was no solution to the problem. Between 1923 and 1925, the United States reached agreements with its debtor nations scaling down the size of the debt, but it was not enough. When the depression struck the world in 1929, all hopes of paying the war debts died. On December 15, 1932, six nations, including Belgium and France, formally defaulted on their debts, and on June

15, 1934, the rest of them defaulted, except Finland, which paid her debt. (H. G. Moulton and Leo Pasvolsky, *War Debts and World Prosperity*, 1932.)

WAR FINANCE CORPORATION. Congress created the War Finance Corporation (WFC) in 1918 to strengthen the private capital investment markets and to make loans to industries engaged in wartime production. In addition to stabilizing the money markets, the WFC sustained the government's financial program by periodically purchasing federal bonds. During World War I, the WFC loaned funds to a wide variety of enterprises, including public utilities, electric power plants, mining and chemical concerns, railroads, and banks. In the postwar years, the WFC underwent several important changes. During the depression of 1920–1922, Congress transformed the WFC into a peacetime, emergency finance corporation, authorizing it to lend money to exporters and to grant agricultural loans to individuals, banks, and local credit agencies. The Agricultural Credits Act of 1921 converted the WFC into an agricultural finance agency capable of providing farmers with intermediate credit to renew or to extend their existing obligations. By 1924 the WFC had loaned over $300 million for agricultural purposes. Congress considered its activities so successful that the Agricultural Credits Act of 1923* established the Federal Intermediate Credit Bank System to assume many of the duties and responsibilities of the War Finance Corporation. The government began to liquidate the WFC in 1924, and five years later Congress officially dissolved it. By the fall of 1931, private bankers were clamoring for its reincarnation, and in 1932 Congress re-established it as the Reconstruction Finance Corporation.* (James S. Olson, *Herbert Hoover and the Reconstruction Finance Corporation, 1931–1933*, 1977.)

WARNER, ALBERT. See WARNER BROTHERS

WARNER BROTHERS. The famous motion picture family, the Warner brothers, came from a working-class family. Harry Morris Warner was born near Warsaw, Poland, on December 12, 1881, and his brother Albert was born there on July 23, 1884. The family immigrated to the United States in 1885, and Samuel Lewis Warner was born in Baltimore Maryland, on August 10, 1887. The family then moved to London, Ontario, Canada, where Jack Leonard Warner was born on August 2, 1892. They all then moved to Youngstown, Ohio, in 1894. After working at odd jobs, the brothers eventually bought themselves a small movie projecter and began to display films for a fee. At first, they travelled from town to town showing a movie until the audience dwindled and then they moved on. In 1903 they moved to New Castle, Pennsylvania, where they opened their first theater.

Because of the difficulties in securing enough film rentals, they moved to New York City and began to produce films themselves. In 1918 they moved their production facilities to Sunset Boulevard in Hollywood, California. Warner Brothers became a household word in 1927 when they produced the first commercially successful "talking" picture—Al Jolson's* *The Jazz Singer.* By 1930, the Warner Brothers company was worth more than $250 million, an empire which included more than 500 theaters, a music publishing firm, a radio factory, and controlling interest in First National Pictures. Their early films included *Kismet* and *Little Caesar* (1930), *Five Star Final* (1931), and *I Am a Fugitive from a Chain Gang* (1932). Samuel Warner died on October 5, 1927, but his brothers kept the enterprise going. During World War II, they produced a number of famous war films, including *Destination Tokyo* (1943) and *Casablanca* (1942). After the war, Warner Brothers diversified into the record and music business, cable television, and electronic games. Harry Warner died on July 25, 1958, Albert on November 26, 1967, and Jack on September 2, 1978. (*New York Times,* July 26, 1958, December 2, 1967, and September 3, 1978; Ted Sennett, *Warner Brothers Presents,* 1971; Jack L. Warner, *Jack of All Trades,* 1975.)

WARNER, HARRY MORRIS. See WARNER BROTHERS

WARNER, JACK LEONARD. See WARNER BROTHERS

WARNER, SAMUEL LEWIS. See WARNER BROTHERS

WASHINGTON NAVAL CONFERENCE. In the years immediately following the close of World War I, world tensions again escalated, particularly in the Far East and Pacific. Two major factors accounted for the mounting tension: Japanese aggression against the Republic of China and the beginning of a dangerous naval arms race among the United States, Great Britain, and Japan. Against this backdrop of increasing tension and public concern over the arms race, President Warren G. Harding* invited the nations of the world to participate in a naval disarmament conference in Washington, D.C. Secretary of State Charles Evans Hughes* presided over the conference, which met between November 12, 1921, and February 6, 1922.

The three major participants—the United States, Great Britain, and Japan—each had its own reasons for participating. Britain had realized that, after World War I, the United States was poised to become the world's largest naval power, supplanting the British in that role. Great Britain knew she could not hope to compete against the vast resources and wealth of the United States. The United States entered the conference hoping to curb Japan's aggressive tendencies toward China. Japan was eager to slow the naval arms race, which was straining her economy.

At the conference, Hughes proposed a ten-year moratorium on the building of new capital ships (those over 10,000 tons displacement or armed with larger than eight-inch guns) and the scrapping of some existing ones. The United States agreed to scrap thirty ships; the British, nineteen; and the Japanese, seventeen. Hughes's proposal was accepted. The five leading naval powers also agreed to limit the tonnage of existing capital ships to a ratio of five for the United States and Great Britain, three for Japan, and 1.67 for France and Italy. They also agreed to a separate treaty among the five powers subjecting submarines to the usual international rules of naval warfare and outlawing the use of gas warfare; to the Four Power Treaty;* to the Nine Power Treaty;* and to guarantees of American cable rights on the island of Yap and reallocation of German cable rights in the Pacific, expanding Chinese control over its own customs offices; and to a Japanese agreement to restore Kiachow and the Shantung peninsula to China. The United States Senate ratified the treaties. (Thomas H. Buckley, *The United States and the Washington Conference, 1921–1922,* 1970.)

WASHINGTON RACE RIOT OF 1919. During World War I, employment opportunities in the nation's capital expanded rapidly; whites took the best of the civil service jobs and blacks assumed their former jobs in the private sector. Blacks in the city enjoyed economic growth in the city, but they still resented President Woodrow Wilson's* decision in 1913 to segregate blacks in the civil service. Fears of radicalism and the Red Scare* were also running rampant in Washington, D.C., in the summer of 1919. In mid-July, rumors of black rapes of white women began to circulate, as did press charges that the police were not investigating the crimes vigorously. On July 20, massive violence erupted when white servicemen began indiscriminately attacking black men and women. Federal troops were called in to stop the rioting, and after four days the tension began to ease. The Washington, D.C., race riot, however, was only a prelude to the more violent riot that occurred in Chicago a week later. (Lloyd M. Abernathy, ''The Washington Race War of July, 1919,'' *Maryland Historical Magazine* 58 [December 1963], 366–91; Arthur I. Waskow, *From Race Riot to Sit-In: 1919 and the 1960s,* 1966.)

WATER POWER ACT OF 1920. See FEDERAL POWER COMMISSION

WEBB-POMERENE ACT OF 1918. Passed on April 10, 1918, the Webb-Pomerene Act was designed to open international markets to American corporations after World War I. Specifically, the act waived antitrust regulations for American trade associations and corporations selling abroad by allowing them to integrate vertically and allocate markets regionally. On December 24, 1919, Congress passed supplementary legislation known as the Edge Act, which allowed banks to combine their capital to finance American business abroad. The Edge Act also permitted chartered corporations to make long-term loans to foreign governments and businesses. Although both the Webb-Pomerene Act and the Edge Act were designed to increase American exports, their effectiveness in the 1920s was abrogated by the protective tariff policies of the Harding,* Coolidge,* and Hoover* administrations, which strangled international trade and contributed to the onset of the Great Depression. (Carl P. Parrini, *Heir to Empire: United States Economic Diplomacy, 1916–1923,* 1969.)

WEIR, ERNEST TENER. Ernest Weir was born on August 1, 1875, in Pittsburgh, Pennsylvania. Weir's father died in 1890, and Ernest quit school and went to work as an office boy. In 1892 he went to work as an office boy for the Oliver Wire Company, and in 1901 he was named chief clerk of the Monongahela Tin Plate mills. Two years later, Weir became superintendent of the Monessen mills for United States Steel Company. In 1905 Weir bought an old tin plate company in Clarksburg, West Virginia, and by 1916 the Weirton Steel Company was well known in the industry. Weir concentrated on the production of light sheet metal steel, and when the automobile* industry boomed in the 1920s, creating enormous demand for such products, Weirton Steel had an advantage over older companies still tied to heavy products for railroads and bridges. In 1931 Weirton Steel merged with several other small companies to form the National Steel Company. Weir headed the new company.

During the Great Depression, Weir was noted for paying high wages to workers and bitterly opposing labor union activities. He became an implacable foe of Franklin D. Roosevelt* and the New Deal. In 1940 and 1941, Weir was active in the America First Committee to keep the United States out of World War II, and he served as chairman of the Republican National Committee. Ernest Weir died on June 26, 1957. (*New York Times*, June 27, 1957; Gertrude Schroeder, *The Growth of Major American Steel Companies*, 1953; Robert Sobel, *The Age of Giant Corporations*, 1972.)

WELFARE CAPITALISM. See OPEN SHOP MOVEMENT

WEST, ROY OWEN. Roy Owen West was born in Georgetown, Illinois, on October 27, 1868. He graduated from DePauw University in 1890 and that same year was admitted to the bar after studying law privately. West practiced law in Chicago and became active in the state Republican Party.* He served as assistant attorney of Cook County in 1893 and then two years as city attorney for Chicago between 1895 and 1897. Between 1904 and 1914, West was chairman of the Illinois Republican state central committee and was secretary of the Republican state central committee from 1924 to 1928. West was appointed secretary of the interior in 1928, where he served until Calvin Coolidge* left the White House in 1929. During the presidency of Herbert Hoover,* West served as national chairman of the Republican Party.* Roy Owen West died on November 29, 1958. (*New York Times*, November 30, 1958; *Who's Who in America, 1928–1929*, 1929.)

"WET." During the 1920s, when prohibition* was in effect, the term "wet" was used to describe individuals who opposed the Eighteenth Amendment* and who wanted to legalize the production and consumption of alcoholic beverages. The term "dry"* was used to describe people in favor of prohibition. (Norman H. Clark, *Deliver Us from Evil: An Interpretation of American Prohibition*, 1976.)

WHARTON, EDITH. Edith Wharton was born in New York City in 1862. From early in her life, she was influenced by the writing and philosophy of Henry James, whom she knew as a child and young adult. Wharton was a member and critic of New York high society until her divorce in 1907, when she moved to Paris. During her career, she wrote forty-seven books. Her first novel, *The House of Mirth* (1905), was the story of a young woman's attempt to make it into high society. During the 1920s, in the wake of World War I, Wharton felt a keen despair about the human potential, and those feelings came through in her novels: *The Age of Innocence* (1920), *A Son at the Front* (1923), and *The Children* (1928). Edith Wharton died on August 11, 1937. (Martin Seymour-Smith, *Who's Who in Twentieth Century Literature,* 1976; Edith Wharton, *A Backward Glance,* 1934.)

WHEELER, BURTON KENDALL. Born on February 27, 1882, in Hudson, Massachusetts, Burton K. Wheeler received a law degree from the University of Michigan in 1905 and was admitted to the Montana bar. In 1910 he was elected to the Montana legislature and served there until 1913, when President Woodrow Wilson* appointed him U.S. attorney for Montana. In 1918 Wheeler resigned to prepare a campaign for the governorship of Montana in 1920. He lost in the general election, but he was elected a United States senator from Montana in 1922 and served continuously until 1947. He was defeated for renomination in the primary of 1946.

During the 1920s, Wheeler emerged as a progressive Democrat, and in the election of 1924* he refused to support John W. Davis* as the party's presidential nominee. Davis was just too conservative for Wheeler. Instead, he accepted the vice-presidential nomination of the Progressive Party* and campaigned with presidential nominee Robert M. La Follette.* La Follette and Wheeler called for vigorous anti-trust action against industrial monopolies, public ownership of water power, gradual government takeover of the railroads, abolition of anti-labor injunctions, federal guarantees of collective bargaining, election of federal judges to ten-year terms, and armaments reductions. In the general election, they carried only 16 percent of the popular vote, and in 1925 Wheeler returned to the Democratic Party.*

During the early New Deal, Wheeler was a vigorous supporter of Franklin D. Roosevelt* and a strong advocate of free coinage of silver and inflation. Later in the 1930s, however, Wheeler turned against Roosevelt, especially over the court-packing scheme. After 1937 he voted against every major New Deal legislation. He opposed Roosevelt's bid for a third term in 1940, announced his own candidacy for the presidency, and tried to get the Democratic Party to pledge not to ''send our boys outside the United States unless the country was attacked.'' Wheeler bitterly opposed the Selective Service Act of 1940 and the Lend Lease bill, primarily because he saw both of them leading the country into war. After his defeat for the Senate in 1946, Wheeler operated a private law firm in Washington, D.C. He died there on January 7, 1975. (Kenneth C. MacKay, *The*

Progressive Movement of 1924, 1947; *New York Times,* January 8, 1975; James T. Patterson, *Congressional Convervatism and the New Deal,* 1967.)

WHITE, EDWARD DOUGLASS. Edward D. White was born on November 3, 1845, in Lafourche Parish, Louisiana. He read law privately in New Orleans, was admitted to the Louisiana bar in 1868, and established a highly lucrative practice there. White was active in Democratic politics, served in the state senate in 1874, and in 1878 was appointed to the Louisiana Supreme Court. In 1888, White was appointed to a vacant seat in the United States Senate, where he served until 1894. That year, President Grover Cleveland appointed him to the United States Supreme Court. In 1910, President William Howard Taft* appointed him chief justice. A judicial conservative, White served as chief justice until his death on May 19, 1921. (*New York Times,* May 22, 1921.)

WHITE, HENRY. Henry White was born on March 29, 1850, in Baltimore, Maryland, to a wealthy family. He studied under private tutors, usually in Europe, and, in 1883, he joined the Diplomatic Service, serving in Vienna and then in London. Until he was replaced for political reasons in 1893, White served as first secretary of the American delegation in London, and he returned to that post in 1897 when William McKinley and the Republicans came to power in Washington, D.C. During that tenure in London, White played critical roles in the Hay-Pauncefote Treaty, the Venezuelan controversy, the Alaskan boundary dispute, and the development of the Open Door notes. He served as ambassador to Italy between 1905 and 1907, and ambassador to France between 1907 and 1909. In 1919 President Woodrow Wilson* appointed White as the only Republican to the Paris Peace Conference* ending World War I, and White became a strong advocate of the League of Nations.* He continued to campaign for American participation in the League of Nations and in the World Court* until his death on July 15, 1927. (Allan Nevins, *Henry White: Thirty Years of American Diplomacy,* 1930; *New York Times,* July 16, 1927.)

WHITE, WILLIAM ALLEN. William Allen White was born in Emporia, Kansas, on February 10, 1868, and he kept Emporia his home during his illustrious career. He attended the University of Kansas to study journalism, and in 1895 he became the owner and editor of the *Emporia Daily and Weekly Gazette.* A gifted writer and syndicated columnist, White wrote a number of books, including *The Life of Woodrow Wilson* (1924), *The Old Order Changeth* (1910), *The Life of Calvin Coolidge* (1925), and *Masks in a Pageant* (1928). He was an observer at the Paris Peace Conference of 1919* and a committed internationalist, opposing the obstructionism of his own Republican Party* in foreign affairs. Politics was his specialty, and he wrote with a passion. A loyal and progressive Republican during the 1920s and 1930s, White found himself in a difficult position, pushing the Republican Party toward the left without losing their support. During the New Deal, he was particularly challenged because he agreed with so much of what Franklin D. Roosevelt* was doing. He wrote that unemployment insurance, work relief, progressive taxation, social security, and collective bargaining were a "attempt[s] to bring the American people up to the modern standards of English-speaking countries." White also firmly believed that the Republican Old Guard* would have to give way to new leadership if the party was going to survive.

White's personal relationship with Franklin D. Roosevelt was a cordial one, one in which the president accused him of being a good friend for "three-and-a-half years out of every four." In 1936 White endorsed Alf Landon for president and unsuccessfully tried an independent run for the Kansas governorship. By the late 1930s, he had grown suspicious of Roosevelt's court-packing scheme, but he was more concerned about the isolationist wing of his own party. He wrote *A Puritan in Babylon* in 1938, and in 1940 he chaired the Committee to Defend America by Aiding the Allies. William Allen White died on January 29, 1944. (David Hinshaw, *A Man from Kansas: The Story of William Allen White*, 1945; *New York Times*, January 30, 1944.)

WHITNEY, RICHARD. Richard Whitney was born in Beverly, Massachusetts, on August 1, 1888. He attended Groton and then graduated from Harvard in 1911. After leaving Harvard, Whitney worked for J. P. Morgan & Company and then entered the family securities business, eventually becoming president of Richard Whitney & Company, a major Wall Street investment firm. Shortly after the stock market crash of 1929,* he became head of the New York Stock Exchange and presided over it during the sensational Pecora investigations of the early 1930s. Despite all the revelations of stock fraud and manipulation of the public, Whitney remained a staunch defender of the securities industry in the United States and just as staunch an opponent of government regulation, including the Securities Act of 1933 and the Securities Exchange Act (SEC) of 1934. Whitney resigned as president of the New York Stock Exchange in 1935 and returned to private business. In 1938 his opposition to government regulation became more understandable after the SEC forced disclosure of his corporate condition, exposing embezzlement of funds from the New York Stock Exchange and the New York Yacht Club and forcing him into bankruptcy. Whitney spent more than three years in prison after he was convicted for fraud. He died on December 5, 1974. (*New York Times*, December 6, 1974; Michael Parrish, *Securities Regulation and the New Deal*, 1970.)

WICKERSHAM, GEORGE WOODWARD. George Wickersham was born in Pittsburgh, Pennsylvania, on September 19, 1858. He studied civil engineering at Lehigh University and then took a law degree at the University of Pennsylvania in 1880. Wickersham practiced law in Philadelphia and later in New York City. He served as attorney general in the cabinet of William Howard Taft* between 1909 and 1913, and then returned to his law practice. He supported Woodrow Wilson's* internationalism and advocated American entry into the League of

Nations.* Late in 1922, Wickersham helped found the League of Nations Non-Partisan Association, and he became president of the organization in 1928. In 1929 President Herbert Hoover* appointed Wickersham head of the National Commission on Law Observance and Enforcement to make a careful study of the problems created by prohibition.* Although Wickersham thought prohibition unenforceable, the commission's conclusions proposed stricter obedience to the law and larger appropriations to the Internal Revenue Service to enforce the law. George Wickersham died on January 25, 1936. (*Dictionary of American Biography,* Supp. 2 [1944], 713–15; *New York Times,* January 26, 1936; Henry F. Pringle, *The Life and Times of William H. Taft,* 1939.)

WICKHAM, CARL ERIC. Carl Wickham was born on August 7, 1887, in Sweden, and he immigrated to the United States in 1905. He worked at a number of jobs in Minnesota, and, beginning in 1914, he began to drive miners from Hibbing to nearby towns in an automobile taxi. With another Swedish immigrant friend, Andrew Anderson, Wickham began to make regularly scheduled runs. Demand for the service was so heavy that he formed the Mesaba Transportation Company and began to buy buses. By 1918 the company had eighteen buses and was covering routes throughout northern Minnesota. Wickham sold out of the business in 1925 and became president of the Northland Transportation Company, a bus subsidiary of the Great Northern Railroad. Wickham moved to Duluth, Minnesota, to run the new firm and began aggressively purchasing smaller bus lines. In 1926 Wickham established the Motor Transit Corporation as a holding company for several dozen bus lines, and in 1930 he changed the name of the company to the Greyhound Corporation. Under Wickham's direction, Greyhound came to dominate the industry. He resigned as president of the company in 1946, and he died on February 5, 1954. (Milton Moscowitz, *Everybody's Business,* 1980; *New York Times,* February 6, 1954.)

WIGGIN, ALBERT HENRY. Albert Henry Wiggin was born in Medfield, Massachusetts, on February 21, 1868. After graduating from high school in Boston in 1885, Wiggin found a job with the Commonwealth Bank of Boston. In 1891 he joined the federal government as a bank examiner, but he lost the job when Grover Cleveland and the Democrats came back into office after the election of 1892. He went to work for the Third National Bank of Boston, and in 1897 he became the vice-president of the Eliot National Bank. In 1899 Wiggin became vice-president of the National Park Bank in New York City. His banking career made its big jump in 1904 when he helped organize the Bankers Trust Company of New York, and in 1905 he became vice-president of the Chase National Bank. Wiggin became president of Chase in 1911 and chairman of the board in 1917. During his tenure at Chase National, the bank's assets increased from $250 million to $2.5 billion, primarily through judicious investments and equally judicious mergers.

A prominent Republican, Wiggin assumed a visible role in national finance after the the stock market crash of 1929.* Wiggin tried to put together a consortium of money to stop the liquidation of the stock markets, but he failed. He also played a prominent role in the formation of the National Credit Corporation* in 1931, a private association of bankers hoping to funnel money into troubled banks. It too failed. At that point, Wiggin's career dissolved. In 1932 Winthrop Aldrich, the new president of Chase National and the representative of the Rockefeller family, which now had controlling interest in Chase, forced Wiggin to resign because of speculative investments and the mixing of his personal funds with bank investments. In 1933, the revelations of the Senate's Pecora committee demonstrated that Wiggin had intentionally used affiliated companies to help Chase avoid federal stock market regulations, had used Chase money to finance his own economic ventures, and had sold short on his own stock during the 1929 securities panic. Wiggin unwittingly had become a symbol of the speculative mania and questionable ethics common on Wall Street in the 1920s. Albert Wiggin died on May 21, 1951. (John Kenneth Galbraith, *The Great Crash*, 1955; Matthew Josephson, *The Money Lords*, 1972; *New York Times*, May 22, 1951; Marjorie Wiggin, *New England Son*, 1949.)

WILBUR, RAY LYMAN. Ray Lyman Wilbur was born in Boonesboro, Iowa, on April 13, 1875. He graduated from Stanford University in 1896, where he became a close associate of future president Herbert Hoover.* Wilbur took a master's degree from Stanford in 1897 and then earned his medical degree from Cooper Medical College in 1899. Wilbur practiced medicine for a while, but his real interests were academic, and in 1911 he returned to Stanford as a dean. In 1916 Wilbur was named president of Stanford University, a position he held until 1943. In 1929 President Herbert Hoover named Wilbur the new secretary of the interior. During his four years in that post, Wilbur saw to it that no new leases on naval oil reserve land were issued, and he settled the dispute between Arizona and California over use of Colorado River water. He had Charles J. Rhoads, former head of the Indian Rights Association, appointed commissioner of Indian affairs, and he doubled federal spending in that area. Wilbur also initiated the philosophical change in federal Indian programs away from assimilation toward tribal independence and cultural pluralism. In 1943 Wilbur was elected "chancellor for life" by the trustees of Stanford University. He died on June 26, 1949. (David Burner, *Herbert Hoover: A Public Life*, 1979; *New York Times*, June 27, 1949; Edgar Eugene Robinson and Paul Carrol Edwards, eds., *Ray Lyman Wilbur*, 1960.)

WILLIAMS, HARRISON CHARLES. Harrison C. Williams was born on March 16, 1873, in Avon, Ohio. After high school, he worked as a bookkeeper until he moved to Pittsburgh in 1890, where he started several small businesses. Along with his brother-in-law, Williams began to invest in electric utilities, the most rapidly growing industry in the country, and in 1906 he helped form the

American Gas and Electric Company, a holding company for several other public utilities. In 1912 he created another utility holding company—the Central States Electric Corporation. By the 1920s, he had a utility empire which rivaled that of Samuel Insull.* Between 1921 and 1929, Williams built that empire through corporate pyramiding, until his personal holdings were valued at more than $600 million. The stock market crash of 1929,* although it did not completely wipe out Williams's holdings, was a real blow, reducing his assets to less than $10 million. Later in the 1930s, a Securities and Exchange Commission investigation charged Williams with building a holding company which by 1929 controlled 17 percent of the nation's $15 billion utility industry. The Public Utility Holding Company Act of 1935 forced Williams to reduce his holdings in each company he controlled, and in 1942 the Central States Electric Corporation declared bankruptcy. Harrison Williams died on November 10, 1953. (Matthew Josephson, *The Money Lords,* 1972; *New York Times,* November 11, 1953.)

WILSON, THOMAS WOODROW. Woodrow Wilson was born on December 28, 1856, in Staunton, Virginia. He graduated from Princeton in 1879; he received his law and master's degrees from the University of Virginia in 1881 and 1882, respectively; and he earned a Ph.D. in history and government at Johns Hopkins University in 1886. Wilson practiced law briefly in Atlanta in 1882 and 1883 before accepting an appointment as an associate professor at Bryn Mawr College in 1885. Wilson went to Wesleyan University in 1888 and then accepted a full professorship at Princeton in 1890. In 1902, Wilson became president of Princeton University. A progressive Democrat, he was elected governor of New Jersey in 1910, and in 1912, when the Republicans split into two parties, one supporting President William Howard Taft* and the other backing former president Theodore Roosevelt, Wilson was elected president of the United States. During his first term in office, Wilson supported the progressive measures which resulted in the reduced rates of the Underwood Tariff, the Federal Reserve Act of 1913, creation of the Federal Trade Commission, and the Clayton Act of 1914.

Wilson was a strong idealist committed to international peace based on democratic principles, and when he led the United States into World War I in 1917, he hoped to "make the world safe for democracy." When he went to Paris in 1919 to help negotiate the Treaty of Versailles,* Wilson was committed to his Fourteen Points,* a vision of the postwar world based on disarmament, freedom of the seas, free trade, national self-determination, and a League of Nations.* He chaired the commission at Paris which drafted the covenant of the League of Nations, the only one of his Fourteen Points that European leaders ever really supported.

But the great irony of his life was that the United States Senate never ratified the treaty. Although most Americans approved of the idea of the League of Nations, they feared it might be too powerful, that it might try to interfere with the country's immigration or tariff policies or limit United States control of the

Western Hemisphere. After the election of 1918,* Republicans controlled both the Senate and the House of Representatives, and Henry Cabot Lodge* of Massachusetts chaired the Senate Foreign Relations Committee. Lodge attached a number of reservations to the treaty designed to make sure that the League of Nations did not have the power to interfere with American foreign or domestic policy, and Wilson refused to accept the reservations. Wilson appealed to the American public to throw their support behind the Treaty of Versailles without reservations, and he travelled widely throughout the country campaigning for its ratification, suffering a debilitating stroke in the process. In the end, Wilson would not agree to the reservations, and Lodge and the Republicans would not agree to withdraw them; on March 19, 1920, the Senate failed by seven votes to approve the treaty. His health destroyed along with his vision of a world order, Wilson left the White House at the end of his term in 1921. He died on February 3, 1924. (Thomas A. Bailey, *Woodrow Wilson and the Lost Peace*, 1944; N. Gordon Levin, Jr., *Woodrow Wilson and World Politics: America's Response to War and Revolution*, 1968; Arthur S. Link, *Wilson the Diplomat*, 1957.)

WILSON, WILLIAM BAUCHOP. William B. Wilson was born in Blantyre, Scotland, on April 2, 1862. He immigrated to Arnot, Pennsylvania, in 1870, and he went to work in the coal mines. Wilson became active in labor union politics and played an important role in the organization of the United Mine Workers (UMW) in 1890. Between 1900 and 1908, he was the national secretary-treasurer of the UMW, and in 1906, he was elected as a Democrat to Congress. In 1913, Wilson left Congress to become secretary of labor in the cabinet of President Woodrow Wilson.* William B. Wilson died on May 25, 1934. (R. W. Babson, *William B. Wilson and the Department of Labor*, 1919; *New York Times*, May 26, 1934.)

WINSOR, ROBERT. Robert Winsor was born on May 28, 1858, in Salem, Massachusetts. He was educated at Phillips Exeter Academy, and he graduated from Harvard in 1880. Winsor immediately went to work for the Boston investment bank of Kidder, Peabody and Company. He became a partner in the firm in 1894. He saw to it that Kidder, Peabody expanded in public transportation, and he helped form the National Shawmut Bank of Boston, a consolidation of several commercial banks. In his role as a partner with Kidder, Peabody, Winsor helped form the Anaconda Copper Company and the United States Steel Company. In the process, Winsor became one of the most prominent investment bankers in the country. As head of Kidder, Peabody after 1919, Winsor was widely known as the "J. P. Morgan" of Boston. But the stock market crash of 1929* exposed serious weaknesses in the Kidder, Peabody financial position. When Winsor died on January 7, 1930, the firm was loaded with frozen, unmarketable assets. Even a $15 million loan from J. P. Morgan* could not save the company from reorganization, which took place in 1931. (Vincent P. Carosso,

More Than a Century of Investment Banking: The Kidder, Peabody Story, 1979; *New York Times,* January 8, 1930.)

WISE, STEPHEN SAMUEL. Stephen Wise was born on March 14, 1874, in Budapest, Hungary. He immigrated to the United States as a child, and in 1892, he graduated from Columbia University. He then studied for the rabbinate and served as an assistant rabbi before earning a Ph.D. from Columbia in 1902. Between 1906 and 1949, Wise was rabbi of the Free Synagogue of New York; between 1922 and 1948, he was president of the Jewish Institute of Religion. A leading exponent of Reform Judaism, Wise was a founder of the National Association for the Advancement of Colored People* in 1909 and of the American Civil Liberties Union* in 1920. A leading Zionist in the United States, Wise hoped to see the creation of a Jewish state in Palestine, and he was the leader of the American Jewish Congress from 1916 to 1949 and of the World Jewish Congress from 1936 to 1949. He campaigned actively for peace and internationalism in the 1920s and 1930s, but, late in the 1930s, he had to call for an end to Nazi aggression. When he died on April 19, 1949, Wise was a happy man, primarily because his dream of a Jewish state had been realized. (Melvin I. Urofsky, *A Voice that Spoke for Justice: The Life and Times of Stephen S. Wise,* 1981.)

WOLFE, THOMAS. Thomas Wolfe was born on October 3, 1900 in Asheville, North Carolina. In 1929, he wrote his first and best novel, *Look Homeward Angel,* an autobiographical account of his own life, with the fictional town of Altamount substituting for Asheville and the main character, Eugene Gant, a symbol of himself. In the second novel, *Of Time and the River* (1935), Wolfe followed Eugene Gant through college and his travels in Europe and New York. Wolfe's last two novels were published posthumously: *The Web and the Rock* (1939) and *You Can't Go Home Again* (1940). Wolfe's personal life was unhappy, and he was never able to emotionally overcome the estrangement of his parents. Both his father, a stonecutter, and his mother, a boarding house operator, lived in Asheville, but Wolfe lived with his authoritarian father. Thomas Wolfe fell ill with pneumonia in 1938 which led to tuberculosis of the brain and his death on September 15, 1938. (Richard S. Kennedy, *The Window of Memory: The Literary Career of Thomas Wolfe,* 1962.)

WOMEN'S JOINT CONGRESSIONAL COMMITTEE. See NATIONAL WOMAN'S PARTY

WOMEN'S ORGANIZATION FOR NATIONAL PROHIBITION RE-FORM. The Women's Organization for National Prohibition Reform was established in 1929 by prominent women Democrats, and was led by Pauline Morton Sabin. They demanded repeal of the Eighteenth Amendment* on the grounds that prohibition* was a violation of state rights, was unenforceable, and was a major source of corruption and organized crime. Its membership in 1932 totaled more than 1.5 million women, and they endorsed Franklin D. Roosevelt* for president. When the Twenty-First Amendment* went into effect, the organization disbanded. (David E. Kyvig, "Women against Prohibition," *American Quarterly* 28 [Fall 1976], 465–82.)

WOMEN'S RIGHTS. See NATIONAL WOMAN'S PARTY or NINE-TEENTH AMENDMENT

WOOD, LEONARD. Leonard Wood was born on October 9, 1860, in Winchester, New Hampshire. He graduated from the Harvard Medical School in 1884 and joined the United States Army. In 1897 Wood became the personal physician to President William McKinley, and he developed a close friendship with Theodore Roosevelt. Wood helped Roosevelt organize the "Rough Riders" during the Spanish-American War. Between 1899 and 1902, Wood served as military governor of Cuba, and in 1903 Roosevelt sent him to the Philippines to help suppress remaining vestiges of the Filipino rebellion. Wood rose to the rank of major general, and in 1910 President William Howard Taft* named him army chief of staff. He remained in that post until 1914. Wood was a Republican candidate for the party's presidential nomination in 1920, but he lost out to Warren G. Harding* of Ohio. After that, he did a tour in the Philippines as military governor, and he remained an enemy of Filipino nationalism. Leonard Wood died on August 7, 1927. (Herman Hagedorn, *Leonard Wood,* 1931; *New York Times,* August 8, 1927.)

WOOD, ROBERT ELKINGTON. Robert Wood was born on June 13, 1879, in Kansas City, Missouri. Wood graduated from the United States Military Academy at West Point in 1900 and then served with the army in the Panama Canal Zone between 1905 and 1915. He left the army in 1915 only to be recalled to service in 1917 to serve with the 42nd "Rainbow" Division in France. By 1918 he had earned the rank of brigadier general, and he was serving as quartermaster general of the U.S. Army. When he left the army in 1919, Wood became a manager with Montgomery Ward and Company. Immediately recognizing the change that the automobile* was bringing to American shopping patterns, Wood tried to convinced Montgomery Ward executives to follow the lead of J. C. Penney and Company in building retail chain stores in small towns to supplement the mail-order business. When they refused, he quit and joined Sears, Roebuck and Company in 1924. Julius Rosenwald* named him president of Sears in 1928. With farm income and mail-order volume way down, Wood gave Sears the same advice he had given Montgomery Ward: Aggressively move into chain store retailing, especially in large cities. The company followed his advice and by 1939 had built more than 500 such stores. Gross sales that year totaled more than $575 million. In 1931 Wood also got Sears into the insurance business by establishing the Allstate Insurance Company to handle automobile insurance. Under Wood's leadership, Sears became the largest retailing business in the world. During the 1930s, although he was a Republican, Wood supported Franklin D. Roosevelt* and much of the New Deal. He was a member of the America First Committee opposing American involvement in World War II, and, after the war, Wood was an active anti-Communist and financer of Senator Joseph McCarthy. Wood retired in 1954 and died on November 6, 1969. (Leon Harris, *Merchant Princes,* 1979; Tom Mahoney and Leonard Sloan, *The Great Merchants,* 1955; *New York Times,* November 7, 1969; Gordon L. Weil, *Sears, Roebuck, U.S.A.,* 1977.)

WOODRUFF, ROBERT WINSHIP. Robert Woodruff was born on December 6, 1889, in Columbus, Georgia. His father, Ernest, was a prominent Atlanta businessman who, along with several other investors, purchased the Coca-Cola Bottling Company in 1919. Robert Woodruff attended Emory University between 1908 and 1910 but then began a career as a salesman for a variety of firms. In 1919 he was named vice-president and in 1923 general manager of the White Motor Company in Cleveland. When Coca-Cola sales dropped between 1920 and 1923, the board of directors invited Woodruff to assume the presidency of the company. Almost immediately, he shelved all plans to acquire competing bottling companies and soft drink establishments; instead he focused on a brilliant sales campaign to market Coca-Cola. Using the phrase "The pause that refreshes," the company made Coca-Cola as American as baseball, hot dogs, and apple pie. Profits soared from $4.5 million in 1923 to $13 million in 1930, and Coca-Cola became the most widely recognized consumer product in the country. When he resigned as president in 1939, profits had climbed to over $38 million, in spite of the Great Depression. After World War II, as chairman of the board, Woodruff led Coca-Cola into the international market, making it a global consumer product, with 1987 sales totaling more than $4.8 billion. Woodruff retired as chairman of the board in 1955. Woodruff died on March 7, 1985. (E. J. Kahn, *The Big Drink,* 1959; *New York Times,* March 8, 1985.)

WORLD COURT. When the United States refused to ratify the Treaty of Versailles* in 1919, all realistic hopes of American participation in the League of Nations* died. Throughout the 1920s, however, internationalists hoped to secure American participation in the Permanent Court of International Justice, or World Court. Secretary of State Charles Evans Hughes* favored the idea, although he had to be quite politic about it for fear of raising the wrath of Republican isolationists in the Senate. In 1923 President Warren G. Harding* came out in favor of joining the World Court, arguing that the World Court and the League of Nations were separate entities. He backtracked from that position when Senators Henry Cabot Lodge* and William E. Borah* raised serious objections. After Harding's death, Calvin Coolidge* endorsed the idea, but not with much enthusiasm because of the upcoming elections of 1924. The Harding scandals were bad enough; Coolidge did not want to give the Democrats another issue.

In 1926 the Senate voted to join the World Court, but only with major reservations giving the United States complete independence from all court decisions and an effective veto on court proposals. One reservation even gave the United States the right to veto court examination of any issue at all, including those to which the United States was not a party. The World Court and the League of Nations refused to sanction the reservations, and the United States did not join. President Herbert Hoover* proposed American entry into the World Court in his inaugural address in 1929, but, once again, when the issue reached the Senate floor, Borah held it up. Franklin D. Roosevelt* also urged ratification of a treaty providing for United States participation in the World Court, but in 1935 the Senate, this time led by Senator Huey Long of Louisiana, rejected membership by a vote of fifty-two to thirty-five. (L. Ethan Ellis, *Republican Foreign Policy, 1921–1933,* 1968.)

WORLD DISARMAMENT CONFERENCE. When the World Disarmament Conference opened on February 2, 1932, representatives from fifty-nine countries gathered to try to reach an agreement to reduce land armaments. The American delegation consisted of Norman H. Davis,* Hugh S. Gibson,* Senator Claude Swanson of Virginia, Hugh Wilson, and Mary E. Wooley. The conference was complicated by the Franco-German rivalry and the Japanese invasion of Manchuria in 1931, and in 1933 the conference was shattered when Adolf Hitler announced that Germany would rearm in defiance of the Treaty of Versailles.* The World Disarmament Conference continued to hold sessions into 1934, but it ended without achieving any tangible results. (L. Ethan Ellis, *Republican Foreign Policy, 1921–1933,* 1968; Robert H. Ferrell, *American Diplomacy in the Great Depression,* 1967.)

WRIGLEY, WILLIAM, JR. William Wrigley, Jr., was born on September 30, 1861, in Philadelphia, Pennsylvania. Even though his father owned a relatively prosperous soap manufacturing company, Wrigley ran away from home at the age of ten to work for a soap factory; at the age of thirteen, he was travelling by train across the country selling soap. In 1891, with a $5,000 loan from his grandfather, Wrigley started his own soap company in Chicago and soon added the production of chewing gum. By the mid-1890s, the soap was dropped, and he concentrated on selling chewing gum. In 1899 Wrigley added ''Spearmint'' gum to the line and advertised it widely, making it, by 1910, the biggest selling gum in the United States. By the 1920s, the William Wrigley Jr., Company was selling gum in European, Asian, and Latin American markets as well. By 1932 sales had exceeded $75 million annually. William Wrigley was an avid baseball* fan and a loyal fan of the Chicago Cubs. Between 1916 and 1921, he purchased controlling interest in the franchise, and attended games regularly until his death on January 26, 1932. (Paul M. Angle, *Philip K. Wrigley*, 1975; *New York Times,* January 27, 1932.)

Y

YOUNG, OWEN D. Owen D. Young was born on October 27, 1874, in Van Hornesville, New York. He graduated from St. Lawrence University in 1894, and then he earned a law degree at Boston University in 1896. He practiced law privately in Boston, specializing in public utility negotiations. In 1912 he went to work for General Electric and became general counsel in 1913. In 1919, working closely with acting Secretary of the Navy Franklin D. Roosevelt,* Young established the Radio Corporation of America (RCA) to take control of all radio patents owned by General Electric (GE), American Telephone and Telegraph, General Motors, United Fruit Company, and Westinghouse. In 1922 Young became chairman of the board of General Electric, while holding the same post with RCA. He retired from RCA in 1929 and from GE in 1939.

During the 1920s, Owen Young was also active in public affairs. An active Democrat, Young nevertheless served on President Warren G. Harding's* Conference on Unemployment as well as on the international committee to evaluate German reparations.* The Dawes Plan* emerged from those conferences in 1924, and in 1928 Young developed his own program for reduction of German reparations, which the allied powers accepted. The Young Plan* remained in effect until the Hoover moratorium* in 1931 and the Lausanne Conference of 1932.* Owen D. Young died on July 11, 1962. (Erik Barnouw, *A History of Broadcasting in the United States,* vol. 1, *A Tower in Babel: To 1933,* 1966; *New York Times,* July 12, 1962; Ida M. Tarbell, *Owen D. Young,* 1932.)

YOUNG PLAN. During the first five years of the Dawes Plan,* Germany managed to meet her reparations* payments, but her success rested on her ability to borrow money from the United States. By July 1, 1931, the United States had also collected a total of $2.6 billion in war debts* from the allied nations. It became obvious to even the most casual observers that a capital flow triangle existed: American loans to Germany allowed the Germans to make their reparations payments to the allied nations of Europe, which, in turn, allowed them to make their debt payments to the United States. Unless the United States was willing to continue exporting sufficient capital to Germany, the loan-reparations-debt triangle would collapse.

In February 1929, the Committee on German Reparations met in Paris to re-evaluate the five-year-old Dawes Plan. Owen D. Young,* an original member of the Dawes Commission, was a member of the committee, and was elected chairman of the committee. The proposals of the committee, which became known as the Young Plan, were to reduce the outstanding reparations debt to just over $8 billion and to allow Germany to repay the note over a fifty-eight-year period at a 5.5 percent annual interest rate. A clause in the agreement also provided for further reductions in the German debt if the United States would agree to reduce the allied war debts. Although the German debt reduction provision of the Young Plan went into effect, the onset of the Great Depression soon destroyed it. At the Lausanne Conference of 1932,* more than 90 percent of the remaining German reparations were cancelled. (Derek Aldcroft, *From Versailles to Wall Street*, 1977; Charles P. Kindleberger, *The World in Depression, 1929–1939*, 1973; Broadus Mitchell, *Depression Decade: From New Era through the New Deal, 1929–1941*, 1947.)

Z

ZEMURRAY, SAMUEL. Samuel Zemurray was born in Bessarabia, Russia, on January 18, 1877. His family immigrated to the United States in 1892 and settled in Alabama. Zemurray worked as a peddlar for several years, and in 1899 he moved to Mobile, Alabama, and went into the fruit business, primarily buying and distributing bananas to small stores. Soon the United Fruit Company in New Orleans gave him a contract to sell their ripening bananas to small dealers and peddlars. In 1900 Zemurray joined with Ashbell Hubbard and began to make bulk purchases of bananas from plantations in Honduras and to sell them in the United States. In 1910, Zemurray and Hubbard bought 5,000 acres of plantation land in Honduras and formed the Cuyamel Fruit Company. The company expanded rapidly as Zemurray bought more and more land and built railroad lines between his plantations to ship the bananas to market. He bought a steamship company in 1922 to bring the bananas in from Honduras and Nicaragua. Throughout the 1920s, the Cuyamel Fruit Company prospered. In 1930 Zemurray sold the Cuyamel Fruit Company to the United Fruit Company and became United's largest stockholder. With his profit of $30 million, Zemurray retired. When United's stock continued to fall after the stock market crash of 1929,* Zemurray gathered up proxies and took control of United, becoming its president in 1938. Under Zemurray's leadership, United Fruit again prospered, expanding beyond bananas to sugar, cocao, and tropical fruit products, and becoming a political and economic force in Central America. Zemurray frequently intervened in local politics in order to protect United Fruit's interests from revolutionary takeovers. He stepped down as president of United Fruit in 1951. Samuel Zemurray died on November 30, 1961. (Stacy May and Galo Plaza, *The United Fruit Company in Latin America,* 1958; *New York Times,* December 1, 1961; Stephen Whitfield, "Strange Fruit: The Career of Samuel Zemurray," *American Jewish History* 73 [March 1984] 79–94.)

ZIEGFELD, FLORENZ. Florenz Ziegfeld was born on March 21, 1869, in Chicago, Illinois. He entered the theatrical business in 1892 when he brought several European military bands to the United States to perform at the Chicago

World's Fair. Ziegfeld profited from the venture and went into theatrical productions. He became a household word after 1907 when he produced the famous "Ziegfeld Follies," grand musical productions which packed Broadway theaters. Ziegfeld was also the producer of such popular Broadway plays as *Papa's Wife, The French Maid, The Little Duchess, The Parisian Model, Miss Innocence, The Pink Lady, Sally,* and *Kid Boots.* Ziegfeld was famous for his "Ziegfeld Girls," beautiful young women who adorned his elaborate stage productions. He died on July 22, 1932. (Robert H. Badrig, *Florenz Ziegfeld: Twentieth Century Showman,* 1972.)

ZIEGFELD FOLLIES. See ZIEGFELD, FLORENZ

"ZIEGFELD FOLLIES OF THE AIR." On April 3, 1932, Florenz Ziegfeld brought his "Ziegfield Follies of the Air" to CBS radio.* Built around such Ziegfeld stars as Will Rogers,* Fanny Brice,* Billie Burke, and Jack Pearl, the format was a weekly sixty-minute program of musical comedy. The show folded late in the summer of 1932, only to be revived in 1936. (Jack Dunning, *Tune in Yesterday: The Ultimate Encyclopedia of Old-Time Radio, 1925–1976,* 1976.)

ZUKOR, ADOLPH. Adolph Zukor was born on January 7, 1873, in Ricse, Hungary. He immigrated to the United States in 1888, where he worked at odd jobs during the day and attended English-language classes and business school at night. By 1892 he had started his own business after inventing a fur clasp. After seeing a short film in a New York arcade in 1903, Zukor became convinced that movies had unlimited commercial potential, and that year, along with Marcus Loew,* he established the Automatic Vaudeville Company and a chain of penny arcades, known as Loew's Enterprises, across the country. Zukor also owned several theaters on his own. To bring the middle classes to the theaters, Zukor began to produce feature films in 1912, and he signed such future stars as Mary Pickford,* Douglas Fairbanks,* and Minnie Maddine Fisk to contracts. Along with the films, Zukor upgraded the theaters to the high-class, ornate palaces which became prominent in the 1920s. In 1916, Zukor took over Paramount Pictures Corporation, a movie distributing firm which also financed new productions. By 1919, Paramount Pictures had purchased 600 theaters across the country to show its films. Zukor added another 300 theaters during the 1920s. In 1921 he was one of the founders of the Motion Picture Producers and Distributors of America, an industry trade association. In 1926, Zukor built the Paramount Theater on Times Square in New York as its showcase theater. Although Paramount underwent bankruptcy and reorganization during the 1930s, Zukor remained president. In 1949 he was named chairman of the board. Adolph Zukor died on June 10, 1976. (*New York Times,* June 11, 1976; Robert Sklar, *Movie-Made America,* 1975; Adolph Zukor, *The Public Is Never Wrong,* 1953.)

CHRONOLOGY

1919

January

18 Paris Peace Conference ending World War I began.

25 Work began on the draft of the Covenant of the League of Nations

February

 6 Seattle general strike began.

14 Draft of the Covenant of the League of Nations was completed at the Paris Peace Conference.

March

 3 Supreme Court decided the *Schenck* v. *United States* case.

May

 7 Treaty of Versailles was presented to Germans.

June

28 Germany signed the Treaty of Versailles.

July

 8 President Woodrow Wilson returned to the United States.

10 Treaty of Versailles was presented to the Senate.

August

19 Wilson agreed with Senate to accept minor reservations not requiring consent of the other parties to the Treaty of Versailles.

September

 4 Wilson started a 9,500–mile tour of the western states to promote the idea of Senate ratification of the Treaty of Versailles.

 9 Boston police strike began.

10 Senators Hiram Johnson and William Borah began their own speaking tour opposing American entry into the League of Nations.

October

2   President Wilson suffered a stroke.

6   First Industrial Conference convened.

27 President Wilson vetoed the Volstead Act.

28 Congress overrode President Wilson's veto of the Volstead Act.

November

1   Coal strike began.

6   Senator Henry Cabot Lodge claimed that ratification of the Treaty of Versailles with fourteen reservations did not weaken the League of Nations.

18 Woodrow Wilson claimed that the Lodge resolutions nullified the treaty.

19 Wilson Democrats and irreconcilable Republicans defeated the Lodge resolutions on the Treaty of Versailles.

December

1   Second Industrial Conference convened.

10 Coal strike ended.

22 U.S. transport *Buford,* also known as the "Soviet Ark," left the United States, deporting 249 political radicals.

24 President Woodrow Wilson announced that the federal government would return the railroads to private control on March 1, 1920.

1920

January

2   Under the influence of the Red Scare, the Department of Justice conducted mass arrests of suspected Communists and Socialists, taking 2,700 people into custody.

8   In a speech at the Jackson Day Dinner, President Wilson insisted that the Treaty of Versailles must not be rewritten by the Senate.

10 League of Nations formally began operations.

16 Volstead Act enforcing prohibition went into effect.

February

9   Senate referred the Treaty of Versailles back to the foreign relations committee, which reported it the following day with reservations intact.

13 Secretary of State Robert Lansing resigned.

25 Mineral Leasing Act became law.

28 Transportation Act became law.

March

8   Wilson restated his opposition to the Lodge reservations to the Treaty of Versailles.

19 The Senate defeated the Lodge reservations to the Treaty of Versailles by a vote of forty-nine to thirty-five.

April

1   United States troops were withdrawn from Siberia.

May

5   Socialist Labor Party nominated W. W. Cox for president and August Gilhaus for vice-president.

8   Socialist Party of America nominated Eugene V. Debs for president.

20 By joint resolution, Congress declared an end to the war with Germany. President Woodrow Wilson vetoed the resolution.

June

5   Merchant Marine Act became law.

8   Republican Party began its presidential nominating convention in Chicago. Warren Harding received the presidential nomination on the tenth ballot. Calvin Coolidge was nominated for vice-president.

10 Water Power Act became law.

28 Democratic Convention met in San Francisco. James Cox was nominated for president on the forty-fourth ballot. Franklin D. Roosevelt was nominated for vice-president.

July

2   By a joint resolution, Congress terminated war with Germany and Austria-Hungary, reserving for the United States any rights secured by the armistice, the Versailles Treaty, or as a result of the war.

11 Farmer-Labor Party nominated Parley Christiansen for president and Max S. Hayes for vice-president.

12 Single Tax Party nominated Robert Macauley for president and Richard Barnum for vice-president.

21 Prohibition Party nominated A. S. Watkins for president.

August

26 Nineteenth Amendment to the Constitution was ratified.

September

5   Alvarao Obregon was elected president of Mexico.

22 Steel strike began.

October

18 Treaties concluding peace with Germany, Austria, and Hungary were ratified.

November

2   Warren G. Harding defeated James Cox in the presidential election.

December

14 Senator William Borah called on President-elect Warren G. Harding to convene an international conference for reduction of naval weapons.

1921

January

3   Supreme Court decided the *Duplex Printing Press Company* v. *Deering* case.

April

20 United States and Colombia reached agreement regarding the Panama dispute of 1903 when the United States fomented revolution in Panama against Colombia. Senate recommended ratifiction of a treaty paying Colombia $25 million.

27 Allied Reparations Commission fixed German reparations at 132 billion gold marks.

May

2 Supreme Court decided the *Newberry* v. *United States* case.

19 Emergency Quota Act became law.

27 Emergency Tariff Act became law.

June

10 Budget and Accounting Act became law.

21 Charles G. Dawes became the first director of the budget.

August

9 Packers and Stockyards Act became law.

24 Capper-Tincher Act became law.

25 Treaty of Berlin was signed.

September

21 Unemployment Conference began.

November

12 Washington Naval Conference convened.

23 Sheppard-Towner Act became law.

Revenue Act of 1921 became law.

December

13 Four-Power Treaty among United States, Britain, France, and Japan, agreeing to respect mutual rights in the Pacific, signed.

1922

February

6 Five-Power Treaty signed.

Nine-Power Treaty signed.

Naval Arms Reduction Treaty signed.

Washington Naval Conference ended.

9 World War Foreign Debt Commission established.

April

7 Secretary of the Interior Albert Fall secretly leased Teapot Dome naval oil reserves to Harry F. Sinclair.

25 Secretary of the Interior Albert Fall secretly leased Elk Hills naval oil reserves to Edward L. Doheny.

May

15   Supreme Court decided the *Bailey* v. *Drexel Furniture Company* case.

31   Allied Reparations Commission granted Germany a moratorium for the remainder of the year.

June

30   Agreement on evacuation procedure in Dominican Republic was worked out by the State Department with a group of Dominican political leaders.

Secretary of the Interior Albert Fall was indicted for bribery and conspiracy.

August

1   Great Britain promised not to ask more from her debtors than was necessary to pay her creditors, primarily the United States.

September

1   Attorney General Harry Daugherty secured a federal court injunction outlawing the railroad strike.

19   President Warren G. Harding veoted the veterans' bonus bill.

21   A second Grain Futures Act became law.

Fordney-McCumber Tariff became law.

22   Cable Act became law granting married women United States citizenship regardless of their husbands' legal status.

December

4   Second Central American Conference convened in Washington, D.C., to settle issues between Nicaragua and Honduras.

26   Germany was declared in default on reparations payments.

1923

January

9   Germany again declared in default on reparations payments.

February

7   Second Central American Conference concluded its meeting.

27   Secretary of State Charles Evans Hughes wrote President Warren Harding advocating U.S. membership in the World Court without any involvement in the League of Nations.

March

4   Federal Intermediate Credit Act became law.

25   Fifth International Conference (Santiago Conference) convened in Santiago, Chile.

April

9   Supreme Court decided the *Adkins* v. *Children's Hospital* case.

August

2   President Warren G. Harding died in San Francisco, California.

3   Calvin Coolidge became president of the United States.

31 Treaty of Bucareli was signed.

December

15 President Coolidge announced that Charles G. Dawes, Henry M. Robinson, and Owen D. Young would serve as experts on a commission to investigate German finances.

1924

January

16 McNary-Haugen Bill was introduced in both houses of Congress.

April

9   Dawes Plan was proposed.

16 Dawes Plan was accepted by Germany and adopted at a London Conference (16 July–16 August).

23 Adjusted Compensation Act approved by the Senate.

May

11 Socialist Labor Party nominated Frank R. Johns for president and Verne L. Reynolds for vice-president.

15 President Coolidge vetoed the Adjusted Compensation Act.

19 Congress overrode the veto, and the Adjusted Compensation Act became law.

24 Rogers Act became law.

26 National Origins Act became law.

June

2   Revenue Act of 1924 became law. Snyder Act (Indian Citizenship) became law.

3   American Party nominated Gilbert Nations for president and Charles Randall for vice-president.

5   Prohibition Party nominated Herman Faris for president and Marie Brehm for vice-president.

10 Republican Party nominated Calvin Coolidge for president and Charles G. Dawes for vice-president.

12 Secretary of State Frank Kellogg warned Mexico that the United States would continue its support only as long as Mexico protected American lives and American property rights.

July

4   Conference for Progressive Political Action launched the Progressive Party and nominated Robert M. La Follette for president and Burton K. Wheeler for vice-president.

9   Democratic Party nominated John W. Davis for president and Charles W. Bryan for vice-president.

11   Communist Party nominated William Z. Foster for president and Benjamin Gitlow for vice-president.

August

24   Agricultural Credits Act became law.

September

1   Dawes Plan went into effect.

November

4   Calvin Coolidge defeated John W. Davis for president.

1925

January

7–14   Interallied Financial Conference at Paris decided that the United States should receive 2.254 percent of annual German reparations to satisfy American claims arising from the cost of World War I.

30   Floyd Collins entered the Sand Cave in Barren County, Kentucky.

February

4   Charles Forbes, former head of the Veterans' Bureau, was indicted for fraud, conspiracy, and bribery.

27   New treaty between United States and Dominican Republic provided for a permanent evacuation of American troops.

March

3   House supported resolution of adherence by a vote of 303 to 28 for U.S. membership in the World Court.

June

8   Supreme Court decided the *Gitlow* v. *New York* case.

18   Robert M. La Follette died.

July

10   ''Monkey Trial'' began in Dayton, Tennessee.

21   ''Monkey Trial'' ended in Dayton, Tennessee.

26   William Jennings Bryan died in Dayton, Tennessee.

October

25   The government of Emiliano Chamorro in Nicaragua assumed power.

December

1   Locarno Treaty was signed.

1926

January

14   Emiliano Chamorro became president of Nicaragua.

27   Senate approved U.S. membership in the World Court by a vote of seventy-six to seventeen if certain reservations were provided.

February

26   Revenue Act of 1926 became law.

May

 9   Richard Byrd flew over the North Pole.

20   Railway Labor Act became law.

September

18   Hurricane struck South Florida, ending the great real estate boom.

November

 2   Congressional elections held.

1927

January

27   U.S. Senate resolution unanimously recommended arbitration of the dispute with
     Mexico.

February

10   President Coolidge called for an international conference at Geneva to consider
     limits on the construction of cruisers, destroyers, and submarines, not curbed at
     the Washington Naval Conference.

11   McNary-Haugen Bill was passed by the Senate.

17   McNary-Haugen Bill was passed by the House.

25   President Coolidge vetoed the McNary-Haugen Bill.

March

 7   Supreme Court decided the *Nixon* v. *Herndon* case.

April

 6   French foreign minister Aristide Briand proposed an international agreement to
     outlaw war.

25   President Nicholas Murray Butler of Columbia University made a formal ac-
     knowledgment of Briand's proposal.

May

 4   President Coolidge sent Henry L. Stimson to Nicaragua to resolve the factional
     dispute between General Augustino Sandino and Adolfo Diaz.

21   Charles Lindbergh arrived in Paris.

June

20   Aristide Briand submitted a draft treaty outlawing war to the United States.

August

 2   President Calvin Coolidge announced he would not seek re-election.

23   Nicola Sacco and Bartolomeo Vanzetti were executed.

December

28   Secretary of State Frank B. Kellogg substituted a multinational for a bilateral
     agreement in a note.

1928

January

11 Kellogg published a draft treaty.

16 President Coolidge opened the Havana Conference.

April

13 Kellogg's draft treaty was brought to the attention of other powers.
    Socialist Party of America nominated Norman Thomas for president and James Maurer for vice-president.

May

15 Flood Control Act became law.

21 Boulder Canyon Project Act became law.

22 Merchant Marine Act became law.

25 Congress passed the Muscle Shoals Bill, but President Calvin Coolidge vetoed it.

27 Communist Party nominated William Z. Foster for president and Benjamin Gitlow for vice-president.

29 Revenue Act of 1928 became law.

June

12 Republican Party nominated Herbert Hoover for president and Charles Curtis for vice-president.

26 Democratic Party nominated Al Smith for president and Joseph T. Robinson for vice-president.

August

27 Fourteen nations signed the Kellogg-Briand Pact.

November

 6 Herbert Hoover defeated Al Smith for president.

19 Through January 6, 1929, Hoover embarked on a goodwill tour of eleven Latin American contries.

December

17 Clark Memorandum to the Monroe Doctrine released.

1929

January

19 Owen D. Young and J. P. Morgan named as American experts on a Committee on German Reparations.

February

11 Committee on German Reparations met in Paris to revise the Dawes Plan; Owen D. Young was designated as chairman of the committee.

March

 4 Hoover urged membership in the World Court in his inaugural address.

June

15   Agricultural Marketing Act became law.

July

21   In ratifying the debt settlement agreement with the United States, France said that war debts payments to the United States should be covered by German reparations payments.

October

 7   Great Britain issued a formal invitation to the other four major naval powers to the London Naval Conference.

24   Stock market crash began in the United States.

1930

January

21   London Naval Conference convened.

April

22   London Naval Conference concluded.

June

17   Hawley-Smoot Tariff became law.

July

21   President Hoover called a special session of Congress to secure favorable action by the Senate on the London Naval Conference. Senate ratified the London Naval Treaty.

November

 4   Congressional elections held.

1931

January

19   Wickersham Report was released.

February

23   Moses-Linthicum Act became law.

26   President Herbert Hoover vetoed congressional bill providing for early payment on veterans' bonuses under the Adjusted Compensation Act.

March

 3   Congress passed the Muscle Shoals Bill, but President Herbert Hoover vetoed it.

May

11   Austrian Credit-Anstalt failed.

June

16   Bank of England advanced 150,000,000 shillings to the Austrian National Bank.

20   President Hoover proposed a one-year moratorium on both interallied debts and reparations.

July

6   Hoover's moratorium was accepted, delayed by French opposition which contributed to the closing of all German banks by mid-July.

September

18   Japan invaded Manchuria.

21   Great Britain abandoned the gold standard.

October

16   League of Nations attempted to end hostilities in the Far East by formally inviting the United States to appoint a representative to sit with the Council in considering the Manchurian crisis.

23–25 French Premier Pierre Laval met at the White House with President Hoover to present the French position on the European debt/reparations crisis.

December

10   League of Nations appointed the Lytton Commission to investigate the Manchurian crisis.

1932

January

4   Military control of South Manchuria was completed.

7   Stimson Doctrine was released by the United States.

29   Naval and military intervention by the Japanese took place at Shanghai.

February

2   General disarmament conference assembled at Geneva with U.S. participation.

    Reconstruction Finance Corporation Act became law.

27   Glass-Steagall Act became law.

March

3   Chinese forces were expelled at Shanghai.

11   League of Nations Assembly unanimously adopted a resolution incorporating the Stimson Doctrine.

23   Norris–La Guardia Labor Relations Act became law.

April

30   Socialist Labor Party nominated Verne Reynolds for president and J.W. Aiken for vice-president.

May

2   Supreme Court decided the *Nixon* v. *Condon* case.

21   Socialist Party nominated Norman Thomas for president and James H. Maurer for vice-president.

28   Communist Party nominated William Z. Foster for president and James W. Ford for vice-president.

31   Japan withdrew from Shanghai.

June

  6 Revenue Act of 1932 became law.

 16 Lausanne Conference canceled over 90 percent of German reparations required under the Young Plan.

July

  5 Prohibition Party nominated William Upshaw for president and Frank Regan for vice-president.

  9 Farmer-Labor Party nominated Jacob S. Coxey for president.

 21 Emergency Relief and Construction Act became law.

 22 Federal Home Loan Bank Act became law.

 28 Bonus Army demonstrations in Washington, D.C., were dispersed by federal troops.

August

 17 Liberty Party nominated W. H. Harvey for president and Frank Hemenway for vice-president.

September

 15 Japan formally recognized the new puppet state of Manchukuo.

October

  4 Lytton Report condemned Japan but proposed a settlement recognizing Japan's special interest in Manchuria, which was to become an automonous state under Chinese sovereignty but Japanese control.

November

  8 Franklin D. Roosevelt defeated Herbert Hoover for president.

December

 15 Six allied nations, including Belgium and France, defaulted on their World War I debts to the United States.

1933

January

  5 Calvin Coolidge died.

 13 Hawes-Cutting Act became law.

February

  3 Twentieth Amendment to the Constitution was ratified.

 24 Lytton Report was adopted by the League of Nations.

March

  4 Franklin D. Roosevelt inaugurated president of the United States.

SELECTED
BIBLIOGRAPHY

AGRICULTURE

Anderson, Clifford B. "Agrarian Attitudes toward the City, Business, and Labor in the 1920s and 1930s." *Mississippi Quarterly,* 14 (Fall 1961).
———. "The Metamorphosis of American Agrarian Idealism in the 1920s and 1930s." *Agricultural History,* 35 (October 1961).
Best, Gary Dean. "Food Relief as Price Support: Hoover and American Pork, January–March 1919." *Agricultural History,* 44 (October 1970).
Case, H.C.M. "Farm Debt Adjustment during the Early 1930s." *Agricultural History,* 34 (October 1960).
Chambers, Clarke A. "The Cooperative League of the United States of America, 1916–1961: A Study of Social Theory and Social Action." *Agricultural History,* 36 (April 1962).
Danbom, David B. *The Resisted Revolution: Urban America and the Industrialization of Agriculture, 1900–1930.* 1979.
Daniel, Pete. *Deep'n As It Come: The 1927 Mississippi River Flood.* 1977.
Dyson, Lowell K. "Radical Farm Organizations and Periodicals in America, 1920–1960." *Agricultural History,* 45 (April 1971).
Erwin, Carl C. "The Dark Tobacco Growers Association, 1922–1926." *Business History Review,* 40 (Winter 1966).
Fausold, Martin L. "President Hoover's Farm Policies 1929–1933." *Agricultural History,* 51 (April 1977).
Fite, Gilbert C. *Farm to Factory: A History of the Consumers Cooperative Association.* 1965.
Fuller, Wayne E. *RFD: The Changing Face of Rural America.* 1964.
Grant, Philip A., Jr. " 'Save the Farmer': Oklahoma Congressmen and Farm Relief Legislation, 1924–1928." *Chronicles of Oklahoma,* 64 (Spring 1986).
———. "Southern Congressmen and Agriculture, 1921–1932." *Agricultural History,* 53 (January 1979).
Guth, James L. "Farmer Monopolies, Cooperatives, and the Intent of Congress: Origins of the Capper-Volstead Act." *Agricultural History,* 56 (January 1982).
Guttenberg, Albert Z. "The Land Utilization Movement of the 1920s." *Agricultural History,* 50 (July 1976).
Higgs, Robert. "The Boll Weevil, the Cotton Economy, and Black Migration, 1910–1930." *Agricultural History,* 50 (April 1976).
Koerselman, Gary H. "Secretary Hoover and National Farm Policy: Problems of Leadership." *Agricultural History,* 51 (April 1977).
Leflar, Robert A. "The Bankers' Agricultural Revolt of 1919." *Arkansas Historical Quarterly,* 58 (Winter 1968).
Lowitt, Richard. "Progressive Farm Leaders and Hoover's Moratorium." *Mid-America,* 50 (July 1968).
Martinson, Henry R. "The New Day in North Dakota: The Nonpartisan League and the Politics of Negative Revolution." *North Dakota History,* 40 (Spring 1973).
Robson, George L., Jr. "The Farmers' Union in Mississippi." *Journal of Mississippi History,* 27 (November 1965).
Rowley, William D. *M. L. Wilson and the Campaign for the Domestic Allotment.* 1970.

Saloutos, Theodore. *Farm Movements in the South, 1865–1933*. 1960.
Schlichter, Gertrude Almy. "Franklin D. Roosevelt's Farm Policy as Governor of New York State, 1928–1932." *Agricultural History*, 33 (October 1959).
Shideler, James H. "Flappers and Philosophers, and Farmers: Rural Tensions of the Twenties." *Agricultural History*, 47 (October 1973).
Shover, John L. "The Farmers' Holiday Association Strike, August 1932." *Agricultural History*, 39 (October 1965).
Wik, Reynold M. "Henry Ford's Tractors and American Agriculture." *Agricultural History*, 38 (April 1964).
Wilson, Joan Hoff. "Hoover's Agricultural Policies, 1921–1928." *Agricultural History*, 51 (April 1977).

BIOGRAPHY

Adams, Larry L. *Walter Lippmann*. 1977.
Adelman, Lynn. "A Study of James Weldon Johnson." *Journal of Negro History*, 52 (April 1967).
Alexander, Charles C. *Ty Cobb*. 1984.
Anderson, Donald E. *William Howard Taft: A Conservative's Conception of the Presidency*. 1973.
Arnold, Peri E. "The 'Great Engineer' as Administrator: Herbert Hoover and Modern Bureaucracy." *Review of Politics*, 42 (July 1980).
Billington, Monroe Lee. *Thomas P. Gore: The Blind Senator from Oklahoma*. 1967.
Blumberg, Dorothy Rose. *Florence Kelley: The Making of a Social Pioneer*. 1966.
Broesamle, John J. *William Gibbs McAdoo: A Passion for Change, 1863–1917*. 1973.
Brown, Richard J. "John Dewey and the League for Independent Political Action." *Social Studies*, 59 (March 1968).
Burner, David. *Herbert Hoover: A Public Life*. 1979.
Burns, James MacGregor. *Roosevelt: The Lion and the Fox*. 1956.
Burns, Vincent Godfrey. *The Man Who Broke a Thousand Chains: The Story of Social Reformation of the Prisons of the South*. 1968.
Burton, David H. *Oliver Wendell Holmes, Jr.* 1980.
Calkins, David L. "Billy Sunday's Cincinnati Crusade." *Cincinnati Historical Society Bulletin*, 27 (Winter 1969).
Capeci, Dominic J. "Al Capone: Symbol of a Ballyhoo Society." *Journal of Ethnic Studies*, 2 (Fall 1974).
Carr, Virginia Spencer. *Dos Passos: A Life*. 1984.
Cherney, Robert W. *A Righteous Cause: The Life of William Jennings Bryan*. 1985.
Coben, Stanley. *A. Mitchell Palmer: Politician*. 1963.
Coletta, Paolo E. *William Jennings Bryan. Vol. III: A Political Puritan, 1915–1925*. 1969.
Cooper, John Milton, Jr. "Robert M. LaFollette: Political Prophet." *Wisconsin Magazine of History*, 69 (Winter 1985–1986).
Costin, Lela. *Two Sisters for Social Justice: A Biography of Grace and Edith Abbott*. 1983.
Coughlan, Neil. *Young John Dewey: An Essay in American Intellectual History*. 1975.
Cramer, C. H. *Newton D. Baker: A Biography*. 1961.

Crunden, Robert M. *A Hero in Spite of Himself: Brand Whitlock in Art, Politics, and War.* 1969.

Currie, Harold W. *Eugene V. Debs.* 1976.

Cywar, Alan. "John Dewey: Toward Domestic Reconstruction, 1915–1920." *Journal of the History of Ideas,* 30 (July–September 1969).

Dalstrom, Harl Adams. *Eugene C. Eppley: His Life and Legacy.* 1969.

Davis, Burke. *The Billy Mitchell Affair.* 1967.

Davis, Kenneth S. *FDR: The New York Years, 1928–1933.* 1985.

Douglas, George H. *H. L. Mencken: Critic of American Life.* 1978.

Dow, Eddy. "Van Wyck Brooks and Lewis Mumford: A Confluence in the Twenties." *American Literature,* 45 (November 1973).

Downes, Randolph C. "The Harding Muckfest: Warren G. Harding—Chief Victim of the Muck-for-Muck's-Sake Writers and Readers." *Northwest Ohio Quarterly,* 39 (Summer 1967).

———. *The Rise of Warren Gamaliel Harding: 1865–1920.* 1970.

Drinnon, Richard. *Rebel in Paradise: A Biography of Emma Goldman.* 1961.

Duram, James C. *Norman Thomas.* 1974.

Eckley, Wilton. *Herbert Hoover.* 1980.

Fausold, Martin L. *James W. Wadsworth, Jr.: The Gentleman from New York.* 1975.

Ferrell, Robert H., ed. *Frank B. Kellogg/Henry L. Stimson.* 1963.

———. *Woodrow Wilson and World War I, 1917–1921.* 1985.

Flynt, Wayne. *Duncan Upshaw Fletcher: Dixie's Reluctant Progressive.* 1971.

Fox, Frank W. *J. Reuben Clark: The Public Years.* 1980.

Freidel, Frank. *Franklin D. Roosevelt: Launching the New Deal.* 1973.

Gal, Allon. *Brandeis of Boston.* 1980.

Garraty, John A. *Right-Hand Man: The Life of George W. Perkins.* 1960.

Giglio, James N. *H. M. Daugherty and the Politics of Expediency.* 1978.

Gottfried, Alex. *Boss Cermak of Chicago: A Study of Political Leadership.* 1962.

Handlin, Oscar. *Al Smith and His America.* 1958.

Harbaugh, William H. *Lawyer's Lawyer: The Life of John W. Davis.* 1973.

Hareven, Tamara R. *Eleanor Roosevelt: An American Conscience.* 1968.

Hawkes, Robert T., Jr. "The Emergence of a Leader: Harry Flood Byrd, Governor of Virginia, 1926–1930." *Virginia Magazine of History and Biography,* 82 (April 1974).

Hawley, Ellis W. *Herbert Hoover as Secretary of Commerce: Studies in New Era Thought and Practice.* 1981.

Hobson, Fred C., Jr. *Serpent in Eden: H. L. Mencken and the South.* 1974.

Holt, Rackham. *Mary McLeod Bethune: A Biography.* 1964.

Hoopes, James. *Van Wyck Brooks: In Search of American Culture.* 1977.

Hovey, Richard B. *John Jay Chapman: An American Mind.* 1959.

Howlett, Charles F. *Troubled Philosopher: John Dewey and the Struggle for World Peace.* 1977.

Humes, D. Joy. *Oswald Garrison Villard, Liberal of the 1920s.* 1960.

Huthmacher, J. Joseph. *Senator Robert F. Wagner and the Rise of Urban Liberalism.* 1968.

Israel, Fred L. *Nevada's Key Pittman.* 1963.

Johnpoll, Bernard K. *Pacifist's Progress: Norman Thomas and the Decline of American Socialism.* 1970.

Josephson, Harold. *James T. Shotwell and the Rise of Internationalism in America*. 1975.

Josephson, Matthew, and Hannah Josephson. *Al Smith: Hero of the Cities: A Political Portrait Drawing on the Papers of Frances Perkins*. 1969.

Keller, Morton. *In Defense of Yesterday: James M. Beck and the Politics of Conservatism, 1861–1936*. 1958.

Kreuter, Kent, and Gretchen Kreuter. *An American Dissenter: The Life of Algie Martin Simons, 1870–1950*. 1969.

Kuehl, Warren F. *Hamilton Holt: Journalist, Internationalist, Educator*. 1960.

Lamson, Peggy. *Roger Baldwin: Founder of the American Civil Liberties Union*. 1976.

Landsberg, Melvin. *Dos Passos' Path to U.S.A.: A Political Biography, 1912–1936*. 1972.

Larson, Bruce L. *Lindbergh of Minnesota: A Political Biography*. 1973.

Lash, Joseph P. *Eleanor and Franklin*. 1971.

Lea, James. "Sinclair Lewis and the Implied America." *Clio*, 3 (October 1973).

Levine, Lawrence W. *Defender of the Faith: William Jennings Bryan: The Last Decade, 1915–1925*. 1965.

Levy, David W. *Herbert Croly of the New Republic: The Life and Thought of an American Progressive*. 1985.

Lowitt, Richard. *George W. Norris: The Making of a Progressive, 1861–1912*. 1963.

———. *George W. Norris: The Persistence of a Progressive, 1913–1933*. 1971.

———. *George W. Norris: The Triumph of a Progressive, 1933–1944*. 1978.

McCoy, Donald R. *Calvin Coolidge: The Quiet President*. 1967.

McDonald, Forrest. *Insull*. 1962.

McKenna, Marian C. *Borah*. 1961.

Mandel, Bernard. *Samuel Gompers: A Biography*. 1963.

Maney, Patrick J. *"Young Bob" La Follette: A Biography of Robert M. La Follette, Jr., 1895–1953*. 1978.

Mann, Arthur. *La Guardia: A Fighter against His Times, 1882–1933*. 1959.

Mason, Alpheus Thomas. *William Howard Taft: Chief Justice*. 1965.

Maurer, Maurer, and Calvin F. Senning. "Billy Mitchell, the Air Service and the Mingo War." *West Virginia History*, 30 (October 1968).

Montgomery, Edrene S. "Bruce Barton's *The Man Nobody Knows*: A Popular Advertising Illusion." *Journal of Popular Culture*, 19 (Winter 1985).

Moore, John Robert. *Senator Joseph William Bailey of North Carolina: A Political Biography*. 1968.

Morgan, H. Wayne. *Eugene V. Debs: Socialist for President*. 1962.

Morison, Elting E. *Turmoil and Tradition: A Study of the Life and Times of Henry L. Stimson*. 1960.

Nethers, John L. *Simeon D. Fess: Educator & Politician*. 1973.

Nevins, Allan. *James Truslow Adams: Historian of the American Dream*. 1968.

O'Brien, Patrick G. "William H. McMaster: An Agrarian Dissenter during 'Normalcy.' " *Emporia State Research Studies*, 20 (June 1972).

Orr, Oliver H., Jr. *Charles Brantley Aycock*. 1961.

Pratt, Norma Fain. *Morris Hillquit: A Political History of an American Jewish Socialist*. 1979.

Quint, Howard, and Robert H. Ferrell, eds. *The Talkative President: The Off-the-Record Press Conferences of Calvin Coolidge*. 1964.

Rader, Frank J. "Harry L. Hopkins, The Ambitious Crusader: An Historical Analysis of the Major Influences on His Career." *Annals of Iowa,* 44 (Fall 1977).

Roberts, Randy. "Jack Dempsey: An American Hero in the 1920's." *Journal of Popular Culture,* 8 (Fall 1974).

———. *Jack Dempsey: The Manassa Mauler.* 1979.

Robinson, Edgar Eugene, and Vaughn Davis Bornet. *Herbert Hoover: President of the United States.* 1975.

Rudwick, Elliott M. *W.E.B. Du Bois: A Study in Minority Group Leadership.* 1960.

Russell, Francis. *The Shadow of Blooming Grove: Warren G. Harding in His Times.* 1968.

Rylance, Daniel. "A Controversial Career: Gerald P. Nye, 1925–1946." *North Dakota Quarterly,* 36 (Winter 1968).

Schapsmeier, Edward L., and Frederick H. Schapsmeier. "Paul H. Douglas: From Pacifist to Soldier-Statesman." *Journal of the Illinois State Historical Society,* 67 (June 1974).

Schapsmeier, Edward L., and Frederick H. Schapsmeier. *Henry A. Wallace of Iowa: The Agrarian Years, 1910–1940.* 1968.

Schwarz, Jordan A. *The Speculator: Bernard M. Baruch in Washington, 1917–1965.* 1981.

Seidler, Murray B. *Norman Thomas: Respectable Rebel.* 1961.

Shaw, Peter. "[Lewis] Mumford in Retrospect." *Commentary,* 56 (September 1973).

Sinclair, Andrew. *The Available Man: The Life behind the Masks of Warren Gamaliel Harding.* 1965.

Smelser, Marshall. *The Life That Ruth Built: A Biography.* 1975.

Socolofsky, Homer E. *Arthur Capper: Publisher, Politician, and Philanthropist.* 1962.

Stenerson, Douglas C. *H. L. Mencken: Iconoclast from Baltimore.* 1971.

Stern, Sheldon. "The Evolution of a Reactionary: Louis Arthur Coolidge, 1900–1925." *Mid-America,* 57 (April 1975).

Strum, Philippa. *Louis D. Brandeis: Justice for the People.* 1984.

Swanberg, W. A. *Norman Thomas: The Last Idealist.* 1976.

Thelen, David P. *Robert M. La Follette and the Insurgent Spirit.* 1976.

Todd, A. L. *Justice on Trial: The Case of Louis D. Brandeis.* 1964.

Trani, Eugene P. "Charles Evans Hughes: The First Good Neighbor." *Northwest Ohio Quarterly,* 40 (Fall 1968).

———. "Hubert Work and the Department of the Interior." *Pacific Northwest Quarterly,* 61 (January 1970).

Urofsky, Melvin I. *Louis D. Brandeis and the Progressive Tradition.* 1981.

Uya, Okon Edet. *From Slavery to Public Service: Robert Smalls, 1839–1915.* 1971.

Wade, Louise C. *Graham Taylor: Pioneer for Social Justice, 1851–1938.* 1964.

Walker, J. Samuel. "Henry A. Wallace as Agrarian Isolationist, 1921–1930." *Agricultural History,* 49 (April 1975).

Walker, Kenneth R., and Randolph G. Downes. "The Death of Warren G. Harding." *Northwest Ohio Quarterly,* 54 (Winter 1962–1963).

Waller, Robert A. *Rainey of Illinois: A Political Biography, 1903–34.* 1977.

Weiss, Nancy Joan. *Charles Francis Murphy, 1858–1924: Respectability and Responsibility in Tammany Politics.* 1968.

Wesser, Robert F. "Charles Evans Hughes and the Urban Sources of Political Progressivism." *New York Historical Quarterly,* 47 (October 1966).

Wexler, Alice. *Emma Goldman: An Intimate Life.* 1984.
Wik, Reynold M. *Henry Ford and Grass-Roots America.* 1972.
Williams, W.H.A. *H. L. Mencken.* 1977.
Wilson, Joan Hoff, and Marjorie Ligniman, eds. *Without Precedent: The Life and Career of Eleanor Roosevelt.* 1984.
Zucker, Norman L. *George W. Norris: Gentle Knight of American Democracy.* 1966.

BUSINESS

Abrahams, Paul P. "American Bankers and the Economic Tactics of Peace: 1919." *Journal of American History,* 56 (December 1969).
Barnouw, Erik. *A Tower in Babel: A History of Broadcasting in the United States. Vol. 1, to 1933.* 1966.
Bilstein, Roger E. *Flight Patterns: Trends of Aeronautical Development in the United States, 1918–1929.* 1983.
———. "Technology and Commerce: Aviation in the Conduct of American Business, 1918–29." *Technology and Culture,* 10 (January 1969).
Burrow, James G. *AMA: Voice of American Medicine.* 1963.
Cochran, Thomas C. *American Business in the Twentieth Century.* 1972.
Costigliola, Frank. "The Other Side of Isolationism: The Establishment of the First World Bank, 1929–1930." *Journal of American History,* 59 (December 1972).
Cowing, Cedric B. *Populists, Plungers, and Progressives: A Social History of Stock and Commodity Speculation, 1890–1936.* 1965.
Galambos, Louis. *Competition & Cooperation: The Emergence of a National Trade Association.* 1966.
George, Paul S. "Brokers, Binders, and Builders: Greater Miami's Boom of the Mid-1920s." *Florida Historical Quarterly,* 65 (July 1986).
Gleason, John Philip. "The Attitude of the Business Community toward Agriculture during the McNary-Haugen Period." *Agricultural History,* 32 (April 1958).
Groth, Clarence W. "Sowing and Reaping: Montana Banking—1910–25." *Montana: The Magazine of Western History,* 20 (October 1970).
Hawley, Ellis W. "Secretary Hoover and the Bituminous Coal Problem, 1921–1928." *Business History Review,* 42 (Autumn 1968).
Heald, Morrell. "Business Thought in the Twenties: Social Responsibility." *American Quarterly,* 13 (Summer 1961).
Himmelberg, Robert F. "Business, Antitrust Policy, and the Industrial Board of the Department of Commerce, 1919." *Business History Review,* 42 (Spring 1968).
Johnson, H. Thomas. "Management Accounting in an Early Multidivisional Organization: General Motors in the 1920s." *Business History Review,* 52 (Winter 1978).
Karnes, Thomas L. *Tropical Enterprise: The Standard Fruit and Steamship Company in Latin America.* 1978.
Kennedy, Susan Estabrook. *The Banking Crisis of 1933.* 1973.
———. "The Michigan Banking Crisis of 1933." *Michigan History,* 57 (Fall 1973).
Kirkendall, Richard S. "A. A. Berle, Jr., Student of the Corporation, 1917–1932." *Business History Review,* 35 (Spring, 1961).
Knapp, Joseph G. *The Advance of American Cooperative Enterprise: 1920–1945.* 1973.
Larson, Henrietta M., and Kenneth Wiggins Porter. *History of Humble Oil and Refining Company: A Study in Industrial Growth.* 1959.

Lee, David D. "Herbert Hoover and the Development of Commercial Aviation, 1921–1926." *Business History Review*, 58 (Spring 1984).

McQuaid, Kim. "Corporate Liberalism in the American Business Community, 1920–1940." *Business History Review*, 52 (Autumn 1978).

Marchand, Roland. *Advertising the American Dream: Making Way for Modernity, 1920–1940*. 1985.

Massie, Joseph L. *Blazer and Ashland Oil: A Study in Management*. 1960.

Meyer, Richard Hemmig. *Bankers' Diplomacy: Monetary Stabilization in the Twenties*. 1970.

Nuechterlein, James A. "Bruce Barton and the Business Ethos of the 1920's." *South Atlantic Quarterly*, 76 (Summer 1977).

Olson, James S. "The End of Voluntarism: Herbert Hoover and the National Credit Corporation." *Annals of Iowa*, 41 (Fall 1972).

Pease, Otis. *The Responsibilities of American Advertising: Private Control and Public Influence, 1920–1940*. 1958.

Raucher, Alan R. *Public Relations and Business, 1900–1929*. 1968.

Ribuffo, Leo P. "Jesus Christ as Business Statesman: Bruce Barton and the Selling of Corporate Capitalism." *American Quarterly*, 33 (Summer 1981).

Sears, Marian V. and Irving Katz. *Investment Banking in America*. 1970.

Severson, Robert F., Jr. "The American Manufacturing Frontier, 1870–1940." *Business History Review*, 34 (Autumn 1960).

Sirkin, Gerald. "The Stock Market of 1929 Revisited: A Note." *Business History Review*, 49 (Summer 1975).

Smiley, Gene. "Did Incomes for Most of the Population Fall from 1923 through 1929?" *Journal of Economic History*, 43 (March 1983).

Sobel, Robert. *The Great Bull Market: Wall Street in the 1920s*. 1968.

White, Eugene Nelson. "The Merger Movement in Banking, 1919–1933." *Journal of Economic History*, 45 (June 1985).

———. "State-Sponsored Insurance of Bank Deposits in the United States, 1907–1929." *Journal of Economic History*, 41 (September 1981).

Wicker, Elmus. "A Reconsideration of the Causes of the Banking Panic of 1930." *Journal of Economic History*, 40 (September 1980).

Wilkins, Mira. *The Maturing of Multinational Enterprise: American Business Abroad from 1914 to 1970*. 1974.

Williamson, Harold. *The American Petroleum Industry: The Age of Energy, 1899–1959*. 1963.

Wilson, Joan Hoff. *American Business and Foreign Policy: 1920–1933*. 1971.

Wilson, J. H. "American Business and the Recognition of the Soviet Union." *Social Science Quarterly*, 52 (September 1971).

Wood, Norman J. "Industrial Relations Policies of American Management, 1900–1933." *Business History Review*, 34 (Winter 1960).

CONSERVATION

Bates, J. Leonard. *The Origins of Teapot Dome: Progressives, Parties, and Petroleum, 1909–1921*. 1963.

Clements, Kendrick A. "Herbert Hoover and Conservation, 1921–1933." *American Historical Review*, 89 (February 1984).

Dunlap, Thomas R. "Values for Varmints: Predator Control and Environmental Ideas, 1920–1939." *Pacific Historical Review,* 53 (May 1984).

Horan, John F., Jr. "Will Carson and the Virginia Conservation Commission, 1926–1934." *Virginia Magazine of History and Biography,* 92 (October 1984).

Parsons, Malcolm B. "Origins of the Colorado River Controversy in Arizona Politics, 1922–1923." *Arizona and the West,* 4 (Spring 1962).

Stratton, David H. "Two Western Senators and Teapot Dome: Thomas J. Walsh and Albert B. Fall." *Pacific Northwest Quarterly,* 65 (April 1974).

Swain, Donald C. *Federal Conservation Policy, 1921–1933.* 1963.

CULTURE

Aitken, Hugh G. J. *The Continuous Wave: Technology and American Radio, 1900–1932.* 1985.

Rochester, Stuart I. *American Liberal Disillusionment in the Wake of World War I.* 1977.

Singal, David Joseph. *The War Within: From Victorian to Modernist Thought in the South, 1919–1945.* 1982.

Tawa, Nicholas. *Serenading the Reluctant Eagle: American Musical Life, 1925–1945.* 1984.

ECONOMIC POLICY

Alchon, Guy. *The Invisible Hand of Planning: Capitalism, Social Science, and the State in the 1920s.* 1985.

Barber, William J. *From New Era to New Deal: Herbert Hoover, the Economists, and American Economic Policy, 1921–1933.* 1985.

Brandes, Joseph. *Herbert Hoover and Economic Diplomacy: Department of Commerce Policy, 1921–1928.* 1962.

Burdick, Frank. "Woodrow Wilson and the Underwood Tariff." *Mid-America,* 50 (October 1968).

Burke, Bernard V. "American Economic Diplomacy and the Weimar Republic." *Mid-America* 54 (October 1972).

Burnham, John Chynoweth. "The Gasoline Tax and the Automobile Revolution." *The Mississippi Valley Historical Review,* 48 (December 1961).

Carroll, John M. "The Paris Bankers' Conference of 1922 and America's Design for a Peaceful Europe." *International Review of History and Political Science,* 10 (August 1973).

Costigliola, Frank C. "Anglo-American Financial Rivalry in the 1920s." *Journal of Economic History,* 37 (September 1977).

Critchlow, Donald T. *The Brookings Institution, 1916–1952: Expertise and the Public Interest in a Democratic Society,* 1985.

Davis, Joseph S. *The World between the Wars, 1919–39: An Economist's View.* 1975.

Falkus, M. E. "United States Economic Policy and the 'Dollar Gap' of the 1920's." *Economic History Review,* 24 (November 1971).

Gardolfi, Arthur E. "Stability of the Demand for Money during the Great Contraction—1929–1933." *Journal of Political Economy,* 82 (September/October 1974).

Glynn, Sean, and Alan L. Loughed. "A Comment on United States Economic Policy and the 'Dollar Gap' of the 1920's." *Economic History Review*, 26 (November 1973).

Godfrey, Aaron Austin. *Government Operation of the Railroads: Its Necessity, Success, and Consequences, 1918–1920*. 1974.

Golembe, Carter H. "The Deposit Insurance Legislation of 1933: An Examination of Its Antecedents and Its Purposes." *Political Science Quarterly*, 75 (June 1960).

Hawley, Ellis W. "Herbert Hoover, the Commerce Secretariat, and the Vision of an 'Associative State,' 1921–1928." *Journal of American History*, 56 (June 1974).

Hawley, Ellis W., Murray N. Rothbard, Robert F. Himmelberg, and Gerald D. Nash. *Herbert Hoover and the Crisis of American Capitalism*. 1973.

Himmelberg, Robert F. *The Origins of the National Recovery Administration: Business, Government, and the Trade Association Issue, 1921–1933*. 1976.

Hubbard, Preston J. *Origins of the TVA: The Muscle Shoals Controversy, 1920–1932*. 1961.

Hurvitz, Haggai. "Ideology and Industrial Conflict, President Wilson's First Industrial Conference of October, 1919." *Labor History*, 18 (Fall 1977).

Johnson, Arthur M. "The Federal Trade Commission: The Early Years, 1915–1935." In Joseph R. Frese, et al., *Business and Government*. 1985.

Johnson, H. Thomas. "Postwar Optimism and the Rural Financial Crisis of the 1920's." *Explorations in Economic History*, 11 (Winter 1973–1974).

Kane, N. Stephen. "Bankers and Diplomats: The Diplomacy of the Dollar in Mexico, 1921–1924." *Business History Review*, 47 (Autumn 1973).

Keller, Robert. "Factor Income Distribution in the United States during the 1920's: A Reexamination of Fact and Theory." *Journal of Economic History*, 33 (March 1973).

Kutler, Stanley I. "Chief Justice Taft, National Regulation, and the Commerce Power." *The Journal of American History*, 51 (March 1965), 651–68.

Leffler, Melvy. "The Origins of Republican War Debt Policy, 1921–1923: A Case Study in the Applicability of the Open Door Interpretation." *Journal of American History*, 59 (December 1972).

McQuaid, Kim. "An American Owenite: Edward A. Filene and the Parameters of Industrial Reform, 1890–1937." *American Journal of Economics and Sociology*, 35 (January 1976).

Nash, Gerald D. "Government and Business: A Case Study of State Regulation of Corporate Securities, 1850–1933." *Business History Review*, 38 (Summer 1964).

Nordhauser, Norman E. *The Quest for Stability: Domestic Oil Regulation, 1917–1935*. 1979.

Olson, James S. "The Depths of the Great Depression: Economic Collapse in West Virginia, 1932–1933." *West Virginia History*, 38 (April 1977).

———. "Rehearsal for Disaster: Hoover, the R.F.C., and the Banking Crisis in Nevada, 1932–1933." *Western Historical Quarterly*, 6 (April 1975).

Parrini, Carl P. *Heir to Empire: United States Economic Diplomacy, 1916–1923*. 1969.

Potter, Jim. *The American Economy between the World Wars*. 1974.

Rhodes, Benjamin D. "Herbert Hoover and the War Debts, 1919–1933." *Prologue*, 6 (Summer 1974).

———. "Reassessing 'Uncle Shylock': The United States and the French War Debt, 1917–1929." *Journal of American History*, 55 (March 1969).

Snyder, J. Richard. "William S. Culbertson and the Formation of Modern American Commercial Policy, 1917–1925." *Kansas Historical Quarterly*, 35 (Winter 1969).

Temin, Peter. *Did Monetary Forces Cause the Great Depression?* 1976.
West, Robert Craig. *Banking Reform and the Federal Reserve 1863–1923.* 1977.
White, Eugene Nelson. *The Regulation and Reform of the American Banking System, 1900–1929.* 1983.
Whitnah, Donald R. *Safer Skyways: Federal Control of Aviation, 1926–1966.* 1966.
Wicker, Elmus. *Federal Reserve Monetary Policy, 1917–1933.* 1966.
———. "A Reconsideration of Federal Reserve Policy during the 1920–1921 Depression." *Journal of Economic History,* 26 (June 1966).
Wilson, David A. "Principles and Profits: Standard Oil Responds to Chinese Nationalism, 1925–1927." *Pacific Historical Review,* 46 (November 1977).
Wilson, Joan Hoff. *Ideology and Economics: U.S. Relations with the Soviet Union, 1918–1933.* 1974.
Wilson, William H. "The Alaska Railroad and Coal: Development of a Federal Policy, 1914–1939." *Pacific Northwest Quarterly,* 73 (April 1982).
Zieger, Robert H. "Herbert Hoover, the Wage-Earner, and the 'New Economic System,' 1919–1929." *Business History Review,* 51 (Summer 1977).

ELECTIONS

Allen, Lee N. "The McAdoo Campaign for the Presidential Nomination of 1924." *Journal of Southern History,* 32 (May 1963).
———. "The Underwood Presidential Movement of 1924." *Alabama Review,* 15 (April 1962).
Bagby, Wesley M. *The Road to Normalcy: The Presidential Campaign and Election of 1920.* 1962.
Best, Gary Dean. "The Hoover-for-President Boom of 1920." *Mid-America,* 53 (October 1971).
Bornet, Vaughn Davis. *Labor Politics in a Democratic Republic: Moderation, Division, and Disruption in the Presidential Election of 1928.* 1964.
Burner, David. "The Brown Derby Campaign." *New York History,* 46 (October 1965).
———. "The Democratic Party in the Election of 1924." *Mid-America,* 46 (April 1964).
Carter, Paul A. "The Campaign of 1928 Re-examined: A Study in Political Folklore." *Wisconsin Magazine of History,* 46 (Summer 1963).
———. "The Other Catholic Candidate: The 1928 Presidential Bid of Thomas J. Walsh." *Pacific Northwest Quarterly,* 55 (January 1964).
Edmonson, Ben G. "Pat Harrison and Mississippi in the Presidential Elections of 1924 and 1928." *Journal of Mississippi History,* 33 (November 1971).
Feinman, Ronald L. "The Progressive Republican Senate Block and the Presidential Election of 1932." *Mid-America,* 59 (April–July 1977).
Fry, Joseph A., and Brent Tarter. "The Redemption of the Fighting Ninth: The 1922 Congressional Election in the Ninth District of Virginia and the Origins of the Byrd Organization." *South Atlantic Quarterly,* 77 (Summer 1978).
Grant, Philip A., Jr. "The Presidential Election of 1932 in Michigan." *Michigan Historical Review,* 12 (Spring 1986).
Greenberg, Irwin F. "Pinchot, Prohibition and Public Utilities: The Pennsylvania Election of 1930." *Pennsylvania History,* 39 (October 1972).
Hall, Alvin L. "Virginia Back in the Fold: The Gubernatorial Campaign and Election of 1929." *Virginia Magazine of History and Biography,* 73 (July 1965).

Johnson, Evans C. "Oscar W. Underwood and the Senatorial Campaign of 1920." *Alabama Review*, 21 (January 1968).

Johnston, Scott D. "Robert La Follette and the Socialists: Aspects of the 1924 Presidential Campaign Re-examined." *Social Science*, 50 (Spring 1975).

Kelley, Donald Brooks. "Deep South Dilemma: The Mississippi Press in the Presidential Election of 1928." *Journal of Mississippi History*, 25 (April 1963).

Ledbetter, Cal, Jr. "Joe T. Robinson and the Presidential Campaign of 1928." *Arkansas Historical Quarterly*, 45 (Summer 1986).

Levin, James. "Governor Albert C. Ritchie and the Democratic Convention of 1932." *Maryland Historical Magazine*, 67 (Fall 1972).

Lichtman, Allan J. *Prejudice and the Old Politics: The Presidential Election of 1928.* 1979.

Ludwig, E. Jeffrey. "Pennsylvania: The National Election of 1932." *Pennsylvania History*, 31 (July 1964).

Maderas, Lawrence H. "Theodore Roosevelt, Jr., versus Al Smith: The New York Gubernatorial Election of 1924." *New York History*, 47 (October 1966).

Margulies, Herbert F. "Irvine L. Lenroot and the Republican Vice-Presidential Nomination of 1920." *Wisconsin Magazine of History*, 61 (Autumn 1977).

Melcher, Daniel P. "The Challenge to Normalcy: The 1924 Election in California." *Southern California Quarterly*, 60 (Summer 1978).

Moore, John Robert. "The Shaping of a Political Leader: Josiah W. Bailey and the Gubernatorial Campaign of 1924." *North Carolina Historical Review*, 41 (April 1964).

Murray, Lawrence L. "General John J. Pershing's Bid for the Presidency in 1920—The Boys Will Never Call Him 'Papa.' " *Nebraska History*, 53 (Summer 1972).

Murray, Robert K. *The 103rd Ballot: Democrats and the Disaster in Madison Square Garden.* 1976.

Ortquist, Richard T. "Depression Politics in Michigan: The Election of 1932." *Michigan Academician*, 2 (Spring 1970).

Prude, James C. "William Gibbs McAdoo and the Democratic National Convention of 1924." *Journal of Southern History*, 38 (November 1972).

Reagan, Hugh D. "Race As a Factor in the Presidential Election of 1928 in Alabama." *Alabama Review*, 19 (January 1966).

Reichard, Gary W. "The Aberration of 1920: An Analysis of Harding's Victory in Tennessee." *Journal of Southern History*, 36 (February 1970).

Stratton, David H. "Splattered with Oil: William G. McAdoo and the 1924 Democratic Presidential Nomination." *Southwestern Social Science Quarterly*, 25 (June 1963).

Traylor, Jack Wayne. "William Allen White's 1924 Gubernatorial Campaign." *Kansas Historical Quarterly*, 42 (Summer 1976).

Tyson, Carl N. " 'I'm Off to Coolidge's Follies': Will Rogers and the Presidential Nominations, 1924–1932." *Chronicles of Oklahoma*, 54 (Summer 1976).

Watson, Richard L. "A Southern Democratic Primary: Simmons vs. Bailey in 1930." *North Carolina Historical Review*, 41 (Autumn 1964).

Williams, Donald E. "Dawes and the 1924 Republican Vice Presidential Nomination." *Mid-America* 44 (January 1962).

Zink, Steven D. "Cultural Conflict and the 1928 Presidential Campaign in Louisiana." *Southern Studies*, 8 (Summer 1978).

FOREIGN POLICY

Accinelli, Robert D. "Was There a 'New' Harding? Warren G. Harding and the World Court Issue, 1920–1923." *Ohio History*, 84 (Autumn 1975).

Adler, Selig. *The Uncertain Giant: 1921–1941, American Foreign Policy between the Wars.* 1965.

Ambrosius, Lloyd E. "Wilson, the Republicans, and French Security after World War I." *Journal of American History*, 59 (September 1972).

Asada, Sadao. "Japan's 'Special Interests' and the Washington Conference, 1921–22." *American Historical Review*, 66 (October 1961).

Baker, George. "The Wilson Administration and Cuba, 1913–1921." *Mid-America*, 46 (January 1964).

———. "The Woodrow Wilson Administration and El Salvadoran Relations, 1913–1921." *Social Studies*, 56 (February 1965).

Ballentine, Dirk Anthony. "Secrets without Substance: U.S. Intelligence in the Japanese Mandates, 1915–1935." *Journal of Pacific History*, 19 (April 1984).

Beelen, George D. "The Harding Administration and Mexico: Diplomacy by Economic Persuasion." *Americas*, 41 (October 1984).

Bell, Sidney. *Righteous Conquest: Woodrow Wilson and the Evolution of the New Diplomacy.* 1972.

Bendiner, Elmer. *A Time for Angels: The Tragicomic History of the League of Nations.* 1975.

Bolt, Ernest C., Jr. *Ballots before Bullets: The War Referendum Approach to Peace in America, 1914–1941.* 1977.

Boothe, Leon. "Lord Grey, the United States, and the Political Effort for a League of Nations." *Maryland Historical Magazine*, 65 (Spring 1970).

Braeman, John. "Power and Diplomacy: The 1920s Reappraised." *Review of Politics*, 44 (July 1982).

Braisted, William R. "China, the United States Navy, and the Bethlehem Steel Company, 1909–1929." *Business History Review*, 42 (Spring 1968).

———. *The United States Navy in the Pacific, 1909–1922.* 1971.

Broderick, Francis L. "Liberalism and the Mexican Crisis of 1927: A Debate between Norman Thomas and John A. Ryan." *Catholic Historical Review*, 45 (October 1959).

Buckley, Thomas H. *The United States and the Washington Conference: 1921–1922.* 1970.

Buhite, Russell D. *Nelson T. Johnson and American Policy toward China, 1925–1941.* 1968.

Burns, Richard Dean. "International Arms Inspection Policies between World Wars, 1919–1934." *Historian*, 31 (August 1969).

Burns, Richard Dean, and Edward M. Bennett. *Diplomats in Crisis: United States–Chinese–Japanese Relations, 1919–1941.* 1974.

Carlton, David. "Great Britain and the Coolidge Naval Disarmament Conference of 1927." *Political Science Quarterly*, 83 (December 1968).

Carroll, John M. "Henry Cabot Lodge's Contributions to the Shaping of Republican European Diplomacy, 1920–1924." *Capitol Studies*, 3 (Fall 1975).

Castor, Suzy. "The American Occupation of Haiti (1915–34) and the Dominican Republic (1916–24)." *Massachusetts Review*, 15 (Winter–Spring 1974).

Chan, Loren B. "Fighting for the League: President Wilson in Nevada, 1919." *Nevada Historical Society Quarterly,* 22 (Summer 1979).

Cole, Bernard. *Gunboats and Marines: The United States Navy in China, 1925–1928.* 1983.

Cole, Wayne S. *Charles A. Lindbergh and the Battle against American Intervention in World War II.* 1974.

Costigliola, Frank. "American Foreign Policy in the 'Nut Cracker': The United States and Poland in the 1920s." *Pacific Historical Review,* 48 (February 1979).

———. "The Other Side of Isolationism: The Establishment of the First World Bank, 1929–1930." *Journal of American History,* 59 (December 1972).

———. "The United States and the Reconstruction of Germany in the 1920s." *Business History Review,* 50 (Winter 1976).

Crosby, Alfred W., Jr. *Epidemic and Peace, 1918.* 1976.

Daniel, Robert L. "The Armenian Question and American-Turkish Relations, 1914–1927. *The Mississippi Valley Historical Review,* 46 (September 1959).

DeBenedetti, Charles. "Alternative Strategies in the American Peace Movement in the 1920s," *American Studies,* 13 (Spring 1972).

———. "Borah and the Kellogg-Briand Pact." *Pacific Northwest Quarterly,* 63 (January 1972).

———. *Origins of the Modern American Peace Movement, 1915–1929.* 1978.

De Witt, Howard A. "The 'New' Harding and American Foreign Policy: Warren G. Harding, Hiram W. Johnson, and Pragmatic Diplomacy." *Ohio History,* 86 (Spring 1977).

Dingman, Roger. *Power in the Pacific: The Origins of Naval Arms Limitation, 1914–1922.* 1976.

Dubay, Robert Wm. "The Geneva Naval Conference of 1927: A Study of Battleship Diplomacy." *Southern Quarterly,* 8 (January 1970).

Ellis, L. Ethan. *Frank B. Kellogg and American Foreign Relations, 1925–1929.* 1961.

———. *Republican Foreign Policy, 1921–1933.* 1968.

Ferrell, Robert H. "Repudiation of a Reputation." *The Journal of American History,* 51 (March 1965), 669–73.

Fike, Claude E. "The United States and Russian Territorial Problems, 1917–1920." *Historian,* 24 (May 1962).

Filene, Peter G. *Americans and the Soviet Experiment, 1917–1933.* 1967.

Fithian, Floyd J. "Dollars without the Flag: The Case of Sinclair and Sakhalin Oil." *Pacific Historical Review,* 39 (May 1970).

Flack, Bruce C. "Dynamics of Intolerance—Internal and External Models in the Study of Intolerance in the United States during the 1920s." *Illinois Quarterly,* 39 (Winter 1976).

Fogelson, Nancy. "The Tip of the Iceberg: The United States and International Rivalry for the Arctic, 1900–25." *Diplomatic History,* 9 (Spring 1985).

Fry, Michael G. *Illusions of Security: North Atlantic Diplomacy, 1918–22.* 1972.

Gelfand, Lawrence E. *The Inquiry: American Preparations for Peace, 1917–1919.* 1963.

Gellman, Irwin F. "Prelude to Reciprocity: The Abortive United States–Colombian Treaty of 1933." *Historian,* 32 (November 1969).

Girard, Jolyon P. "Congress and Presidential Military Policy: The Occupation of Germany, 1919–1923." *Mid-America,* 56 (October 1974).

Glad, Betty. *Charles Evans Hughes and the Illusions of Innocence: A Study in American Diplomacy.* 1966.

Glaser, David. "1919: William Jenkins, Robert Lansing, and the Mexican Interlude." *Southwestern Historical Quarterly,* 74 (January 1971).

Green, David. *The Containment of Latin America: A History of the Myths and Realities of the Good Neighbor Policy.* 1971.

Grieb, Kenneth J. *The United States and Huerta.* 1969.

Hecht, Robert A. "Great Britain and the Stimson Note of January 7, 1932." *Pacific Historical Review,* 38 (May 1969).

Heinrichs, Waldo H., Jr. *American Ambassador: Joseph C. Grew and the Development of the United States Diplomatic Tradition.* 1966.

Holsinger, M. Paul. "The 'I'm Alone' Controversy: A Study in Inter-American Diplomacy, 1929–1935." *Mid-America,* 50 (October 1968).

Howlett, Charles F. *Troubled Philosopher: John Dewey and the Struggle for World Peace.* 1977.

Hoyt, Frederick B. "The Summer of '30: American Policy and Chinese Communism." *Pacific Historical Review,* 46 (May 1977).

Ichioka, Yuji. "Japanese Associations and the Japanese Government: A Special Relationship, 1909–1926." *Pacific Historical Review,* 66 (August 1977).

Kamman, William. *A Search for Stability: United States Diplomacy toward Nicaragua, 1925–1933.* 1968.

Kasurak, Peter. "American Foreign Policy Officials and Canada, 1927–1941: A Look through Bureaucratic Glasses." *International Journal,* 32 (Summer 1977).

Kaufman, Burton I. *Efficiency and Expansion: Foreign Trade Organization in the Wilson Administration, 1913–1921.* 1974.

———. "The Organizational Dimension of United States Economic Foreign Policy, 1900–1920." *Business History Review,* 46 (Spring 1972).

———. "Wilson's 'War Bureaucracy' and Foreign Trade Expansion, 1917–21." *Prologue,* 6 (Spring 1974).

Klein, Ira. "Whitehall, Washington, and the Anglo-Japanese Alliance, 1919–1921." *Pacific Historical Review,* 41 (November 1972).

Komons, Nick A. *Bonfires to Beacons: Federal Civil Aviation Policy under the Air Commerce Act, 1926–1938.* 1978.

Koppes, Clayton R. "The Good Neighbor Policy and the Nationalization of Mexican Oil: A Reinterpretation." *Journal of American History,* 69 (June 1982).

Kuehl, Warren F. *Seeking World Order: The United States and International Organization to 1920.* 1969.

Kuklick, Bruce. "The Division of Germany and American Policy on Reparations." *Western Political Quarterly,* 23 (June 1970).

Lawrence, James R. "The American Federation of Labor and the Philippine Independence Question, 1920–1935." *Labor History,* 7 (Winter 1966).

Leffler, Melvyn P. "American Policy Making and European Stability, 1921–1933." *Pacific Historical Review,* 46 (May 1977).

———. "The Origins of Republican War Debt Policy, 1921–1923: A Case Study in the Applicability of the Open Door Interpretation." *Journal of American History,* 59 (December 1972).

———. "Political Isolationism, Economic Expansionism, or Diplomatic Realism: American Policy toward Western Europe 1921–1933.'' *Perspectives in American History,* 8 (1974).

Levin, N. Gordon, Jr. *Woodrow Wilson and World Politics: America's Response to War and Revolution.* 1968.

Libbey, James K. *Alexander Gumberg and Soviet-American Relations, 1917–1933.* 1977.

Little, Douglas. ''Antibolshevism and American Foreign Policy, 1919–1939: The Diplomacy of Self-Delusion.'' *American Quarterly,* 35 (Fall 1983).

Long, John W. ''American Intervention in Russia: The North-Russian Expedition, 1918–19.'' *Diplomatic History,* 6 (Winter 1982).

Machado, Manuel A., Jr., and James T. Judge. ''Tempest in a Teapot? The Mexican–United States Intervention Crisis of 1919.'' *Southwestern Historical Quarterly,* 74 (July 1970).

Maddox, Robert James. ''Another Look at the Legend of Isolationism in the 1920's.'' *Mid-America,* 53 (January 1970).

———. *The Unknown War with Russia: Wilson's Siberian Intervention.* 1977.

———. ''Woodrow Wilson, the Russian Embassy, and Siberian Intervention.'' *Pacific Historical Review,* 36 (November 1967).

Maga, Timothy P. ''Prelude to War? The United States, Japan, and the Yap Crisis, 1918–1922.'' *Diplomatic History,* 9 (Summer 1985).

Margulies, Herbert F. ''The Senate and the World Court.'' *Capitol Studies,* 4 (Fall 1976).

Marks, Sally, and Denis Dulude. ''German-American Relations 1918–1921.'' *Mid-America* 53 (October 1971).

Mitchell, Kell F., Jr. ''Diplomacy and Prejudice: The Morris-Shidehara Negotiations, 1920–1921.'' *Pacific Historical Review,* 39 (February 1970).

Munro, Dana G. ''The American Withdrawal from Haiti, 1929–1934.'' *Hispanic American Historical Review,* 49 (February 1969).

———. *Intervention and Dollar Diplomacy in the Caribbean, 1900–1921.* 1964.

———. *The United States and the Caribbean Republics, 1921–1933.* 1974.

Murphy, Francis J. ''The Poet and the Pact: Paul Claudel and the Kellogg-Briand Pacts.'' *Mid-America,* 60 (April 1978).

Parsons, Edward B. *Wilsonian Diplomacy: Allied-American Rivalries in War and Peace.* 1978.

Pugach, Noel. ''Making the Open Door Work: Paul S. Reinsch in China, 1913–1919.'' *Pacific Historical Review,* 38 (May 1969).

Rabe, Stephen G. ''Anglo-American Rivalry for Venezuelan Oil 1919–1929.'' *Mid-America,* 58 (April–July 1976).

———. *The Road to OPEC: United States Relations with Venezuela, 1919–1976.* 1982.

Radosh, Ronald. ''John Spargo and Wilson's Russian Policy, 1920.'' *The Journal of American History,* 52 (December 1965), 548–65.

Randall, Stephen J. ''The Barco Concession in Colombian-American Relations, 1926–1932.'' *Americas,* 33 (July 1976).

———. *The Diplomacy of Modernization: Colombian-American Relations, 1920–1940.* 1977.

———. ''The International Corporation and American Foreign Policy: The United States and Colombian Petroleum, 1920–1940.'' *Canadian Journal of History,* 9 (August 1974).

Rappaport, Armin. *Henry L. Stimson and Japan, 1931–1933.* 1963.

Rhodes, Benjamin D. "The Origins of Finnish-American Friendship, 1919–1941." *Mid-America*, 54 (January 1972).

Rice, Elizabeth Ann. *The Diplomatic Relations between the United States and Mexico, As Affected by the Struggle for Religious Liberty in Mexico, 1925–1929*. 1959.

Ross, Stanley Robert. "Dwight Morrow and the Mexican Revolution." *Hispanic American Historical Review*, 46 (November 1958).

Safford, Jeffrey J. "Edward Hurley and American Shipping Policy: An Elaboration of Wilsonian Diplomacy, 1918–1919." *Historian*, 35 (August 1973).

Schmidt, Royal J. *Versailles and the Ruhr: Seedbed of World War II*. 1968.

Schmitt, Bernadotte E. "The Peace Treaties of 1919–1920." *Proceedings of the American Philosophical Society*, (February 1960).

Schwabe, Klaus. *Woodrow Wilson, Revolutionary Germany, and Peacemaking, 1918–1919: Missionary Diplomacy and the Realities of Power*. 1985.

Sellen, Robert W. "Why Presidents Fail in Foreign Policy: The Case of Woodrow Wilson." *Social Studies*, 44 (February 1973).

Sessions, Gene A. "The Clark Memorandum Myth." *Americas*, 34 (July 1977).

Sherwood, Morgan. "The Versailles Treaty and Irish-Americans." *Journal of American History*, 55 (December 1968).

Siverson, Randolph, and Charles McCarty. "Alliances in the Interwar Era, 1919–1939: A Reexamination." *Western Political Quarterly*, 35 (March 1982).

Smith, Daniel M. *Aftermath of War: Bainbridge Colby and Wilsonian Diplomacy, 1920–1921*. 1970.

———. "Bainbridge Colby and the Good Neighbor Policy, 1920–1921." *The Mississippi Valley Historical Review*, 50 (June 1963).

Smith, Douglas L. "The Millspaugh Mission and American Corporate Diplomacy in Persia, 1922–1927." *Southern Quarterly*, 14 (January 1976).

Smith, Robert F. *The United States and Cuba: Business and Diplomacy, 1917–1960*. 1960.

———. *The United States and Revolutionary Nationalism in Mexico, 1916–1932*. 1972.

Spector, Robert M. *W. Cameron Forbes and the Hoover Commissions to Haiti (1930)*. 1985.

Stivers, William. *Supremacy and Oil: Iraq, Turkey, and the Anglo-American World Order, 1918–1930*. 1982.

Stone, Ralph A. "The Irreconcilables' Alternatives to the League of Nations." *Mid-America*, 49 (July 1967).

———. *The Irreconcilables: The Fight against the League of Nations*. 1970.

Strakhovsky, Leonid I. *American Opinion about Russia, 1917–1920*. 1961.

Tillman, Seth P. *Anglo-American Relations at the Paris Peace Conference of 1919*. 1961.

Trani, Eugene P. "Woodrow Wilson and the Decision to Intervene in Russia: A Reconsideration." *Military Affairs*, 40 (October 1976).

Trask, Roger R. *The United States Response to Turkish Nationalism and Reform 1914–1939*. 1971.

Trimble, William F. "Admiral Hilary P. Jones and the 1927 Geneva Naval Conference." *Military Affairs*, 63 (February 1979).

Trow, Clifford W. "Woodrow Wilson and the Mexican Interventionist Movement of 1919." *Journal of American History*, 58 (June 1971).

Tulchin, Joseph S. *The Aftermath of War: World War I and U.S. Policy toward Latin America*. 1971.

Valaik, J. David. "American Catholics and the Second Spanish Republic, 1911–1936." *Journal of Church and State,* 10 (Winter 1968).

Van Meter, Robert H., Jr. "The Washington Conference of 1921–1922: A New Look." *Pacific Historical Review,* 46 (November 1977).

Vinson, J. Chal. "The Imperial Conference of 1921 and the Anglo-Japanese Alliance." *Pacific Historical Review,* 33 (August 1962).

Walworth, Arthur. *America's Movement: 1918. American Diplomacy at the End of World War I.* 1977.

Wank, Solomon, ed. *Doves and Diplomats: Foreign Offices and Peace Movements in Europe and America in the Twentieth Century.* 1978.

Ward, Robert D. "Against the Tide: The Preparedness Movement of 1923–1924." *Military Affairs,* 38 (April 1974).

Weissman, Benjamin M. *Herbert Hoover and Famine Relief to Soviet Russia, 1921–1923.* 1974.

Weston, Rubin Francis. *Racism in U.S. Imperialism: The Influence of Racial Assumptions on American Foreign Policy, 1893–1946.* 1972.

Wheeler, Gerald E. "Isolated Japan: Anglo-American Diplomatic Co-operation, 1927–1936." *Pacific Historical Review,* (May 1961).

———. "Republican Philippine Policy, 1921–1933." *Pacific Historical Review,* 4 (November 1959).

Williams, William A. "American Intervention in Russia, 1917–1920." *Studies on the Left,* 3 (Fall 1963).

———. "American Intervention in Russia, 1917–1920." Part II. *Studies on the Left,* 3 (Winter 1964).

Wimer, Kurt, and Sarah Wimer. "The Harding Administration, the League of Nations, and the Separate Peace Treaty." *Review of Politics,* 29 (January 1967).

Winkler, Fred H. "The War Department and Disarmament, 1926–1935." *The Historian,* 28 (May 1966).

Winterrle, John. "John Dewey and the League of Nations." *North Dakota Quarterly,* 34 (Summer 1966).

Wood, Bryce. *The Making of the Good Neighbor Policy.* 1961.

Zivojinovic, Dragan R. *America, Italy, and the Birth of Yugoslavia.* 1973.

GENERAL

Aldridge, John W. "Afterthoughts on the 20's." *Commentary,* 56 (September 1973).

Braeman, John, Robert H. Bremner, and David Brody, eds. *Change and Continuity in Twentieth-Century America: The 1920s.* 1968.

Carter, Paul A. *Another Part of the Twenties.* 1977.

———. *The Twenties in America.* 1968.

Daniels, Jonathan. *The Time between the Wars: Armistice to Pearl Harbor.* 1966.

Diamond, Sander A. "The Years of Waiting: National Socialism in the United States, 1922–1933." *American Jewish Historical Quarterly,* 59 (March 1970).

Hawley, Ellis W. *The Great War and the Search for a Modern Order: A History of the American People and Their Institutions, 1917–1933.* 1979.

Hicks, John D. *Republican Ascendancy, 1921–1933.* 1960.

Kindleberger, Charles P. *The World in Depression, 1929–1939.* 1973.

Noggle, Burl. *Into the Twenties: The United States from Armistice to Normalcy.* 1974.

————. "The Twenties: A New Historiographical Frontier." *The Journal of American History*, 53 (September 1966).

Stevenson, Elizabeth. *Babbitts and Bohemians: The American 1920s*. 1967.

IMMIGRATION

Ansheles, Walter, and Jill Louise Ansheles. "The Role of the Caribbean Immigrant in the Harlem Renaissance." *Afro-Americans in New York Life and History*, 1 (January 1977).

Carrott, M. Browning. "Prejudice Goes to Court: The Japanese and the Supreme Court in the 1920s." *California History*, 62 (Summer 1983).

Christiansen, John B. "The Split Labor Market Theory and Filipino Exclusion, 1927–1934." *Phylon*, 40 (March 1979).

Cuddy, Edward. "The Irish Question and the Revival of Anti-Catholicism in the 1920's." *Catholic Historical Review*, 67 (April 1981).

Folsom, Burton W., Jr. "Immigrant Voters and the Nonpartisan League in Nebraska, 1917–1920." *Great Plains Quarterly*, 1 (Summer 1981).

Hellwig, David J. "Black Leaders and United States Immigration Policy, 1917–1929." *Journal of Negro History*, 66 (Summer 1981).

Ichioka, Yuji. "The Early Japanese Immigrant Quest for Citizenship: The Background of the 1922 Ozawa Case." *Amerasia Journal*, 4, 2 (1977).

————. "Japanese Immigrant Response to the 1920 California Alien Land Law." *Agricultural History*, 58 (April 1984).

Joselit, Jenna Weissman. *Our Gang: Jewish Crime and the New York Jewish Community, 1900–1940*. 1983.

Klayman, Richard. *The First Jew: Prejudice and Politics in an American Community, 1900–1932*. 1985.

Ludmerer, Kenneth M. "Genetics, Eugenics, and the Immigration Restriction Act of 1924." *Bulletin of the History of Medicine*, 45 (November–December 1971).

Matthews, Fred H. "White Community and 'Yellow Peril'." *Mississippi Valley Historical Review*, 50 (March 1964), 612–33.

O'Grady, Joseph P., ed. *The Immigrants' Influence on Wilson's Peace Policies*. 1967.

Raat, W. Dirk. *Revoltosos: Mexico's Rebels in the United States, 1903–1923*. 1981.

Reisler, Mark. "Always the Laborer, Never the Citizen: Anglo Perceptions of the Mexican Immigrant during the 1920s." *Pacific Historical Review*, 45 (May 1976).

————. *By the Sweat of Their Brow: Mexican Immigrant Labor in the United States, 1900–1940*. 1976.

Rosales, Francisco Arturo, and Daniel T. Simon. "The Mexican Immigrant Experience in the Urban Midwest: East Chicago, Indiana, 1919–1945." *Indiana Magazine of History*, 77 (December 1981).

Sullivan, Margaret. "Fighting for Irish Freedom: St. Louis Irish-Americans." *Missouri Historical Review*, 65 (January 1971).

Urganski, Adam. "Immigration Restriction and the Polish American Press: The Response of Wiadomosci Codzienne, 1921–1924." *Polish American Studies*, 28 (Autumn 1971).

Wang, Peter H. "The Immigration Act of 1924 and the Problem of Assimilation." *Journal of Ethnic Studies*, 2 (Fall 1974).

LABOR

Baskin, Alex. "The Ford Hunger March—1932." *Labor History*, 13 (Summer 1972).

Bayard, Charles J. "The 1927–1928 Colorado Coal Strike." *Pacific Historical Review*, 34 (August 1963).

Bernstein, Irving. *The Lean Years: A History of the American Worker, 1920–1933*. 1960.

Best, Gary Dean. "President Wilson's Second Industrial Conference, 1919–1920." *Labor History*, 16 (Fall 1975).

Brody, David. *Steelworkers in America: The Nonunion Era*. 1960.

Bubka, Tony. "The Harlan County [Kentucky] Coal Strike of 1921." *Labor History*, 11 (Winter 1970).

Cary, Lorin Lee. "The Reorganized United Mine Workers of America, 1930–1931." *Journal of the Illinois State Historical Society*, 66 (Autumn 1973).

Dubofsky, Melvyn. *We Shall Be All: A History of the Industrial Workers of the World*. 1969.

Fox, Bonnie R. "Unemployment Relief in Philadelphia, 1930–1932: A Study of the Depression's Impact on Voluntarism." *Pennsylvania Magazine of History and Biography*, 93 (January 1969).

Freidheim, Robert L. "Prologue to a General Strike: The Seattle Shipyard Strike of 1919." *Labor History*, 6 (Spring 1965).

———. *The Seattle General Strike*. 1964.

———. "The Seattle General Strike of 1919." *Pacific Northwest Quarterly*, 52 (July 1961).

Freidheim, Robert L., and Robin Freidheim. "The Seattle Labor Movement, 1919–1920." *Pacific Northwest Quarterly*, 55 (October 1964).

Gieske, Millard L. *Minnesota Farmer-Laborism: The Third-Party Alternative*. 1979.

Grubbs, Frank L., Jr. "Council and Alliance Labor Propaganda, 1917–1919." *Labor History*, 7 (Spring 1966).

———. *The Struggle for Labor Loyalty: Gompers, the A.F.L., and the Pacifists, 1917–1920*. 1968.

Harris, William H. *Keeping the Faith: A. Philip Randolph, Milton P. Webster, and the Brotherhood of Sleeping Car Porters, 1925–1937*. 1977.

Hurvitz, Haggai. "Ideology and Industrial Conflict, President Wilson's First Industrial Conference of October, 1919." *Labor History*, 18 (Fall 1977).

Kanarek, Harold K. "Disaster for Hard Coal: The Anthracite Strike of 1925–1926." *Labor History*, 15 (Fall 1973).

———. "The Pennsylvania Anthracite Strike of 1922." *Pennsylvania Magazine of History and Biography*, 99 (April 1975).

Keeran, Roger R. "Communist Influence in the Automobile Industry, 1920–1933: Paving the Way for an Industrial Union." *Labor History*, 20 (Spring 1979).

Kerr, K. Austin. *American Railroad Politics, 1914–1920: Rates, Wages, and Efficiency*. 1968.

Long, Durward. "The Open-Closed Shop Battle in Tampa's Cigar Industry, 1919–1921." *Florida Historical Quarterly*, 47 (October 1968).

Montgomery, David. "Immigrants, Industrial Unions, and Social Reconstruction in the United States, 1916–1923." *Labour*, 13 (Spring 1984).

———. "The 'New Unionism' and the Transformation of Workers' Consciousness in America, 1909–22." *Journal of Social History*, 7 (Summer 1974).

Murphy, Paul L., Kermit Hall, and David Klaassen. *The Passaic Textile Strike of 1926.* 1974.

Nelson, Daniel. *Unemployment Insurance: The American Experience, 1915–1935.* 1969.

———. " 'While Waiting for the Government': The Needle Trades Unemployment Insurance Plans, 1919–28." *Labor History,* 11 (Fall 1970).

Nyden, Linda. "Black Miners in Western Pennsylvania, 1925–1931: The National Miners Union and the United Mine Workers of America." *Science & Society,* 41 (Spring 1977).

Peterson, Joyce Shaw. "Auto Workers and Their Work, 1900–1933." *Labor History,* 22 (Spring 1981).

———. "Black Automobile Workers in Detroit, 1910–1930." *Journal of Negro History,* 44 (Spring 1979).

Powell, Allan Kent. "Utah and the Nationwide Coal Miners' Strike of 1922." *Utah Historical Quarterly,* 45 (Spring 1977).

Rosenzweig, Roy. "Organizing the Unemployed: The Early Years of the Great Depression, 1929–1933." *Radical America,* 10 (July–August 1976).

Schacht, John N. *The Making of Telephone Unionism, 1920–1947.* 1985.

Scheuerman, William E. "Canton and the Great Steel Strike of 1919: A Marriage of Nativism and Politics." *Ohio History,* 93 (Spring 1984).

Smith, Michael M. "Beyond the Borderlands: Mexican Labor in the Central Plains, 1900–1930." *Great Plains Quarterly,* 1 (Fall 1981).

Starobin, Robert S. *Industrial Slavery in the Old South.* 1970.

Straw, Richard A. "An Act of Faith: Southeastern Ohio Miners in the Coal Strike of 1927." *Labor History,* 21 (Spring 1980).

———. "The United Mine Workers of America and the 1920 Coal Strike in Alabama." *Alabama Review,* 28 (April 1975).

Stricker, Frank. "Affluence for Whom?—Another Look at Prosperity and the Working Classes in the 1920s." *Labor History,* 24 (Winter, 1983).

Trattner, Walter I. *Crusade for the Children: A History of the National Child Labor Committee and Child Labor Reform in America.* 1970.

Tripp, Joseph F. "Toward an Efficient and Moral Society: Washington State Minimum-Wage Law, 1913–1925." *Pacific Northwest Quarterly,* 67 (July 1976).

Urofsky, Melvin I. *Big Steel and the Wilson Administration.* 1969.

Wakstein, Allen M. "The National Association of Manufacturers and Labor Relations in the 1920s." *Labor History,* 10 (Spring 1969).

———. "The Origins of the Open-Shop Movement, 1919–1920." *Journal of American History,* 51 (December 1964).

Walker, Roger W. "The A.F.L. and Child-Labor Legislation: An Exercise in Frustration." *Labor History,* 11 (Summer 1970).

Wollenberg, Charles. "Huelga, 1928 Style: The Imperial Valley Cantaloupe Workers' Strike." *Pacific Historical Review,* 37 (November 1968).

Zahavi, Gerald. "Negotiated Loyalty: Welfare Capitalism and the Shoeworkers of Endicott Johnson, 1920–1940." *Journal of American History,* 70 (December 1983).

Zerzan, John. "Understanding the Anti-Radicalism of the National Civic Federation." *International Review of Social History,* 19, part 2 (1974).

Zieger, Robert H. *American Workers, American Unions, 1920–1985.* 1986.

———. "From Hostility to Moderation: Railroad Labor Policy in the 1920s." *Labor History,* 9 (Winter 1968).

————. "Herbert Hoover, the Wage-Earner, and the 'New Economic System,' 1919–1929." *Business History Review*, 51 (Summer 1977).

————. "Pennsylvania Coal and Politics: The Anthracite Strike of 1925–1926." *Pennsylvania Magazine of History and Biography*, 93 (April 1969).

————. "Pinchot and Coolidge: The Politics of the 1923 Anthracite Crisis." *The Journal of American History*, 52 (December 1965), 566–81.

————. *Republicans and Labor: 1919–1929.* 1969.

"Senator George Wharton Pepper and Labor Issues in the 1920s." *Labor History*, 9 (Spring 1968).

MINORITIES

Abernathy, Lloyd M. "The Washington Race War of July, 1919." *Maryland Historical Magazine*, 58 (December 1963).

Allswang, John M. "The Chicago Negro Voter and the Democratic Consensus: A Case Study, 1918–1936." *Journal of the Illinois State Historical Society*, 60 (Summer 1967).

Bodnar, John, Michael Weber, and Roger Simon. "Migration, Kinship, and Urban Adjustment: Blacks and Poles in Pittsburgh, 1900–1930." *Journal of American History*, 66 (December 1979).

Buni, Andrew. *Robert L. Vann of the Pittsburgh Courier: Politics and Black Journalism.* 1974.

Carlson, Leonard. "Federal Policy and Indian Land: Economic Interests and the Sale of Indian Allotments, 1900–1934." *Agricultural History*, 57 (January 1983).

Critchlow, Donald T. "Lewis Meriam, Expertise, and Indian Reform." *Historian*, 43 (May 1981).

Dickerson, Dennis C. "Black Ecumenism: Efforts to Establish a United Methodist Episcopal Church, 1918–1932." *Church History*, 52 (December 1983).

Eisenberg, Bernard. "Only for the Bourgeois? James Weldon Johnson and the NAACP, 1916–1930." *Phylon*, 43 (June 1982).

Ellis, Richard N., ed. " 'The Apache Chronicle.' " *New Mexico Historical Review*, 47 (July 1972).

Frizzell, George E. "The Politics of Cherokee Citizenship, 1898–1930." *North Carolina Historical Review*, 61 (April 1984).

Giffin, William. "Black Insurgency in the Republican Party of Ohio, 1920–1932." *Ohio History*, 82 (Winter–Spring 1973).

Gonzalez, Gilbert G. "Racism, Education, and the Mexican Community in Los Angeles, 1920–30." *Societas—A Review of Social History*, 4 (Autumn 1974).

Hellwig, David J. "Afro-American Reactions to the Japanese and the Anti-Japanese Movement, 1906–1924." *Phylon*, 38 (March 1977).

Henri, Florette. *Black Migration: Movement North, 1900–1920.* 1975.

Hertzberg, Hazel W. *The Search for an American Indian Identity: Modern Pan-Indian Movements.* 1971.

Hill, Robert A. "The Foremost Radical among His Race: Marcus Garvey and the Black Scare, 1918–1921." *Prologue*, 16 (Winter 1984).

Hine, Darlene Clark. "The NAACP and the Supreme Court: Walter F. White and the Defeat of Judge John J. Parker, 1930." *Negro History Bulletin*, 40 (September–October 1977).

Hoffman, Abraham. *Unwanted Mexican Americans in the Great Depression: Repatriation Pressures, 1929–1939.* 1974.

Huggins, Nathan Irvin. *Harlem Renaissance.* 1971.

Katznelson, Ira. *Black Men, White Cities: Race, Politics, and Migration in the United States, 1900–30, and Britain, 1948–68.* 1973.

Kelly, Lawrence C. *The Navajo Indians and Federal Indian Policy, 1900–1935.* 1968.

Kornweibel, Theodore, Jr. "An Economic Profile of Black Life in the Twenties." *Journal of Black Studies,* 6 (June 1976).

Larner, John. "Braddock's Congressman M. Clyde Kelly and Indian Policy Reform, 1919–1928." *Western Pennsylvania Historical Magazine,* 66 (April 1983).

Leab, Daniel J. " 'All-Colored'—But Not Much Different: Films Made for Negro Ghetto Audiences 1913–1928." *Phylon,* 36 (September 1975).

Lewis, David Levering. "The Politics of Art: The New Negro, 1920–1935." *Prospects,* 3 (1977).

McMarthy, G. Michael. "Smith vs. Hoover—The Politics of Race in West Tennessee." *Phylon,* 39 (June 1978).

Martin, Charles H. "Negro Leaders, the Republican Party, and the Election of 1932." *Phylon,* 32 (Spring 1971).

Martin, Tony. *Race First: The Ideological and Organizational Struggles of Marcus Garvey and the Universal Negro Improvement Association.* 1976.

Miller, Frederic. "The Black Migration to Philadelphia: A 1924 Profile." *Pennsylvania Magazine of History and Biography,* 108 (July 1984).

Murray, Hugh T., Jr. "Aspects of the Scottsboro Campaign." *Science and Society,* 35 (Summer 1971).

Nelli, Humbert S. *The Business of Crime: Italians and Syndicate Crime in the United States.* 1976.

Osofsky, Gilbert. "Symbols of the Jazz Age: The New Negro and Harlem Discovered." *American Quarterly,* 17 (Summer 1965).

Parker, Russell D. "The Black Community in a Company Town: Alcoa, Tennessee, 1919–1939." *Tennessee Historical Quarterly,* 37 (Summer 1978).

Parris, Guichard, and Lester Brooks. *Blacks in the City: A History of the National Urban League.* 1971.

Philp, Kenneth R. "Albert B. Fall and the Protest from the Pueblos 1921–1923." *Arizona and the West,* 12 (Autumn 1970).

———. *John Collier's Crusade for Indian Reform, 1920–1954.* 1977.

Reisler, Mark. "Mexican Unionization in California Agriculture, 1927–1936." *Labor History,* 14 (Fall 1973).

Rippley, La Vern J. "Conflict in the Classroom: AntiGermanism in Minnesota Schools, 1917–19." *Minnesota History,* 47 (Spring 1981).

Robbins, William G. "Herbert Hoover's Indian Reformers under Attack: The Failures of Administrative Reform." *Mid-America,* 63 (October 1981).

Roos, Philip D., Dowell H. Smith, Stephen Langley, and James McDonald. "The Impact of the American Indian Movement on the Pine Ridge Indian Reservation." *Phylon,* 41 (March 1980).

Ross, B. Joyce. *J. E. Spingarn and the Rise of the NAACP, 1911–1939.* 1972.

Schaefer, Richard T. "The Ku Klux Klan: Continuity and Change." *Phylon,* 32 (Spring 1971).

Scheiner, Seth M. *Negro Mecca: A History of the Negro in New York City, 1865–1920.* 1965.

Sherman, Richard B. "Johnstown v. the Negro: Southern Migrants and the Exodus of 1923." *Pennsylvania History,* 30 (October 1963).

Singleton, Gregory Holmes. "Birth, Rebirth, and the 'New Negro' of the 1920s." *Phylon* 43 (March 1982).

Sochen, June. *The Unbridgeable Gap: Blacks and Their Quest for the American Dream, 1900–1930.* 1972.

Szasz, Margaret. *Education and the American Indian: The Road to Self-Determination, 1928–1973.* 1974.

Tucker, David M. "Black Pride and Negro Business in the 1920's: George Washington Lee of Memphis." *Business History Review,* 43 (Winter 1969).

Tuttle, William M., Jr. *Race Riot: Chicago in the Red Summer of 1919.* 1970.

———. "Views of a Negro During 'The Red Summer' of 1919." *Journal of Negro History,* 51 (July 1966).

Vincent, Theodore G. *Black Power and the Garvey Movement.* 1971.

Watkins, Ralph. "The Marcus Garvey Movement in Buffalo, New York." *Afro-Americans in New York Life and History,* 1 (January 1977).

Williams, Henry. *Black Response to the American Left: 1917–1929.* 1973.

Williams, Lillian. "Afro-Americans in Buffalo, 1900–1930: A Study in Community Formation." *Afro-Americans in New York Life and History,* 8 (July 1984).

Wolters, Raymond. *Negroes and the Great Depression: The Problem of Economic Recovery.* 1970.

———. *The New Negro on Campus: Black College Rebellions of the 1920s.* 1975.

POLITICS

Best, Gary Dean. *The Politics of American Individualism: Herbert Hoover in Transition, 1918–1921.* 1975.

Bicha, Karel Denis. "Liberalism Frustrated: The League for Independent Political Action, 1928–1933." *Mid-America,* 48 (January 1966).

Burner, David. *The Politics of Provincialism: The Democratic Party in Transition, 1918–1932.* 1968.

Cravens, Hamilton. "The Emergence of the Farmer-Labor Party in Washington Politics, 1919–20." *Pacific Northwest Quarterly,* 57 (October 1966).

Daniels, Pete. *Deep'n As It Come: The 1927 Mississippi River Flood.* 1977.

Daniels, Roger. *The Bonus March: An Episode of the Great Depression.* 1971.

Elenbas, Jack D. "The Boss of the Better Class: Henry Leland and the Detroit Citizens League, 1912–1924." *Michigan History,* 58 (Summer 1974).

Fausold, Martin L. *The Presidency of Herbert C. Hoover.* 1985.

Fragnoli, Raymond R. *The Transformation of Reform: Progressivism in Detroit—And After, 1912–1933.* 1982.

Fry, Joseph A. "Senior Adviser to the Democratic 'Organization': William Thomas Reed and Virginia Politics, 1925–1935." *Virginia Magazine of History and Biography,* 85 (October 1977).

Grant, Philip A., Jr. "Congressional Leaders from the Great Plains, 1921–1932." *North Dakota History,* 46 (Winter 1979).

Hamilton, David E. "Herbert Hoover and the Great Drought of 1930." *Journal of American History,* 68 (March 1982).

Hendrickson, Kenneth E., Jr. "The Pro-War Socialists, the Social Democratic League and the Ill-Fated Drive for Industrial Democracy in America, 1917–1920." *Labor History,* 11 (Summer 1970).

Holsinger, M. Paul. "The Appointment of Supreme Court Justice Van Devanter: A Study of Political Preferment." *American Journal of Legal History,* 12 (October 1968).

Hundley, Norris, Jr. *Water and the West: The Colorado River Compact and the Politics of Water in the American West.* 1975.

Huthmacher, J. Joseph. *Massachusetts People and Politics, 1919–1933.* 1959.

Israel, Fred. "The Fulfillment of Bryan's Dream: Key Pittman and Silver Politics, 1918–1933." *Pacific Historical Review,* 32 (November 1961).

Johnson, Donald. *The Challenge to American Freedoms: World War I and the Rise of the American Civil Liberties Union.* 1963.

Johnson, Walter. *1600 Pennsylvania Avenue: Presidents and the People, 1929–1959.* 1960.

Kerr, K. Austin. "Organizing for Reform: The Anti-Saloon League and Innovation in Politics." *American Quarterly,* 32 (Spring 1980).

Lambert, Roger. "Hoover and the Red Cross in the Arkansas Drought of 1930." *Arkansas Historical Quarterly,* 29 (Spring 1970).

Lee, David D. *Tennessee in Turmoil: Politics in the Volunteer States, 1920–1932.* 1979.

Lisio, Donald. *The President and Protest: Hoover, Conspiracy, and the Bonus Riot.* 1974.

Lohof, Bruce. "Herbert Hoover, Spokesman of Humane Efficiency: The Mississippi Flood of 1927." *American Quarterly,* 22 (Fall 1970).

Margulies, Herbert F. "The Collaboration of Herbert Hoover and Irvine Lenroot, 1921–1928." *North Dakota Quarterly,* 45 (Summer 1977).

Minot, Rodney G. *Peerless Patriots: Organized Veterans and the Spirit of Americanism.* 1962.

Moeller, Beverly Bowen. *Phil Swing and Boulder Dam.* 1971.

Murray, Lawrence L. "The Mellons, Their Money, and the Mythical Machine: Organizational Politics in the Republican Twenties." *Pennsylvania History,* 42 (July 1975).

Murray, Robert K. *The Harding Era: Warren G. Harding and His Administration.* 1969.

Neal, Donn C. *The World beyond the Hudson: Alfred E. Smith and National Politics, 1918–1928.* 1983.

Noggle, Burl. *Teapot Dome: Oil and Politics in the 1920s.* 1962.

Olson, James S. "The Philosophy of Herbert Hoover: A Contemporary Perspective." *Annals of Iowa,* 43 (Winter 1976).

Preston, William, Jr. *Aliens and Dissenters: Federal Suppression of Radicals, 1903–1933.* 1963.

Puryear, Elmer L. *Democratic Party Dissension in North Carolina, 1928–1936.* 1962.

Romasco, Albert. *The Poverty of Abundance: Hoover, the Nation, and the Depression.* 1965.

Rosen, Elliot A. *Hoover, Roosevelt, and the Brains Trust: From Depression to New Deal.* 1977.

Schwarz, Jordan A. *The Interregnum of Despair: Hoover, Congress, and the Depression.* 1970.

Shapiro, Stanley. " 'Hand and Brain': The Farmer-Labor Party of 1920." *Labor History*, 26 (Summer 1985).

Sinclair, Barbara D. "Party Realignment and the Transformation of the Political Agenda: The House of Representatives, 1925–1938." *American Political Science Review*, 71 (September 1977).

Smith, Daniel M. "Robert Lansing and the Wilson Interregnum." *Historian*, 21 (February 1959).

Stratton, David H. "The Shadow of Blooming Grove." *Pacific Northwest Quarterly*, 61 (January 1970).

Warren, Harris Gaylord. *Herbert Hoover and the Great Depression*. 1959.

Watson, Richard L., Jr. "The Defeat of Judge Parker: A Study in Pressure Groups and Politics." *The Mississippi Valley Historical Review*, 50 (September 1963).

Weaver, John C. "Lawyers, Lodges, and Kinfolk: The Workings of a South Carolina Political Organization, 1920–1936." *South Carolina Historical Magazine*, 78 (October 1977).

Werner, M. R., and John Starr. *Teapot Dome*. 1959.

Williams, David. "The Bureau of Investigation and Its Critics, 1919–1921: The Origins of Federal Political Surveillance." *Journal of American History*, 68 (December 1981).

————. " 'They Never Stopped Watching Us': FBI Political Surveillance, 1924–1936." *UCLA Historical Journal*, 2 (1981).

Wimer, Kurt. "Woodrow Wilson's Plan for a Vote of Confidence." *Pennsylvania History*, 28 (July 1961).

POPULAR CULTURE

Barnouw, Erik. *The Golden Web: A History of Broadcasting in the United States. Vol. II: 1933 to 1953*. 1968.

Brazil, John R. "Murder Trials, Murder, and Twenties America." *American Quarterly*, 33 (Summer 1981).

Cravens, Hamilton. *The Triumph of Evolution: American Scientists and the Heredity-Environment Controversy, 1900–1941*. 1978.

Davidson, Abraham A. *Early American Modernist Painting, 1910–1935*. 1981.

Flink, James J. *The Car Culture*. 1975.

Hausdorff, Don. "Magazine Humor and Popular Monthly, 1929–1934." *Journalism Quarterly*, (Summer 1964).

Hearn, Charles R. *The American Dream in the Great Depression*. 1977.

Higham, Charles. *Warner Brothers*. 1975.

Kendall, Elizabeth. *Where She Danced*. 1979.

Kihlstedt, Folke T. "The Automobile and the Transformation of the American House, 1910–1935." *Michigan Quarterly Review*, 19–20 (Fall 1980–Winter 1981).

Koppes, Clayton R. "The Social Destiny of the Radio: Hope and Disillusionment in the 1920's." *South Atlantic Quarterly*, 68 (Summer 1969).

Krug, Edward A. *The Shaping of the American High School. Vol. 2: 1920–1941*. 1972.

Leonard, Neil. *Jazz and the White Americans: The Acceptance of a New Art Form*. 1962.

Lesy, Michael. "Dark Carnival: The Death and Transfiguration of Floyd Collins." *American Heritage*, 27 (October 1976).

Ludmerer, Kenneth M. "American Geneticists and the Eugenics Movement: 1905–1935." *Journal of the History of Biology*, 2 (Fall 1969).

Pursell, Carroll. *The American Ideology of National Science, 1919–1930*. 1971.

Rae, John B. *The Road and the Car in American Life*. 1971.

Rosen, Philip T. *The Modern Censors: Radio Broadcasters and the Federal Government, 1920–1934*. 1980.

Ruyter, Nancy Lee Chalfa. *Reformers and Visionaries: The Americanization of the Art of Dance*. 1979.

Seymour, Harold. *Baseball: The Golden Age*. 1971.

Shankman, Arnold. "Black Pride and Protest: The Amos 'n' Andy Crusade of 1931." *Journal of Popular Culture*, 12 (Fall 1979).

Siegel, Marcia B. *The Shapes of Change: Images of American Dance*. 1979.

Smith, Dean. "The Black Sox Scandal." *American History Illustrated*, 11 (January 1977).

Soderbergh, Peter A. "Aux Armes!: The Rise of the Hollywood War Film, 1916–1930." *South Atlantic Quarterly*, 65 (Autumn 1966).

Stanley, Douglas. "The Social Impact of the Radio." *Historical Journal of Western Massachusetts*, 1 (Fall 1972).

Tobey, Ronald C. *The American Ideology of National Science, 1919–1930*. 1971.

Wik, Reynold M. "The Radio in Rural America during the 1920's." *Agricultural History*, 55 (October 1981).

———. "Radio in the 1920s: A Social Force in South Dakota." *South Dakota History*, 11 (Spring 1981).

PROGRESSIVISM

Buenker, John D. "The Progressive Era: A Search for a Synthesis." *Mid-America*, 51 (July 1969).

———. *Urban Liberalism and Progressive Reform*. 1973.

Chambers, Clarke A. *Seedtime of Reform. American Social Service and Social Action, 1918–1933*. 1963.

Flannagan, John H., Jr. "The Disillusionment of a Progressive: U.S. Senator David I. Walsh and the League of Nations Issue, 1919–1941." *New England Quarterly*, 41 (December 1968).

Forcey, Charles. *The Crossroads of Liberalism: Croly, Weyl, Lippmann, and the Progressive Era, 1900–1925*. 1961.

Glad, Paul W. "Progressives and the Business Culture of the 1920s." *Journal of American History*, 53 (June 1966).

Graham, Otis L., Jr. *The Great Campaigns: Reform and War in America, 1900–1928*. 1971.

Greenbaum, Fred. *Fighting Progressive: A Biography of Edward P. Costigan*. 1971.

Havig, Alan R. "A Disputed Legacy: Roosevelt Progressives and the LaFollette Campaign of 1924." *Mid-America*, 52 (October 1970).

Lemons, J. Stanley. "The Sheppard-Towner Act: Progressivism in the 1920s." *Journal of American History*, 55 (March 1969).

Link, Arthur S. "What Ever Happened to the Progressive Movement in the 1920s?" *American Historical Review*, 64 (July 1959).

Madison, Charles A. *Leaders and Liberals in 20th Century America*. 1961.

Marguiles, Herbert. "Recent Opinion on the Decline of the Progressive Movement." *Mid-America,* 45 (October 1963).

Olssen, Erik. "The Progressive Group in Congress, 1922–1929." *Historian,* 42 (February 1980).

Putnam, Jackson K. "The Persistence of Progressivism in the 1920s: The Case of California." *Pacific Historical Review,* 35 (November 1966).

Robertson, James O. "Progressives Elect Will H. Hays Republican National Chairman, 1918." *Indiana Magazine of History,* 64 (September 1968).

Shover, John L. "The California Progressives and the 1924 Campaign." *California Historical Quarterly,* 50 (December 1971).

Winters, Donald L. "The Persistence of Progressivism: Henry Cantwell Wallace and the Movement for Agricultural Economics." *Agricultural History,* 41 (April 1967).

PROHIBITION

Bader, Robert. *Prohibition in Kansas. A History.* 1986.

Burnham, J. C. "New Perspectives on the Prohibition 'Experiment' of the 1920's." *Journal of Social History,* 2 (Fall 1968).

Clark, Norman H. *Deliver Us from Evil: An Interpretation of American Prohibition.* 1976.

———. *The Dry Years: Prohibition and Social Change in Washington.* 1965.

Franklin, Jimmie L. "That Noble Experiment: Prohibition in Oklahoma." *Chronicles of Oklahoma,* 43 (Spring 1965).

Jackson, Joy J. "Prohibition in New Orleans: The Unlikeliest Crusade." *Louisiana History,* 19 (Summer 1978).

Jones, Bartlett C. "Nullification and Prohibition, 1920–1933." *Southwestern Social Science Quarterly,* 12 (March 1964).

———. "Prohibition and Prosperity, 1920–1930." *Social Science,* 50 (Spring 1975).

Kerr, K. Austin. *Organized for Prohibition: A New History of the Anti-Saloon League.* 1985.

Mennell, S. J. "Prohibition: A Sociological View." *Journal of American Studies,* 3 (December 1969).

Timberlake, James H. *Prohibition and the Progressive Movement, 1900–1920.* 1963.

RADICALISM

Asher, Robert. "Radicalism and Reform: State Insurance of Workmen's Compensation in Minnesota, 1910–1933." *Labor History,* 13 (Fall 1972).

Burbank, Garin. "Agrarian Radicals and Their Opponents: Political Conflict in Southern Oklahoma, 1910–1924." *Journal of American History,* 58 (June 1971).

———. *When Farmers Voted Red: The Gospel of Socialism in the Oklahoma Countryside, 1910–1924.* 1976.

Candeloro, Dominic. "Louis F. Post and the Red Scare of 1920." *Prologue,* 11 (Spring 1979).

Colburn, David R. "Govenor Alfred E. Smith and the Red Scare, 1919–20." *Political Science Quarterly,* 88 (September 1973).

Conlin, Joseph R. *Big Bill Haywood and the Radical Union Movement.* 1969.

Cook, Philip I. "Red Scare in Denver." *Colorado Magazine,* 43 (Fall 1966).

DeWitt, Howard A. *Images of Ethnic and Radical Violence in California Politics, 1917–1930.* 1975.

Felix, David. *Protest: Sacco-Vanzetti and the Intellectuals.* 1965.

Flynt, Wayne. "Florida Labor and Political 'Radicalism,' 1919–1920." *Labor History,* 9 (Winter 1968).

Gilbert, James Burkhart. *Writers and Partisans: A History of Literary Radicalism in America.* 1968.

Green, James R. *Grass-Roots Socialism: Radical Movements in the Southwest, 1895–1943.* 1978.

Jaffe, Julian F. *Crusade against Radicalism: New York during the Red Scare, 1914–1924.* 1972.

Josephson, Harold. "The Dynamics of Repression: New York during the Red Scare." *Mid-America,* 59 (October 1977).

Lisio, Donald J. *The President and Protest: Hoover, Conspiracy, and the Bonus Riot.* 1974.

Lovin, Hugh T. "Idaho and the 'Reds,' 1919–1926." *Pacific Northwest Quarterly,* 69 (July 1978).

Myers, Constance Ashton. *The Prophet's Army: Trotskyists in America, 1928–1941.* 1977.

Nelson, John K. *The Peace Prophets: American Pacifist Thought, 1918–1941.* 1967.

Pells, Richard H. *Radical Visions and American Dreams: Culture and Social Thought in the Depression Years.* 1973.

Pernicone, Nunzio. "Carlo Tresca and the Sacco-Vanzetti Case." *Journal of American History,* 66 (December 1979).

Russell, Francis. "How I Changed My Mind about the Sacco-Vanzetti Case." *Antioch Review,* (Winter 1965–1966).

Shafer, Ralph E. "Communism in California, 1919–1924: 'Orders from Moscow' or Independent Western Radicalism?" *Science and Society,* 34 (Winter 1970).

Szajkowski, Zosa. *Jews, Wars, and Communism. Vol. II: The Impact of the 1919–20 Red Scare on American Jewish Life.* 1974.

Tyler, Robert L. *Rebels of the Woods: The I.W.W. in the Pacific Northwest.* 1967.

Weinstein, James. *The Decline of Socialism in America, 1912–1925.* 1967.

———. "Radicalism in the Midst of Normalcy." *The Journal of American History,* 52 (March 1966).

RELIGION

Abell, Aaron I. *American Catholicism and Social Action: A Search for Social Justice, 1865–1950.* 1960.

Berenbaum, May. " 'The Greatest Show That Ever Came to Town'—An Account of the Billy Sunday Crusade in Buffalo, New York, January 27–March 25, 1917." *Niagara Frontier,* 22 (Autumn 1975).

Birnschein, Alan. "The Nature and Function of the Board of Directors of the Lutheran Church—Missouri Synod from 1917 to 1935." *Concordia Historical Insititute Quarterly,* 43 (August 1970).

Brod, Donald F. "The Scopes Trial: A Look at Press Coverage after Forty Years." *Journalism Quarterly,* (Spring 1965).

Brown, Thomas Elton. "Patriotism or Religion: Compulsory Education and Michigan's Roman Catholic Church, 1920–1924." *Michigan History,* 64 (July/August 1980).

Buczek, Daniel S. "Polish American Priests and the American Catholic Hierarchy: A View from the Twenties." *Polish American Studies,* 33 (Spring 1976).

Burkett, Randall K. *Garveyism As a Religious Movement: The Institutionalization of a Black Civil Religion.* 1978.

Chatfield, Charles. *For Peace and Justice: Pacifism in America, 1914–1941.* 1971.

Curry, Lerond. *Protestant-Catholic Relations in America: World War I through Vatican II.* 1972.

Davis, Mollie C. "American Religions and Religious Reaction to Mexico's Church-State Conflict, 1926–1927: Background to the Morrow Mission." *Journal of Church and State,* 13 (Winter 1971).

de Camp, L. Sprague. *The Great Monkey Trial.* 1968.

Engelmann, Larry D. "Billy Sunday: 'God, You've Got a Job on Your Hands in Detroit.' " *Michigan History,* 55 (Spring 1971).

Ernst, Eldon G. "The Interchurch World Movement and the Great Steel Strike of 1919–1920." *Church History,* 39 (June 1970).

Gatewood, Willard B. "Embattled Scholar: Howard W. Odum and the Fundamentalists, 1925–1927." *Journal of Southern History,* 34 (November 1965).

———. "The Evolution Controversy in North Carolina, 1920–1927." *Mississippi Quarterly,* 17 (Fall 1964).

———. "From Scopes to Creation Science: The Decline and Revival of the Evolution Controversy." *South Atlantic Quarterly,* 83 (Autumn 1984).

———. "North Carolina Methodism and the Fundamentalist Controversy, 1920–1927." *Wesleyan Quarterly Review,* 2 (May 1965).

———. *Preachers, Pedagogues, & Politicians: The Evolution Controversy in North Carolina, 1920–1927.* 1966.

Grabill, Joseph L. *Protestant Diplomacy and the Near East: Missionary Influence on American Policy, 1810–1927.* 1971.

Gray, Virginia. "Anti-Evolution Sentiment and Behavior: The Case of Arkansas." *Journal of American History,* 57 (September 1970).

Halsey, William M. *The Survival of American Innocence: Catholicism in an Era of Disillusionment, 1920–1940.* 1980.

Handy, Robert T. "The American Religious Depression, 1925–1935." *Church History,* 29 (March 1960).

Harvey, Charles E. "John D. Rockefeller, Jr., and the Interchurch World Movement of 1919–1920: A Different Angle on the Ecumenical Movement." *Church History,* 51 (June 1982).

Holsinger, M. Paul. "The Oregon School Bill Controversy, 1922–1925." *Pacific Historical Review,* 37 (August 1968).

Johnson, Gwen Mills. "Churches and Evangelism in Jackson, Mississippi, 1920–1929." *Journal of Mississippi History,* 34 (November 1972).

Johnson, Niel M. "The Missouri Synod Lutherans and the War against the German Language, 1917–1923." *Nebraska History,* 56 (Spring 1975).

Jorgenson, Lloyd P. "The Oregon School Law of 1922: Passage and Sequel." *Catholic Historical Review,* 56 (October 1968).

Lankford, John E. "The Impact of the New Era Movement on the Presbyterian Church in the United States of America, 1918–1925.'' *Journal of Presbyterian History*, 40 (December 1962).

———. ''The Impact of the Religious Depression upon Protestant Benevolence, 1925–1935.'' *Journal of Presbyterian History*, 42 (June 1964).

Ledbetter, Cal. ''The Antievolution Law: Church and State in Arkansas.'' *Arkansas Historical Quarterly*, 38 (Winter 1979).

Ledbetter, Patsy. ''Defense of the Faith: J. Frank Norris and Texas Fundamentalism, 1920–1929.'' *Arizona and the West*, 15 (Spring 1973).

Meyer, Donald B. *The Protestant Search for Political Realism, 1919–1941*. 1960.

Miller, Robert Moats. *American Protestantism and Social Issues, 1919–1939*. 1958.

Moorhead, James H. ''The Erosion of Postmillennialism in American Religious Thought, 1865–1925.'' *Church History*, 53 (March 1984).

Sappington, Roger E. *Brethren Social Policy, 1908–1958*. 1961.

Scopes, John T., and James Presley. *Center of the Storm: Memoirs of John T. Scopes*. 1967.

Smylie, James H. ''The Roman Catholic Church, the State, and Al Smith.'' *Church History*, 29 (September 1960).

Stange, Douglas C. ''Al Smith and the Republican Party at Prayer: The Lutheran Vote—1928.'' *Review of Politics*, 32 (July 1970).

———. ''Lutherans and Presidential Politics: The NLEA Statement of 1928.'' *Concordia Historical Institute Quarterly*, 41 (November 1968).

Street, T. Watson. ''The Evolution Controversy in the Southern Presbyterian Church with Attention to the Theological and Ecclesiastical Issues Raised.'' *Journal of the Presbyterian Historical Society*, 37 (December 1959).

Szasz, Ferenc M. ''The Scopes Trial in Perspective.'' *Tennessee Historical Quarterly*, 30 (Fall 1971).

———. ''William Jennings Bryan, Evolution, and the Fundamentalist-Modernist Controversy.'' *Nebraska History*, 56 (Summer 1975).

Thompson, James J. ''Southern Baptists and Anti-Catholicism in the 1920's.'' *Mississippi Quarterly*, 32 (Fall 1979).

———. ''Southern Baptists and the Antievolution Controversy of the 1920's.'' *Mississippi Quarterly*, 29 (Winter 1975–76).

———. ''Southern Baptists and Postwar Disillusioniment, 1918–1919.'' *Foundations*, 21 (April–June 1978).

Tomkins, Jerry R., ed. *D-Day at Dayton: Reflections on the Scopes Trial*. 1965.

Trani, Eugene. ''Woodrow Wilson, China, and the Missionaries, 1913–1921.'' *Journal of Presbyterian History*, 49 (Winter 1971).

Vinea, Robert. ''The American Catholic Reaction to the Persecution of the Church in Mexico from 1926–1936.'' *Records of the American Catholic Historical Society of Philadelphia*, 79 (March 1968).

SOCIAL CONFLICT

Abbey, Sue Wilson. ''The Ku Klux Klan in Arizona, 1921–1925.'' *Journal of Arizona History*, 14 (Spring 1973).

Akin, William E. *Technocracy and the American Dream: The Technocrat Movement, 1900–1941*. 1977.

Alexander, Charles C. "Defeat, Decline, Disintegration: The Ku Klux Klan in Arkansas, 1924 and After." *Arkansas Historical Quarterly*, 22 (Winter 1963).
———. "Kleagles and Cash: The Ku Klux Klan As a Business Organization, 1915–1930." *Business History Review*, 39 (Autumn 1965).
———. *The Ku Klux Klan in the Southwest.* 1965.
———. "Secrecy Bids for Power: The Ku Klux Klan in Texas Politics in the 1920s." *Mid-America*, 46 (January 1964).
———. "White Robes in Politics: The Ku Klux Klan in Arkansas, 1922–1924." *Arkansas Historical Quarterly*, 22 (Fall 1963).
Bayor, Ronald H. *Neighbors in Conflict: The Irish, Germans, Jews, and Italians of New York City, 1929–1941.* 1978.
Cantor, Louis. *A Prologue to the Protest Movement: The Missouri Sharecropper Roadside Demonstration of 1939.* 1969.
Carlson, Robert A. "Americanization as an Early Twentieth-Century Adult Education Movement." *History of Education Quarterly*, 10 (Winter 1970).
Chalmers, David. "The Ku Klux Klan in the Sunshine State: The 1920's." *Florida Historical Quarterly*, 43 (January 1964).
Coben, Stanley. "A Study in Nativism: The American Red Scare of 1919–20." *Political Science Quarterly*, 79 (March 1964).
Daniels, Roger. *The Politics of Prejudice: The Anti-Japanese Movement in California and the Struggle for Japanese Exclusion.* 1962.
Ellsworth, Scott. *Death in a Promised Land: The Tulsa Race Riot of 1921.* 1982.
Flack, Bruce C. "Dynamics of Intolerance—Internal and External Models in the Study of Intolerance in the United States during the 1920s." *Illinois Quarterly*, 39 (Winter 1976).
Goldberg, Robert A. "Beneath the Hood and Robe: A Socioeconomic Analysis of Ku Klux Klan Membership in Denver, Colorado, 1921–1925." *Western Historical Quarterly*, 11 (April 1980).
———. *Hooded Empire: The Ku Klux Klan in Colorado.* 1981.
———. "The Ku Klux Klan in Madison, 1922–1927." *Wisconsin Magazine of History*, 58 (Autumn 1974).
Hux, Roger K. "The Ku Klux Klan in Macon, 1919–1925." *Georgia Historical Quarterly*, 62 (Summer 1978).
Jackson, Kenneth T. *The Ku Klux Klan in the City, 1915–1930.* 1967.
Janick, Herbert. "An Instructive Failure: The Connecticut Peace Movement, 1919–1939." *Peace and Change*, 5 (Spring 1978).
Jenkins, William D. "The Ku Klux Klan in Youngstown, Ohio: Moral Reform in the Twenties." *Historian*, 41 (November 1978).
———. "Moral Reform after the Klan: Joseph Heffernan As Mayor of Youngstown, 1928–1931." *Old Northwest*, 9 (Summer 1983).
Jensen, Joan M. *The Price of Vigilance.* 1968.
Marguiles, Herbert F. "Anti-Catholicism in Wisconsin Politics, 1914–1920." *Mid-America*, 44 (January 1962).
Murphy, Paul L. "Sources and Nature of Intolerance in the 1920s." *Journal of American History*, 51 (June 1964).
Pivar, David J. "Cleansing the Nation: The War on Prostitution." *Prologue* 12 (Spring 1980).
Reitman, Alan. *The Pulse of Freedom: American Liberties: 1920–1970s.* 1975.

Rudwick, Elliott, and August Meier. "Early Boycotts of Segregated Schools: The Case of Springfield, Ohio, 1922–1923." *American Quarterly,* 20 (Winter 1968).

Smith, Norman W. "The Ku Klux Klan in Rhode Island." *Rhode Island History,* 37 (May 1978).

Toy, Eckard V., Jr. "The Ku Klux Klan in Tillamook, Oregon." *Pacific Northwest Quarterly,* 53 (May 1962).

Williams, Lee E., and Lee E. Williams II. *Anatomy of Four Race Riots: Racial Conflict in Knoxville, Elaine (Arkansas), Tulsa and Chicago, 1919–1921.* 1972.

Zink, Steven D. "Cultural Conflict and the 1928 Presidential Campaign in Louisiana." *Southern Studies,* 8 (Summer 1978).

SOCIAL WELFARE

Altmeyer, Arthur J. "The Wisconsin Idea and Social Security." *Wisconsin Magazine of History,* 41 (Autumn 1958).

Baird, Nancy D. "The 'Spanish Lady' [influenza] in Kentucky 1918–1919." *Filson Club History Quarterly,* 50 (July 1976).

Burbank, Lyman B. "Chicago Public Schools and the Depression Years of 1928–1937." *Journal of the Illinois State Historical Society,* 64 (Winter 1971).

Chambers, Clarke A. *Paul U. Kellogg and the Survey: Voices for Social Welfare and Social Justice.* 1971.

———. *Seedtime of Reform: American Social Service and Social Action, 1918–1933.* 1963.

Felt, Jeremy P. *Hostages of Fortune: Child Labor Reform in New York State.* 1965.

Freidel, Frank. *Franklin D. Roosevelt: Launching the New Deal.* 1973.

Lubove, Roy. *The Professional Altruist: The Emergence of Social Work as a Career, 1880–1930.* 1965.

———. *The Struggle for Social Security, 1900–1935.* 1968.

McClymer, John F. *War and Welfare: Social Engineering in America, 1890–1925.* 1980.

Mullins, William H. "Self-Help in Seattle, 1931–1932: Herbert Hoover's Concept of Cooperative Individualism and the Unemployed Citizens' League." *Pacific Northwest Quarterly,* 72 (January 1981).

Olson, James S. "Gifford Pinchot and the Politics of Hunger, 1932–1933." *Pennsylvania Magazine of History and Biography,* 46 (October 1972).

Trolander, Judith Ann. *Settlement Houses and the Great Depression.* 1975.

URBAN LIFE

Brownell, Blaine A. "The Notorious Jitney and the Urban Transportation Crisis in Birmingham in the 1920's." *Alabama Review,* 15 (April 1972).

———. *The Urban Ethos in the South, 1920–1930.* 1975.

Condit, Carl W. *Chicago, 1910–29: Building, Planning, and Urban Technology.* 1973.

Cotner, Robert C., Robert F. Colwell, Dorothy De Moss, Mary Maverick McMillan Fisher, Merry K. Fitzpatrick, John P. Griffin, Lyndon Gayle Knippa, William E. Montgomery, Marion Martin Nordeman, Diane Tredaway Ozment, Robert Ozment, Bradley R. Rice, and Judith Jenkins Turman. *Texas Cities and the Great Depression.* 1973.

Danbom, David B. *The Resisted Revolution: Urban America and the Industrialization of Agriculture, 1900–1930.* 1979.

Foster, Mark S. "The Automobile and the City." *Michigan Quarterly Review*, 19–20 (Fall 1980–Winter 1981).

Hilton, George W., and John F. Due. *The Electric Interurban Railways in America*. 1960.

Huthmacher, J. Joseph. *Senator Robert F. Wagner and the Rise of Urban Liberalism*. 1968.

Kirschner, Don S. *City and Country: Rural Responses to Urbanization in the 1920s*. 1970.

McKelvey, Blake. *Rochester: An Emerging Metropolis, 1925–1961*. 1961.

Preston, Howard L. *Automobile Age Atlanta: The Making of a Southern Metropolis, 1900–1935*. 1979.

Thomas, Richard. "The Detroit Urban League: 1916–1923." *Michigan History*, 60 (Winter 1976).

Wilson, William H. *Coming of Age: Urban America, 1915–1945*. 1974.

VETERANS' AFFAIRS

Reid, Bill G. "Franklin K. Lane's Idea for Veterans' Colonization, 1918–1921." *Pacific Historical Review*, 33 (November 1964).

WOMEN

Baer, Judith A. *The Chains of Protection: The Judicial Response to Women's Labor Legislation*. 1978.

Becker, Susan D. *The Origins of the Equal Rights Amendment: American Feminism between the Wars*. 1981.

Bennett, Mildred R. "Willa Cather and the Prairie." *Nebraska History*, 56 (Summer 1975).

Blocker, Jack S., Jr. "Separate Paths: Suffragists and Women's Temperance Crusade." *Signs*, 10 (Spring 1985).

Chafe, William Henry. *The American Woman: Her Changing Social, Economic, and Political Roles, 1920–1970*. 1972.

Costin, Lela B. "Grace Abbott of Nebraska." *Nebraska History*, 56 (Summer 1975).

Cott, Nancy F. "Feminist Politics in the 1920s: The National Woman's Party." *Journal of American History*, 71 (June 1984).

Davis, Allen F. "The Women's Trade Union League: Origins and Organization." *Labor History*, 5 (Winter 1964).

Freedman, Estelle B. "The New Woman: Changing Views of Women in the 1920s." *Journal of American History*, 61 (September 1974).

Gordon, Felice. *After Winning: The Legacy of the New Jersey Suffragists, 1920–1947*. 1986.

———. "After Winning: The New Jersey Suffragists in the Political Parties, 1920–1930." *New Jersey History*, 101 (Fall/Winter 1983).

Gordon, Linda. *Woman's Body, Woman's Right: A Social History of Birth Control in America*. 1976.

Gripe, Elizabeth Howell. "Women, Restructuring and Unrest in the 1920s." *Journal of Presbyterian History*, 52 (Summer 1974).

Horowitz, Helen Lefkowitz. "Hull House As Women's Space." *Chicago History*, 12 (Winter 1983–1984).

Johnson, Dorothy E. "Organized Women as Lobbyists in the 1920's." *Capitol Studies,* 1 (Spring 1972).

Klaczynska, Barbara. "Why Women Work: A Comparison of Various Groups—Philadelphia, 1910–1930." *Labor History,* 17 (Winter 1976).

Kraditor, Aileen S. *The Ideas of the Woman Suffrage Movement, 1890–1920.* 1965.

Kyvig, David E. "Woman against Prohibition." *American Quarterly,* 28 (Fall 1976).

Larson, T. A. "The Woman Suffrage Movement in Washington." *Pacific Northwest Quarterly,* 67 (April 1976).

Lauter, Paul. "Race and Gender in the Shaping of the American Literary Canon: A Case Study from the Twenties." *Feminist Studies,* 9 (Fall 1983).

Leach, William R. "Transformations in a Culture of Consumption: Women and Department Stores, 1890–1925." *Journal of American History,* 71 (September 1984).

Lemons, J. Stanley. "Social Feminism in the 1920s: Progressive Women and Industrial Legislation." *Labor History,* 14 (Winter 1973).

Levine, Daniel. *Jane Addams and the Liberal Tradition,* 1971.

Louis, James P. "Sue Shelton White and the Woman Suffrage Movement in Tennessee, 1913–1920." *Tennessee Historical Quarterly,* 42 (June 1963).

McFarland, C. K., and Nevin E. Neal. "The Reluctant Reformer: Woodrow Wilson and Woman Suffrage, 1913–1920." *Rocky Mountain Social Science Journal,* 11 (April 1974).

Massa, Ann. "Black Women in the 'White City'." *Journal of American Studies,* 8 (December 1974).

Morgan, David. *Suffragists and Democrats: The Politics of Woman Suffrage in America.* 1972.

Nichols, Carole. *Votes and More for Women: Suffrage and After in Connecticut.* 1983.

O'Neill, William L. *Everyone Was Brave: The Rise and Fall of Feminism in America.* 1969.

Seller, Maxine. "The Education of the Immigrant Woman, 1900–1935." *Journal of Urban History,* 4 (May 1978).

Sheehan, Nancy M. " 'Women Helping Women': The WCTU and the Foreign Population in the West, 1905–1930." *International Journal of Women's Studies,* 6 (November/December 1983).

Strom, Sharon Hartman. "Leadership and Tactics in the American Woman Suffrage Movement: A New Perspective from Massachusetts." *Journal of American History,* 62 (September 1975).

Wandersee, Winifred D. *Women's Work and Family Values: 1920–1940.* 1981.

Wilson, Joan Hoff. " 'Peace Is a Woman's Job . . . ': Jeanette Rankin and American Foreign Policy: Her Lifework As a Pacifist." *Montana, the Magazine of Western History,* 30 (April 1980).

INDEX

Page numbers set in *italic* indicate location of main entry.

General Conference of Women's Clubs, 71

General Federation of Women's Clubs, 247, 271

General Foods, 66

General Motors, 101, 102, 130, 276–77

Geneva Arms Convention of 1925, *145*, 147

Geneva Conference of 1932, *145*, 244

Geneva Naval Conference of 1927, 77, *145*, 147, 244

George, David Lloyd, 36, 263

Gerber, Daniel Frank, Jr., *145–46*

Gershwin, George, *146*

Giannini, Amadeo Peter, *146–47*

Gibson, Hugh Simons, 145, *147*, 219

Gifford, Walter Sherman, *147*, 268–69

Gilbert, Seymour Parker, 88, *147–48*

Gilhaus, August, 105

Gimbel, Bernard, *148*

Gish, Lillian Diana, *148*

Gitlow, Benjamin, 74–75

Gitlow v. *New York*, 148

Glackens, William, 18

Glass, Carter, *149–50*

Glass-Steagall Act of 1932, *149–50*

Glenn, John Mark, *149*

"The Goldbergs," *150*

Goldman, Emma, 151, 308

Goldwyn, Samuel, 218

Gompers, Samuel, 11, 43, *151–52*, 243, 254, 308

Good, James William, *152*

Good Neighbor Policy, 68, 71, 77, *152–53*, 180

Gordon, Anna Adams, *153–54*

Gosden, Freeman, 13

Graham, Martha, *154*

Grain Stabilization Corporation, 6, 123

Grange, Harold, 92, *154–55*

Grant, Madison, 112, *155*

Grant, William Thomas, *155–56*, 246

Gray, Harold, 216

Gray, Judd, 305

Great Depression, *156*, 174, 214

Green, William, 11, *156–57*, 321

Grew, Joseph Clark, *157*

Grey, Zane, *157–58*, 271

Griffith, David Wark, 30, 64, 119, *158*, 163, 200, 238, 267

"Grizzley Bear," 188

Grundy, Joseph, 165

Guggenheim, Harry, 211

Hadley, Lindley, 121

Hagen, Walter, 92, *159*

Hale, Frederick, 259

Hall, Edward, 160

Hall, Joyce Clyde, *159*

Hall, Prescott, 183

Hallmark cards, 159

Hall-Mills murder case, *160*

Hammer v. *Dagenhart*, 24, *160*, 243

Hammett, Samuel Dashiell, *160–61*

Hammond, W. A., 228

Hanna, Mark, 243

"The Happiness Boys," *161*

Harding, Warren Gamaliel, 2, 4, 10, 11, 51, 76, 79, 83, 85, 86, 87, 90, 91, 93, 97, 105–8, 112, 113, 114, 119, 124, 127, 133, 136, 152, 157, *161–63*, 166, 173, 178, 179, 198, 204, 208, 220, 221, 229, 231, 253, 257, 258, 281, 301, 307, 309, 313, 314, 321, 327, 334

Hardy, Oliver, 208–9

Hare, Ernie, 161

Harlem Renaissance, *163*

Harreld, John, 121

Hart, William Surrey, *163–64*, 238

Harvey, William, 215

Haugen, Gilbert Nelson, 164, *227–28*

Hauptmann, Richard Bruno, *164*, 215

Havana Conference of 1928, *165*

Hawes-Cutting Act of 1933, *165*

Hawley, Willis, 121, 165

Hawley-Smoot Tariff, 63, 134, 156, *165–66*

Hayes, Max, 121

Hays, Arthur Garfield, *166*

Hays, William Harrison, *166*

Haywood, William Dudley, 83, *167*

Hearst, William Randolph, 84, 110–11, *167–68*

Hemenway, Frank, 215

Hemingway, Ernest, 117, *168*, 220

About the Author

JAMES S. OLSON is Professor of History at Sam Houston State University, Huntsville, Texas. His earlier works include *Dictionary of the Vietnam War*, *Historical Dictionary of the New Deal: From Inauguration to Preparation for War* (Greenwood Press, 1988, 1985), *Herbert Hoover and the Reconstruction Finance Corporation, 1931–1933*, *The Ethnic Dimension in American History*, *Native Americans in the Twentieth Century*, and numerous articles.